KAS	Atchison, Kans. (USA) — St. Benedict's College Library
KdP	Kendal (Eng.) — Public Library
KdWG	Kendal (Eng.) — Office of *Westmorland Gazette*
KeP	Kensington (Eng.) — Public Library
KiP	Kilmarnock (Scot.) — Dick Institute Public Library
KkKJ	Kilkenny (Eire) — Office of *Kilkenny Journal*
KyLx	Lexington, Ky. (USA) — Public Library
KyU	Lexington, Ky. (USA) — University of Kentucky Library
*L	London (Eng.) — British Museum Library
LAt	London (Eng.) — Athenaeum Club Library
LCM	London (Eng.) — Royal College of Music Library
LCP	London (Eng.) — Royal College of Physicians Library
LDC	London (Eng.) — Dulwich College Library
LE	London (Eng.) — London School of Economics Library
LFS	London (Eng.) — Friends Society Library
LGI	London (Eng.) — Gray's Inn Library
LGU	London (Eng.) — Guildhall Library
LIT	London (Eng.) — Inner Temple Library
LLG	London (Eng.) — Office of *London Gazette*
LLL	London (Eng.) — London Library
LLlL	London (Eng.) — Office of *Lloyd's List and Shipping Gazette*
LLN	London (Eng.) — Lincoln's Inn Library
LLW	London (Eng.) — Law Society Library
LMA	London (Eng.) — British Medical Association Library
LMD	London (Eng.) — Royal Society of Medicine Library
LMT	London (Eng.) — Middle Temple Library
LNHT	New Orleans, La. (USA) — Howard Memorial Library
*LP	London (Eng.) — Patent Office Library
LR	London (Eng.) — Royal Society Library
*LS	London (Eng.) — Royal College of Surgeons Library
LSD	London (Eng.) — Office of *Sunday Dispatch*
LTT	London (Eng.) — Office of *The Times*
*LU	London (Eng.) — London University Library
LUC	London (Eng.) — University College Library
LVA	London (Eng.) — Victoria and Albert Museum Library
LaP	Lambeth (Eng.) — Tate Central Library
LcLC	Leicester (Eng.) — Office of *Illustrated Leicester Chronicle*
LcLM	Leicester (Eng.) — Office of *Leicester Mercury*
LcP	Leicester (Eng.) — Public Library
LdL	Leeds (Eng.) — Leeds Library
LdP	Leeds (Eng.) — Public Library
LdYP	Leeds (Eng.) — Office of *Yorkshire Post*
LmLC	Limerick (Eire) — Office of *Limerick Chronicle*
LmP	Limerick (Eire) — Municipal Public Libraries
LnLR	Lincoln (Eng.) — Office of *Lincoln, Rutland and Stamford Mercury*

LnP	Lincoln (Eng.) — Public Library
LoLS	Londonderry (No. Ire.) — Office of *Londonderry Sentinel*
LoM	Londonderry (No. Ire.) — Magee University College Library
LoP	Londonderry (No. Ire.) — Public Library
LrC	Lismore (Eire) — Waterford County Libraries
LsP	Lancaster (Eng.) — Public Library
LvA	Liverpool (Eng.) — Athenaeum Library
LvP	Liverpool (Eng.) — Public Library
MB	Boston, Mass. (USA) — Public Library
MBAt	Boston, Mass. (USA) — Boston Athenaeum Library
MCh	Manchester (Eng.) — Chetham's Library
MH	Cambridge, Mass. (USA) — Harvard University Library
MH-Z	Cambridge, Mass. (USA) — Harvard Museum of Comparative Zoology
MHi	Boston, Mass. (USA) — Massachusetts Historical Society Library
MMG	Manchester (Eng.) — Office of *Manchester Guardian*
MNS	Northampton, Mass. (USA) — Smith College Library
MP	Manchester (Eng.) — Public Library
MR	Manchester (Eng.) — John Rylands Library
MWA	Worcester, Mass. (USA) — American Antiquarian Society Library
MaP	Maidenhead (Eng.) — Public Library
MdBE	Baltimore, Md. (USA) — Enoch Pratt Free Library
MdBJ	Baltimore, Md. (USA) — The Johns Hopkins University Library
MdBP	Baltimore, Md. (USA) — Peabody Institute Library
MeB	Brunswick, Me. (USA) — Bowdoin College Library
MeHi	Brunswick, Me. (USA) — Maine Historical Society Library
MiD-B	Detroit, Mich. (USA) — Detroit Public Library, Burton Historical Collection
MiU	Ann Arbor, Mich. (USA) — University of Michigan Library
MiU-C	Ann Arbor, Mich. (USA) — University of Michigan Library, William Clements Library of American History
MnU	Minneapolis, Minn. (USA) — University of Minnesota Library
MoM	Montrose (Scot.) — Montrose Library
MoMR	Montrose (Scot.) — Office of *Montrose Review*
MoP	Montrose (Scot.) — Public Library
MoU	Columbia, Mo. (USA) — University of Missouri Library
MsP	Maidstone (Eng.) — Public Library
N	Albany, N. Y. (USA) — New York State Library
NIC	Ithaca, N. Y. (USA) — Cornell University Library
NN	New York, N. Y. (USA) — Public Library
NNC	New York, N. Y. (USA) — Columbia University Library

*NNG	Nottingham (Eng.) — Office of *Nottingham Guardian*
NNHi	New York, N. Y. (USA) — New York Historical Society Library
NNJ	Nottingham (Eng.) — Office of *Nottingham Journal*
NP	Nottingham (Eng.) — Public Library
NPV	Poughkeepsie, N. Y. (USA) — Vassar College Library
NRU	Rochester, N. Y. (USA) — University of Rochester Library
NcD	Durham, N. C. (USA) — Duke University Library
NcU	Chapel Hill, N. C. (USA) — University of North Carolina Library
NjHi	Newark, N. J. (USA) — New Jersey Historical Society Library
NjP	Princeton, N. J. (USA) — Princeton University Library
NjR	New Brunswick, N. J. (USA) — Rutgers University Library
NkP	Newark-on-Trent (Eng.) — Gilstrap Public Library
NoMH	Northampton (Eng.) — Office of *Mercury and Herald*
NoP	Northampton (Eng.) — Public Library
NpP	Newport (Eng.) — Public Library
NrC	Norwich (Eng.) — Private Library of Mrs. Colman (Inquire at NrM or NrP)
NrM	Norwich (Eng.) — Castle Museum Library
NrP	Norwich (Eng.) — Public Library
NwEC	Newcastle-upon-Tyne (Eng.) — Office of *Evening Chronicle*
NwL	Newcastle-upon-Tyne (Eng.) — Literary Philosophical Society Library
NwP	Newcastle-upon-Tyne (Eng.) — Public Library
NwS	Newcastle-upon-Tyne (Eng.) — Society of Antiquaries Library
O	Oxford (Eng.) — Bodleian Library
OC	Cincinnati, O. (USA) — Public Library
OCl	Cleveland, O. (USA) — Public Library
OClWHi	Cleveland, O. (USA) — Western Reserve Historical Society Library
OHi	Columbus, O. (USA) — Ohio State Archaeological and Historical Society Library
OMA	Oxford (Eng.) — Manchester College Library
OPU	Oxford (Eng.) — Public Library
OU	Columbus, O. (USA) — Ohio State University Library
PBr	Bryn Athyn, Pa. (USA) — Academy of the New Church
PHC	Haverford, Pa. (USA) — Haverford College Library
PPAP	Philadelphia, Pa. (USA) — American Philosophical Society Library
PPHi	Philadelphia, Pa. (USA) — Historical Society of Pennsylvania Library
PPL	Philadelphia, Pa. (USA) — Library Company of Philadelphia
PPPrHi	Philadelphia, Pa. (USA) — Presbyterian Historical Society Library

PU	Philadelphia, Pa. (USA) — University of Pennsylvania Library
PeP	Perth (Scot.) — Sandeman Public Library
PePA	Perth (Scot.) — Office of *Perthshire Advertiser*
PlP	Plymouth (Eng.) — Central Library
PmHT	Portsmouth (Eng.) — Office of *Hampshire Telegraph*
PmP	Portsmouth (Eng.) — Public Library
PrH	Preston (Eng.) — Harris Public Library
PsP	Paisley (Scot.) — Public Library
RP	Reading (Eng.) — Public Library
RRM	Reading (Eng.) — Office of the *Reading Mercury*
RdP	Rochdale (Eng.) — Public Library
RiP	Richmond (Eng.) — Public Library
RtP	Rotherham (Eng.) — Public Library
SP	Sheffield (Eng.) — Public Library
SU	Sheffield (Eng.) — Sheffield University Library
SaU	St. Andrews (Scot.) — St. Andrews University Library
SbSW	Salisbury (Eng.) — Office of *Salisbury and Winchester Journal*
ScP	Stockport (Eng.) — Public Library
ScSA	Stockport (Eng.) — Office of *Stockport Advertiser and Guardian*
SfP	Salford (Eng.) — Public Library
SkP	Southwark (Eng.) — Public Library
SnP	Stoke Newington (Eng.) — Public Library
SoP	Southampton (Eng.) — Public Library
SptP	Southport (Eng.) — Public Library
SrP	Shrewsbury (Eng.) — Public Library
SrS	Shrewsbury (Eng.) — Shrewsbury School Library
SrSC	Shrewsbury (Eng.) — Office of *Shrewsbury Chronicle*
SsP	South Shields (Eng.) — Public Library
StP	Stoke-on-Trent (Eng.) — Public Library
StfP	Stafford (Eng.) — Public Library
StfS	Stafford (Eng.) — William Salt Library
StfSA	Stafford (Eng.) — Office of *Staffordshire Advertiser*
SthC	Stonyhurst (Eng.) — Stonyhurst College Library
StlP	Stirling (Scot.) — Public Library
StlSJ	Stirling (Scot.) — Office of *Stirling Journal and Advertiser*
StmLR	Stamford (Eng.) — Office of *Lincoln, Rutland, and Stamford Mercury*
SuP	Sunderland (Eng.) — Public Library
SwI	Swansea (Wales) — Royal Institution of South Wales Library
SwP	Swansea (Wales) — Public Library
SyP	Stepney (Eng.) — Public Libraries
TaP	Taunton (Eng.) — Public Library
TaS	Taunton (Eng.) — Somerset Archaeological and Natural History Society Library
TmP	Tynemouth (Eng.) — Public Library
ToP	Tottenham (Eng.) — Public Library
TrP	Truro (Eng.) — Public Library

CO-OPERATING LIBRARIES†

AAJ	Aberdeen (Scot.) — Office of *Aberdeen Journals*		**BurC**	Bury St. Edmunds (Eng.) — Cullum Library
*AU	Aberdeen (Scot.) — Aberdeen University Library		**BwP**	Barrow-in-Furness (Eng.) — Public Library
ArP	Arbroath (Scot.) — Public Library			
AyAA	Ayr (Scot.) — Office of *Ayr Advertiser & Galloway Journal*		***C**	Cambridge (Eng.) — Cambridge University Library
AyP	Ayr (Scot.) — Public Library		**CPL**	Cambridge (Eng.) — Cambridge Philosophical Society
AybA	Aylesbury (Eng.) — Buckinghamshire Archaeological Society		**CPU**	Cambridge (Eng.) — Public Library

---

NOTE TO USERS OF THIS INDEX

This *Index* is designed for use not only with the *Union List of Serials* (ULS) and the *Union Catalogue of the Periodical Publications in the University Libraries of the British Isles* (UCP) but also with the forthcoming *British Union Catalogue of Periodicals* (BUCOP). Cross references are given to ULS and UCP only, but when BUCOP has been published, the user of this *Index* may assume that the cross references to UCP are valid also for BUCOP. Furthermore, he may assume that in many cases BUCOP, which will list the holdings of many British libraries not covered by UCP, records titles not found in UCP and hence should be consulted even in the absence of a cross reference.

Certain precautions which the user of this *Index* should take when associating symbols with libraries (and especially those preceded by an asterisk) are set forth at the end of this list of co-operating libraries.

BBW	Birmingham (Eng.) — Office of *Birmingham Weekly Post*		**C-S**	San Francisco, Cal. (USA) — California State Library, Sutro Branch
BO	Birmingham (Eng.) — Oscott College Library		**CSmH**	San Marino, Cal. (USA) — Henry Huntington Library
BP	Birmingham (Eng.) — Public Library		**CSt**	Stanford Univ., Cal. (USA) — Stanford University Library
BaA	Barnstaple (Eng.) — North Devon Athenaeum		**CU**	Berkeley, Cal. (USA) — University of California Library
BbP	Blackburn (Eng.) — Public Library			
BdL	Bradford (Eng.) — Bradford Library and Literary Society		**CaK**	Kingston (Canada) — Queen's University Library
BdP	Bradford (Eng.) — Public Library		**CaL**	London (Canada) — University of Western Ontario Library
BddP	Bideford (Eng.) — Public Library			
BedP	Bedford (Eng.) — Public Library		**CaM**	Montreal (Canada) — McGill University Library
BerBA	Berwick-on-Tweed (Scot.) — Office of *Berwick Advertiser*		**CbP**	Camborne (Eng.) — Public Library
BhP	Bath (Eng.) — Municipal Library		**ChlP**	Chelsea (Eng.) — Public Library
BiBH	Brighton (Eng.) — Office of *Brighton & Hove Herald*		**ChsCCh**	Chester (Eng.) — Office of *Chester Chronicle*
BiP	Brighton (Eng.) — Public Library		**ChsCCo**	Chester (Eng.) — Office of *Chester Courant*
BkP	Birkenhead (Eng.) — Public Library		**CiP**	Cirencester (Eng.) — Bingham Public Library
BlBN	Belfast (No. Ire.) — Office of *Belfast News-Letter*			
BlL	Belfast (No. Ire.) — Linen Hall Library		**CmC**	Carmarthen (Wales) — Carmarthenshire County Museum
BlNW	Belfast (No. Ire.) — Office of *Northern Whig and Belfast Post*		**CnP**	Croydon (Eng.) — Public Library
BlP	Belfast (No. Ire.) — Public Library		**CoP**	Cork (Eire) — Municipal Library
BlU	Belfast (No. Ire.) — Queen's University		**ColCG**	Colchester (Eng.) — Office of *Colchester Gazette*
BmP	Bournemouth (Eng.) — Public Library		**ColEC**	Colchester (Eng.) — Office of *Essex County Standard*
BnU	Bangor (Wales) — University College of North Wales Library		**ColP**	Colchester (Eng.) — Public Library
BoP	Bolton (Eng.) — Public Library		**CpFH**	Cupar (Scot.) — Office of *Fife Herald and Journal*
BrBW	Bristol (Eng.) — Office of *Bristol Western Daily Press* &c.		**CrP**	Cardiff (Wales) — Public Library
BrP	Bristol (Eng.) — Public Library		**CsCN**	Carlisle (Eng.) — Office of *Cumberland News*
BrU	Bristol (Eng.) — Bristol University Library		**CsP**	Carlisle (Eng.) — Public Library
BtP	Battersea (Eng.) — Public Library		**CsfP**	Chesterfield (Eng.) — Public Library
BtlP	Bootle (Eng.) — Public Library		**CtHT**	Hartford, Conn. (USA) — Trinity College Library
BuC	Bury (Eng.) — Co-operative Society Library			

† To these libraries should be added those in ULS and UCP which are not listed here, since cross references are given to these volumes. For a full explanation of this fact see the second paragraph of the Foreword.

CtP Cheltenham (Eng.) — Public Library
CtY New Haven, Conn. (USA) — Yale University Library
CvCS Coventry (Eng.) — Office of *Coventry Standard*
CvP Coventry (Eng.) — Public Library
CyKG Canterbury (Eng.) — Office of *Kentish Gazette and Canterbury Press*

D Dublin (Eire) — Trinity College Library
*DA Dublin (Eire) — Royal Irish Academy Library
DCC Dublin (Eire) — Central Catholic Library
DCU Washington, D. C. (USA) — Catholic University of America Library
*DL Dublin (Eire) — National Library of Ireland
DLC Washington, D. C. (USA) — Library of Congress
DLL Dublin (Eire) — King's Inn Law Library
DML Dublin (Eire) — Marsh's Library
DPK Dublin (Eire) — Public Library, Kevin Street
DRC Dublin (Eire) — Representative Church Body Library
DRS Dublin (Eire) — Royal Dublin Society Library
DSA Dublin (Eire) — Royal Society of Antiquaries in Ireland Library
DcDG Doncaster (Eng.) — Office of *Doncaster Gazette*
DcP Doncaster (Eng.) — Public Library
DcrN Dorchester (Eng.) — Dorset Natural History and Archaeological Society Library
DeP Derby (Eng.) — Public Library
DlP Darlington (Eng.) — Edward Pease Public Library
DmP Dunfermline (Scot.) — Public Library
DnCA Dundee (Scot.) — Office of *Courier and Advertiser*
DnP Dundee (Scot.) — Public Library
DrC Durham (Eng.) — County Libraries
DrDC Durham (Eng.) — Office of *Durham County Advertiser*
DrU Durham (Eng.) — Durham University Library
DsD Dumfries (Scot.) — Dumfriesshire Libraries
DuC Duns (Scot.) — Berwickshire County Library
DvW Devizes (Eng.) — Wiltshire Archaeological and Natural History Society Library
DvWG Devizes (Eng.) — Office of *Wiltshire Gazette*

*E Edinburgh (Scot.) — National Library of Scotland
EEG Edinburgh (Scot.) — Office of *Edinburgh Gazette*
EP Edinburgh (Scot.) — Public Library
ER Edinburgh (Scot.) — Royal Society of Edinburgh Library
ESL Edinburgh (Scot.) — Signet Library
ETS Edinburgh (Scot.) — Office of *The Scotsman*
EU Edinburgh (Scot.) — Edinburgh University Library

ElEC Elgin (Scot.) — Office of *Elgin Courant and Courier*
EnnIR Enniskillen (No. Ire.) — Office of *Impartial Reporter and Farmer's Journal*
EtS Eton (Eng.) — School Library
ExD Exeter (Eng.) — Devon and Exeter Institution Library
ExDE Exeter (Eng.) — Office of *Devon and Exeter Gazette*
ExP Exeter (Eng.) — Public Library
ExWT Exeter (Eng.) — Office of *Western Times*

FoP Folkestone (Eng.) — Public Library

GGH Glasgow (Scot.) — Office of the *Glasgow Herald*
GM Glasgow (Scot.) — Mitchell Library
*GU Glasgow (Scot.) — Glasgow University Library
GeG Greenock (Scot.) — Greenock Library
GmP Grimsby (Eng.) — Public Library
GrGJ Gloucester (Eng.) — Office of *Gloucester Journal*
GrP Gloucester (Eng.) — Public Library

HP Hull (Eng.) — Public Library
HdP Hampstead (Eng.) — Central Library
HdS Hampstead (Eng.) — Hampstead Subscription Library
HfP Hereford (Eng.) — Public Library
HlHC Halifax (Eng.) — Office of *Halifax Courier and Guardian*
HlL Halifax (Eng.) — Literary and Philosophical Society Library
HlP Halifax (Eng.) — Public Library
HnA Haddington (Scot.) — East Lothian Antiquarian Society Library
HnP Haddington (Scot.) — Public Library
HsP Hammersmith (Eng.) — Central Carnegie Library
HtHM Hertford (Eng.) — Office of *Hertfordshire Mercury & County Press*
HtP Hertford (Eng.) — Public Library
HwV Harrow (Eng.) — Vaughan Library

ICN Chicago, Ill. (USA) — Newberry Library
ICU Chicago, Ill. (USA) — University of Chicago Library
IHi Springfield, Ill. (USA) — Illinois Historical Society Library
IP Peoria, Ill. (USA) — Public Library
IU Urbana, Ill. (USA) — University of Illinois Library
InIC Inverness (Scot.) — Office of *Inverness Courier*
InP Inverness (Scot.) — Burgh and County Public Library
InR Inverness (Scot.) — Raigmore
IpP Ipswich (Eng.) — Public Library
IpSC Ipswich (Eng.) — Office of *Suffolk Chronicle and Mercury*
IsP Islington (Eng.) — Islington Public Libraries

TrRC	Truro (Eng.) — Office of *Royal Cornwall Gazette and County News*	**WIP**	Wigan (Eng.) — Public Library
TrWB	Truro (Eng.) — Office of *West Briton*	**WmP**	Westminister (Eng.) — Public Library
TuP	Tunbridge Wells (Eng.) — Public Library	**WnP**	Winchester (Eng.) — Public Library
		WoP	Woolwich (Eng.) — Public Library
		WrP	Warrington (Eng.) — Municipal Library
V	Richmond, Va. (USA) — Virginia State Library	**WtLE**	Whitehaven (Eng.) — Lowther Estates Library
VU	Charlottesville, Va. (USA) — University of Virginia	**WtP**	Whitehaven (Eng.) — Public Library
		WtfP	Waterford (Eire) — Municipal Library
		WvP	Wolverhampton (Eng.) — Public Library
WHl	Madison, Wis. (USA) — University of Wisconsin Library	**WwP**	Warwick (Eng.) — Public Library
		WwWW	Warwick (Eng.) — Office of *Warwick and Warwickshire Advertiser*
WcBW	Worcester (Eng.) — Office of *Berrow's Worcester Journal*	**WxC**	Wexford (Eire) — County Libraries
WcP	Worcester (Eng.) — Public Library	**WxOC**	Wexford (Eire) — Office of M. J. O'Connor, Solicitors
WdWS	Windsor (Eng.) — Office of *Windsor, Slough and Eton Express*	**YP**	York (Eng.) — Public Library
WhP	West Ham (Eng.) — Public Library	**YYH**	York (Eng.) — Office of *Yorkshire Herald*
		YeWG	Yeovil (Eng.) — Office of *Western Gazette*

Note 1:

Fortunately my adoption of the library symbols employed by ULS and BUCOP did not lead to a single case of duplication when the American and British libraries co-operating with this *Index* were combined into one list. In seven instances, however, libraries listed in ULS (but not in this *Index*) have the same symbols as other libraries which co-operated with this *Index* and BUCOP. It is unlikely that confusion will arise because of this duplication, but a word of caution can hardly be amiss.

AU	Aberdeen University	is also Alabama University in ULS
C	Cambridge University	is also California State Library in ULS
DA	Royal Irish Academy	is also U.S. Department of Agriculture in ULS
DL	National Library of Ireland	is also U.S. Department of Labor in ULS
GU	Glasgow University	is also University of Georgia in ULS
LU	London University	is also University of Louisiana in ULS
NNG	Office of *Nottingham Guardian*	is also General Theological Seminary in ULS

Note 2:

A possible source of confusion (especially for British users) arises from the fact that the symbols to be used in the forthcoming BUCOP (and hence the symbols in this *Index*) do not always signify the same libraries that they do in UCP. Five of these symbols are used in this *Index*. (When BUCOP is published, this problem, of course, will cease to exist.)

E	National Library of Scotland in this *Index* and BUCOP, but Edinburgh University in UCP
L	British Museum in this *Index* and BUCOP, but London University in UCP
LP	Patent Office in this *Index* and BUCOP, but School of Pharmacy in UCP
LS	Royal College of Surgeons in this *Index* and BUCOP, but School of Slavonic Studies in UCP
LU	London University in this *Index* and BUCOP, but University College in UCP

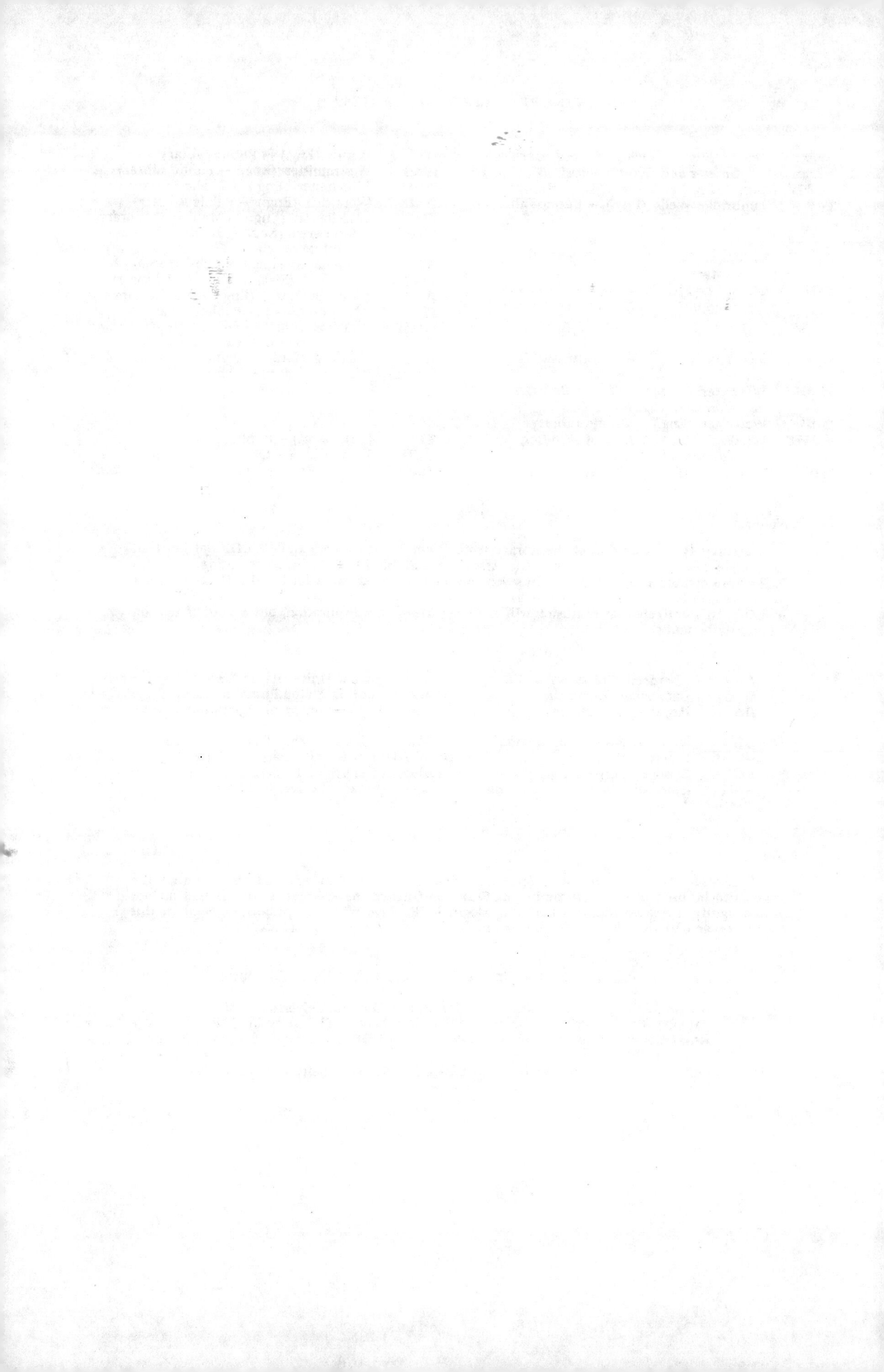

Index and Finding List
of Serials Published
in the British Isles
1789-1832

Index and Finding List of Serials Published in the British Isles 1789-1832

Compiled by

William S. Ward

UNIVERSITY OF KENTUCKY PRESS

LEXINGTON

Publication of this book has been aided by a grant from
the Carl and Lily Pforzheimer Foundation, Inc.

Library of Congress Catalog Card Number: 53-5521

To
Elizabeth S. Ward
and
Margaret Byrn Ward

TABLE OF CONTENTS

FOREWORD

During the past quarter of a century the rapid growth of interest in the periodical literature of the past has emphasized increasingly the need for specialized hand lists. The American *Union List of Serials* and the British *Union Catalogue of the Periodical Publications in the University Libraries of the British Isles* are indispensable and will continue to be so; but to search their pages for periodicals published in the United Kingdom during any given period is a tedious and time-consuming task. Furthermore, even when used in combination with other existing lists these volumes by no means provide a definitive list of newspapers and periodicals. The *ULS*, for example, is far from complete when listing the British newspapers held by libraries in the United States and Canada; the *UCP* limits itself to eighty-three university libraries in the British Isles. And all others are characterized by one sort of limitation or another: Crane and Kaye's *Census* does not go beyond the year 1800; the *Tercentenary Handlist* is based largely on the British Museum and omits Scottish and Irish newspapers and periodicals; Felix Sper's *The Periodical Press of London* is limited to London theatrical and literary periodicals for the years 1800-1830; and the *World List of Scientific Periodicals* and Leiper's *Periodicals of Medicine and Allied Sciences in British Libraries* restrict themselves to periodicals of a scientific character.

Thus it was that while working on a problem requiring an examination of the British periodicals of the English Romantic period I resolved to prepare a finding list of the periodicals published during this period (for which the dates 1789-1832 have been adopted) and to indicate in what libraries, both American and British, they may be found. A seven-month stay in the British Isles in 1938 enabled to me make a substantial start on the list, but teaching duties and a war with its aftermath caused ten years to pass before much more could be done. A return to the British Isles has not been possible, but the friendly co-operation of many people has enabled me to achieve a degree of thoroughness that I dared not hope for at one time. Statistically speaking, more than 260 public and private libraries in the United Kingdom and Eire have been kind enough to respond to my inquiries; and some 94 newspapers whose inception dates lie between 1789 and 1832 have been good enough to reply to my queries about newspaper files. In the United States and Canada approximately 70 libraries with British newspaper holdings have responded to my inquiries; and in the United Kingdom and Eire some 20 university libraries have reported holdings supplementary to *UCP*. To these may be added some 15 principal American libraries and a like number of major metropolitan libraries in the United Kingdom and Eire which I have been able to examine personally. By no means did every one of these 475 libraries and newspaper offices have files for the years 1789-1832, but 359 of them did. Of this number some 280 are represented in no existing finding list; the remainder appear in some list but are repeated here in order to correct errors, give fuller information, or list new holdings. And to these libraries and newspaper offices are to be added the libraries which co-operated with *ULS* and *UCP*, for a cross reference is always given to them when they record library holdings for the periodical in question.

In all, then, when one adds the 600 libraries co-operating in *ULS*, the 475 in my *Index*, and the 83 in *UCP*, some 1080 libraries and newspaper offices (after duplications are allowed for) have been investigated. But even so, a final and definitive list of the periodicals published in the United Kingdom and Eire between 1789 and 1832 has not been achieved. Co-operating libraries, for one thing, are bound to have overlooked a few items; but more important, a number of libraries and newspapers have declined to report their holdings; and in still other cases rare and unique items are certain to exist in private hands or in libraries or newspaper offices of which I am ignorant or to which it did not occur to me to write.

Some inconvenience may arise from the fact that the libraries listed by *ULS* and *UCP* are not relisted here. Instead, a cross reference to these volumes is given whenever a periodical is listed by them. Such a system, of course, usually requires the American student to supplement this volume with the *ULS*, and frequently requires the British student to do likewise with *UCP*. As an explanation and apology for such inconvenience I can only say that any other method than the one employed would have been so costly as to prevent the list from ever being published.

It has just been explained that this list is geared, so to speak, for use with *ULS* and *UCP*. It should be explained also that it may be used in combination with the forthcoming *British Union Catalogue of Periodicals*, publication of which is scheduled for about 1955. In fact, in so far as my list duplicates libraries covered by *BUCOP* I have adopted the symbols to be used in that monumental work; and in choosing symbols for libraries not investigated by *BUCOP* I have been assisted by its editorial staff so that conflicting symbols would be avoided.

One of the painful things about preparing a list such as this is the compiler's constant awareness of its defects. Not only are some good files bound to escape his notice, but errors are certain to occur: in reports from libraries; in transcribing this information; in untangling complicated histories of some newspapers and periodicals; and so on. Occasionally, too, data must remain incomplete. Thus it is sometimes impossible to determine with certainty the dates of the initial and final issues of a given serial, so that in some instances the dates assigned are merely those of the longest runs reported. And besides errors of this sort which are assumed to have occurred, certain other limitations are known to exist. For example, the listing of almanacs, yearbooks, reports, transactions, proceedings, and the like is less definitive than that of newspapers and periodicals in the more usual journalistic sense of those words. No serial of any sort has been omitted intentionally, but responses from libraries make it clear that variant practices were adopted in determining what should be reported. Inversely, some titles almost certainly have been included that should have been omitted. For one thing, it has not always been possible to examine every serial before including it. Again, as observed in another connection, different standards are applied by different libraries in determining what is considered to be a serial and what is not. And still another source of error is the fact that not all of the war damages and losses have been finally assessed. A few libraries which I had investigated in 1938 have had to be re-examined, but it is probably safe to say that in some cases losses have not been discovered, or at least not recorded, and that in others the library's advice that a certain file "will soon be replaced" was based on a hope never actually to be realized.

William S. Ward

Lexington, Kentucky
February 1, 1952

ACKNOWLEDGMENTS

To enumerate all the librarians and others who have assisted me in the preparation of this *Index* would be all but impossible. I can only say that from first to last I encountered a spirit of helpfulness and graciousness that was unfailing. Many times I had little choice but to impose unreasonable requests upon a library or newspaper office; yet almost without exception my embarrassed appeal was met with a warm reception that never ceased to astonish me.

Many, many persons deserve separate mention, but my particular thanks to the few must stand for the many. Especially am I indebted to the following for the practical assistance which they have given me and for their advice and encouragement: Dr. Harry M. Lydenberg, Director Emeritus of the New York Public Library; Mrs. Winifred Gregory Gerould, Editor of the *Union List of Serials*; Dr. R.H. Hayes, Director of the National Library of Ireland; Mr. Robert Bain, late Director of the Mitchell Library, Glasgow; Mr. C.B. Oldman, Principal Keeper, the British Museum; the late Alfred Loewenberg, Editor of the *British Union Catalogue of Periodical Publications*; Mr. James D. Stewart, Dr. Loewenberg's successor, and still Editor of *BUCOP*; and Dr. Hill Shine, Professor of English, and Miss Norma Cass, Reference Librarian, both of the University of Kentucky.

For permission to list holdings as well as for the assistance which they have rendered I am indebted also to every library whose name appears in this *Index*. To the Royal Society in London, therefore, to the London Library, the British Museum, the National Libraries of Scotland and Ireland, the Royal Dublin Society, the Mitchell Library, the John Rylands Library, the Literary and Philosophical Society and the Society of Antiquaries in Newcastle-upon-Tyne, and to the Public Libraries of Birmingham, Bolton, Brighton, Bristol, Cardiff, Dundee, Edinburgh, Gloucester, Leeds, Liverpool, Plymouth, Sheffield, Worcester, and the other public, private, newspaper, church, school, and university libraries that have given me kind assistance I express my thanks.

There are four people in particular to whom I owe a personal debt of gratitude. One of these is the late Newman I. White, of Duke University, who first stimulated my interest in periodicals and who as director of my first serious researches gave me a concept of literary scholarship that extends beyond the footnotes at the bottom of the page. Another is Dr. Sylvia L. England, of London, whom I have met only through the scores of letters we have exchanged, but without whose careful and interested assistance this *Index* would be far more incomplete than it is. And most of all I express my sincere thanks to my wife and my mother for the multitude of ways in which they have given their help. By their encouragement and by their assistance in checking and rechecking the thousands of dates, volume numbers, and library symbols contained in these pages they have made my labors much lighter.

W. S. W.

PROCEDURES, ABBREVIATIONS, AND SYMBOLS

1. The following *ULS* definition of a serial has been adopted: "A publication issued in successive parts, usually at regular intervals, and, as a rule, intended to be continued indefinitely."

2. A serial not published by a society or other institution or agency is entered under the first word, not an article, of the title.

3. A serial published by a society, etc., but having a distinctive title, is entered under the title without reference to the name of the society.

4. The transactions, minutes, reports, proceedings, journals, abstracts, etc., of a society or other institution are entered under the first word, not an article, of the name of the society.

5. Title, place of publication, volume and/or number, initial and final dates, and frequency of publication are given in that order in so far as they are known with reasonable certainty.

6. In cases where there are title changes, the title chosen for the main entry is the one by which the serial was known in 1789 or at the time of its inception if this comes later than 1789. Each changed title is given in alphabetical order, with cross reference to the proper main entry.

7. The inception title and any changes of title prior to 1789 or after 1832 are given in summary form.

8. In general, all title changes have been recorded when they are known. When the change is restricted to minor alterations in the subtitle only, however, this fact is indicated as follows: "subtitle varies slightly." And in a few cases part of a title is placed within parentheses to suggest that the word or words so enclosed were used during only a portion of the serial's history.

9. Libraries reported in *ULS* and *UCP* are repeated only if by doing so an error can be corrected or important fuller information be given.

10. Libraries in the United States and Canada which have holdings follow an italicized lower-case *a*. When the serial in question is listed in the *Union List of Serials* or its *Supplement,* this fact is indicated by writing *ULS* or *ULSup* before listing individual libraries.

11. Libraries in the United Kingdom and Eire which have holdings follow an italicized lower-case *b*. When the serial in question is listed in the *Union Catalogue of Periodical Publications in the University Libraries of the British Isles,* this fact is indicated by writing *UCP* before listing individual libraries.

12. In so far as libraries co-operating with this list duplicate those co-operating with

the forthcoming *British Union Catalogue of Periodicals*, the symbols used in that volume have been adopted.

13. *a.* In indicating the completeness of files for most serials (all except newspapers), the procedure is relatively simple:

(1) If a library symbol stands alone, the file may be assumed to be complete.

(2) Imperfect files are explained individually.

b. In indicating the completeness of newspaper files (in which the frequency of issue makes detailed listings impossible) a fourfold scheme of classification is used:

(1) If a library symbol stands alone, or if it is followed by a date, the file for the period in question may be assumed to be complete or to lack no more than one or two issues.

(2) If a library symbol is followed by a date enclosed within parentheses, it may be assumed that the file is incomplete but that it lacks no more than one-third of the total number of issues for the period indicated.

(3) If a library symbol is followed by a date enclosed within brackets, it may be assumed that the file lacks more than one-third but not more than two-thirds of the total number of issues for the period indicated.

(4) Files with fewer than one-third of the total number of issues are handled as individual cases. If, for example, good or complete runs are rather easily accessible, widely scattered numbers are ignored altogether. If, on the other hand, good sets are rare or nonexistent, broken files are given, but with some such notation as "sc. nos." (scattered numbers) or else some actual listing of the individual numbers themselves.

14. If an initial or final date is unknown, the fact is indicated by means of a question mark within brackets: thus [?]-1806-1818-[?]. When a terminal date is entered but there is reason to consider it doubtfully correct, the fact is indicated by means of a slanting line followed by a question mark: thus 1816-1821/?.

15. If an initial or final date is unknown but can be conjectured with reasonable certainty, the date so assigned is placed within brackets: thus [1797]· 1824.

16. Abbreviations and Symbols:

a.	published annually	f.	published fortnightly
		f.c.	film copy
a:	libraries in the U.S.A. and/or Canada to follow	impf.	imperfect (employed when the extent of imperfection is not known)
b:	libraries of the United Kingdom and/or Eire to follow	inc.	incomplete
		ir.	published at irregular intervals
C & K	*A Census of British Newspapers and Periodicals*, 1620-1800, by R.S. Crane & F.B. Kaye	m.	published monthly
		no.	number
ca.	approximately	n.p.	no place of publication, or place of publication unknown
CBEL	*Cambridge Bibliography of English Literature*	ns	new series
		os	old series
d.	published daily	pt	part
-date	denotes that the serial is still being published	q.	published quarterly
		s	series

s.a.	published semiannually
s.m.	published semimonthly
S N & Q	*Scottish Notes and Queries*
s.w.	published semiweekly
sc.nos.	scattered numbers only
t.w.	published triweekly
UCP	*Union Catalogue of Periodical Publications in the University Libraries of the British Isles*
ULS	*Union List of Serials*
ULSup	*Supplement to Union List of Serials*
v	volume
w	published weekly
+	used in the sense of "and following": thus no.1+
/?	a doubtful termination date
( )	1. When enclosing a library's holdings signifies an imperfect file which is at least 2/3 complete
	2. In all other cases is used conventionally to enclose explanatory matter
[ ]	1. When enclosing a library's holdings signifies an imperfect set which is between 1/3 and 2/3 complete
	2. In all other cases is used to enclose data which are conjectural
Ja	January
F	February
Mr	March
Ap	April
My	May
Je	June
Jl	July
Ag	August
S	September
O	October
N	November
D	December

INDEX AND FINDING LIST OF

BRITISH SERIALS, 1789-1832

ABERDEEN ALMANACK. Aberdeen. 1772-date.
*b:*UCP.

ABERDEEN AUXILIARY SOCIETY for Improving the System of Church Patronage in Scotland. Proceedings. Aberdeen. 1826-36.
a: UCP.

ABERDEEN CENSOR. Aberdeen. Mr 3, 1825-Ja 19, 1827. f.;m.
a: ULS. / *b:* E vl; GM; L no1-19; O vl.

ABERDEEN CHRONICLE. Aberdeen. O 9, 1806-Ag 25, 1832. w. (See S N & Q, sl. I.5, for details.)
a: CSmH Ap 10, 1819. / *b:* AAJ 1806-30; LLL Ap 3, 1819.

ABERDEEN HERALD, and General Advertiser for the Counties of Aberdeen, Banff, and Kincardine. Aberdeen. 1832-76.
b: AU.
(United 1876, with *Weekly Free Press* and continued as *The Herald and Weekly Press.*)

ABERDEEN INDEPENDENT; or Literary, Political, and Commercial Repository. Aberdeen. no1-12, Ag 1830-Jl 1831. m.
b: E no1-2, 9-12.
Continued as
ABERDEEN NEW INDEPENDENT. Aberdeen. no1-3, O-D 1831. m.
b: E.

ABERDEEN INFIRMARY. Reports. Aberdeen. 1829-37.
b: UCP.
(Continued as *Aberdeen Royal Infirmary,* &c., 1838-date.)

ABERDEEN INFIRMARY AND LUNATIC HOSPITAL. Reports. Aberdeen. 1814-19.
b: UCP.

ABERDEEN JOURNAL. Aberdeen. 1748-1876. (Succeeds *Aberdeen's Journal,* 1747-48.)
a: ULS; CSmH Mr 2, 1831; DLC widely sc. nos. 1806 and 1809. / *b:* AAJ (1789-1832); AU.
(Continued as *Aberdeen Weekly Journal,* 1876-1941; as *Weekly Journal,* 1941-date.)

ABERDEEN LANCET. Aberdeen. no1-3, 1831. ir.
a: ULS. / *b:* UCP.

ABERDEEN LUNATIC ASYLUM. Medical Report. Aberdeen. 1831-35.
a: UCP.
(Continued as *Aberdeen Royal Lunatic*

Asylum (afterwards *Mental Hospital) Report,* 1836-date.)

ABERDEEN MAGAZINE. Aberdeen. vl-2, 1831-32.
b: UCP; EP vl; L.

ABERDEEN MAGAZINE; or Universal Repository. Aberdeen. vl-3, 1796-98. m.
a: ULS. / *b:* UCP; E; L vl, 3.

ABERDEEN MAGAZINE, A Literary Chronicle and Review. Aberdeen. vl-4, Ja 17, 1788-D 1791-[?]. (Succeeds *Northern Gazette, Literary Chronicle and Review,* 1787.)
a: ULSup. / *b:* UCP; L vl-3.

ABERDEEN NEW INDEPENDENT.
(See *Aberdeen Independent; or Literary, Political and Commercial Repository.)*

ABERDEEN OBSERVER. A Commercial and Political Journal. Aberdeen. vl, no1-v3,no143, Mr 1829-D 1831. w.
a: CSmH Ja 7, 1830. / *b:* AAJ; E(1829-31).

ABERDEEN STAR. Aberdeen. [?] 1827-[?].
b: AU ns, vl, no1-18.

ABOLITIONIST. Edinburgh. 1832-34.
b: UCP.

Abstracts of . . .
See (1) *Ashmolean Society;* (2) *Royal Society of London;* (3) *Society for the Propagation of the Gospel;* (4) *Treasury Office, London.*

ACADEMIC: A Periodical Publication, comprising Original Essays, Reviews, Poems,&c. Liverpool. no1-22, 1821.
b: L; LvP.

ACADEMIC. Conducted by the Students in the University of Glasgow. Glasgow. vl, Ja 5-Ap 27, 1826.
b: E Ja 5-Mr 30; GM; L; LUC; O.
Continued as
THE COLLEGIAN. Conducted by Students in the University of Glasgow. Glasgow. D 13, 1826-Mr 7, 1827.
b: L.
Continued as
THE COLLEGE ALBUM, a Selection of Original Pieces edited by the Students in the University of Glasgow. 1828-1834.
b: L.
(Continued as *Glasgow University Album,* 1836-59; as *Old College,* 1869; as *New College,* 1874; as *Glasgow University Album,* 1874.)

THE ACADEMIC CHRONICLE. London. no1-2, My 14-21, 1831. w.
a: CSmH no1. / *b:* L no1; O no2.

2

THE ACADEMIC CORRESPONDENT AND MAGAZINE OF EDUCATION. London, v1, 1832.
b: L.

THE ACADEMIC REVIEW, and General Literary Magazine. London. v1, no1, S 1, 1827/?.
a: ULSup.

ACADIAN MAGAZINE. Halifax. Jl 1826-Je 1827.
a: ULS.

AN ACCOUNT of the Different Gooseberry Shews, held in Lancashire, Cheshire, and Other Parts of the Kingdom. Manchester. 1824-26.
b: L.

AN ACCOUNT of the Times and Places of Holding the Meetings for Worship, and the Quarterly and Monthly Meetings of the Society of Friends in Great Britain. (See *Society of Friends in Great Britain*).

ACKERMANN'S JUVENILE FORGET-ME-NOT. London. 1830-32.
a: PP 1832. / *b:* UCP; L; O.
(In 1833 incorporated with *Juvenile Forget-me-not.*)

ACKERMANN'S POETICAL MAGAZINE: Dedicated to the Lovers of the Muse.
(See *Poetical Magazine; dedicated to the Lovers of the Muse.*)

ACKERMANN'S REPOSITORY of Arts, Literature, Manufactures, Fashions, and Politics.
(See Repository of *Arts, Literature, Manufactures, &c.*)

ACKERMANN'S REPOSITORY of Fashions. London. no1-9, 1829.
b: UCP.

ACTING MANAGER, or the Minor Spy. London. no1-4, My 14-Je 18, 1831/?.
a: ULSup.

THE ACTOR. London. no1-15, 1789.
b: O no1,15.

ACTS OF PARLIAMENT OF SCOTLAND. Edinburgh. v1-11, 1814-44.
b: UCP.

ADAMS'S WEEKLY COURANT. Chester. 1730-1793.
b: ChsCCo; L Jl 17, 1792.
Continued as
CHESTER COURANT and Anglo-Welsh Gazette. Chester. 1793-1831.
a: CSmH Ag 9, 1825; CtY 13 sc.nos. 1795-98. / *b:* BnU Ja-Je, 1806; ChsCCo; L.
Continued as
CHESTER COURANT and Advertiser for North Wales. Chester. 1831-date. (Subtitle varies.)
b: ChsCCo; L.

YR ADDYSGYDD. Caerfyrddin. 1823.
b: UCP; CrP.

ADVENTURER AND BONNE BOUCHE: or Olio of History, Anecdote, Wit, Literature, and the Arts. London. no1-17, O 8, 1823-Ja 28, 1824. (Title varies slightly. Formed by uniting (1) *Adventurer of the Nineteenth Century* and (2) *Bonne Bouche.*)
a: ULS.

ADVENTURER OF THE NINETEENTH CENTURY. London. no1-40, Ap 12, 1823-Ja 10, 1824. w. (United with *Bonne Bouche* to form *Adventurer and Bonne Bouche.*
a: ULS. / *b:* L no1-30; O 1823.

ADVERTISER. London. no[1]-34, 1825. w.
b: L no23-34, Jl-O, 1825.
Continued as
GENERAL ADVERTISER. no35-52, O 1825-F 5, 1826. w.
b: L.
Continued as
POST OFFICE REGISTER. London. no53-64, F 12-Ap 30, 1826. w.
b: L.

ADVERTISER'S DAILY MAGAZINE. London. [no1, Ja 29, 1805]-no9, F 8, 1805-[?]. d.
(No issues known. See *CBEL*, III.798)

THE ADVISER. London. v1, 1803.
b: L; O.
Continued as
THE ADVISER; or the Moral and Literary Tribunal. London. v2-4, 1803.
b: L; O.

THE ADVISER: a New Periodical Paper. Edinburgh. no1-16, F 11-My 27, 1797. w.
a: ULS. / *b:* DL no1-7.

THE ADVISER; or Essays to do Good. Boston. no1-32, 1812-13. w.
b: L lacking no 30.

THE ADVISER: or the Moral and Literary Tribunal.
(See *The Adviser.*)

THE ADVOCATE. London. no1-6, 1826.
b: L.

ADVOCATE OF REVEALED TRUTH. London. v1-2, no1-12, Ja-D, 1804. m.
b: UCP.

THE ÆCONOMIST; or, Englishman's Magazine.
(See *The Œconomist; or, Englishman's Magazine.*)

ÆGIS; or, Independent Weekly Expositor. London. no1-12, Jl 13-S 18, 1818. w. (See also *The Blanketeer, and People's Guardian*, which this apparently precedes.)
b: L.

AFFAIRES DU TEMPS. London. no1-23, 1786-89.
a: ULS.

AFFECTION'S GIFT. London. 1830-1844.
(No issues known. See *CBEL*, III.840.)

AFFECTION'S OFFERING: designed as a Christmas and New Year's Gift. London. vl-2, 1830-31.
b: UCP.

AFRICAN ASSOCIATION PROCEEDINGS. London. 1790.
(No issues known. See C & K, 1013.)

AFRICAN INSTITUTION. Reports. London. vl-27, 1807-27.
a: ULS.   /   *b:* UCP;LFS.

AFRICAN RESEARCHES; or, Proceedings of the Association.
(See *Association for Promoting the Discovery of the Interior Parts of Africa. Proceedings.*)

AGE. London. no1-13, 1819. w.
b: L; O.

AGE. London. 1825-1843. w.
a: ULS; CSmH My 29, 1825; CtY 1825-31; N N 9, 1828-Ap 26, 1829. / *b:* L; O no1; TmP Ja 14, 1827.
(Absorbed *The Argus* and continued as *Age and Argus,* 1843-45; as *English Gentleman,* 1845-46.)

AGE OF CIVILIZATION. London. vl, no1-4, 1818.
b: LUC no4.

AGRICULTURAL MAGAZINE (or, *Farmer's Monthly Journal*).
(See *Commercial and Agricultural Magazine.*)

AIKIN'S ANNUAL REVIEW: and History of Literature.
(See *Annual Review and History of Literature.*)

AIR ADVERTISER, or West Country Journal. Air. no1+, Ag 5, 1803-date. w. (Subtitle varies.)
a: CSmH Mr 13, 1828; NN Je 11, 1812. / *b:* AyAA lacking Ag 5-N 24, 1803; AyP (1814-24, 1831-32); DsD My 1827-D 1830.
(Spelling changed to *Ayr* Mr 28, 1839.)

THE AIRDRIE LITERARY ALBUM; or, Weekly Repository of Original and Select Literature. Airdrie. no1-24, 1829. w.
b: E; GM.

THE ALBION. Liverpool. no1+, 1825-1871. w.
a: CSmH Mr 8, 1830; CtY Ja 30, 1832. / *b:* L no59+, Ja 1 1827-32; LvP Jl-D 1832.
(Continued as *Liverpool Weekly Albion,* 1871-87.)

ALBION. London. no1+, N 15, 1830-O 15, 1831. d.
a: DLC [Ap 29-O 15, 1831]. / *b:* L.
Combined with *The Star* and continued as
ALBION AND STAR. London. O 17, 1831-1835. d.
a: DLC [O 17-D 27, 1831]. / *b:* C Mr 19, 1832; L.

ALBION. A New Weekly Paper. London. [?]-1799-1809/?. w. (Subtitle varies: *e.g., Albion and Evening Advertiser.*)
a: CSmH F 19, 1809; NNHi Ap 30, 1800; 46 sc.nos. Ag 23, 1807-Ag 14, 1808. / *b:* UCP; L Ja 9, 1800.

ALBION: or, Tyne and Wear Monthly Advertiser and Literary Record. South Shields. [?]-1831-[?]. m.
b: TmP O 12, 1831.

ALBION AND EVENING ADVERTISER.
(See *The Albion. A New Weekly Paper.*)

ALBION AND STAR.
(See *Albion.*)

THE ALBUM, a Periodical Magazine. London. vl-4, 1822-25. q.
a: ULS. / *b:* UCP; BP; L; LVA.

ALEXANDER'S EAST INDIA MAGAZINE, and Colonial and Commercial Journal. London. vl-23, 1831-42. (Also known as *East India Magazine; and Colonial and Commercial Journal.*)
b: UCP; E; L; LLL.

ALFRED, 1810-11.
(See *Alfred and Westminster Gazette.*)

ALFRED, 1830-31.
(See *Intelligence*)

ALFRED AND WESTMINSTER GAZETTE. London. no1+, Ap 17, 1810-1811-[1833]. d. (Second part of title soon dropped.)
b: BP no34, My 26, 1810; L no22-195, 213-533, My 12-N 30, 1810, D 21, 1810-D 31, 1811; LLL Ap 24-D 28, 1810.

ALFRED LONDON WEEKLY JOURNAL.
(See *Bridgwater and Somersetshire Herald.*)

ALFRED, West of England Journal, and General Advertiser. Exeter. no1-846, Je 6, 1815-Ag 23, 1831. w.
a: CSmH D 16, 1828. / *b:* ExD 1820-32; ExP (1815-30); L; LLL Je 23, 30, Jl 7, 1818.
Continued as
EXETER INDEPENDENT. Exeter. S 6-N 1, 1831. w.
b: L.
(Incorporated with *Western Luminary,* 1831.)

ALLEN'S SPIRITUAL MAGAZINE.
(See *The Spiritual Magazine, or the Christian's Grand Treasure.*)

ALMACK'S. Brighton. no1-9, D 5, 1827-Ja 30, 1828. w.
b: BiP no 1, 6-9.

AN ALMANACK FOR THE USE OF FRIENDS. London. 1795-1807.
b: LFS 1795-99, 1804, 1806-7.

AN ALMANACK FOR THE YEAR OF OUR LORD GOD 1815. London. 1815.
b: LGU.

ALMANACK: Yorkshire, Durham, Northumberland, Westmorland, and Cumberland. London. 1809-1823.
   b: LdP.

AN ALPHABETICAL LIST of the Officers of his Majesty's Marine Forces. London. 1748-1846. (Title varies slightly.)
   b: L 1796, 1820-24, 1826-27.

ALSTON MISCELLANY; or Gentleman's Magazine. Alston. v1-2, 1799-1801. m.
   b: UCP; L lacking no3-4 of v1 and no2, 4-5 of v2.

ALTER ET IDEM, a New Review. For a summer Month in 1794. Reading. no1, 1794.
   a: DLC. / *b:* UCP; L; O; RP.

THE AMARANTH. London. no1-2, 1832.
   b: L.

THE AMATEUR. Perth. no1, N 1828. m.
   b: PeP.

L'AMBIGU: ou, Variétés littéraires et politiques. London. v1-58, 1803-18.
   a: ULS. / *b:* UCP; L; MR; O v1-40, 48-50.

THE AMBULATOR: or the Stranger's Companion in a Tour round London. London. v1-12, 1774-1820.
   b: LGU lacking v6.

THE AMERICAN MONITOR, a Monthly Political, Historical, and Commercial Magazine, particularly devoted to the Affairs of South America. London. v1-2, 1824-25. m.
   a: ULS. / *b:* L; LLL.

AMERICAN RUSH LIGHT. London. no1-4, F 15-Mr 31, 1800/?. f.
   a: ULS.

THE AMETHYST, or Christian's Annual. Edinburgh. v1-3, 1832-34. a.
   b: UCP; L.

THE AMULET. A Christian and Literary Remembrancer. London. v1-11, 1826-36. a. (Subtitle varies.)
   a: ULS; ULSup. / *b:* UCP; L.

ANALECTA. Original Reviews of New Works of Taste and Imagination. Rotherham. no1-5, 1822-23. (Subtitle varies.)
   b: L; LdP no5; RtP no1-4.

ANALYTICAL DIGEST of all the Cases decided and reported in the House of Lords. London. 1831-37.
   b: UCP.

AN ANALYTICAL DIGEST of the Reports of Cases decided in the Courts of Common Law and Equity, of Appeal, &c. London. 1818-55.
   b: L lacking 1818-23.

ANALYTICAL REVIEW: or, History of Literature, Domestic and Foreign. London. v1-28, 1788-98; ns, v1, Ja-Je 1799. m.

   a: ULS. / *b:* UCP; BO; BrP v1-28; L; LdL, v1-26; MoM; NwL v18-28-ns, v1; WcP.

THE ANALYTICAL SOCIETY. Memoirs. Cambridge. v1, 1813.
   a: ULS. / *b:* UCP; LP.

ANCELL'S MONTHLY MILITARY COMPANION.
   (See *Monthly Military Companion.*)

ANDERSON'S QUARTERLY JOURNAL of Medicine and Surgery.
   (See *Quarterly Journal of Foreign (and British) Medicine and Surgery.*)

ANDERSON'S QUARTERLY JOURNAL of the Medical Sciences.
   (See *Quarterly Journal of Foreign (and British) Medicine and Surgery.*)

ANDREWS'S CONSTITUTIONAL PRECEPTOR. v1, no1-8, 1832.
   b: L.

ANDREWS' PENNY ORTHODOX JOURNAL.
   (See *Weekly Orthodox Journal of Entertaining Christian Knowledge.*)

ANGLO-GENEVAN CRITICAL JOURNAL. London. v1-2, 1831.
   b: UCP.

ANGUS AND MEARNS REGISTER. Montrose. 1808-16. (Also called *Smith's Angus and Mearns Register.* For fuller details see S N & Q, sl.III. 7.)
   b: AU 1816.

ANGUS INTELLIGENCER. Dundee. 1799. (May have been one of the early numbers of the *Dundee Advertiser.*)
   (No issues known. For details see S N and Q, sl.III.99.)

ANGUS-SHIRE REGISTER. Dundee. 1799-1802.
   (No issues known. See S N & Q, sl.III.100 and III.117.)

ANNALES POLITIQUES, Civiles et Littéraires du 18e siècle. Paris, London. v1-19, 1777-1792.
   a: ULS. / *b:* MR.

ANNALS OF AGRICULTURE and Other Useful Arts. London. v1-46, 1784-1815. q.
   a: ULS; ULSup. / *b:* UCP; BP v1-45; DRS v1-43; IpP v1-36, 38-44; L; LLL v1-45; LP; WiP v1-45.

ANNALS OF BOTANY. London. v1-2, My 1804-S 1806. a.
   a: ULS; ULSup. / *b:* UCP; L; LLL; LR; NwL.

ANNALS OF CHEMICAL PHILOSOPHY. no1-3, 1828-29.
   b: L.

ANNALS OF HEALTH AND LONG LIFE. London. v1, 1818/?.
   a: ULS.

ANNALS OF MEDICINE.
(See *Medical Commentaries.*)

ANNALS OF MEDICINE; new Medical and Physical Journal. London. v1-10, [?]-1815.
b: UCP; O v9-10.

ANNALS OF MEDICINE AND SURGERY, or Records of the Occurring Improvements, &c. London. v1-2, Mr 1816-D 1817.
a: ULS. / *b:* UCP; LCP v1; LS.

ANNALS OF ORIENTAL LITERATURE. London. v1, no1-3, Je 1820-F 1821. q.; then 5 mos.
a: ULS; ULSup. / *b:* UCP; L.

ANNALS OF PHARMACY AND MATERIA MEDICA. Dublin. 1830.
b: UCP.

ANNALS OF PHILOSOPHY; or Magazine of Chemistry, Mineralogy, Mechanics, Natural History, Agriculture and the Arts. London. v1-16, 1813-20; ns, v1-12, 1821-26. m. (Discontinued after 1826 as a separate publication and united with *The Philosophical Magazine.*)
a: ULS; ULSup. / *b:* UCP; BP; CPL v1-12; CrP ns, v1-12; DRS; GeG; L; LP; LR; LdP ns, v1-12.

ANNALS OF PHILOSOPHY, Natural History, Chemistry, Literature, Agriculture, and the Mechanical and Fine Arts. London. v1-3, 1801-04. a.
a: ULS. / *b:* UCP; GeG v1; L v1-2; LR; NwL.

ANNALS OF SPORTING, and Fancy Gazette; a Magazine entirely appropriated to Sporting Subjects and Fancy Pursuits. London. v1-13, 1822-28.
a: ULS; ULSup. / *b:* UCP; BP v10; L.

ANNALS OF THE FINE ARTS. London. v1-5, 1816-20.
a: ULS. / *b:* UCP; HdP; L; LVA; LdL.

THE ANNIVERSARY: or, Poetry and Prose for 1829. London. 1829. a.
b: UCP; BrP; L.

ANNUAL ABSTRACT OF NEW ACTS AND LAW CASES, being Public General Statutes ..., and an Alphabetical Digest of Law Cases from the Commencement of Michaelmas Term. London. 1828.
b: L.

ANNUAL ANTHOLOGY. Bristol, London. v1-2, 1799-1800. a.
a: ULS. / *b:* UCP.

ANNUAL BIOGRAPHY AND OBITUARY. London, v1-21, 1817-37. a.
a: ULS; ULSup. / *b:* UCP; EP; L; LLL; LLN: LP; LdL; LdP; O; SP.

ANNUAL CABINET of Modern Foreign Voyages and Travels.
(See *Cabinet of Foreign Voyages and Travels.*)

ANNUAL CHRONOLOGY and Historical Record of Important and Interesting Events in 1827. London. 1828.
b: L.

ANNUAL HAMPSHIRE REPOSITORY; or, Historical, Economical, and Literary Miscellany; a Provincial Work, of entirely original Materials, &c. Winchester. v1-2, 1798-1801. a. (Vol. 2 is called *The Hampshire Repository.*)
b: UCP; L; O; PmP; SoP; WnP.

ANNUAL HISTORIAN. A Sketch of the Chief Historical Events of the World for the Year. London. 1831-33. a.
b: UCP; L 1831.

ANNUAL MEDICAL REGISTER. London. v1, 1808. a.
a: ULS. / *b:* UCP; LMD.
Continued as
ANNUAL MEDICAL REVIEW and Register. London. v2, 1809. a.
a: ULS. / *b:* UCP; LMD.

ANNUAL MEDICAL REVIEW AND REGISTER.
(See *Annual Medical Register.*)

ANNUAL MISCELLANY; or, Rational Repository. London. 1812. a.
b: UCP; E; PsP.

ANNUAL MONITOR; or, New Letter-Case and Memorandum Book. York. v1-30, 1813-41. a.
a: ULS; ULSup. / *b:* UCP; CrP v7, 10-15,17, 20-21; GrP 1813-15; 1819; L; LFS; LLL; LdP 1813-32; O.
(Continued as *Annual Monitor; or Obituary of the Society of Friends,* 1842-1920.)

ANNUAL NECROLOGY FOR 1797-98; including also Various Articles of Neglected Biography. London. v1, 1800. a.
b: L; LGU; LdL.

ANNUAL PASTORAL ADDRESS of the General Synod of Ulster.
(See *Pastoral Address from the Ministers of the Synod of Ulster.*)

ANNUAL PEERAGE OF THE BRITISH EMPIRE . . . . The Annual Peerage . . . to which is added the Baronetage, and the Arms of the Peers. London. v1-4, 1827-29. a.
b: L.

ANNUAL RACING CALENDAR. York. v1-23, [?]-1809. a.
b: L v23.

ANNUAL REGISTER; or, a View of the History, Politicks, and Literature for the Year.... London. v1+, 1758-date.
a: ULS; ULSup. / *b:* UCP; BbP; BkP; BmP; BrP; BurC lacking v37, 71; BwP; CrP; CsP 1789-1801, 1825-32; GeG 1789-90, 1798-1807; HfP; HsP; IpP; L; LGI; LGU; LIT; LLL; LLW; LP; LcP; LdP; LvP; MCh 1808-17; MR; MoM; MsP 1789-

1823; NpP; O; PrH; PsP 1789-1809; SP; SnP lacking 1813, 1816; SptP 1789-1827; SwP; WhP; WiP; WmP.

ANNUAL REPORTS.
    See also *Extracts, Minutes, Proceedings, Reports, Transactions,* etc.; and in general see the society, institution, or other group making the report. In UCP, however, entries are commonly under "Annual Report."
    See especially (1) *Auxiliary Bible Society, Leeds;* (2) *Baptist Missionary Society;* (3) *Canterbury Philosophical and Literary Institution;* (4) *Deaf and Dumb Institution;* (5) *Edinburgh Bible Society;* (6) *Edinburgh Institution for the Education of the Deaf and Dumb;* (7) *General Baptist Missionary Society;* (8) *Hull Literary and Philosophical Society;* (9) *Imperial Brazilian Mining Association;* (10) *Leeds Church Missionary Association;* (11) *Leeds Guardian Society;* (12) *Leeds Ladies Auxiliary Society in Aid of the London Society for Promoting Christianity among the Jews;* (13) *London Female Penitentiary;* (14) *London Infirmary for Curing Diseases of the Eye;* (15) *Periodical Accounts relative to the Baptist Missionary Society;* (16) *Royal Institution of Cornwall;* (17) *Royal Zoological Society of Ireland;* (18) *Scarborough Philosophical (and Archaelogical) Society;* (19) *Trinitarian Bible Society;* (20) *United Society for Christian Literature;* (21) *Whitby Literary and Philosophical Society;* (22) *York Retreat;* (23) *Yorkshire Institution for the Education of Deaf and Dumb Children;* (24) *Yorkshire Philosophical Society.*

ANNUAL RETROSPECT OF PUBLIC AFFAIRS. London. v1-2, 1831. a.
    b: LLL.

ANNUAL REVIEW; and History of Literature. London. v1-7. 1802-1808. a. (Also called *Aikin's Annual Review,* &c.)
    a: ULS; ULSup; KyLx v1-6; KyU. / *b:* UCP; BrP; GeG v1-3; L; LGU; LLL; LvP, v5; NwL; O.

ANOMALIAE. Being Desultory Essays on Miscellaneous Subjects. Whitby. no1-34, O 24, 1797-Je 12, 1798. w.
    b: L; LdP.

THE ANONYMOUS. Dublin. v1-2, D 23, 1806-S 10, 1808.
    a: ULSup. / *b:* DA; L; O.

THE ANT. A Periodical Paper. Glasgow. v1-2, no1-26, D 2, 1826-S 29, 1827.
    a: ULS. / *b:* UCP; E; EP; L.

ANTHOLOGIA HIBERNICA; or, Monthly Collections of Science, Belles Lettres, and History. Dublin. v1-4, 1793-94. m.
    a: ULS; ULSup. / *b:* UCP; EP; L; LLL.

THE ANTHOLOGY; an Annual Reward Book for Midsummer and Christmas. London. 1830.
    (No issues known. See CBEL, III.840.)

ANTI-COBBETT; or the Weekly Patriotic Register. (Extracted from the *Day and New Times.* London. v1, no1-8, F 15-Ap 5, 1817. w.
    b: BP no1-4; L; O no1, 8.

ANTI-GALLICAN; or, Standard of British Loyalty, Religion, and Liberty, including a Collection of the Principal Papers, Tracts, Speeches, and Songs, that have been Published on the Threatened Invasion; together with many Original Pieces on the Same Subject. London. no1-12, 1804.
    a: ULS. / *b:* CrP; L; LLL; O.

ANTI-GALLICAN MONITOR. London. no1-22, 1811. w.
    a: IHi. / *b:* UCP; L; MR.
    Continued as
ANTI-GALLICAN MONITOR and Anti-Corsican Chronicle. London. no23-362, 1811-18. w.
    a: ULS; DLC Ja 2, 1814-Ja 8, 1815, Ja 7-D 29, 1816; IHi lacks 9 nos.; MnU lacking 2 nos.; NNHi Jy 12, 1812-D 29, 1816; PPL Je 9, 1811-D 7, 1812, Ja 3, 1813-Je 4, 1815. / *b:* UCP; L; LGU; Ja 8, 1815-D 29, 1816; MR 1811-16.
    Continued as
BRITISH MONITOR. London. 1818-25. w.
    a: ULS. / *b:* L.

ANTI-GALLICAN MONITOR AND ANTI-CORSICAN CHRONICLE.
    (See *Anti-Gallican Monitor.*)

ANTI-GALLICAN SONGSTER. London. no1-2, 1793.
    a: ULS. / *b:* L.

ANTI-INFIDEL. London, v1, 1831.
    b: L.

ANTI-JACOBIN; or, Weekly Examiner. London. v1-2, no1-36, N 1797-Jl 1798. w.
    a: ULS; ULSup; NRU lacking no 1. / *b:* UCP; KeP; L; LA; LLL; LLN; NpP; WmP

ANTI-JACOBIN REVIEW AND MAGAZINE; or, Monthly Political and Literary Censor. London. v1-61, 1798-1821. (Subtitle varies.)
    a: ULS; ULSup. / *b:* UCP; BP; BrP v1-48; EP; L; LGU v1-34; LLL v1-42; LdL lacking v52; MCh v1-42; NwL v14-19, 41-45; WcP v3-55.

ANTI-LANCET: or, Physicians and Doctors Reviewed.
    (See *Multum in Parvo; or, Physicians and Doctors Reviewed.*)

ANTI-LEVELLER. London. no1, Jan. 10, 1793.
    (No issues known.)

ANTI-LEVELLING SONGSTER. London. no1-2, 1793.
    a: ULS. / *b:* L.

ANTI-NEMO. [Edinburgh.] no1-3, 1832/?.
    b: L no3.

ANTI-PATRONAGE REPORTER.
(See *Church Patronage Reporter.*)

ANTI-PATRONAGE SOCIETY OF THE CHURCH OF SCOTLAND.
(See *Society for Improving the System of Church Patronage in Scotland.*)

ANTI-SLAVERY MAGAZINE, and Recorder of the Progress of Christianity in the Countries Connected with Slavery. Derby. no1-12, Ja 31-D 31, 1824.
  a: ULS. / *b:* L no1, 10-12.

ANTI-SLAVERY MONTHLY REPORTER. London. v1-3, 1825-31. m.
  a: ULS; ULSup. / *b:* UCP; L; LFS 1827-31; MR 1827-31.
  Continued as
ANTI-SLAVERY REPORTER. London. v4-6, 1831-33. m.
  a: ULS. / *b:* UCP; L; LFS 1832; MR.
  (Continued to date under changing titles: as *British Emancipator*, 1837-40; as *British and Foreign Anti-Slavery Reporter*, 1840-45; as *Anti-Slavery Reporter*, 1846-date.)

ANTI-SLAVERY RECORD. London. 1832.
  b: LU no7, N 1.

ANTI-SLAVERY REPORTER.
(See *Anti-Slavery Monthly Reporter.*)

ANTI-SLAVERY SOCIETY. Negro Slavery.
(See *Society for the Mitigation and Gradual Abolition of Slavery in the British Dominions.*)

ANTI-TIMES. London. no1-4, N 20-D 11, 1819. w.
  a: ULS. / *b:* L; LLL no1.

ANTI-UNION. Dublin. no1-32, D 27, 1798-Mr 9, 1799. t-w.
  a: ULS. / *b:* UCP; BlU; DRS; L; LLL.

ANTI-UNIONIST, a Weekly Magazine. Dublin. no1-17, Ja 31-My 30, 1818. w.
  b: DL; DRS; O no9, 14.

ANTIBIBLION; or, the Papal Tocsin. London. no1-8, 1817. ir.
  b: L; O no1-3.

ANTICIPATION, in Politics, Commerce, and Finance, during the Present Crisis. London. no1-14, Mr 12-Je 11, 1808. w.
  a: ULS. / *b:* L no2, impf.

ANTIDOTE. Dublin. 1822-25. w. (Subtitle varies, as *or Constitutional Sentinel*; as *or Protestant Guardian.*)
  a: CtY Mr 9-Ap 17, Ag 21-O 12, N 23, 1822-Mr 8, 1823. / *b:* L (Ja 24, 1823-Ap 2, 1825).

L'ANTIDOTE. Par un sujet de Sa Majesté Britannique. London. no1, 1804.
  b: L.

ANTIDOTE TO WEST-INDIAN SKETCHES. (African Institution Publications.) London. no1-7, 1816-17/?.
  a: MB no1-2, 6-7; NIC no2, 4-7.

ANTIQUARIAN. London. no1, My 26, 1832.
  b: O.

ANTIQUARIAN AND TOPOGRAPHICAL CABINET. London. v1-10. 1807-11. m.
  b: UCP; L 1807-08.

ANTIQUARY. London. F 1805/?. m.
  (No issues known. See Nichol's *Illustrations of Literary History*, v8, p. 610.)

ANTIQUARY: or, Curious Gleanings from old Newspapers, Broad Sheets, &c. London. no1, ca. 1800.
  b: BP.

ANTIQUARY'S MAGAZINE; or Archaeological Library. London. v1, no1-3, 1807. m.
  b: L; O.

ANTIQUITIES OF IONIA. Society of Dilettanti, &c.
  (See *Society of Dilettanti, London. Antiquities of Ionia.*)

APOLLO MAGAZINE. Consisting of Original Lyric Pieces, Essays, Reviews, and Miscellaneous Articles. London. v1-2, no1-7, My-D 1823/?. m.
  a: ULS.

APOLLO'S GIFT: or the Musical Souvenir. London. 1830.
  b: UCP.

ABORICULTURAL SOCIETY OF IRELAND. Transactions. Dublin. v1, 1831.
  b: UCP.

ARBROATH MAGAZINE; or Repository of Literature. Arbroath. no1+, O 1799-O 1800. m.
  b: ArP impf. (See also Craig, *Scottish Periodical Press*, p. 96, and S N & Q, sl.II. 66.)

THE ARCADIAN. London. no1, Mr 1, 1820. m.
  a: MB.

ARCANA; or the Museum of Natural History. London. v1, pt1-21, 1810-11.
  a: ULS.

ARCANA OF SCIENCE and Annual Register of the Useful Arts.
  (See *Arcana of Science and Art; or, one thousand Popular Inventions.*)

ARCANA OF SCIENCE AND ART; or, one thousand Popular Inventions and Improvements, abridged from the Transactions of Public Societies and from Scientific Journals. London. v1-1], 1828-31.
  a: ULS; ULSup. / *b:* UCP; BP; GeG; L.
  Continued as
ARCANA OF SCIENCE and Annual Register of the Useful Arts. London. 1832-38.
  a: ULS. / *b:* UCP; BP; GeG; L.

ARCHAEOLOGIA; or, Miscellaneous Tracts relating to Antiquity. (Society of Antiquaries of Newcastle-upon-Tyne.) London. v1+, 1770-date.
    a: ULS; ULSup. / *b:* UCP; BP; ChlP lacking v11; DRS; GrP; IpP; LA; LGU; LR; LVA; LdP; LvP; NwS; PrH; SP; WiP; WmP.

ARCHAEOLOGIA AELIANA: or, Miscellaneous Tracts relating to Antiquity. (Society of Antiquaries of Newcastle-upon-Tyne.) Newcastle-upon-Tyne. v1+, 1822-date.
    a: ULS listed, but no issues for 1789-1832. / *b:* LGU; LR; LVA; LdP; LvP; NwS.

ARCHAEOLOGIA SCOTICA: or Transactions of the Society of Antiquaries of Scotland. Edinburgh. 1792-1890. (Merged into the Society's *Proceedings.*)
    a: ULS; ULSup. / *b:* UCP; C; EP; GeG 1792; LA; LVA; MCh; NwS.

ARCHAEOLOGICAL LIBRARY. London. v1, no1-3, 1807. m.
    b: O.

ARCHAICA. London. no1, Mr 1814/?.
    (No issues known. See Nichol's *Illustrations of Literary History*, v8, p. 610.)

ARCHIVES OF PHILOSOPHICAL KNOWLEDGE. London. v1, 1805.
    b: UCP.

ARCHIVES OF UNIVERSAL SCIENCE. Edinburgh. v1-3, 1809. q.
    a: ULS. / *b:* UCP; L; LP; LU no1-9.

THE ARGO. London. no1-6, N 25, 1822-F 20, 1823.
    a: ULS. / *b:* L.

THE ARGUS. London. [no1, Mr 7, 1789]-no 840, N 1791-[?].
    a: DLC Jl 2, N 22, 23, 1791; ICU Ap 2, 1789; MdBJ S 26, 1791. / *b:* L sc.nos. Ap 11, 1789-N 15, 1791.
    Continued as
ARGUS OF THE CONSTITUTION. [?]-no 930-946-[?], F 28-Mr 17, 1792-[?].
    b: BiP S 21, 1792; L no930-46, F 28-Mr 17, 1792.

THE ARGUS. Dublin. [?]-1827-[?]. w.
    a: CSmH no70, My 12, 1827.

THE ARGUS. London. no1-24, Je 30-Jy 26, 1828.
    a: CSmH no1. / *b:* L; O no1.
    (Incorporated in *Globe and Traveller.*)

THE ARGUS. London. no1, O 6, 1832.
    b: BP; O.

THE ARGUS; or, General Observer: a Political Miscellany, containing the most Important Events of Europe, and the Principal Occurrences in England, from the Meeting of Parliament, October 29, 1795, to its Dissolution, May 18, 1796. London. 1795-96.
    (Running title: *Register of Occurrences and Miscellany.*)

a: ULS. / *b:* UCP; L 1796, pp. iv-648.

THE ARGUS; or, Record of Politics, Literature and the Arts and Sciences. v1, no1-8, F 5-My 21, 1831. f.
    a: ULS. / *b:* L; SoP.

ARGUS; or the Theatrical Observer, containing Strictures on the Merits and Demerits of the Principal Performers of the Theatre Royal, Manchester Manchester. no1-7, 1804-05. m.
    a: ULS. / *b:* L.

ARGUS OF THE CONSTITUTION.
    (See *The Argus*, 1789-1791.)

ARGUS POLITIQUE. London. no1-42, 1818-20.
    a: ULS.
    Continued as
REFLEXIONS HISTORIQUES, morales and politiques. no43-50, 1820-21.
    a: ULS.

ARIS'S BIRMINGHAM GAZETTE. Birmingham. 1741-1888. w. (no1 entitled *Birmingham Gazette; or the General Correspondent.*)
    a: CtY 1793, 1803-17, 1819, 1821-24; ICN 19 sc.nos. 1795-1806, [1812, 1818]. / *b:* UCP; BP; L 1824-32.
    (Incorporated with *Birmingham Daily Gazette*, 1888.)

ARLISS'S POCKET MAGAZINE of Classic and Polite Literature.
    (See *Pocket Magazine of Classic and Polite Literature.*)

ARMAGH, IRELAND. Astronomical Observations Made at the Armagh Observatory. London. v1, no1-3, 1829-32.
    a: ULS. / *b:* UCP.

ARMINIAN MAGAZINE, consisting of Extracts and Original Translations on Universal Redemptions. London. v1-20, 1778-1797. m.
    a: ULS; ULSup. / *b:* UCP; BP; CrP; GrP v4, 10, 12-13, 15-17, 19-20; L; LLL; LdP; MR; SP v12-20.
    Continued as
THE METHODIST MAGAZINE, being a Continuation of the Arminian Magazine. v21-44, 1798-1821. m.
    a: ULS; ULSup. / *b:* UCP; BP; BrP 1810, 1812-13; CrP; GrP v21, 24, 26-28, 31, 33-36, 41-44; L; LLL; LdP; LvP v25, 33, 35, 38, 42-43; MR; SP.
    Continued as
THE WESLEYAN METHODIST MAGAZINE. Third Series. v45-47, 1822-44; &c.-date.
    a: ULS; ULSup. / *b:* UCP; BP; BrP 1823-26; CrP; GrP v45-72, 84-95; L; LLL; LdP; LvP v46-47, 50, 53; MR; SP 1832.

ARMY LIST. List of all the Officers of the Army, &c.
    (See *List of all the Officers of the Army and Royal Marines.*)

ARNOLD'S MAGAZINE OF THE FINE ARTS.
    (See *Library of the Fine Arts.*)

ARTISAN: or, Mechanic's Instructor. London. v1-2, no1-34, 1824-25.
   a: ULS. / *b:* UCP; LP; LR.

THE ARTIST; a Collection of Essays, relative to Painting, Poetry, Sculpture, Architecture, the Drama, Discoveries of Science and Various Other Subjects. London. v1-2, 1807-09. w.
   a: ULS; ULSup. / *b:* UCP; L.

THE ARTIST'S REPOSITORY AND DRAWING MAGAZINE, exhibiting the Principles of the Polite Arts in their Various Branches. London. v1-5, 1788-1794. m.
   a: ULS. / *b:* L.

THE ARTIZAN'S LONDON AND PROVINCIAL CHRONICLE.
   (See *The Journeyman and Artizan's London and Provincial Chronicle.*)

THE ARTIZAN'S MISCELLANY, or Journal of Politics and Literature. Edinburgh. v1, no1-10, 1831.
   b: EP.

ASHMOLEAN SOCIETY. Abstract of the Proceedings. Oxford. v1-3, no1-36, 1832-58.
   b: UCP; LP; LR.
      (Continued under slightly changing titles to 1881.)

ASIATIC ANNUAL REGISTER: or a View of the History of Hindustan and of the Politics, Commerce, and Literature of Asia. v1-12, 1799-1811. a.
   a: ULS; ULSup; KyLx v1-4. / *b:* UCP; CrP v4; GeG 1803; L; LLL; LLW 1799-1805.

ASIATIC JOURNAL AND MONTHLY REGISTER for British India and its Dependencies. London. v1-28, 1816-29; ns, v1-40, 1830-43; s3-s4, 1843-75. m. (Subtitle varies slightly.)
   a: ULS. / *b:* UCP; EP; L; LLL; MCh 1819-24, 30-32; WcP 1827-32.

ASIATIC SOCIETY OF BENGAL, CALCUTTA. Asiatick Researches; or, Transactions of the Society Instituted in Bengal for Inquiring into the History and Antiquities, the Arts, Sciences, and Literature of Asia. London. v1-20, 1799-1839. (Subtitle varies.)
   a: ULS; ULSup. / *b:* UCP; GeG v4-12; LdP v6.

ASIATIC SOCIETY OF BENGAL, CALCUTTA. Journal. London. v1-33, 1832-64.
   a: ULS; ULSup.

ASIATICK RESEARCHES; or, Transactions of the Society Instituted in Bengal, &c.
   (See *Asiatick Society of Bengal*, &c.)

ASMODEUS; or, the Devil in London.
   (See *The Devil's Memorandum Book*, &c.)

ASMODEUS IN LONDON.
   (See *The Devil's Memorandum Book*, &c.)

THE ASS; or, Weekly Beast of Burden, carrying all Men, Things, Opinions, and Facts, for the Period of its Existence. London. no1-16, Ap 1-Jl 16, 1826. w.
   a: ULS. / *b:* UCP; L no1-10, 12-13, 15; O.

ASSISTANT OF EDUCATION; Religious and Literary; intended for the Use of Young Persons from ten to sixteen Years of Age. London. v1-10, 1823-28.
   a: ULS. / *b:* UCP; L v10, impf.

THE ASSOCIATE.
   (See *Associate and Co-operative Mirror.*)

ASSOCIATE AND CO-OPERATIVE MIRROR. London. no1-12, 1829. (Formerly *The Associate.*)
   b: UCP.

ASSOCIATED APOTHECARIES and Surgeon-Apothecaries of England and Wales. Transactions. London. v1, 1823.
   a: ULS. / *b:* UCP; LR; LS.

ASSOCIATION FOR OXFORD and its Vicinity in Aid of the Church Missionary Society. Report. Oxford. v1-22, [?]-1832-47.
   b: UCP.

ASSOCIATION FOR PRESERVING LIBERTY and Property against Republicans and Levellers. Association Papers. London. 1793.
   a: ULS.

ASSOCIATION FOR PRESERVING LIBERTY and Property against Republicans and Levellers. Proceedings. London. v1-2, N 1790-Mr 15, 1793.
   a: ULS.

ASSOCIATION FOR PRESERVING LIBERTY and Property against Republicans and Levellers. Publications. London. no1-14, 1792-93/?.
   a: ULS.

ASSOCIATION FOR PRESERVING LIBERTY and Property against Republicans and Levellers. Tracts. London. no1-13, 1792-93/?.
   a: ULS.

ASSOCIATION FOR PROMOTING the Discovery of the Interior Parts of Africa. Proceedings. v1-2, 1788-1809. (v2 called *African Researches; or, Proceedings of the Association.*)
   a: ULS; ULSup. / *b:* UCP; LR.

ASSOCIATION FOR THE IMPROVEMENT OF PRISONS and of Prison Discipline in Ireland. Reports. Dublin. v1-7, 1819-26.
   b: UCP.

ASSOCIATION FOR THE RELIEF of the Manufacturing and Labouring Poor. Report. London. v1-2, 1815-16.
   b: UCP.

ASSOCIATION OF FELLOWS and Licentiates of the King's and Queen's College of Physicians in Ireland. Transactions. Dublin. v1-5, 1817-28.

b: UCP; LCP v1-4; LS.
Continued as
DUBLIN MEDICAL TRANSACTIONS. A Series of Papers by the Members of the Association of Fellows of King's and Queen's College of Physicians in Ireland. Dublin. 1830.
b: UCP; LMD.

ASSOCIATOR. London. 1792.
(No issues known. See C & K, 1032.)

ASTROLOGER OF THE NINETEENTH CENTURY: or, Compendium of Astrology, Geomancy, and Occult Philosophy. London. no1-22, Je 5-O 30, 1824. w. (Separate nos. for Je 5-Ag 14 called *Straggling Astrologer;* for Ag 21-O 30, *Straggling Astrologer of the Nineteenth Century.*)
a: ULS. / *b:* L; MR.

ASTROLOGER'S MAGAZINE: and Philosophical Miscellany, &c.
(See *Conjuror's Magazine,* &c.)

ASTRONOMICAL OBSERVATIONS MADE AT . . .
(In general, see details under the name of the observatory. But see especially (1) Armagh, (2) Cambridge; (3) Greenwich.)

ASTRONOMICAL SOCIETY OF LONDON. Memoirs.
(See *Royal Astronomical Society of London.*

ASYLUM, or Weekly Mscellany.
(See *Weekly Miscellany of Instruction and Entertainment.*)

ATHENAEUM; a Journal of Literature, Science, the Fine Arts, Music and the Drama. v1-153, 1828-1921. w. (Subtitle varies.)
a: ULS; ULSup. / *b:* BP; CnP 1831-32; CrP 1828, 1832; L; LVA; LdP; MR; NwL; O; WcP 1832.

ATHENAEUM, a Magazine of Literary and Miscellaneous Information. v1-5, 1807-09. m. (Aikin).
a: ULS; ULSup. / *b:* UCP; CrP v2; EP; L; LLL; LP; LvA; MCh; MR; MsP v1-2; NwL; SP v1-3.

ATHENAEUM, a Magazine of Literary and Miscellaneous Information. no1-11, 1823. (Doherty.)
a: ULS. / *b:* L.

ATHENAEUM, an Original Literary Miscellany; edited by the Students in the University of Glasgow. Glasgow. 1830.
b: GM; L.

ATHENAEUM AND LITERARY CHRONICLE.
(See *Athenaeum; a Journal of Literature, Science,* &c.)

ATHLONE HERALD. Athlone. 1785-1827/?.
(Only one issue located. For details, see C & K, 1035a; CBEL, II.736; Richard R. Madden, *History of Irish Periodical Literature,* II.243.)
a: CSmH Je 8, 1827.

ATHLONE SENTINEL. Athlone. 1798-1850/?.
(No issues known. For details, see C & K, 1035b; CBEL, II.736; Richard R. Madden, *History of Irish Periodical Literature,* II.243.)

YR ATHRAW. Merthyr Tyfil. 1828.
b: UCP.

YR ATHRAW. Pontypool. 1829.
b: UCP.

ATHRAW I BLENTYN. Llanrwst. v1-36, 1827-62.
b: UCP.

ATKINSON'S PRICES OF SHARES. London. D 1, 1824-Je 15, 1829.
b: L.

ATLAS: a General Newspaper and Journal of Literature. London. no1+, 1826-1862.
a: ULS; CtY; DLC Ja 7, 1827-D 25, 1831; IU; NN 1832; OClWHi Ja-Ap-[My-Je]-Jl-Ag, 1832. / *b:* L; NpP Ag 3-D 28, 1828; O 1830-31, impf.
(Continued as *Englishmen,* 1862-65; *Atlas,* 1865-69; *Atlas and Public Schools Chronicle,* 1869; *Public Schools Chronicle,* 1869.)

ATTIC MISCELLANY. London, v1, no1, O 1824.
a: ULS. / *b:* UCP; L.

ATTIC MISCELLANY; Or, Characteristic Mirror of Men and Things. London. v1-3, 1789-1792/?.
a: ULS. / *b:* UCP; L v1-2.

ATTIC STORIES; or the Opinions of E. Hazelrig, Glasgow. no1-26, Ja 13, 1817-Ja 20, 1818. f.
b: GM; L; O.

AUCTION REGISTER and Law Chronicle. London. no1-146, 1813-15. w.
a: ULS. / *b:* UCP; L.
Continued as
LAW CHRONICLE and Estate Advertiser. no147-448, 1815-20. w.
a: MH. / *b:* L.
Continued as
LAW CHRONICLE, Commercial and Bankruptcy Register. London. no449-2747, 1820-47. w.
a: MH. / *b:* L.

THE AUGUSTAN REVIEW: a Monthly Production. London. v1-3, 1815-16. m.
b: UCP; L.

AUGUSTI LIBERALIS. London. no1-6, My-O, 1823. m.
a: ULS. / *b:* L.

THE AURIST; or, Medical Guide for the Deaf . . . with Translations and an Analysis of Foreign Works on the Subject. London. no1-3, 1825.
b: L.

THE AURORA; or, Dawn of Genuine Truth, being a Repository of Spiritual, Rational, and Useful Knowledge, designed for the Benefit of every Serious Enquirer after True Wisdom. London. vl-2, no1-24, My 1799-Mr 1801.
   a: PBr. / *b:* L; O.

AURORA and British Imperial Reporter. London. no1+, Ja 19,1807-Ja 29,1808-[?]. d.
   a: MBAt My 12, 1807; NNHi D 7, 1807; Ja 1-29, 1808. / *b:* L Ja 19, My 20, 26, 28-30, Je 6, 8, 1807.

AURORA BOREALIS. London. no1-45, Mr 25-D 30, 1821. w.
   a: CSmH no20, Ag 12, 1821. / *b:* L. (On Ja 6, 1822, incorporated with *Observer of the Times* and continued as *Observer of the Times and Aurora Borealis.* For details, see *Observer of the Times.*)

AUTHENTIC MEMOIRS OF THE GREEN ROOM, involving Sketches, Biographical, Critical, and Characteristic of the Performers of the Theatres-Royal, Drury Lane, Covent-Garden, and the Haymarket. London. ptl-4, 1801-04. a. (a new edn. in 1806.)
   a: PPL. / *b:* L; LLL ptl, 3-4.

AUXILIARY BIBLE SOCIETY. LEEDS. Annual Reports. Leeds. 1809-date.
   b: LdP 1809-29.

AUXILIARY BIBLE SOCIETY, Stirlingshire Report. Stirling. [?]-1828-[?].
   b: UCP.

AXE LAID TO THE ROOT, or a Fatal Blow to Oppressors. London. no1-5, 1817.
   b: L.

AYR ADVERTISER.
(See *Air Advertiser.*)

AYR AND WIGTONSHIRE COURIER. Ayr. 1820-25. w.
   a: CSmH no356, N 22, 1825. / *b:* AyP Je 8, Ag 28, 1820.

AYR CORRESPONDENT. Ayr. no1-13, 1824-25.
   b: GM; L.

AYR OBSERVER. Ayr. no1+, My 1, 1832-1927/?. w.
   b: AyP My 1, 1832.

AYRE'S SUNDAY LONDON GAZETTE and Weekly Monitor. London. no1+, 1783-1795-[1800?]. w. (Also called *Sunday London Gazette.*)
   a: CtY N 21, 1790; MH 1789-91, lacking Jl 5, O 18, 1789. / *b:* UCP; L Ag 14, 1791; Mr 22, 1795; MR 1793.

AYRSHIRE INDEPENDENT and Literary Gleaner. Ayr. no1-4, 1825.
   b: GM; L.

AYRSHIRE MAGAZINE and West Country Monthly Repository. Irvine. vl-2, Ag 1815-Jl 1817. m.
   b: AyP; E vl; L vl.

AYRSHIRE MAGNET, a Collection of Literary and Miscellaneous Articles, Original and Selected. Ayr. vl-2, no1-8, 1826.
   b: L.

AYRSHIRE MIRROR, a Miscellany of Useful, Entertaining and Instructive Information. Kilmarnock. no1-8, N 1820-Je 1821. m.
   b: AyP; GM; L.

AYRSHIRE MISCELLANY; or, Kilmarnock Literary Expositor. Kilmarnock. vl-20, 1817-22. (Also called *Kilmarnock Literary Expositor.*)
   b: GM, lacking no 1 of v20; L v4, 7-10, 12, 14-17.

THE BABBLER; or, Weekly Literary and Scientific Intelligencer. Leeds. vl-2, O 31, 1821-My 14, 1822. w.
   b: UCP; L O 31, 1821-Ap 23, 1822; LdL O 31, 1821-Ap 23, 1822; LdP.

THE BAGATELLE. Cork. no1-13, 1821.
(No issues known. See John Power, *Irish Literary Periodical Publications,* p. 10.)

BALDWIN'S LONDON JOURNAL; or, Bristol Chronicle. London. no1+, 1762-[?]. w.
(No issues for 1789 or later known.)
Continued as
BALDWIN'S LONDON WEEKLY JOURNAL. London. [?]-1791-1836. w.
(Also called *Baldwin's Weekly Journal and Craftsman. Philanthropic Gazette* incorporated with this S 1823.)
   a: CSmH Ag 5, 1826. / *b:* BP D 17, 1791; My 16, 1818; L D 10, 1803-1832.

BALDWIN'S LONDON MAGAZINE.
(See *London Magazine,* 1820-29.)

BALDWIN'S LONDON WEEKLY JOURNAL.
(See *Baldwin's London Journal,* &c.)

BALLINA IMPARTIAL; or, Tyrawly Advertiser. Ballina. no1+, Ja 13, 1823-1835. w.
   a: CSmH no226, My 7, 1827; NIC Mr 15, 1830. / *b:* L lacking 1826.

BALLITORE MAGAZINE, consisting of Original Pieces and Communications. Dublin. no1-4, Ap-Jl 1820; ns, no1-6, Ag 1820-Ja 1821. m.
   a: ULS. / *b:* UCP.

BALLOT. London. no1-97, Ja 2, 1831-N 4, 1832. (*Political Letter* was incorporated with this Ag 20, 1831.)
   a: CSmH no7. / *b:* L; O no2.

BALLYSHANNON HERALD and Donegal Advertiser. Ballyshannon. [1831]-1832-73. (Subtitle varies.)
   a: CSmH v2, no30, D 28, 1832. / *b:* L 1832.

BANKERS' CIRCULAR. London. no1-7, Jl 25-S 5, 1828. w.
   a: ULS. / *b:* UCP; L.
Continued as

CIRCULAR TO BANKERS. London. no8-1417, S 12, 1828-1853. w.
a: ULS. / *b:* UCP; L.
(Continued as *Bankers' Circular*, 1854-58; as *Monetary Times and Bankers' Circular*, 1858-59; as *Bankers' Circular and Monetary Times*, 1860.)

BANNATYNE CLUB. Publications. Edinburgh. v1-120, 1823-67.
a: ULS. / *b:* UCP; EP lacking 1824.

BANNATYNE MISCELLANY, containing Original Papers and Tracts, chiefly relating to the History and Literature of Scotland. Edinburgh. v1, 1827.
b: NwS.

BAPTIST ANNUAL REGISTER, including Sketches of the State of Religion among Different Denominations of Good Men at Home and Abroad. London. v1-4, 1790-1802. a.
a: ULS; ULSup. / *b:* UCP; L; O.

BAPTIST CHILDREN'S MAGAZINE and Sabbath Scholar's Reward. Loughborough; London; Leicester. 1827-34. (Generally listed as *Baptist Reporter*.)
a: ULS; ULSup.
(Continued as *Baptist Tract Magazine, &c.*, 1835-37; as *Baptist Reporter and Tract Magazine*, 1838-43; as *Baptist Reporter*, 1844-57; as *British Baptist Reporter, &c.*, 1858-63; as *Baptist Reporter and Missionary Intelligencer*, 1864.)

BAPTIST MAGAZINE. Tiverton, London. v1-96, 1809-1904. (Also numbered in series.)
a: ULS; ULSup. / *b:* UCP; BP; CrP v7, 11-12, 14, 16, 18-19, 21, 23; EP v2, 4-16, 18, 20+; L lacking v10-11.

BAPTIST MISSIONARY SOCIETY. Annual Reports.
(See *Baptist Missionary Society. Periodical Accounts.*)

BAPTIST MISSIONARY SOCIETY. Periodical Accounts. London. v1-6, 1791-1819.
a: ULS.
Continued as
BAPTIST MISSIONARY SOCIETY. Annual Reports. London. 1820-date. (v46 is the first numbered volume.)
a: ULS; ULSup.

BAPTIST REPORTER.
(See *Baptist Children's Magazine and Sabbath Scholar's Reward.*)

BAPTIST UNION. Proceedings. London. ?/1813-51. (Title varies).
a: ULS.

THE BARD, being a selection of Original Poetry. London. no1-8, O 9-D 7, 1822. w.
b: L; O.

BARNSTAPLE MISCELLANY. Barnstaple. no1-22, O 3, 1823-Mr 26, 1824. f.: w.
b: BddP.

BARRISTER. London. no1-4, My 1824. w.
a: ULS.

BARRY'S BRISTOL CHRONICLE. Bristol. 1818. w.
a: CSmH v1, no6, Je 6, 1818.

BATH AND BRISTOL MAGAZINE; or Western Miscellany. Bath. v1-3, 1832-34.
a: ULS; ULSup. / *b:* BhP; BrP; L; LP; TaP.

BATH AND CHELTENHAM GAZETTE, and General Advertiser. Bath. no1+, 1812-97. w. (Incorporated with *Bath Herald*.)
a: CSmH S 11, 1827; MiU-C N 23, 1824. / *b:* BhP; CtP 1812-15, 1827-28; L 1825-32.

BATH AND WEST AND SOUTHERN COUNTIES SOCIETY. Letters and Papers on Agriculture, Planting, &c. Bath, London. v1-14, 1780-1816; v15, pt1, 1829. (Also known as *Bath and West of England Society for the Encouragement of Agriculture, Arts, Manufactures, and Commerce.*)
a: ULS: ULSup. / *b:* UCP; BhP 1789-96; CrP 1789-99; DRS v1-12; L; LP.
(Continued as *Bath and West and Southern Counties Society. Journal*, 1853-68.)

BATH AND WEST OF ENGLAND SOCIETY, &c.
(See *Bath and West and Southern Counties Society, &c.*)

BATH CHRONICLE. Bath. 1770-1925. w. (Preceded by *Bath Advertiser*, 1755-1760-[?]; *Bath Chronicle or Universal Register*, [?]-1761-[?]; *Martin's Bath Chronicle*, [?]-1763-[?]; *Pope's Bath Chronicle*, [?]-1768; *Archer's Bath Chronicle*, 1768; *Bath and Bristol Chronicle*, 1768-70.)
a: CSmH Je 5, 1823. / *b:* UCP; BhP; BrP (1801, 1808, 1814-15); L 1789, 1825-32.
(Continued as *Bath Chronicle and Herald*, 1925-date.)

BATH HERALD.
(See *Bath Herald and General Advertiser.*)

BATH HERALD AND GENERAL ADVERTISER Bath. no1+, 1792-93. w.
b: L.
Absorbed *Bath Register and General Advertiser* and continued as
BATH HERALD AND REGISTER. Bath. 1793-1800. w.
b: L.
Continued as
BATH HERALD. Bath. 1800-1925. w.
b: L.
(Amalgamated with *Bath Chronicle and Herald*, 1925.)

BATH HERALD AND REGISTER.
(See *Bath Herald and General Advertiser.*)

BATH JOURNAL. Bath. 1773-Ja 1822. w. (Preceded by *Bath Journal*, 1744-53-[?]; *Boddely's Bath Journal*, [?]-1756-73.)

b: BP My 28, 1804; BhP; L Ja 9, D 31, 1792, Ja 7, 1793; D 19, 1803.
Continued as
KEENE'S BATH JOURNAL. Bath. Ja 1822-1916. w.
a: CSmH Jl 16, 1827. / *b:* BhP; L 1825-32.
(Incorporated with *Bath Herald.*)

BATH REGISTER AND GENERAL ADVERTISER. Bath. 1792-93. (Amalgamated with *Bath Herald.*)
(No issues known. For further details, see CBEL, II.720; C & K 1046a; and *Bath Herald,* above.)

BATH THEATRICAL REVIEW, a Series of Criticisms on the Performers and Drama in General, for the Season 1822-23. Bath. no1-25, 1822-23; ns, no1-2, 1823-24. (Running title, *Theatrical Review.*)
a: ULS. / *b:* L; O 1823.

THE BAZAAR, or Literary and Scientific Repository. Birmingham. no1-47, 1823-24. (Page heading up to no27, *The Birmingham Bazaar.*)
b: BP; O no1.

THE BEACON. Edinburgh. no1-38, Ja 6-S 22, 1821. w.
a: ULS. / *b:* E; EP; GM; L; MoP; O lacking no28.

BEACON. London. no1-7, Ap 21-Je 2, 1822. w.
b: L.

BEACON-LIGHT; or, Occasional Researches in Politics, Morals, Literature, &c. Edinburgh. no1-4, Ag 1810-Ja 1811. f.
a: ULS.

LE BEAU MONDE; or, Literary and Fashionable Magazine. London. v1-5, 1806-09. (v5 called "Novel Series.")
a: ULS. / *b:* BP v1-3; DL v2, 4; L v1-4, lacking O 1808; LVA v1-4.
Continued as
LE BEAU MONDE, and Monthly Register. London. v1-2, no1-13, Ap 1809-Ap 1810/?. m.
a: ULS. / *b:* L no1-10; LLL no1-9.

BEAU MONDE MAGAZINE; or Monthly Journal of Fashion. London. 1831-43. m.
a: ULS. / *b:* O.
(Continued as *Nouveau Beau Monde,* 1844-46; *London and Paris Ladies Magazine of Fashion, Polite Literature,* 1847-1891/?.)

LE BEAU MONDE, and Monthly Register.
(See *Beau Monde; or, Literary and Fashionable Magazine.*)

THE BEAUTIES OF THE MAGAZINES and Spirit of the Times.
(See *Spirit of the Times, &c.*)

THE BEAUTIES OF THE MAGAZINES, Reviews, and other Periodical Publications. Edinburgh. Ja 1788-Mr 1789.
b: PeP.

THE BEDFORD CHRONICLE. Herts and Huntington Register Weekly. Bedford. 1831/?.
a: CSmH no13, Jl 21, 1831.

THE BEE. Liverpool. no1-24, 1820-21.
b: LvP.

THE BEE. Liverpool. no1, 1832.
b: L.

THE BEE. Whitehaven. Mr 7-F 27, 1822.
b: CsP.

THE BEE; Fireside Companion, and Evening Tales. Liverpool, London. v1, 1820.
a: ULS. / *b:* L; O.
Continued as
THE QUEEN BEE; or, Monarch of the Hive. London. v2, 1821.
b: L.
Continued as
THE WORKING BEE; or, Caterer for the Hive. London. v3, 1822.
b: L.

THE BEE: or, Literary Weekly Intelligencer. Edinburgh. v1-18, 1790-94. w.
a: ULS; ULSup. / *b:* UCP; BP; BoP; EP 1791-93; L; LLL; NwL.

THE BEE; or, Stamford Herald and County Chronicle. Stamford. no1-113, 1830-33. w.
a: CSmH no39, Jl 29, 1831. / *b:* L.
(Continued as *Stamford Bee and County Press for Lincoln,* 1833.)

THE BEE-HIVE; or, Chester Magazine. Chester. v1, F 28-Ag 15, 1798. f.
b: UCP; DPK.

BELFAST ALMANACK. Belfast. 1786-1849.
b: UCP.

BELFAST COMMERCIAL CHRONICLE. Belfast. F 18, 1805-55. t-w.
a: CSmH Ap 21, 1821; CtY S 23, 1829; MB 1806; N Jl 31, Ag 7, 14, 21, 24, 28, S 4, 1822. / *b:* UCP; BlL 1805-10, 1812-14, 1816, 1826; BlP (1817, 1820-22); L 1823-27, 1832.

BELFAST CO-OPERATIVE ADVOCATE, and Miscellany of Useful Knowledge. Belfast. no1-2, Ja-Mr 1830/?
a: ULS. / *b:* UCP; BlL.

THE BELFAST LITERARY JOURNAL. Belfast. v1, Ap 1-Je 10, 1816. f.
b. BlL.

BELFAST LITERARY SOCIETY. Select Papers. Belfast. 1808.
b: UCP.

BELFAST MAGAZINE, and Literary Journal. Belfast. v1, no1-6, F-Jl 1825. m.
a: ULS. / *b:* UCP; BlL; DL; L.

BELFAST MERCANTILE REGISTER.
(See *Taggart's Mercantile Journal.*)

BELFAST MONTHLY MAGAZINE. Belfast. v1-13, 1808-14. m.
a: ULS; ULSup. / *b:* UCP; L.

BELFAST NEWS-LETTER. Belfast. no1+, 1796-date. s.w. (Preceded by *Belfast News-Letter and General Advertiser.* 1737-69.)
   a: NN Jl 3, D 14, 1795; NNHi Ja 3, 1792-D 30, 1796. / *b:* UCP; BlL; BlBN lacking Ja-Mr 20, 1795, Ja-Mr 1799; BlP (1789-1801, 1806-09, 1811-15), 1819, 1827, 1829-30; L 1828-32.

BELLAMY'S PICTURESQUE MAGAZINE, and Literary Museum. London. v1, 1793/?.
   a: ULS.

LA BELLE ASSEMBLÉE; or, Bell's Court and Fashionable Magazine. London. v1-7, 1806-10; ns, v1-30, 1810-24; s3, v1-15, 1825-32. m.
   a: ULS; ULSup. / *b:* UCP; BP v1-7; ns, v1-4, 7-13, 15-16; s3, v11-15; CoC; CtP v1-7; ns, v15-20, 23-30; s3, v1-12; DL; KeP lacking ns, v8-18; s3, v11-15; L v1-7; ns, v29-30; s3, v9, 11-15; LLL lacking ns, v5, 9-13, 21; s3, v7-10; 14; LVA v2-3; ns, v1-11, 13. 15-16, 19-20, 27-30; s3, v1-15.
   Continued as
THE COURT MAGAZINE and Belle Assemblée. London. v1-9, 1832-36. m.
   a: ULS; ULSup. / *b:* UCP; CoP; DL; EP; L; LVA.
      (Continued as *The Court Magazine and Monthly Critic,* 1837-48.)

BELL'S ANNUAL MESSENGER. London. 1798-99. a. (Reprinted from *Bell's Weekly Messenger.)* a.
   a: MBAt. / *b:* UCP.

BELL'S COMMERCIAL AND AGRICULTURAL REGISTER and Universal Price Current. London. no1-8, Jl 17-S 22, 1821.
   b: L.

BELL'S LIFE IN LONDON and Sporting Chronicle. London. no1-3799, 1822-86. w. *(Pierce Egan's Life in London and Sporting Chronicle* incorporated with this, N 4, 1827.)
   a: CtY [D 1827-D 1830]. / *b:* BP S 7, 1823; F 10, 25, 1827; L; TmP Ag 12,1827.

BELL'S NEW WEEKLY MESSENGER. London. no1-1288, Ja 1, 1832-55. w.
   a: CSmH no1. / *b:* L.
      (Incorporated with *News of the World,* 1855.)

BELL'S PARLIAMENTARY DEBATES, and Biographical Sketches of Senatorial Characters. London. 1807.
   b: L Prospectus only.

BELL'S SUNDAY DISPATCH. London. no1+, Ap 16, 1815-[?]. w.
   (No issues known. Bell edited this paper during his exclusion from the *Weekly Dispatch.* For details, see CBEL, III.811.)

BELL'S UNIVERSAL ADVERTISER. London. 1805. w. (This paper weekly with a copy of *Bell's Weekly Messenger.)*
   a: CSmH no2, F 2, 1805; MBAt Ja 19, F 16, 1805. / *b:* L Prospectus only.

BELL'S WEEKLY DISPATCH.
   (See *Weekly Dispatch.)*

BELL'S WEEKLY MARKET REGISTER. London. 1820.
   a: CSmH My 15, 1820.

BELL'S WEEKLY MESSENGER. London. no1+, My 1, 1796-1896. w.
   a: ULS; ULSup.; CaK Ag 10, 1828-D 27. 1829; CaM Ag 14, 1814-Mr 3, 1816; CtY My 1, 1796-D 1797; 4 sc.nos. 1798; Ja 6-My 5, 1799; Ap 27-S 21, 1800; N 16-D 28, 1801; 1806; 1813; (F 27-D 25, 1814); 1815; 9 sc.nos. 1817-19; 9 sc.nos. 1821; 1823; 1825; DLC Ja 5, 1800-D 29, 1811; Ap 12, 1812-Ap 24, 1813; Ja 7, 1816-D 30, 1821; Jl 7, 1822-D 30, 1827; Je 3-D, 1832; ICN 1805-24; IU My 1, 1796-1817; 1821-23; MB S 3, 1809-S 30, 1810; N 19-D 17, 1810; Ja 4, F 4-Je 24, 1811; MBAt Mr 22-Ap 5, 1807; Ja 1824-Je 1827; O 18, 1830-32; MnU My 1, 1796-97; 1799-1804; Ap 30,1809-1812; 1814-15; NcD 1805-06; NN S 25-D 25, 1808; 1809-14; Ag 10-D 28, 1817; Ja 4, 18-F 8, 1818; O 24, 1819-O 24, 1824; 1828-29; NNHi 1824-26, 1828; NjR Ja 6-D 29, 1811; OHi (1813-15, Jl 30, 1826-Jl 23, 1827); PPHi 1829-31. / *b:* UCP; IpP Ja 22, 1804-D 29, 1820; L; LGU 1796-1819; LLL 1804-05; 1809-1810; 1812-O 1813; 1820; MR 1796-1813; SaU 1812; SptP sc.nos. 1811-23.
      (Continued as *Country Sport and Messenger of Agriculture,* 1896-1904.)

BELVOIR FOXHOUNDS. Journal of the Operations. London. 1812-23. a.
   b: L lacking vol. for 1819-20.

BENEFIT SOCIETIES' PENNY MAGAZINE. London. no1, N 17, 1832. w.
   b: BP; O.

BENEVOLENT AND RELIGIOUS ORANGE REPORTER. Dublin. v1, 1826.
   b: UCP.

BENGAL CALENDAR. London. [?]-1789-1796-[?]. (Issued with *London Kalendar.)*
   b: DA 1789, 1791-93, 1796.

BENNET'S GLASGOW MAGAZINE. Glasgow. v1, 1832-33.
   b: GM.

BENT'S MONTHLY LIST OF NEW PUBLICATIONS.
   (See *A Monthly List of New Publications.)*

BENT'S MONTHLY LITERARY ADVERTISER (and Register of Engravings.)
   (See *A Monthly List of New Publications.)*

BERKSHIRE CHRONICLE; or, the Gentleman's, Sportsman's, Tradesman's Repository. Faringdon. v1, no1, Ja 2, 1798. w.
   b: UCP.

BERKSHIRE CHRONICLE, and Forest, Vale, and General Advertiser. Reading. no1+, Ja 29, 1825-date. w. (Subtitle varies.)

a: CSmH no28, Ag 6, 1825; CtY. / *b:* L
Ja 1829-32; RP; RRM.

BERKSHIRE REPOSITORY. Maidenhead.
v1, 1797.
   a: CtY. / *b:* O.

BERROW'S WORCESTER JOURNAL. Worcester. 1753-date. w. (Preceded by *Worcester
News-sheet,* 1690-1709; *Worcester Post-man,*
1709-1722; *Worcester Post or Western Journal,* 1722-25; *Weekly Worcester Journal,* 1725-
48; *Worcester Journal,* 1748-53.)
   a: ULS; CSmH Ja 20, 1831; CtY [1799]-
   1800-02, 1805-32. / *b:* BP 1799-1800;
   L 1808-14; 1816; 1818-20; 1822-32; WcP
   (1789-1832); WcBW.

BERTHOLD'S POLITICAL HANDKERCHIEF.
London. no1-10. 1831.
   a: ULS. / *b:* UCP; L; O no1-5, 7.

BERWICK ADVERTISER.
   (See *British Gazette and Berwick Advertiser.*)

BERWICKSHIRE NATURALISTS CLUB. History. Alnwick. 1831-1908. (Individual numbers called *Proceedings.*)
   a: ULS. / *b:* DuC; LR.

BERWICKSHIRE NATURALISTS CLUB.
Journal. Alnwick. v1, 1831/?.
   b: DuC; NwS.

BERWICKSHIRE NATURALISTS CLUB. Proceedings.
   (See *Berwickshire Naturalists Club. History.*)

BERWICKSHIRE NATURALISTS CLUB.
Transactions. Alnwick. 1831-1935/?.
   b: EP.

**BESLEY'S EXETER NEWS and Devon Coun-
ty Chronicle.** Exeter. [no1]-273-287, [1822]-
D 30, 1826-Ap 14, 1827. w.
   a: CSmH D 30, 1826. / *b:* L Ja 6-Ap 14,
   1827.
   Continued as
**DEVONSHIRE CHRONICLE and Exeter
News.** Exeter. no288+, Ap 21, 1827-1837.
   a: CSmH O 6, 1827. / *b:* ExD 1831-32; L.
      (Continued as *Besley's Devonshire
      Chronicle and Exeter News,* 1837-51;
      as *Devonshire Chronicle and Exeter
      News,* 1851-53.)

**BETHELL'S LIFE IN LONDON and Liver-
pool Sporting Register.** Liverpool. v1-2, [?]-
1826.
   b: L v2, no69.

**BIBLE CHRISTIAN, designed to Advocate
the Sufficiency of the Scripture, and the
Right of Private Judgment in Matters of
Faith.** Belfast. v1-6, 1830-36, ns, v1-3, 1837-
39; s3, v1-7, 1840-45.
   a: ULS. / *b:* UCP; L.
      (Continued as *Irish Unitarian Maga-
      zine,* &c., 1846-47.)

**BIBLE CHRISTIAN MAGAZINE . . . being a
Continuation of the Arminian Magazine.** London. Shebbear. 1822-1907. (The "Bible
Christians" broke away from the Wesleyan
Methodists and continued the *Arminian Magazine* under this title and in competition with
the *Wesleyan Methodist Magazine.*)
   a: ULS; ULSup.
      (Superseded by *United Methodist Mag-
      azine.*)

BIBLE MAGAZINE and Theological Review.
London. 1815-19. v1-5. m.
   a: ULS. / *b:* UCP; L lacking pp.1-522 of
   v3.

**BIBLICAL CABINET; or Hermeneutical, Ex-
egetical, and Philosophical Library.** Edinburgh. v1-45, 1832-44; ns, v1-3, 1844-45.
   a: ULS; ULSup.

**THE BIBLICAL MAGAZINE, intended to
Promote the Knowledge and Belief of the
Sacred Scriptures.** Clipstone. v1-5, 1801-05.
a.
   a: ULS. / *b.* L v1-2.
      (United with *Theological Magazine
      and Review* and continued as *Theolog-
      ical and Biblical Magazine.* See *Theo-
      logical Magazine and Review* for de-
      tails.)

THE BIBLICAL REGISTER. London. no1-6,
Ja-Je, 1818. m.
   a: ULS. / *b:* L.

**BIBLIOGRAPHIANA . . . originally Pub-
lished in the Manchester Exchange Herald.**
Manchester. no1-34, 1817.
   a: ULS.

**BIBLIOGRAPHICAL AND RETROSPECTIVE
MISCELLANY.** London. no1-4, 1830.
   a: ULS; ULSup. / *b:* UCP; EP; L; MR; O.

**BIBLIOGRAPHICAL MEMORANDA, in Illus-
tration of Early English Literature.** Bristol.
no1-5/6, 1814-16.
   a: ULS.

**LA BIBLIOTECA AMERICANA, o Miscel-
anea de Literatura Artes i Ciencias.** London. v1-2, 1823.
   a: ULS. / *b:* L.

BIBLIOTHECA JURIDICA. London. 1830.
   b: L.

**BIBLIOTHECA TOPOGRAPHICA BRITAN-
NICA.** London. v1-8, 1780-90.
   a: ULS. / *b:* UCP.
   Continued as
MISCELLANEOUS ANTIQUITIES. London.
1791-93.
   a: ULS.

**BIJOU; or, Annual of Literature and the
Arts.** London. v1-3, 1828-30. a.
   a: ULS. / *b:* UCP; BrP 1828; L.

BILLINGE'S LIVERPOOL ADVERTISER.
   (See *Williamson's Liverpool Advertiser.*)

BINGLEY'S LONDON JOURNAL. London. 1772-[1790]. w. (Succeeds *Bingley's Journal; or, the Universal Gazette,* 1770-71; *Bingley's Journal,* 1771-72.)
(No issues known after 1775. For details, see CBEL, II.715.)

THE BIOGRAPHICAL AND IMPERIAL MAGAZINE, containing History, Philosophy, &c. v1-5, 1789-92. (Monthly parts entitled *The Imperial Magazine.*)
a: ULS. / *b:* UCP; L.

THE BIOGRAPHICAL MAGAZINE, containing Portraits and Characters of Eminent and Ingenious Persons of Every Age and Nation. London. 1794.
a: ULS; ULSup. / *b:* UCP.

BIOGRAPHICAL MAGAZINE: containing Portraits of Eminent and Ingenious Persons of every Age and Nation. London. v1-2, 1819-20.
a: ULS; ULSup. / *b:* UCP.

THE BIRCH. Humbly Dedicated to the Magistrates of the City of Oxford. Oxford. no1-5, 1795-96.
b: UCP; L.

BIRMINGHAM AND COVENTRY FREE PRESS. Birmingham. no1+, Ap 15-My 20, 1830.
b: L.

THE BIRMINGHAM ARGUS. Birmingham. 1818-19. w.
a: CSmH v2, no38, S 18, 1819. / *b:* L v1, no3, O 31, 1818.

BIRMINGHAM ARGUS AND PUBLIC CENSOR. Birmingham. v1-2, 1828-29. (From v2, no6, called *Birmingham Monthly Argus and Public Censor.*)
b: BP.
Continued as
MONTHLY ARGUS AND PUBLIC CENSOR. Birmingham. ns, v1-4, 1829-32.
b: BP; L v1-3, lacking all before p.105 of v1.)

THE BIRMINGHAM BAZAAR.
(See *The Bazaar, or Literary and Scientific Repository.*)

BIRMINGHAM CHRONICLE.
(See *Swinney's Birmingham Chronicle.*)

BIRMINGHAM COMMERCIAL HERALD. Birmingham. [?]-1806-1820-[?]. (Subtitle varies.)
a: CSmH My 1, 1819. / *b:* BP sc.nos., 1806-1809; complete 1812-15, 1817-18, 1820; L Je 5, 1809.

BIRMINGHAM CO-OPERATIVE HERALD. Birmingham. no1-9, 1829.
b: UCP.

BIRMINGHAM GAZETTE.
(See *Aris's Birmingham Gazette.*)

BIRMINGHAM INDEPENDENT; a Monthly Publication on Parochial and other Local Subjects. Birmingham. no1-12, 1827-28. m.
b: BP.

BIRMINGHAM INSPECTOR, a Periodical Work published in the Year 1817. Birmingham. no1-16, Ja 4-Ag 23, 1817. f.
a: ULS. / *b:* UCP; BP.

BIRMINGHAM JOURNAL. Birmingham. no1+, Je 4, 1825-1869. w.
a: CSmH D 27, 1828. / *b:* BBW; BP sc. nos. 1825-29; L.
(Incorporated with *Midland Representative and Birmingham Herald,* 1832. Incorporated with *Birmingham Daily Post* in 1869 and continued to date as *Birmingham Weekly Post.*)

BIRMINGHAM MAGAZINE; or Literary, Scientific and Theological Repository. Birmingham. v1, no1-9, N 1827-Jl 1828. m. (Subtitle varies slightly.)
a: ULS. / *b:* BP.

BIRMINGHAM MERCURY and Warwickshire and Staffordshire Advertiser. Birmingham. no1+, 1820-21. w.
a: CSmH O 29, 1821. / *b:* BP Ja 29, Je 4, 1821.

BIRMINGHAM MONTHLY ARGUS and Public Censor.
(See *Birmingham Argus and Public Censor.*)

BIRMINGHAM REPORTER, and Theatrical Review; or, the Opinions, Doubts, and Perplexities of Humphrey Digbeth, Manufacturer, and Others. Birmingham. v1, no1-14, Je 19-S 18, 1823. w.
a: ULS. / *b:* BP no1-3, 5-7, 10-12.

BIRMINGHAM REVIEW. Birmingham. 1824.
b: BP Ag 7, 14.

BIRMINGHAM SCHOLASTIC TICKLER. Birmingham. no1-6, 1829.
b: BP.
Continued as
JENKINSON'S SCHOLASTIC TICKLER. Birmingham. no7-9, 1829.
b: BP.

BIRMINGHAM SPECTATOR, a Miscellany of Literature and Dramatic Criticism. Birmingham. no1-24, My 29-N 6, 1824. w.
a: ULS. / *b:* UCP; BP; L.

THE BLACK DWARF. London. v1-12, 1817-24. w.
a: ULS. / *b:* UCP; BP; BrP (1817-20); CrP v1; L v1-12, but v6, 11 impf.; LLL v2-4; NwP.

BLACKBURN ALFRED. no1-129, Ag 6, 1832-Ja 7, 1835. w.
b: BdP; L.

BLACKBURN GAZETTE.
(See *Blackburn Mail.*)

BLACKBURN MAIL. Blackburn. 1793-1829. w. (Subtitle varies.)
a: CSmH D 10, 1828. / *b:* BP N 27, 1805;

BbP My 29, 1793-O 1, 1828; L Ja, 1826-Ag 12, 1829.
Continued as
BLACKBURN GAZETTE. Blackburn. Ag 22, 1829-1843. w.
    a: CSmH Ap 20, 1831. / *b:* BbP; L.

BLACKWOOD'S EDINBURGH MAGAZINE. Edinburgh. no1+, 1817-date. (No1-6 as *Edinburgh Monthly Magazine.*)
    a: ULS; ULSup. / *b:* UCP; BP; BrP; CnP; CrP; EP; ExP; GeG; GrP lacking v1-18; L; LLL; LLW; LdL; LdP; LvA; LvP; MR; MoM; MsP lacking v1-13; NpP; NwL; NwP; PeP; PrH; PsP; WcP; WmP.

BLAGDON'S WEEKLY POLITICAL REGISTER. London. v1-3, O 4, 1809-Ja 23, 1811.w.
    a: ULS. / *b:* UCP; L a Prospectus only.

THE BLANKETEER, and People's Guardian; a New Moral and Political Work. Leeds. no1-5, 1819. w. (Apparently first appeared as *Ægis.*)
    b: L no5.

BLOSSOMS AT CHRISTMAS and First Flowers of the New Year. London. 1824. a.
    b: UCP; L.

THE BLUE DWARF. Yarmouth. no1-6, 1820/?.
    b: L.

BLYTH MONTHLY GLEANER. Blyth. Je-Ag 1819. m.
    a: ULS.

BOARD OF AGRICULTURE. Communications to.
    (See *Communications to the Board of Agriculture.*)

BOHEMIAN. London. 1817.
(No issues known. Listed in Muddiman's *Tercentenary Handlist.*)

BOLG AN TSOLAIR; or Gaelic Magazine. Belfast. no1. 1795.
    b: BlL.

BOLSTER'S QUARTERLY MAGAZINE. Cork, Dublin, London. v1-3, 1826-31.
    a: ULS. / *b:* UCP; CoP; DM v1-2; L.

BOLTON CHRONICLE. Bolton. no1+, O 9, 1824-1917.
    a: CSmH S 26, 1829. / *b:* BoP sc.nos. 1825-26; (1827-31);L Ja 8, 1831-32.

BOLTON EXPRESS, and Lancashire General Advertiser. Bolton. Jl 5, 1823-Je 26, 1827. w.
    a: CSmH Je 23, 1827. / *b:* BoP Jl 5, 1823-Je 26, 1824; N 6, 1824; Je 4, 1825; Je 17, 1826.

BOLTON HERALD. Bolton. no1-2, My 1-8, 1813/?. w.
    b: BoP no2.

BOLTON LITERARY JOURNAL. Bolton. v1, O 16, 1830-Ap 9, 1831.
    b: BoP.

BOLTON REFLECTOR. Bolton. v1, no1-19, Jl 12-N 22, 1823. w.
    b: BoP.

THE BON TON GAZETTE.
    (See *Crim. Con. Gazette, &c.*)

THE BON TON MAGAZINE; or Microscope of Fashion and Folly. London. v1-5, 1791-96. m.
    a: ULS. / *b:* UCP; L v1; LLL.

BONNE BOUCHE, or Olio of History, Anecdote, Wit, Literature and the Arts. London. no1-14, 1823.
    a: ULS.
    (United with *Adventurer of the Nineteenth Century* to form *Adventurer and Bonne Bouche.* For details, see *Adventurer of the Nineteenth Century.*)

BONNER AND MIDDLETON'S BRISTOL JOURNAL. Bristol. no1+, 1774-1803. w.
    b: BrP; L Ag 21, 1790; Mr 19, 1791.
    Continued as
FENLEY AND SHEPARD'S Bristol Journal. Bristol. Ja 7-Ap 7, 1804. w.
    b: BrP; L Ja 7, 1804.
    Continued as
(BRISTOL) MIRROR, late Bonner and Midleton's Journal. Bristol. Ap 14, 1804-1864. w.
    a: CSmH Ag 23, 1823. / *b:* BrP; L Ja 2, 1819-1832+.

BOOK FOR THE PEOPLE. London. no1, 1831.
    b: L.

THE BOOKWORM. Stafford. no1-13, 1820. w.
    b: BP; StfS.

BORDER MAGAZINE. Berwick. v1-2, 1831-32.
    a: ULS. / *b:* EP.

BOSTON GAZETTE and Lincolnshire Advertiser. Boston. Jl 2, 1811-O 30, 1832. w.
    a: CSmH Je 25, 1822. / *b:* L Jl 2, Ag 20, N 12, 1811; Ap-Ag 1814; My-Ag, 1815; Ja 6, 1829-O 30, 1832.

BOSTON, LINCOLN, AND LOUTH HERALD.
    (See *Lincoln Herald, and County Advertiser.*)

BOSTON, LOUTH, NEWARK, STAMFORD, AND RUTLAND CHAMPION.
    (See *Champion of the East.*)

BOTANIC ANNUAL. London. 1832.
    b: UCP.

BOTANIC GARDEN. London. v1-13, 1824-50.
    a: ULS. / *b:* UCP.

BOTANICAL CABINET, Consisting of Coloured Delineations of Plants, from all Countries, with a Short Account of Each. London. v1-20, 1817-33.
    a: ULS; ULSup. / *b:* UCP; DRS; L; LGU; MR 1817-18; O v7-20.

BOTANICAL MAGAZINE; or, Flower Garden
Displayed: in which the most Ornamental
Foreign Plants... will be Accurately Repre-
sented. London. v1-14, 1787-1800. m.
  a: ULS; ULSup. / b: BP; BkP; BoP; CrP;
  DRS; L; LGU; LLL; LP; LU; LVA; LvP;
  NwL; NwP v3-14; RiP; WiP.
Continued as
CURTIS'S BOTANICAL MAGAZINE; or
Flower Garden Displayed. London. s1-3+,
1801-date. m.
  a: ULS; ULSup. / b: UCP; BP; BoP;
  CrP 1801-15; DRS; L; LGU; LLL 1801-09;
  LP; LU; LVA; LvP; NwL; NwP; RiP
  1801-25; WiP.

BOTANICAL MISCELLANY, containing Figures and Descriptions of such Plants as
Recommended Themselves by their Novelty,
Rarity, or History, or the Use to which they
may be Applied. London. v1-3, 1830-33.
  a: ULS. / b: UCP; DRS; L; LP; NwL.
      (Continued as Journal of Botany,
      1834-42; as London Journal of Bot-
      any, 1842-57.)

BOTANICAL REGISTER; consisting of Coloured Figures of Exotic Plants, cultivated in
British Gardens, with Their Treatment. London. v1-14, 1815-28. a.
  a: ULS; ULSup. / b: UCP; BP; CrP v1-
  9; DRS; L; LLL v13-14; MR.
Continued as
EDWARD'S BOTANICAL REGISTER; or Ornamental Flower-Garden and Shrubbery, &c.
London. v15-33, 1829-47.
  a: ULS; ULSup. / b: UCP; BP; L; LLL;
  MR.

BOTANICAL REVIEW. London. v1, 1790/?.
  a: ULS.

BOTANISTS' REPOSITORY for New and
Rare Plants. v1-10, 1797-1815.
  a: ULS. / b: UCP; NwL.

THE BOUDOIR, or British Magazine. London. v1, 1832.
  b: UCP; L.

THE BOUQUET. A Collection of Tales, Essays, and Poems, Original and Select. London. v1-3, 1831-33.
  b: UCP; L.

THE BOUQUET; or, Blossoms of Fancy.
London. v1-2, 1795-96.
  b: UCP; L v2.

THE BOUQUET OF POPULAR LITERA-
TURE. London. no1, 1822.
  b: L.

BOYLE'S COURT AND COUNTRY GUIDE.
London. 1806-23. a.
  b: UCP.
Continued as
BOYLE'S FASHIONABLE COURT and
Country Guide. London. 1824-1925.
  b: UCP.

BOYLE'S FASHIONABLE COURT and Country Guide.
  (See Boyle's Court and Country Guide.)

BOYLE'S MAGAZINE. London. 1807.
  b: UCP.

BOYS' AND GIRLS' PENNY MAGAZINE.
London. no1-34, S 15, 1832-Ap 27, 1833/?.
(Also numbered as no1-10; ns, no1-24.)
  a: ULS. / b: L no9, 17-18.

BRADFORD AND HUDDERSFIELD COURIER,
and General West-Riding Advertiser. Bradford. [?]-1827-[?]. w.
  a: CSmH v3, no21, N 1, 1827.

THE BRADFORD INSTRUCTIVE and Entertaining Miscellany. Bradford. no1-9, 1818. w.
  b: L.

THE BRAZEN HEAD. London. no1-4, 1826.
  b: L.

THE BRAZEN TRUMPET. London. no1-6,
F 10-My 17, 1798. m.
  a: ULS. / b: UCP.

BREAKFAST TABLE; or, Ladies' Pocket
Library. London. no1, O 1808/?.
  (No issues known. See John Nichol, Illus-
  trations of Literary History, v8, p.610.)

BRICE AND CO'S OLD EXETER JOURNAL.
  (See Brice's Old Exeter Journal, &c.)

BRICE'S OLD EXETER JOURNAL; or, Western Advertiser. Exeter. [?]-1789. (Preceded
by The Postmaster; or, The Loyal Mercury,
[?]-1718-1725; as Brice's Weekly Journal,
1725-30-[?]; as Old Exeter Journal, [?]-1755-
1788-[?].
  (No issues known. Data from CBEL, II.723.)
Continued as
BRICE AND CO'S Old Exeter Journal. Exeter. 1789-1791/?.
  (No issues known. Data from CBEL, II.723.)

BRIDGWATER AND SOMERSETSHIRE HER-
ALD. Bridgwater. no[?]-264-358, [?]-1829-31.
  a: CSmH no264, Je 17, 1829. / b: L no
  328-58, Ja 5-Ag 3, 1831.
Continued as
ALFRED LONDON WEEKLY JOURNAL.
Bridgwater, no1-126, Ag 10, 1831-D 30,
1833.
  b: L.

BRIGHTON AND SUSSEX MIRROR. Brighton.
no1-12, Ag 30-N 15, 1823.
  b: BiP.

BRIGHTON FASHIONABLE and Local Register. Brighton. 1823. f.
  b: BiP no1-4, S 15-O 27, 1823.

BRIGHTON GAZETTE. Brighton. 1821-1926.
w. (Subtitle varies.)
  a: CSmH Ja 13, 1831. / b: BIP; L no
  203+, 1825-32.
      (Continued as Southern Weekly News,
      1926-33; as Brighton Gazette, 1933-
      date.)

BRIGHTON GLEANER; or General Repository of Literary Selections. Brighton. v1-2,
1822-23.
  b: BiP; L lacking pp. 67-70 of v1.

BRIGHTON GUARDIAN. Brighton. no1+, Ja 31, 1827-1901. w.
   a: CSmH D 10, 1828. / *b:* BiP no2+, F 7, 1827-D 24, 1828; L.

BRIGHTON GUIDE. Brighton. 1797/?.
(No issues known. See C & K, 1059a.)

BRIGHTON HERALD. Brighton. S 6, 1806-1922. w. (Subtitle varies.)
   a: CSmH S 22, 1827; CtY 1809. / *b:* BiBH 1812-32+; BiP S 6-D 27, 1806; 1807; O 25, D 16, 1815; Ag 18, 1821; O 7, 1826-D 29, 1827; 1828-31; L no961+, 1825-1832+.
   (Continued as *Brighton and Hove Herald*, 1922-date.)

BRIGHTON KALEIDOSCOPE; or Sussex Literary and Scientific Journal. Brighton. [?]-1830.
   b: BiP no17, F 6, 1830.

BRIGHTON LITERARY JOURNAL, or Monthly Magazine. Brighton. 1823.
   b: BiP Jl 1, 1823.

BRIGHTON MAGAZINE. London. v1-2. Ja-Ag 1822. m.
   a: ULS. / *b:* UCP; BiP; L.

BRISTOL AUXILIARY, British and Foreign School Society. Report. Bristol. 1815-19.
   b: UCP.

BRISTOL, BATH, GLO'STER, West of England, and South Wales General Advertiser. Bristol. no1-2, Ap 16-23, 1831. w.
   b: BrP.

BRISTOL CORNUCOPIA. Bristol. no1-2, Ap-My 1823. m.
   b: BrP; L.

BRISTOL GAZETTE and Public Advertiser. Bristol. no1+, 1767-1872. w.
   a: CSmH N 14, 1822; MHi Jl 28, 1791. / *b:* UCP; BrP (1789-1832); L 1789; 21 sc.nos. for 1790-1817; complete 1819-1832+.

BRISTOL HERALD. Bristol. no1-5, Je 27, Jl 25, 1829. w. (Subtitle varies.)
   a: CSmH no1, Je 27, 1829. / *b:* L.

BRISTOL INSTITUTION. Proceedings of the Annual Meeting. Bristol. v1-13, 1822-36. a.
   a: ULS.

BRISTOL JOB NOTT; or, Labouring Man's Friend. Bristol. no1-107, D 15, 1831-1833.w.
   a: ULS. / *b:* UCP; BrP; L; O:

BRISTOL JOURNAL.
(See *Bonner and Middleton's Bristol Journal.*)

BRISTOL LIBERAL. Bristol. no1-33, Jl 23, 1831-Mr 3, 1832. w.
   b: L.

BRISTOL MEMORIALIST. Bristol. no1-4, Mr 1816-Je 15, 1823. q. (no1-3, Mr-S 1816; no4, Je 1823. After being suspended for almost

7 years, the periodical was renewed with no 4 so that the previous nos. might be brought into a whole and published.)
   a: ULS. / *b:* UCP; BrP; L.

BRISTOL MERCURY and Universal Advertiser. Bristol. 1790-1877. w.
   a: CSmH Ja 27, 1823. / *b:* BrP 1790-1832, impf.; GrP Mr 1, 1790; Mr 3, 1821; L S 15, 1806; Ja 4, 1819.
   (Continued as *Bristol Mercury and Daily Post*, 1878-1901; as *Bristol Daily Mercury*, 1901-09.)

BRISTOL MIRROR.
(See *Bonner and Middleton's Bristol Journal.*)

BRISTOL OBSERVER. Bristol. [?]-1819-23. w.
   a: CSmH Mr. 4, 1819. / *b:* L no75+, Ja 7, 1819-O 1, 1823.

BRISTOL PRESENTMENTS; Exports for the Year 1770 . . . Bristol. no1+, 1770-1808-[?]. w.
   (No issues known. For details, see CBEL, II.719.)

BRISTOL REVIEW. Bristol. no1, 1829.
   b: O.

BRISTOL SPECTATOR. Bristol. 1800. w.
   b: BrP O 30, N 6, 1800.

BRISTOL, West of England and South Wales Magazine..
(See *West of England and South Wales Magazine.*)

BRISTOLIAN. Bristol. 1827-31. d. (Subtitle varies through 9 series.)
   a: CSmH Ap 11, 1828. / *b:* BrP no1-8, My 28-Je 5, 1827; no1-11, Je 6-18, 1827; v1-2, Je 20-S 1, 1827; v1, no2-3, 6-7, Mr 28-My 2, 1838; N 15, 1828-Ja 21, 1829; no4-8, F 14-Ap 4, 1829; v1-5 impf., Ap 25, 1829-My 25, 1831; v1, no1, F 23, 1832; BrU no1-8, My 28-Je 5, 1827; no1-11, Je 6-18, 1827; 1829-30; L v1, no1-13-v2, no1-9-ns, no1-20, 1827-29; v1-3, 1829-30; lacking no1-33 of v1; v1, no7, Ap 24, 1830; O no1, O 31, 1829.

BRISTOLIAN; Daily Literary Publication.
(See *Bristolian.*)

BRISTOLIAN; or, Memoirs and Correspondence of James Acland.
(See *Bristolian.*)

BRISTOLIAN IN MONMOUTHSHIRE.
(See *Bristolian.*)

BRITANNIC MAGAZINE; or Entertaining Repository of Heroic Adventures. London. v1-12, 1793-1807. m.
   a: ULS; ULSup. / *b:* UCP; BP v1-8; DL; L; MsP v1-2; O v1-8.
   Continued as
BRITANNIC MAGAZINE and Chronological Repository. London. v13, D 1807-D 1809. m.
   b: C.

BRITANNIC MAGAZINE and Chronological
Repository.
(See *Britannic Magazine; or Entertaining
Repository*, &c.)

BRITANNICA; or, the Sunday Fashionable
Literary and Commercial Advertiser. London.
no1-45, 1807-08/?. w.
b: C no45, Ja 24, 1808.

BRITISH ACADEMY; or, Ancient and Modern
School of Fine Arts. London. 1807.
b: L   Prospectus only.

BRITISH ALMANAC and Glasgow Register.
Edinburgh. 1808.
b: GU.

BRITISH ALMANAC and Universal Scots
Register. Edinburgh. 1802-08.
b: UCP.

BRITISH ALMANAC of the Society for the
Diffusion of Useful Knowledge. London.
1828-88. a.
b: UCP; BbP; BkP; CrP; GeG 1828-32;
IpP; LP; LdP; NpP 1831; SP.
(Continued as *British Almanac and
Companion*, &c., 1889-1914.)

BRITISH AND COLONIAL Weekly Register.
London. no1-39, Ja 3-S 25, 1824. w.
b: L.

BRITISH AND FOREIGN BIBLE SOCIETY.
Monthly Extracts from the Correspondence.
London. 1817-58. m.
a: ULS.
(Continued as *Monthly Reporter of the
British and Foreign Bible Society*,
1858-1904.)

BRITISH AND FOREIGN BIBLE SOCIETY.
Quarterly Extracts. London. v1, 1824/?. q.
a: ULS.

BRITISH AND FOREIGN BIBLE SOCIETY.
Reports. London. v1, 1804/05-date.
a: ULS. / *b:* UCP; CrP; GeG 1812; LFS;
LdP 1814-17.

BRITISH AND FOREIGN PRICE CURRENT.
(See *London Price Current*.)

BRITISH AND FOREIGN SCHOOL SOCIETY.
Quarterly Extracts from the Correspondence.
London. no1-74, 1825-45/?.
a: ULS.

BRITISH AND FOREIGN SCHOOL SOCIETY.
Report. London. 1810/14-date.
a: ULS; ULSup. / *b:* UCP.

BRITISH AND FOREIGN STATE PAPERS.
(Foreign Office.) London. v1+, 1812-date.
a: ULS. / *b:* UCP; EP.

BRITISH AND FOREIGN Temperance Herald.
London. v1-4, 1832-35.
a: ULSup. / *b:* UCP; L.

BRITISH AND INDIAN OBSERVER. London.
no1-31, D 14, 1823-Jl 11, 1824. w.
b: L.

BRITISH AND IRISH LADIES' SOCIETY for
Improving the Conditions . . . of the Female
Peasantry of Ireland. Report. London. v1-3,
[?]-1823-24/?.
b: UCP.

BRITISH ASSOCIATION for Promoting Cooperative Knowledge. Report of the Proceedings. London. [?]-1829-30/?.
a: ULS.

BRITISH ASSOCIATION for the Advancement
of Science. Reports. London. v1-108, 1831-
1938.
a: ULS; ULSup. / *b:* CrP; DRS; LGU; LdP
(Superseded by *Advancement of
Science*.)

BRITISH BIBLIOGRAPHER.
(See *Censura Literaria*.)

BRITISH CHRONICLE, or Pugh's Hereford
Journal. Hereford. no1+, 1770-1792. w.
a: NcD My 16, 1792. / *b:* GrP; HfP.
Continued as
HEREFORD JOURNAL. Hereford. 1793-
1925.
a: NcD 30 sc.nos. 1793-1802. / *b:* GrP;
HfP; L 1830-32.
(Incorporated with *Hereford Observer*
and continued as *Hereford Journal
Observer*, 1926-32. Incorporated with
Hereford Times.)

BRITISH CHRONICLE, or Union Gazette.
Kelso. 1784-1803; 1832-[?]. w. (Discontinued
in 1803; resumed 1832. Preceded by *Kelso
Chronicle*, 1783-84.)
a: MdBJ Jl 12, 1798-N 20, 1800; PPL Ag
27, 1790-Ag 17, 1792; O 24, 1794-O 19,
1797. / *b:* EP Ja-Mr 20, Ap 3-D 4, 1789;
Je 24, 1791.

BRITISH COOPERATOR; or, Record and
Review of Co-operative and Entertaining
Knowledge. London. no1-7, 1830.
a: ULS. / *b:* UCP.

BRITISH CRITIC, a New Review. London.
v1-42, 1793-1813; ns, v1-23, 1814-25; s3,
v1-3, 1825-26. m.
a: ULS; ULSup. KyLx v1-30. / *b:* UCP;
BO s3, v1-3; BrP; CrP v12, 33, ns, v11;
GeG v13-42; ns, v1-5; GrP; L; LLL; LLW
v1-42; LdL; LdP ns, v21-22; LvP v6, 12,
27, 35, 40; ns, v8, 11, 19; MCh; MoM
1804-13; PrH; SP 1793-98; SthC v1-32;
WcP lacking v1; s3, v3.
(United with *Quarterly Theological Review* and continued as
BRITISH CRITIC. Quarterly Theological
Review and Ecclesiastical Record. London.
v1-34, 1827-43. q. (After v22 *Ecclesiastical Record* was dropped from the title.)
a: ULS; ULSup. / *b:* UCP; BO; BrP; CrP
v1-10; GrP; L; LLL; LdL; LvP v1-10; MCh.

BRITISH CRITIC, Quarterly Theological Review, and Ecclesiastical Record.
(See *British Critic, a New Review*.)

BRITISH DRAMA and Literary Humorist.
London. no1-2, 1832.
b: L.

BRITISH ENTOMOLOGY. London. v1, 1824-25.
  b: UCP.

BRITISH FARMER'S CHRONICLE, and Commercial Gazette. London. [?]-1827-[?]. w.
  a: CSmH no224, Ag 13, 1827.

BRITISH FARMER'S MAGAZINE. London. no1, Je 1811/?.
  b: L Prospectus only. (For other details, see Nichol's *Illustrations of Literary History*, v8, p.610.)

BRITISH FARMER'S MAGAZINE, exclusively devoted to Agricultural and Rural Affairs. London. v1-10, 1826-36; ns, v1-78, 1837-80.
  a: ULS; ULSup. / *b:* UCP; CrP v2-3; E; L.

BRITISH FLOWER-GARDEN. London. 1823-28, v1-s2, v4.
  b: UCP.

BRITISH FOREIGN PRICE CURRENT.
  (See *London Price Current*.)

BRITISH FREEHOLDER and Saturday Evening Journal. London. no1-175, 1820-23. w.
  a: MnU Jl 22, 1820. / *b:* L; O no1.

BRITISH GAZETTE and Berwick Advertiser. Berwick. no1+, Ja 2, 1808-N 22, 1823. w.
  a: CSmH O 28, 1826; CtY 1812-13; (1814): sc.nos. 1815; (1816-22); 1823. / *b:* BerBA.
  Continued as
BERWICK ADVERTISER. Berwick, N 29, 1823-date. w.
  a: CSmH O 28, 1826. / *b:* BerBA; L Ja 1825-32.

BRITISH GAZETTE and Public Advertiser. London. [?]-1776-97-[?].
  b: UCP.

BRITISH GUARDIAN. London. [?]-1809-[?].
  a: CSmH no76, D 24, 1809.

BRITISH GUARDIAN and Protestant Advocate. London. no1-116, Ja 7, 1824-Mr 22, 1826. w.
  a: CSmH N 30, 1825. / *b:* BP Jl 7, 1824; L.

BRITISH IMPERIAL CALENDAR; or General Directory of the United British Empire. London. 1809.
  b: O.
  Continued as
BRITISH IMPERIAL CALENDAR, or General Register of the United Kingdom. London. 1810-date.
  b: UCP; O 1810, 1812-14, 1817, 1819-20, 1824-29, 1832.

BRITISH LABOURER'S PROTECTOR and Factory Child's Friend. Leeds. no1-31, S 21, 1832-1833. w.
  a: ULS. / *b:* UCP.

BRITISH LADY'S MAGAZINE and Monthly Miscellany. London. v1-5, ns, v1-2, 1815-18. m.

a: ULS. / *b:* UCP; L.
  Continued as
NEW BRITISH LADY'S MAGAZINE; or Monthly Mirror of Literature and Fashion. London. s3, v1-3, 1819. m.
  a: ULS.

BRITISH LION. London. no1-11, Ap 3-Je 12, 1825. w.
  a: CSmH no10, Je 5, 1825. / *b:* L; O ,no1.

BRITISH LUMINARY. London. no1+, Ja 4-S 26, 1818. w.
  a: DLC Jl 4-S 26, 1818. / *b:* L no3-38. (Incorporated O 3, 1818, with *Weekly Intelligencer* and continued as *Weekly Intelligencer and British Luminary*. For details, see *Weekly Intelligencer*.)

BRITISH LUMINARY and Weekly Intelligencer.
  (See *Weekly Intelligencer*.)

BRITISH LYRE; or, Muses Repository . . . containing a Collection of New Songs. London. 1793. a.
  a: MH. / *b:* UCP; L.

BRITISH MAGAZINE. London. v1-2, Ja 1800-Ja 1801. m.
  a: ULS; DLC; ICN v2, no7-9; PPL. / *b:* UCP; L.

BRITISH MAGAZINE. London. no1-3, Ja-Mr 1825. m.
  a: L.

BRITISH MAGAZINE. London. v1-12, 1828-37.
  a: CtY v1, 11-12.

BRITISH MAGAZINE; a Continuation of "The Spirit and Manners of the Age."
  (See *The Spirit and Manners of the Age*.)

BRITISH MAGAZINE; a Monthly Journal of Literature, Science, and Art. London. v1-2, 1830.
  a: ULS. / *b:* UCP; L.

BRITISH MAGAZINE; or, Monthly Magazine of Polite Literature, comprehending an Analysis of Modern Publications with Extracts. London. v1, 1823. m.
  b: UCP; DL no1-2; L.

BRITISH MAGAZINE and Monthly Register of Religious and Ecclesiastical Information, Parochial History, &c. London. v1-36, 1832-49.
  a: ULS; ULSup. / *b:* UCP; BwP; EP; GrP; L; MCh.

BRITISH MAGAZINE and Periodical Gleaner, or Depository for Hints and Suggestions calculated to Promote the Comfort and Happiness of Men. Glasgow. v1, no1-10, O 1818-Jl 1819. m.
  b: GM lacking no1.

BRITISH MAGAZINE of Literature, Religion, and Philosophy. London. v1, no1-3, Ja-Mr 1828. m.
  a: ULSup. / *b:* L.

BRITISH MEDICAL JOURNAL.London.1798.
  b: L Prospectus only.

BRITISH MERCURY; or, Historical and Critical Views of the Events of the Present
Times. London. v1-5, 1797-1800. s.m.
  a: ULS. / b: UCP; BrP; L v1; MR 1798-
99.

BRITISH MERCURY; or Wednesday Evening
Post. London. [?]-1814-25. w.
  a: CSmH ns, no18, S 10, 1823; DLC Ja 6,
1819-D 27, 1820. / b: L no412+, Mr 30,
O 12, 19, 1814; Ja 7, 1818-Jl 13, 1825.

BRITISH MILITARY JOURNAL. London.
v1, no1-6, O 1798-Mr 1799. m.
  a: ULS.

BRITISH MILITARY LIBRARY; or Journal,
comprehending a Complete Body of Military
Knowledge. London. v1-2, 1798-1801. m.
  a: ULS. / b: L.

BRITISH MINERALOGY. London. [?]-1808-
[?]. m.
  (No issues known. See Literary Annual
  Register, or Records of Literature, F
  1808, p. 72, where it is stated that 42
  nos. have appeared.)

BRITISH MISCELLANY. London.[?]-1808/?.
m.
  (No issues known. See Literary Annual
  Register, or Records of Literature, F
  1808, pp. 67-75, for details.)

BRITISH MONITOR.
  (See Anti-Gallican Monitor.)

BRITISH MUSE; or Cabinet of Harmony.
London. v1, no1, Ja 1818. m.
  b: O.

BRITISH NAVAL MAGAZINE; or, Maritime
Journal.
  (See Naval Magazine; or, Maritime Miscel-
  lany.)

BRITISH NEPTUNE. London. no1+, Ja 1803-
1823. w.
  a: CSmH no15, Ap 11, 1803. / b:L no904-
3395, Ja 4, 1818-My 12, 1823.

BRITISH NEPTUNE; or, Naval, Military, and
Fashionable Advertiser. London. [?]-1808-
[?]. w.
  b: L no269, Mr 6, 1808.

BRITISH POETICAL MISCELLANY. Huddersfield. no1-30, 1797. w.
  a: ULS. / b: UCP; L.

BRITISH POLITICAL GAZETTE. London.
no1-6, Je 14-Jl 19, 1828. w.
  b: L.

BRITISH PREACHER. London. v1-3, 1831-
32.
  b: UCP.

BRITISH PRESS; or, Morning Literary Advertiser. London. Ja 1, 1803-O 31, 1826. d.

  a: CSmH Ja 27, 1824; CtY 11 sc.nos. 1806-
09; DLC (O 15-27, 1821); MB 1803; F 22,
Ap 10, 1812; MiU-C F 4, 1814; MnU S 7,
1820; O 12, 1825; NNC (Jl-D 1810); NNHi
S 1, 1804-My 31, 1805; Ja 1, 1806-Je 30,
1807; Ja 30, 1808-D 30, 1809; Jl 2, 1810-
Je 29, 1811; NjR 7 sc.nos. Jl 1811; 2 sc.
nos. Ap-My 1812; 26 sc.nos. Mr-Jl 1814;
7 sc.nos. Jl-D 1815; WHi 14 sc.nos. 1805-
06. / b: BiP Je 28, 1814; F 3, 1820; BlU
5 sc.nos. 1805; 15 sc.nos. 1815; L no1,
Ja 1, 1803; no22+, Ja 26, 1803-O 31, 1826,
lacking D 31, 1810-Ja 1, 1818; LLL Je 20,
1818; O 1804-09, impf.; TmP Mr 22-24,
1820.

BRITISH PUBLIC CHARACTERS.
  (See Public Characters.)

BRITISH PULPIT. London. v1-6, 1832-36.
  b: UCP.

BRITISH REVIEW and London Critical Journal. London. v1-23, 1811-25. q.
  a: ULS. / b: UCP; BP; L; LLL lacking
v22-23; NwL v16-21; WcP.

BRITISH SEAMAN'S ADVOCATE. London.
v1-2, 1825.
  b: UCP.

BRITISH SEAMAN'S MAGAZINE; or, Church
of England Maritime Guardian. London. v1,
no1, F 1831.
  b: BP.

BRITISH SOCIETY for Promoting the Religious Principles of the Reformation. London
Quarterly Extracts. London. 1828-31.
  a: ULS.

BRITISH SOCIETY for Promoting the Religious Principles of the Reformation. Reports.
London. 1828-31.
  b: UCP.

BRITISH STAGE AND LITERARY CABINET.
London. v1-6, 1817-22. m.
  a: ULS. / b: L v1-6, v1-2 impf.

BRITISH STAGE, or Dramatic Censor. London. v1, no1-3, Ap-Je, 1831/?. m.
  a: ULS.

BRITISH STATESMAN. London. no1-262, F
10-D 11, 1819. d.
  a: CSmH no148, Jl 31, 1819. / b: L.

BRITISH TARIFF. London. v1-34, 1829-62.
  b: UCP; L.

BRITISH THALIA; or, Jacks of Newbury's
Delight. London. no1-3, 182?.
  b: LGU.

BRITISH THEATRE. London. 1800-[?].
  (No issues known. See C & K, 1082.)

BRITISH TRAVELLER. London. no1-3703,
1821-33. d.
  a: CSmH Ag 11, 1821; DLC 6 sc.nos. O-D
1826; 21 sc.nos. Ja-Je 1827. / b: L.

BRITISH TRIDENT; or Register of Naval Actions. London. 1804-09.
  b: DL.

BRITISH UNIVERSALIST. Glasgow. 1829.
  b: UCP.

BRITISH VOLUNTEER and Manchester Weekly Express. Manchester. no 2, 1804-1825-[?]. w.
  a: CSmH N 14, 1818; MBAt Mr 1, 1806; MHi D 30, 1809; 9 sc.nos. 1810. / *b:* BP 12 sc.nos. 1805-15; L no 28-182, Ja 5, 1805-D 6, 1807; MP no576-938, Ag 5, 1815-Ag 3, 1822; SfP O 8, 1825.

BRITISH VOLUNTEER, and Sunday Naval Chronicle. London. no1+, 1804-1806-[?]. w.
  a: MBAt 1 no.1806. / *b:* C no108, Mr 30, 1806.

BRITISH YEOMAN AND RURAL GAZETTE. London. no1-14, 1832.
  b: L.

THE BRITON. Newark. v1, no1-54, Ja 23, 1793-F 12, 1794. w.
  b: BP; L; NP.

THE BRITON. London. no1-9, 1819. w.
  a: ULS. / *b:* L.

THE BRITON'S FRIEND; or, Moral and Oeconomical Register. London. no1-4, S 5-26, 1807. w.
  b: O.

BROWNE'S GENERAL LAW-LIST, being an Alphabetical Register of the Names and Residence of all the Judges, Sergeants, Counsellors . . . and Attornies, &c. London. 1777-1797/?.
  b: L 1789-90, 1792-97.

Y BRUD A SYLWYDD; sef cyfrwng o wybodiaeth gyffredinawl. Caerfyrddin, Liverpool. no1-8, 1828.
  b: UCP; L no1-7.

BRUNSWICK; or, True Blue. London. no1-18. Ja 28-My 28, 1821.
  b: L.

BRYDGES' BRITISH BIBLIOGRAPHER.
  (See *Censura Literaria*.)

BUCKINGHAMSHIRE, Bedfordshire and Hertfordshire Chronicle. Aylesbury. [?]-1820-1829/?. w.
  a: CSmH S 13, 1828. / *b:* AybA 1820-25; L no122-436, N 20, 1822-Ja 3, 1829, lacking Je 28-S 6, 1828.

BUCKS GAZETTE, Windsor and Eton Express and Reading Journal. Windsor, Aylesbury. no1+, 1812-1849. (Subtitle varies.) w.
  a: CSmH no674, Je 18, 1825; no937, Jl 3, 1830. / *b:* L no866+, F 21, 1829-32.

BUCKS HERALD. Aylesbury. no1+, Ja 7, 1832-date.
  b: L.

THE BUDGET.
  (See *Paddy Kelly's Budget; or, a Pennyworth of Fun*.)

BUILDER'S PRICE BOOK. London. 1776-1806.
  b: L 1805-06; LP 1792, 1801.
  Continued as
TAYLOR'S BUILDER'S PRICE BOOK. London. 1808-31-[?].
  b: C 1825; L 1808-31; LP 1822, 1827, 1830.
  (Continued as *Taylor's Original and Improved Price Book*, [?]-1854/?.)

THE BULL DOG, A WEEKLY EXPOSITOR OF HUMBUG. London. no1-4, Ag 26-S 16, 1826. w.
  b: L.

BULLETINS OF STATE INTELLIGENCE.
  (See *Bulletins of the Campaign*.)

BULLETINS OF THE CAMPAIGN. London. v1-23, 1793-1815. (Compiled from *The London Gazette*.)
  a: ULS; ULSup; IHi. / *b:* UCP; BP; C; L; LU.
  Continued as
BULLETINS OF STATE INTELLIGENCE. London. v1-33, 1817-49. (Compiled from *The London Gazette*.)
  a: ULS; ULSup; IHi. / *b:* UCP; BP; L; LU.
  (Continued as *Bulletins and other State Intelligence*, 1849-date.)

THE BURNISHER. no1-11, D 20, 1800-F 28, 1801. w.
  b: UCP.

BURY AND NORWICH POST. Bury St. Edmunds. [?]-1787-1931. w. (Preceded by *Bury Post; or Suffolk and Norfolk Advertiser*, 1782-1785-[?]. (Also has varying subtitle.)
  a: ICU 30 sc.nos. 1798-1808; S 6-N 29, 1809; Ja 31-Mr 7, Ap 4-S 26, O 24-D 26, 1810; Ja 2-30, F 13-D 25, 1811. / *b:* BurC; C (Ja 31, 1810-D 15, 1813); sc.nos. 1823; (Mr 16, 1825-S 26, 1827); [1828]; 1829-32; L My 21, 1794-1832; NrP 1802-30.

BURY AND SUFFOLK HERALD.
  (See *Suffolk Herald*.)

BURY AND SUFFOLK PRESS. Bury St. Edmunds. no1-69, Mr 21, 1832-1833.
  a: CSmH no8, My 9, 1832. / *b:* L.

BURY GAZETTE; or Bury, Ipswich and Norwich Advertiser for the Counties of Suffolk, Norwich, &c. Bury St. Edmunds. no1+, 1821-27. w.
  a: CSmH S 18, 1822. / *b:* BurC; C; L Ja 9, Ap 3, 1822.

THE BURY PHILOSOPHIC ALBUM, including a Variety of Original Articles. Bury St. Edmunds. 1827.
  b: L.

BUSINESS OF THE DIAGNOSTIC SOCIETY. Edinburgh University.

(See *Edinburgh University. Business of the Diagnostic Society.*)

THE BUSY BODY; a Collection of Periodical Essays, Moral, Whimsical, Comic and Sentimental. London. v1-2, 1787-89.
  b: UCP; L; MR.

THE BUSY BODY; or, Men and Manners. London. v1-4, 1816-18. m.
  a: ULS. / *b:* L no1-5; LGU v1-2; O.

THE BUTTERFLY, a Series of Literary Papers. Warrington. no1-25, D 31, 1825-Ap 21, 1827.
  a: ULS. / *b:* L no1-19, 21-25; O; WrP.

THE BY-STANDER; or, Universal Weekly Expositor. London. v1, no1-26, Ag 15, 1789-F 6, 1790. w.
  a: ULS; MdBJ. / *b:* UCP; L.

THE CAB. London. no1-19, Mr 3-Jl 7, 1832.
  a: ULS. / *b:* BP no1-4, 6-8; L no1-17; O no1, 5.

THE CABINET. London. no1-36, Ja 2-F 11, 1792-[?].
  a: MdBJ sc.nos. Ja-F 1792. / *b:* L Ja 2, 4, 1792; MR no15-16.

THE CABINET. Norwich. v1-3, 1794-95.
  a: ULS. / *b:* L; LLL.

CABINET. London. no1-12, Ap 16-Jl 2, 1803. w.
  a: ULS. / *b:* L.

CABINET; or, Monthly Report of Polite Literature. London. v1-6, F 1807-Ag 1809. m.
  a: ULS. / *b:* BP v1, 3; GM; L v1-4; O v1-4; SP.

CABINET; or, the Selected Beauties of Literature. Edinburgh. v1-2, 1824-25/?.
  a: ULS.

THE CABINET ANNUAL REGISTER, and Historical, Political, Biographical, and Miscellaneous Chronicle. v1-3, 1831-33. a.
  b: UCP; L; O 1831-32.

THE CABINET HISTORIAN; a Series of Summaries of the History of each Country. v1, pt1, 1825.
  b: L.

CABINET MAGAZINE; or Literary Olio. London. v1-2, 1796-97.
  a: ULS. / *b:* UCP; L lacking Je 1797.

CABINET OF CURIOSITIES; or, Wonders of the World Displayed. London. no1-34. 1824. w.
  b: DL; SoP no1-27.

CABINET OF FOREIGN VOYAGES and Travels; or Annual Selections from the latest Works of that Description, which have not yet Appeared in English. London. v1, 1825. a.
  b: UCP; L.
    Continued as
ANNUAL CABINET OF MODERN FOREIGN Voyages and Travels. London. v2, 1826.
  b: UCP; L.

THE CABINET OF LIFE, Wit, and Humour. Liverpool. no1-8, 1829.
  b: L no1; O no1, 8.

CAERNARVON ADVERTISER. Caernarvon. Ja 5-Mr 30, 1822.
  b: BnU.

CAERNARVON HERALD and North Wales Advertiser. Caernarvon. no1-262, Ja 1, 1831-1836. w.
  a: CSmH no37, S 10, 1831. / *b:* BnU (1831-32); L.
  (Continued as *Caernarvon and Denbigh Herald and North and South Wales Independent*, 1836-1900.)

THE CALEDONIAN. Glasgow. no1-31, Ap 11-N 7, 1807. w.
  b: GM lacking no23.

THE CALEDONIAN.
  (See *The Caledonian; or, Donald's Letters to his Country-Folk.*)

THE CALEDONIAN, a Quarterly Journal. Dundee. no1-6, 1820-21. q.
  a: ULS. / *b:* UCP; DnP; EP; GM no1-5; L; SaU.

THE CALEDONIAN; or, Donald's Letters to his Country-Folk on Borough Politics, Political Economy, &c. Aberdeen. no1, Ap 17, 1818.
  (No issues known. See S N & Q. s1.I.20.)
    Continued as
THE CALEDONIAN. Aberdeen. no[?]-4, [?]-My 8, 1818.
  (No issues known. See S N & Q, s1.I.20.)

CALEDONIAN; or, Scottish Literary and Political Investigator. London. 1819. w.
  a: CSmH no2, Ja 9, 1819. / *b:* L no5-15, Ja 30-Ap 10, 1819; O no1, Ja 2, 1819.

CALEDONIAN CANAL REPORTS. n.p. v1-95, 1803-1919.
  b: UCP.

CALEDONIAN CHRONICLE. Edinburgh. no1+, O 9, 1792-Je 25, 1793. s.w.
  a: MiD-B Ja 8, 1793.

CALEDONIAN HORTICULTURAL SOCIETY. Memoirs. Edinburgh. v1-5, 1814-32.
  a: ULS. / *b:* UCP.

CALEDONIAN LITERARY AND POLITICAL Museum. Aberdeen. no1-7, Ap 10-Jl 3, 1815.f.
  b: AU.

CALEDONIAN MAGAZINE: or Aberdeen Repository. Aberdeen. v1-ns, v5, 1786-90. f.
  b: UCP; L v1, 3.

CALEDONIAN MAGAZINE AND REVIEW.
  (See *Dundee Magazine and Caledonian Review.*)

CALEDONIAN MERCURY. Edinburgh. 1720-1867. t.w.
  a: ULS; C-S Ag 15,20,22,25,27, 1791; S 11-D 9, 1824; CSmH D 10, 1803; CtY F 28, 1795; DLC (Ja-Je 9, 1800); TxU 37 sc.nos.

Mr 27-Ag 28, 1790. / b: UCP; C Jl 10, 1802; E; EP 1790-91, 1800-08, 1815-16; ESL 1789-1800; Je 1, 1801-My 31, 1802; Je 2, 1803-My 31, 1804; Je 3, 1805-My 31, 1806; GeG 1820-25; L 1789-1832, lacking 5 nos. for 1828.

CALENDAR OF CRIME and General Advertiser. London. no1-3, 1832.
   b: BP; O no1.

CALM OBSERVER'S LETTERS. London. 1793.
   b: O.

CAMBRIAN, or General Weekly Advertiser for the Principality of Wales. Swansea. 1804-1930. w.
   a: CSmH O 10, 1818; CtY 1817; 9 sc.nos. 1822. / b: UCP; CrP 1804-32 impf.; L 1818-27; 1830-32; SwI (1804-32); SwP 1804-31.
   (Merged with *Herald of Wales* from 1930.)

CAMBRIAN AND CALEDONIAN Quarterly Magazine and Celtic Repertory.
   (See *Cambrian Quarterly Magazine, and Celtic Repertory*.)

CAMBRIAN MAGAZINE.
   (See *Cambrian Visitor; a Monthly Miscellany*.)

CAMBRIAN QUARTERLY MAGAZINE, and Celtic Repertory. London. v1-4, 1829-33. q.
   a: ULS. / b: UCP; CrP; DLL lacking v3; L; SwP.
   (Continued as *Cambrian and Caledonian Quarterly Magazine and Celtic Repertory*.)

CAMBRIAN REGISTER. London. v1-3, 1796-1818.
   a: ULS. / b: UCP; CrP; L; LLL lacking v3.

CAMBRIAN VISITOR; a Monthly Miscellany. Swansea. 1813. m.
   a: ULS. / b: UCP; CrP; L; O.
   Continued as
   CAMBRIAN MAGAZINE. Swansea. no1-2, 1813. m.
   a: ULS. / b: UCP; L.

CAMBRIDGE, ENGLAND. University Astronomical Observatory. Astronomical Observations. Cambridge. v1-26, 1828-1928.
   a: ULS.

CAMBRIDGE CHRONICLE AND JOURNAL. Cambridge. no1+, 1762-1848. w.
   a: CSmH S 21, 1827. / b: C; L F 25, D 8 1804; Ja 30, Jl 2, 1808; Ja 28, 1809; O 26, N 2-D 28, 1810; 1811-32.
   (Continued as *Cambridge Chronicle and University Journal*, 1849-1934; in 1934 incorporated with *Cambridge Independent Press*.)

CAMBRIDGE INTELLIGENCER. Cambridge. 1793-1803. w.
   a: ULS; NcD (Jl-D 1793), 1794, (1795-96, Ja-S 1797, 1800); ICU Ja-O 1798. / b: C (1799-1803); CPU Jl 20, 1793-D 31, 1796; sc.nos. Ja 1797-Je 1803; L (1798-D 1800).

CAMBRIDGE MAGAZINE. Cambridge. no1-2, Mr 11-25, 1829. f.
   b: UCP.

CAMBRIDGE MONTHLY REPOSITORY. Cambridge. no1, D 1819. m.
   b: UCP.

CAMBRIDGE PHILOSOPHICAL SOCIETY. Transactions. Cambridge. v1-23, 1820-1928.
   a: ULS; ULSup. / b: BP v1-4; CPL; DRS v1-5; LR.

CAMBRIDGE QUARTERLY REVIEW, and Academical Register. London. v1-2, 1824.
   b: UCP; L v1.

THE CAMBRO-BRITON, and General Celtic Repository. London. v1-3, no1-22, S 1819-Je 1822. m. (Suspended Jl-O 1821.)
   a: ULS. / b: UCP; BP; CrP; L; LLL; O v1-2, SwP.

THE CAMEO. London. 1831. a.
   (No issues known. See CBEL, III.840.)

CAMERA OBSCURA; or, Life in Glasgow. Glasgow. v1-2, [?]-1831. m.
   b: E v2, no57-58, Ap-My 1831.

O CAMPEAO PORTUGUEZ; ou, O Amigo do Rei e do Povo, Jornal Politico. London. v1-4, no1-36, Jl 1819-Jl 1821. m.
   a: ULS. / b: L.

CANAL BOATMAN'S MAGAZINE. Nottingham. 1830-31. m.
   b: NP v1, no2, 4; ns, no1.

CANAL BOATMEN'S MAGAZINE. London. v1; ns, v1-3, 1829-32. (The head title of v1 reads *Paddington Canal Boatmen's Magazine*.)
   b: UCP; L; NP ns, v1, no3.

CANTERBURY Philosophical and Literary Institution. Annual Report. Canterbury. 1830.
   a: ULS.

CANTON MISCELLANY. London. no1-5, 1831.
   b: UCP.

THE CAP OF LIBERTY, a Political Publication. London. v1, S 8, 1819-Jl 4, 1820. w.
   a: ULS. / b: UCP; L; O.
   (Incorporated with *The Medusa; or Penny Politician*, Ja 5, 1820.)

CAPTAIN ROCK; or the Chieftain's Gazette. London, Dublin. 1827. (According to John Power's *Irish Literary Periodical Publications*, p. 12, this was an unsuccessful attempt to revive an 1825-26 publication of similar title.)
   b: DL.

CAPTAIN ROCK IN LONDON; or, the Chieftain's Weekly Gazette. London. no1-94, Mr 5, 1825-D 16, 1826. w.
   a: ULS; ULSup. / b: UCP; BiP; DA; DL; DM no1-44; L.

CAREY'S GENERAL EVENING POST.
   (See *General Evening Post* of Dublin.)

CATHOLIC ANNUAL. London. 1827-30.
  b: UCP; O 1830.

CATHOLIC ASSOCIATION in Dublin. Proceedings. London. My 13, 1823-F 11, 1825.
  b: UCP.

CATHOLIC GENTLEMAN'S MAGAZINE. London. no1-9, Ja-S 1818. m.
  b: UCP; L no1-8.

CATHOLIC JOURNAL. London. no1-55, Mr 1, 1828-Mr 15, 1829. w.
  a: CSmH Mr 15, 1829. / *b:* L.

CATHOLIC MAGAZINE. London. no1-6, Je-D 1812/?. m.
  a: ULS. / *b:* UCP.

CATHOLIC MAGAZINE.
  (See *Edinburgh Catholic Magazine.*)

CATHOLIC MAGAZINE and Reflector. Liverpool. no1-2, 1801.
  a: ULS.

CATHOLIC MAGAZINE and Review. London. v1, no1-4, Ja-Ap 1813. m.
  b: UCP.

CATHOLIC MAGAZINE and Review. Birmingham. v1-6, 1831-35; s2-s3, 1836-43/?.
  a: ULS. / *b:* UCP; BO; BP; L; SthC.

CATHOLIC MISCELLANY; and Monthly Repository of Information. London. v1-9, ns, v1-3, 1822-30.
  a: ULS. / *b:* UCP; DCC v7; L v4-12; SthC.

CATHOLIC OR CHRISTIANITY not Popery. Manchester. no1-20, 1821-22.
  b: BP.

CATHOLIC PHENIX; or Papal Scourge. [Manchester]. no1-6, 1822.
  b: BP.

CATHOLIC SPECTATOR, Selector, and Monitor; or Catholicon.
  (See *Catholicon; or, the Christian Philosopher.*)

CATHOLIC VINDICATOR, a Weekly Paper, in Reply to "The Protestant." London. no1-52, 1818-19. w.
  a: ULS. / *b:* UCP; L.

CATHOLICON; or, the Christian Philosopher; a Roman Catholic Magazine. London. v1-5, 1815-18; ns, v1, 1818. m. (Individual nos. in v1 appeared as *The Publicist.*)
  a: ULS. / *b:* UCP; DCC 1815-16; L.
  Continued as
  CATHOLIC SPECTATOR, Selector, and Monitor; or Catholicon. London. s3, v1-4, 1823-26.
  a: ULS. / *b:* UCP; L v1.

CELESTIAL ATLAS. London. 1805-90.
  (No issues known. Issues for 1820, 1824-32, once held by LUC, but destroyed by fire as result of bombing.)

THE CENSOR. London. v1, Ja-D 1803. m.
  b: L.

THE CENSOR. Oxford. no1-5, My 15-Je 19, 1813. w.
  b: O.

THE CENSOR: an entirely original Work, devoted to Literature, Poetry, and the Drama. London. no1-16, S 6, 1828-Ap 4, 1829. f.
  a: ULS; CSmH. / *b:* L; O no1, 16.

CENSOR AMERICANO. London. v1, Jl-O 1820.
  a: ULS.

CENSURA LITERARIA. London. v1-10, 1805-09.
  a: ULS; ULSup. / *b:* WmP.
  Continued as
  BRITISH BIBLIOGRAPHER. London. v1-4, 1810-14. (Also called *Brydges' British Bibliographer*)
  a: ULS. / *b:* WmP.
  Continued as
  RESTITUTA; or, Titles, Extracts, and Characters of old Books in English Literature, revived. London. v1-4, 1814-16.
  a: ULS; ULSup.

THE CERBERUS; or Tartarean Review. London. v1, no1, My 1, 1830.
  b: BoP.

CHALMERS'S JOURNAL, and Monthly Miscellany of Arts and Sciences. n.p. 1827.
  b: GM.

CHALMERS'S JOURNAL of Useful Knowledge. Edinburgh. v1, 1827.
  b: UCP.

CHAMBERS'S EDINBURGH JOURNAL. Edinburgh, London. v1-12, 1832-44; ns, v1-20, 1844-54. w.
  a: ULS; ULSup. / *b:* UCP; BP; DL; E; EP; GeG; GrP; L; LLL; PrH; SptP.

CHAMBERS'S HISTORICAL NEWSPAPER. A Monthly Record of Intelligence. Edinburgh. no1-39, N 1832-D 1835. m.
  a: ULS. / *b:* BP; EP; L; LLL; O no1.

CHAMELEON. London. s1-s2, 1832-33.
  a: ULS. / *b:* UCP; EP; GM; O.

CHAMPION. A Weekly Political and Literary Journal.
  (See *Drakard's Paper.*)

CHAMPION. Weekly Review of Politics and Political Economy. London. 1813-1821-[?].w.
  b: L no464, N 25, 1821; O no452, S 2, 1821.

CHAMPION AND SUNDAY REVIEW of Weekly News, Literature and Arts.
  (See *Drakard's Paper.*)

CHAMPION OF THE EAST. Stamford. no1-4, Ja 5-26, 1830. w.
  b: L.
  Continued as

BOSTON, LOUTH, NEWARK, STAMFORD, and Rutland Champion. Stamford. no5-52, F 2-D 28, 1830. w.
  a: CSmH no6, F 9, 1830. / *b:* L.
  Continued as
STAMFORD CHAMPION. Stamford. no53-104, Ja 4-D 27, 1831. w.
  b: L.
  Continued as
LINCOLN AND NEWARK TIMES, Stamford Champion, &c. Stamford. no105-107, Ja 4-18, 1832. w.
  a: CSmH Jl 6, 1831. / *b:* L.
  (Incorporated with *Drakard's Stamford News.*)

THE CHANGELING. London. no1, O 31, 1813. w.
  a: DLC.

THE CHANTICLEER. London. no1, My 28, 1829.
  b: LU.

THE CHARLES JAMES FOX. London. no1-29, 1814-15. w.
  a: ULS. / *b:* L.

CHART AND COMPASS. (British and Foreign Sailors' Society.) London. v1+, 1808-date.
  a: ULS.

THE CHAT OF THE WEEK; or, Compendium of all Topics of Public Interest, &c.
  (See *The Chat of the Week and Gazette of Literature.* &c.)

THE CHAT OF THE WEEK and Gazette of Literature, Fine Arts, and Theatricals. London. no1-13, Je 5-Ag 28, 1830. w. (no1-7 known as *The Chat of the Week; or Compendium of all Topics of Public Interest, Original and Select.*)
  a: ULS. / *b:* L.

THE CHEAP MAGAZINE; or Poor Man's Fireside Companion. Haddington. v1-2, Ja 1813-D 1814. m.
  a: ULS. / *b:* UCP; EP; GM; HnP; L.
  Continued as
MONTHLY MONITOR and Philanthropic Museum; being a Cheap Repository for Hints, Suggestions, Facts and Discoveries interesting to Humanity. Haddington. v1-2, Ja-D 1815. m.
  a: ULS. / *b:* UCP; DL v1; EP v1; HnA; HnP; O.

THE CHEILEAD; or University Coterie; being Violent Ebullitions and Graphomaniacs, affected by cacoethes scribendi, and fama-e sacra fames. Edinburgh. no1-16, O 1826-F 16, 1827. w.
  a: ULS. / *b:* AU; EP; EU; L.

CHELMSFORD CHRONICLE. Chelmsford. no1+, 1771-1884. w. (Preceded by *Chelmsford and Colchester Chronicle*, 1764-71.)
  a: CSmH S 7, 1821; CtY [Ja 2-N 27, 1789], 1790; ICU Ja 1, 8, Mr 5-Ap 23, 1799. / *b:* L Je 24, 1791; Je 1, 1832+.
  (Continued as *Essex County Chronicle*, 1884-1919; as *Essex Chronicle*, 1920-date.)

CHELMSFORD GAZETTE. Chelmsford. 1822-1825. w.
  b: L no71-169; Ja 2, 1824-D 30, 1825.

THE CHELSEA GAZETTE; containing Reports of Proceedings in Vestry, and Letters on Miscellaneous Subjects. Chelsea. no1-8, 1822.
  b: L.

CHELTENHAM ALBUM. Cheltenham. Jl-O 1828.
  b: BP.

CHELTENHAM CHRONICLE and Gloucester Advertiser. Cheltenham. no1+, My 4, 1809-date. w. (Subtitle varies.)
  a: CSmH N 13, 1828. / *b:* CtP My 4, 1809-D 27, 1810; My 12, 1814-D 30, 1819; L Ap 26, My 3, 17, 1810; S 16, 1813; Ja 4, 1827-32.

CHELTENHAM JOURNAL. Cheltenham. 1824-1868. w. (Subtitle varies.)
  a: CSmH Ja 28, 1828. / *b:* GrP F 7, 1825; Mr 28, 1825; Ja 16, 1826; D 31, 1827; L Ja 1, 1827-1832, lacking 1829; D 7-28, 1830; Ap 19, Jl 19, D 13, 1831; Ag 15, 1832.

THE CHEMIST. London. v1-2, Mr 13, 1824-Ap 16, 1825. w.
  a: ULS. / *b:* UCP; L.

CHESHIRE AND NORTH WALES MAGAZINE. Chester. v1, no1, 1813.
  b: UCP.

CHESTER CHRONICLE; or Commercial Intelligencer. Chester. 1775-date. w. (Subtitle varies.)
  a: CSmH D 31, 1819; CtY (1791). / *b:* BP Ag 24, 1804; BnU 1810-13, 1818-25; ChsCCh; CrP 1812-22 impf.; L (Jl 29, 1791-92), 1825-32.

CHESTER COURANT and Advertiser for North Wales.
  (See *Adams' Weekly Courant.*)

CHESTER COURANT and Anglo-Welsh Gazette.
  (See *Adams' Weekly Courant.*)

CHESTER GLEANER; a Cheshire, Lancashire, Shropshire and North Wales Monthly Magazine. Chester. no1, 1824.
  b: L.

CHESTER GUARDIAN. Chester. [?]-1822-[?].
  b: L no241, Ap 25, 1822.

CHESTERFIELD GAZETTE, and Scarsdale and High Peak Advertiser. Chesterfield. 1828-29.
  a: CSmH no52, D 27, 1828. / *b:* DeP.

THE CHILDREN'S FRIEND. Kirby Lonsdale. 1824-93/?.
  a: ULS; ULSup. / *b:* L lacking 1824-25; Jl-Ag 1826; F-My 1827; Mr 1830.

THE CHILDREN'S MAGAZINE; or Monthly Repository of Instruction and Delight. London. 1799-1800. m.
  a: ULS. / *b:* L.

THE CHILD'S COMPANION; or, Sunday Scholar's Reward. London. v1-9, 1824-31; ns, v1-6, 1832-37; s3, v1-7, 1838-44.
  b: L.
  (Continued as *Child's Companion and Juvenile Instructor*, 1846-date.)

THE CHILD'S MAGAZINE and Sunday Scholar's Companion. London. 1832-45/?.
  a: ULS. / *b:* L v2, 4-6 &c.

CHIMNEY CORNER COMPANION. London. v1, 1827.
  b: UCP; L; O.

THE CHOLERA GAZETTE, consisting of Documents Communicated by the Central Board of Health. London. no1-16, 1832.
  a: ULS. / *b:* UCP; C no1-6; L no1-6; LMD no1-6, 15-16; LS no1-6.

THE CHRISTIAN. By the Association for the Refutation of Infidel Publications. London. v1-2, no1-33, N 15, 1819-Jl 8, 1820. w.
  a: ULS. / *b:* UCP.

THE CHRISTIAN ADVOCATE and Weekly Record of Literature, Science, Agriculture, Commerce, and Polite Occurrences. London. no1-505, 1830-39. w.
  a: CSmH Ja 3, 1831. / *b:* L.

THE CHRISTIAN AMBASSADOR. Edinburgh. v1, 1824.
  b: UCP.

THE CHRISTIAN CHAMPION. London. no1-3, 1819.
  b: L no2-3.

THE CHRISTIAN CORRECTOR. London. 1829-32.
  b: GM impf.

THE CHRISTIAN EXAMINER and Church of Ireland Magazine. Dublin. v1-11, 1825-31; ns, v1-4, 1832-35; s3-s6, 1836-69.
  a: ULS. / *b:* UCP; BP; L; O.

THE CHRISTIAN FREEMAN. Belfast. v1-3, 1832-35.
  b: BlL.

THE CHRISTIAN GLEANER. London. v1-2, 1823.
  b: GM.

THE CHRISTIAN GLEANER and Missionary Museum. Dublin. [?]-1835.
  (No issues before 1833 known; L has v? 5, 1833-35.)

THE CHRISTIAN GUARDIAN, &c.
  (See *Zion's Trumpet, a Theological Miscellany.*)

THE CHRISTIAN HERALD.
  (See *The Missionary Magazine.*)

THE CHRISTIAN HERALD: a Monthly [afterwards. quarterly] Magazine, Chiefly on Subjects connected with Prophecy. Dublin. v1-5, 1830-35. m.; q.
  b: L.

THE CHRISTIAN INSTRUCTOR; or Occasional Expositor. Kendal. no1-12, 1825.
  b: L.

CHRISTIAN INVESTIGATOR. Aberdeen. v1, 1830-31.
  b: UCP.

CHRISTIAN KNOWLEDGE SOCIETY. Report of. London. 1814-23.
  (No issues known. Held by LGU until destroyed during bombing raid.)

THE CHRISTIAN LADY'S FRIEND and Family Repository. London. v1-2, 1832-33.
  b: L.

THE CHRISTIAN MAGAZINE; or, Evangelical Repository. Edinburgh. v1-10; ns, v1-14, 1797-1820. m.
  a: ULS. / *b:* UCP; EP 1817.
  United with *Christian Repository and Religious Register* and continued as
THE CHRISTIAN MONITOR and Religious Register. Edinburgh. 1821-25.
  a: ULS. / *b:* UCP.
  (Probably continued as *Edinburgh Theological Magazine*, but for details see under this title.)

THE CHRISTIAN MARINER'S JOURNAL; or, a Series of Observations and Reflections, on a Ship, the Sea, Sailors. the Works of God, &c. London. 1829.
  b: E; O.

THE CHRISTIAN MIRROR; exhibiting some of the Excellencies and Defects of the Religious World. London. no1-27, 1805.
  b: L.

THE CHRISTIAN MISCELLANY. London. v1-2, no1-24, 1816-17. m.
  b: LLL.

THE CHRISTIAN MISCELLANY; or, Religious and Moral Magazine. London. v1-3, 1792.
  a: ULS. / *b:* UCP; C; L.

CHRISTIAN MISCELLANY and Herald of Union. Perth. v1-2, [?]-1832/?.
  a: ULSup.

THE CHRISTIAN MODERATOR. London. v1-3, My 1826-D 1828.
  b: UCP; L.

THE CHRISTIAN MONITOR and Family Friend.
  (See *The Christian Monitor and Theological Review.*)

CHRISTIAN MONITOR and Religious Register.
  (See *Christian Magazine; or, Evangelical Repository.*)

THE CHRISTIAN MONITOR and Theological Review. London. v1-2, 1826-27.
  b: UCP; L.
  Continued as
THE CHRISTIAN MONITOR and Family Friend. London. v1-2, 1827-28.
  b: L.

THE CHRISTIAN MORALIST. London. no1, Ja 1, 1820. w.
  b: O.

THE CHRISTIAN OBSERVER, conducted by the Members of the Established Church. London. v1-74, 1802-74. m.
  a: ULS; ULSup. / b: UCP; GeG; L; LLL lacking 1818; SthC.
  (Continued as Christian Observer and Advocate, 1875-77.)

THE CHRISTIAN PIONEER, intended to uphold the Great Doctrines of the Reformation, the Sufficiency of Scripture, the Right of Individual Judgment, and of Fearless Free Inquiry. Glasgow, Edinburgh, Newcastle-upon-Tyne. v1-19, 1826-45.
  a: ULS; ULSup. / b: UCP; GM; L.

THE CHRISTIAN RECORDER. York. v1-2, Mr 1819-F 1821.
  a: ULS.

THE CHRISTIAN RECORDER. London. no1-25, Ja-Jl 1829. w.
  a: ULS.

THE CHRISTIAN RECORDER, and British and Foreign Religious Intelligencer. Glasgow. v1-3, Ja 1821-Ap 1822/?.
  a: ULS. / b: UCP; GM v1-2.

THE CHRISTIAN REFLECTOR and Theological Inquirer. Liverpool. v1-10, 1820-29. (Also v1-5; ns, v1-5.) m.
  a: ULS. / b: UCP; L; LvP 1821.

THE CHRISTIAN REFORMER; or New Evangelical Miscellany. Hackney. v1-19, 1815-33. m.
  a: ULS. / b: UCP; BP lacking v11; L.
  (Continued as Christian Reformer; or Unitarian Magazine and Review, 1834-63.)

THE CHRISTIAN REGISTER, or General Record of the Several Religious Metropolitan Meetings. London. 1829-30.
  b: L.

THE CHRISTIAN REMEMBRANCER; or the Churchman's Biblical, Ecclesiastical and Literary Miscellany. London. v1-22, 1819-40. m.; q.
  a: ULS. / b: UCP; BrP lacking v2-9; CrP v1; L; MCh; O.
  (Continued as Christian Remembrancer, a Monthly Magazine and Review, 1840-68.)

CHRISTIAN REPORTER. London. no1+, Ja 3, 1820-F 11, 1822. w.
  a: CSmH Jl 2, 1821. / b: L.
  (Incorporated with Philanthropic Gazette, F 20, 1822.)

THE CHRISTIAN REPORTER; or, Tract Missionary and Sabbath School Magazine. Dundee. v1-7, 1829-35.
  b: DnP.
  (Continued as Dundee Christian Reporter, 1836.)

THE CHRISTIAN REPOSITORY; a Magazine and Review, conducted chiefly by Members of the Baptist Denomination. London. v1-2, 1825-26.
  b: UCP; L.

CHRISTIAN REPOSITORY, and Religious Register. Edinburgh. v1-5, 1816-20.
  a: ULS. / b: UCP.
  (United in 1820 with Christian Magazine; or, Evangelical Repository, and continued as Christian Monitor and Religious Register. For details, see the former.)

THE CHRISTIAN REVIEW and Clerical Magazine. London. v1-3, 1827-29.
  a: ULS. / b: UCP; C; E; L.

CHRISTIAN SELECTOR, a Periodical Compilation, designed to Subserve the Interests of Religion and Morality. Paisley. ?/1810-1815/?.
  a: ULS.

CHRISTIAN SPECTATOR. London. no1, 1823.
  b: L.

CHRISTIAN VISITANT. Belfast. v1-2, 1825-27.
  a: ULS.

THE CHRISTIAN VISITOR. Glasgow. no1-4, 1827-28.
  b: GM lacking no4.

THE CHRISTIAN WATCHMAN; or Theological Inspector.
  (See The Watchman; or Theological Inspector.)

THE CHRISTIAN'S FRIEND. Huntingdon. no1-6, 1819-20.
  b: UCP; L.

THE CHRISTIAN'S MAGAZINE; or, Gospel Repository. Being a Compendium of Doctrinal and Experimental Religion. London. v1-3, 1790-92.
  a: ULS. / b: UCP; L.

THE CHRISTIAN'S MAGAZINE; or Weekly Miscellany of Religious Essays, Anecdotes, Literature, Biography, Intelligence, and Poetry. London. v1, F 26-Mr 26, 1831/?.
  a: ULS. / b: UCP; L.

THE CHRISTIAN'S PENNY MAGAZINE. A Weekly Miscellany conducted upon Principles of Protestant Reformation. London. v1-5; ns, v1-2, 1832-37.
  a: ULS. / b: UCP; CrP; L.

THE CHRISTIAN'S POCKET MAGAZINE, and Anti-Sceptic.
  (See The Christian's Pocket Magazine, and Theological Critic.)

THE CHRISTIAN'S POCKET MAGAZINE, and Theological Critic. London. v1-6, 1819-22. m.
  b: L.
  Continued as
THE CHRISTIAN'S POCKET MAGAZINE, and Anti-Sceptic. London. v7-9, 1822-23. m. (Also called ns, v1-3.)
  a: ULS. / b: L; O 1823.

THE CHRISTMAS BOX; an Annual Present for Children. London. 1828-29. a.
  b: UCP; O.
  Continued as
MARSHALL'S CHRISTMAS BOX. London. 1831-32. a.
  b: UCP; L; O.

THE CHRONICLE OF BRISTOL. Bristol. no1-6, Ag 1, 1829-Ja 1, 1830. m.
  b: BrP; L.

CHRONICLE OF THE TIMES and Provincial Magazine. Manchester. v1, 1815. m.
  a: ULS. / b: UCP; L; MCh; MP; MR; RdP.
  Continued as
THE MANCHESTER MAGAZINE; or Provincial Chronicle for the Courties of Chester, Derby, Lancaster, Stafford, and York. Manchester. v2, 1816. m. (Also called Manchester Magazine, the Chronicle of the Times, and Provincial Magazine.)
  a: ULS. / b: UCP; L; MCh; MP; MR; RdP.

CHRONICLER OF THE TIMES; or, Hypocrisy Unmasked. London. v1, 1832.
  b: UCP.

CHRONIQUE DE PARIS, imprimée à Londres, ouvrage Périodique. London. v1-2, 1816-17.
  b: L.
  Continued as
MEMOIRES SECRETS, ou Chronique de Paris. London. no10, 1817.
  b: L.

CHURCH EXAMINER and Ecclesiastical Record. London. v1, no1-21, My 19-D 1, 1832.
  a: ULS. / b: L; O lacking no19.

CHURCH MISSIONARY RECORD; detailing the Proceedings of the Church Missionary Society. London. v1-46, 1830-90.
  a: ULS. / b: UCP; L.
  (In 1876-78 was published with Christian Missionary Intelligencer, into which it merged in 1879.)

CHURCH MISSIONARY SOCIETY. Proceedings. London. v1+, 1801-date.
  a: ULS.

CHURCH MISSIONARY SOCIETY REPORT. (See Missionary Society. Report.)

CHURCH OF ENGLAND BULWARK, and Clergyman's Protector. London. v1, 1828.
  b: UCP; C; L.

CHURCH OF ENGLAND REVIEW. (Listed by ULS as running 1819-44, but 1837 is really the inception date.)

CHURCH OF ENGLAND-MAN'S EXPOSITOR. (See Expositor and Sunday Family Instructor.)

CHURCH OF SCOTLAND. (See Register of the Actings and Proceedings of the General Assembly of the Church of Scotland.)

CHURCH PATRONAGE REPORTER. Edinburgh. no1-13, 1829-32.
  a: ULS. / b: L no8-13.
  (Continued as Anti-Patronage Reporter, 1833-34, under which it is listed in ULS.)

CHURCH REFORMER'S MAGAZINE for England and Ireland. London. v1, F-Jl, 1832.
  b: E; L.

THE CHURCHMAN; a Magazine. London. v1-8, [?]-1829-43.
  b: E v2-8.

THE CHURCHMAN'S REMEMBRANCER, being a Collection of Scarce and Valuable Tracts in Defence of the Doctrine and Discipline of the Church of England. London. v1-2, 1803-08.
  a: ULS. / b: L.

CHUTE'S WESTERN HERALD and Kerry Advertiser. Tralee. 1805-35.
  a: CSmH Je 6, 1827. / b: L Ag 27, 1812; 1828-32.

THE CIGAR. London. v1-2, 1825.
  a: ULSup. / b: L.

THE CIRCULAR LETTER, from the Ministers and Messengers of the Baptist Congregational Churches statedly meeting at Alcester, Warwickshire. Oxford. 1806-32.
  b: BP sc.nos. 1806-32.

CIRCULAR TO BANKERS. (See Bankers' Circular.)

CIRCULATOR OF USEFUL KNOWLEDGE, Literature, Amusements, and General Information. London. no1-26, 1825. w.
  a: ULS. / b: UCP; L; LP.

THE CITIZEN. London. 1809.
  b: L Prospectus only.

THE CITIZEN. Cork. 1813.
  b: O no5, Je 24, 1813.

THE CITIZEN. Edinburgh. 1832.
  b: BP no1, Ja 9, 1832; L Prospectus only.

THE CITIZEN; a Fortnightly Periodical. Carlisle. 1821-33.
  b: CsP N 9, 1821-O 23, 1824; N 25, 1825-F 1, 1831; Mr 20-D 1832.

CIVIC SERMONS TO THE PEOPLE. Dundee. no1, 1792.
  b: E.

THE CLARE JOURNAL. Ennis. [1777]-1827-
[?]. s.w.; w. (Subtitle varies.)
  a: CSmH Ap 26, 1827. / *b:* C v18, no4,
for 1795.
  (Continued as *Ennis Journal and Clare
Advertiser,* [?]-1917. Incorporated in *Saturday Record.*)

CLARKE'S NEW LAW LIST.
  (See *New Law List.*)

THE CLASSIC WREATH. London. no1-2,
1832.
  b: L.

THE CLASSICAL JOURNAL. London. v1-40,
1810-29.
  a: ULS; ULSup. / *b:* UCP; BP; BrP; CrP
lacking v21; L; LLL; LvA v1-21; MCh.

THE CLERICAL REVIEW. Edinburgh. no1-2,
N 10-17, 1799. w.
  b: UCP.

THE CLERICAL REVIEW. n.p. v1-4, 1823.
  b: UCP.

THE CLERICAL REVIEW; or, Impartial Report of Sermons. Edinburgh. v1-2, 1800. w.
(May be the predecessor of *The Orthodox
Churchman's Magazine.*)
  a: PPL.

CLONMEL ADVERTISER. Clonmel. [?]-
1823-38.
  a: CSmH no1649, My 19, 1827. / *b:* D
no222; L no1714+, Ja 2, 1828-32.

THE CLONMEL GAZETTE.
  (See *Hibernian Gazette, or Universal Advertiser.*)

THE CLONMEL HERALD.
  (See *The Herald.*)

CLYDE COMMERCIAL ADVERTISER. Glasgow. 1807/?.
  a: MBAt Mr 11, 1807.

CLYDESDALE HORSE SOCIETY of the
United Kingdom of Great Britain and Ireland.
London, Glasgow. v1+, 1830/78-date.
  a: ULS.

CLYDESDALE JOURNAL.
  (See *Glasgow Sentinel.* Probably was formerly *Clydesdale Journal.*)

THE CLYDESDALE MAGAZINE. Lanark.
v1, no1-8, My-D 1818. m.
  b: GM lacking no1.

COASTING TRADE. London. 1817.
  a: NcD O 29-30, 1817.

COATES'S HERD BOOK
  (See *General Short-horned Herd-Book.*)

COBBETT'S ANNUAL REGISTER. London.
v1-5, 1802-04. w.
  a: ULS; ULSup. / *b:* UCP; BP; BdL; CrP;
L; LGU; LLL; LVA; MoM; WcP.

Continued as
COBBETT'S POLITICAL REGISTER. London. v5-89, 1804-35. w. (Also called *Cobbett's Weekly Political Register* and *Cobbett's Weekly Register.*)
  a: ULS; ULSup. / *b:* UCP; BP; BdL;
CrP lacking v25, 67; L lacking v29; LGU;
LLL; LVA; MoM; WcP v30-34, 36-40, 46-
48, 51-56, 60-64, 67, 69.

COBBETT'S COTTAGE ECONOMY. London.
no1-3, Ag-O 1821. m.
  b: O.

COBBETT'S EQUITABLE ADJUSTER; and
Norfolk Gazette Extraordinary. London. 1823.
  a: CSmH Je 1823, number extraordinary.

COBBETT'S EVENING POST. London. no1-
55, Ja 29-Ap 1, 1820. d.
  a: CSmH no31, Mr 4, 1820; ICU Ja 29, F
4, Mr 4, 1820. / *b:* L.

COBBETT'S GENUINE TWO-PENNY TRASH
for the Month of February 1831. London.
1831. [Not by Cobbett.]
  b: L.

COBBETT'S MONTHLY RELIGIOUS TRACTS.
London. no1-11, 1821-22. (No4 called *Cobbett's Monthly Sermons.*)
  b: KeP lacking no10; L no1-4.

COBBETT'S MONTHLY SERMONS.
  (See *Cobbett's Monthly Religious Tracts.*)

COBBETT'S PAPER AGAINST GOLD. London. Ag 30, 1810-S 12, 1815.
  b: LGU.

COBBETT'S PARLIAMENTARY DEBATES.
London. v1-22, 1803-12.
  b: UCP; CrP; EP; LIT; LdP; SP.
  Continued as
PARLIAMENTARY DEBATES. London. v
23-ns, v20, 1812-29. (Absorbed *Cobbett's
Parliamentary History of England* in 1820.)
  b: UCP; CrP; EP; LIT; LdP; SP.
  Continued as
HANSARD'S PARLIAMENTARY DEBATES.
London. ns, v21-s3, v356, 1829-91.
  b: UCP; CrP; EP; LIT; LdP; SP 1829-30.
  (Continued as *Parliamentary Debates,*
1892-date.)

COBBETT'S PARLIAMENTARY HISTORY
of England. London. v1-36, 1806-20.
  b: UCP; CrP; EP.
  (Absorbed by *Parliamentary Debates* in
1820.)

COBBETT'S PENNY TRASH. London. no1-
3, F-Ap 1831. m.
  a: ULS. / *b:* UCP; L; MR; O.

COBBETT'S POLITICAL REGISTER.
  (See *Cobbett's Annual Register.*)

COBBETT'S POOR MAN'S FRIEND; or Useful Information and Advice for the Working
Class. London. no1-5, Ag 1826-O 18, 1827.
  a: ULS.

COBBETT'S SPIRIT of the Public Journals.
London. v1, 1804.
  a: ULS. / *b:* UCP.

COBBETT'S TWO-PENNY TRASH; or, Politics for the Poor. London. v1-2, 1830-32.
(Title varies slightly.)
  a: ULS. / *b:* UCP; BP; KeP; L; LLL.

COBBETT'S WEEKLY POLITICAL REGIS-
TER.
  (See *Cobbett's Annual Register.*)

COBBETT'S WEEKLY REGISTER.
  (See *Cobbett's Annual Register.*)

COCHRAN'S PERIODICAL CATALOGUE,
Theological and Literary. London. no1-2,
My-D 1830.
  b: L.

THE COFFEE-ROOM; or, Weekly Register
of Political Opinions. Glasgow. no1-5, O 16-
N 20, 1819. w.
  b: ESL.

THE COILA REPOSITORY, and Kilmarnock
Monthly Magazine. Kilmarnock. Ag 1817-Ag
1818. m. (Also called *Kilmarnock Monthly
Magazine.*)
  a: ULS. / *b:* E; GM lacking Ag 1817; L.

COLBURN'S LITERARY GAZETTE.
  (See *Literary Gazette, and Journal of
  Belles Lettres.*)

COLCHESTER COURIER.
  (See *Sickle.*)

COLCHESTER GAZETTE. Colchester. 1814-
37. w.
  a: CSmH no458, O 5, 1822. / *b:* BP no
  399-400, Ag 18, 25, 1821; ColCG 1814-21,
  [1822-32]; ColP 1816-19, 1822-25; L Ja
  6, 1821-32, lacking 1822.
  (Incorporated with *Essex Independent,*
  1832-33. Continued as *Essex and Suffolk
  Times,* 1837-41; later as *Colchester Gazette,* to date.)

COLLECTANEA BOTANICA; or Figures and
Botanical Illustrations of Rare and Curious
Exotic Plants, &c. London. no1-8, 1821.
  b: L.

A COLLECTION OF MODERN AND CONTEM-
PORARY VOYAGES AND TRAVELS. London.
v1-10, 1805-09. ir.
  b: L.

COLLECTION OF THE LOCAL AND PER-
SONAL ACTS. London. 1798-1869.
  b: UCP.

COLLECTION OF THE PUBLIC GENERAL
STATUTES. London. 1798-1865.
  b: UCP.

COLLECTION OF THE PUBLIC LOCAL
AND PERSONAL STATUTES. London. 1798-
date.
  b: UCP.

COLLECTITIA; or, Pieces, Religious, Moral,
and Miscellaneous, adapted to the Society of
Friends. York, v1, 1824.
  a: PHC. / *b:* L; O.

COLLEGE ALBUM, a Selection of Original
Pieces, &c.
  (See *The Academic.*)

THE COLLEGE MAGAZINE. Windsor. 1819.
  (No issues known. See CBEL, III.838.)

COLLEGE OBSERVER. Edinburgh, no1-23,
N 20, 1827-F 15, 1828. s.w.
  b: EP.
  Continued as
THE REFLECTOR. Edinburgh. 1828.
  b: EP.

THE COLLEGE REPOSITORY. York. v1-10,
ns, v1-7, 1815-40. w. (A manuscript copy.)
  b: OMA lacking 1828-29.

THE COLLEGE TATLER. Edinburgh. 1824-
25.
  b: EP.

THE COLLEGIAN.
  (See *The Academic.*)

THE COLLOQUIST. Newport-Pagnel. no1-6,
S 10-F 1, 1825-26.
  b: O.

THE COLONIAL JOURNAL. London. v1-3,
1816-17. q.
  a: ULS. / *b:* L; O v1, impf.

THE COLONIAL REGISTER, and West Indian
Journal. London. v1, 1824.
  b: L; LU no1-2; O.

COLONIST and Commercial Weekly Advertiser. no1-8, F 24-Mr 21, 1824. w.
  b: L.
  Continued as
COLONIST and Weekly Courier. London.
no9-39, Mr 28-O 24, 1824. w.
  b: L.
  Continued as
SUNDAY HERALD. London. no1-69, O 31,
1824-My 22, 1825.
  b: L.

THE COLONIST and Weekly Courier.
  (See *Colonist and Commercial Weekly Advertiser.*)

COLUMBINE, or Dramatic Mirror.
  (See *Columbine and Weekly Review of Literature, &c.*)

COLUMBINE, and Weekly Review of Literature, the Sciences, Fine Arts, Theatricals,
&c. London. no1-19, Jl 4, 1829-Ap 17, 1830.
w.
  a: MB; MH. / *b:* L S 26, 1829-Ap 17, 1830.
  Continued as
COLUMBINE, or Dramatic Mirror. London.
no1-27, Ap 24, 1830-Je 18, 1831. w.
  a: CSmH no1- 12; MB lacking no3, 6, 8-26;
  MH lacking no21, 24-27. / *b:* L Ap 24-
  S 25, 1830.

THE COMET. London. [?]-1791-[?].
  No issues known. See CBEL, II.711.)

THE COMET. Paisley. no1-8, Mr 7-Je 14,
1823.
  b: PsP.

THE COMET. Dublin. no1+, My 1, 1831-1833.
  a: CSmH Jl 22, 1832; NN Ag 21, O 9, N 20-
  D 4, 25, 1831; Ja 15, F, Mr 25, My 13,
  Je 3-17, Jl 1-15, Ag 12-S 23, O 21-N 1832.
  / b: DA (no14-50); L.

THE COMET, or Evening Gazette. London?.
1790/?.
  a: MBAt Je 14-16, 1790.

THE COMET; or, Falvey's Liverpool Observer. Liverpool. no1-6, 1832.
  b: L no1; O no2, 6.

THE COMET; or, Literary Wanderer. Birmingham. no1-4, 1819-20.
  b: BP; L.

COMIC ANNUAL. London. v1-11, 1830-42. a.
  a: ULSup. / b: UCP; HdP; L; SP 1831.

COMIC MAGAZINE. London. v1-4, 1832-34.
  a: ULS. / b: UCP; L.

COMIC OFFERING; or Ladies' Melange of
Literary Mirth. London. v1-5, 1831-35. a.
  a: ULS. / b: UCP; GM; L.

THE COMICK MAGAZINE; or, Compleat Library of Mirth, Humour, Wit, Gaity and Entertainment. London. v1, 1796.
  a: MdBJ. / b: L.

COMMENTATOR. London. no1-20, Mr 29-
Ag 7, 1828.
  a: CSmH no13, Je 19, 1828. / b: L.

COMMENTATOR. A Weekly Publication.
London. no1, F 14, 1818. w.
  b: L; O.

COMMERCIAL AND AGRICULTURAL MAG-
AZINE. London. no1-19, 1799-1802. m.
  a: ULS. / b: UCP; BP; DRS no1-4; L;
  LP.
  Continued as
AGRICULTURAL MAGAZINE. London. v1-
14, 1802-06; ns, v1-2, 1806-07. m.
  a: ULS; ULSup. / b: UCP; BP; L.
  Continued as
AGRICULTURAL MAGAZINE, or Farmer's
Monthly Journal. London. v1-11, 1807-12;
ns, v1-6, 1813-15; s3, v1, 1816. m.
  a: ULS. / b: UCP; BP; L.

COMMERCIAL CHRONICLE. London. [?]-
1805-1823. t.w.
  a: CSmH S 19, 1812. / b: WcBW S 17,
  1805; L S 28, 1815-Mr 22, 1823.
  (Incorporated with London Chronicle, Mr
  29, 1823.)

COMMERCIAL DIRECTOR. Manchester. [?]-
1814-19-[?].
  b: LdP 1814-15, 1818-19.

COMMERCIALIST and Weekly Advertiser.
London. 1832. w.
  a: CSmH no1, Ja 1, 1832.

COMMISSIONERS. Report from . . . on the
Public Records of Ireland. London. v1-10,
1810-20.
  b: UCP.

COMMISSIONERS of H.M.'s Woods, Forests
and Land Revenues (afterwards Commissioners of Crown Lands). Report. London. 1812-
date.
  a: UCP.

COMMISSIONERS of the Board of Education
(afterwards of National Education) in Ireland.
Report. London, Dublin. 1809-date.
  b: UCP.

COMMITTEE FOR THE ABOLITION OF
SLAVERY. Report. London. v1-3, 1824-26.
  b: UCP.

COMMITTEE OF THE GENERAL ASSEMBLY
for Increasing the Means of Education and
Religious Instruction in Scotland. Report of.
Edinburgh. 1829-34.
  b: UCP.

COMMITTEES OF THE HOUSE OF COMMONS.
Reports from.
  (See House of Commons, &c.)

COMMON SENSE. London. no1-80, Ag 1,
1824-Mr 27, 1825.
  b: L.
  (Incorporated Mr 27, 1825, with Weekly
  Globe and continued as
COMMON SENSE AND WEEKLY GLOBE.
London. Mr 27, 1825-F 5, 1826. w.
  a: CSmH Mr 27, 1825. / b: L.

COMMON SENSE AND WEEKLY GLOBE.
(See Common Sense.)

COMMON SENSE BOOK. London. no1-3, 1824.
  b: L.

COMMON SENSE: Vox Populi. London. no1-
5, 1830.
  b: UCP.

COMMUNICATIONS to the Board of Agriculture. London. v1-7, 1797-1811.
  b: UCP; CrP v1-3.

THE COMPANION. London. no1-29, 1828.
  a: ULS. / b: UCP; BP; L; O.

COMPANION TO THE ALMANAC . . . Published under the Superintendence of the Society for the Diffusion of Useful Knowledge.
London. 1828-88.
  b: UCP; GeG; MCh.

COMPANION TO THE GENTLEMAN'S DIARY;
or a Preparative to that Useful Work. London. 1797.
  b: L; LR.
  (May be continued as Gentleman's Mathematical Companion.)

THE COMPILER; or Literary Banquet. Consisting of interesting Extracts from the most Popular, Scarce, and Expensive Works. London. v1-2, 1807-08. f.
  b: L; O.

A COMPLETE HISTORICAL DETAIL, &c.
  (See An Historical Detail, &c.)

CONFERENCE OF METHODISTS. Minutes of.
  (See Methodists. Minutes of the Conference of.)

CONGREGATIONAL MAGAZINE.
  (See London Christian Instructor, &c.)

THE CONJURER. Glasgow. no1-16, 1825-26.
  b: GM; L.

THE CONJUROR'S MAGAZINE, or Magical and Physiognomical Mirror. London. v1-2, 1791-93.
  a: ULS; ULSup. / b: UCP; L; LLL; MR.
  Continued as
ASTROLOGER'S MAGAZINE; and Philosophical Miscellany. London. v3, 1794. (Also called ns, v1.)
  a: ULS; ULSup. / b: L; MR.

CONNAUGHT ADVERTISER. Tuam. 1774-96.
  b: UCP.
  (May be continued as Western Chronicle and Connaught Advertiser. For further details see Galway Reader, v1, no2, p. 14; v1, no3, p. 31.

CONNAUGHT GAZETTE. Loughrea. 1797.
  (No issues known. See C & K, 1138a; CBEL, II.738; Galway Reader, v1, no3, p. 32.)

CONNAUGHT JOURNAL; or, Galway Advertiser. Galway. no1+, 1754-1840. s.w. (Also known as Martin Burke's Connaught Journal. Subtitle varies.)
  a: CSmH My 29, 1828. / b: C Je 27, 1805; L My 24, 1813-1832, lacking D 1822.
  (For further details see Galway Reader, v1, no3, pp. 30, 31; v1, no2, p. 14; v1, no4, p. 40.)

CONNOISSEUR. Advertisements for Wednesday. [London]. no1, Mr 2, 1814/?.
  b: BP.

CONNOISSEUR; or Dublin Weekly Gazette. Dublin, no1-5, S 15-O 13, 1827. w. (No1 has title My Tablets; or, the Dublin Weekly Gazette.)
  b: DA no1-2, DL; LVA.

THE CONSTITUTION. London. no1+, 1812-23. w.
  a: CSmH S 29, 1822; CtY N 3-D 20, 1812; (1813); Ja 2-My 8, 1814; DLC (Ja 12, 1812-Mr 20, 1814). / b: L Ja 5, 1812; Ja 4, 1818-Ja 5, 1823.
  Observer of the Times incorporated in The Constitution and continued as
OBSERVER OF THE TIMES and Constitution. London. Ja 12-Ap 6, 1823.
  b: L.
  (Incorporated with Englishman, Ap 13, 1823.)

CONSTITUTION. London. no1-17, F 4-My 27, 1827.
  b: L.

CONSTITUTION. London. no1-33, Ap 3, 1831-Ja 22, 1832.
  b: L.
  (Incorporated with Plain Dealer, Ja 22, 1832.)

CONSTITUTION; or, Anti-Union Evening Post. Dublin. no1-101, D 9, 1799-Jl 31, 1800. t.w.
  a: ICU D 12-28, 1799; Ja 2-4, 9, 11, 14, 18-F 25, Mr 1-8, 13-15, 20-Ap 5, 1800. / b: C; DLL; L no78; O no1-94.

CONSTITUTION, or Cork Advertiser. no1+, 1822-73. t.w. (Subtitle varies.)
  a: CSmH N 27, 1827; NN Je 28, 1828. / b: CoP Ja 3-Mr 4, 1825; D 1822, 1824-25, 1827; L S 15, 1823; Ja 3, 1826-32.

CONSTITUTION and Sunday Evening Gazette. London. 1806.
  b: L Prospectus only.

CONSTITUTIONAL ADVISER. London. no1-7, 1819.
  b: L no4-7, O 30-N 20, 1819.

CONSTITUTIONAL AND DUNDEE COURIER.
  (See Dundee Weekly Courier, &c.)

CONSTITUTIONAL LETTERS. Edinburgh. no1-8, Je 4-Jl 23, 1792. w.
  (No issues known. See C & K, 1141, and W.J. Couper, The Edinburgh Periodical Press, v2, p. 189.)

CONSTITUTIONAL MAGAZINE, and True Briton's Friend; containing a Weekly Register of Public Affairs, Foreign and Domestic. London. v1, 1793/?.
  a: ULS.

CONSTITUTIONAL REVIEW. London. v1, 1809/?.
  a: ULS. / b: L Prospectus only.

LE CONSTITUTIONNEL DE LONDRES. London. 1832.
  b: O no1, N 18, 1832.

THE CONTEMPLATIST; a Series of Essays upon Morals and Literature. London. no1-21, Je 9-O 27, 1810. w. (Also called Mudford's Contemplatist.)
  a: ULS. / b: O.

CONTINENTAL ANNUAL and Romantic Cabinet. London. 1832. a.
  b: UCP; BiP; L; O.

CONTINENTAL SOCIETY. Reports. London. 1819-29.
  b: UCP.

CONTINENTAL SOCIETY for the Diffusion of Religious Knowledge.
  (See European Missionary Society.)

THE CONTRASTING MAGAZINE of Errors and Truths; intended to direct the Attention

of Thinkers to the Errors of the Leading Opinions of the Day. London. no 1-18. 1827.
  b: L.

THE CONTROVERSIAL REVIEW. London.
1804.
  a: ULS.

CO-OPERATIVE CONGRESS. Proceedings.
London, Manchester. 183[?]-date.
  b: UCP.

**THE CO-OPERATIVE MAGAZINE and Month-
ly Herald.** London. v1-3, 1826-29. m.
  a: ULS; ULSup. / *b:* UCP; C; L.
  Continued as
  THE LONDON CO-OPERATIVE MAGAZINE.
  London. v4, no1-3, 1830.
  b: UCP; L.

**CO-OPERATIVE MISCELLANY; or Magazine
of Useful Knowledge.** Maidstone. no 1-10, Ja-
O 1830. m.
  b: O.

THE CO-OPERATOR. Brighton. no 1-28, 1828-
30. m.
  a: ULS. / *b:* UCP; BiP; L; O.

COOPER'S JOHN BULL. London. no 1-19, Ja
1-My 8, 1826. w.
  b: L.
  Continued as
  JOHN BULL. London. no20-23, My 14-Je 5,
  1826.
  b: L.

**THE COPPER-PLATE MAGAZINE, or Month-
ly Cabinet of Picturesque Prints consisting
of Sublime and Interesting Views of Great
Britain and Ireland.** London. v1-5, 1792-1802.
m.
  a: ULS; ULSup. / *b:* UCP; DL; L.

**CORK ADVERTISER: or Commercial Adver-
tiser.** Cork. no 1+, 1799-1824. t.w.
  a: IU Je 4, 1799. / *b:* C Ag 28, 1802; CoP
  1807; D Je 20, 1799; DA Je 12, D 13, 1800;
  Je 18, S 10, D 3, 1803; Je 27, 1812; Ja 4,
  1814; L My 29, 1813; S 16, 1823; Mr 16,
  1824.
  (Incorporated with *The Cork Constitution*.)

CORK ALMANAC. Cork. 1824-25.
  b: UCP.

CORK COURIER. Cork. no1, Jl 23, 1794-
1795-[?].
  b: UCP.

CORK EVENING POST. Cork. no 1+, 1754-
91. s.w.
  b: UCP.
  Continued as
  NEW CORK EVENING POST. Cork. 1791-
  1810-[?]. s.w.
  a: CtY 1799 impf.; NN (Mr-D 1799). / *b:*
  UCP; DA Ap 9, 1789; Jl 5, 1798; 10 sc.
  nos. Je-S, 1803.

  CORK GAZETTE. Cork. 1772-95.
  b: UCP.

CORK GAZETTEER; or, General Advertiser.
Cork. 1789-97. s.w.
  (No issues known. See C & K, 1157h, and
  CBEL, II.737. May be the same as *Cork
  Gazette* above.)

CORK HERALD; or, Munster Advertiser.
Cork. no 1+, F 10, 1798-Ja 10, 1799. s.w.
  a: IU F 17-Je 9, 16-S 22, 1798. / *b:* UCP.
  (Incorporated with *The Cork Constitution*.)

**CORK MAGAZINE or Miscellany of Litera-
ture, Arts, Politics, and Notable Occurrences.** Cork. no 1-4, Je 10-Jl 21, 1819.
  b: DRS.

CORK MERCANTILE CHRONICLE.
  (See *Hibernian Chronicle*.)

CORK MORNING INTELLIGENCER. Cork.
[?]-1815-21-[?]. s.w.
  b: D no669-916, for 1815-17; DL Ja 16-D
  22, 1821.

THE CORK PACKET. Cork. 1793. s.w.
  b: UCP.

THE CORK RELIGIOUS MISCELLANY. Cork.
1814.
  (No issues known. See John Power, *Irish
  Literary Periodical Publications*.)

CORK SENTINEL. Cork. 1830-31.
  b: L no11-17, Ja 19-S 3, 1831.

CORN TRADE CIRCULAR. London. no 1-402,
O 24, 1825-1833.
  b: L.

THE CORNISH MAGAZINE.
  (See *The Selector, or Cornish Magazine*.)

CORNUBIAN. Falmouth. no 1-378, O 1, 1830-
37. w.
  a: CSmH O 8, 1830. / *b:* L.
  (Incorporated with *Falmouth Express*.)

**THE CORNUCOPIA; or Literary and Dra-
matic Bouquet.**
  (See *The Cornucopia; or Literary and Dramatic Mirror*.)

**THE CORNUCOPIA; or, Literary and Dra-
matic Mirror, containing Critical Notices of
the Drama, and a Variety of Interesting Subjects under the Head of Miscellanies.** London. v1, S 1820-S 1821. m. (No1-2 called *The
Cornucopia; or Literary and Dramatic Bouquet.*)
  a: ULS; ULSup. / *b:* BP; L.

CORNUCOPIA BRITANNICA.
  (See *Edinburgh Cornucopia*.)

**CORNWALL GAZETTE and Falmouth Pack-
et.** Falmouth. no 1+, Mr 7, 1801-O 16, 1802.
  b: TaP (1801-02).
  Ceased until Jl 2, 1803, and continued as
  ROYAL CORNWALL GAZETTE, Falmouth
  Packet, and Plymouth Journal. Jl 2, 1803-
  date. (Subtitle varies.)
  a: CSmH N 14, 1818. / *b:* L (Mr 6, 1811-
  17), 1818-32; TaP (Jl 2, 1803-D 1806); TrP
  Jl 2, 1803-Ja 1809; TrRC.

CORPORATION REGISTER and Civic and Parochial Reporter. London. v1, no1-2, 1832.
   b: L.

A CORRECT LIST OF SHIPS and Steam Vessels Registered in the Port of Newcastle. Newcastle-upon-Tyne. 1830-43.
   b: L.

THE CORRECTOR; or, Dramatic Intelligencer, containing Original Criticisms on the Performances and Performers of the Theatre-Royal, Liverpool, for the Summer Season, 1816. Liverpool. no1-8, 1816.
   b: L.

CORREIO BRAZILIENSE, ou Armazen Literario. London. v1-29, 1808-22.
   a: ULS. / *b:* L.

CORREIO LITERARIO y Politico de Londres; Periodico Trimestre.
   (See *Variedades; ó mensagero de Londres.*)

CORRESPONDANCE FRANCAIS, ou Tableau de l'Europe. London. no1, 1793. t.w.
   a: ULS. / *b:* L; LLL.
   Continued as
   CORRESPONDANCE POLITIQUE, ou Tableau de l'Europe. London. no2-118, N 1793-Ag 2, 1794. t.w.
   a: ULS. / *b:* L; LLL.

CORRESPONDANCE POLITIQUE, ou Tableau de l'Europe.
   (See *Correspondance Francais, ou Tableau de l'Europe.*)

CORRESPONDANCE SECRÈTE, politique et littéraire. London. v1-18, 1787-90. (Really a reprint of *Correspondance littéraire secrète,* 1774-85.)
   a: ULS. / *b:* MR.

CORRESPONDENCE OF THE BATH and West of England Agricultural Society.
   (See *Bath and West and Southern Counties Society.*)

CORRESPONDENT. Dublin. no1+, 1806-20. d.
   a: NNC Ja 7, 1812-Ap 30, 1813, uncollated. / *b:* UCP; D N 10, 1806-Ag 12, 1808; DA sc.nos. for the years 1810, 1817, 1820-21; DLL Ja 7-Je 30, 1808; L N 8, 1806-20, lacking D 1809; 1810; Jl 25-O 26, 1811; 1812-13; Ja-N 1814; Je-D 1815; Ja-Mr 14, Jl 19-D 1816; 1817-20.
   Continued as
   DUBLIN CORRESPONDENT. Dublin. 1820-27. d.
   a: CSmH My 10, 1827; DLC Ag 16, 25, 1820. / *b:* D Ja 26, 1818-D 30, 1830; DA 1821 impf.; Ag 19, 1823; S 4, 1824; L Ja-D 1823; sc.nos. 1824-26.
   Continued as
   EVENING PACKET and Correspondent. Dublin. no1+, Ja 22, 1828-54. t.w.
   a: CSmH Ja 26, 1828. / *b:* D.

CORRESPONDENT.
   (See *Dissenter.*)

CORRESPONDENT. London. no1+, Mr 27-D 25, 1819.
   b: L.

THE CORRESPONDENT; consisting of Letters, Moral, Political and Literary, between Eminent Writers in France and England. London. no1-3, 1817.
   a: ULS. / *b:* L; NwL.

CORRESPONDENT AND PUBLIC CAUSE.
   (See *Dissenter.*)

THE COSMOPOLITE. A London Weekly Newspaper. London. 1832-33. w.
   a: CSmH no6, Ap 14, 1832. / *b:* L; LU v1, no25; O no1.

THE COSMOPOLITE, a Periodical Paper, consisting of Familiar Essays on Men, Manners, and Literature. no1-14, Ap 2-O 1, 1812. f.
   a: ULS. / *b:* L; O no6.

THE COTTAGE MAGAZINE; or, Plain Christian's Library. London, Wakefield. v1-21, 1812-32; ns, v1-2, 1846-47. m.
   a: ULS; ULSup. / *b:* L v1-17, 20-21; LdP v1.

COTTAGE REGISTER; or, Juvenile Review. Edinburgh. v1-2, 1825-26/?. (Ja-My 1825 incorrectly dated Ja-My 1824.)
   a: ULS.

THE COTTAGER'S MONTHLY VISITOR. London. v1-36, 1821-56. m.
   a: ULS. / *b:* UCP; L.

COULTER'S COUNTRY MISCELLANY and Literary Selector.
   (See *County Miscellany and Literary Selector.*)

COUNCIL OF TEN. London. v1-3, Je 1822-My 1824. m.
   a: ULS. / *b:* UCP; L; LLL.

COUNTRY. London. v1-13, 1783-89.
   b: UCP.

COUNTRY CHRONICLE. London. [?]-1796-[?].
   b: UCP.

COUNTRY CONSTITUTIONAL GUARDIAN and Literary Magazine. Bristol. v1, 1822. (Also called *Gutch's Country Constitutional Guardian.*)
   b: UCP; L lacking no5.

COUNTRY LITERARY CHRONICLE and Weekly Review.
   (See *Literary Chronicle and Weekly Review.*)

COUNTRY MAGAZINE; or Fire-side Companion. London. no1-26, 1817-18/?.
   a: ULS.

COUNTRY MAGAZINE, and Quarterly Chronicle for Hull and the East Riding of Yorkshire. Hull. v1, no1-3, 1813. q.
   b: L.

COUNTRY MISCELLANY. London. no 1-7, 1832.
    b: UCP.

COUNTRY SPECTATOR. Gainsborough. no 1-33, O 9, 1792-My 21, 1793. w.
    a: ULS; ULSup. / *b:* UCP; L.

COUNTRY TIMES.
    (See *Country Times and Agricultural and Commercial Advertiser.*)

COUNTRY TIMES and Agricultural and Commercial Advertiser. London. no 1-102, Ja 4, 1830-D 26, 1831. w. (After no 7 *Agricultural* was dropped from the title; after no 13 the title was *Country Times.*)
    a: CSmH no 4. / *b:* BtP no 1-66; L.

COUNTRY TIMES and Commercial Advertiser.
    (See *Country Times and Agricultural and Commercial Advertiser.*)

COUNTY AND NORTH DEVON ADVERTISER, and Weekly Chronicle of Politics, Commerce, Agriculture, and Literature. Barnstaple. no 1-898, 1832-48. w.
    b: L.

COUNTY ANNUAL REGISTER. London. v 1-2, 1810-11. a. (The word *Imperial* added to the title in v2.)
    b: L.

COUNTY CHRONICLE and Weekly Advertiser for Essex, Herts, Kent, Surrey, &c. London, Lewes. 1787-1841. w.
    a: CSmH Jl 21, 1827. / *b:* UCP; ColP 1811-12; L 1798, 1818-32; LLL Ag 19, 1794-Ja 16, 1798.
    (Continued as *County Chronicle, Surrey Herald, and Weekly Advertiser for Kent,* 1841-69; as *County Chronicle and Mark Lane Journal,* 1870-1902.)

COUNTY MISCELLANY and Literary Selector. Sittingbourne. no 1-7, 1832. (The title on some of the wrappers reads *Coulter's Country Miscellany and Literary Selector.*)
    b: UCP; L.

COUNTY PRESS for Herts, Beds, Bucks, Huntingdon, Cambs, Essex and Middlesex. Hertford. no 1-287, Jl 12, 1831-36. w.
    a: CSmH no 3. / *b:* HtP.

COUNTY PRESS, for Northamptonshire, Bedfordshire, Buckinghamshire, and Huntingdonshire. Northampton. no 1-179, Ja 23, 1808-Je 26, 1811. w.
    b: AybA 1808-09; L.

COURIER (and Evening Gazette). London. 1792-1842. d.
    a: ULS; ULSup; C-S Ja-Ap, O-D 1796, 1797-1805; CaK (Ap 23, 1805-F 3, 1806); CtY (1795); [1798]; Ja 2-O 12, 1801; Je 18-D 31, 1804; Ja 17-D 31, 1806; 1807-32; DLC (1804-08); sc.nos. 1809-10; (1811-28); [1831-32]; ICN (1815, Ap 8, 1825-26); ICU sc.nos. 1794-97, 1800-02; (1810, 1812, Ag 16-D 31, 1814, 1818); 1819-22; (Jl-D 1823); 1824-25; (Jl-D 1826); (Jl-D 31, 1827-1828);

sc.nos. 1829; IU [1823]; MB sc.nos. 1800-06; MBAt N 29, 1803-Je 30, 1804; Ag 29, 1805-O 9, 1806; D 24, 1806-O 30, 1807; Mr 25, 1808-O 27, 1809; Ja 1814-1832; MH (1807-09; My 1-D 31, 1811; F 1-My 20, 1812; My 1-D 29, 1813); sc.nos. 1814-16, 1818; (1819-20; Ja 1-Je 29, 1822; F-D 1823, 1824, 1826-27, 1830); MHi 1809-32, lacking Ja-Je 1827; MNu Jl 31-S 18, 1800; 1811; 1813; 1818-20; NIC sc.nos. 1810-12; NN [Ap-D 1798; O 9-D 26, 1799; Ja-Ap 1800]; sc.nos. 1801-02; complete Ja 19-D 31, 1811; F 8, 1812-O 20, 1820; 1823-26; My 6, 1831-32; NNHi 1804-25; 1828-32; NcD 1809-10; (1812-20); 1822-28; NjR sc.nos. 1806, 1811, 1814-15; PPHi My 18-D 31, 1818; WHi sc.nos. 1805, 1806. / *b:* UCP; BP Jl-D 1795; F 4-5, 1800; D 21, 1804-32; BiP sc.nos. 1794, 1797, 1799, 1808-09, 1815, 1825; DlP 1814-16; E Jl 3, 1804-Jl 25, 1806; 1810-16; 1818; 1823-32; L 27 sc.nos. 1792-95; complete for Mr 12, 1800-32; LGU S 4, 1800-1820; NwS (1795-96).

COURIER; or, Manchester Advertiser. Manchester. v 1-3, 1817-19. w. (With no 20 or 21 the title became *Saturday's Manchester Courier.*)
    b: MP (v 1-3).

COURIER AND ARGUS. Nethergate. S 20, 1816-50-[?]. w.
    (No issues known before 1850.)

COURIER D'ANGLETERRE. Tous les Actes du Gouvernement Britannique contenus dans le Courier D'Angleterre seront traduits de la Gazette de Londres. London. no 1-1011, 1805-14.
    a: ULS. / *b:* L.

COURIER DE LONDRES. London. 1788-1805. s.w. (Preceded by *Courier de l'Europe,* 1777; *Courier Politique et Littéraire,* 1777-1778.)
    a: ULS; C-S S 10-N 5, 1790. / *b:* UCP.
    Continued as
GAZETTE DE LA GRANDE BRETAGNE. London. 1805-07. s.w.
    b: UCP.
    Continued as
COURIER DE LONDRES. London. 1807-26. s.w.
    a: ULS. / *b:* UCP; L 1818-25.

COURSE OF THE EXCHANGE. London. 1697-1908. w.; s.w.
    b: UCP; L Mr 11, 1825-32.

COURT AND CITY ENGLISH REGISTER.
    (See *English Registry,* &c.)

COURT AND CITY REGISTER. (Rider's British Merlin Royal Kalendar.) London. 1747-1893. (Also known as *London Kalendar.*)
    a: ULS; PPL 1791, 1794, 1797. / *b:* UCP; DA 1789-92, 1794, 1796-97, 1799-1800, 1802, 1804, 1806; LGU 1783-1816.

COURT AND COUNTRY GUIDE. London. 1816-18.
    b: C Ja 1816, Ap 1818.

COURT CIRCULAR. London. no1+, My 2, 1829-1911.
(No issues known. See CBEL, III.813.)

COURT JOURNAL. A Record of Manners, Literature, Science, Art, and Fashion. London. no1+, 1829-date. w.
a: ULS; CSmH O 30, 1830. / *b:* E no4; LLL Ja-D 1830, lacking no62; StfS.

COURT MAGAZINE and Belle Assemblée. (See *La Belle Assemblée,&c.*)

COURT OF COMMON PLEAS and Exchequer Chamber. Report of Cases argued and determined. London. v1-2, 1788-96.
b: LGU.

COVENANTER. Belfast, Londonderry. v1-3, 1830-34; s2-s4, 1834-99/?.
a: ULS. / *b:* UCP; B1L; GM.

COVENT GARDEN JOURNAL. London. v1-2, 1810.
a: ULS; ULSup; NRU. / *b:* MR.

COVENT GARDEN MONTHLY RECORDER. London. 1792. m.
(No issues known. See C & K, 1171a; CBEL, II.682.)

COVENT GARDEN THEATRICAL GAZETTE. A Complete Analysis of the Evening's Entertainment, with the Names of the Characters, Performers, &c. London. no1-148, 1816-17. d.
a: ULS. / *b:* L no1-140.

COVENTRY HERALD AND OBSERVER. (See *Coventry Herald and Weekly Advertiser.*)

COVENTRY HERALD and Weekly Advertiser. Coventry. no1+, Ap 22, 1808-30. w.
a: CSmH O 29, 1824. / *b:* BP 6 sc.nos. 1808-21; CvP 13 sc.nos. 1808-30; L Ja 2, 1824-Mr 1830.
Continued as
COVENTRY HERALD and Observer. Coventry. Ap 1830-63. w.
b: L.
(Continued as *Coventry Herald and Free Press,* 1863-date.)

COVENTRY MERCURY. Coventry. 1787-1836. (Preceded by *Coventry Mercury; or, the Weekly Country Journal,* 1741-43; *Jopson's Coventry and Northampton Mercury,* 1743; *Jopson's Coventry and Warwick Mercury,* 1743-87.) (Subtitle varies.)
a: CtY (1824), 1825-27. / *b:* CvCS 1803; CvP 107 sc.nos. 1789-1831; L 1789-1823 impf.
(Continued as *Coventry Standard,* 1836-date.)

COVENTRY OBSERVER. Coventry. no1-129, 1827-30. w.
b: CvP 21 sc.nos.; L.
(Incorporated with *Coventry Herald.*)

COWDROY'S MANCHESTER GAZETTE. (See *Manchester Gazette.*)

THE CRACKER, and other Explosions which have Gone Off during the Election. Leeds. no1-7, 1832.
b: LdP.

THE CRAFTSMAN; or, Say's Weekly Journal. London. no1+, 1758-1810. w.
b: UCP; L sc.nos. 1791-92; complete Ja 7, 1797-D 28, 1799; O 11, 1800-My 10, 1801; Ag 7, 1802.
(Incorporated in *Baldwin's London Journal,* 1810.)

CRELL'S CHEMICAL JOURNAL. London. v1-3, 1791-93. (English edition of *Chemische annalen für die Freunde der Naturlehre.*)
a: ULS. / *b:* UCP; L; LCP; LP.

THE CRIM. CON. GAZETTE; or, Diurnal Register of the Freaks and Follies of the Present Day. London. no1-7, 1830-31.
b: L.
Continued as
THE BON TON GAZETTE. London. no8-18, 1831.
b: L.

THE CRIPPLEGATE GAZETTE. London. no1-3, F-D 1830.
b: LGU.

THE CRISIS. London. 1806. d.
a: CtY Ap 17, 26, 1806. / *b:* L Prospectus only.

THE CRISIS; a Collection of Essays. London. no1-41, 1792-93.
a: CtY. / *b:* UCP.

CRISIS; or Star to the Great Northern Union. Preston. 1830/?.
a: ULS.

THE CRISIS; or, the Change from Error and Misery to Truth and Happiness. London. v1-4, 1832-34. (After no15 the title was changed to *The Crisis, and National Cooperative Trades Union . . . Gazette.*) (Title varies slightly.)
a: ULS. / *b:* UCP; BP; L lacking v2, no6; LLL.

THE CRISIS, and National Cooperative Trades Union . . . Gazette.
(See *The Crisis; or, the Change from Error and Misery to Truth and Happiness.*)

THE CRITIC, a Monthly Magazine. London. no1-2, 1832.
b: L.

THE CRITIC; or Weekly Theatrical Reporter. London. no1-7, Jl 22-S 2, 1820. w.
a: ULS.

CRITICA BIBLICA. London. v1-4, 1824-27.
b: UCP.

THE CRITICAL FIGARO in Paris and London, containing every thing relative to Literature, the Fine Arts, Music, &c. London. no1-3, 1832/?. w.
b: C no3, F 4, 1832; O no1, Ja 21, 1832.

CRITICAL OBSERVATIONS on Books Antient and Modern. London. v1-4, 1776-1811.
b: UCP.

CRITICAL REVIEW; or, Annals of Literature. London. v1-70, 1756-90; ns, v1-39, 1791-1803; s3, v1-24, 1804-11; s4, v1-6, 1812-14; s5, v1-5, 1815-17. m.
a: ULS; ULSup. / *b:* UCP; BrP lacking s5, v2-5; DL; E; EP ns, v3-4, 13-24, 26-31; 35-36; GrP 1792-97, 1805-08; L; LdL 1789-1808; MCh 1789-96; MoM 1789-99; WcP.

Y CRONICL CENHADOL. Caerfyrddin. 1816-1904.
a: ULSup. / *b:* UCP; CrP 1816-23.

CROSBY'S BUILDER'S NEW PRICE BOOK. London. [?]-1806-20/?.
b: L 1806, 1809, 1817; LP 1807, 1820.

O CRUZEIRO; ou, a estrella constitucional dos Portuguezes. London. no1-12, N 1826-D 1827; 1829-31/?.
a: ULS; / *b:* L 1826-27.

THE CRYPT; or, Receptacle for Things Past: an Antiquarian, Literary and Miscellaneous Journal. Ringwood. v1-3, Ag 3, 1827-D 1, 1828. m.; q.
a: ULS. / *b:* UCP; EP; L; LAt; LLL; NwS v1-2; PmP; WnP.
Absorbed *Wheeler's Hampshire and West of England Magazine* and continued as THE CRYPT, or Receptacle for Things Past, and West of England Magazine. Winchester. ns, v1, Ja-D 1829. (No nos. issued Jl-Ag, O-N.)
a: ULS; ULSup. / *b:* UCP; L; WnP.

THE CULLER. Glasgow. v1, no1-20, Ag 12-D 23, 1795. m.
a: ULS; ULSup. / *b:* UCP; BP; EP; GM.

CUMBERLAND PACQUET and Ware's Whitehaven Advertiser. Whitehaven. 1744-1896. w.
a: CSmH Jl 7, 1829. / *b:* CsP sc.nos. 1789-97; [1798]; sc.nos. 1799-1800; [1801]; sc.nos. 1802-06; (1807); (1809); Je-D 1811; 1812; (1813-14); 1815-20; (1822-23, 1826-31); 1832; L Ja 1829-32; LLL (My 16, 1820-D 31, 1821); NwS 106 sc.nos. 1795, 1811-16; WtLE; WtP 1819-32.
(Continued as *West Cumberland Post,* 1897-98; *Cumberland Pacquet,* 1898-1915.)

THE CUMBRIAN. Carlisle. no1+, D 7, 1824-F 19, 1829/?.
b: CsCN no7-8; CsP no1.

THE CUMBRIAN. Carlisle. no1, Ja 1, 1825.
b: CsP.

CUPAR HERALD, or Fife, Kinross, Strathearn & Clackmannan Advertiser. Cupar. no1-53, Mr 14, 1822-Mr 13, 1823.
b: CpFH.
Continued as
FIFE HERALD, and Kinross, Strathearn & Clackmannan Advertiser. Cupar. no54+, Mr 20, 1823-81.
a: CSmH N 25, 1830. / *b:* CpFH; SaU D 9, 1830-32, impf.

(Continued as *Fife Herald,* 1881-93; absorbed *Fifeshire Journal* in 1893 and continued as *Fife Herald and Journal,* 1893-date.)

THE CURIOUS MAN. A Daily Paper. London. no1-24, Ap 8-My 4, 1822. d.
b: O.

CURTIS'S BOTANICAL MAGAZINE.
(See *Botanical Magazine; or, Flower Garden Displayed.*)

CYCLOPAEDIAN MAGAZINE, and Dublin Monthly Register of History, Literature, and Arts, Sciences, &c. Dublin. v1-3, 1807-09. m.
a: ULS. / *b:* UCP; DL; L.

CYDYMAITH YR IEUENGCTID, neu drysorfa o amrywiaeth o bethau difyr a buddiol. Llanrwst. 1826-27.
b: UCP; CrP.

CYFAILL Y CYMRO. Bala. v1, 1822.
b: UCP.

CYFRINACH Y BEDYDDWYR am y flwyddyn. Maesycwmwr. 1827.
b: UCP.
(United with *Greal y Bedyddwyr.*)

CYLCHGRAWN CYMRU. Chester. v1-4, 1814-15.
b: UCP; CrP.

Y CYLCHGRAWN CYNMRAEG, neu Drysorfa gwybodaeth. Trevecca. 1793-95.
a: ULS. / *b:* UCP; CrP 1793-94.

THE CYMMRODORION, or Metropolitan Cambrian Institution. Transactions. London. v1+, 1822-43; 1892-date. (No transactions published 1843-91.)
a: ULS. / *b:* UCP; CrP; LLN.
(After 1892 known as the *Honourable Society of Cymmrodorion.*)

Y CYMRO, neu drysorfa celfyddyd a gwybodaeth fuddiol a chyffredi. Llundain. no1+, 1830-32.
b: UCP; CrP.

DAILY ADVERTISER. London. 1730-98. d.
a: ULS; C-S 5 sc.nos. 1790-92; CtY 1789-95 f.c.; DLC 1789-95 f.c.; ICU 1789-95 f. c; MH 1789-95 f.c.; MoU 1789-95 f.c.; NNC 1789-95 f.c. / *b:* UCP; L 16 sc.nos. 1789-95; complete for 1796; MR sc. nos. 1792-93; O Jl 17, 1789-98, lacking Je 1790; SptP Ja 15, 1795-98.
Incorporated with *Oracle and Public Advertiser* in 1798 and continued as
ORACLE AND DAILY ADVERTISER. London. S 10, 1798-M 24, 1802. d.
a: ULS; CtY [1798; Jl 19-N 16, 1800; 1801-02; Jl 1803-Je 1804]; (F-Jl 12, 1805; Ja 16-Jl 15, 1806); Ja 11-Je 1808. / *b:* L; O; SptP 1798-D 31, 1799.
Continued as
DAILY ADVERTISER AND ORACLE. London. Mr 25, 1802-D 25, 1803. d.
a: ULS; CtY Mr 24, 1802-1803; ICN (Ja 1-Je 30, 1803). / *b:* L.

Incorporated with *True Briton* and continued as
DAILY ADVERTISER, Oracle, and True Briton. London. D 26, 1803-Je 8, 1809. d.
a: ULS; CSmH Ja 2-Je 30, 1806; [Ja 1, 1807-D 31, 1808]; NNHi F 23, O 28-31, 1807. / *b:* L.

DAILY ADVERTISER AND ORACLE.
(See *Daily Advertiser.*)

DAILY ADVERTISER, Oracle, and True Briton.
(See *Daily Advertiser.*)

DAILY MAGAZINE and Parlour Library. London. no1-9, 1823.
b: L.
Continued as
UNIVERSAL MAGAZINE and Parlour Library. London. no10-13, 1823.
b: L.

DAILY STATEMENT of the Packet Boats.
(See *General Post Office. Daily Statement of the Packet Boats.*)

DAILY VISITER; or, Companion for the Breakfast Table, forming a Quarterly Review, containing Original Essays, &c. Dublin. v1, no1-79, N 1, 1822-F 1, 1823. d.
a: ULS. / *b:* DA; DL.

DAILY WORDS of the Brethren's Congregation(s). London. ?/1777-1821/?.
b: UCP.

THE DAWN OF LIGHT and Theological Inspector. London. 1825.
b: L.

THE DAY. London. Ja 2, 1809-17. d. (Absorbed by *The New Times* in 1817 and for a short while ran as *The Day and New Times.*)
a: DLC Ja-D 1815, lacking Je 6; NcD Ja-N 1810 lacking O5. / *b:* BP; L Ja 1-D 20, 1809.

THE DAY, a Journal of Literature, Fine Arts, Fashions, &c. Glasgow. v1-2, no1-112, 1832. d.
a: ULS; ULSup. / *b:* E; GM; L.

THE DAY AND NEW TIMES.
(See *The New Times.*)

DEAF AND DUMB INSTITUTION. Reports. Edinburgh. [?]-1814-23-[?].
b: EP 1814, 1817, 1823.

DECISIONS OF THE COURT OF SESSION. Edinburgh. 1796-1841.
b: UCP; EP 1796-1825.

THE DEIST: or, Moral Philosopher. London. no1-2, 1819/?.
a: ULS.

THE DÉJEUNÉ; or, Companion for the Breakfast Table. London. v1-2, no1-56, O 21-D 30, 1820. d. (no 50 never published.)
a: ULS. / *b:* L no1-49.

LE DELIZE DELLE DAME FILARMONICHE. London. [?]-1808-[?]. m.
(No issues known. See *Literary Annual Register, or Records of Literature,* 2 (F 1808) 73.

THE DEMOCRATIC RECORDER, and Reformers' Guide, a London Weekly Publication. London. no1-4, O 2-N 1819. w.
b: BP no1; O no1.

DEPUTY CLERK REGISTER of Scotland. Report. Edinburgh. v1-7, 1807-13.
b: UCP.

DERBY AND CHESTERFIELD REPORTER.
(See *Derby Reporter and General Advertiser.*)

DERBY HERALD; or, Derby, Nottingham, and Leicester Advertiser. Derby. 1792.
b: DeP.

DERBY MERCURY. Derby. [?]-1789-1933. w.
(Preceded by *Derby Mercury,* 1733-1769; *Drewry's Derby Mercury,* 1769-[?].)
a: CSmH D 23, 1829; CtY Mr 8, 1826; ICU 1801-02. / *b:* DeP; L 1789-1832, lacking Jl 16, 1795; Ag 31-S 7, 1797; Ja-O 1798. (Incorporated with *Derbyshire Advertiser,* 1933.)

DERBY REPORTER and General Advertiser. Derby. 1823-27-[?]. w.
a: CSmH no2, Ja 9, 1823. / *b:* DeP.
Continued as
DERBY AND CHESTERFIELD REPORTER. Derby. [?]-1829-1930. w.
b: DeP Jl 30, 1829-32; L Ja 6, 1831-1832.

DERBYSHIRE CHRONICLE and Universal Weekly Advertiser. Derby. [?]-1813-[?]. w.
b: DeP 1813.

DERBYSHIRE COURIER. Chesterfield. 1828-1922. w.
a: CSmH no103, D 19, 1929. / *b:* L no 157+, Ja 1, 1831-32.
(Incorporated with *Derbyshire Times.*)

THE DETECTER, an Occasional Paper. London. no1, Ja 1817.
b: O.

DETECTOR. Dublin. 1800. s.w.
a: ICU no1, &c., Ja 30, F 1, 11, 18, 20, 22, Mr 1, 4, 11, 18, 22, Ap 3, 19, 22, 1800. / *b:* L no1-36, Ja 30-My 20, 1800, lacking no7-8, 12, 14-16, 23.

THE DETECTOR; or a Series of Periodical Observations on Human Knowledge and Manners in the Present Age. London. 1803.
b: UCP. (But UCP is in error; should be no4 instead of no2 in the Bodleian.)

DER DEUTSCH-ENGLISCHE ANZEIGER. London. no1-17, 1832.
b: L.

THE DEVIL IN LONDON.
(See *The Devil's Memorandum Book.*)

THE DEVIL'S MEMORANDUM BOOK; being
all the Wit, Whim, and Waggery contained in
the Collected Numbers of Asmodeus in London. London. no1-37, F 29-N 10, 1832. (no1-
7 called *The Devil in London;* no8-24 called
Asmodeus; or, the Devil in London; no25-
37 called *Asmodeus in London.)*
  a: ULS; ULSup. / *b:* UCP; BoP; L; O.

THE DEVIL'S PULPIT, containing Astro-
nomico-Theological Discourses. London.
v1-2, 1831-32.
  b: MR; O no1.

THE DEVIL'S WALK. London. no1-3, 1832.
  a: ULS. / *b:* UCP; O no1.

DEVIZES AND WILTSHIRE GAZETTE.
(See *Simpson's Salisbury Gazette.)*

DEVON AND EXETER GAZETTE. Exeter.
[?]-1792-94-[?]. w.
  a: CtY 4 sc.nos. 1792-94.

DEVONPORT ADVERTISER WEEKLY NEWS.
Devonport. no1-2, 1826.
  (No issues known. This information from
  Plymouth Public Library.)

THE DEVONSHIRE ADVENTURER. Tavi-
stock. no1-12, 1814-15. m.
  b: L no1-11.

DEVONSHIRE CHRONICLE and Exeter News.
(See *Besley's Exeter News and Devon
County Chronicle.)*

DEVONSHIRE FREEHOLDER, and Plymouth,
Devonport, and West of England General Advertiser. Plymouth. 1821-24-[?]. w.
  a: CSmH no71, F 28, 1823. / *b:* PlP no
  155, S 18, 1824; no207-08, S 17, 24, 1825.
  Continued as
PLYMOUTH HERALD and Devonshire Freeholder, or West of England General Advertiser. Plymouth. [?]-1825-27-[?]. w.
  a: CSmH no229, Je 30, 1827. / *b:* PlP
  (no241, My 13, 1826-My 31, 1828).

DIAMOND MAGAZINE. London. v1-2, no1-
12, 1831-32.
  a: ULS. / *b:* UCP; DL; L.

DIARIA BRITANNICA. Birmingham. 1787-95.
  b: UCP.

THE DIARY; or, Woodfall's Register. London. 1789-93. d.
  a: C-S Mr 30-Ag 8, 1789; Ja-Ag 1790; Ja-
  Jl 1790; CtY Ap 16-D 30, 1789; 12 sc.nos.
  1790; ICU (Ap 6-Jl 18, 1789); My 27, N
  23-D 25, 1790; Ap 6-12, My 17, 21, 28-Je
  3, 1791; My 31-Ag 15, 1792; MBAt Ap 6-
  18, 27, 1789-Je 15, 1790; NcD (Ap 18-O
  31, 1789; Ja-My 1, 1790; Ja 3-Je 28, 1791;
  Ja 4-D 1792); WHi (Je 15-Ag 26, 1789);
  sc.nos. N-D 1790, Ag-D 1791. / *b:* UCP;
  L no1-60, 152, 239-1452, Mr 30-Je 6, S
  1789, Ja 1, 1790-Ag 31, 1793.

T. DIBDIN'S PENNY TRUMPET. To be
Blown Weekly (not Weakly) throughout the
British Empire!!! and farther if Required.

London. no1-5, O 20-N 17, 1832/?. w.
  a: ULS. / *b:* L no1-4; O no1-4.

THE DILIGENT OBSERVER. London. v1,
no1-4, Ag 2-23, 1817. w.
  b: L no1; O no2-4.

THE DIRECTOR; a Weekly Literary Journal:
containing I. Essays, on Subjects of Literature, the Fine Arts and Manners. II. Bibliographiana . . . . III. Royal Institution.
Analysis of Lectures. . . . IV. British Gallery. Description of Principal Pictures. London. v1-2, no1-24, Ja 24-Jl 4, 1807. w.
  a: ULS; ULSup. / *b:* UCP; BP; L; LLL;
  LdL; MR.

THE DISSECTOR. London. v1, 1829.
  b: UCP; L lacking no2.

THE DISSENTER. London. no1-26, Ja 1-
Je 24, 1812. w.
  a: CSmH no16. / *b:* L.
  Continued as
CORRESPONDENT. London. no1-14, Jl 1-
S 30, 1812. w.
  b: L.
  Continued as
CORRESPONDENT AND PUBLIC CAUSE.
London. 1812-14/?. w.
  a: CSmH no2, O 12, 1814. / *b:* L no1, O
  7, 1812.

DISSENTER'S GAZETTE of Politics, Commerce, Literature, and General Information.
London. no1-20, Ja 4-My 17, 1826. w.
  a: CSmH no1. / *b:* L.
  Continued as
WEDNESDAY TIMES. London. no1-9, My
24-Jl 19, 1826. w.
  a: CSmH no6. / *b:* L.

DISSENTER'S MAGAZINE for Yorkshire and
Lancashire. London. no1-6, 1832-33.
  b: L.

THE DOCTOR: a Medical Penny Magazine,
adapted for the Use of Clergymen, Heads of
Families, Nurses, &c. London. v1-4, 1832-
36; ns, no1-64, 1838. w.
  a: ULS. / *b:* L; LCP.

DOLBY'S PARLIAMENTARY REGISTER.
London. no1-67, Ja-Je 1819.
  b: BP; L; O no1.

DOMESTIC CHRONICLE. London. no1-2, N
3-10, 1821. w.
  b: L.

DOMESTIC GARDENER'S MANUAL. London.
no1, 1829.
  b: O.

DOMESTIC GAZETTE; or, Weekly Record
of the Stage, Music, Public Exhibitions, &c.
London. v1, no1-12, O 9, 1830-Ja 1, 1831/?.
w.
  a: MB.

THE DOMESTIC MAGAZINE. London. no1-
2, Jl-Ag, 1814. m.
  b: L.

THE DOMESTIC MISCELLANY; and Poor Man's Friend. Leeds. no1-7, S 21-D 21, 1819. f.; ir.
  a: ULSup. / *b:* L; LdL.

THE DOMESTIC VISITOR. London. v1-4, 1828-31. q.
  b: L.

DONCASTER JOURNAL. Doncaster. [?]-1792-[?]. w.
  (No issues known, but listed by C & K, 1205a, and CBEL, II.723. Probably a confusion, however, with *Yorkshire Journal,* founded in 1786 and absorbed by *Doncaster Gazette* at some time subsequent to 1794.)

DONCASTER, Nottingham and Lincoln Gazette.
  (See *Yorkshire, Nottinghamshire and Lincolnshire Gazette and Universal Advertiser.)*

DONCASTER, Retford and Gainsborough Gazette.
  (See *Yorkshire, Nottinghamshire and Lincolnshire Gazette and Universal Advertiser.)*

DONOVAN'S NATURALISTS' REPOSITORY. London. v1-5, 1823-26.
  b: UCP.

DORCHESTER and Sherborne Journal and Western Advertiser. Sherborne. [?]-1792-1825-[?]. w. (Succeeds *Cruttwell's Sherborne Journal,* 1764-65-[?]; *Sherborne Journal,* [?]-1773-[?].)
  a: DLC 1792-94, lacking Mr 15, 1793. / *b:* DcrN Je 1796-D 1804; 1809-16; 1824-25.
  Continued as
THE SHERBORNE, Dorchester and Taunton Journal. Sherborne. [?]-Ja 3, 1827-1886. w. (Subtitle varies slightly.)
  a: CSmH D 11, 1828. / *b:* L 1829-32; YeWG 1827-32.

DORSET COUNTY CHRONICLE. Dorchester. no1+, 1822-date. w. (Subtitle varies.)
  a: CSmH Jl 9, 1829. / *b:* DcrN 1825-26, 1828-29; 1831-32; L 1829-32.

DOUGLAS REFLECTOR and Isle of Man Magazine of Classic and Polite Literature. Douglas. no1-6, 1821.
  b: L.

DRAKARD'S PAPER. London. no1-51, Ja 10-D 26, 1813. w.
  a: ULS; CSmH D 19, 1813. / *b:* BiP; EP lacking no15; L.
  Continued as
CHAMPION. London. no52-491, Ja 2, 1814-Je 2, 1822. w. (Subtitle varies.)
  a: ULS; CtY (1814-21); NN 1814-17. / *b:* EU no52-156, 1814-15; L; LGU 1818-21; LLL no157-259, for 1816-17; O no339-62, Jl 4-D 26, 1819.
  Continued as
INVESTIGATOR. London. Je 9, 1822-[?]. w. (No issues known. See CBEL, III.811.)

DRAKARD'S STAMFORD NEWS, and General Advertiser, for the Counties of Lincoln, Rutland, Northampton, &c. Stamford. 1809-34. w.
  a: ULS; CSmH Ag 15, 1823. / *b:* L O 1809-D 28, 1827; F 6-S 4, 1829; F 26, 1830-1832.
  (Incorporated with *Lincoln Gazette.)*

DRAMA, a Daily Register of Histrionic Performances on the Dublin Stage; and Critical Review of General Dramatic Literature. Dublin. v1, no1-42, O 23-D 10, 1821. d.
  a: ULS.

DRAMA; or, Theatrical Pocket Magazine. London. v1-7, 1821-25; ns, v1-2, 1825-26.
  a: ULS. / *b:* UCP; BP v1-3; CrP v4-5, 7; L lacking ns, v2; MR 1821-24.

DRAMATIC AND LITERARY CENSOR. (See *Dramatic Censor; or, Weekly Theatrical Report.)*

DRAMATIC ANNUAL. London. 1831.
  b: UCP.

DRAMATIC ARGUS. Dublin. v1-2, 1824-25.
  a: ULS. / *b:* L.

DRAMATIC CENSOR. Edinburgh. no1-38, S 23-D 12, 1829. d.; s.w.
  b: EP lacking no30, 35.

DRAMATIC CENSOR; or, Critical and Biographical Illustrations of the British Stage. London. v1, Ja-N 1811. m.
  a: ULS. / *b:* BP; L; O.

DRAMATIC CENSOR, or Monthly Epitome of Taste, Fashion, and Manners. (See *Dramatic Censor; or, Weekly Theatrical Report.)*

DRAMATIC CENSOR; or, Weekly Theatrical Report. London. v1-2, no1-26, Ja 4-Je 28, 1800. w.
  a: ULS. / *b:* UCP; L.
  Continued as
DRAMATIC CENSOR, or Monthly Epitome of Taste, Fashion, and Manners. London. v3-4, no27-38, Jl 1800-Je 1801. m.
  a: ULS. / *b:* UCP; L.
  Continued as
DRAMATIC AND LITERARY CENSOR. London. v4-5, no39-50, Jl-D 4, 1801. m.; w.
  a: ULS. / *b:* UCP; L.

DRAMATIC CORRESPONDENT and Amateur's Placebook. London. no1-21, 1828-29/?. w.
  a: ULS.

THE DRAMATIC GAZETTE; or Weekly Record of the Stage; Music, Public Exhibitions; &c. London. no1-12, O 9, 1830-Ja 1, 1831. w.
  a: ULS. / *b:* L.

DRAMATIC MAGAZINE, embellished with Numerous Engravings of the Principal Performers. London. v1-3, 1829-31. m.
  a: ULS; ULSup; MB. / *b:* UCP; L; LLL v3.

DRAMATIC MANUAL.
(See *The Theatrical Gazette*.)

DRAMATIC MISCELLANY and Medley of Literature. London. no 1, Ap 8, 1820.
  b: L.

DRAMATIC OBSERVER and Musical Review. London. no 1, Ap 14, 1823/?.
  a: MH.

DRAMATIC REVIEW. Dublin. 1821.
  (No issues known. See John Power, *Irish Periodical Publications*, p. 10.)

DRAMATIC REVIEW; or, Mirror of the Stage. London. 1795.
  (No issues known. See C & K, 1206.)

DRAMATIC SPECULUM. Liverpool. no 1, 1826.
  b: L.

DRAMATIC TATLER; or, Companion to the Theatre. Edinburgh. no 1-17, Mr 30-Ap 17, 1829. d.
  a: ULS.

DRAMATICAL AND MUSICAL MAGAZINE. London. 1823/?. m.
  a: ULS.

DRAWING ROOM SCRAP BOOK. London. 1832-36.
  b: BkP.

DRAWING ROOM SCRAP SHEET. London. no 1-26, 1831-32.
  b: L.

DREWRY'S DERBY MERCURY.
(See *Derby Mercury*.)

DROGHEDA JOURNAL; or, Meath and Louth Advertiser. Drogheda. [1775]-1843.
  a: CSmH Ag 20, 1828. / *b:* C Ja 23, 1796; L 1823-32.

THE DROGHEDA NEWS LETTER. Drogheda. [?]-1800-1813-[?]. s.w.
  b: DL 7 sc.nos. 1808-09; L My 29, 1813.

THE DRUIDS' MAGAZINE, a Compendium of Druidical Proceedings. London. v1-4, 1830-33.
  b: CrP v1; L lacking v1 and v2, no1, 3.
  (Continued as *Druids' Monthly Magazine and Literary Journal*, 1834-39.)

DRURY LANE THEATRICAL GAZETTE. London. no 1-140, S 7, 1816-Mr 20, 1817. s.w.
  b: L.

DRY TOAST, prepared for the Sunday Morning Repast. London. no 1-9, Je 7-Ag 2, 1823/?. w.
  a: ULS. / *b:* UCP; L no1-3.

Y DRYCH. Caerfyrddin. 1826.
  b: UCP.

Y DRYSORFA. Treffynnon. 1813-1930.
  b: UCP.

Y DRYSORFA. Caerlleon. 1831-date.
  a: ULS. / *b:* UCP; CrP; L; SwP.

Y DRYSORFA.
(See *Trysorfa Ysprydol*.)

Y DRYSORFA GYMMYSGEDIG. Caerfyrddin. v1, 1795.
  b: UCP.

Y DRYSORFA YSPRYDOL. Chester. v1-4, 1799-1827.
  b: UCP.

DUBLIN AND LONDON MAGAZINE. London. v1-2, 1825-26.
  a: ULS; KyU v1. / *b:* UCP; DL; L.
  Continued as
ROBIN'S LONDON AND DUBLIN MAGAZINE. London. v3-4, 1827-28.
  a: ULS. / *b:* UCP; BlP; L v3.

DUBLIN CHRISTIAN INSTRUCTOR, and Repertory of Education. Dublin. v1-2, Ja 1818-D 1819. m.
  b: DL lacking Je-Jl, O 1818 and Mr-Ap, Je, S, N-D 1819.

DUBLIN CHRONICLE. Dublin. no1-1043, 1787-93. t.w.
  a: ULS; CtY (1789-D 31, 1791); TxU 11 sc. nos. 1789-92. / *b:* UCP; DA 1789-My 1, 1792; DL Ja-My 1, 1789; L 1789-O 31, 1793, lacking My 1792-Ap 1793.

DUBLIN CHRONICLE.
(See *Hunter's Dublin Chronicle*.)

DUBLIN CORRESPONDENT.
(See *Correspondent*.)

DUBLIN EVENING EXPRESS. Dublin. [?]-1811-24-[?]. t.w.
  b: L Jl 13, 1811; Mr 22, 1824.

DUBLIN EVENING HERALD. Dublin. no1+, Ja 30, 1821-Ja 29, 1822.
  a: MiU-C Ja 26, F 18, 1807. / *b:* L.

DUBLIN EVENING MAIL. Dublin. no1+, F 3, 1823-1928. t.w.; d.
  a: CtY; DLC F-Jl 1823. / *b:* D N 17, 1826-32; L.
  (Continued as *Evening Mail*, 1928-date.)

DUBLIN EVENING PACKET (afterwards *Town; or Dublin Evening Packet*.) Dublin. 1788-1794/?.
  b: UCP.

DUBLIN EVENING POST. Dublin. no1+, 1732-1875. t.w.; d.
  a: CtY 1801-04, 1806, 1809-20; 1822-24; 1826-32; ICU 19 sc.nos. 1794-1804; KkKJ sc.nos. 1791-96; NNHi (Ap-My 1806); WHi 1803; Ja-Ag 1810. / *b:* UCP; BlL Mr 6-Ap 3, 1798; Ja 6, 1831-Mr 6, 1832; DA 1791-93; DL 1807-08; L 1789-90, 1792, 1794, 1796-97, N 1805-1810, 1815-25, F 1826-1832.

DUBLIN EXAMINER, or Monthly Journal of Science, Literature, and Art. Dublin. v1-2,

no1-9, My 1816-Ja 1817. m. (Last no. dated
Ja but published in Ap.)
  a: ULS; ULSup. / *b:* UCP; L.

**DUBLIN FAMILY MAGAZINE; or, Literary
and Religious Miscellany.** Dublin. no1-6, Ap-
S 1829. m. (Also called *Dublin Juvenile Magazine.*)
  a: ULS; ULSup. / *b:* DA; DL; L.
  (May be continued as *Dublin Monthly
  Magazine.*)

DUBLIN GAZETTE. Dublin. 1705-1922. t.w.
  a: CSmH Ag 11, 1827. / *b:* UCP; DL 1790,
  1792-1832; DLL Je 1815-32; L 1793-1811;
  MR O 22-24, 1811. (Continued as *Iris Oifi-
  giúil,* 1922-date.)

DUBLIN HALFPENNY JOURNAL. Dublin.
v1, no1-4, N 3-24, 1832. w.
  b: O.

DUBLIN HOSPITAL. Reports and Communications in Medicine and Surgery. Dublin, London. v1-5, 1817-30.
  a: ULS. / *b:* UCP; LS.

DUBLIN IMPERIAL MAGAZINE. Dublin. no
1, Je 2, 1827.
  b: DL.

DUBLIN INFIRMARY for Skin Diseases. Report. Dublin. v1, 1820.
  b: UCP.

DUBLIN INQUISITOR. Dublin. v1-2, Ja-Ag
1821.
  a: ULS. / *b:* UCP; DA; DL; DLL; L.

DUBLIN JOURNAL.
  (See *Faulkner's Dublin Journal.*)

**DUBLIN JOURNAL of Medical and Chemical
Science.** Dublin. v1-28, 1832-45.
  a: ULS. / *b:* C; DLL; L; LMA; LCP; LS;
  LUC.
  (Continued as *Dublin Quarterly Journal of
  Medical Science,* 1846-71; as *Dublin
  Journal of Medical Science,* 1872-1920; as
  Irish Journal of Medical Science, 1922-
  date.)

**DUBLIN JOURNAL OF SCIENCE, Literature
and Art.** Dublin. 1816.
  b: DLL.

DUBLIN JUVENILE MAGAZINE.
  (See *Dublin Family Magazine; or, Literary
  and Religious Miscellany.*)

DUBLIN LIST OF IMPORTS AND EXPORTS.
Dublin. [?]-1800-36-[?].
  (No issues known. See CBEL, II.719.)

DUBLIN LITERARY CENSOR. London. 1810.
  (No issues known. See John Power, *Irish
  Literary Periodical Publications,* p. 8.)

**DUBLIN LITERARY GAZETTE, or Weekly
Chronicle of Criticism, Belles Lettres, and
Fine Arts.** Dublin. v1, no1-6, Ja 2-Je 26,
1830. w.

  a: ULS; ULSup. / *b:* UCP; DL; L; LLL;
  LVA.
  Continued as
NATIONAL MAGAZINE. Dublin. v1, Jl-D
1830. m.
  a: ULS. / *b:* UCP; DL; L.
  Continued as
**NATIONAL MAGAZINE and Dublin Liter-
ary Gazette.** Dublin. v1-2, 1830-31. m.
  a: ULS. / *b:* UCP; BlL; DL; L.

**DUBLIN MAGAZINE; or General Repository
of Philosophy, Belles-Lettres, &c.** Dublin.
v1-2, 1820. m.
  a: ULS. / *b:* UCP; DL; L.

**DUBLIN. MAGAZINE, or Monthly Memorialist,
a Work Sacred to the Preservation of Fugitive
Genius, National Events, and Important Discoveries.** Dublin. v1, 1812-13. m.
  a: ULS. / *b:* BlL; DL; L.

**DUBLIN MAGAZINE and Irish Monthly Reg-
ister.** Dublin. v1-5, 1798-1800. m.
  a: ULS; ULSup. / *b:* UCP; CoP v4-5; L.

DUBLIN MEDICAL AND PHYSICAL ESSAYS.
Dublin. v1-2, 1807-08.
  a: ULS. / *b:* UCP; LMD.

DUBLIN MEDICAL TRANSACTIONS.
  (See *Association of Fellows and Licentiates.*)

DUBLIN MERCANTILE ADVERTISER. Dublin. [?]-1823-65.
  a: CSmH My 14, 1827. / *b:* L no110+, Ja
  6, 1823-32.

DUBLIN MONTHLY MAGAZINE. Dublin. no
1-6, Ja-Je 1830. m.
  a: ULS. / *b:* UCP; DLL; L; O no1.
  (May succeed *Dublin Family Magazine;
  or Literary and Religious Miscellany.*)

**DUBLIN MONTHLY MAGAZINE; or, Irish
Sentinel.** Dublin. 1826.
  b: DL Ag 1826.

**DUBLIN MONTHLY MAGAZINE, and Polit-
ical Register.** Dublin. v1, no1-3, Ja-Mr 1810.
m.
  b: UCP; L no1-2.
  Continued as
POLITICAL REGISTER. Dublin. v1-3, 1810-
12. m.
  a: ULS. / *b:* UCP; DL lacking v3, no2;
  L v1-2, no1.

DUBLIN MORNING POST. Dublin. [?]-1824-
32. d.
  a: CSmH no4087, Je 11, 1823. / *b:* D
  1825-30; L no4300, &c., F 16, 1824; My 11,
  1825; Jl 1, S 2, 4, 1826; Ja 1, 1830-My 5,
  1832.
  (Incorporated with *Dublin Times.*)

**DUBLIN MUSEUM, or Entertaining Pocket
Companion.** Dublin. v1, Ja-D 1807. m. (First
no. has title *New Magazine. The Dublin Museum.*)
  b: DL.

DUBLIN OBSERVER.
(See *Sunday Observer.*)

DUBLIN PENNY JOURNAL. Dublin. v1-4, 1832-36. w.
  a: ULS; ULSup. / *b:* UCP; CoP; CrP; DA; DCC; DL; DRS; DSA; GM; L; LLL.

DUBLIN PHILOSOPHICAL JOURNAL and Scientific Review. Dublin. v1-2, 1825-26.
  a: ULS; ULSup. / *b:* UCP; C; DL; DRS; L; LR v1.

DUBLIN POLITICAL REVIEW. Dublin. no1-13, F 6-My 1, 1813. w.
  b: DL.

DUBLIN SATIRIST. Dublin. v1, N 1809-Mr 1810. m.
  b: DL; DRS; L; MR.

DUBLIN TEMPERANCE GAZETTE. Dublin. v1, 1832-33/?.
  a: ULS.

DUBLIN TIMES. Dublin. no1+, Mr 16, 1831-1833.
  a: CSmH Je 29, 1831. / *b:* D My 3-D 31, 1832; L.
  (Incorporated with *Dublin Morning Post.*)

DUBLIN WEEKLY GAZETTE; or Weekly Chronicle of Literature, Belles Lettres, and Fine Arts. Dublin. no1-30, 1830.
  (No issues known. See John Power, *Irish Literary Periodical Publications*, p. 13.)

DUBLIN WEEKLY JOURNAL. Dublin. [?]-1795-[?].
  b: L v10, no7, F 14, 1795.

DUBLIN WEEKLY JOURNAL, a Repository of Music, Literature, and Entertaining Knowledge. Dublin. v1, no1-30, N 1832-1833. (Subtitle varies slightly.)
  a: ULS. / *b:* UCP; DLL; O no1.

DUBLIN WEEKLY MESSENGER. Dublin. 1808-13. w.
  b: UCP; L no17, 29, 32, for Mr 6, My 1, 29, 1813.

DUBLIN WEEKLY REGISTER. Dublin. no1+, O 24, 1818-50. w.
  a: CSmH My 12, 1827. / *b:* L 1818-22, 1827-32.

DUCKETT'S DISPATCH. London. no1+, 1816-18. w.
  b: L no85-97, Ja 4-Mr 29, 1818.
  Continued as
DUCKETT'S PAPER. London. no1-4, Ap 12-My 3, 1818. w.
  b: L.

DUCKETT'S PAPER.
(See *Duckett's Dispatch.*)

DUMFRIES AND GALLOWAY COURIER. Dumfries. 1809-1939. w. (In latter years called *Dumfries and Galloway Courier and Herald.*)
  a: CSmH D 29, 1829. / *b:* DsD.

DUMFRIES MONTHLY MAGAZINE and Literary Compendium. Dumfries. v1-3, 1825-26. m.
  a: ULS. / *b:* DsD; E; EP; EUv1; L; LP.

DUMFRIES WEEKLY JOURNAL. Dumfries. no1+, 1777-1835. w.   (Succeeds *Dumfries Weekly Magazine*, 1773-77.)
  a: CSmH N 28, 1826. / *b:* DsD 1789; O 1793-D 1795; Ja 1797-D 1803; N 1809-D 1815; Jl 1822-D 1831.

DUMFRIESSHIRE AND GALLOWAY Monthly Magazine. Dumfries. v1, Jl 1821-Je 1822. m.
  b: DsD.

DUNDEE AND PERTH Weekly Advertiser and Angusshire Intelligencer.
(See *Dundee Weekly Advertiser.*)

DUNDEE COURIER.
(See *Dundee Weekly Courier and Forfarshire . . . Advertiser.*)

DUNDEE COURIER AND ARGUS. Dundee. 1816.
  (No issues known. See S N & Q, sl.III. 136.)

DUNDEE COURIER and Forfarshire Agricultural and Commercial Advertiser.
(See *Dundee Weekly Courier and Forfarshire . . . Advertiser.*)

DUNDEE DIRECTORY . . . containing a Short Statistical Account of the Town. Dundee. 1809. a.
  b: DnP.

DUNDEE DIRECTORY . . . containing Lists of Names, Public Bodies, Charitable Institutions, Public Offices, &c. Dundee. 1818. a.
  b: DnP.

DUNDEE DIRECTORY AND REGISTER . . . to which is added a Directory for Broughty Ferry. Dundee. 1829.
  b: DnP.

DUNDEE LUNATIC ASYLUM. Report. Dundee. 1826-36.
  b: UCP.
  (Continued as *Report of the . . . Dundee Royal Asylum for Lunatics;* 1839-58.)

DUNDEE MAGAZINE and Caledonian Review. Dundee. no1-4, Jl-O 1822. m.
  a: ULS. / *b:* DnP no1-2; E; L.
  Continued as
CALEDONIAN MAGAZINE and Review. Dundee. no5-8, N 1822-Ap 1823.
  b: DnP no5-6, 8; E; L.

DUNDEE MAGAZINE and Journal of the Times. Dundee. v1-4, 1799-1802; ns, v1, 1815. m.
  b: DnP.

DUNDEE MAIL. Dundee. no1+, 1798-[?]. s.w.
  (No issues known. See C & K, 1232; S N & Q, sl.III.99: M.E. Craig, *Scottish Periodical Press*, p. 97.)

DUNDEE MERCURY, or Angus, Mearns, Perth, Fife, Stirling, and Kinross Shires General Advertiser. Dundee. no1-262, Je 1, 1805-Je 13, 1810. w.
  b: DnCA no176-262.
  Continued as
DUNDEE MERCURY and Commercial Advertiser. Dundee. 1810-12.
  b: DnCA.

DUNDEE MERCURY and Commercial Advertiser.
  (See *Dundee Mercury, or Angus, Mearns... Advertiser.*)

DUNDEE MISCELLANY. Dundee. no1-2, Ja-F 1829. m.
  b: DnP.

DUNDEE, PERTH, and Cupar Advertiser.
  (See *Dundee Weekly Advertiser.*)

DUNDEE RECORDER. Dundee. 1831.
  b: DnP.

DUNDEE REGISTER AND DIRECTORY. Containing Lists of Public Bodies, Companies, Shipping, Tables of Dues, &c. Dundee. 1824-25.
  b: DnP.

DUNDEE REPOSITORY of Political and Miscellaneous Information. Dundee. v1-2, F 15, 1793-F 21, 1794. w.
  b: DnP; GM F 15-Ag 9, 1793.

DUNDEE THEATRICAL REVIEW. Dundee. 1826.
  (No issues known. S N & Q, sl.III.150-51.)

DUNDEE WEEKLY ADVERTISER, and Angusshire Intelligencer. Dundee. Ja 16, 1801-Jl 1802. w.
  b: DnCA; E no1.
  Continued as
DUNDEE AND PERTH Weekly Advertiser and Angusshire Intelligencer. Dundee. Jl 1802-My 1803. w.
  b: DnCA.
  Continued as
DUNDEE, PERTH, AND CUPAR Advertiser (; or, Perth, Fife and Angusshire Intelligencer.) My 1803-21. w.
  b: DnCA; DnP F 1812-D 1819; Ja 1819-21.
  Continued as
NEW DUNDEE, PERTH AND CUPAR Advertiser. Dundee. 1821. w.
  b: DnCA; DnP.
  Continued as
DUNDEE, PERTH AND CUPAR Advertiser. Dundee. 1821-61. w.
  a: CSmH Jl 13, 1826. / *b:* DnCA; DnP 1821-23; 1830-32; L F 22, 1827.
  (Continued as *Dundee Advertiser,* 1861-1926; amalgamated with *Dundee Courier* and continued as *Dundee Courier and Advertiser,* 1926-date.)

DUNDEE WEEKLY COURIER and Forfarshire Agricultural and Commercial Advertiser. Dundee. no1+, S 20, 1816-1817. w.
  b: L no1.

Continued as
DUNDEE COURIER (and Forfarshire Agricultural and Commercial Advertiser). Dundee. 1817-32. w.
  a: CSmH no457, Je 16, 1825.
  Continued as
CONSTITUTIONAL AND DUNDEE COURIER. Dundee. 1832-34. w.
  (No issues known. For details on this and preceding title changes see S N & Q, sl. III.136-37.)
  (Continued as *Dundee Courier,* 1834-61; as *Dundee Courier and Argus,* 1861-1926: amalgamated with *Dundee Advertiser* and continued as *Dundee Courier and Advertiser,* 1926-date.)

DUNGANNON WEEKLY MAGAZINE. Dungannon. 1800.
  (No issues known. See C & K, 1235, and CBEL, II.688.)

DURHAM ADVERTISER.
  (See *Durham County Advertiser.*)

DURHAM CHRONICLE; or, General Northern Advertiser. Durham. 1819-1930. w.
  a: CSmH D 16, 1820; Ap 25, 1829. / *b:* L no201+, N 1, 1823-32; SuP Mr 16-D 1832; TmP 58 sc.nos. 1820-27.
  (Incorporated with *Durham County Advertiser.*)

DURHAM COUNTY ADVERTISER. Durham. no1+, 1814-30. w.
  a: CSmH D 5, 1829; CtY D 24, 1825; DLC F 4, 1815. / *b:* DrDC; L no478+, N 1, 1823-Jl 3, 1830; NwS sc.nos. 1814, 1817; TmP 47 sc.nos. 1816-27.
  (*Durham County Advertiser* succeeds *Newcastle Advertiser.* See the latter for details.)
  Continued as
DURHAM ADVERTISER. Durham. 1830-54.
  b: DrDC; L.
  (Continued as *Durham County Advertiser,* 1855-date.)

DUSTER. Derby. no1-4, 1832. f.
  b: DeP no2, 4.

Y DYSGEDYDD CREFYDDOL, am flwyddn. Dolgelly. no1+, Ja 1, 1822-date. (Title varies slightly.)
  a: ULS. / *b:* UCP; CrP; L; SwP.

E. JOHNSON'S BRITISH GAZETTE and Sunday Monitor.
  (See *Johnson's British Gazette and Sunday Monitor.*)

EAST ANGLIAN. Norwich. no1-132, O 12, 1830-1833. w.
  a: CSmH O 19, 1830. / *b:* L; NrP.
  (Incorporated with *Bury and Norwich Post.*)

EAST ANGLIAN: a Magazine of Literary and Miscellaneous Information for the Counties of Suffolk, Norfolk, Essex, and Cambridge. Ipswich. 1814-15. m.
  b: IpP.

EAST INDIA MAGAZINE; and Colonial and Commercial Journal.
  (See *Alexander's East India Magazine,* &c.)

EAST-INDIA REGISTER AND DIRECTOR. London. 1803-44. a.
  b: UCP; EP 1822, 1824-25, 1828, 1830; L; LGU lacking 1809; LU 1805, 1808-09.
  (Continued as *East-India Register and Army List,* 1845-60; *Indian Army and Civil Service List,* 1861-76; *India List, Civil and Military,* 1877-95; *India List and India Office List,* 1896-1906; *India Office List,* 1907-date.)

EAST LOTHIAN BIBLE SOCIETY. Report. Haddington. 1820.
  b: UCP.

EAST LOTHIAN Literary and Statistical Journal. Haddington. v1, no1-12, Jl 1830-Je 1831. m.
  b: HnP; L 1830.

EAST-LOTHIAN MAGAZINE; or, Literary and Statistical Journal. Haddington. v1, Ap-D 1822.
  b: E; EP.

EATON CHRONICLE; or the Salt-Box. Chester. no1-20, 1789.
  a: ULS. / *b:* UCP;·L.

THE ECCENTRIC.
  (See *The Eccentric Magazine; or, Lives and Portraits of Remarkable Characters.)*

THE ECCENTRIC MAGAZINE; a Collection of Anecdotes, Epitaphs, Bon Mots, &c., Selected from Reviews, Magazines, and other Publications. Aberdeen. v1-2, 1820-21.
  b: UCP; E.

THE ECCENTRIC MAGAZINE; or, Lives and Portraits of Remarkable Characters. London. v1-2, 1812-13. (No1 called *The Eccentric.*)
  a: ULS; ULSup. / *b:* BkP; L.

ECCENTRICITIES OF LITERATURE AND LIFE; or the Recreative Magazine.
  (See *Recreative Magazine, or Eccentricities of Literature and Life.)*

THE ECCLESIASTIC. London. no1-7, Ja 31-Mr 14, 1829. w.
  a: CSmH Ja 31, 1829. / *b:* L no2-7.

THE ECCLESIASTICAL AND UNIVERSITY Annual Register .... With an Appendix containing an Index to the English Rectories, Vicarages, Curacies, &c. London. v1-3, 1809-11. a.
  b: UCP; CrP v1-2; L.

THE ECCLESIASTICAL OBSERVER, and Reformed Presbyterian's Intelligencer; or
the Elucidator of the Spirit of the Reformation. Edinburgh. 1824.
  (No issues known. See SN & Q, s3.XI.181.)

THE ECHO. London. no1, Ja 3, 1807.
  (No issues known. See John Nichols, *Illustrations of Literary History,* v8, p. 610.)

ECHO DES FEUILLES Politiques et Littéraires.
  (See *Esprit des Gazettes.)*

ECLECTIC REVIEW. London. v1-10, 1805-13; s2, v1-30, 1814-28; s3, v1-16, 1829-36; s4-s6, 1837-68. m.
  a: ULS. / *b:* UCP; BP lacking s3, v4, 7-8; BrP v1-10; s2, v1-6; GeG s2, v7-26; L; LGU 1819-32; LLL; LdL; MCh; SP 1831-32.

ECLIPSE. London. no1-78, O 4, 1824-Ja 1, 1825.
  b: L.

THE ECLIPSES; or, Luminaries Involved in Darkness; an Universal Repository for Enigmatical, Critical, Philosophical and Mathematical Questions. Newmarket, Bury St. Edmunds. 1795-97.
  a: PPL 1795. / *b:* UCP; L 1795.

THE ECONOMIST. A Periodical Paper, explanatory of the New System of Society projected by Robert Owen, Esq.; and a Plan of Association for Improving the Condition of the Working Classes. London. v1-2, no1-52, 1821-22.
  a: ULS. / *b:* UCP; L lacking no27; O.

THE ECONOMIST; or, Englishman's Magazine. Newcastle-upon-Tyne. no1-10, 1798/?.
  b: NwL no1, 10.

ECONOMIST AND GENERAL ADVISER, containing important Papers on the following Subjects: The Markets, Marketing. Drunkenness. Gardening. Cookery. Travelling. Housekeeping. Management of Income. Distilling. Baking. Brewing. London. v1-2, 1824-25.
  a: ULS; ULSup. / *b:* UCP; L; LE v1.
  Continued as
HOUSEKEEPER'S MAGAZINE and Family Economist. London. v1, 1825-26.
  a: ULS. / *b:* UCP; L.

EDINBURGH ACADEMY. Report by the Directors. Edinburgh. 1825-46.
  b: UCP.

EDINBURGH ADVERTISER. Edinburgh. no1+, 1764-1859.
  a: ULS; C-S v57-60, 1792-93; v63-64, 1795; CaL Ap 1, 1800-D 1802; CtY 1789-95; 1798; (1799); S 13, 1817-D 29, 1818; ICU (F 26-D 31, 1793); 1815; 1822-23; MeHi My 31-Je 1789; MnU 1789-1802; N (1795); NN 3 sc.nos. 1823; PPL Ap 9, 1793-Ap 14, 1795. / *b:* UCP; E 1800; 1807-14; EP 1789-90; 1793; 1795-1832; ESL; GM 1797-1803; 1814; 1816-29 impf.; L lacking 1815; 1825-32.
  (Incorporated with *Edinburgh Evening Courant.)*

EDINBURGH ALMANACK. Edinburgh. 1744-
1836. (Second half of title varies: . . . *and
Scots Register;* . . . *and Imperial Register;
or Universal Scots and Imperial Register.*
Also called *Oliver and Boyd's Edinburgh
Almanac.*)
    b: UCP; EP 1832; LGU 1810-32; O 1791,
    1794-1800, 1802, 1804, 1806-08.

EDINBURGH AND LEITH ADVERTISER.
Edinburgh. no1-62, 1825-26.
    b: EP.
    (Incorporated with *The Star,* Ag 12, 1826.)

**EDINBURGH AND LEITH ORKNEY and Zet-
land Society. Report.** Edinburgh. 1823-29.
    b: UCP.

EDINBURGH ANNUAL REGISTER. Edinburgh. v1-19, 1808-26. a.
    a: ULS; ULSup; KyLx v1-7. / *b:* UCP;
    EP v1-18; GeG v1-4, 12-19; L; LLL v1-
    18; LdP.

**EDINBURGH ASSOCIATION for Relief of
Destitute Imprisoned Debtors. Report.** Edinburgh. v1-11, [?]-1824-25.
    b: UCP.

**EDINBURGH ASYLUM for Relief of the In-
digent and Industrious Blind. Report of the
State of.** Edinburgh. 1797-1816-[?].
    b: UCP.
    Continued as
ROYAL BLIND ASYLUM. Report. Edinburgh.
[?]-1829-45.
    b: UCP.

**EDINBURGH BIBLE SOCIETY. Annual Re-
ports.** Edinburgh. [?]-1826-61. a.
    b: EP 1826, 1828-31.
    (Continued as *National Bible Society,*
    1862-date.)

EDINBURGH CATHOLIC MAGAZINE. Edinburgh. s1, 1832-37; s2, 1837-42.
    a: ULS. / *b:* GM; L.
    (Revived as *Catholic Magazine,* 1843-44.
    Listed in ULS under this title.)

EDINBURGH CHRISTIAN INSTRUCTOR.
Edinburgh, Glasgow, s1, v1-31, 1810-31; s2,
v1-4, 1832-35; s3-s4, 1836-40. m.
    a: ULS; ULSup. / *b:* UCP; EP; GeG lack-
    ing v1-13; L lacking s1, v1-14, 24, 27-31.

**EDINBURGH CLERICAL REVIEW or Weekly
Report of the Different Sermons preached
every Sunday by the Established Clergy of
Edinburgh.** Edinburgh. 1799. w.
    b: EP.

EDINBURGH COLLEGE OBSERVER. Edinburgh. 1827-28.
    b: EP.

EDINBURGH CORNUCOPIA. Edinburgh. v1,
no1-9, O 1-N 19, 1831. w.
    b: EP.
    Continued as
CORNUCOPIA BRITANNICA. Edinburgh.
v1, N 26, 1831-Mr 3, 1832. w.
    a: ICU D 10, 17, 24, 31, 1831; Ja 7, 1832.
    / *b:* EP.

EDINBURGH CORRESPONDENT. Edinburgh.
no1+, 1810-22, s.w.; t.w. (Suspended Jl 6,
resumed N 26, 1818.)
    a: CSmH Jl 17, 1820. / *b:* E My 12, 1814
    Je 27, 1816 impf.; EP 3 sc.nos. 1815; EU
    1821-22 impf.; InIC 1814-16, 1818, 1822
    impf.; L My 25, 1822.
    Continued as
EDINBURGH OBSERVER. Edinburgh. 1822-
45.
    a: CSmH O 28, 1825. / *b:* E 1824; EP
    no1173-1252, Jl 23, 1832-Ap 5, 1833, lack-
    ing no1179, 1184; GM; L.

**EDINBURGH DRAMATIC AND MUSICAL
Magazine.** Edinburgh. no1-3, N 18-D 3, 1827.
w.
    a: ULS.

**EDINBURGH DRAMATIC JOURNAL; or, The-
atrical Observer.** Edinburgh. no1-11, O 11-
N 29, 1828. w; s.w.
    a: ULS. / *b:* EP.

EDINBURGH DRAMATIC RECORDER. Edinburgh. no1-12, Ja 29/F 5-Ap 23/30, 1825. w.
    a: ULS. / *b:* E.

EDINBURGH DRAMATIC REVIEW. Edinburgh. v1-9, 1822-24; ns, v1-5, 1824-25.
    a: ULS; ULSup. / *b:* E v1-5; EP lacking
    ns, v4-5; L O 7, 1822-F 11, 1823.

**EDINBURGH DRAMATIC REVIEW and Thes-
pian Inquisitor.** Edinburgh. no1-50, O 22-D
31, 1827. d.
    b: E no24, 32; EP.
    (Issue suspended for O 29-N 12 and for
    D 25.)

**EDINBURGH DRAMATIC TETE-A-TETE; or,
Companion to the Theatre.** Edinburgh. v1,
no1-42, Mr 20-My 7, 1828. d.
    a: ULS. / *b:* EP no14.

**EDINBURGH ECHO; or Weekly Register of
Remarkable Events and Repository of Wit.**
Edinburgh. no1-6, Ag 27-O 22, 1831.
    b: EP.
    Suspended for a time and revived as
**EDINBURGH ECHO; or Weekly Register of
Remarkable Events in Scottish History.** Ed-
inburgh. no7-11. Dates not known.
    (No issues known. For details. see S N &
    Q, s3. X. 105.)

EDINBURGH EVANGELICAL MAGAZINE.
Edinburgh. v1-3, Ja 1803-D 1805. m.
    a: ULS. / *b:* UCP.

EDINBURGH EVENING COURANT. Edinburgh. no1+, 1718-1860. t.w.
    a: ULS; C-S no11,020-174 for 1789; no11,
    802-955 for 1794; CU S 21, 1811-Jl 8, 1820;
    CtY Ja 1, 1816-Je 18, 1818, lacking 6 nos.;
    DLC 1798; ICU (D 1794), 1795, 1797. / *b:*
    UCP; E; EP; ESL 1789-D 29, 1796; Ja 4,
    1798-1818; GM 1795-1832, lacking 1798,
    1801-02; L 1789, [1799] (1800-01, 1803),
    1804, (1805-10), 1814, (1815), 1816-17,
    (1818-20), 1821, (1822), 1823, (1824), 1825-
    27, (1828), 1829-32.
    (Continued as *Daily Courant,* 1860; *Edin-*

burgh Evening Courant, 1860-71; *Edinburgh Courant,* 1871-86. Incorporated in *Scottish News* (Glasgow), under which it is listed by ULS.)

EDINBURGH EVENING POST. Edinburgh. 1827-32-[?].
  a: CSmH v3, no104, My 2, 1829; IU Mr 24, 1832.
  (Merged with the *Courant* about 1850-60. See S N & Q, s1.VI.37.)

EDINBURGH EVENING POST and Scottish Literary Gazette. Edinburgh. v1-13, 1830-41.
  b: EP v1-3, 7, 13, some vols. impf.

THE EDINBURGH EXAMINER. Edinburgh. [?]-1829-[?].
  a: CSmH Je 13, 1829.

EDINBURGH GAZETTE. Edinburgh. no1+, Jl 2, 1793-date. s.w.
  a: CSmH F 19, 1828; MnU Ag 10-S 3, 1822; NN Jl 2, 9-O 29, N 5-D 31, 1793; 1794. / *b:* E 1794-1802; 1804-32; EEG; L 1797.

EDINBURGH GAZETTEER. Edinburgh. N 16, 1792-F 1794. s.w.; w.
  a: PPHi N 23, 1792-My 31, 1793. / *b:* L D 25, 1792; Ja 15, Mr 8, 1793.

EDINBURGH GLEANER.
  (See *Edinbury·Gleaner.*)

EDINBURGH HERALD. Edinburgh. no1+, Mr 15, 1790-Ja 2, 1797. t.w.
  a: C-S Ap 2-D 27, 1790; NN Ap 2, 5, 12, 23-Je 2, 1790. / *b:* ESL Mr 15, 1790-D 30, 1791; L (1790-92).
  Continued as
HERALD AND CHRONICLE. Edinburgh. Ja 2, 1797-Ag 29, 1806. t.w.; w.
  a: DLC 1797; NN sc.nos. F-D 1800; Ja 28, 1805. / *b:* E.

EDINBURGH INSTITUTION for the Education of the Deaf and Dumb. Annual Reports. Edinburgh. [?]-1818-48-[?]. a.
  b: EP 1818, 1820, 1824.

EDINBURGH INSTITUTION for the Encouragement of Sacred Music. Report. Edinburgh. v1, 1817.
  a: ULS. / *b:* UCP; EP.

EDINBURGH JOURNAL of Medical Science. Edinburgh. v1-3, Ja 1826-Ap 1827.
  a: ULS. / *b:* UCP; DRS; E; L; LS.

EDINBURGH JOURNAL of Natural and Geographical Science. Edinburgh. v1-3, 1829-31.
  a: ULS. / *b:* UCP; CPL; L; LR, v1-8, with v3 impf.; LUC.

EDINBURGH JOURNAL OF SCIENCE. Edinburgh. v1-10, 1824-29; ns, v1-6, 1829-32. (Has varying subtitles.)
  a: ULS; ULSup. / *b:* UCP; CPL; DRS; EP; L; LLL lacking ns, v3; LP; LR.
  (Merged into *Philosophical Magazine;* later *London, Edinburgh, and Dublin Philosophical Magazine and Journal of Science.*)

EDINBURGH LAW JOURNAL. Edinburgh. v1-2, 1831-37.
  a: ULS. / *b:* UCP; L no1-4.

EDINBURGH, Leith, Glasgow, and North British Commercial and Literary Advertiser. Edinburgh. [?]-1827-28-[?].
  a: CSmH no98, S 13, 1828. / *b:* EP 1827.

EDINBURGH LITERARY ALMANAC.
  (See *Janus; or, the Edinburgh Literary Almanac.*)

EDINBURGH LITERARY GAZETTE. Edinburgh. v1-2, no1-61, 1829-30.
  b: UCP; E v1; EP no1-26; L.

EDINBURGH LITERARY GAZETTE, or Weekly Cyclopedia. Edinburgh. no1-62, 1823-24/?. (With no17 the subtitle was dropped.)
  a: ULS. / *b:* E v1, F 8-My 17, 1823; EU no10; GM v1, F 8-My 17, 1823; L no16-62.

EDINBURGH LITERARY JOURNAL; or Weekly Register of Criticism and Belles Lettres. v1-6, 1828-32.
  a: ULS. / *b:* UCP; BP; EP; GeG 1828-29; L; LLL; PeP.

EDINBURGH LUNATIC ASYLUM. Report. Edinburgh. 1832-70.
  b: UCP.
  (Afterwards *Royal Edinburgh Asylum for the Insane.*)

EDINBURGH MAGAZINE, or Literary Miscellany. Edinburgh. v1-13, 1785-91; ns, v1-22, 1793-1803. m.
  a: ULS. / *b:* UCP; E; EU ns, v13, 15-22; L.
  (Merged with *Scots Magazine* and continued as *Scots Magazine and Edinburgh Miscellany.* See the latter for details.)

EDINBURGH MAGAZINE, and Literary Miscellany.
  (See *Scots Magazine.*)

EDINBURGH MAGDALENE ASYLUM. Report. Edinburgh. 1823-48.
  b: UCP.

EDINBURGH MEDICAL AND SURGICAL Journal.
  (See *Medical Commentaries.*)

EDINBURGH MISSIONARY SOCIETY. Report. Edinburgh. [?]-1818-[?].
  b: EP 1818.

EDINBURGH MONTHLY INTELLIGENCER. Edinburgh. 1792-[?].
  (No issues known. See C & K, 1255. May be a confusion with *Historical Register; or Edinburgh Monthly Intelligencer.*)

EDINBURGH MONTHLY MAGAZINE.
  (See *Blackwood's Edinburgh Magazine.*)

EDINBURGH MONTHLY MAGAZINE and Review. Edinburgh. My 1810-Mr 1811. m.
  a: ULS; NN v1, no1-2, 7-8, My-Je, N-D 1810.
  Continued as

EDINBURGH QUARTERLY MAGAZINE and
Review. Edinburgh. v1, no1, Mr 1811. q.
  a: UCP; E.
  Continued as
EDINBURGH QUARTERLY REVIEW and
Magazine. Edinburgh. v1, no2-4, Je-D 1811.
q.
  b: UCP; E.
  Continued as
EDINBURGH QUARTERLY REVIEW. Edin-
burgh. v1, no5-6, Mr-Je, 1812. q.
  b: E no5.
  Continued as
SCOTISH REVIEW. Edinburgh. S 1812-Mr
1814. q.
  b: E S 1812.
  (A new series begins Mr 1814, but no is-
  sues are known. See S N & Q, s2.VI.101.)

EDINBURGH MONTHLY REVIEW. Edinburgh.
v1-5, 1819-21. m.
  a: ULS. / *b:* UCP; L; LLL; NwL v2-3.
  Continued as
NEW EDINBURGH REVIEW. Edinburgh. v1-
4, 1821-23. q.
  a: ULS. / *b:* UCP; E; L; LLL; O v1-2.

EDINBURGH MUSICAL MISCELLANY. Edinburgh. 1804.
  b: GM.

EDINBURGH NEW PHILOSOPHICAL Journal.
  (See *Edinburgh Philosophical Journal.*)

EDINBURGH OBSERVER.
  (See *Edinburgh Correspondent.*)

EDINBURGH OBSERVER; or, Town and
Country Magazine. Edinburgh. no1-11, S 13,
1817-Mr 7, 1818. f.
  b: UCP; EP; L no1-3; O no1.

EDINBURGH PHILOSOPHICAL JOURNAL.
Edinburgh. v1-14, 1819-26.
  a: ULS; ULSup. / *b:* BrP; C; CPL; EP
  v1-10; GeG; L; LCP; LP; LR; NwL; O.
  Continued as
EDINBURGH NEW PHILOSOPHICAL Jour-
nal. Edinburgh. v1-4, 1826-28; ns, v5-57,
1828-54; s3, v1-19, 1855-64.
  a: ULS; ULSup. / *b:* BrP; C; CPL; DL;
  GeG; L; LCP; LP; LR; NwL; O.
  (Incorporated with *Quarterly Journal of
  Science.*)

EDINBURGH PRACTICE of Physic, Surgery
and Midwifery. Edinburgh. v1-4, 1803.
  b: UCP.

EDINBURGH QUARTERLY MAGAZINE, intended to promote the Knowledge, Belief, and
Influence of Divine Revelation. Edinburgh.
v1-3, Mr 31, 1798-Je 28, 1800/?. q.
  a: ULS. / *b:* UCP; EP v1-2; GeG; L;
  MR 1798.

EDINBURGH QUARTERLY MAGAZINE and
Review.
  (See *Edinburgh Monthly Magazine and Re-
  view.*)

EDINBURGH QUARTERLY REVIEW (and
Magazine).
  (See *Edinburgh Monthly Magazine and Re-
  view.*)

EDINBURGH REFLECTOR. A Weekly Political and Literary Miscellany. Edinburgh. no1-
27, Jl 1-D 30, 1818; ns, no1-8, Ja 6-Mr 3,
1819. w.
  b: BP no1-3; EP; O.

EDINBURGH REPOSITORY for Polite Literature. Edinburgh. 1792.
  a: PPL.

EDINBURGH REVIEW. Edinburgh. 1773-99.
  (Listed by C & K 202, as being in the University of Texas Library, but a letter from
  this library reports that this is a "bibliographical ghost.")

EDINBURGH REVIEW, or Critical Journal.
Edinburgh. v1-250, 1802-1929.
  a: ULS; ULSup; KyLx. / *b:* UCP; BO;
  BP; BdL; BiP; BtP; BwP; CPU; CrP; EP;
  ExP; GeP; GrP: HP; KeP; L; LAt; LDC;
  LGU; LLL; LLN: LLW; LMT; LVA; LaP;
  LcP; LdL; LdP; LvA; LvP; MCh; MR;
  NpP lacking v43-4, 51-2, 55; NwL; NwP;
  O; PeP lacking v24; PrH; PsP; RP v5-
  28; SP; SthC; WcP; WhP; WmP; YP.

EDINBURGH REVIEW and the West Indies.
Edinburgh. no1-39, 1816. ir.
  b: C; E.

EDINBURGH SATURDAY POST. Edinburgh.
no1-52, My 12, 1827-My 3, 1828.
  a: CSmH S 22, 1827. / *b:* L.

EDINBURGH SATURDAY REGISTER. Edinburgh. no1-20, D 3, 1831-Ap 14, 1832. w.
  a: EP lacking no18-20; ESL no4-6, 14,
  18-20; GM.

EDINBURGH SOCIETY for Promoting the
Mitigation and Ultimate Abolition of Negro
Slavery. Report. Edinburgh. v1-2, 1824-25/?.
  a: ULS.

EDINBURGH SOCIETY for the Relief of the
Destitute Sick. Report. Edinburgh. 1816-67.
  b: UCP.

EDINBURGH SPECTATOR, a Journal of
Literature and the Fine Arts. Edinburgh.
no1-10, F 15-Ap 7, 1832. s.w.; w.
  a: ULS. / *b:* E; EP; L.

EDINBURGH SPY. Edinburgh. no1, 1810.
  b: GM.

EDINBURGH SPY. Edinburgh. no1-19, Je 11,
1825-Je 1828. f.; ir.
  (No issues known. Data from S N & Q, s3.
  X.88-89.)

EDINBURGH STAR. Edinburgh. S 16, 1808-
1826. s.w.
  a: C-S Ag 1809-Jl 1811; S 1813-16; PPL
  F 16, Mr 9, 20, 24, 1810. / *b:* EP 1811-
  12; InIC (1812-13, 1817, 1824-26); L S 16,
  1808-Mr 1817; sc.nos. Ap 1817-Ag 1819;
  WcBW D 16, 1808.
  (United with *Northern Reporter*, Jl 8, 1826,
  and continued as
EDINBURGH STAR and Northern Reporter.
Edinburgh. 1826-[?].
  (No issues known. Data from S N & Q, s2.
  VI.86-87.)

EDINBURGH STAR and Northern Reporter.
(See *Edinburgh Star*.)

EDINBURGH THEATRICAL CASKET. Edinburgh. no1, Jl 1832.
(No issues known. Data from S N & Q
s2.VII.4.)

EDINBURGH THEATRICAL CENSOR. Edinburgh. no1-12, Mr 21-Jl 28, 1803. w.
a: ULS. / *b:* EP no1-6.

EDINBURGH THEATRICAL OBSERVER,
and Musical Review. Edinburgh. v1-2, no1-
55, Jl 15, 1823-Mr 30, 1824/?. d.
a: ULS. / *b:* EP v1; L v1.

EDINBURGH THEOLOGICAL MAGAZINE.
Edinburgh. v1-7, 1826-32/?. (Probably succeeds *Christian Monitor and Religious Register*.)
a: ULS; / *b:* UCP; EP v1-2; L v1-4.
(Continued as *United Secession Magazine*, 1833-46; as *United Secession and Relief Magazine*, 1847; as *United Presbyterian Magazine*, 1847-1900; as *Union Magazine*, 1900-04.)

EDINBURGH TIMES. Edinburgh. 1825-26. w.
a: CSmH no22, Je 18, 1825.
(United with *Northern Reporter* in spring of 1826. For further information, see S N & Q, s2.VI.167.)

EDINBURGH UNIVERSITY. Business of the
Diagnostic Society. Edinburgh. 1823-24.
b: UCP.

EDINBURGH UNIVERSITY JOURNAL and
Critical Review. Edinburgh. no1-12, 1823.
b: E; EP no1-2; EU.

EDINBURGH UNIVERSITY MAGAZINE. Edinburgh. no1-4, Ja-Ap 1831/?. m.
a: ULS. / *b:* E no4; EP; EU no1.

EDINBURGH WEEKLY CENSOR.
(See *Letter Box; or Edinburgh Weekly Censor*.)

EDINBURGH WEEKLY CHRONICLE. Edinburgh. 1808-48. w. (Incorporated March 1828
with *Edinburgh News*.)
a: C-S Ap 7-D 29, 1832; CSmH D 1, 1819. /
b: EU [1810-13]; L no45+, O 11, 1809-N 1, 1815.

EDINBURGH WEEKLY ESSAYIST.
(See *Mentor; or, Edinburgh Weekly Essayist*.)

EDINBURGH WEEKLY JOURNAL. Edinburgh.
1757-1847. w.
a: C-S Ja 3-D 25, 1798; ICU (S 3, 1800-Ja 2, 1805). / *b:* UCP; AU 1818-20; 1824-29; E 1801-02, 1807-19, 1821-26, 1829-32; EP 1801-05, 1818-21, 1824-25, 1827-31; EU (F 8-D 1832); L Ja 1807-32.

EDINBURGH WEEKLY MISCELLANY. Edinburgh. v1, no1-14, N 1831-F 1832.
b: GM.

EDINBURGH WEEKLY REGISTER. Edinburgh. no1-57, N 1808-D 1809. w.
a: ULS; CtY D 21, 1808-Ja 4, Mr 1-8, Je 7-S 20, 1809. / *b:* EP.

EDINBURY GLEANER. Being a Collection
of Anecdotes, &c., for the Amusement of
Youth. Edina [Edinburgh]. no1-17, 1828(?).
b: BP lacking no5, 8, 13-15; L lacking no 5, 8, 13-14, 16.

EDMOND'S WEEKLY RECORDER and Saturday's Advertiser. Birmingham. no1-8, Je 26-Ag 14, 1819. w. (No6-8 dropped *and Saturday's Advertiser* from the title.)
b: BP; LU.
Continued as
EDMOND'S WEEKLY REGISTER. Birmingham. no1-19, Ag 26, 1819-Ja 8, 1820. w.
b: BP; LU.
Continued as
SATURDAY REGISTER. Birmingham. no1-7, 1820.
b: BP.

EDMOND'S WEEKLY REGISTER.
(See *Edmond's Weekly Recorder and Saturday's Advertiser*.)

EDUCATIONAL REVIEW AND MAGAZINE.
London. v1-2, 1826-27.
b: UCP; L.

EDWARD'S BOTANICAL REGISTER.
(See *Botanical Register, consisting of Coloured Figures of Exotic Plants*.)

YR EFANGYLYDD. Llandovery. v1-5, 1831-35.
b: UCP; CrP; SwP.

ELECTIONEERING and Parliamentary Review. London. v1, no1, 1795.
b: UCP.

THE ELECTOR'S GUIDE. Addressed to the
Freeholders of the County of York. York. no 1-7, Ja-Ap 1826.
b: UCP; L.

ELECTOR'S REMEMBRANCER. London. v1-2, 1822.
b: UCP; L.

ELGIN COURIER. Elgin. 1827-74.
a: CSmH O 12, 1827. / *b:* ElEC (1827-32).
(Combined with *Elgin Courant* and continued as *Elgin Courant and Courier*, 1874-date.)

ELGIN LITERARY MAGAZINE. Elgin. 1831.
b: E; O.

ELLIS'S BRITISH TARIFF; contains the
Duties payable on Foreign Goods imported
into Great Britain and Ireland. London. 1832-35.
b: C.
(Continued as *British Tariff*.)

EMERALD, a Weekly Miscellany of Literature, Politics, and Fashion. Dublin. no1-2, 1822.
  b: DL no1.

EMERALD; and Annual Keepsake of Beauty, Art, and Literature. London. 1830(?). a.
  b: L.

EMERALD FOR 1831. A New Year's Gift. Dublin. 1831. a.
  b: L.

EMMANUEL: a Christian Tribute of Affection. London. 1830.
  b: UCP; L.

THE EMMET, a Selection of Original Essays. Glasgow. v1-2, 1823-24/?. w.
  a: ULS. / b: GM; L no2, 4, 6-8; O no1-26.

EMPIRE. Dublin. no1-60, Je 18-N 2, 1832.
  b: L.

EMPORIUM OF LITERATURE, Science, and Belles Lettres. London. v1, 1831.
  b: L.

ENDLESS ENTERTAINMENT; or, Comic, Terrific, and Legendary Tales. London. v1, 1825.
  b: L lacking no1-2, 18.

ENGINEER, a Periodical Work. Glasgow. no 1-16, 1821/?.
  (No issues known. Listed in the first edition of ULS, but no libraries listed.)

ENGLISH BOTANY; or, Coloured Figures of British Plants. London. v1-36, 1790-1814. m. (Also called Sowerby's English Botany.)
  a: ICU v2; MH. / b: DRS.

ENGLISH CATALOGUE OF BOOKS.
  (See London Catalogue of Books.)

ENGLISH CENSOR.
  (See English Censor; or, National Satirist.)

ENGLISH CENSOR; or, National Satirist. London. v1, no1-3, Ja-Mr 1808. m. (Running title, English Censor.)
  a: ULS. / b: L Prospectus only.

ENGLISH CHRONICLE and Universal Evening Post. London. 1781-1801. t.w. (Subtitle varies. Succeeds English Chronicle, 1779-81.)
  a: ULS; ICU Jl 16-18, 1789; 4 sc.nos. 1795. / b: UCP; L 1789-Ap 1, 1793, Je 18, Jl 16, D 31, 1793-D 29, 1801; O [1789-96].
  Incorporated with Whitehall Evening Post and continued as
ENGLISH CHRONICLE and Whitehall Evening Post. London. Ja 1, 1802-43. t.w.
  a: ULS; CtY Ja-Jl 16, 1789; (1811-12); DLC 8 sc.nos. 1812-19; ICU Ag 5/8, 1809; Jl 15/17, 24/27, 1819; NcU 98 sc.nos. 1812-19; OCIWHi (1814); Ja-Ag 22, 1815. / b: BP sc.nos. 1790-91, 1794, 1796-1800,

1814-15, 1819, 1827; BnU 1806; C S 28, 1819-D 28, 1820 impf.; L 1802-32, early years very impf.

ENGLISH FIGARO. London. no1-2, 1832/?.
  a: ULS. / b: UCP; L.

ENGLISH FREEHOLDER. London. no1-21, Je 1-N 20, 1791/?. w.
  a: ULS. / b: UCP; L no1-14; LE.

ENGLISH GENTLEMAN. London. no1-153. 1824-27. w. (British Monitor incorporated with this Ap 1825.)
  a: CSmH Ag 7, 1825. / b: L.
  Continued as
NIMROD. London. no154+, N 25, 1827-Ja 13, 1828. w.
  a: CSmH Ja 13, 1828. / b: L.

ENGLISH HISTORICAL SOCIETY. Publications. London. v1-29, 1828-56.
  b: EP.

ENGLISH MAGAZINE and Commercial Repository. London. v1-2, 1796-97.
  b: L.

ENGLISH MUSICAL GAZETTE; or, Monthly Intelligencer. London. no1-7, Ja-Jl 1819. m.
  a: ULS. / b: UCP; L; O.

ENGLISH REGISTRY. Dublin. 1751-1844. (The number for 1799 called Court and City English Register. Also called London Calendar.)
  b: DA 1789-94, 1796-1800, 1802, 1804; L 1789-1801, 1803-21, 1823-28, 1830, 1832; LGU 1789-1831.

ENGLISH REVIEW; or, an Abstract of English and Foreign Literature. London. v1-26, 1783-95.
  a: ULS. / b: UCP; GrP v2-14, 16; L; MoM 1789-92.
  Continued as
ENGLISH REVIEW OF LITERATURE, Science, Discoveries, Inventions, and Practical Controversies and Contests. London. v27-28, 1795-96.
  a: ULS. / b: L.
  (Merged in Analytical Review.)

ENGLISH REVIEW OF LITERATURE, Science, Discoveries, &c.
  (See English Review; or, an Abstract of English and Foreign Literature.)

ENGLISH SPY: an Original Work, Characteristic, Satirical, and Humorous. London. v1-2, pt1-34, 1825-26. m.
  b: L.
  Continued as
ST. JAMES'S ROYAL MAGAZINE, and Monthly Gazette of Fashion. London. no1-2, Mr-Ap 1826. m.
  b: L.

ENGLISHMAN. London. no1+, 1803-34. w. (Varying subtitles. Observer of the Times and Constitution merged with this Ap 13, 1823.)

a: CSmH D 13, 1807; DLC F 6, 1820; ICU Mr 23, 1806. / *b:* L Ap 13, 1823-32; O Ja 1, 1815-D 22, 1817; 12 sc.nos. 1821-31.

ENGLISHMAN and Observer of the Times.
(See *Englishman;* see also *Constitution.)*

ENGLISHMAN'S ALMANACK. London. 1829-36.
b: LGU 1829.

ENGLISHMAN'S FIRE-SIDE. A Monthly Periodical Work. Oundle. v1, 1820. m.
a: ULS; ULSup. / *b:* L; O.

ENGLISHMAN'S FIRE-SIDE; or weekly Penny. Oundle. v1, 1819. w.
b: L no5.

ENGLISHMAN'S MAGAZINE. London. v1-2, 1830-31.
a: ULS. / *b:* UCP.

ENGLISHMAN'S REGISTER. London. no1-9, My 7-Jl 2, 1831. w.
a: ULS. / *b:* UCP; L.

ENIGMATICAL ENTERTAINER and Mathematical Associate.
(See *Gentleman's Mathematical Companion,* &c.)

ENIGMATICAL REPOSITORY, or Museum of Entertainment. Norwich. v1, 1828.
b: L.

ENNIS CHRONICLE.
(See *Ennis Chronicle and Clare Advertiser.)*

ENNIS CHRONICLE and Clare Advertiser. Ennis. 1782-1831. s.w. (Second half of title was dropped after a time.)
a: CSmH My 5, 1827. / *b:* UCP; E Ja 2-D 29, 1794.

ENNIS GAZETTE. Ennis. [?]-1813-[?]. s.w.
b: L no302, My 26, 1813.

ENNISKILLEN CHRONICLE and Erne Packet. Enniskillen. [?]-1812-49. w.
a: CSmH My 3, 1827. / *b:* BIL 1812-32 impf.; L My 27, 1813; 1824-32.
(Continued as *Fermanagh Mail,* 1849-93.)

THE ENNISKILLENER; or, Fermanagh Constitution. Enniskillen. 1830.
b: CSmH no15, My 22, 1830.

THE ENQUIRER, a Periodical Work. Glasgow. no1-16, O 11, 1820-My 9, 1821. f.
a: ULS. / *b:* EP; GM; L; O; PsP.

THE ENQUIRER; or Literary, Mathematical, and Philosophical Repository. London. v1-3, 1811-13. q.
a: ULS. / *b:* UCP; L v1-2; LP.

THE ENQUIRER; or, Philosophical and Mathematical Repository. Liverpool. 1825.
b: LvP no2, Ap 1825.

ENTERTAINING ECHO. Edinburgh. 1831.
(No issues known. Data from S N & Q, s3. X.105.)

ENTERTAINING MAGAZINE; or New Elegant Extracts in Prose and Verse, containing Tales, Essays, Anecdotes, Poems, etc., by the most celebrated Authors. London. no1-12, 1803. (Also known as *Entertaining Magazine; or, Polite Repository of Elegant Amusement.)*
b: UCP; L.

ENTERTAINING MAGAZINE; or, Repository of General Knowledge. London. v1-3, 1813-15. m.
a: ULS; ULSup. / *b:* DL; L; O.

ENTERTAINING PRESS, and Journal of Advertisements. London. no1-12, 1831-32.
b: L lacking no8, 11; O no9.

ENTOMOLOGICAL MAGAZINE. London, v1-5, 1832-38.
a: ULS; ULSup. / *b:* UCP; CrP.
(Continued as *Entomologist,* 1840-date.)

ENTOMOLOGICAL SOCIETY OF LONDON. Transactions. London. no1-17, 1806-12.
a: ULS.

EPHEMERA. Elgin. v1-2, 1822-23.
b: UCP; GM.

EPHEMERIDES. Edinburgh. no1-8, Mr 13-My 8, 1813. w. (No issues for week of Ap 10.)
b: EP.

THE EPICURE'S ALMANACK; or Calendar of good Living: containing a Directory of the Taverns, Coffee-Houses, Inns, Eating Houses, and other Places of Alimentary Resort in the British Metropolis and its Environs. London. 1815.
b: UCP; L; LGU.

EPISCOPAL GAZETTE; a Journal of Priestcraft and Knavery. London. no1, 1832.
b: BP; O.

EL ESPANOL. London. v1-8, 1810-14.
a: ULS; ULSup. / *b:* UCP; L; LAt.

EL ESPANOL CONSTITUCIONAL; ó miscelánea de politica, ciencias y artes, literatura. Periódico Mensual. London. v1-4, 1818-20; s2, v1-5, 1821-25. m.
a: ULS; ULSup. / *b:* L no21, 24.

ESPELHO POLITICO E MORAL. London. no1-41, 1813-14.
a: ULS. / *b:* UCP.

ESPRIT DES GAZETTES. London, Brussels. v1-35, 1780-97.
a: ULS.
Continued as
ECHO DES FEUILLES POLITIQUES et littéraires. London, Brussels. v36-38, 1798-99.
a: ULS.

L'ESPRIT DU JOUR, papier francois . . . par in Société de Gens de Lettres. London. 1792.
b: L Prospectus only.

ESSAI HISTORIQUE sur la destruction de ligue et de la liberté helvétiques.
(See *Mercure Britannique.)*

ESSAYISTS' SOCIETY MAGAZINE. Dundee. no1, My 1828. m.
(No issues known. Data from S N & Q, sl, III.151.)

ESSAYS on the Formation of Human Character. London. 1832.
b: C no2.

ESSEX AND SUFFOLK PRESS. Chelmsford. no1+, Je 26-Ag 7, 1832.
a: CSmH Je 26, 1832. / *b:* L.
(Incorporated with *Essex Independent.*)

ESSEX HERALD and Weekly Advertiser, for Suffolk, &c. Chelmsford. no1+, 1800-date. w. (Subtitle varies.)
a: CSmH S 25, 1821; ICU [Je 17, 1806-S 1, 1807]. / *b:* L D 22, 27, 1812.

ESSEX INDEPENDENT. Chelmsford. no1+, 1832-33. w.
b: L no22-27, Je 1, 1832-Je 21, 1833.
(*Essex and Suffolk Press* incorporated with this. Incorporated with *Colchester Gazette*, 1833.)

ESSEX STANDARD. Chelmsford. no1+, Ja 7, 1831-92. w.
a: CSmH Ja 7, 1831. / *b:* ColEC; L no 36+, S 10, 1831-32.
(Continued as *Essex County Standard*, 1892-date.)

ETON COLLEGE MAGAZINE. Eton. no1-8, Je 25-N 19, 1832.
a: ULS. / *b:* EtS; L; LLL.
(Superseded by *Kaleidoscope*, 1833.)

ETON MISCELLANY. Eton. v1-2, 1827. w.
a: ULS. / *b:* C; L: MR; O v1.

THE ETONIAN. Windsor. v1-2, O 1820-Ag 1821. m.
a: ULS; ULSup. / *b:* C; EtS; L; O.

YR EURGRAWN CYMRAEG. Caernarvon. 1807-08.
b: UCP.

EURGRAWN MON, neu Drysorfa Hanesyddawl, am y flwyddyn. Caergybi. 1825-26.
b: UCP; CrP: L.

YR EURGRAWN WESLEYAIDD, neu Drysorfa o Wybodaeth ddwyfol ac iachusol, am y flwyddyn. Llanidloes. 1809-date.
a: ULS. / *b:* CrP; L lacking v6, 18, 20, 25.

EUROPEAN MAGAZINE and London Review. London. v1-87, 1782-1825. ns, v1-2, 1825-26. m. (After v2 of ns united with *Monthly Magazine.*)
a: ULS; ULSup; KyLx 1801-10. / *b:* UCP; BP; BhP; BwP v1-82, lacking v65-66; CrP v15, 17-18, 24-25, 36-74; EP 1789-90; GrP 1793; L; LGU; LLL; LLW; LVA; LaP; LdL lacking v16, 20, 54; LvP v1-62; MCh; SwP v24, 31-34, 45-46, 53, 65, 81-82; WcP.

EUROPEAN MISSIONARY SOCIETY. Extracts of Correspondence. London. 1818-

37/?. (To 1835 as *Continental Society for the Diffusion of Religious Knowledge.*)
a: ULS.

EUROPEAN MISSIONARY SOCIETY. Proceedings. London. v1-20, 1819-38/?. (Title varies.)
a: ULS.

EUROPEAN REPERTORY. London. [?]-1800. (No issues known. Data from C & K, 1285. May be the same as the magazine of identical title published in Hamburg, no1-2, Ja-F 1800.)

EUROPEAN REVIEW; or, Mind and its Productions, in Britain, France, Italy, Germany, &c. London. no1-6, 1824-26.
b: UCP; L.

EVANGELICAL GLEANER: containing interesting Narratives . . . Anecdotes . . . Original and Selected. v1-2, Ag 16, 1823-Mr 6, 1824. (Running title of v1, *Sussex Evangelical Gleaner.*)
b: L.

EVANGELICAL MAGAZINE. London. v1-20, 1793-1812. m.
a: ULS; ULSup. / *b:* UCP; L: LGU v9-10, 16-20; LLL; MR.
Continued as
EVANGELICAL MAGAZINE and Missionary Chronicle. London. v21-30, 1813-22; ns, v1-36, 1823-58; s3-s5, 1859-date. m.
a: ULS; ULSup. / *b:* UCP; CrP; L; LGU v22-29; ns, v3-18; LLL; MR.

EVANGELICAL MAGAZINE and Missionary Chronicle.
(See *Evangelical Magazine.*)

EVANGELICAL MAGAZINE and Theological Review.
(See *New Evangelical Magazine and Theological Review.*)

EVANGELICAL PENNY MAGAZINE and Bible Illustrator. London. no1-10, 1832. w.
b: L; O no1.

EVANGELICAL PULPIT; or, Christian's Weekly Magazine, containing Sermons by the most eminent Ministers of the Day. London. no1-24, Ja 10-Je 19, 1824. w.
a: ULS.
(Merged into *Pulpit.*)

EVANGELICAL RAMBLER. London. v1-3, no1-108, 1822-25.
a: ULS. / *b:* UCP; L.

EVANGELICAL REGISTER; or, Magazine for the Connexion of the late Countess of Huntingdon. London. v1-4, 1825-31; ns, v5-14, 1832-43.
a: ULS. / *b:* UCP; L.

EVANGELICAL SPECTATOR. London. v1-3, 1829-31.
a: ULS. / *b:* UCP; L; O.

EVANS AND RUFFY'S Farmer's Journal.
(See *Farmer's Journal.*)

EVENING AMUSEMENTS; or, the Beauty of the Heavens Displayed. London. 1804-30. (Also called *Frend's Evening Amusements*, &c.)
    b: UCP; L 1804-22; MsP 1804-22; O 1804-19, 1822.

EVENING CHRONICLE. London. no1-30, F 4-Mr 19, 1824.
    b: L.
    (Incorporated in *The Globe*.)

EVENING FREEMAN. Dublin. no1+, Ja 18, 1831-71.
    b: L.
    (Incorporated with *Evening Telegraph*.)

EVENING HERALD. Dublin. 1806-13. t.w.
    a: MiU-C Ja 26, F 18, 1807. / b: L 7 sc. nos. 1807; 6 sc.nos. 1811; 2 sc.nos. Ap-My 1813.

EVENING HERALD; or, General Advertiser. Dublin. 1786-89/?. t.w.
    b: L 1789.

EVENING MAIL. London. 1789-1868. t.w.
    a: C-S N 28, 1794-D 1795; CtY (Mr-Jl 1789); D 30, 1791-My 28, 1794; D 30, 1795-D 28, 1796; DLC (1794-My 3, 1797); Ja 1-Ag 30, 1802; 3 sc.nos. 1824; ICU sc.nos. Mr-Je 1789; 6 sc.nos. for the years 1807, 1817, 1819; MH (O 11, 1793-F 12, 1794); MHi (1802-Ja 1811); NN F 14, Je 23, 1794. / b: UCP; L (1801-32); MR 4 sc.nos. 1792-94; RiP Ag 24, 1796; TmP My 6, 1818.
    (Continued as *The Mail*, 1868-date.)

EVENING PACKET AND CORRESPONDENT. (See *Correspondent*.)

EVENING STANDARD. (See *The Standard*.)

EVENING TIMES. London. no1-46, N 14, 1825-Ja 5, 1826. t.w.
    b: L.

EVERY-DAY BOOK; or Everlasting Calendar of Popular Amusements . . . forming a complete History of the Year, Month, and Seasons. London. v1-2, 1825-26. w.
    b: HdS; LVA.
    Continued as
    THE TABLE BOOK. London. v1-2, 1827-28. w.
    b: HdS.

EVERY DAY BOOK, Table Book, and Year Book. London. v1-4, 1830-32.
    b: O.

EVERY FAMILY'S BOOK FOR 1828; containing Every Thing that is most Useful and Necessary to be known by Females. London. 1828. a.
    b: L.

EVERY MAN'S BOOK FOR 1826(-30). London. no1-5, 1826-30. a.
    b: L lacking no3.

EVERY MAN'S PAPER of Useful and Entertaining Intelligence. London. no1-3, 1832. w.
    b: L; O no1.

EVERY NIGHT BOOK. London. 1827.
    b: O.

THE EXAMINER. [Monday Edition.] London. 1818-27.
    b: L.

EXAMINER; a Sunday Paper, on Politics, Domestic Economy, and Theatricals. London. no1+, 1808-81. (Subtitle varies slightly.) w.
    a: ULS; CU 1808-26, 1829-30; MB 1808-16, Ja-Je, N-D 1819; MnU Ja 2-D 21, 1820; NN 1808-16; (1817); 1818-19; (1820); 1821-24; (1825-27); 1828-30; NNHi Ja 7, 1810-Ap 14, 1811; Ja 3-D 1813. / b: UCP; BP; BiP; GM 1815; HdP 1808-18, 1821-23; L 1808-28, (1829), 1830-32; LLL lacking 1820; MR 1819; O 1808-30.

EXCHANGE HERALD, Aston's Manchester Commercial Advertiser. Manchester. no1-1030, S 30, 1809-Ag 23, 1825. w.
    a: CSmH Jl 4, 1814; CtY 1814-20; DLC Ja 4, 1814-Ag 23, 1825; MnU Ja 4, 1814-1815, 1818, 1820. / b: L 1809-1825, lacking Ja-Ap, My 20, Jl 1, 1817; My 18, 24, 1819; Ap 25, 1820; S 25-O 2, 1821; Mr 5, 1822; Mr 23, Ap 13, Je 8, 1824; MP.
    Continued as
    HERALD, Aston's Manchester Commercial Advertiser. Manchester. no1031-1087. S 1, 1825-S 28, 1826. w.
    a: DLC S 1-D 29, 1825; Ja 12-S 28, 1826. / b: L; MP.

THE EXCITEMENT; or, a Book to Induce Young People to Read. Edinburgh. 1830-41.
    b: UCP; L.

EXETER FLYING POST. (See *Trewman's Exeter Flying Post*.)

EXETER GAZETTE. (See *Woolmer's Exeter and Plymouth Gazette*.)

EXETER INDEPENDENT. (See *Alfred, West of England Journal, and General Advertiser*.)

EXETER JOURNAL. Exeter. [?]-1792-1877-[?]. w.
    b: ExP 1816, 1825, 1827-28, 1830-32.

EXETER WEEKLY TIMES. Exeter. no1-65, O 6, 1827-D 27, 1828. w.
    a: CSmH F 9, 1828. / b: ExP (1827-28); ExWT; L.
    Continued as
    WESTERN TIMES. Exeter. no66+, Ja 3, 1829-date. w.
    a: CSmH Ja 10, 1829. / b: ExD 1831-32; ExP 1829-30; ExWT; L.

EXHIBITIONS. (In general, see the society or other group concerned. See also *Catalogues of Exhibitions*.)

EXLEY AND DIMSDALE Corn Exchange Circular. London. no1-94, Ja 1, 1824-O 10, 1825.
    b: L.
    Continued as

EXLEY, DIMSDALE, and Hopkinson's Corn Exchange. London. no95-306, O 17, 1825-D 28, 1829.
b: L.

EXLEY, DIMSDALE, and Hopkinson's Corn Exchange.
(See *Exley and Dimsdale Corn Exchange Circular.*)

EXOTIC BOTANY. London. [?]-1808-[?]. q.
(No issues known. Data from *Literary Annual Register*, 2 (F 1808) 69.)

THE EXPLORATOR. London. 1811.
b: L no1-2.

EXPOSITOR and Sunday Family Instructor; a Periodical Work, being an Illustration of the Liturgy . . . with Sermons, and private Devotions. London. v1-2, 1812. w. (Also known as *Frizell's Expositor.*)
b: UCP; L.
Continued as
CHURCH OF ENGLAND-Man's Expositor. London. v3, 1814. w.
b: L.

EXPOSURE OF HYPOCRISY AND BIGOTRY; in an Address to the Society formed for Promoting Christianity among the Jews. London. no1-7, 1822.
b: L.

EXPRESS. Dublin. no1+, O 8, 1832-F 2, 1833.
b: L.

EXPRESS AND EVENING CHRONICLE. London. no1+, [S 1794]-1798-[?].
b: L no439, Jl 6/8, 1797.
Continued as
EXPRESS AND LONDON CHRONICLE. London. [?]-1799-[?].
b: MR sc.nos. 1799.

EXPRESS AND THE LONDON CHRONICLE.
(See *Express and Evening Chronicle.*)

EXSHAW'S GENTLEMAN'S and London Magazine. London. 1791-94. (May succeed *London Magazine, enlarged and improved.*)
b: UCP; DL.

EXTRACTOR; or, Universal Repertorium of Literature, Science, and the Arts; comprehending . . . the whole of the Instructive and Amusing Articles from all the Reviews, Magazines, and Journals. London. v1-3, N 1828-Jl 1829. q.
a: ULS. / *b:* UCP; L; LP.
Continued as
THE POLAR STAR. London. v1-10, 1829-32.
a: ULS. / *b:* UCP; L.
Continued as
THE POLAR STAR and Extractor of Entertainment. London. v1, 1832.
a: ULS. / *b:* L.

EXTRACTS . . .
(See also *Annual Reports, Minutes, Proceedings, Reports,* &c.; and in general see the society, institution, or other group making the extracts. In UCP, however, entries are commonly under *Extracts.*)
See especially *(1) European Missionary Society; (2) Holderness Agricultural Society; (3) Irish Society for promoting the Education of the Native Irish,* &c.; *(4) United Brethren's Society for Propagating the Gospel,* &c.

THE EYE OF REASON . . . Being a Paper of Essays on the most Popular Political Subjects that have occurred between January 3 and May 30, 1807. London. no1-27, 1807.
b: L; O.

FACTS AND ILLUSTRATIONS, demonstrating the Important Benefits . . . derived by Labourers from Possessing small Portions of Land. London. v1-14, no1-160, 1831-44; ns, v1+, 1844-84. (After O 1834 known as *Labourer's Friend Magazine.* In ULS under this title.)
a: ULS; ULSup. / *b:* UCP; L no1-18, 20, 23.

FALCON; or, Journal of Literature. Manchester. no1-4, N 5-26, 1831. w.
b: MP; MR no1.

FALKIRK MONTHLY MAGAZINE. Falkirk. no1-4, 1827. m.
b: EP; L.

FALKIRK NEW MONTHLY MAGAZINE. Falkirk. 1828.
b: EP.

FALMOUTH PACKET and Cornish Herald. Falmouth. no1+, Ap 4, 1829-date. w. (Subtitle varies.)
a: CSmH Ap 17, 1830.
(Ultimately becomes *Lake's Falmouth Packet, Cornwall Advertiser, and Visitor's List.*)

FALSTAFF'S ANNUAL.
(See *New Comic Annual.*)

FAMILY GAZETTE: a Weekly Register of Politics, Agriculture, Commerce, Literature, Miscellanies, &c. London. no1-14, Ja 2-Ap 3, 1809. w.
b: UCP; L Prospectus only.

FAMILY GAZETTE; and Literary and Philanthropic Journal. London. no1-35, O 6, 1821-Je 1, 1822. w.
b: UCP; DL.

FAMILY LIBRARY. London. [?]-1791-[?].
(No issues known. Data from C & K, 1306a.)

FAMILY MAGAZINE. London. 1825.
b: UCP.

FAMILY MAGAZINE. London. v1-2, 1830.
b: UCP; L.

FAMILY MAGAZINE; or, a Repository of Religious Instruction and Rational Amusement. Designed to Counteract the Pernicious

Tendency of Immoral Books. London. v1-3, Ja 1788-Je 1789. m.
  a: ICU. / *b:* UCP; L; LVA.

FAMILY MONITOR. London. no1-12, 1831. (No1-3 has running title of *Family Monitor and Servants' Guide.)*
  b: UCP; L; O impf.

FAMILY MONITOR and Servants' Guide.
  (See *Family Monitor.)*

FAMILY NEWSPAPER and Weekly Advertiser. London. 1809. w.
  b: L Prospectus only.

FAMILY ORACLE of Health, Economy, Medicine, and good Living; adapted to all ranks of society, from the Palace to the Cottage. London. v1-6, 1824-28.
  a: ULS. / *b:* UCP; L.

THE FANCY, or True Sportsman's Guide: being authentic Memoirs of the Lives, Actions, Prowess, and Battles of the leading Pugilists from the Days of Figg and Brought-on to the Championship of Ward. London. v1-2, 1821-26.
  a: ULSup. / *b:* L.

FARLEY'S BRISTOL JOURNAL.
  (See *Felix Farley's Bristol Journal.* See also *Sarah Farley's Bristol Journal.)*

FARMER'S CALENDAR or Monthly Monitor. Montrose. 1828. m.
  (No issues known. Data from S N & Q, s1. III.25-26.)

FARMERS' EXPRESS.
  (See *Mark Lane Express.)*

FARMER'S JOURNAL, (and Manufacturer's and Trader's Register). London. Ag 15, 1807-Ap 17, 1809. w. (Subtitle varies slightly).
  a: NNHi. / *b:* L.
  Continued as
EVANS AND RUFFY'S Farmer's Journal. London. Ap 24, 1809-Jl 16, 1832. w. (Also with varying subtitles.)
  a: CSmH My 1, 1809; NNHi lacking 1830-32. / *b:* L.
  (Incorporated in *Bell's Weekly Messenger.)*

FARMER'S MAGAZINE. London. v1-2, 1832-33.
  a: ULS. / *b:* UCP; L; StfS.

FARMER'S MAGAZINE, a Periodical Work exclusively devoted to Agricultural and Rural Affairs. Edinburgh. v1-26, 1800-25. q.
  a: ULS; ULSup. / *b:* UCP; BP v1-22; CrP v14-26; DRS; HnA v3-4, 6-7, 12, 14; IpP v1-12; L; LP v1-24, lacking v1, no2-4, v2-3; NwL.

FARMER'S REGISTER; and Monthly Magazine of Agriculture and Rural Affairs; with a Summary of Foreign and Domestic Political Events. Glasgow. v1-2, 1827-28.
  a: ULS. / *b:* GM.

THE FARRAGO. London. v1-2, 1792.
  b: UCP.

THE FARRAGO; or, the Lucubrations of Counsellor Bickerton, Esquire. Oxford. no1-2, Je 17-18, 1816. d.
  b: L; O.

FARRIER AND NATURALIST. London. v1, 1828.
  a: ULS. / *b:* UCP; L.
  Continued as
FARRIER AND NATURALIST, or Horseman's Chronicle. London. v1-2, 1829.
  a: ULS. / *b:* UCP; L.
  Continued as
HIPPIATRIST, and Veterinary Journal. London. v1-3, 1830.
  a: ULS. / *b:* UCP; L; LP v3.

FARRIER AND NATURALIST, or Horseman's Chronicle.
  (See *Farrier and Naturalist.)*

FASHIONS OF LONDON AND PARIS. London. v1, 1798-1801. ir.
  b: DL.

FAULKNER'S DUBLIN JOURNAL. Dublin. [?]-1745-1825. s.w.; t.w. (Preceded by *Dublin Journal,* 1725-[?].)
  a: CSmH Ap 14, 1823; CtY Ag 11, 1804; ICU Ja 2, 4, 6, 9, 1798; IU sc.nos. Ja-My 1799; sc.nos. Ag-S 1819; sc.nos. My-Je 1820; sc.nos. Ja-F, Ag-D 1821; sc.nos. O-D 1822; sc.nos. Ja, My 1823; sc.nos. Ap-My 1824; NN Ja 28-D 29, 1792; D 30, 1794; S 23, 1802. / *b:* UCP; DA Ap 1791-Jl 1793; DL; DLL Ja 2, 1794-N 14, 1807; KkKJ sc.nos. 1791-96; L 1796; Je 23, 1798; Ja 24-Ap 13, 1799; Ag 4, 1803; O 27-D 29, 1804; 1805-10; Ap 22, Je 1, 1813; D 31, 1819; 1820-21; O 6, 1823; O 4, 1824; LLL [1797-98]; MR 1792.

FELIX FARLEY'S Bristol Journal. Bristol. 1752-1853. w.
  b: BrP; L 1789; S 25, 1790; Mr 13, 1802; 1808; N 9, 1811; Ag 20, 1814; Ap 13, Jl 13, 1816; N 29, 1817; S 26, 1818; 1819-32. (Incorporated in *The Bristol Times.)*

FEMALE MENTOR; or, Select Conversations. London. 1793.
  b: UCP; DL.

FEMALE PRECEPTOR. London. v1-3, 1813-14.
  a: ULS. / *b:* DL.

FENLEY AND SHEPARD's Bristol Journal.
  (See *Bonner and Middleton's Bristol Journal.)*

FERRAR'S LIMERICK CHRONICLE. Limerick. 1768-date. s.w.
  b: L Ja 11, 1794; My 26, 1813; F 23, 1825; 1826-29; 1832.

FIFE AND KINROSS REGISTER . . . containing accurate Lists of Public Offices, Office-Bearers, &c. within these Counties. Cupar. [?]-1814-76-[?].
  b: EP 1814, 1829-32; L 1818, 1828.

FIFE CABINET; or, Literary Gleaner. Kirkcaldy. 1828.
  b: E pt5-6.

FIFE HERALD.
(See *Cupar Herald, or Fife, Kinross, Strathearn, &c.*)

FIGARO IN CHESTERFIELD. Chesterfield. v1-2, 1832-35.
  a: ULS. / *b:* CsfP.

FIGARO IN LONDON. London. v1-8, no1-402, 1831-39. w.
  a: ULS; ULSup. / *b:* UCP; BP no8, 28; BoP; L; LGU; LLL; WiP impf.

FIGARO IN SHEFFIELD. Sheffield. v1-6, 1832-38.
  b: SP.

FIGARO'S MONTHLY NEWSPAPER. London. 1832/?. m.
  (No issues known. Data from *Figaro in London*, 2 (D 29, 1832) 224, which states that an issue has just been published.)

FINANCE ACCOUNTS OF GREAT BRITAIN. (Treasury.) London. 1805-date.
  b: UCP.

FINANCIAL AND COMMERCIAL RECORD. London. no[1]-612-2820, [?]-N 2, 1824-45.
  b: L N 2, 1824-32 impf.

FINANCIAL PAMPHLETS. London. no1-37, 1796-1885/?.
  a: ULS.

FINN'S LEINSTER JOURNAL. Kilkenny. no1+, 1766-Mr 10, 1830. s.w.; w. (Changed title to *Leinster Journal* at some time during the 1790's.)
  a: CSmH Mr 29, 1828; NN D 25, 28, 1799; Ja 18, 25, F 5, Ap 12, 1800. / *b:* UCP; D v9, no78-v10, no77, 1811-12; KkKJ 1789, 1792, 1794-97, 1802-06, 1808, 1812; L v11, no43, My 29, 1813.
  Continued as
KILKENNY JOURNAL and Leinster Commercial Advertiser. Kilkenny. Mr 17, 1830-date. s.w. (Subtitle varies.)
  a: CSmH Je 25, 1831. / *b:* KkKJ 1830-32; L 1832.

FIRESIDE MAGAZINE; and Monthly Epitome.
(See *Fireside Magazine; or, Monthly Entertainer.*)

FIRESIDE MAGAZINE; or, Monthly Entertainer. Stamford. v1, 1819. m. (Running title for Jan., *Fireside Magazine; or, Monthly Epitome;* for Feb.-Sept., *Fireside Magazine; and Monthly Epitome;* for Oct.-Dec., *Fireside Magazine; or, Monthly Entertainer.*)
  b: L.

FIRESIDE MAGAZINE; or, Monthly Epitome.
(See *Fireside Magazine; or, Monthly Entertainer.*)

FISHER'S DRAWING ROOM SCRAP BOOK. London. v1-26, 1831-54. a. (Volume for 1832 exact duplicate of 1831 except date on title page.)
  a: ULS; ULSup. / *b:* UCP; L.

THE FISHER'S GARLAND. Newcastle-upon-Tyne. no1-11, 1821-31.
  b: L.

THE FLAGELLANT. London. no1-9, 1792. w.
  a: ULS. / *b:* L.

THE FLAPPER. A Periodical Work. Dublin. v1-2, no1-75, F 2, 1796-S 10, 1797. s.w.
  a: ULS. / *b:* UCP; DL; L.

FLEMING'S BRITISH FARMER'S Chronicle.
(See *Fleming's Weekly Express.*)

FLEMING'S WEEKLY EXPRESS. London. no1-167, My 4, 1823-Jl 9, 1826. w.
  a: CSmH My 4, 1823. / *b:* L.
  Continued as
FLEMING'S BRITISH FARMER'S Chronicle. London. Jl 10, 1826-Ja 26, 1829. w.
  b: L.

FLINDELL'S WESTERN LUMINARY.
(See *Western Luminary: the Family Newspaper, &c.*)

FLORIST'S GAZETTE, containing an Account of the Different Ranunculus, Pink and Carnation Meetings, held in Lancashire, Cheshire, Yorkshire, and other Parts of the Kingdom. Manchester. 1824.
  b: L pt2.

FLORIST'S GUIDE. London. v1-2, 1827-32.
  b: UCP.

FLOWERS OF LITERATURE . . . of Characteristic Sketches of Human Nature and Modern Manners. London. pt1-7, 1803-10.
  b: L.

FLOWER'S POLITICAL REVIEW and Monthly Register. Harlow. v1-9, 1807-11. m.
  a: ULS. / *b:* UCP; BrP v4-9; L.
  Continued as
POLITICAL REVIEW and Monthly Mirror of the Times. Harlow. v1-4, 1812-13. m. (Also called *Political Mirror of the Times.*)
  a: ULS. / *b:* UCP; BrP v1.

FLUTICON; or Flute Player's Monthly Companion. London. no1-5, Mr-Jl 1832/?. m.
  (No issues known. Data from *Figaro in London*, 1 (Mr 24, 1832) 64.)

FLUTIST'S MAGAZINE; and Musical Miscellany. London. v1, pt1-2, 1827.
  a: ULS. / *b:* L.

FLYNN'S HIBERNIAN CHRONICLE. Cork. 1768-1801. s.w. (Also known as *Hibernian Chronicle.*)
  b: UCP.
  Incorporated with *Cork Mercantile Chronicle* and continued as
CORK MERCANTILE CHRONICLE. Cork. 1801-35. s.w.
  a: CSmH Mr 26, 1828; NNHi 18 sc.nos. F 1812-Jl 1814. / *b:* UCP; CoP 1820; DA S 3, 1802; Jl 27, 1803; O 5, 1810; DL (Ap 27, 1803-Ap 25, 1804); L My 28, 1813; O 1, 1823; F 14, Ap 22, 27, 1825; 1832.

THE FOCUS OF PHILOSOPHY, Science and Art. London. v1, no1-9, no3-5, 1821-22. (No1-9 published weekly, D 1, 1821-Ja 26, 1822. These were followed by 3 monthly numbers dated Mr 1, Ap 1, My 1, and number no3-5.)
  a: ULS; ULSup. / *b:* L; LP v1, no5

FOREIGN LITERARY GAZETTE, and Weekly Epitome of Continental Literature, Sciences, Arts. London. no1-13, Ja 6-Mr 31, 1830. w.
  b: UCP; DL; L; LdL.

FOREIGN OFFICE. British and Foreign State Papers.
  (See *British and Foreign State Papers. Foreign Office.*)

FOREIGN QUARTERLY REVIEW. London. v1-37, 1827-47. q.
  a: ULS; ULSup. / *b:* UCP; BP; BrP; CrP; DL; E; GeG; L; LLL; LLN; LdL; LdP; LvA; MCh; MR.
  (Merged into *Westminster Review,* 1846.)

FOREIGN REVIEW and Continental Miscellany. London. v1-5, 1828-30
  a: ULS. / *b:* UCP; DL; L; LLL; LVA; LdL; MR; SwP.

FORGET-ME-NOT. London. v1-25, 1823-47. a.
  b: UCP; L.

THE "FORLORN HOPE," or a Call to the Supine. London. no1-3, 1817.
  b: L.

FOWLER'S COMMERCIAL DIRECTORY of the Lower Ward of Renfrewshire. n.p. 1831-32.
  b: GeG.

FOXHOUND KENNEL STUD BOOK. London. 1800-date.
  a: ULS.

LA FRANCE ET L'ANGLETERRE, ouvrage périodique, publié le 1 et 15 de chaque mois. London. v1-4, 1817-18.
  b: L; MR v1-3.

FRASER'S MAGAZINE (for Town and Country). London. v1-80, 1830-69; ns, v1-26, 1870-82. (Dropped second half of title after 1869.)
  a: ULS; ULSup. / *b:* UCP; BP; BrP 1831-32; CrP; EP; L; LLL; LdL; MR; NwP; PrH.
  (Superseded by *Longman's Magazine.*)

FREE ENQUIRER into the Rights, Privileges . . . Funds, etc., of the Fraternity of Merchant Tailors. London. no1-8, 1831.
  b: L.

FREEBOOTER. London. v1, no1-28, O 11, 1823-My 1, 1824. w.
  a: ULS; ULSup. / *b:* L; O no1-26.

FREEHOLDER. Cork. no1-80-[?], 1813-15.
  b: O no14, Ap 18, 1813; no80, F 4, 1815.
  Continued as
  FREEHOLDER; or, Eighth-Day Magazine. Cork. no[?]-89-148-[?], 1815-18-[?].
  b: O no89 O 29, 1815; no115-17, D 6-20, 1816; no139, Je 18, 1817; no145, Ag 13, 1817; no148, S 30, 1817.
  Continued as
  FREEHOLDER. Cork. [?]-1818-27-[?].
  a: CSmH no1, F 22, 1818. / *b:* O Jl 12,

1822; O 31, 1825; My 23, Jl 14, O 27, 1827. (Continued as *Freeholder and Cork Magazine,* [?]-1835-36.)

FREEHOLDER; or, Eighth-day Magazine. (See *Freeholder.*)

FREEMAN'S JOURNAL.
  (See *Public Register; or, Freeman's Journal.*)

FREEMASON'S JOURNAL; or, Pasley's Universal Intelligencer. Dublin. 1795-97.
  b: UCP; DA sc.nos. 1795-97.

FREEMASON'S MAGAZINE, or General and Complete Library. London. v1-11, 1793-98. m. (Single nos. for 1798 called *Scientific Magazine and Freemason's Repository.*)
  a: ULS. / *b:* UCP; DL; L lacking v9; LLL v8.

FREETHINKING CHRISTIAN'S MAGAZINE, intended for the Promotion of Rational Religion and Free Inquiry. London. v1-4, 1811-14. m.
  a: ULS. / *b:* UCP; L; LLL.

FREETHINKING CHRISTIAN'S Quarterly Register. London. v1-2, 1823-25. q.
  a: ULS. / *b:* UCP; L; LLL.

FREE-TRADE WEEKLY EXPRESS. London. no1-6, Jl 3-Ag 7, 1831. w.
  a: CSmH no1. / *b:* L.

FRENCH SENATOR; or, exact weekly Journal of the Debates of the National Assembly of France, to Commence from the Escape of the King. London. 1792. w.
  b: L Prospectus only.

FREND'S EVENING AMUSEMENTS; or, the Beauty of the Heavens Displayed.
  (See *Evening Amusements; or, the Beauty of the Heavens Displayed.*)

THE FRIEND. Dublin. no1-10, 1829-30.
  b: L.

THE FRIEND: a Literary, Moral, and Political Weekly Paper. London. no1-27, 1809-10. w.
  a: ULS. / *b:* UCP; CsP; LVA; O no1-23.

THE FRIEND, a Weekly Essay. London. no1-23, 1796. w.
  b: L; O.

FRIEND OF THE PEOPLE. London. no1-6, 1816-17.
  a: ULS.

FRIEND OF THE PEOPLE. London. no1, My 23, 1818.
  b: O.

FRIENDLY SOCIETY of Iron Founders of England, Ireland, and Wales. Monthly Report. London. v1+, 1809-date.
  a: ULS.

FRIENDLY SOCIETY of Iron Founders of England, Ireland, and Wales. Report. London. v1+, 1810-1910/?.
  a: ULS.

FRIENDLY VISITOR. Kirkby Lonsdale. v1, 1819. m.
  b: LdP.

FRIENDS LIBRARY. Lindfield. 1832-37.
  b: LFS.

FRIENDS' MAGAZINE.
  (See *Friends' Monthly Magazine.*)

FRIENDS MEETINGS chiefly within the Compass of London and Middlesex. Quarterly Meeting. London. 1822-24.
  b: LFS.

FRIENDS MEETINGS in Durham. Quarterly Meeting. Durham. 1820.
  b: LFS.

FRIENDS' MONTHLY MAGAZINE. Bristol. v1-2, 1830-31. m. (Caption title of v2, *Friends' Magazine.*)
  a: ULS. / *b:* BrP; DlP; EU v1, no13-14; v2, no1; GM; GrP; L; LFS.

FRIENDSHIP'S OFFERING; a Literary Album.
  (See *Friendship's Offering; or, the Annual Remembrancer.*)

FRIENDSHIP'S OFFERING; or, the Annual Remembrancer; a Christmas Present or New-Year's Gift. London. 1824-25. a.
  b: UCP; CrP; L.
  Continued as
FRIENDSHIP'S OFFERING; a Literary Album. London. 1826-44.
  b: UCP; CrP; L.

FRIZELL'S EXPOSITOR.
  (See *The Expositor and Sunday Family Instructor, &c.*)

FUND FOR THE RELIEF of Widows and Children of Burgh and Parochial Schoolmasters in Scotland. Proceedings. Edinburgh. 1822-1922.
  b: UCP.

FUND FOR THE WIDOWS AND CHILDREN of the Ministers of the Church of Scotland. Report. Edinburgh. 1749-1850.
  b: UCP.

THE GABERLUNZIE. Ayr. no1-13, 1827-28.
  b: L.

THE GABERLUNZIE, a Periodical Publication. Paisley. no1-2, 1825.
  b: GM; L.

THE GABERLUNZIE, a Periodical Publication. Paisley. no1-12, 1826.
  b: PsP.

GAELIC SOCIETY OF DUBLIN. Transactions. Dublin. v1, 1808.
  a: ULS. / *b:* UCP; CrP.

THE GALLANT. For God, the King, and the Fair. London. no1, My 10, 1823.
  b: O.

GALLERY OF FASHION. London. v1-9, 1794-1803. m.
  a: ULS. / *b:* L; LLL.

THE GALVANIST, a Periodical Paper. Cambridge. no1-11, 1804.
  b: C; L.

GALWAY CHRONICLE. Galway. [?]-1775-1818-[?]. (At one time known as *Galway Chronicle and Western Intelligence.*)
  (No issues known. Data from *Galway Reader*, v1, no3 (Winter 1948) 30, 31.)

GALWAY CHRONICLE and Western Intelligence.
  (See *Galway Chronicle.*)

GALWAY EVENING POST. Galway. [?] 1782-91-[?].
  (No issues known. Data from *Galway Reader*, v1, no3 (Winter 1948) 30.)

GALWAY FREE PRESS. Galway. v1, no1, 1832.
  (No issues known. Data from *Galway Reader*, v1, no4 (Spring 1949) 40.)

GALWAY INDEPENDENT PAPER. Galway. [?]-1829-1832.
  b: L v5, no1-v8, no27, Ja 3, 1829-Mr 31, 1832.

GALWAY WEEKLY ADVERTISER. Galway. [?]-1819-31-[?]. w.
  a: CSmH v13, no26, Je 25, 1831.
  (Additional data from *Galway Reader*, v1, no3 (Winter 1948) 31.)

GAMING HOUSE EXPOSITOR. London. no1-15, 1825-26.
  b: L.

GARDENER'S MAGAZINE, and Register of Rural and Domestic Improvement. London. v1-19, 1826-44.
  a: ULS; ULSup. / *b:* UCP; BP; BurC; CrP v1-2; DRS; GeG v2-6; L; LLL; LP.

THE GASOMETER; or, Dunfermline Literary Magazine. Dunfermline. Ja-D 1831.
  b: E; L.

GAZETTE DE LA GRANDE BRETAGNE.
  (See *Courier de l'Europe.*)

GAZETTE NATIONALE, ou le Moniteur Universel. London. v1-4, 1797. (Actually appeared in 1792.)
  b: UCP.

GAZETTE OF FASHION and Magazine of the Fine Arts, and Belles Lettres. London. no1-13, F 2-Jl 27, 1822. w.; m.; q.
  a: ULS. / *b:* L.

GAZETTE OF HEALTH.
(See *Monthly Gazette of Health.*)

GAZETTE OF THE EXCHANGE BAZAARS.
London. no1-9, S 29-N 24, 1832/?. w.
a: ULS.

GAZETTEER and New Daily Advertiser.
London. 1764-97. (Preceded by *London Ga-zetteer,* 1748-55?; as *Gazetteer and London Daily Advertiser,* 1755?-64.)
a: CtY 3 sc.nos. 1789; Ap-D 1790; Ja-S 8, 1791; ICU My 2, Jl 11, 1789; D 18, 1790; (Ap-My 1791); (My 25-Ag 15, 1792); MBAt F 6, 1790; D 20, 1792; MdBJ 5 sc.nos. 1791-92; NNHi 7 sc.nos. 1789-91; 25 sc. nos. 1794-97; PPL (1789-93). / *b:* BiP F 25, 1790; L sc.nos. 1789-96; LLL 1789-93 impf.; MR sc.nos. 1792-94.

Y GEIRGRAWN; neu Drysorfa Gwybodaeth.
Chester. 1796.
a: ULS. / *b:* UCP; L.

THE GEM; a Literary Annual.
(See *The Pledge of Friendship.*)

GENERAL ADVERTISER. London. [1784]-May 1789. (Preceded by *General Advertiser and Morning Intelligencer,* [1776]-1780-[1782]; *Parker's General Advertiser and Morning Intelligencer,* [1782]-1783-[1784].)
b: L.
Continued as
PATRIOT AND GENERAL ADVERTISER.
London. Je 3, 1789-Ag 16, 1790-[?].
b: L Je 3, 1789-Ag 16, 1790.

GENERAL ADVERTISER.
(See *Advertiser.*)

GENERAL ADVERTISER; or, Limerick Gazette. Limerick. no1+, S 17, 1804-N 10, 1820. s.w.
b: C S 24, 1804; DL Je 1809-1818; L; LmP 28 sc.nos. Ap 19-N 22, 1814.

GENERAL ALMANACK of Scotland and British Register. Edinburgh. 1809-15.
b: UCP; LGU 1810, 1812-14.

A GENERAL AND HERALDIC DICTIONARY of the Peerage and Baronetage of the United Kingdom. London. 1826-37.
b: L.
(Continued as *A Genealogical and Heraldic Dictionary of the Peerage and Baronetage of the British Empire,* 1839-date.)

GENERAL BAPTIST ADVOCATE. London. v1-6, 1831-36,
b: UCP.

GENERAL BAPTIST HOME MISSIONARY Register, Tract Repository, and Teacher's Magazine. Loughbrough. 1828-31/?. (Also known as *Home Missionary Register, Tract Repository, and Teacher's Magazine.*)
a: ULS. / *b:* BP N 1829; Je 1830.

GENERAL BAPTIST MAGAZINE. London. v1-3, 1798-1800. m.
a: ULS. / *b:* BP Ja 1800; L.

GENERAL BAPTIST MISSIONARY SOCIETY. Annual Report. London. no1-75, 1818-91/?. a.
a: ULS.

GENERAL BAPTIST MISSIONARY SOCIETY. Quarterly Papers. London. no1-65, 1825-34/?.
a: ULS.

GENERAL BAPTIST REPOSITORY. London. v1-10, 1802-21. q.
a: ULS; ULSup. / *b:* L.
Continued as
GENERAL BAPTIST REPOSITORY and Missionary Observer. London. v1-32, 1822-53. q.
a: ULS. / *b:* UCP; BP 1822, 1824-26; 1828-32; L.
(Continued as *General Baptist Magazine,* 1854-91; *Baptist Union Magazine,* 1892-95; *Church and Household,* 1896-1901.)

GENERAL BAPTIST REPOSITORY and Missionary Observer.
(See *General Baptist Repository.*)

GENERAL BAPTIST YEAR BOOK. London. 1787-date. a.
b: L.

GENERAL CHRONICLE and Literary Magazine. London. v1-6, 1811-12. m.
a: ULS. / *b:* UCP; L.

GENERAL ELECTION GUIDE. London. 1832.
b: L First sheet only.

GENERAL EVENING POST. London. no1+, 1733-F 1, 1822. t.w.; d.
a: ULS; CtY 1792-94; 1799; DLC (1792-94; 1797); ICU sc.nos. 1789; sc.nos. 1794; (1795); sc.nos. 1796-1807; MBAt Je 4, 1789-N 30, 1790; MnU Mr 15, 1791-Ja 2, 1821; NcD F 20-My 16, 1820, lacking Mr 7-11, 16-18. / *b:* UCP; BP sc.nos. 1790-1808; L lacking D 7, 1812-D 30, 1817; MR sc.nos. 1792-93.
(Incorporated with *St. James Chronicle,* F 2, 1822.)

GENERAL EVENING POST. Dublin. no1+, 1781-1784-[?]. t.w.
(No issues known after 1784. Data from CBEL,II.736.)
Possibly continued as
CAREY'S GENERAL EVENING POST. Dublin. [?]-1797-[?]. t.w.
(No issues known. Data from CBEL,II.736.)

GENERAL MAGAZINE; or, Epitome of Useful Knowledge. London. 1793. m.
(No issues known. Data from C & K, 1351, and CBEL,II.682.)

GENERAL MAGAZINE; or, Political and Literary Reporter. London. v1, no1-2, Ja-F 1810. m.
a: ULS.

GENERAL MAGAZINE and Impartial Review, Including a History of the Present Times and an Account of New Publications, interspersed with . . . Tales, Essays, Biography, Poetry, &c. London. v1-6, 1787-92.
a: ULS. / *b:* UCP; EP v6; L v1-5.

GENERAL POST OFFICE. Daily Statement of the Packet Boats. London. [1798]-1808-17-[1837?]. d. (Also known as *Daily Statement of the Packet Boats*.)
  a: NcD 1808-12, 1816-17, lacking 33 sc. nos.

GENERAL REGISTER of Philosophy, Literature, and Politics. London. 1791.
  b: L Prospectus only.

GENERAL REVIEW; or Weekly Literary Epitome. London. v1, no1-2, Je 12-19, 1819/?. w.
  a: ULS.

GENERAL REVIEW of British and Foreign Literature. London. v1, no1-6, Ja-Je 1806. m.
  b: L.

GENERAL SHIPPING and Commercial List. London. [?]-1802-17-[?].
  a: NNHi N 6, 1802-F 14, 1807; NcD (1809-14, 1817).

GENERAL SHORT-HORNED HERD-BOOK. Otley. v1, 1822.
  a: ULS; ULSup. / *b:* UCP.
  Continued as
  COATES'S HERD BOOK. Otley. 1822-date.
  a: ULS; ULSup. / *b:* UCP.

GENERAL STATE OF NATIONAL ACCOUNT. Dublin. 1788-92.
  b: UCP.

GENERAL STUD BOOK, containing Pedigrees of English Race Horses, from the Earliest Accounts, &c. London. 1808-date. (Issued every four years with a yearly supplement.)
  a: ULS. / *b:* L.

GENERAL WEEKLY REGISTER of News, Literature, Law, Politics, and Commerce. London. no1-13, Ap 7-Je 30, 1822. w.
  b: UCP; L.

THE GENIUS OF ALBION; or, Weekly Biographical, Political, Law, and Literary Repository. London. 1790. w.
  b: UCP.

THE GENIUS OF KENT; or, County Miscellany. Canterbury, Margate. no1-28, 1792-95. (Suspended Ap-D 1793.)
  b: UCP; L.

GENTLEMAN'S AND CITIZEN'S ALMANACK. Dublin. 1750-1833/?. a.
  b: UCP; LGU.

GENTLEMAN'S and London Magazine and Monthly Chronicler. Dublin. 1755-94. m. (Preceded by *London Magazine and Monthly Chronicler*, 1751-54.)
  a: ULS. / *b:* UCP.

GENTLEMAN'S DIARY, or Mathematical Repository. London. v1-100, 1741-1840. a.
  a: ULS; ULSup. / *b:* UCP; L 1814; LGU 1827-30; LR 1789-1800.
  (United with *Ladies Diary* to form *Lady's and Gentleman's Diary*.)

GENTLEMAN'S GAZETTE; or, London Magazine of Fashion. London. 1832.
  b: L Ja 1832.

GENTLEMAN'S MAGAZINE; or Monthly Intelligencer. London. v1-103, 1731-1833; s2-s4, 1834-68. m. (Subtitle varies; finally dropped.)
  a: ULS; ULSup. / *b:* UCP; BO 1789-1802; BP; BedP; BhP; BiP; BoP; BrP; BtP; BurC; BwP; ChlP; ColP; CrP; CsP; CtP; FoP; GrP; HP lacking v73, pt1; v78, pt1; HfP; HsP; IpP; L; LAt; LCP; LGU; LIT; LLL; LLW; LMT; LVA 1789-1808; LaP; LcP; LdL; LdP; LnP; LvA; LvP; MCh; MR; MsP; NpP; NwL lacking pt 1, 1793; NwP; NwS 1813-32; OPU; SP; SnP; SptP; StfS; SthC 1789-98; TuP 1789-1818; WcP; WiP; WmP; WnP 1789; 1790, pt2; 1791-1805; 1806, pt1; 1807; 1808, pt1; 1809, pt 2; 1810-11; 1812, pt1; 1813-32; WwP 1814-32; YP.

GENTLEMAN'S MAGAZINE of Fashion, Fancy Costumes, and the Regimentals of the Army. London. v1-11, 1828-38; s2-s3, 1839-94.
  a: ULS. / *b:* UCP; L; LLL lacking v3.
  (Merged into *London Tailor and Record of Fashion*.)

GENTLEMAN'S MATHEMATIC COMPANION . . . containing new Enigmas, Rebuses, Charades, &c. London. no1-30, 1798-1827. a.
  a: ULS. / *b:* UCP; L; LR; NwL.
  Continued as
  ENIGMATICAL ENTERTAINER and Mathematical Associate. London. no1-4, 1827-30. (Each issue in two parts: *Enigmatical Entertainer* and *Mathematical Associate*.)
  a: ULS. / *b:* L; O.

GENTLEMAN'S MONTHLY MISCELLANY. London. no1-5, Ja-My 1803. m.
  b: UCP; L no1-2.

GENTLEMAN'S POCKET MAGAZINE and Album of Literature and the Fine Arts. London. v1-4, 1827-30.
  a: ULS. / *b:* UCP; BP 1827-29; L.

GEOGRAPHICAL MAGAZINE; or the Universe Display'd. London. v1-3, 1790-92.
  b: UCP.

GEOLOGICAL SOCIETY OF LONDON. Proceedings. London. v1-4, no1-104, 1826-45.
  a: ULS. / *b:* UCP; WiP.
  (Superseded by *Quarterly Journal of the Geological Society of London*.)

GEOLOGICAL SOCIETY OF LONDON. Transactions. London. v1-5, 1811-21; s2, v1-7, 1822-56.
  a: ULS; ULSup. / *b:* UCP; CPL; LP; LR; WiP.

THE GEORGIUM SIDUS and Patriotic Censor. Tralee. v1, no1-6, O 9-D 18, 1819. w.
  b: O no1, 6.

GERMAN MUSEUM, or Monthly Repository of the Literature of Germany, the North and

the Continent in General. London. v1-3, Ja
1800-Je 1801. m.
  a: ULS. / *b:* UCP; L; LLL.

THE GHOST. Edinburgh. no1-46, Ap 26-N
16, 1796. s.w.
  a: ULS. / *b:* UCP; EP; L.

THE GHOST OF JUNIUS. London. no1, N
13, 1819.
  b: LU.

GHOST OF THE FREE PRESS. Dublin. no1,
1810. w.
  b: DL.

GHOST OF THE RUSHLIGHT. Belfast. no1,
1826.
  b: DL.

GILES AND SIDGWICK'S Mark Lane Circular.
London. S 26, 1825-Ja 16, 1826.
  b: L.

**GILL'S Technological and Microscopic Re-
pository.**
  (See *Technical Repository, containing
  Practical Information on Subjects connected with Discoveries, &c.*)

**GIOVANNI IN LONDON: a Journal of Liter-
ature, Anecdotes, Wit and Satire, Poetry,
Fine Arts, and Theatricals.** London. v1, no
1-6, F 18-Mr 24, 1832. w.
  a: ULS. / *b:* BoP; O.

GIRLS' AND BOYS' PENNY MAGAZINE.
London. v1, 1832-33.
  b: L.

GLASGOW ACADEMIC. Glasgow. v1, 1826.
  b: GM.

**GLASGOW ADVERTISER (and Evening In-
telligencer.)** Glasgow. no1+, 1783-O 29, 1802.
s.w. (Second half of title added Je 28, 1789;
dropped Ja 21, 1794.)
  b: GGH [Ja-Mr, 1789]; Jl 3, 1789-Jl 25,
  1791; F 10, 1792-D 26, 1794; 1798; Ja 2-
  Je 26, 1801; L 1789-1800.
  Continued as
HERALD AND ADVERTISER. Glasgow. N
1, 1802-Ag 21, 1805. s.w.
  b: GGH; GM 1802-03.
  Continued as
GLASGOW HERALD. Glasgow. Ag 23, 1805-
date. s.w.
  a: CSmH D 1, 1817; NN 3 sc.nos. 1832. /
  b: E Ja 8, 1808; My 15, 1815; GGH; GM;
  GU (1810-16); 1819-31; L F 4, 1820-Ja
  1827, lacking 1823 and Ja 1824.

GLASGOW ALMANACK. Glasgow. [?]-1787-
96-[?].
  b: EP 1795-96.

GLASGOW (ROYAL) ASYLUM for Lunatics.
Report. Glasgow. v1-41, 1815-55.
  b: UCP.

GLASGOW CHRONICLE. Glasgow. 1811-30.
t.w.
  a: CSmH Je 30, 1830; CtY F 1-D 31, 1816.
  / *b:* GM 1811-14, 1816, 1820; GU Ap 1814-
  D 1817.

**GLASGOW CITY POOR, Suppression of Men-
dicity, and Principles of Plan for New Hospital. Report.** Glasgow. 1818.
  b: GeG.

GLASGOW COLONIAL SOCIETY.
  (See *Glasgow North American Colonial
  Society. Report.*)

GLASGOW CORNUCOPIA. Glasgow. 1831.
  b: GM N 19.

GLASGOW COURIER. Glasgow. no1+, S 1,
1791-1866. w.; t.w.
  a: ULS; CSmH D 29, 1829; CtY Mr 28-D
  28, 1799; (1807); (1812); 1821; ICU (Je 6-
  D 30, 1797); 1798-1800; MBAt S 17, 1805;
  NNHi Ja 17, 1801. / *b:* C O 3, 1793; E
  S 1, 1791-Ag 30, 1792; 1797-1821; GM
  1791-95, 1797-1800, 1803-07, 1809-21,
  1823-24, 1831-32; GU 1791-94; (Ja 1-S 5,
  1795); GeG 1821-22, 1826-28, 1830.

**GLASGOW EVENING POST, and Paisley and
Renfrewshire Reformer.** Glasgow. [?]-1831-
37/?.
  a: CSmH no228, Je 25, 1831. / *b:* GM
  1831-32 impf.

GLASGOW FREE PRESS. Glasgow. v1-13,
1823-35. s.w.
  a: CSmH Ag 19, 1829. / *b:* GM v1-4, 1823-
  26.

GLASGOW HERALD.
  (See *Glasgow Advertiser (and Evening Intelligencer).*)

GLASGOW JOURNAL. Glasgow. 1729-1841.
w.
  a: CSmH Je 17, 1825; NcD F 22, 1822. /
  b: GM Je 10, 1818.
  (Incorporated with *Glasgow Chronicle.*)

GLASGOW LOOKING GLASS. Glasgow. v1,
no1-5, Je-Ag 1825.
  a: ULS. / *b:* E; GM; LLL.
  Continued as
**NORTHERN LOOKING GLASS, or Litho-
graphic Album.** Glasgow. v1, no6-ns, v1-2,
1825-26.
  a: ULS. / *b:* E v1, no6-16; GM; LLL.

GLASGOW MAGAZINE. Glasgow. v1, 1795.
  b: GM.

GLASGOW MAGAZINE. Glasgow. v1, no1, O
1820. m.
  b: E.

**GLASGOW MAGAZINE and Clydesdale Month-
ly Register.** Glasgow. v1-3, 1810-12. m.
  b: GM.

GLASGOW MAGAZINE OF WIT. Glasgow.
1803.
  b: GM.

**GLASGOW MECHANICS MAGAZINE and An-
nals of Philosophy.** Glasgow. v1-5, 1824-26.
  a: ULS; ULSup. / *b:* UCP; DmP v1-4;
  GM; GeG v2; HnP v1; L; LGU; LP.

GLASGOW MEDICAL EXAMINER. Glasgow. v1-2, 1831-32.
a: ULS. / b: C; GM; LMD; LS.

GLASGOW MEDICAL JOURNAL. Glasgow. v1-5, 1828-32; s2-s7, 1833-date.
a: ULS; ULSup. / b: GM v1-3; L; LMA; LMD; LS.

GLASGOW MERCURY. Glasgow. v1-20, 1778-1796.
b: GM; L 1790, 1793.

GLASGOW MISCELLANY. Glasgow. v1-2, [?]-1800/?.
b: UCP.

GLASGOW MONTHLY REPOSITORY of Religious, Political, and Miscellaneous Intelligence. Glasgow. v1, 1813. m.
b: GM.

GLASGOW NORTH AMERICAN COLONIAL Society. Report. Glasgow. v1-8, 1826-35/?. (Title varies. Also called *Glasgow Colonial Society*.)
a: ULS.

GLASGOW PUNCH, a Weekly Pennyworth of Fun and Frolic, Whim and Whipping. Glasgow. no1-9, 1832.
b: GM.

GLASGOW REGISTER. Glasgow. N 16-D 8, 1803.
(No issues known. Data from *Transactions of the Edinburgh Bibliographical Society*, I.5.Sec.10.)

GLASGOW REPOSITORY OF LITERATURE. Glasgow. no1-4, Ja-Ap 1805. m.
b: GM.

GLASGOW SENTINEL. Glasgow. 1809-10. w.
b: GM no2, 50, 126, 213.

GLASGOW SENTINEL. Glasgow. 1821-77. (Apparently was preceded by *Clydesdale Journal*.)
b: GM v1-2, 1821-23; L no1, 5-9, 12-39, 41-47, 49-68 for 1821-22.

GLASGOW THEATRICAL OBSERVER. Glasgow. v1, 1824.
b: GM.

GLASGOW THEATRICAL REGISTER. Glasgow. 1803-05.
b: GM N 16-D 8, 1803.
(Additional data in *Transactions of the Edinburgh Bibliographical Society*, I.2. sec.24.)

GLASGOW THEOLOGICAL ACADEMY. Report. Edinburgh, Glasgow. v1-22, [?]-1823-36.
b: UCP.

GLASGOW UNIVERSALIST'S MISCELLANY.
(See *Vehicle of Free Inquiry*,&c.)

GLASGOW UNIVERSITY JOURNAL. Glasgow. no1, 1832.
b: GM.

GLASGOW WEEKLY MAGAZINE. Glasgow. no1-3, 1824.
b: GM no3.

GLASGOW YOUTH'S SOCIETY for Schools in the Highlands. Report. Glasgow. [?]-1821-33.
b: UCP.

GLEANER. London. no1-6, 1793.
b: UCP.

GLEANER. London. no1-3, 1797.
b: UCP.

GLEANER. London. v1-4, 1811.
b: DLL.

GLEANER; a Cheshire, Lancashire, Shropshire and North Wales Monthly Magazine. Chester. no1, 1824. m.
b: L.

GLEANER, consisting of Pieces, Moral, Literary and Humorous. Glasgow. 1806.
b: GM.

GLEANER: containing original Essays in Prose and Verse, with Extracts from Various Publications. Edinburgh. no1, F 14, 1795.
b: EP.

GLEANER, or Cirencester Weekly Magazine . . . containing Original Communications on various Subjects, and Selections from some of the most approved Authors. Cirencester. 1816. w.
a: ULS. / b: CiP; L.

GLEANER; or Economical Pocket Magazine, and Weekly Miscellany. Liverpool. no1-26, 1822-23. w.
b: L Titlepage, Preface, Table of Contents, and pp. 218-26; LvP no1-15, 18, 20, 25-26.

GLEANER; or, Entertainment for the Fireside: consisting of Tales, &c. Salford. v1-2, 1805-06. w.
b: L.
Continued as
HARVEST HOME; or Instruction and Amusement for the Fireside: consisting of Tales, &c. Salford. v1-2, 1807-08. w.
b: L; MR.
Continued as
NEW GLEANER; or Entertainment for the Fire-side. Salford. v1-2, 1809-10. w.
a: PP. / b: DL; L; MR.

GLEANER; or, Farmer's and Tradesman's Weekly Miscellany. Belfast. no1-10, 1821. w.
b: BlL no10.

GLEANER; or Lady's and Gentleman's Instructive and Entertaining Magazine for Youth and Age, the Merry, Wise, and Pious, of every Sect and Party. Dublin. v1-2, Ja 6-Ap 28, 1821.
a: ULS. / b: DL.

GLEANER; or, Weekly Historical Register: containing Modern Voyages, Travels, Historical Events, Tales, &c. London. v1-2, Ap 30, 1823-Je 16, 1824. w.
a: ULS. / b: DL; L.

GLEANER; or Youth's Miscellany. Leeds. 1825.
b: HlP; LdP.

GLEANER, and Irish Observer. Dublin. no1, 1806.
b: DA; L.

GLEANER and Spirit of the Public Journals; or, Fashionable Monthly Miscellany. London. no1-2, Ja-F 1822. m.
b: DL.

GLEANER'S PORT-FOLIO, or Provincial Magazine; containing Original Essays on various Subjects, with Extracts from the most approved Authors. Lewes. no1-4, Ag-D 1819. m. (Originally published in numbers as *The Provincial Magazine.*)
b: BiP; CrP; L; O.

GLEANINGS OF LITERATURE; or, the Miscellany of Taste. Dublin. v1, 1805.
(No issues known. Data from John Power, *Irish Literary Periodical Publications.*)

GLOBE. London. no1+, 1803-22. d.
a: CSmH Ja 31, 1806-Je 29, 1816; S 5, 1820; CtY Ja 1-D 20, 1806; Ap 29, 1808-1814; ICU O 9, 1804; 1809-16; F 14, Jl 30, 1817; F 17, 25, Mr 6, My 1, Je 15, Jl 17, 27, 1819; Ap 18, 1820; MnU S 8, 28, O 4, 1820; NNHi (Jl 5-S 14, 1810; Ag 10-S 21, 1819); NcD (1811). / *b:* UCP; EP Jl-D 1810; N 21, 23, 1812; L 35 sc.nos. 1807-16; complete 1818-22; SptP Je 26-D 13, 1815.
Absorbed *Traveller* and continued as
GLOBE AND TRAVELLER. London. 1822-1921. d.
a: ULS; CSmH 1822-32 impf.; DLC 94 sc. nos. 1810-24; ICN (Ja 10-Je 29, 1824; Jl 1-D 29, 1825); IU Mr 22-27, 1824. / *b:* C 1828-32; E 1832; L.
(Absorbed *Statesman,* F 1824; *Evening Chronicle,* Mr 1824; *Nation,* Jl 1824; *Argus,* Jl 1828. Incorporated in *Evening Standard,* 1922.)

GLOBE AND TRAVELLER.
(See *Globe.*)

GLOCESTER JOURNAL.
(See *Gloucester Journal.*)

GLOUCESTER AND CHELTENHAM Herald.
(See *Gloucester Herald.*)

GLOUCESTER AND CHELTENHAM Standard. Gloucester. v1, no1-8, 1832. w.
b: GrP.

GLOUCESTER GAZETTE. no1+, [1782]-96-[?]. (Has varying subtitles.)
b: GrP Ap 13, 1792-N 18, 1796; MR no 193 for 1792.

GLOUCESTER HERALD. Gloucester. 1802-23-[?].
b: BP Jl 2, 1814; GrP (1802-23).
Continued as
GLOUCESTER AND CHELTENHAM Herald. Gloucester. [?]-1826-28-[?].

a: CSmH S 10, 1827. / *b:* GrP sc.nos. 1826-28; L Ja 1, 1827-Je 9, 1828.

GLOUCESTER JOURNAL. Gloucester. 1722-date. w.
a: ULS; CSmH Jl 28,1823; CtY Ja 3, 1791-Ap 8, 1793; WHi 1789-1805. / *b:* CrP 1789-90; CtP Ja 7, 1789-D 27, 1824; GrP; L.

GLOUCESTER MERCURY. Gloucester. no1-34, Ag 6, 1828-Mr 25, 1829. w.
b: L.

GLOUCESTERSHIRE REPOSITORY; or, Literary and Political Miscellany. Stroud. 1817-22.
a: ULS. / *b:* GrP v1; ns, v2; L lacking pp. 331-34 of v2.

GOGGINS' ULSTER MAGAZINE. A Weekly Journal. Monaghan. 1798-1800. w.
b: DL Ja 3-D 5, 1800, lacking F 28, Mr 14-28, Je 20, S 19.

GOLD'S LONDON MAGAZINE.
(See *London Magazine; and Monthly Critical Dramatic Review.*)

GOLEUAD CYMRU; sef Cylchgrawn Gwybodaeth.
(See *Goleuad Gwynedd.*)

GOLEUAD GWYNEDD, neu 'n hytrach Goleuad Cymru; sef Cylchgrawn Gwybodaeth; yn cynnwys cynnulliad o fyrdraethiadau, hyspyiadau, addysgiadau . . . ynghyd ag amrywiol gyfansoddiadau mewn barddoniaeth. Chester. v1-2, no1-26, 1818-20.
b: UCP; CrP; L.
Continued as
GOLEUAD CYMRU; sef Cylchgrawn Gwybodaeth, &c. Chester. 1820-30.
b: UCP; CrP; L.

THE GOOD CITIZEN; a Political and Literary Miscellany. Nottingham. no1, D 10, 1831.
b: NP.

GOOD OLD TIMES! A New Light for the People of England.
(See *Good Old Times; or, the Poor Man's History of England.*)

GOOD OLD TIMES; or, the Poor Man's History of England from the Earliest Period down to the Present Time. London. no1-28, Mr 1-S 13, 1817. w. (Running title, *Good Old Times! A New Light for the People of England.*)
a: ULS. / *b:* UCP; L; O.

GORDON'S MERRY CHRONICLE and Universal Advertiser. Newry. 1795.
b: UCP.

GORE'S GENERAL ADVERTISER. Liverpool. [?]-1788-1876. w. (Preceded by *General Advertiser,* 1765-79-[?].)
a: CSmH Ag 29, 1822; MBAt Jl-Ag 7, 1806; Je 8, Jl 13, 1820; WHi Jl 31, 1806. / *b:* L Ja-Jl 1800; 1805; 1822-23; 1826-32.

THE GORGON; a Weekly Political Publication. London. no1-49, My 23, 1818-Ap 24, 1819. w.
   a: ULS. / *b:* UCP; L; O.

GOSPEL COMMUNICATOR, or Philanthropists' Journal. Glasgow. v1-3, 1823-27/?.
   a: ULS. / *b:* L.

GOSPEL MAGAZINE; and Theological Review. London. v1-10, 1796-1805; ns, v1-10, 1806-15; s3, v1-10, 1816-25; s4, v1-10, 1826-35; s5-s11, 1836-date. m.
   a: ULS. / *b:* UCP; BrP v1-10; ns, v1-5; s3, v4-5; L.

THE GOSSIP; a Series of Original Essays and Letters, Literary, Historical, and Critical; Descriptive Sketches, Anecdotes, and Original Poetry. Kentish Town. no1-18, Mr 3-Je 30, 1821. w.
   a: ULS; CSmH. / *b:* L; O.
   Continued as
   LITERARY GOSSIP, a Series of Original Essays and Poems. London. no19-24, Jl 7-Ag 11, 1821. w.
   a: ULS; CSmH. / *b:* L; O.

GOVERNMENT BULLETINS on the Irish Rebellion of 1798. Dublin. 1798.
   b: UCP.

GOWNSMAN.
   (See *The Snob: a Literary and Scientific Journal.*)

THE GRACCHUS; or, Advocate of the People. A Political and Literary Journal. London. no1, Je 27, 1818. w.
   b: O.

THE GRACES, or Literary Souvenir. London. 1823-24. a.
   b: UCP; L.

GRANA UILLE'S MONTHLY JOURNAL. Dublin. 1817.
   b: DL Jl, 1817.

GRANGER'S New, Original and Complete Wonderful Museum, &c.
   (See *New, Original and Complete Wonderful Museum and Magazine Extraordinary.*)

GRAPHIC AND HISTORICAL Illustrator. London. v1, 1832-34.
   a: ULS.

GRATIS SABBATH SCHOOL SOCIETY, Edinburgh. Report. Edinburgh. v1-30, [1797]-1827.
   b: UCP.

Y GREAL. Chester. 1800.
   b: UCP.

Y GREAL; sev Cynnulliad o orchestion ein hynaviaid, a llofion o amryw van-govion y cyn-oesodd. Llundain. 1805-07.
   b: UCP; CrP; L.

Y GREAL NEU EURGRAWN, sef Trysorfa Gwybodaeth. Chester. v1, 1800.
   b: UCP; CrP no1.

GREAL Y BEDYDDWYR. Swansea. 1817.
   b: BnU; CrP.

GREAL Y BEDYDDWYR; neu Ystorfa Efengylaidd . . . y gyhoeddwyd dan olygiad J. Herring. . . . Aberteifi; Cardigan. v1-67, 1827-1918.
   a: ULS. / *b:* UCP; L lacking v2, 4.

THE GRECIAN. London. no1-4, 1832.
   a: ULS. / *b:* L.

THE GREEN MAN; and Independent Weekly Expositor.
   (See *The Green Man; or Periodical Expositor.*)

THE GREEN MAN; or Periodical Expositor. London. v1-3, O 31, 1818-Jl 24, 1819. w.
   b: BP v1-2; L; O no1.
   Continued as
   THE GREEN MAN; and Independent Weekly Expositor. London. no1-3, Ag 21-S 11, 1819. w.
   b: L.

GREENOCK ADVERTISER, and Clyde and West Country Chronicle.
   (See *Greenock Advertiser, Clyde and Renfrewshire Chronicle.*)

GREENOCK ADVERTISER and Clyde Commercial Herald.
   (See *Greenock Advertiser, Clyde and Renfrewshire Chronicle.*)

GREENOCK ADVERTISER, Clyde and Renfrewshire Chronicle. Greenock. 1802-84. (Second half of title varies: . . . *and Clyde and West Country Chronicle;* . . . *and Clyde Commercial Herald;* . . . *and Clyde Commercial Journal.*)
   b: C Mr 30, 1802; E 1805; 1808; Mr 1813-F 17, 1818; My 26, 1820-23; Je 1829-1832; GeG.

GREENWICH. Astronomical Observations made at the Royal Observatory. v1-2, 1750-65; s2, v1-4, 1765-1810; s3, v1-5, 1811-24; s4, v1-12, 1825-35; s5+, 1836-date.
   a: ULS; ULSup. / *b:* UCP.

THE GRIDIRON. Dublin. 1823-24.
   (No issues known. Data from John Power, *Irish Literary Periodical Publications,* p. 11).

THE GRIDIRON; or, Cook's Weekly Register. London. no1-3, 1822. w.
   b: DRS no1; L.

THE GRUMBLER. London. 1791.
   b: UCP.

THE GUARDIAN. Belfast. no1+, Je 19, 1827-36.
   b: L.

THE GUARDIAN; or, Historical and Literary Recorder. London. no1+, D 12, 1819-Ap 25, 1824. w. (Subtitle varies.)
  a: CSmH D 8, 1822; NNHi (D 1, 1822-Ja 25, 1824). / *b:* L.

THE GUARDIAN. Advertisements for Tuesday. London. 1814.
  b: BP no1, Mr 1, 1814.

GUARDIAN and Constitutional Advocate. Belfast. v1-9, no1-883, 1827-36.
  a: CSmH Jl 8, 1828. / *b:* UCP.

GUARDIAN and Public Ledger. London. [?]-1832/?.
  a: CSmH v72, no53, S 28, 1832.

THE GUARDIAN OF EDUCATION; a Periodical Work: consisting of a Practical Essay on Christian Education . . . and a Copious Examination of Modern Systems of Education, Children's Books, and Books for Young Persons. London. v1-5, 1802-06, suspended S-D 1803. m.; q.
  a: ULS. / *b:* UCP; BP; L; WmP v2-5.

THE GUIDE, a Moral and Economical Weekly Family Paper. London. no1-25, 1808.
  b: L.

GUIDE COMMERCIAL DE GIBSON, et Prix Courant Général. London. 1816.
  b: L F 6, 1816.

GUIDE TO KNOWLEDGE. London. v1, no1-6, Jl-Ag 1832.
  b: E.

GUILFORD JOURNAL and General Advertiser. Guilford. 1831.
  a: CSmH no6, S 10, 1831.

GUTCH'S COUNTRY Constitutional Guardian.
  (See *Country Constitutional Guardian and Literary Magazine.*)

GWYLIEDYDD; sef, Cylchgrawn o wybodaeth fuddiol, er budd i'r cymro uniaith. Bala. v1-14, 1822-37.
  a: ULS. / *b:* UCP; CrP; SwP.

THE HALFPENNY LIBRARY, or Magazine for the Diffusion of Useful and Entertaining Knowledge. London. no1-17, 1832/?. s.w.
  b: BP; O no1, 3-5.

THE HALFPENNY MAGAZINE; a Miscellany of Original Articles, and Selections from the Best Authors, in Prose and Verse. London. no1-19, My 5-S 8, 1832. w.
  a: ULS. / *b:* L; O no1, 3-4.

THE HALF-PENNY MAGAZINE; or Cheap Repository of Amusement and Instruction. Edinburgh. v1, no1-50, 1832. s.w.
  b: E no1-44; EP; GM; L.

THE HALFPENNY MAGAZINE, or the Witness. Leeds. no1-32, 1832. w.
  b: L; LdP no1-25; O no3-4, 11.

HALIFAX AND HUDDERSFIELD EXPRESS. Halifax. no1+, F 12, 1831-41.
  a: CSmH F 19, 1831. / *b:* HlHC; L.

HALIFAX COMMERCIAL CHRONICLE, and Yorkshire and Lancashire Advertiser. Halifax. no1-79, Jl 4, 1829-D 24, 1830. w.
  a: CSmH D 19, 1829. / *b:* HlHC Jl 11, 1829-D 25, 1830; HlP; L.

HALIFAX GUARDIAN, and Huddersfield and Bradford Advertiser. Halifax. no1+, D 1, 1832-1921. (Subtitle varies.)
  b: HlHC (1832); HlL; HlP lacking no1-3; L.
  (Incorporated with *Halifax Courier,* 1921, and continued as *Halifax Courier and Guardian,* 1921-date.)

HALIFAX JOURNAL and Yorkshire and Lancashire Advertiser. Halifax. no1+, Je 6, 1801-F 23, 1811.
  b: HlHC O 24, 1801-Je 16, 1804; My 11, 1805-Je 20, 1807; HlP.

HAMPSHIRE ADVERTISER. Southampton. [?]-1828-date. (Probably succeeds *Southampton Town and County Herald.* See F.A. Edwards, "A List of Hampshire Newspapers," *Hampshire Antiquary and Naturalist,* I (1891) 96.)
  a: CSmH D 6, 1828. / *b:* L no307+, Je 6, 1829-32.

HAMPSHIRE CHRONICLE. Winchester. 1789-1820. w. (Subtitle varies.)
  b: L Jl 1-D 1816; WnHC.
  Incorporated with *Hampshire Courier,* 1816; continued as
HAMPSHIRE CHRONICLE AND COURIER. Winchester. 1820-60. w. (Subtitle varies.)
  a: CSmH Jl 7, 1828. / *b:* L 1830-32; WnHC.
  (Continued as *Hampshire Chronicle,* with varying subtitles, 1860-date.)

HAMPSHIRE CHRONICLE AND COURIER.
  (See *Hampshire Chronicle.*)

HAMPSHIRE COURIER.
  (Hampshire Chronicle was published under this title, Sept. 1814.)

HAMPSHIRE COURIER; or, Portsmouth, Portsea, Gosport, and Chichester Advertiser. Portsmouth. 1810-16. w.
  a: CSmH Mr 25, 1816. / *b:* L no3-313, Jl 16, 1810-Je 24, 1816; SoP O 19, 1812-Je 24, 1816.
  (Incorporated in *Hampshire Chronicle.*)

HAMPSHIRE JOURNAL and County Register. Winchester. no1+, Mr 6, 1790-1792-[?]. w.
  b: WnP no1-46, Mr 6, 1790-Ja 15, 1791.

HAMPSHIRE REPOSITORY.
  (See *Annual Hampshire Repository,* &c.)

HAMPSHIRE TELEGRAPH
  (See *Portsmouth Telegraph; or, Mottley's Naval and Military Journal.*)

YR HANESYDD CENADAWL. Llundain. 1827-31.
  b: UCP.

HANSARD'S PARLIAMENTARY DEBATES.
  (See *Cobbett's Parliamentary History of England.*)

HARLEQUIN. A Journal of the Drama. London. no 1-9, My 11-Jl 16, 1829. w.
  a: ULS; ULSup. / *b:* L; LLL no 1-6.

HARMONIC MAGAZINE, and Weekly Miscellany of Amusement and Instruction. London. v1, no 1-12, Ja 8-Mr 26, 1821/?. w.
  a: ULSup.

THE HARMONICON, a Journal of Music. London. v1-11, 1823-33. (Dropped subtitle after 1827.)
  a: ULS. / *b:* UCP; BkP 1823-28; EP; L; LdP.

THE HARP. London. no 1-10, D 2, 1810-F 3, 1811. w.
  b: DL.

THE HARP OF ERIN. Cork. no 1-4, Mr 7-17, 1798. s.w.
  b: C no3, Mr 14, 1798.

THE HARP OF ERIN; or, Compleat Vocal Library. Cork. no 1-4, 1810-12.
  b: DL.

THE HARP OF ERIN; or, Faithful Irishman. London. no 1, Mr 1818. m.
  b: L; O.

THE HARROVIAN. A Collection of Poems, Essays, and Translations. London. no 1-6, Mr-Ag 1828. m.
  a: CtY. / *b:* HwV; L; O.

HARTFORD MERCURY. Hertford. 1772-1832-[?].
  b: HtHM (1789-1832).
  (Continued as *Hertford Mercury and Reformer*, 1844-71; as *Hertfordshire Mercury and County Press*, 1872-date.)

HARVEST HOME; or Instruction and Amusement for the Fire-side.
  (See *Gleaner; or, Entertainment for the Fireside.*)

HASTINGS and Cinque Ports Iris. Hastings. no 1-37, O 23, 1830-Jl 2, 1831. (Also has varying subtitles.)
  a: CSmH no10, D 25, 1830. / *b:* L.

HAZELWOOD MAGAZINE. Hazelwood School, Birmingham. v1-8, 1822-30.
  b: BP v1-2, 5-8; ToP v5-8.

HEART OF OAK, and Union Advertiser. London. 1800.
  b: L Prospectus only.

THE HEATHERY; or, a Monograph on the Genus Erica. London. no 1-35, [?]-1808/?. m.
  (No issues known. Data from *Literary Annual Register*, 2 (F 1808) 69.)

HEATH'S PICTURESQUE ANNUAL. London. v1-14, 1832-45. a.
  b: UCP.

HEAVEN AND HELL MAGAZINE. London. v1-2, 1790-91.
  b: O.

HELICONIA. London. no1, Mr 1814.
  (No issues known. Data from John Nichol, *Illustrations of Literary History*, v8, p. 610.)

THE HELICONIAN GAZETTE [of Edinburgh University]. Edinburgh. no 1-4, N 12-19, 1828.
  (No issues known. Data from S N & Q, s2. II.89.)

THE HERALD. Clonmel. 1800-02. s.w.
  (No issues known. Data from CBEL, II. 737.)
  Continued as
CLONMEL HERALD. Clonmel. 1802-41. s.w.
  a: CSmH My 19, 1827. / *b:* C no9, Je 30, 1802; D Ja 3, 1815-D 28, 1816; L My 26, 1813; F 16, 1825; Ja 1828-32.

HERALD AND ADVERTISER.
  (See *Glasgow Advertiser.*)

HERALD AND CHRONICLE.
  (See *Edinburgh Herald.*)

HERALD, Aston's Manchester Commercial Advertiser.
  (See *Exchange Herald, Aston's Manchester Commercial Advertiser.*)

HERALD OF PEACE. London. v1-3, 1819-21; ns, v1-10, 1822-35; s3-s5+, 1836-date. m.
  a: ULS. / *b:* UCP; L; LFS 1822-24; SP 1820-21.

HERALD OF THE TRADES' ADVOCATE, and Co-operative Journal. Glasgow. S 25, 1830-My 28, 1831. w.
  a: ULS. / *b:* UCP; GM.

HERALD OF TRUTH; or, Friend of Religion, Literature, and Science. Liverpool. no1, 1828.
  b: L.

HEREFORD INDEPENDENT; and Monmouth and South Wales Literary, Commercial and Political Chronicle. Hereford. 1824-28.
  a: CSmH Ag 6, 1825. / *b:* BP no1-13, 15-54, 57-82, for 1824-26; HfP O 2, 1824-Jl 26, 1828; L N 19, 1825.

HEREFORD JOURNAL.
  (See *British Chronicle, or Pugh's Hereford Journal.*)

HEREFORD TIMES, General Advertiser for the United Kingdom. Hereford. 1832-date.
  b: HfP.

THE HERMES; a Literary, Moral, and Scientific Journal. Liverpool. v1, no1-28, N 1822-My 1823. w.
  b: L; O no1, 3-4, 6-21, 23-28.

HERTFORD, Huntingdon, Bedford, . . . Mercury.
  (See *Herts Mercury.*)

HERTFORD MERCURY.
  (See *Hartford Mercury.*)

THE HERTFORDIAN. Hertford. no1-5, 1822.
  b: L.

HERTS MERCURY. Hertford. no1-146, Jl 2, 1825-Ap 12, 1828.
  b: HtP; L.
  Continued as
HERTFORD, Huntingdon, Bedford, Cambridge, and Isle of Ely Mercury. Hertford. no147-397, Ap 19, 1828-F 2, 1833. (Title varies slightly.)
  a: CSmH D 20, 1828. / *b:* HtP no147-83, Ap 19-D 1828; L 1828-30.
  (Incorporated with *Essex Mercury.*)

HIBERNIA MAGAZINE. Dublin. v1, Ja-Je 1810. m.
  a: ULS; ULSup. / *b:* UCP; DA; L.
  Incorporated with *Monthly Panorama* and continued as
HIBERNIA MAGAZINE and Monthly Panorama. Dublin. v2-3, Jl 1810-Je 1811. m. (Individual parts called *Hibernia Magazine and Dublin Monthly Panorama.*)
  a: ULS; ULSup. / *b:* DA; L.

HIBERNIA MAGAZINE and Dublin Monthly Panorama.
  (See *Hibernia Magazine.*)

HIBERNIA MAGAZINE and Monthly Panorama.
  (See *Hibernia Magazine.*)

HIBERNIA AUXILIARY. Church Missionary Society. Report. Dublin. 1815-36.
  b: UCP.

HIBERNIAN BIBLE SOCIETY. Monthly Extracts. Dublin. [?]-1832.
  b: UCP.

HIBERNIAN BIBLE SOCIETY. Quarterly Extracts from the Correspondence. Dublin. no1-28, 1832-39.
  b: UCP.

HIBERNIAN BIBLE SOCIETY. Report. Dublin. v1-46, 1804-52.
  b: UCP.

HIBERNIAN CHRONICLE.
  (See *Flynn's Hibernian Chronicle.*)

HIBERNIAN CONSTITUTIONAL MAGAZINE. Dublin. c.1829.
  (No issues known. Data from John Power, *Irish Literary Periodical Publications,* p.12.)

HIBERNIAN EVANGELICAL MAGAZINE. Dublin. v1-2, Ja 1815-D 1816. m.
  b: DL.

HIBERNIAN EVANGELICAL MAGAZINE, or Gospel Repository.
  (See *Hibernian Magazine, or Gospel Repository.*)

HIBERNIAN GAZETTE, or Universal Advertiser. Clonmel. [1772]-[?].
  (No issues known. Data from CBEL, II. 737.)
  Continued as
CLONMEL GAZETTE. Clonmel. [?]-1790-1796-[?].
  b: KkKJ sc.nos. 1791-96.

HIBERNIAN JOURNAL; or Chronicle of Liberty. Dublin. 1773-1820. t.w.; d.
  a: CaM Ja 3-D 30, 1820; ICU S 16, 1793; Ja 3-5, Je 13-15, 1798; O 31, 1800; F 15, 1802; Ap 10, 1804; NN N 27-28, 1801; Mr 1-2, 23-24, Ap 2, 10, 24, Ag 11, O 8, 1802. / *b:* UCP; BiP F 6, 1793; DA 1789-O 28, 1793; sc.nos. 1791-92; 1800; DL 1789-97, 1800-07; KkKJ sc.nos. 1791-96; L 1801; 1803-08; 2 sc.nos. 1813; 9 sc.nos. 1820.

HIBERNIAN MAGAZINE or Gospel Repository. Dublin. v1, 1802-Ap 1803. m. (Also known as *Hibernian Evangelical Magazine, or Gospel Repository.*)
  b: BIL; DL.

HIBERNIAN MUSICAL REVIEW. London. no 1, 1822.
  b: UCP.

HIBERNIAN REVIEW. Dublin. no1-7, 1830. (First published under the title of *Moon Review.*)
  b: DA no4-6; L.

HIBERNIAN SOCIETY for the Diffusion of Knowledge in Ireland. Report. Shacklewell. 1810-11.
  b: UCP.

HIBERNIAN SUNDAY SCHOOL SOCIETY. Report. Dublin. v1-8, 1810-18.
  b: UCP.

HIBERNIAN TELEGRAPH; or Morning Star. Dublin. [?]-1795-1803/?. d.
  a: ICU F 3, 1802; My 4, 1803. / *b:* C no 322, Mr 25, 1795; D Mr 18, 1795; My 29, 1801.

HIBERNO-CELTIC SOCIETY.
  (See *Iberno-Celtic Society.*)

HIGH COURT (and Circuit Courts) of Justiciary in Scotland. Reports of Cases before. Edinburgh. 1819-1916.
  b: UCP.

HIGH LIFE and Sunday Fashionable Post.
  (See *High Life In London.*)

HIGH LIFE IN LONDON. London. no1-11, D 23, 1827-Mr 2, 1828. w.

a: CSmH no8, F 10, 1828. / *b:* L.
   Continued as
HIGH LIFE and Sunday Fashionable Post.
London. no12-14, Mr 9-23, 1828. w.
   b: L.

HIGHLAND AGRICULTURAL SOCIETY of
Scotland. Prize Essays and Transactions.
Edinburgh. no1+, 1799-date. (The society
known as *Highland Society of Scotland*
through 1832.)
   a: ULS; ULSup. / *b:* UCP; GeG 1799-
1820; LR 1799-1824.

HIGHLAND SOCIETY OF SCOTLAND.
   (See *Highland Agricultural Society of Scotland.*)

THE HIPPIATRIST, and Veterinary Journal.
   (See *Farrier and Naturalist.*)

HISTORICAL, Biographical, Literary and
Scientific Magazine. London. v1-2, 1799-
1800. m.
   a: ULS. / *b:* UCP; CrP v1; L; MsP v1.

AN HISTORICAL DETAIL of the most Re-
markable Public Occurrences. London. no1-
2, 1796. w.
   (No issues known. Data from CBEL,II.716.)
   Continued as
A COMPLETE HISTORICAL DETAIL of the
most Remarkable Public Occurrences. London. no3+, 1796-[?].
   (No issues known. See CBEL,II.716.)

HISTORICAL GALLERY of Portraits and
Paintings; or, Biographical Review. London.
1807.
   b: L Prospectus only.

HISTORICAL MAGAZINE; or, Classical Li-
brary of Public Events. London. v1-5, 1789-
92. m.
   a: ULS. / *b:* UCP; DL; L.

HISTORICAL MISCELLANY of the Curiosi-
ties and Rarities in Nature and Art. London.
v1-5, 1794-1800/?. (Individual nos. called
*History of the Curiosities and Rarities in
Nature and Art.)*
   a: ULS.

HISTORICAL REGISTER; or Edinburgh
Monthly Intelligencer. Edinburgh. 1791-92. m.
   b: EP no11-12; GeG.
   Continued as
UNIVERSAL MONTHLY INTELLIGENCER.
Edinburgh. 1792.
   (No issues known.)

HISTORICAL REGISTER; or, Monthly Polit-
ical Review. Dublin. no1-2, 1807. m.
   b: DA.

HISTORICAL SKETCHES of Politics and
Public Men. London. [?]-1812-14-[?]. a.
   b: L 1814; LLL 1812.

HISTORY of the Berwickshire Naturalists
Club.
   (See *Berwickshire Naturalists Club.*)

HISTORY of the Curiosities and Rarities in
Nature and Art.
   (See *Historical Miscellany of the Curiosi-
ties and Rarities in Nature and Art.*)

THE HIVE. A Hebdomadal Selection of Lit-
erary Tracts. London. no1-10, Je-N 1789.
   b: UCP; L.

THE HIVE, or Weekly Entertaining Register,
comprising curious and valuable Papers on
Interesting Subjects, &c. London. v1-4, no1-
117, Ag 1822-D 1824. w. (Subtitle varies
slightly. Caption title, *The Hive; or Weekly
Register of Remarkable Events.)*
   a: ULS; ULSup. / *b:* UCP; DL; L.
   (Merged into *Portfolio of Entertaining and
Instructive Varieties in History, &c.*)

THE HOBBY. London. no1-3, Mr 21-23, 1822.
d.
   b: O.

HODGE'S BIBLICAL REPOSITORY. London.
v1, 1825.
   b: O.

HOG'S WASH.
   (See *Hog's Wash; or, a Salmagundy for
Swine.*)

HOG'S WASH; or, a Salmagundy for Swine.
London. no1-4, 1793. w.
   a: ULS. / *b:* UCP; L.
   Continued as
HOG'S WASH. London. no5, 1793. w.
   a: ULS. / *b:* UCP; L.
   Continued as
HOG'S WASH; or, Politics for the People.
London. no6, 1793. w.
   a: ULS. / *b:* UCP; L.
   Continued as
POLITICS FOR THE PEOPLE; or, Hog's
Wash. London. no7-9, 1793. w.
   a: ULS. / *b:* UCP; L.
   Continued as
POLITICS FOR THE PEOPLE. London.
no10-15; ns, no1-14, 1794-95. w.
   a: ULS; ULSup. / *b:* UCP; BP v2, no2;
L.

HOG'S WASH; or, Politics for the People.
   (See *Hog's Wash; or, a Salmagundy for
Swine.*)

HOLDEN'S ANNUAL DIRECTORY . . . Mer-
chants, Ship Owners, Bankers, &c. London.
1816.
   b: LU.

HOLDEN'S ANNUAL LIST of Coaches, Wag-
gons, Carts, Vessels, &c., from London to
all Parts of England. London. 1802-09.
   b: L.

HOLDERNESS AGRICULTURAL SOCIETY.
Extracts from the Minutes. Kingston-upon-
Hull. [?]-1795-1850-[?].
   b: LP.

HOME MISSIONARY MAGAZINE; or, Record
of the Transactions of the Home Missionary

Board. London. v1-16, 1820-35; ns-s3+, 1836-
date. (Also known as *Record of the Transactions of the Home Missionary Board.*)
  a: ULS. / *b:* UCP; L lacking v1-4.

**HOME MISSIONARY REGISTER, Tract Re-
pository and Teachers' Magazine.**
  (See *General Baptist Home Missionary
Register.* &c.)

HOMMAGE AUX DAMES. London. 1825.
  b: UCP.

HONE'S REFORMIST'S REGISTER.
  (See *Reformist's Register and Weekly Commentary.*)

HONE'S WEEKLY COMMENTARY. London.
no1-2, Ja 18-25, 1817. w.
  (No issues known. See *Reformist's Register and Weekly Commentary*, 1817, for evidence of its existence.)

**THE HONEYCOMB. A Weekly Literary Jour-
nal.** London. no1-10, Je 17-Ag 19, 1820. w.
  a: ULS. / *b:* O no10.

HORAE JUVENILES. Chelsea. no1-9, Ap 23-
Je 18, 1830. w.
  b: L.

HORAE SALISBURIENSIS. Salisbury. no1-5,
1827-28.
  b: UCP.

**HORTICULTURAL REGISTER and General
Magazine.** London, Sheffield. v1-5, 1831-36.
  a: ULS. / *b:* UCP; L; LLL; LR.

**HORTICULTURAL SOCIETY of London.
Transactions.**
  (See *Royal Horticultural Society of Lon-
don.*)

HOUSE OF COMMONS.
  (See *Journals of the House of Commons.*)

**HOUSE OF COMMONS. Reports from Com-
mittees.** London. 1803-06.
  b: UCP; SP.

**THE HOUSE OF INDUSTRY, established in
Edinburgh for the Benefit of the Poor. Report.** Edinburgh. 1801-35.
  b: UCP.

HOUSE OF LORDS.
  (See *Journals of the House of Lords.*)

**HOUSE OF RECOVERY and Fever Hospital,
Dublin. Report.** Dublin. v1-8, 1806-13.
  b: UCP.

**HOUSE OF RECOVERY of the City of Cork.
Report.** Cork. 1802-03.
  b: UCP.

**HOUSE OF REFUGE for Juvenile Offenders.
Reports.** Edinburgh. [?]-1820-24-[?].
  b: EP 1820, 1824.

**HOUSEKEEPER'S MAGAZINE and Family
Economist.**
  (See *Economist and General Adviser.*)

HOW DO YOU DO? London. no1-8, Jl 30-N
5, 1796. f.
  a: ULS. / *b:* UCP; BP; L.

HOXTON SAUSAGE, and Jerry-Wag's Journal.
London. no1-5, 1832. (Sometimes called
Jerry-Wag's Journal.)
  b: L.

HUE AND CRY and Police Gazette. London.
no1-634, 1794-1827. Every three weeks.
  a: ULS. / *b:* UCP; L Ja 17, 1818-D 29,
1827; MaP no457-58, 462-66, 469-70, for
1817-18.
  Continued as
POLICE GAZETTE; or, Hue and Cry. London. 1828-34. Every three weeks.
  a: ULS. / *b:* LGU.

HULL AND LINCOLN CHRONICLE. Hull.
no1-119, My 20-S 23, 1807. w.
  b: L.
  Continued as
LINCOLN AND HULL CHRONICLE. Hull.
O 2, 1807-Jl 6, 1810. w.
  b: L.

HULL ADVERTISER and Exchange Gazette.
Hull. no1+, 1794-1867. w.
  a: CtY Jl 14, 1820; ICU Ja 4-D 27, 1800,
lacking Je 21, S 13; MdBJ v1-2, Jl 5,1794-
Jl 2, 1796. / *b:* HP 1794-1808, 1810-32;
L (1799-1802), 1803-Mr 1821, 1823, 1826-
32; NwS 44 sc.nos. 1799-1800.

**HULL, East Rising and North Lincolnshire
Literary and Scientific Panorama.** Hull. no1,
1812.
  b: L.

**HULL Literary and Philosophical Society.
Annual Report . . . and Transactions.** Hull.
1824-date.
  a: ULS; ULSup.

HULL PACKET. Hull. no1+, 1787-1886. w.
  a: CSmH D 18, 1820. / *b:* HP D 2, 1794-
D 27, 1796; N 25, 1800-D 29, 1807; L
(1800-03), 1804, (1805-08), 1809-19, 1823,
1826-32.
  (Incorporated with *Hull Daily Mail.*)

**HULL POLISH RECORD. (Hull Literary As-
sociation of the Friends of Poland.)** Hull.
no1-5, Ag 1832-Je 1833/?.
  a: ULS.

**HULL PORTFOLIO; or, Memoirs and Cor-
respondence of J. Acland, its Proprietor and
Editor.** Hull. v1-4, 1831-33/?. w.
  a: ULS. / *b:* UCP; L lacking no4 of v1;
LdP v1-3.

**HULL, Rockingham, and Yorkshire and Lin-
colnshire Gazette.**
  (See *Rockingham and Hull Weekly Advertiser.*)

**HULL WESLEYAN METHODIST Missionary
Auxiliary Society.**
  (See *Wesleyan Methodist Missionary So-
ciety (of Hull).*)

HUMBER MERCURY. Hull. no1-47, My 2, 1805-Mr 20, 1806. w.
  b: L.

HUMMING BIRD; or, Morsels of Information on the Subject of Slavery, with Various Miscellaneous Articles. Leicester. v1, no1-12, D 1824-N 1825. m.
  a: ULS. / *b:* UCP; L; O.

THE HUMORIST, a Companion for the Christmas Fireside. London. 1831-32.
  b: L.

HUMOROUS DELINEATOR; or, Vehicle of Genius, Literature, Science Information, &c. London. no1-26, 1824. w. (Individual numbers called *Vehicle of Genius, Literature, Science, Information . . . and the Humorous Delineator.*)
  a: CtY no2. / *b:* DL; L no1-25; O 1824.

HUNTER'S DUBLIN CHRONICLE. Dublin. 1815-17. t.w. (Also known as *Dublin Chronicle.*)
  b: L no82+, Ja 1, 1816-Ap 20, 1817.

HUNTINGDON, Bedford, and Cambridge Weekly Journal. Huntingdon. no1-163, F 26, 1825-Ap 12, 1828. w.
  b: L.

HUNTINGDON, Bedford, and Peterborough Gazette, &c.
  (See *Huntingdon, Bedford, Cambridge and Peterborough Gazette.*)

HUNTINGDON, Bedford, Cambridge and Peterborough Gazette. Huntingdon. no1+, [?]-1815-19. w.
  b: CPU Je 1815-D 1817; 1818; My 1819-Je 1820; 1828-29; L no222+, Ja 3, 1818-Mr 27, 1819; LLL Ag 29, S 5, 12, 19, 1818.
  Continued as
HUNTINGDON, Bedford and Peterborough Gazette, and Cambridge and Hertford Independent Press. Huntingdon. 1819-39. w.
  a: CSmH Ag 18, 1827. / *b:* L 1825-32.
  (Continued as *Cambridge Independent Press*, with varying subtitles, 1839-date.)

HYGEIA; or Essays Moral and Medical on the Causes affecting the Personal State of our affluent Classes. London. v1-3, no1-11, 1802-03.
  a: ULS; LS.

HYGEIAN JOURNAL. London, Glasgow. v1, no1-12, N 6, 1832-O 1, 1833. m.
  a: ULS.

IBERNO-CELTIC SOCIETY. Transactions. Dublin. v1, 1820. (Also called *Hiberno-Celtic Society.*)
  a: ULS; ULSup. / *b:* UCP; CrP; NwS.

THE IDLER. London. no1, My 24, 1832.
  b: O.

THE IMMORTAL MEMORY MAGAZINE, or Monthly Protestant Register of Important Facts. Dublin. no1-6, 1823.
  b: UCP; L.

IMPARTIAL REPORT of the Debates that Occur in the Two Houses of Parliament. London. 1794-1802. (Also known as *Woodfall's Parliamentary Reports.*)
  b: UCP; GeG 1794-97; MsP Ja-S, 1794; Ja-Ag 1795; Ja-Jl 1796; N 1796-Ag 1797.
  Continued as
PARLIAMENTARY REGISTER; or, an Impartial Report of the Debates that Occur in the Two Houses of Parliament. London. v1-5, 1803-04.
  b: UCP.

IMPARTIAL REPORTER, or Fermanagh Farmer's Journal. Enniskillen. no1+, My 1825-29. w.
  a: CSmH My 3, 1827; IU Ja 8, 1829. / *b:* BlL 1830-32; EnnIR.

IMPERIAL AND COUNTY Annual Register. London. 1810.
  b: CrP.

IMPERIAL BRAZILIAN Mining Association. Annual Report. London. v1-2, [?]-1827/?.
  a: ULSup.

IMPERIAL GAZETTE.
  (See *Imperial Weekly Gazette.*)

IMPERIAL MAGAZINE.
  (See *Biographical and Imperial Magazine, &c.*)

IMPERIAL MAGAZINE, or Compendium of Religious, Moral, and Philosophical Knowledge. Liverpool, London. v1-12, 1819-30; ns, v1-4, 1831-34. m. (Subtitle varies.)
  a: ULS; ULSup. / *b:* UCP; CrP v1-2, 9-10; DL; L; LvP v1-3.

IMPERIAL REVIEW; or, London and Dublin Literary Journal. London. v1-3, 1804-05. m.
  a: ULS. / *b:* UCP; DL; L; LdL.
  Continued as
IMPERIAL REVIEW; or, London, Edinburgh, and Dublin Literary Journal. London. v4-5, 1805. m.
  a: ULS. / *b:* UCP; DL; L; LdL.

IMPERIAL REVIEW; or, London, Edinburgh, and Dublin Literary Journal.
  (See *Imperial Review; or, London and Dublin Literary Journal.*)

IMPERIAL WEEKLY GAZETTE. London. no1+, 1804-11-[?]. w.
  a: CSmH no373, Ap 6, 1811; DLC no188, S 19, 1807. / *b:* L F 20-Ap 30, 1808; Ja 6-Je 2, 1810.
  Incorporated with *Westminster Journal and London Political Miscellany* and continued as
IMPERIAL WEEKLY GAZETTE and Westminster Journal. London. [?]-1818-23. w.
  b: L no3997+, Ja 3, 1818-F 8, 1823.
  Continued as
IMPERIAL GAZETTE. London. 1823-25. w.
  b: L no4158+, F 15, 1823-Ja 22, 1825.

IMPERIAL WEEKLY GAZETTE and West-minster Journal.
(See *Imperial Weekly Gazette*.)

IMPORTS AND EXPORTS. London. 1817. d.
a: NcD Ap 15-D 31, 1817, lacking 9 sc.nos.

IMPROVED BUILDER'S PRICE BOOK; con-taining upwards of seven thousand Prices, founded upon actual Calculations . . . Also the Workman's Prices for Labor only. Lon-don. 1828.
b: L.

INCORPORATED SOCIETY for Clothing, Maintaining, and Educating Poor Orphans of Clergymen. Report. London. 1831-40.
b: UCP.

INCORPORATED SOCIETY for the Propaga-tion of the Gospel in Foreign Parts. Proceed-ings. London. F 1820-F 1821.
b: UCP.

THE INDEPENDENT. Edinburgh. no1+, 1824-26. w.
(No issues known. United with *Northern Reporter*, spring of 1826; merged in *Edin-burgh Star*, Jl 8, 1826. Data from S N & Q, s2.VI.166.)

THE INDEPENDENT. London. no1-7, My 8-Je 19, 1830. w.
b: L.

THE INDEPENDENT; a London Literary and Political Review. London. no1-22, Ja 6-Je 2, 1821. w.
b: L; O no1.

THE INDEPENDENT; or Dundee Periodical Journal of Literature and Criticism, History and Politics, Agriculture and Commerce. Dundee. v1, no1-3, Mr-S, 1816. q.
a: ULS. / *b:* DnP; L.

INDEPENDENT OBSERVER
(See *New Observer*.)

INDEPENDENT REVIEW. London. no1-4, Ag 1-22, 1807. w.
b: O no1, 4.

INDEPENDENT THEATRICAL OBSERVER. Dublin. v10-11, Je 17-Ag 14, 1822/?. (Num-bering begins with v10 since this publication was to supersede *Original Theatrical Ob-server*, which, however, did not cease.)
a: ULS.

INDEPENDENT WHIG. London. no1-793, Ja 5, 1806-Mr 25, 1821. w.
a: C-S no105-260, for 1808-10; CSmH Ap 24, 1814; CtY Ja 4, 1807-Je 29, 1817; DLC 1810-13; ICU Ag 17-D 28, 1806, lacking Ag 24, N 30; NNHi Jl 24, 1808; NcD Ap 20, My 21, Je 4-D 31, 1815, lacking 5 sc. nos.; WHi no169-417, Mr 26, 1809-D 26, 1813. / *b:* UCP; BP D 28, 1817; Ja 18, 25, F 1, 1818; CsP F 21, 1808-09; L no6+, F 9, 1806-1810; O-D 1811; 1816; Jl 1817-21.

INDEPENDENT WHIG. London. no1, My 30, 1826/?.
b: O.

THE INDIAN. London. no1, Ja 14, 1816.
b: O.

THE INDICATOR. London. v1-2, no1-100, O 13, 1819-O 13, 1821. w. (Temporary sus-pension at no76.)
a: ULS; ULSup. / *b:* UCP; BP no1-76; BrP; CrP v1; HdP; L; O.

INFANT SCHOOL SOCIETY. Report. v1-5, 1832-44.
b: UCP.

INFIRMARY AND DISPENSARY in Man-chester. Report on the State of. Manchester. 1815-29.
b: UCP.
Continued as
REPORT of the State of the Manchester Royal Infirmary, Dispensary, (and the Roy-al) Lunatic Hospital, and Asylum. Man-chester. 1830-date.
b: UCP.

THE INQUIRER. Dublin. v1-2, 1804-05.
b: DLL.

THE INQUIRER. London. v1-2, 1822-23. q.
a: ULS. / *b:* UCP; DLL; L.

THE INQUIRER; a Periodical Paper pub-lished at Aberdeen, from December 5, 1804, to March 13, 1805. Aberdeen. no1-15, 1805. w.
b: UCP; EP; L.

THE INQUIRER; or Literary Miscellany. Lon-don. no1-3, 1814-15. q.
b: L; O.

INQUISITOR. London. no1+, O 18, 1808-O 31, 1809/?. t.w.
a: CSmH no161, O 31, 1809. / *b:* L no 129, Ag 15, 1809.

THE INQUISITOR. London. no1-26, N 21, 1821-My 15, 1822. w.
a: MH. / *b:* L no1-25; O.

INSOLVENCY REGISTER. London. no1, D 21, 1822.
b: O.

THE INSPECTOR. Bath. no1-5, O 22-N 19, 1825.
b: LVA.

THE INSPECTOR, a Weekly Dramatic Paper. London. no1-4, Ja 2-23, 1819. w.
b: L; O no1.

INSPECTOR AND LITERARY REVIEW. Lon-don. v1, My-O 1826. (Caption title of no1, *Inspector and West of England Review*.)
a: ULS. / *b:* UCP; L.
Continued as
INSPECTOR, Literary Magazine and Re-view. London. v2-3, N 1826-My 1827.
a: ULS. / *b:* UCP; L.

Absorbed *National Magazine and General Review* and continued as
INSPECTOR and National Magazine. London. v3, Je-Ag 1827.
a: ULS. / *b:* UCP.

INSPECTOR AND NATIONAL MAGAZINE.
(See *Inspector and Literary Review.*)

INSPECTOR and West of England Review.
(See *Inspector and Literary Review.*)

THE INSPECTOR . . . consisting of Narratives, Dialogues, and Essays. London, Aylesbury. no1, Jl 1807. q.
b: L.

INSPECTOR, Literary Magazine and Review.
(See *Inspector and Literary Review.*)

INSTITUTION FOR THE EDUCATION of Deaf and Dumb Children. Reports. Edinburgh. 1815-27.
b: UCP.

INSTRUCTIVE MAGAZINE, a Library of Interesting Knowledge, Rational Entertainment, and useful Information. London. no1-39, My 5, 1832-Ja 26, 1833. w.
a: ULS. / *b:* L no1-4; O no1.

INSTRUCTOR. London. 1808-09. w.
a: CtY Ja 6, 1808-D 27, 1809. / *b:* GeG.

INSTRUCTOR and Select Weekly Advertiser. London. no1+, 1807-14/?. w.
a: CSmH no384, D 21, 1814.

INTELLECTUAL REPOSITORY and New Jerusalem Magazine.
(See *Intellectual Repository for the New Church.*)

INTELLECTUAL REPOSITORY for the New Church. London. v1-6, no1-48, 1814-23; ns, v1-3, 1824-29. q.
a: ULS; PBr. / *b:* UCP; L no12-14, 18-20, 40; ns, v1-3; MR.
Continued as
INTELLECTUAL REPOSITORY and New Jerusalem Magazine. London. v1-5, 1830-39; ns-s3+, 1840-81. q.
a: ULS; PBr. / *b:* UCP; L; MR.
(Continued as *New Church Magazine*, 1881-date.)

INTELLIGENCE. London. Mr 21, 1830-Jl 30, 1831. w.
a: CSmH no7, My 2, 1830. / *b:* L.
Incorporated with *Paul Pry*, Mr 20, 1831.
Continued as
ALFRED. London. Jl 31, 1831-Ap 23, 1833. w.
a: CSmH no1. / *b:* L.
(Incorporated with *Old England*, Ap 28, 1833.)

INTRUDER; a Periodical Paper. Aberdeen. no1-36, Ja 1-O 22, 1802. w.; f.
a: ULS; ULSup. / *b:* UCP; E; O no1-26.

INVASION. Glasgow. no1-5, c.1804.
b: MR.

INVERNESS COURIER, and General Advertiser for the Counties of Inverness, Ross, Moray, Nairn, Cromarty, Sutherland and Caithness. Inverness. no1+, D 4, 1817-date. w.
a: CSmH Je 16, 1825. / *b:* InIC lacking D 18, 25, 1823.

INVERNESS JOURNAL and Northern Advertiser. Inverness. 1807-48. w.
a: CSmH Ap 15, 1831. / *b:* AU 1813-22; EP 1815, 1828; InIC 1807-25 impf.; InR; L no251+, My 22, 1812-21.

INVESTIGADOR PORTUGUEZ em Inglaterra, ou Journal Literario, Politico, &c. London. v1-23, 1811-19.
a: ULS; ULSup. / *b:* L.

THE INVESTIGATOR. London. 1796.
b: O no1, 5.

THE INVESTIGATOR. London. v1-8, 1820-24. q. (v3-8 entitled *The Investigator; or Quarterly Magazine*.)
a: ULS. / *b:* UCP; L.

INVESTIGATOR.
(See *Drakard's Paper*.)

INVESTIGATOR; or, Monthly Expositor and Register on Prophecy. London. v1-5, 1831-36. m.
a: ULS. / *b:* L lacks pp. 241-48 of v4.

INVESTIGATOR; or Quarterly Magazine.
(See *Investigator*, 1820-24.)

IONIAN ANTIQUITIES.
(See *Society of Dilettanti, London.*)

IPSWICH JOURNAL. Ipswich. 1720-1886. w. (Slight variation in title prior to 1789.)
a: ULS; CtY (1811-13); ICU Mr 28, 1795-1796; 1797, lacking My 20, 27; 1798, lacking Je 23; (1799); 1801-12; (1813); 1814-17; (1818); 1819-20; 1821, lacking Ja 27-F 10; 1822-26; 1827, lacking Ja 6, 13; 1828-32. / *b:* UCP; BP Ag 18, 25, 1821; BurC 1823-24, 1826-27; ColP 1794-1808; 1812-17; 1821-26; IpP; IpSC 1789-96, 1800-28, 1830-32; L 1789-93; D 27, 1794; 1795-1802, lacking Jl 25, 1795; (1803-06); 1807-28; 1830.
(Continued as *Daily Ipswich Journal*, 1886-87; as *Daily Journal*, 1887-88; as *Ipswich Journal*, 1888-1902.)

IPSWICH JOURNAL. A Critical Review of the Ipswich Journal; or candid Remarks on the Disputes, both Religious and Political, which occur in that Paper . . . . Ipswich. no1-3, Ja-Mr, 1790. m.
b: L.

IPSWICH MAGAZINE. Ipswich. F 1799-F 1800-[?]. m.
b: UCP; IpP F 1799-F 1800; L F 1799-Ja 1800.

IPSWICH, Yarmouth, and Lynn Herald; or Weekly Advertiser for Suffolk, Norfolk, Es-

sex and Cambridgeshire. Ipswich. 1804-06. w.
  a: CSmH no34, Je 29, 1805; CtY N 10,
  1804-Mr 15, 1806.

IRELAND'S MIRROR; or, a Chronicle of the
Times. Dublin. v1-2, 1804-05. m. (On titlepage, New Magazine. Ireland's Mirror; or, a
Chronicle of the Times.)
  a: ULS. / b: UCP; BlL; D; L; MR v2.
  Continued as
  IRELAND'S MIRROR; or, the Masonic Magazine. Dublin. v3, Ja-Ap 1806. m.
  b: BlL.

IRELAND'S MIRROR; or, the Masonic Magazine.
  (See Ireland's Mirror; or, a Chronicle of
  the Times.)

IRIS; a Journal of Literature, Science, and
the Fine Arts. London. v1-2, no1-54, 1825-
26. w. (Single numbers entitled Iris; a London Weekly Review, and Journal of Literature, Science and the Fine Arts.
  a: ULS. / b: UCP; L.

IRIS; a Literary and Religious Offering. London. 1830-31. a.
  b: UCP; L 1830.

IRIS, a Literary Magazine. Birmingham. v1,
no1-9, Jl 1-O 21, 1830/?. f.
  a: ULS.

IRIS; a London Weekly Review, &c.
  (See Iris; a Journal of Literature, Science,
  &c.)

IRIS; or Norwich and Norfolk Weekly Advertiser. Norwich. no1-100, F 5, 1803-D 29,
1804. w.
  a: CSmH no48, D 31, 1803; CtY no100, D
  29, 1804; MdBJ. / b: C no3, 35, 43-100;
  L.

IRIS; or, Sheffield Advertiser.
  (See Sheffield Register, Yorkshire, Derbyshire and Nottinghamshire General Advertiser.)

IRISH AGRICULTURAL MAGAZINE. Dublin. 1798-1801. ir.
  a: ULS. / b: UCP; DRS; L.

IRISH AUXILIARY, London Society for Promoting Christianity among the Jews. Reports.
London. 1819-38.
  b: UCP.

IRISH CATHOLIC MAGAZINE. Cork. v1,
1829/?.
  a: ULS. / b: DL no1-2.

IRISH CATHOLIC MAGAZINE and Monthly
Asylum for Neglected Biography.
  (See Irish Magazine and Monthly Asylum
  for Neglected Biography.)

IRISH DRAMATIC CENSOR. Dublin. no1-6,
1811-12.
  a: ULS. / b: L.

IRISH ECCLESIASTICAL REGISTER. Dublin. 1817. a.
  b: UCP.

IRISH EVANGELICAL SOCIETY. Report.
London. v1-29, 1814-43.
  b: UCP.

IRISH FARMER'S JOURNAL and Weekly Intelligencer. Dublin. v1-15, 1812-26. w.
  a: ULS. / b: UCP; BlL v1-3; DL; L
  v3-15.

IRISH MAGAZINE.
  (See Bolster's Quarterly Magazine.)

IRISH MAGAZINE and Monthly Asylum for
neglected Biography. Dublin. v1-9, 1807-15.
m. (Issue for Ja 1808 has caption title,
Irish Catholic Magazine and Monthly Asylum
for Neglected Biography.)
  a: ULS; ULSup. / b: UCP; BlL; L; LLL.

IRISH MONTHLY MAGAZINE of Politics
and Literature. Dublin. v1-3, 1832-34. m.
  a: ULS. / b: UCP; DL lacking no17, 19-
  20 of v2.

IRISH OBSERVER. Limerick. 1824-25. s.w.
  a: CSmH v2, no105, Ja 29, 1825. / b: L
  My 1, 1824.

IRISH PACKET. Dublin. 1807-08. t.w.
  b: C no284, D 24, 1808; L O 27, 29, D
  10, 1807.

IRISH PROTESTANT, and Faithful Examiner. Dublin. v1, no1-20, N 15-D 30, 1822.
  a: ULS. / b: DA; DL; O no1-13.

IRISH PULPIT. Dublin. v1, no1, Ja 26, 1828.
  b: D.

IRISH RACING CALENDAR. Dublin. 1790-
date.
  b: DL 1790, 1798-1817, 1820-23, 1829,
  1831-32.

IRISH RUSH LIGHT; a Magazine of Political
and Miscellaneous Information for the ''Mil-
lions.'' Dublin. Ap-N 1831.
  a: ULS. / b: UCP; DL.

IRISH SABBATH SCHOOL MAGAZINE. Belfast. v1-2, 1832-34.
  b: BlL.

IRISH SENTINEL, and Liberal Magazine.
Dublin. no1-8, Ag 1828-O 1830.
  b: DA; DL no1-5.

IRISH SOCIETY for Promoting the Scriptural
Education of the Native Irish through the
Medium of their own Language. Quarterly
Extracts. Dublin. no1-44, 1819-33/?.
  a: ULS.

IRISH SOCIETY for Promoting the Scriptural
Education of the Native Irish through the
Medium of their own Language. Reports.
Dublin. 1819-99/?.
  a: ULS. / b: UCP.

IRISH TIMES. Dublin. no1+, O 15, 1823-Jl
18, 1825.
  a: CSmH no286, Je 10, 1825. / b: L no1+,
  O 15, 1823; D 1, 6, 8, 13, 17, 22, 24, 1824;
  Ja 3-Jl 18, 1825.

IRISH UNITARIAN CHRISTIAN SOCIETY.
Report . . . with the Proceedings of the Annual General Meeting. Dublin. v1-2, 1831-32.
  b: UCP.

IRISHMAN. Belfast. [?]-1819-1824/?. w.
  a: CSmH v4, no191, Ja 24, 1823; DLC F
  1820-Je 1822; N Je 26, Ag 16, S 6, 13,
  1822. / b: BIL 1819-N 21, 1823; BlP
  1820-24 impf.

IRISHMAN. London. no1-5, F 27-Mr 27, 1831.
w.
  a: CSmH no4, Mr 20, 1831. / b: L.

IRON.
  (See Mechanics Magazine.)

IRON-MASTERS OF YORK AND DERBY.
Minutes of Meetings. Bradford. 1800. 2 pts.
  b: LP.

THE IRVINE AND COUNTY OF AYR Miscellany. Irvine. S 1814-Jl 1815. m.
  b: AyP; GM.

THE ISIS. A London Weekly Publication.
London. no1-39, F 11-D 15, 1832. w.
  a: ULS. / b: UCP; BP no1; CrP; L; O.

ISLINGTON GAZETTE, or Monthly Miscellany of Local Intelligence. London. no1-3,
1828. m.
  b: IsP no1, Ja 1828.

ISLINGTON POPULAR LIBRARY of Religious Knowledge. London. no1-6, [?]-1832.
  b: IsP no5-6, Ap-My 1832.

ITALIAN MAGAZINE. London. no1-2, N-D
1795.
  (No issues known. Data from CBEL, II.
  682.)
  Continued as
ITALIAN TRACTS. London. 1796.
  b: L.

L'ITALICO, ossia giornale politico, letterario e miscellaneo, da una Società d'Italiani.
London. v1-3, 1813-14.
  b: L.

JACKSON'S OXFORD JOURNAL. Oxford.
1753-date. w. (Later as Oxford Journal.)
  a: ULS; CSmH Ag 16, 1823; CtY Ag 27,
  1791; Je 23, 1792-1832; DLC (F 23, 1793-
  Je 5, 1802: 15 nos lacking); (Ja 5, 1805-
  D 27, 1806: 2 nos missing). / b: L [1789-
  90]; sc.nos. 1791; [1792]; sc.nos. 1793-
  94; O (1789-1800); OPU lacking 1792,
  1794-98; WcBW My 11, Jl 20, 1811; Ap
  18, My 9, 1812.

JAMES MURRAY'S Royal Asylum for Lunatics. Report of the Directors. Perth. v1+,
1828-date.
  b: UCP.

JANUS: or, the Edinburgh Literary Almanack.
Edinburgh. 1826. (Also called Edinburgh Literary Almanack.)
  b: UCP; EP; L; LLL.

JENKINSON'S SCHOLASTIC TICKLER.
  (See Birmingham Scholastic Tickler.)

JERRY-WAG'S JOURNAL.
  (See Hoxton Sausage, and Jerry-Wag's
  Journal.)

THE JESTER; or, Paisley Magazine of Wit.
Greenock. 1805.
  b: PsP.

JEWISH EXPOSITOR, and Friend of Israel.
  (See Jewish Repository, or Monthly Communications respecting the Jews.)

JEWISH REPOSITORY, or Monthly Communications respecting the Jews and the Proceedings of the London Society. London.
v1-3, 1813-15. m.
  a: ULS. / b: UCP; L v1-2.
  Continued as
JEWISH EXPOSITOR, and Friend of Israel;
containing Monthly Communications respecting the Jews, and the Proceedings of
the London Society. London. v1-16, 1816-
31. m.
  a: ULS; ULSup. / b: UCP; L v1-14.

JOHN BULL. London. no1-3739, D 17, 1820-
1892. w.
  a: ULS; ULSup; C-S 1820-28; CU 1820-
  24; NNHi; NjP 1820-21, 1823-28; OClWHi
  1820-25; PP. / b: UCP; BiP (1820-32);
  DcrN 1825, 1832; EP; IpP 1820-30; L;
  LLL; LVA lacking 20 sc.nos.; MR 1821-27;
  NwS sc.nos. 1822; 1823; sc.nos. 1824-25.

JOHN BULL.
  (See Cooper's John Bull.)

JOHN BULL MAGAZINE and Literary Recorder. London. v1, no1-6, Jl-D 1824/?. m.
(Title varies slightly.)
  a: ULS. / b: UCP; BP; L.

JOHN BULL'S BRITISH JOURNAL. London.
no1-3, F 25-Mr 11, 1821. w.
  b: L.

JOHN BULL'S PAPER. London. no1-15, Je
13-S 19, 1813. w.
  a: ULS. / b: O no2-15.

JOHN BULL'S PICTURE GALLERY. Political, Satirical, and Humourous. London. no1-
4, My-Je, 1832.
  b: O.

JOHN HILLARY'S PUE'S OCCURRENCES.
Dublin. [1788]-1792/?. s.w. (Preceded by
Impartial Occurrences, Foreign and Domestick, [1703]-1706-[?]; Pue's Occurrences,
[?]-1731-[1763]; John Roe's Pue's Occurrences, [1763]-[1787].)
  (No issues known for years 1789-1832; but
  listed by ULS and UCP. Data also from
  CBEL, II.733.)

THE JOHN KNOX; or Religious Reformer of
Scotland. Glasgow. no1-8, 1824.
  b: GM.

E. JOHNSON'S BRITISH GAZETTE and Sunday Monitor. London. [?]-1784-1805. w. (Pre-

ceded by *British Gazette and Sunday Monitor*, 1780-83-[?].)
  a: C-S Mr 27, Ap 3, 17, My 1, N 20, 1791;
  CtY F 7, 18, 28-Je 27, 1790; DLC Jl 3-
  D 25, 1791, lacking Jl 31, O 13, D 4; ICU
  1802-04, lacking Ag 12, 1804; 26 nos. mutilated; NNHi (1789-My 1797); Je 1797-
  1798; NNU-H Ap 3-24, 1791; V [1792-93];
  5 sc.nos. 1794. / *b:* UCP; L [1789-91];
  1792-S 22, 1805.
    Continued as
JOHNSON'S SUNDAY MONITOR and British Gazette. London. no 2341-2877, S 29,
1805-F 20, 1814. w.
  b: L.
    Continued as
SUNDAY MONITOR, and London Recorder.
London. no 2878-2912, F 27-D 25, 1814. w.
  b: L.
    Continued as
SUNDAY MONITOR. London. no 2913-4670,
Ja 1, 1815-Ja 25, 1829. w.
  a: CSmH Ag 7, 1825; DLC D 13, 1818. /
  b: L.

JOHNSON'S RACING CALENDAR. York.
1828-66.
  b: L no 9+, Ag 2, 1828-32, lacking 1831.

JOHNSON'S SUNDAY MONITOR and British Gazette.
  (See *E. Johnson's British Gazette and Sunday Monitor*.)

JOHNSTONE'S MONTHLY REGISTER of Public Events and Monthly Scottish Lists.
Edinburgh. no 1-3, Ag-O, 1832.
  a: ULS; ULSup.
    Was begun as supplement to *The Schoolmaster, and Edinburgh Weekly Magazine*.
    With no 3 it assumed a separate existence
    and was continued as
JOHNSTONE'S POLITICAL REGISTER,and Monthly Chronicle of Public Events, Scottish Lists, &c. Edinburgh. no 4-11, 1832-33.
  a: ULS.

JOHNSTONE'S POLITICAL REGISTER,and Monthly Chronicle of Public Events, &c.
  (See *Johnstone's Monthly Register of Public Events*, &c.)

JONES'S ANNUAL, and the only Complete Family Account Book. London. [1823.]
  b: L.

JONES'S LITERARY GAZETTE. Manchester. no 1-6, Mr 7-Ap 11, 1829/?. w.
  a: ULS.

JONES'S SENTIMENTAL AND MASONIC Magazine. Dublin. [?]-1793/?. m.
  a: DLC v3, Jl-D 1793.

JORDAN'S PARLIAMENTARY JOURNAL.
London. v1-9, 1792-95.
  a: ULS. / *b:* UCP; L v1.

JOURNAL OF . . .
  In general, see the society, institution, or other group concerned. In using UCP, however, see under *Journal of*.
    See especially (1) *Asiatic Society of Ben-*

gal, Calcutta; (2) *Belvoir Foxhounds;* (3)
Berwickshire Naturalists Club; (4) *Journal of Science and Arts;* (5) *Quarterly Journal of Agriculture;* (6) *Royal Geographical Society;* (7) *Royal Institution of Cornwall;* (8) *Society for the Preservation of Public Footpaths.*

JOURNAL CLINIQUE. London. v1-8, 1825-
28.
  b: UCP.

JOURNAL DE FRANCE et d'Angleterre.
London. no 1-3, 1797.
  b: UCP; MR no1.

JOURNAL DE L'EUROPE. London. no 1-16,
Ag 4-S 25, 1789/?. s.w.
  b: L no1, 16.

JOURNAL DE MIDDLESEX. London. no 1+,
Ap 15-My 3, 1791/?. s.w.
  a: MBAt Ap 15-My 3, 1791.

JOURNAL DES. DAMES. London. no 1-104,
1817-19. w.
  a: ULS.

JOURNAL OF AGRICULTURE. Edinburgh.
v1-13, 1828-43; ns-s3+, 1843-68.
  a: ULSup.

JOURNAL OF COMMERCE and Shipping Telegraph. Liverpool. 1826-1921/?. d.
  (No issues before 1833. Data from DLC card catalogue.)

**JOURNAL OF ELEMENTAL LOCOMOTION,
or Monthly Advocate of the Advantages to arise from the Substitution of inanimate for animate Power.** London. no 1-6, 1832-33.
  a: ULS. / *b:* UCP; GM; L.

JOURNAL OF FACTS. London. Ja-Je 1829.
  b: UCP.

JOURNAL OF FASHIONS. London. 1829-30.
  b: O.

**JOURNAL OF ITINERATING EXERTIONS
in some of the more Destitute Parts of Scotland.** Edinburgh. v1, no 1-6, 1814-16/?.
  a: ULS.

**JOURNAL OF MORBID ANATOMY, ophthalmic Medicine and pharmaceutical Analysis;
with Medico-botanical Transactions, communicated by the Medico-botanical Society of London.** London. v1, no1, 1828.
  a: ULS. / *b:* UCP; L; LS; O.

**A JOURNAL OF NATURAL PHILOSOPHY,
Chemistry and the Arts.** London. v1-5, 1797-
1802; ns, v1-36, 1802-13. m. (Also called
Nicholson's Journal.)
  a: ULS; ULSup. / *b:* UCP; CPL; DRS;
  GeG; GrP 1802-06; L; LCP v1-5; LGU
  v1-5; LR; LaP ns, v9-36; NpP v1-5.
  (Merged into *Philosophical Magazine*.)

JOURNAL OF POPULAR MEDICINE.
  (See *A Monthly Journal of Popular Medicine*.)

JOURNAL OF PUBLIC HEALTH. London.
v1-2, 1823-24/?
  a: ULS.

JOURNAL OF SCIENCE AND ARTS. London. v1-6, 1816-19. q.
  a: ULS; ULSup. / *b:* UCP; BdP 1817-19; CPL; DRS; GeG 1818-19; GrP; L; LGU; LP; LR; MCh; NwP; SthC.
  Continued as
QUARTERLY JOURNAL OF LITERATURE, Science and the Arts. London. v7-22, 1819-27. q.
  a: ULS; ULSup. / *b:* UCP; BdP 1819-22, 1827; CPL; DRS; GeG; GrP; L; LGU; LP; LR; MCh; NwP; SthC v7-13.
  Continued as
QUARTERLY JOURNAL OF SCIENCE, Literature, and the Arts. London. ns, v1-7, 1827-30. q.
  a: ULS; ULSup. / *b:* UCP; CPL; DRS; GeG; L; LGU; LR; LVA; MCh; NwP.
  Continued as
JOURNAL OF THE ROYAL INSTITUTION of Great Britain. London. v1-2, 1830-31.
  a: ULS. / *b:* UCP; CPL; L; LGU v1; LR; MCh.
  (Merged into *London and Edinburgh Philosophical Magazine.*)

JOURNAL OF TRADE AND COMMERCE; or, Merchant and Manufacturers Magazine. London. v1-2, no1-14, 1818-19.
  a: ULS.

JOURNALS OF THE HOUSE OF COMMONS. London. 1742-date.
  b: UCP; CrP 1795-1806; SP.

JOURNALS OF THE HOUSE OF COMMONS of the Kingdom of Ireland. Dublin. v1-28, 1782-1791.
  b: UCP.

JOURNALS OF THE HOUSE OF LORDS. London. 1509-date.
  b: UCP; CrP; SP 1817-32.

JOURNALS OF THE HOUSE OF LORDS, Ireland. Dublin. 1779-1800.
  b: UCP.

JOURNALS OF THE ROYAL INSTITUTION of Great Britain. London. v1-2, 1802-03.
  b: UCP.

JOURNEYMAN AND ARTIZAN'S London and Provincial Chronicle. London. no1-13, Je 12-S 4, 1825. (No5-7 entitled *Artizan's London and Provincial Chronicle;* no8-13 entitled *Mechanic's Newspaper.*)
  a: CSmH no12. / *b:* L; O no1.

THE JUDGMENT SEAT OF CHRIST. London. no1-17, 1831.
  b: L lacking no9-12.

THE JUDICIAL REGISTER. Edinburgh. N 1828-Ja 1829/?. w.; m.
  (No issues known. Data from S N & Q, s2.VI.181.)

JURIDICAL SOCIETY, Edinburgh. Law Cases and Speculative Questions for Discussion. Edinburgh. 1817-94.
  a: ULS. / *b:* UCP listed under *Law Cases.*

JURIST; or, Quarterly Journal of Jurisprudence and Legislation. London. v1-4, 1827-33.
  a: ULS. / *b:* UCP; L; LLN; LLW.

THE JUVENAL. A Periodical Paper. Edinburgh. no1-8, F 4-My 14, 1805. f.
  a: ULS. / *b:* EP.

JUVENILE CABINET; or Magazine of Entertainment and Instruction for British Youth. Coventry. v1-2, Jl 1808-Je 1809. m.
  b: CvP.

JUVENILE CABINET, or Magazine of Entertainment and Instruction. Birmingham. v1-2, 1816.
  b: BP v2.

JUVENILE DEAF AND DUMB ASSOCIATION. Report. London. 1829-37.
  b: UCP.

JUVENILE ENCYCLOPEDIA.
  (See *Monthly Preceptor; or, Juvenile Library.*)

JUVENILE FORGET-ME-NOT (Ackermann's).
  (See *Ackermann's Juvenile Forget-Me-Not.*)

JUVENILE FORGET-ME-NOT. London. v1-9, 1829-37. a.
  b: UCP; L; O 1829, 1831-32.

JUVENILE KEEPSAKE. London. v1-2, 1829-30. a.
  b: UCP.

JUVENILE LIBRARY.
  (See *Monthly Preceptor; or, Juvenile Library.*)

JUVENILE MAGAZINE. Limerick. v1, no1-6, Ja-Je 1814. m.
  b: DA.

JUVENILE OLIO, or Monthly Medley London. Ja-D 1796. m.
  b: O.

JUVENILE SOUVENIR and New Year's Gift. London. 1829-33. a.
  b: O 1829.

KALEIDOSCOPE; or Edinburgh Literary Amusements. Edinburgh. no1-12, O 6, 1821-Ja 12, 1822. f.
  b: EP no1-8.

KALEIDOSCOPE; or, Literary and Scientific Mirror. Liverpool. v1-2, 1818-20; ns, v1-11, 1820-31. w. (Subtitle varies.)
  a: ULS. / *b:* UCP; BtlP 1822-31; EP no1-53, 1820-21; L; LLL lacking v1-2; LvP; O v1-2; WiP ns, v1-7.

KEARSLEY'S ANNUAL TAX TABLES. London. 1793-1840/?. a. (Title varies: *Kearsley's Annual Ten-penny Tax Tables; Kearsley's Tax Tables; Kearsley's Correct Tax Tables,* &c.)
  b: UCP; L.

KEENE'S BATH JOURNAL.
  (See *Bath Journal.*)

KEEPSAKE. London. v1-30, 1828-57. a.
  a: ULSup. / *b:* UCP; BP; BiP 1831; BrP v1-3; CrP; EP; L; LLL 1828; 1832; MR; O.

KEEPSAKE FOR THE YOUNG. London. 1830. a.
  b: L.

LE KEEPSAKE FRANCAIS. Paris, London. 1831.
  b: UCP.

KELSO MAIL. Kelso. no1+, Ap 13, 1797-1934. s.w.
  a: CSmH D 4, 1826. / *b:* E 1802-31; L Ap 2, 1810-Jl 1811.
  (Continued as *Border Mail,* 1934-date.)

KELSO WEEKLY JOURNAL. Kelso. 1806-29.
  (No issues known. Data from Craig, *Scottish Periodical Press,* p. 73.)

KENDAL NEWS. Kendal. [?]-1820-23-[?].
  b: KdWG 1820-23.

KENT AND ESSEX MERCURY. London. no1-536, O 15, 1822-33. w.
  a: CSmH S 11, 1827. / *b:* L.
  (Continued as *Essex and Herts. Mercury,* 1833-36; as *Essex, Herts., and Kent Mercury,* 1836-43; as *Essex, Herts., and Suffolk Mercury,* 1843.)

KENT COUNTY HERALD. Canterbury. [1802]-1808-10. w. (Probably the same as *Kentish Herald.*)
  b: L S 22, 1808; Ja 5, 1809; Jl 25, 1810.

KENT HERALD.
  (See *Kentish Herald.*)

KENTISH CHRONICLE and Canterbury Journal. Canterbury. 1788-Je 7, 1791. w. (Succeeds *Kentish Weekly Post; or, Canterbury Journal,* 1768-69; *Kentish Post and Canterbury Journal,* 1769-70; *Canterbury Journal,* 1770-88.)
  a: ULS. / *b:* L.
  Continued as
  KENTISH CHRONICLE. Canterbury. Je 17, 1791-1838. s.w.
  a: ULS; CSmH My 20, 1828; NNHi 1831-32. / *b:* UCP; L.

KENTISH GAZETTE. Canterbury. no1+, My 4, 1768-date. (Preceded by *Kentish Post,* 1717-68.)
  a: CSmH My 23, 1828; CtY [1789-92]; sc. nos. 1795; (Ja-F 1796); Mr 1796-1799; MBAt Jl 6, 1804. / *b:* CyP; L 1789-92;

[1793] (1794); 1795-98; (1799); 1800-01; 2 sc.nos. 1802; (1803); 1804-20; 1830-32; LLL F 7, 1826-D 19, 1828; MsP 1789-1832.

KENTISH HERALD. Canterbury. no1+, Ap 8, 1802-D 1823. w. (See also *Kent County Herald,* which may be the same as this paper.)
  b: L lacking Jl 8-Ag 6, 1802; Ap 21, My 19, Jl 7, S 1-8, O 13-27, 1803; 1804-23.
  Continued as
  KENT HERALD. Canterbury. Ja 1824-date.
  a: CSmH D 13, 1827. / *b:* L.

KENTISH HERALD, and Universal Register.
  (No issues known. Probably precedes *Kentish Herald.* Data from CBEL, II.722.

KENTISH MISCELLANY and Literary Album, comprising Original Essays, Poetry, Biography, Anecdotes, Jeux d'Esprit, Sketches of Society and Manners. Canterbury. no1-17, My 13-D 13, 1828.
  a: ULS.

KENTISH OBSERVER. Canterbury. no1+, O 4, 1832-date.
  (No issues known. Files in *Kentish Observer* office destroyed during the late war.)

KENTISH REGISTER, and Monthly Miscellany. Canterbury. v1-3, 1793-95. m.
  a: ULS. / *b:* UCP; CyP; L; LLL; WoP.

KENT'S ORIGINAL TRADESMAN'S Assistant.
  (See *Shopkeeper's and Tradesman's Assistant.*)

KENT'S SHOPKEEPER'S and Tradesman's Assistant.
  (See *Shopkeeper's and Tradesman's Assistant.*)

KENT'S WEEKLY DISPATCH and Sporting Mercury. London. 1816 20. w.
  a: CtY 2 sc.nos. 1817, 1819. / *b:* L no 98-192, Ap 5, 1818-Ja 23, 1820.

KERR EVENING POST. Tralee. 1827/?.
  a: CSmH Je 6, 1827.

KERRY CHRONICLE, and Tralee Advertiser. Tralee. [?]-1790-[?].
  b: UCP.

KERRY EVENING POST. Tralee. [1774]-1793-1917. s.w.
  a: CSmH Je 6, 1827. / *b:* UCP; L My 24, 1813; D 22, 1824; 1828-32.

KILDARE PLACE SOCIETY for Promoting the Education of the Poor of Ireland. Report. Dublin. 1825-37.
  b: UCP.

KILKENNY CHRONICLE. Kilkenny. 1812-13/?. w.
  b: L no98, My 29, 1813.

KILKENNY INDEPENDENT. Kilkenny. 1826-27/?. s.w.
    a: CSmH no115, My 26, 1827.

KILKENNY JOURNAL and Leinster Commercial Advertiser.
    (See *Finn's Leinster Journal.*)

KILKENNY MODERATOR. Kilkenny. [?]-1825-1919. s.w.
    a: CSmH no1843, My 5, 1827. / *b:* L no1627+, F 19, 1825; Ja 2, 1828-1832.
    (Continued as *The Moderator*, 1920-25.)

KILMARNOCK CHRONICLE, and Ayrshire Advertiser. Kilmarnock. [?]-1832/?.
    a: CSmH no64, My 22, 1832.

KILMARNOCK LITERARY EXPOSITOR.
    (See *Ayrshire Miscellany; or, Kilmarnock Literary Expositor.*)

KILMARNOCK MIRROR and Literary Gleaner. Kilmarnock. v1-2, no1-16, O 1818-Ja 1820. m.
    a: ULS. / *b:* UCP; GM; L no1-8.

KILMARNOCK MONTHLY MAGAZINE.
    (See *Coila Repository, and Kilmarnock Monthly Magazine.*)

KING'S BENCH GAZETTE. London. v1, no1-5.
    b: BrP.

KINGS AND QUEENS COLLEGE of Physicians in Ireland. Transactions. Dublin. v1-5, 1817-28.
    b: DRS.

KIRBY'S Wonderful and Eccentric Museum, or Magazine of Remarkable Characters. London. v1-6, 1803-20. (v1 also called *Wonderful and Scientific Museum, or Magazine of Remarkable Characters;* v2 also called *Kirby's Wonderful and Scientific Museum, or Magazine of Remarkable Characters.*)
    a: ULS; ULSup. / *b:* LGU lacking v4; O v1-2.

KIRBY'S Wonderful and Scientific Museum, &c.
    (See *Kirby's Wonderful and Eccentric Museum.*)

KNIGHT ERRANT; a Literary Miscellany, consisting of Original Prose and Verse, with Occasional Notices of New Books, Drama, &c. London. v1, no1-5, Jl 5-Ag 16, 1817. ir.
    b: L.

KNIGHT'S PENNY MAGAZINE.
    (See *Penny Magazine of the Society for the Diffusion of Useful Knowledge.*)

KNIGHT'S QUARTERLY MAGAZINE. London. v1-3, 1823-24. q.
    a: ULS; ULSup. / *b:* UCP; BP; BiP; C; CrP; GM; L; LdL; NwP.
    Continued as
    QUARTERLY MAGAZINE. London. ns, no1, 1825. q.
    a: ULS. / *b:* UCP; GM; L.

LABOURER'S FRIEND and Handicrafts Chronicle. London. v1, no1-12, Ja-D 1821; ns, v1-3, no6, 1822-24/?.
    a: ULS. / *b:* UCP; L no1.

LABOURER'S FRIEND MAGAZINE.
    (See *Facts and Illustrations.*)

LABOURER'S FRIEND SOCIETY.
    (See *Society for Improving the Conditions of the Labouring Classes.*)

LADIES' CABINET of Fashion, Music, and Romance. London. v1-14, 1832-38; s2-s4, 1839-70.
    a: ULS; ULSup. / *b:* UCP; BP Ja-Je 1832; L.

LADIES DIARY. London. v1-137, 1704-1840. a.
    a: ULS; DLC lacking 1796; MH 1794-95; 1797-1804; 1806; 1808; 1827; 1831-32; NjP 1789-92; 1797-1832. / *b:* UCP; LGU 1815.
    (In 1840 united with *Gentleman's Diary* to form *Lady's and Gentleman's Diary*, 1841-71.)

LADIES' FASHIONABLE REPOSITORY. Ipswich. [?]-1809-95-[?].
    b: IpP 1809-32.

LADIES MAGAZINE and Museum of Belles Lettres.
    (See *Lady's Magazine; or entertaining Companion for the Fair Sex.*)

LADIES' MONTHLY MUSEUM.
    (See *Lady's Monthly Museum, or Polite Repository of Amusement and Instruction.*)

LADIES' MUSEUM.
    (See *Lady's Monthly Museum, or Polite Repository of Amusement and Instruction.*)

LADIES' PENNY GAZETTE; or, Mirror of Fashion and Miscellany of Instruction and Amusement. London. no1-59, 1832-33/?.
    a: ULS. / *b:* L no1-10, 13-19, 21, 23-42, 44-54, 59; O no1, 7.

LADIES POCKET MAGAZINE. London. v1-15, 1824-40.
    a: ULS. / *b:* UCP; BP 1830-31; KeP; L; LGU 1824.

LADIES SOCIETY for Promoting the early Education and Improvement of the Children of Negroes and of People of Colour in the British West Indies. London. v1-4, 1826-29/?.
    a: ULSup.

LADY'S GAZETTE, and Evening Advertiser. London. no1-12, My 5-Je 13, 1789/?.
    a: CtY no1, My 5, 1789. / *b:* UCP.

LADY'S MAGAZINE; or Entertaining Companion for the Fair Sex. London. v1-50, 1770-1819; ns, v1-10, 1820-29; s3, v1-5, 1830-32. m.
    a: ULS; ULSup. / *b:* UCP; BP v20-24, 29, 38, 43, 46, 48, all vols. impf.; CrP

1789-95; 1800-14; GrP 1794, 1807-08, 1810; L v1-2, 4-7, 9-34, 36-49; ns, v1, 4-10; s3, v1-5; LLL 1789-97, 1799-1814, 1816-24, 1830.
Incorporated with *Lady's Museum* and continued as
LADY'S MAGAZINE and Museum of Belles Lettres. London. v1-11, 1832-37. m.
   a: ULS. / *b:* UCP; EP; L.
   (United with *Court Magazine and Monthly Critic* and continued as *Court Magazine and Monthly Critic, and Ladies Magazine and Museum of Belles Lettres*, 1838-47.)

LADY'S MONTHLY MUSEUM; or Polite Repository of Amusement and Instruction. London. v1-16, ns, v1-17, 1798-1814. m.
   a: ULS. / *b:* UCP; BiP v4, 6, 8-9; BrP v1-11; DL v1-9, 11-16; ns, v1-17; HfP 1811-14; L v1-16; ns, v2-10; LLL, lacking ns, v11; NpP v1; SoP v1-12.
   Continued as
LADIES' MONTHLY MUSEUM. Improved Series. London. s3, v1-28, 1815-28. m.
   a: ULS; CaK v27-28. / *b:* UCP; DL; HfP 1815-16; L v5-6, 19-28; LLL lacking s3, v8, 12, 22; SoP 1815-20.
   Continued as
LADIES' MUSEUM. London. s4, v1-4, 1829-30; s5, v1-3, 1831-32. m.
   a: ULS; ULSup; CaK 1829-31. / *b:* UCP; DL; L 1829-30; LLL.
   (In 1832 incorporated with *Lady's Magazine* and continued as *Lady's Magazine and Museum of Belles-Lettres*, 1833-37.)

LADY'S New and Elegant Pocket Magazine; or Polite and Entertaining Companion for the Fair Sex. London. v1, 1795.
   b: L.

LANCASHIRE AND YORKSHIRE Co-operator; or, Useful Classes Advocate.
   (See *Lancashire Co-operator.*)

LANCASHIRE CO-OPERATOR. Manchester. no1-6, 1831.
   a: ULS. / *b:* UCP; L.
   Continued as
LANCASHIRE AND YORKSHIRE Co-operator; or, Useful Classes Advocate. Manchester. no1-12; ns, no1-12, 1831-32.
   b: UCP; L.

LANCASHIRE LITERARY MUSEUM. Liverpool. v1-2, 1827-28.
   b: L lacking no5, 9, 44 of v1, and no11 of v2. No 5, 9, 44 impf.

LANCASHIRE OMNIBUS, a Journal of Literature and Amusement. Liverpool. no1, 1832.
   b: L.

LANCASTER GAZETTE.
   (See *Lancaster Gazetteer.*)

LANCASTER GAZETTEER, and General Advertiser for Lancashire, Westmorland, &c. Lancaster, no1-132, Je 20, 1801-D 24, 1803. w.
   b: L; LsP.
   Continued as

LANCASTER GAZETTE, and General Advertiser for Lancashire, Westmorland, &c. Lancaster. no133-6498, D 31, 1803-1894. w.
   a: CSmH Je 18, 1825. / *b:* L; LsP.

LANCASTER HERALD, and Town and County Advertiser. Lancaster. no1-118, Ja 15, 1831-1833. w.
   a: CSmH no1, Ja 15, 1831. / *b:* L; LsP.

LANCASTER MAGAZINE, or the Provincial Repository. Lancaster. no1-3, Je-Ag 1824. m.
   b: LsP.

THE LANCET. A Journal of British and Foreign Medical and Chemical Science, Criticism, Literature and News. London. v1-12, 1823-27; v13-45, 1827-44; &c.-date.
   a: ULS; ULSup. / *b:* BP; C; L; LMA; LCP; LP; LS; LvP (1823-32); O v1-8.

LANDSCAPE ANNUAL. London. v1-5, 1830-34. a.
   b: UCP; L; MR.
   (Continued as *Jenning's Landscape Annual*, 1835-39.)

LANDSCAPE MAGAZINE, containing Preceptive Principles of Landscapes. London. no1-12, ca. 1800/?.
   a: ULS.

LANTERN. Dublin. no1-6, F 26-Mr 9, 1799. t.w.
   a: ULSup. / *b:* UCP.

LAPSUS LINGUAE; or, the College Tatler. Edinburgh. no1-50, 1823-24.
   b: EP; EU.
   Continued as
NEW LAPSUS LINGUAE; or, the College Tatler. Edinburgh. no1-50, 1824-25; ns, no1-18, 1825-26.
   b: EP no1-50; EU; L 1825.

THE LARGS MAGAZINE of Literature and Amusement. Largs. no1, Ja 1826/?.
   b: GM.

LAUGHABLE MAGAZINE, or Cabinet of Humour. London. 1808/?. f.
   (No issues known. Data from *Literary Annual Register, or Records of Literature*, 2 (Ja 1808) 34.)

LAUGHING PHILOSOPHER. London. no1-3, 1832. w.
   b: LU no2; O no3.

LAW ADVERTISER. London. v1-9, Mr 13, 1823-D 29, 1831. (A supplement to *Law Journal*.)
   a: ULS. / *b:* L; LLW v1-8.

LAW AND COMMERCIAL Remembrancer. London. 1832.
   b: L.

LAW CASES. A Register of Law Publications, &c. London. 1790.
   b: L.

LAW CASES and Speculative Questions for the Discussion of the Juridical Society of Edinburgh. Edinburgh. 1822-43.
 b: UCP.

LAW CASES and Speculative Questions for the Discussion of the Scots Law Society.
 (See *Juridical Society, Edinburgh.*)

LAW CHRONICLE. London. v1, no1-63, 1811-12. w.
 a: ULS.

LAW CHRONICLE; or, Journal of Jurisprudence and Legislation. Edinburgh. v1-5, 1829-33. (v1, no1-4, called *Scots Law Chronicle.*)
 a: ULS; ULSup. / *b:* UCP; L.

LAW CHRONICLE and Estate Advertiser.
 (See *Auction Register and Law Chronicle.*)

LAW CHRONICLE, Commercial and Bankruptcy Register.
 (See *Auction Register and Law Chronicle.*)

LAW GAZETTE. London. no1-1146, 1822-47. w.
 a: CSmH no504, Jl 14, 1831. / *b:* L.

LAW JOURNAL. (Morgan and Williams.) London. v1-2, 1803-04. (See also *Law Journal,* by Smith.)
 a: ULS.

LAW JOURNAL. (Smith.) London. v1-3, 1804-06. (v1 was begun as v3 of *Law Journal,* by Morgan and Williams.)
 a: ULS; / *b:* L.

LAW JOURNAL. Tracts. London. v1-2, 1825-29.
 a: ULS. / *b:* LLN.

LAW JOURNAL. An Analytical Digest of the Cases published in the Law Journal, and in all the Reports from 1822-28. &c. London. 1823-date.
 b: L; LP; LdP.

LAW JOURNAL . . . comprising Reports of Cases in the Courts of Chancery, King's Bench and Common Pleas. London. v1-12, 1822-34.
 a: ULS. / *b:* UCP; CnP; L; LP; LdP.
 (Continued as *Law Journal Reports,* 1835-date.)

LAW MAGAZINE, or Quarterly Review of Jurisprudence. London. v1-31, ns, v32-55, 1828-56. q.
 a: ULS; ULSup. / *b:* UCP; L; LLL; LLN; LLW; LMT.
 (Continued as *Law Magazine and Law Review,* 1856-71; as *Law Magazine and Review,* 1872-75; as *Law Magazine and Review and Quarterly Digest of all Reported Cases,* 1876-date.)

LAW RECORDER, containing Reports of Cases and Proceedings in the Courts of Law and Equity . . . at Dublin, and Elsewhere. Dublin. v1-4, 1828-31.

 b: UCP; L; LLN.
 (Continued as New Series, 1833-38; in 1838 divided and continued as *Irish Equity Reports,* 1838-50; and *Irish Law Reports,* 1838-50.)

LAW REPORTER, consisting of early Reports of Cases heard in Banco and at Nisi Prius. London. v1, 1821.
 b: L.

LAWYER'S AND MAGISTRATE'S MAGAZINE; in which is included an Account of every important Proceeding in the Courts at Westminster. With the Decisions of the Judges in their own Words. London. v1-6, 1790-94. (v1-3 reprinted in Dublin and sometimes called *Lawyer's Magazine.*)
 a: ULS; ULSup. / *b:* UCP; L; LGU v1-5; LLN; LLW v1-4; LMT 1792, 1794.

LAWYER'S MAGAZINE.
 (See *Lawyer's and Magistrate's Magazine.*)

THE LAYMAN'S PRESERVATIVE against Popery. Aberdeen. no1-8, D 15, 1830-Ap 2, 1831.
 (No issues known. Data from S N & Q, s1. I.21.)

THE LEADING ARTICLE. An Antidote to the Misleading Articles of the Newspapers. London. no1-12, 1822-23.
 b: L.

LEAMINGTON SPA COURIER. Leamington. no1-525, Ag 9, 1828-38. w.
 a: CSmH no3, Ag 23, 1828. / *b:* BP Ap 14, 1832; L.
 (Continued as *Royal Leamington Spa Courier,* 1838-78; as *Leamington Spa Courier,* 1878-1913; as *Royal Leamington Spa Courier,* 1914-date.)

LEDBURY DIARY; or, Weekly Magazine. Ledbury. no1-5, Mr 31-Ap 29, 1817.
 b: HfP.

LEEDS AND YORKSHIRE ALMANACK. Leeds. [?]-1825-34-[?].
 b: LdP 1825-32.

LEEDS AUXILIARY BIBLE SOCIETY.
 (See *Auxiliary Bible Society, Leeds. Annual Reports.*)

LEEDS CHURCH MISSIONARY Association. Annual Reports. Leeds. [?]-1814-18-[?]. a.
 b: LdP 1814-18.

LEEDS CORRESPONDENT, a Literary, Mathematical, and Philosophical Miscellany. Leeds, London. v1-5, 1814-23.
 a: ULS; ULSup. / *b:* UCP; C v1-3; HlP v2-3; L v1-4; LdL; LdP; NwL.

LEEDS GAZETTE, and Commercial and Agricultural Advertiser. Leeds. 1820.
 a: CSmH v1, no6, F 9, 1820.

LEEDS GUARDIAN SOCIETY. Annual Reports. Leeds. [?]-1822-1908-[?].
 b: LdP 1822-32.

LEEDS INDEPENDENT and York County Advertiser. Leeds. 1819-25/?. w.
  a: CtY 10 sc.nos. 1819-21, 1823. / *b:* L no98, N 16, 1820; no105-365, Ja 4, 1821-D 27, 1825; LdP Ja 7-Je 10, Jl 22-Ag 12, Ag 26-O 21, N 4-D 30, 1819; (1820-21); [1825].

LEEDS INTELLIGENCER. Leeds. no1+, 1754-1866. w. (Also known as *Wright's Leeds Intelligencer.*)
  a: ULS; CSmH Mr 6, 1820; CtY Ja 14, 1793-D 14, 1795; Ja 1798-Je 30, 1800; 15 sc. nos. 1796; 9 sc.nos. 1797; 10 sc. nos. 1819-23; ICU 9 sc.nos. 1816 & 1821-23. / *b:* HIHC (Mr 11, 1816-1832); L (1789-91); 1792-97; [1798]; 1799-1813; 12 sc. nos. 1814; complete 1815-32; LdL 1819-32; LdP 1789; Ja 5-Ag 3, 17, 31, S 14-D 28, 1790; 1791-92; Ja 7-28, F 11-Je 17, Jl 15-D 30, 1793; 1794-98; (1799); 1800; 1 no. for 1801; [S-D 1805]; (1806); 2 sc. nos. 1810; [Je-D 1811]; (1812-13); sc.nos. 1814-19; 1820-21; (1822-23); 1824-25; (1826); sc.nos. 1827-30; 1831; [1832]; LdYP 1789-95, 1801-26.
  (Continued as *Yorkshire Post*, 1866-date.)

LEEDS LADIES' AUXILIARY SOCIETY in Aid of the London Society for Promoting Christianity amongst the Jews. First Annual Report. Leeds. 1815.
  b: LdP.

LEEDS LITERARY OBSERVER. Leeds. v1, no1-9, Ja-S 1819. m.
  a: ULS. / *b:* L; LdL; LdP; O no1.

LEEDS MERCURY. Leeds. no1+, 1718-1901. w.; d.
  a: CSmH Ap 21, 1827; CtY 1790-92; ICU Je 17, 1809; (Ja 6, 1821-D 27, 1823); MiD-B Ag 24, 1799. / *b:* HIHC sc.nos. 1810-31; L 1804-05; 1807-14; Ap 1815-S 1817; 1821-32; LLL Je 14, 21, 1817; LdL 1802-05, 1826-32; LdP; LdYP 1819-21, 1823, 1825.
  (Continued as *Leeds and Yorkshire Mercury*, 1901-39; merged with *Yorkshire Post*, 1939.)

LEEDS MERCURY Extraordinary. Leeds. [?]-1812-13-[?].
  b: L Ag 18, 1812; Jl 5, Ag 16, N 5, 1813.

LEEDS MONTHLY MAGAZINE. London. v1, no1-10, Mr-D 1829. m.
  a: ULSup. / *b:* LdL; LdP.

LEEDS PATRIOT and Yorkshire Advertiser. Leeds. no1+, 1825-33. w.
  a: CSmH no323, My 29, 1830. / *b:* L no 250-467, Ja 3, 1829-32.

LEEDS PHILOSOPHICAL and Literary Society. Report of the Council. London. v1+, 1820-date.
  a: ULS; ULSup. / *b:* EP v6; LdP 1822/23-date.

LEEDS PHILOSOPHICAL and Literary Society. Transactions. London. 1824-36.
  a: PPAP.

LEEDS PITT DINNER: Songs and Glees to be sung at the Leeds Pitt Dinner, at the Music Hall, Leeds. Leeds. [?]-1815-17-[?].
  b: LdP 1815-17.

LEEDS TEMPERANCE SOCIETY. Reports. Leeds. [?]-1831-1900-[?].
  b: LdP.

LEGAL AND MERCANTILE JOURNAL. London. 1819. w.
  b: L no1-7, Ag 6-S 17, 1819.

LEGAL EXAMINER. London. v1-3, 1831-33.
  a: ULS. / *b:* UCP; L; LLN.
  (Continued as *Legal Examiner and Law Chronicle*, 1833-35; as *Westminster Hall Chronicle and Legal Examiner*, 1835-36.)

LEGAL OBSERVER, or Journal of Jurisprudence. London. v1-32, 1831-46. w.
  a: ULS; ULSup. / *b:* UCP; BP; L; LLN; LLW.
  (Continued as *Legal Observer, Digest, and Journal of Jurisprudence*, 1847-53; as *Legal Observer and Solicitor's Journal*, 1854-56.)

LEGAL REFORMER. London. no1-10, N 7, 1819-Ja 9, 1820. w.
  b: L.

LEGAL REGISTER. London. no1-134, 1807-08.
  a: ULS.

LEGAL REVIEW. London. v1, N 1812-Jl 1813. 3 times a year.
  a: ULS. / *b:* LLN.

LEGISLATOR. London. 1817-18. w.
  b: L no49-61, Ja 4-Mr 28, 1818.

LEICESTER AND NOTTINGHAM Journal. (See *Leicester Journal.*)

LEICESTER CHRONICLE. Leicester. no1+, 1812-1915. w. (Also called *Leicester Chronicle and Mercury*. Subtitle varies.)
  b: L no842+, Ja 6, 1827-32; LcLC; LcP 1812-13; 1815-17; (1818-32).

LEICESTER CHRONICLE AND MERCURY. (See *Leicester Chronicle.*)

LEICESTER HERALD. Leicester. 1792-95.
  b: LcP; MR sc.nos. 1793-95.

LEICESTER HERALD. (See *Leicestershire Herald.*)

LEICESTER JOURNAL. Leicester. no1+, 1753-1920. w. (Dropped *and Nottingham* from title, perhaps in 1787. For a time called *Leicestershire Journal, and Midland Counties General Advertiser.*)
  a: CSmH O 29, 1824; NN My 21, Jl 16, 30, Ag 6, S 10, O 8, 1790; NNHi Ag 16, S 6, 27, 1805. / *b:* BP Jl 28, 1809; Mr 15, 1812; N 17, 1815; L O 26, 1805; My 6, 1808; S 13, 1811; 1827-32; LcLM; LcP; O 1789-1832 impf.

LEICESTERSHIRE HERALD, and General Advertiser. Leicester. no1-52, Jl 18, 1827-Jl 9, 1828. w.
   a: CSmH no52, Jl 9, 1828. / *b:* L; LcP.
   Continued as
LEICESTER HERALD. Leicester. no53+, Jl 16, 1828-1842.
   b: L; LcP.

LEICESTERSHIRE JOURNAL, and Midland Counties General Advertiser.
   (See *Leicester Journal.*)

LEINSTER CHRONICLE, or Parsontown Gazette. Parsontown. 1812/?.
   b: L no44, D 12, 1812.

LEINSTER EXPRESS. Maryborough. no1+, S 24, 1831-date. w.
   b: L.

LEINSTER JOURNAL.
   (See *Finn's Leinster Journal.*)

LEITH AND EDINBURGH TELEGRAPH. Leith. no1+, 1808-12. s.w.
   b: L no47-463, Ja 1809-D 1812, lacking 1810-11.

LEITH COMMERCIAL LIST. London. 1797-1905-[?].
   b: EP 1813-32.

LEITH DISPENSARY and Humane Society. Report. Leith. v1-2, 1827-28.
   b: UCP.
   Continued as
LEITH DISPENSARY and Edinburgh and Leith Humane Society. Report. Leith. v3-8, 1829-34.
   b: UCP.
   (Continued as *Edinburgh and Leith Humane Society, Dispensary and Casualty Hospital*, 1836.)

LEODIENSIAN: or Leeds Grammar School Magazine. Leeds. no1-12, Ag 1827-S 1828.
   b: L; LdL; LdP; O.

LESSON SYSTEM MAGAZINE, for Parents and Sunday School Teachers. Edinburgh. v1-2, 1831-35.
   a: ULS.

LETTER-BOX.
   (See *Letter-Box; or Edinburgh Weekly Censor.*)

LETTER BOX. London. no1-4, 1818.
   b: O no1, 4.

LETTER-BOX; or Edinburgh Weekly Censor. Edinburgh. no1-3, F 7, Mr 7, 1818. w. (Sometimes called *Edinburgh Weekly Censor.*)
   a: ULS. / *b:* EP.
   Continued as
LETTER-Box. Edinburgh. no4-20, Mr 21-Jl 4, 1818. w.
   a: ULS. / *b:* EP.

LETTERS; or a Review of the Political State of Europe. London. 1792.
   b: O.

LETTERS AND PAPERS on Agriculture, Planting, &c.
   (See *Bath and West and Southern Counties Society.*)

LETTERS FOR LITERARY LADIES. London. 1799.
   b: UCP.

LETTRES A MONSIEUR LE COMTE DE B... sur la révolution. London, Paris, v1-7, no1-51, Jl 12, 1789-Mr 28, 1790.
   a: ULS.
   (Superseded by *Courier Extraordinaire*, pub. in Paris.)

LETTRES AU REDACTEUR du Courier de Londres. London. no1-4, 1801.
   a: ULS.

THE LEWES AND BRIGHTHELMSTON Pacquet, and Weekly Advertiser for the County of Sussex. Lewes. 1789-90.
   b: BiP.

LEWIS'S COVENTRY RECORDER; or the Freeman's Advocate. Coventry. 1819.
   b: CvP [no1-8].

THE LIBERAL.
   (See *Weekly Times.*)

THE LIBERAL. Sheffield. no1, N 17, 1832.
   b: SP.

THE LIBERAL. Verse and Prose from the South. London. v1-2, 1822-23.
   a: ULS; ULSup. / *b:* UCP; BP; EU; HdP v1; L; LVA; MR; O.

THE LIBRARIAN; being an Account of Scarce, Valuable and Useful English Books, Manuscript Libraries, Public Records, &c. London. v1-4, no1-19, Jl 1808-Ja 1810. m. (Subtitle did not appear on v1-2.)
   a: ULS. / *b:* UCP; EP; KeP v1-3; L; LLL v1-3; TaP no1-12; WmP.

LIBRARY FOR THE PEOPLE. London. v1-3, 1826-27.
   b: O.

LIBRARY NEWSPAPER and Musical Journal. London. no1-6, N 1-D 6, 1806. w.
   b: L no1, 3-6.

LIBRARY OF ECCLESIASTICAL Knowledge. London. 1831-36. (*Miscellaneous Series*, v1-4, 1831-34; *Historical Series*, v1-2, 1831-36; *Critical Series*, v1, 1834; *Biographical Series*, v1, 1832.)
   b: L.

LIBRARY OF THE FINE ARTS; or Repertory of Painting, Sculpture, Architecture, and Engraving. London. v1-4, 1831-32. (Sometimes called *Arnold's Magazine of the Fine Arts.*)
   a: ULS. / *b:* UCP; C; EP; L; LGU; WmP.
   (Continued as *Arnold's Library of the Fine Arts*, 1833; as *Arnold's Magazine of the Fine Arts*, 1833-34.)

LICHFIELD MERCURY. Lichfield. no1+, 1815-33. (Subtitle varies.)
  a: CSmH Ap 22, 1828. / *b:* L no219+, Ja 1, 1830-1832; StfS (1815-19, 1823-27); sc. nos. 1828-31.
  (Continued with varying subtitles, 1833-date.)

LIFE IN LONDON. London. no1-23, Ja 13-Je 16, 1822. w.
  b: L.
  (Incorporated in *Bell's Life in London*)

LIFE IN LONDON. Liverpool. N 1824-O 1827.
  b: LvP N 1824-O 1827 impf.

LIGHT FROM THE WEST; or, the Cornish Parochial Visitor. London, Launceston. v1-17, 1832-48.
  a: ULS. / *b:* UCP; L.

LIGHT IN THE HOME and Tract Magazine.
  (See *Tract Magazine; or Christian Miscellany.*)

LIMERICK CHRONICLE. Limerick. 1768-date. s.w. (Called *Watson's Limerick Chronicle* for a time, apparently 1793-95.)
  a: CSmH S 17, 1823; MBAt Ap 6, 1805; MH sc.nos. 1813-14; / *b:* UCP; C Mr 28, 1792; L Ap 26, 1790; Ja 11, 1794; LmLC 1792; Ja 5-D 18, 1793; Ja 9, 1796-D 30, 1797; Ja 9, 1799-D 24, 1806; F 8, 1809-D 15, 1810; F 1, 1812-D 15, 1827; Ja 6, 1830-D 29, 1832; LmP Ja 1-Ap 5, N 5, 1794; Ja 7, Mr 14, 1795.

LIMERICK EVENING POST (and Clare Sentinel). Limerick. 1811-33. s.w. (Subtitle added 1828. Must temporarily have ceased publication for a time before 1821, as an advertisement in *Limerick Chronicle*, Mr 5, 1821, announces that publication will be resumed.)
  a: CSmH Je 5, 1827. / *b:* DL 1811-18; L 1828-32; LmP Jl 27, 31, 1820.
  (Continued as *Limerick Star and Evening Post*, 1834-38.)

LIMERICK HERALD. Limerick. no1+, Ap 18, 1831-1833.
  b: L.
  (Continued as *Limerick Evening Herald*, 1833-35; incorporated with *Limerick Times*, Ap 14, 1835.)

LIMERICK HERALD and Munster Advertiser. Limerick. My 29, 1788-D 19, 1795-[?].
  b: C Jl 8, 1790; D 19, 1795; DA sc.nos. 1789; LmP Ag 12, 1790.

LIMERICK JOURNAL. Limerick. 1779-1819/?. s.w.
  b: UCP; LmLC Ja 31-N 7, 1791; Je 12, Jl 10, 1802; LmP My 19, D 25, 1794; N 17, 1798; Ag 10, 1799.
  (For further bibliographical data see Robert Herbert's *Limerick Printers and Printing*, p. 52.)

LIMERICK MONTHLY MAGAZINE. Limerick. no1, Mr 1830.
  b: DL; O.

LIMERICK NEWS. Limerick. F 18, 1822-F 20, 1823. s.w.
  b: DA no2-106, F 21, 1822-F 20, 1823.

LIMERICK WEEKLY MAGAZINE; or Miscellaneous Repository. Limerick. 1790.
  b: DL no1-25, Je-D 1790.

LINCOLN AND HULL CHRONICLE.
  (See *Hull and Lincoln Chronicle.*)

LINCOLN AND LINCOLNSHIRE CABINET and Annual Intelligence . . . with a Monthly Retrospect of the Principal Events of the Country for 1826. Lincoln. 1827-29.
  b: L.

LINCOLN AND NEWARK TIMES.
  (See *Newark Times.*)

LINCOLN AND NEWARK TIMES, Stamford Champion, &c.
  (See *Champion of the East.*)

THE LINCOLN CABINET. Lincoln. v1, no1-12, F 1-Ap 18, 1832. w.
  b: L no4, 7-8; LnP.

LINCOLN DRAMATIC CENSOR. Lincoln. no1-4, O 21-N 18, 1809/?.
  a: ULS.

LINCOLN HERALD, and County Advertiser. no1+, June 1828-Ja 27, 1832. w.
  a: CSmH D 18, 1829. / *b:* L; LnP.
  Continued as
BOSTON, LINCOLN, AND LOUTH Herald. Boston, no189+, F 7, 1832-1835. w.
  b: L.
  (Continued as *Boston, Lincoln, Louth and Spalding Herald*, 1836-43; as *Boston Stamford, and Lincolnshire Herald*, 1843-53; as *Lincolnshire Herald*, 1854-94.)

LINCOLN MIRROR. Lincoln. v1, no1-7, S 26-N 7, 1832. w.
  b: LnP.

LINCOLN, RUTLAND AND STAMFORD Mercury. Stamford. 1784-date. w. (Preceded by *Stamford Mercury*, [1709-1732]; *Howgrave's Stamford Mercury*, [1732]-1736; *Stamford Mercury*, 1736-84.)
  a: CSmH N 16, 1832; CtY Ja 24, 1794-1832; MH 9 sc.nos. 1827-28; MeHi sc.nos. 1798. / *b:* GmP 1802-32; L 1789-94, 1799-1802, 1804-32; LLL 1805; LnLR; LnP 1793-1832.

LINCOLNSHIRE CHRONICLE and Leader. Lincoln. [?]-1832-date. w.
  (No issues before 1833 known. Data from Office of *Lincolnshire Chronicle*.)

LINCOLNSHIRE INDEPENDENT. The Whig for the Counties of Lincoln, Nottingham, &c. Lincoln. no1-3, Ja 4-18, 1832. w.
  b: L.

LINCOLNSHIRE MAGAZINE and Provincial Literary Repository.
  (See *Provincial Literary Repository.*)

THE LINGUIST; or Weekly Instructions in the French and German Languages. London. v1-2, 1825-26/?.
  a: ULS. / *b:* UCP; BP; O.

LINNEAN SOCIETY OF LONDON. Transactions. London. v1-30, 1791-1875; s2+, 1875-date.
  a: ULS; ULSup. / *b:* BP; C; CPL; DRS; IpP lacking v6; LCP; LR; WiP.

LION. London. v1-4, 1828-29.
  a: ULS. / *b:* UCP; BrP v1; GM; L.

LIST OF ALL THE OFFICERS of the Army and Royal Marines. London. 1756-1881. m. (Also known as *Army List.*)
  b: UCP; O 1812-date.
  (Continued as *Monthly Army List*, 1881-date.)

LIST OF BROKERS of the City of London. London. 1797-1885.
  b: LGU 1797, 1816, 1821-32.

LIST OF COMMUNICATIONS of the Literary and Philosophical Society of Liverpool.
  (See *Literary and Philosophical Society of Liverpool.*)

A LIST OF FLAG OFFICERS (and other Commissioned Officers) of his Majesty's Fleet, with the dates of their . . . Commissions. London. 1780-1861.
  b: UCP; L 1795-1832 impf.
  (Continued as *Active List of Flag-Officers, &c.*, 1862-date.)

LIST OF MEMBERS of the Royal Company of Archers, Edinburgh.
  (See *Royal Company of Archers, Edinburgh.*)

LIST OF OFFICE-BEARERS. . . [and] Report. Edinburgh and Leith Seaman's Friend Society. Leith. v1-2, 1820-23.
  b: UCP.
  Continued as
REPORT. Edinburgh and Leith Seaman's Friend Society. Leith. v3-4, 1824-27.
  b: UCP.

LIST OF OFFICERS of H.M. Marine Forces. London. 1783-date.
  b: UCP.

LIST OF THE BANKRUPTS, with their Dividends and Certificates. London. v1-2, 1794-95.
  b: L.

LIST OF THE [EAST INDIA] COMPANY'S Civil Servants, at their Settlements in the East Indies, the Island of St. Helena, and China. London. pt1-2, 1782-90.
  b: L.

LIST OF THE GENERAL AND FIELD Officers as they Rank in the Army, &c. London. 1754-1868.
  b: L.

LIST OF THE MASTERS, Medical Officers, and Pursers of His Majesty's Fleet. With the

Date of their First Warrants. London. 1827-30.
  b: L lacking 1828.

LIST OF THE OFFICERS of the Several District Corps of Ireland, together with Dates of their Respective Commissions and an Alphabetical Index. Dublin. 1797.
  b: L.

LIST OF THE OFFICERS of the Several Regiments and Battalions of Militia, and of the Several Regiments of Fencible Cavalry and Infantry upon the Establishment of Ireland. Dublin. v1-4, 1797-1800.
  b: L.

LIST OF THE OFFICERS of the Several Regiments and Corps of Fencible Cavalry and Infantry: of the Officers of the Militia of the Corps and Troops of Gentlemen and Yeomanry; and of the Corps and Companies of Volunteer Infantry. London. 1797-1800.
  b: L lacking 1798.

LIST OF THE OFFICERS of the Several Regiments and Corps of Militia: also of the several Fencible Regiments and of the New Independent Companies. London. 1793-1825.
  b: L lacking 1798, 1802, 1806, 1818-19, 1821-24.

LITERARY AND ANTIQUARIAN SOCIETY of Perth. Transactions. Perth. v1, 1827.
  a: ULS. / *b:* UCP; EP; NwS; PeP.

LITERARY AND BIOGRAPHICAL Magazine and British Review.
  (See *Literary Magazine and British Review.*)

LITERARY AND MASONIC MAGAZINE. Dublin. v1, Mr-D, 1802.
  b: DL.

LITERARY AND PHILOSOPHICAL Society of Liverpool. List of Communications. Liverpool. 1812-21.
  b: LP.

LITERARY AND PHILOSOPHICAL Society of Manchester. Memoirs. Manchester, v1-5, 1785-1802; s2, v1-15, 1805-60; s3, v1-10, 1862-87.
  a: ULS; ULSup. / *b:* UCP; BP; CPL; DRS; GeG 1789-1802; LP; LR.
  (Continued as *Memoirs and Proceedings, &c.*, 1888-date.)

LITERARY AND PHILOSOPHICAL Society of Newcastle-upon-Tyne. Reports. Newcastle-upon-Tyne. 1793-date.
  a: ULS.

LITERARY AND PHILOSOPHICAL Society of Portsmouth and Portsea. n.p. [?]-1827-1832/?.
  a: ULS.

LITERARY AND PHILOSOPHICAL Society of Sheffield. Reports. Sheffield. v1-65, 1824-88.
  b: LP.

LITERARY AND POLITICAL EXAMINER.
Cork. no1-4, Ja-My 1818. m.
  a: ULS. / *b:* DL no1-3; L no1.

LITERARY AND STATISTICAL Magazine
for Scotland. Edinburgh. v1-4, 1817-20. q.
  a: ULS. / *b:* UCP; DL; E; GM; L.
  Continued as
SCOTTISH EPISCOPAL REVIEW and Magazine. Edinburgh. v1-3, 1820-22. q.
  a: ULS. / *b:* L.

**LITERARY ANNUAL REGISTER; or, Rec-
ords of Literature, Domestic and Foreign.**
London. v1-2, 1807-08. a.; m. (Running title
for v1, *Records of Literature.*)
  a: ULS. / *b:* L.
  (Merged with *Literary Panorama.*)

**LITERARY BEACON; a Guide to Books, the
Drama, Music, and the Fine Arts.** London.
no1-12, Je 18-S 3, 1831; ns, no1-3, S 10-24,
1831. w.
  a: ULS. / *b:* L; O no1-3.

LITERARY BEE: or the New Family Library.
London. no1, 1817.
  b: L.

**LITERARY BLUE BOOK; or, Kalendar of
Literature, Science, and Art.** London. 1830.
  b: UCP; L; O.

LITERARY CABINET. Glasgow. no1-4, 1831.
  b: GM no4.

**LITERARY CABINET, and Journal of Belles-
Lettres, Fine Arts, Drama, &c.** London. no1-
3, F 17-Mr 3, 1827. w.
  b: L.

**LITERARY CHRONICLE and General Mis-
cellany of Science, Arts, History, Politics,
Morals, Manners, Fashions, and Amusements.**
London. 1818. w. (This magazine identical
with *Literary Journal, and General Miscellany of Science,* except that there is a variation in the dating of the issues.)
  b: L no6-16.

LITERARY CHRONICLE and Weekly Review.
London. v1-10, no1-471, 1819-29. w. (As
*Country Literary Chronicle and Weekly Re-
view,* 1819-24.)
  a: ULS. / *b:* UCP; E 1826; L; LLL no1-
96; O 1822-28.
  (Incorporated with *Athenaeum.*)

LITERARY CORONAL. Glasgow. 1825-28.
  b: DL; GM lacking 1827; L 1828.

LITERARY CYNOSURE. Edinburgh. no1,
1824.
  b: EP.

**LITERARY EXAMINER; consisting of the
Indicator, a Review of Books, and Miscellaneous Pieces in Prose and Verse.** London.
v1, no1-26, 1823. w.
  a: ULS; ULSup. / *b:* UCP; EU; L; LLL;
O.

**LITERARY EXPOSÉ and Fashionable Pro-
teus.**
  (See *Literary Humbug; or, Weekly Take-in.*)

**LITERARY GAZETTE, and Journal of Belles
Lettres.** London. no1-8, Ja 18-Mr 15, 1817.
w. (Also known as *Colburn's Literary Ga-
zette.*)
  a: ULS; ULSup. / *b:* UCP; BP; L; LLL;
LdL; MCh; NwL; SwP.
  Continued as
**LITERARY GAZETTE, Journal of Belles
Lettres, Politics, and Fashion.** London.
no9-28, Mr 22-Ag 2, 1817. w.
  a: ULS. / *b:* UCP; BP; L; LLL; LdL;
MCh; NwL; SwP.
  Continued as
**LITERARY GAZETTE, Journal of Belles
Lettres, Arts, Politics, &c.** London. v1-42;
ns, v1-8, 1817-62. w.
  a: ULS. / *b:* UCP; BP; CrP 1824-32; EP
1826-32; HdP 1829; L; LLL; LdL; MCh;
MR 1827-32; NwL lacking 1818, 1832; StfS
no259-362 for 1822-23; SwP; WcP My 2,
1829-1832.
  (Incorporated with *The Parthenon.*)

**LITERARY GAZETTE, Journal of Belles
Lettres, Arts, Politics, &c.**
  (See *Literary Gazette, and Journal of
Belles Lettres.*)

LITERARY GEM. London. 1830.
  b: UCP.

**LITERARY GOSSIP, a Series of Original
Essays and Poems.**
  (See *Gossip: a Series of Original Essays
and Letters.*)

**LITERARY GUARDIAN, and Spectator of
Books, Science, Fine Arts, the Drama, &c.**
London. v1-2, no1-45, 1831-32. (Subtitle varies.)
  a: ULS. / *b:* UCP; L; O no1.

LITERARY HUMBUG; or Weekly Take-in.
London. no1-6, My 14-Je 18, 1823. w.
  a: ULS. / *b:* BP; L; O.
  Continued as
**LITERARY EXPOSE and Fashionable Pro-
teus.** London. no7-13, My 21-S 10, 1823. w.
  a: ULS. / *b:* BP; L; O.

LITERARY JANUS. Kington. 1829.
  b: HfP; O.

**LITERARY JORDAN and Gazette of Belles
Lettres, Arts, Sciences, &c.** London. 1825.
(A lampoon on *The Literary Gazette.*)
  b: L.

**LITERARY JOURNAL; a Review of Domestic
and Foreign Literature.**
  (See *Literary Journal; a Review of Literature, Science,* &c.)

**LITERARY JOURNAL, a Review of Litera-
ture, Science, Manners, Politics.** London.
v1-5, 1803-05. w.; m.
  a: ULS. / *b:* UCP; EP v1; L; NwL v1;
SyP (1803-04).
  Continued as
**LITERARY JOURNAL; a Review of Domes-
tic and Foreign Literature, Science, Manners, Politics.** London. ns, v1-2, 1806. m.
  a: ULS. / *b:* UCP; L; NwL.

LITERARY JOURNAL. A Weekly Review. London. no 1-40, Ja 5-O 4, 1828. w.
   a: PP. / *b:* L.

LITERARY JOURNAL, and General Miscellany of Science, Arts, History, Politics, &c. London. v 1-2, no 1-59, Mr 29, 1818-My 8, 1819. w. (See *Literary Chronicle,* which is identical with this magazine except for slight variation in dates.)
   a: ULS. / *b:* L; O.

LITERARY LEISURE; or, the Recreations of Solomon Saunter, Esq. London. v 1-2, no 1-60, S 26, 1799-D 18, 1800. w.
   a: ULS. / *b:* O.

LITERARY LOUNGER. London. v 1, Ja-S 1826. m.
   a: ULS. / *b:* L no 1-3, 5-7; O.

LITERARY MAGAZINE, or Monthly Epitome of British Literature.
   (See *Monthly Epitome and Catalogue of New Publications.*)

LITERARY MAGAZINE and British Review. London. v 1-12, 1788-94. m. (Separate parts have title, *Literary and Biographical Magazine and British Review.*)
   a: ULS; ULSup. / *b:* UCP; BP v 9-12; BdP 1789-90; 1791, pt 1; 1793, pt 2; CrP v 3, 12; L; O v 1.

LITERARY MAGNET, or Monthly Journal of the Belles Lettres.
   (See *Literary Magnet of the Belles Lettres, Science,* &c.)

LITERARY MAGNET of the Belles Lettres, Science, and the Fine Arts. London. v 1-4, 1824-26. w. (Pt 1 has title, *Weekly Literary Magnet.*)
   a: ULS. / *b:* UCP; DL F-O 1824; L; LVA v 1-2.
Continued as
LITERARY MAGNET or Monthly Journal of the Belles Lettres. London. ns, v 1-4, 1826-28. m. (ULS erroneously gives ns, v 1-5.) (Also known as *Wright's Literary Magnet.*)
   a: ULS. / *b:* UCP; L.

LITERARY MELANGE; or Weekly Register of Literature and the Arts. Glasgow, v 1-2, 1822-23. w.
   b: GM v 1; O.

LITERARY MIRROR. Montrose. 1793-1815. a.
   b: O 1810.
   (Additional data in S N & Q, s 1, III. 6-7, & III.55.)

LITERARY MIRROR; or British and Continental Magazine. London. no 1, N 1802. m.
   b: O.

LITERARY MISCELLANY; or, Selections and Extracts, Classical and Scientific. Stourport, Poughnill. v 1-21, 1801-12. ir.
   a: ULS; CtY; ICU. / *b:* UCP.

LITERARY MUSEUM; containing copious Extracts from and a Review of all the Books of acknowledged Merit of the Present Day. London. F-O 1828. m. (Running title, *Monthly Literary Journal.*)
   b: L.

LITERARY MUSEUM; or, Weekly Magazine. Belfast. 1793.
   b: BlL no 2-5.

LITERARY MUSEUM and Critical Review. Glasgow. v 1-2, 1830-32.
   b: GM v 1; L v 2.

LITERARY MUSEUM and Register of Arts, Sciences, &c.
   (See *Museum; or, Record of Literature, Fine Arts,* &c.)

LITERARY OLIO. Dundee. no 1-14, Ja 10-Jl 1824. f.
   b: DnP lacking no 12-13.

LITERARY OMNIBUS; or Journal of Literature, Criticism, &c. Edinburgh?. no 1-4, N 12-D 3, 1831. w.
   b: ESL.

LITERARY PANORAMA. London. v 1-15, 1806-14; ns, v 1-9, 1814-19. m. (*Literary Annual Register, or Records of Literature* merged with this in 1809. After v 9 incorporated with *New Monthly Magazine.* Subtitle varies.)
   a: ULS. / *b:* UCP; L.

LITERARY PANORAMA, and National Register, &c.
   (See *Literary Panorama.*)

LITERARY PANORAMA, being a Compendium of National Papers, &c.
   (See *Literary Panorama.*)

LITERARY PHOENIX. Birmingham. v 1, no 1-4, N 1829-F 1830. m.
   a: ULS. / *b:* UCP; BP.

LITERARY POCKET-BOOK; or, Companion for the Lover of Nature and Art. London. 1818.
   b: L.

LITERARY RAMBLER, a Magazine of Literature, Science, and Art. Glasgow. 1832.
   a: ULS. / *b:* UCP; E no 1-7; GM.

LITERARY REGISTER of the Fine Arts, Sciences, and Belles Lettres. London. no 1-56, Jl 6, 1822-Jl 26, 1823. w. (Also known as *Weekly Register of the Fine Arts, Sciences, and Belles Lettres.*)
   a: CtY no 1-44, lacking no 37-39. / *b:* CrP no 27-52; L; O no 1.

LITERARY REPORTER; or, Weekly Miscellany. Glasgow. v 1-2, 1822-23.
   b: GM v 1, lacking no 14; v 2, lacking pp. 411-30.

LITERARY REVIEW and Historical Journal. London. v 1-3, 1794-95.
   b: UCP.

LITERARY REVIEW and Political Journal.
London. no1-15, O 1, 1794-My 15, 1795. f.
(No issues known. Data from CBEL, II.
682. May be a confusion with *Literary Review and Historical Journal*.)

**LITERARY SKETCH-BOOK, consisting of
Reviews of Popular Works; Original Sketches
of Characters, Manners and Society, &c.** London. v1, no1-37, Ag 16, 1823-Ap 28, 1824/?.w.
a: ULS; CtY no1-26. / *b:* UCP; L.

LITERARY SOCIETY OF BOMBAY. Bombay
Branch of the Royal Asiatic Society of Great
Britain and Ireland. Transactions. London.
v1-3, 1819-23. (In ULS under *Royal Asiatic
Society of Great Britain and Ireland.*)
a: ULS. / *b:* UCP.

LITERARY SOCIETY OF MADRAS. Transactions. London. 1827.
a: ULS. / *b:* UCP.

**LITERARY SOUVENIR, or Cabinet of Poetry
and Romance.** London. v1-10, 1825-34. a.
a: ULS; ULSup. / *b:* UCP; BP v5; CrP
1827-31; L; LLL 1830-32.
(Continued as *Literary Souvenir, and Cabinet of Modern Art*, 1835; as *Cabinet of
Modern Art, and Literary Souvenir*, 1836-
37.)

LITERARY SPECULUM. London. v1-3, 1821-
23. m.
a: ULS. / *b:* DL; L v1-2; O v1-2.

LITERARY SPECULUM. London. v1-2, no1-
42, 1824.
b: O.

**LITERARY TEST; a Liberal, Moral, and Independent Weekly Review of Books, the Stage
and the Fine Arts.** London. no1-5, 1832.
(Subtitle varies.)
b: UCP; O no1.

THE LIVER, a Record of Minor Letters, Suggestions . . . respecting the Town of Liverpool. Liverpool. Jl 1824-F 1825.
b: L no1-2, 6; LvP.

THE LIVERPOOL and Lancaster Herald.
Liverpool. 1788-[1789]. w.
(No issues known. Data from CBEL, II.
725.)
Possibly continued as
LIVERPOOL WEEKLY HERALD. Liverpool. [?]-1792-[?]. w.
(No issues known. Data from CBEL, II.725
and C & K 1516a.)

LIVERPOOL and Manchester Quarterly Magazine. Liverpool. no1+, Mr 18, 1818-1819. q.
(First published as *Liverpool Quarterly Magazine.*)
b: LvP.
Continued as
ROYAL MAGAZINE. Liverpool. Mr-D 1820.
b: LvP.

LIVERPOOL APOLLONIUS; or, the Geometrical and Philosophical Repository. London.
v1-2, 1823-24.
a: ULS. / *b:* UCP.

LIVERPOOL CHRONICLE.
(See *Liverpool Commercial Chronicle.*)

LIVERPOOL CHRONICLE; or, Political Intelligencer, &c.
(See *Liverpool Chronicle and Commercial
Advertiser.*)

**LIVERPOOL CHRONICLE and Commercial
Advertiser.** Liverpool. Ja 1804-D 1807. w.
a: MBAt N 7, 1804; Ap 9, 1806. / *b:* LvP.
Continued as
LIVERPOOL CHRONICLE; or, Political Intelligencer and Commercial Advertiser. Liverpool. D 9-30, 1807. w.
b: LvP.

LIVERPOOL COMMERCIAL CHRONICLE.
Liverpool. no1-109, D 17, 1825-Ja 12, 1828.
w.
a: CSmH Mr 17, 1827; CtY Je 16, 1827. /
b: L; LvP.
Continued as
LIVERPOOL CHRONICLE. Liverpool. no
110-5092. Ja 19, 1828-S 26, 1868.
a: CSmH Mr 29, 1828; DLC Ap 16, 1831;
MH 4 sc.nos. 1830-31. / *b:* L; LvP.

**LIVERPOOL COURIER (and Commercial
Register).** Liverpool. no1+, 1808-63. w. (Subtitle varies.)
a: CSmH Ag 13, 1828; CtY F 8, 1832; DLC
Ap 28, 1820; S 16, 1829; MeB 1802-13 &
1816-19 impf. / *b:* L no1, Ja 6, 1808;
no940+, Ja 4, 1826-32.
(Continued as *Daily Courier*, 1863-82;
Liverpool Courier, 1882-1922; *Daily Courier*, 1922-29.)

**LIVERPOOL DRAMATIC CENSOR; or Theatrical Recorder; containing Strictures on Actors and Actresses, and a Critical Analysis
of every Popular Dramatic Composition represented at the Theatre Royal, in this Town,
during the Season.** Liverpool. no1-4, Je 8-Jl
1, 1806. ir.
a: ULS. / *b:* LvP.

LIVERPOOL DRAMATIC JOURNAL. Liverpool. no1, 1832.
b: L.

LIVERPOOL EXAMINER, a Monthly Magazine. Liverpool. no1, 1832.
b: L.

LIVERPOOL FREEMAN; or Weekly Magazine. Liverpool. no1-6, 1816. w.
b: L no1, 3-4,6.

**LIVERPOOL GENERAL ADVERTISER; or,
the Commercial Register.** Liverpool. no1+,
1765-1832-[?].
b: LvP 1789-98, My 1814-1832.

LIVERPOOL GLEANER. Liverpool. no1-2,
Mr 25-Ap 1, 1817. w.
b: L; LvP.

LIVERPOOL HERALD. Liverpool. 1831. w.
a: CSmH no1, Ja 6, 1831.

**LIVERPOOL JOURNAL, and Lancashire
Weekly Express.** Liverpool. no1-2722, Ja 2,

1830-1884. w. (Subtitle varies.)
   a: CSmH Jl 17, 1830; PPL Mr 3, Ap 14, Ag 4, 1832. / *b:* L.

LIVERPOOL LADIES' MAGAZINE; or, Lancashire Witch. Liverpool. no1, 1829.
   b: L.

LIVERPOOL MAGAZINE and General Provincial Miscellany. Liverpool. Ja-N 1816. m.
   a: ULS. / *b:* L; LvP.

LIVERPOOL MERCANTILE GAZETTE. Liverpool. 1804. t.w.
   a: MBAt Mr 3, 1804.

LIVERPOOL MERCURY. Liverpool. no1+, 1811-1904. w.;d. (Subtitles vary: ...*and Lancashire General Advertiser; ...or, Commercial, Literary, and Political Herald.*)
   a: ULSup; CtY Jl 5, 1811-1832; DLC Jl 5, 1811-1825; Ja 5, 1827-D 24, 1830; MH Ag 19, 1814; MnU Jl 1811-Jl 1821; Jl 1822-Je 1823; D 1825-1832; NNHi Jl 5, 1811-D 26, 1828; NcD Jl 1818-Je 1819. / *b:* BkP Jl 1811-D 1813; BtlP 1812-14; L; LvP Jl 5, 1811-Je 1823; Mr 1827-D 1832; WiP 1816-18.
   (Amalgamated with *Liverpool Daily Post.*)

LIVERPOOL MONTHLY MAGAZINE. Liverpool. v1, no1-2, 1817. m.
   b: L.

LIVERPOOL PHOENIX. Liverpool. 1790-92-[?]. w.
   (No issues known. Data from CBEL,II. 725 and C & K, 1515b.)

LIVERPOOL QUARTERLY MAGAZINE.
   (See *Liverpool and Manchester Quarterly Magazine.*)

LIVERPOOL REPOSITORY of Literature, Philosophy, and Commerce. Liverpool. Ja-D 1826.
   a: ULS. / *b:* L; LvP.

LIVERPOOL SATURDAY'S ADVERTISER. Liverpool. 1805-28. w.
   a: CSmH My 18, 1822; CtY F 7, 1818; MBAt Mr 15, O 11, 1806; WHi My 11, Jl 27, 1805; Jl 26, Ag 16, O 25, N 1, 1806. / *b:* L no1698+, Ja 4-D 1823, lacking O4; D 3, 10, 1825; 1826-Ag 2, 1828.
   Continued as
SATURDAY'S ADVERTISER. Liverpool. no1990+, Ag 9, 1828-Mr 9, 1833. w.
   a: MH 3 sc.nos. 1830-32. / *b:* L.

LIVERPOOL SPECTATOR, a Weekly Periodical. Liverpool. 1830.
   b: L no1.

LIVERPOOL STANDARD. Liverpool. no1-1739, N 23, 1832-1856. w.
   b: L.

LIVERPOOL TEACHERS' MAGAZINE; or, Museum of Science and Literature. Liverpool. 1826.
   b: L no1.

LIVERPOOL THEATRICAL INVESTIGATOR and Review of Amusements. Liverpool. v1-2, 1821-22/?. (Title varies slightly.)
   a: ULS; ULSup. / *b:* LLL My 29-D 1, 1821; LvP My-D 1821; Je-N 1822.

LIVERPOOL TIMES, and Billinge's Advertiser.
   (See *Williamson's Liverpool Advertiser.*)

LIVERPOOL TRADE LIST. Liverpool. [1794]-1798-1800. w.
   a: L no234-305, Jl 26, 1798-Ja 5, 1800.

LIVERPOOL WEEKLY HERALD.
   (See *Liverpool and Lancaster Herald.*)

LIVERSEY'S MORAL REFORMER.
   (See *Moral Reformer and Protector against the Vices, Abuses, and Corruptions of the Age.*)

LLEUAD YR OES; neu amgeueddfa fisol o wybodaeth mewn crefydd, moes, athroniaeth, a hanes am 1827(-1830). Abertawy, Aberystwyth, Llanymddyfri. v1-4, 1827-30.
   a: ULS. / *b:* UCP; CrP; L.

LLOYD'S EVENING POST (and British Chronicle). London. 1757-1808-[1815?]. t.w.
   a: DLC Ja 28, 1793; Jl 18, 1800; ICU (Ja 3-Je 22, 1791); MB N 25, 1791-Ap 7, 1794; Ja 1795-N 10, 1797; MBAt O 23, 1789; MnU (D 30, 1789-D 31, 1790). / *b:* UCP; L 1790-1805; LGU 1789-N 16, 1808; NwS [1797].

LLOYD'S LIST. London. 1762-1884. s.w. (Also with subtitle after 1872.)
   a: NNHi Ja 1, 1796-D 11, 1798; Ja 10, 1800-D 28, 1802; NcD (1806, 1809-13, 1820). / *b:* L 1790-1832.
   (Continued as *Shipping and Mercantile Gazette and Lloyd's List,* 1884-1914; as *Lloyd's List (and Shipping Gazette),* 1914-date.)

LOCAL ACTS. London. 1815-date.
   b: UCP.

LOCAL REGISTER, a Chronological Account of Occurrences and Facts connected with the Town and Neighborhood of Sheffield from the earliest Period to the Year 1829, [1868-72]. Sheffield, 1830, 1868-72. a. (Discontinued 1830-67).
   b: L; SP.

LODGE'S PEERAGE.
   (See *Peerage (and Baronetage) of the British Empire.*)

LOG BOOK; or, Nautical Miscellany. London. no1-31, 1830.
   b: UCP.

LOITERER. London. v1-2, 1792.
   b: UCP; DL.

THE LOITERER, a Periodical Work. Oxford. v1-2, no1-60, Ja 31, 1789-Mr 20, 1790. w.
   a: ULS; ULSup. / *b:* UCP.

THE LOITERER; or Universal Essayist.
London. no 1-8, N 12-D 31, 1796.
  b: UCP; L no 1-2.

LONDON ALFRED; or, People's Recorder.
London. no 1-12, Ag 25-N 17, 1819. w.
  a: ULS. / b: UCP.

LONDON ALMANACK. London. 1734-1895.
  b: LGU.

LONDON AND EDINBURGH Philosophical
Magazine, and Journal of Science.
(See *Philosophical Magazine.*).

LONDON AND PARIS Ladies Magazine of
Fashion, &c.)
  (See *Beau Monde Magazine; or Monthly
Journal of Fashion.*)

LONDON AND PROVINCIAL Sunday Gazette. London. [1808]-1810-23. w.
  a: CSmH Mr 25, 1810. / b: L no 488-589,
Ja 6, 1818-My 11, 1823; O Je 24, 1810.

LONDON, BRITISH AND FOREIGN Price
Current.
(See *London Price Current.*)

LONDON CALENDAR, or Court and City
Register.
(See *English Registry, &c.*)

LONDON CATALOGUE OF BOOKS. London.
1700-1855, [printed 1773-1855]. (Also known
as *English Catalogue of Books.* United with
British Catalogue of Books and with *English
Catalogue of Books.*)
  b: UCP; EP 1801-32; GeG 1800-22; HdP
1801-32; LP; LU 1801-32; SP 1801-32;
SptP 1801-32.

LONDON CHRISTIAN INSTRUCTOR; or Congregational Magazine. London. v1-7, 1818-
24. m.
  a: ULS. / b: UCP; L; MR.
  Continued as
CONGREGATIONAL   MAGAZINE.   New
Series. London. v1-12, 1825-36; ns, v1-9,
1837-45.
  a: ULS; ULSup. / b: UCP; E v3-5,7; L;
MR.
  (Continued as *Biblical Review and Congregational Magazine,* 1846-50.)

LONDON CHRONICLE. London. 1765-1823.
t.w. (Preceded by *London Chronicle; or, Universal Evening Post,* 1757-65.)
  a: ULS; ULSup; C-S 83 sc nos. 1789-92;
complete Ja-Je 1793; CU Ja-Je 1789; 1790;
Jl 1791-1805; 1807-11, 1816-19; 1821-22;
CtY 1789-Jl 15, 1822; DLC (Ja-O 29, 1796;
1797-1800); 1801-Je 29, 1807; 1808; Ag
28-D 29, 1809; (Ja 1-Je 29, 1812); 1813-
16; ICN 1789-90; ICU 1800-Ap 28, 1823,
lacking 15 sc.nos.; IU 1789-91; MB Ja-
Mr 1789; 1793; 1813-20; MBAt Jl 1, 1790-
Je 30, 1791; 1793; Jl-D 1794; Ja 13, 15,
31, 1795; Ja-Je 1796; Ja-Je 1797; MiD-B
1796-97; Je 1798-1803, 6 nos. missing;
MiU (1792,1797-99, Ja-O 1800); MnU 1789-
Je 1812; NN 1789; Ja 2-F 25, Mr 2-30,
1790; 1791-92; Jl 2-D 31, 1793; Ja 2-Je

28, 1794; (1797); Ja 6-Ag 18, 25-29, 1798;
NNHi 1789-95; NcD Ja-Je 1789; 1790-1806;
NjP 1809-14; OClWHi Jl-D 10, 1799; PPHi
D 31, 1795-Je 30, 1796; Ag 13-D 31, 1796;
PPL Je 29-D 31, 1793; PU D 30, 1790-
Je 30, 1791; TxU (1790-99). / b: UCP;
BP v67 for 1790; v69-70 for 1791; BdP
1819; BiP Ja 31-My 2, 5-14, 19-30, Je 6-
9, 1789; Ap 17-21, 28-My 3, 1792; D 17-
20, 1792; EP sc.nos. 1789-93; ExP (S
1789-D 1795); L [1789-96, 1798-1802,
1818-23]; LGU 1789-Ap 28, 1823; LLL D
31, 1796-Je 29, 1797; MR 1789-92; NwS
53 sc.nos. 1795; PlP Ap 17, 19, 1792;
PrH 1789-Je 1804.
  (In 1824 united with *London Packet* and
continued as *London Packet; or New
Lloyd's Evening Post.* See *London Packet* for details.)

LONDON COAL MARKET. Newcastle-upon-
Tyne. Je 26, 1822-D 30, 1831.
  b: L.
  Continued as
PRICES OF COAL at the London Coal Market. Newcastle-upon-Tyne. Ja 2, 1832-1834.
  b: L.
  (Continued as *An Account of Coals, etc.,*
at *London Market offered for Sale,* 1834-
41.)

LONDON CO-OPERATIVE MAGAZINE.
(See *Co-operative Magazine and Monthly
Herald.*)

LONDON CORRESPONDING SOCIETY. Publications. London. [?]-1792-95/?.
  a: MB (1792-95); PPHi O 26, 1795.

LONDON, EDINBURGH, AND DUBLIN Philosophical Magazine and Journal of Science.
(See *Philosophical Magazine, &c.*)

LONDON EVENING CHRONICLE. London.
no 1-133, Ag 2, 1824-N 7, 1825.
  b: L.

LONDON EVENING POST. London. no 1-
8553, 1727-1806. t.w. (Subtitle varies).
  a: ULS; ICU 73 sc.nos. 1789-93; NN N 23,
26, 1805. / b: UCP; L 1789-1806 impf.;
LGU D 26-29, 1789; Ap 5-7, 1792; Ap 28-
My 1, 1792; MR sc.nos. 1792-1801; NpP
Ag 27-29, 1805.

LONDON FEMALE PENITENTIARY. Annual Reports. London. [1808]-1811-14. a.
  b: LGU 1811, 1814.

LONDON FREE PRESS. London. no 1-24, F
11, Jl 22, 1827. w.
  a: CSmH no 1, F 11, 1827. / b: L.

LONDON GAZETTE. London. no 24+, 1666-
date. (Preceded by *Oxford Gazette,* 1665-66.
Numerous issues were called *Supplement to
the London Gazette;* others, *London Gazette
Extraordinary.*)
  a: ULS; CSmH (1789-1832); CSt D 27,
1808-32; CtY (1790); 1802-06; Jl 1807-Je
1808; 1809-32; MB; MBAt; MnU (1789-
1832); NN; TxU 56 sc.nos. 1789-98. / b:
BP; EP My 31, 1803-1832 impf.; L lack-

ing Ja 3-D 28, 1824; LGU; LIT; LLG; LLW; LMT; LdL; LvP (1814-24); NwS sc. nos. 1811-12; sc.nos. 1816-19; sc.nos. 1822-26; sc.nos. 1829-30; sc.nos. 1832.

LONDON GAZETTE EXTRAORDINARY. Published by Anticipation. London. [?]-1681-1817-[?].
 a: ULS. / b: L N 8, 1803.

LONDON GAZETTEER. London. 1809.
 b: L Prospectus only.

LONDON HERALD and Evening Post. London. [1796]-1799-[?]. s.w.
 b: L no400-402, F 9-16, 1799; MR sc.nos. 1799.
 (Perhaps incorporated with *Express and Evening Chronicle.*)

LONDON HIBERNIAN SOCIETY. Report. London. v1-41, [1806]-47.
 b: UCP.

LONDON IMPORTED. London. [?]-[1683]-1794-1817-[1838?]. d.
 a: NcD (1794, 1808-09, 1811-Ap 12, 1817).
 (Perhaps continued as *London Customs Bill of Entry*, 1839-date. Data from CBEL, II.718.)

LONDON INFIRMARY for Curing Diseases of the Eye. [Later *London Ophthalmic Hospital.*] Annual Reports. London. v1-30, [?]-1807-1834.
 b: LCP lacking v1-2.

LONDON JOURNAL of Arts and Sciences; containing Reports of all new Patents, &c. London. v1-14, 1820-27; ns, v1-9, 1828-32. m.
 a: ULS; ULSup. / b: UCP; DRS ns, v1-9; GM ns, v4-6; L; LP; LdP lacking v1-4, 9.
 Continued as
LONDON JOURNAL of Arts and Sciences, and Repertory of Patent Inventions. Conjoined Series. London. v1-45, 1832-54.
 a: ULS; ULSup. / b: UCP; L; LP; LdP.
 (Continued as *Newton's London Journal of Arts and Sciences*, 1855-66.)

LONDON JOURNAL OF LITERATURE. London. no1-2, My 5-12, 1821. w.
 b: L.

LONDON KALENDAR.
 (See *Court and City Register.*)

LONDON LITERARY CHRONICLE. London. v1, 1828.
 a: ULS.
 (Merged into *Athenaeum.*)

LONDON MAGAZINE. (Baldwin's). London. v1-10, 1820-24; ns, v1-10, 1825-28; s3, v1-3, 1828-29. m. (The first two vols. of s2 has title, *London Magazine and Review*. Sometimes called *Baldwin's London Magazine* to distinguish it from *Gold's London Magazine.*)
 a: ULS; ULSup. / b: UCP; BdP 1820-21, 1825-29; HdP 1821-22; Ja-Ap 1825; L; LGU; LLL; LVA v1-10; LdL 1823-28; LvP v1-7, 10; SwP v1-10; ns, v1-2; WcP v1-10.

LONDON MAGAZINE; and Monthly Critical and Dramatic Review. (Gold's). London. v1-2, 1820. m. (Also called Gold's *London Magazine* to distinguish it from *Baldwin's London Magazine.*)
 a: ULS. / b: UCP; L; LLL.
 United with *Theatrical Inquisitor; or, Literary Mirror* and continued as
LONDON MAGAZINE and Theatrical Inquisitor. London. v3-4, 1821. m. (From F 1821 the numbers are entitled *Gold's London Magazine and Theatrical Inquisitor.*)
 a: ULS. / b: UCP; L; LLL v3.

LONDON MAGAZINE AND REVIEW.
 (See *London Magazine (Baldwin's.)*)

LONDON MAGAZINE and Theatrical Inquisitor.
 (See *London Magazine; and Monthly Critical Dramatic Review.*)

LONDON MECHANICS' MAGAZINE, Museum, Register, Journal, and Gazette. London. 1829-38.
 b: L lacking Jl, Ag 8, 1829-Ja 1830; F 13-27, Jl 17, 31, 1830.

LONDON MECHANICS' REGISTER. London. v1-4, 1824-26.
 a: ULS; ULSup. / b: UCP; L; LGU; O.
 Continued as
NEW LONDON MECHANICS' REGISTER, and Magazine of Science and the Useful Arts, embracing exclusive and authentic Reports of the Lectures delivered at the London Mechanics Institution. London. v1-2, 1827-28.
 a: ULS. / b: UCP; L; LGU.

LONDON MEDICAL and Physical Journal.
 (See *Medical and Physical Journal.*)

LONDON MEDICAL and Surgical Journal. London. v1-2, 1828-29.
 a: ULS. / b: UCP; L.
 Incorporated with *London Medical Repository, Monthly Journal, and Review* and continued as
LONDON MEDICAL and Surgical Journal, including the London Medical Repository. London. v3-7, 1829-31; ns, v1-8, 1832-36; s3, v1-11, 1832-37.
 a: ULS. / b: UCP; L; LS; O.

LONDON MEDICAL and Surgical Spectator; or, Monthly Register of the Modern State and Improvements of Medicine. London. v1-3, no1-14, 1808-09/?. m.
 a: ULS. / b: UCP; LS v1-2.

LONDON MEDICAL GAZETTE; being a Weekly Journal of Medicine and the Collateral Sciences. London. v1-35, 1827-45; ns, v1-13, 1845-51. w. (Incorporated with *Medical Times.*)
 a: ULS; ULSup. / b: UCP; L; LMA; LCP; LS.

LONDON MEDICAL JOURNAL. London. v1-11, 1781-90. q.
 a: ULS; ULSup. / b: UCP; L; LMA; LCP.
 Continued as

MEDICAL FACTS and Observations. London. v1-8, 1791-1800. q.
  a: ULS; ULSup. / *b:* UCP; L; LS.

LONDON MEDICAL REPOSITORY, Monthly Journal and Review.
  (See *London Medical, Surgical, and Pharmaceutical Repository.*)

LONDON MEDICAL REVIEW. London. v1-5, 1808-12.
  a: ULS. / *b:* UCP; LMA v1-4; LS.

LONDON MEDICAL REVIEW.
  (See *London Medical Review and Magazine.*)

LONDON MEDICAL REVIEW and Magazine. London. v1-6, 1799-1801. m.
  a: ULS. / *b:* UCP; L; LCP; LS.
  Continued as
LONDON MEDICAL REVIEW. London. v7-8, 1802. m.
  a: ULS. / *b:* UCP; LCP v1; LS.

LONDON MEDICAL, Surgical, and Pharmaceutical Repository. London. v1, 1814. m.
  a: ULS. / *b:* UCP; L; LCP; LS; MCh.
  Continued as
LONDON MEDICAL REPOSITORY, Monthly Journal and Review. London. v2-20, 1815-23; ns, v1-3, 1824-25; s3, v1-6, 1825-28. m.
  a: ULS. / *b:* UCP; L lacking pp. 1-96 or v2; part of v6; v7-9; part of v10; LCP; LS; MCh v2-20; ns, v1-2.
  Incorporated with *London Medical and Surgical Journal* and continued as
LONDON MEDICAL and Surgical Journal, including the London Medical Repository. London. v3-7, 1829-31; ns, v1-8, 1832-36; s3, v1-11, 1832-37.
  a: ULS. / *b:* C; L; LCP; O.

LONDON MERCANTILE JOURNAL.
  (See *Mercantile Journal.*)

LONDON MERCANTILE PRICE CURRENT. London. [?]-1818-1864. s.w.
  a: CSmH My 25, 1830. / *b:* L Mr 18, 1828.

LONDON MERCURY. London. no1+, Ag 12-D 23, 1826. w.
  a: CSmH no4, S 2, 1826. / *b:* BP S 30, 1826; L.

LONDON MERCURY. London. no1-41, Ja 2-Jl 6, 1828. s.w.
  b: L.

LONDON MISCELLANY. London. no1-7, 1829.
  b: O.

LONDON MISCELLANY, a Repertorium of Useful Information, Instruction, and Amusement, &c. London. no1-7, [1825?].
  b: L; O.

LONDON MISSIONARY SOCIETY. Quarterly Chronicle of the Transactions. London. v1-3, no1-64, 1815-32.
  a: ULS.

LONDON MODERATOR and National Adviser. London. 1813-23. w.
  a: CtY S 9, 23, 1818; Jl 14, 28, 1819; DLC ns, v5, no314, Ag 5, 1818. / *b:* L (1813-14); Ja 7, 1818-My 6, 1823.

LONDON MONTHLY REGISTER. London. 1805.
  b: L Prospectus only.

LONDON MONTHLY REVIEW. London. 1787-1809.
  (Recorded by ULS, CBEL, and C & K, but really a confusion of titles. Should be *Monthly Review*, the error arising from the fact that Georgetown University Library's set of *Monthly Review* has *London Monthly Review* on the spines of the various volumes.)

LONDON MUSEUM; or Record of Literature, Fine Arts, &c.
  (See *Museum; or, Record of Literature, Fine Arts, &c.*)

LONDON NEW PRICE CURRENT. London. 1814-70. w.
  a: CSmH O 16, 1829. / *b:* L Ag 2, 1814; S 2, 1817; Ja 2, 1818-1831.

LONDON OLIO. London. no1-10, Ja 6-Mr 9, 1816. w.
  a: ULS. / *b:* L; O.

LONDON OPHTHALMIC HOSPITAL.
  (See *London Infirmary for Curing Diseases of the Eye.*)

LONDON ORIENTAL INSTITUTION. Report. London. v1, 1828.
  b: UCP.

LONDON PACKET; or New Lloyd's Evening Post. London. [?]-1776-1836. t.w. (Title varies slightly. Preceded by *London Packet*, [1769]-1771; *London Packet; or New Evening Post*, 1771-[1772]; *London Packet and General Hue and Cry*, [1772]-[?].
  a: ULS; CtY (Ja 21-Mr 13, 1789; 1800-01); 3 sc.nos. 1820-21; Ja 2-Je 21, 1826; (1831); DLC (Ap 18-D 31, 1800); (1802, many nos. mutilated); ICN Jl 26, 1799-Ja 1, 1802, lacking 6 nos; ICU Ap 10-13, 1789; IU 1808, 1813-14, 1818, 1820; MBAt F 14-17, 21-24, 1794; MHi Mr 7, 9, 12, 1804; D 1805; (My-D 1811); (1812-O 1814; Ap 19-D 1815). / *b:* UCP; L 1791-1832 impf.; LGU N 18, 1808-1811; 1813-16; 1818-27.

LONDON PACKET AND CHRONICLE, and Lloyd's Evening Post.
  (See *London Packet; or, New Lloyd's Evening Post.*)

LONDON PACKET and Lloyd's Evening Post.
  (See *London Packet; or, New Lloyd's Evening Post.*)

LONDON PENNY JOURNAL. London. My 12-Jl 7, 1832.
  b: L; O no1.

LONDON PILOT. London. 1809.
  a: IP Ag 17, 1809.

LONDON POLITICIAN. London. no1, My 31,
1815. w.
  b: O.

LONDON PRICE CURRENT. London. no1-
220, Ja 1, 1822-Mr 28, 1826.
  b: L.
  Continued as
BRITISH AND FOREIGN PRICE CURRENT.
London. no221-288, Ap 4, 1826-Jl 17, 1827.
w.
  b: L. ·
  Continued as
LONDON PRICE CURRENT. London. no
289-294, Jl 24-Ag 28, 1827. w.
  b: L. .
  Continued as
LONDON, BRITISH, AND FOREIGN Price
Current. no295-329, S 4, 1827-Ap 29, 1828.
w.
  b: L.
  Continued as
BRITISH FOREIGN PRICE CURRENT.
London. no330-525, My 6, 1828-Je 21, 1832.
w.
  b: L.

LONDON PRICE CURRENT. London. [1776]-
1789-[?]. w.
  b: L no700, S 11, 1789; no704, O 8, 1789.
  Continued as
PRINCE'S LONDON PRICE CURRENT.
London. [?]-1796-1880. w.
  a: PPL 1823-24. / b: C Ja 6, 1809; L
  1796-99; LE no2441-2545 for 1823-24; LU
  no1917-69, for 1813.
  (United with London Price Current, prior
  to 1825.)

LONDON RECORDER and Sunday Gazette.
London. no1+, 1783-1809. w. (In 1796 absorbed Sunday Reformer and Universal Register and became London Recorder and Sunday
Reformer.)
  a: CSmH Mr 31, 1793. / b: BP 1790-93
  impf.; L 1789-1809 impf.; SU Ag 16, 23,
  1807; F 21, 1808.
  (Perhaps incorporated with Johnson's
  Sunday Monitor.)

LONDON RECORDER and Sunday Reformer.
  (See London Recorder and Sunday Gazette.)

LONDON REGISTER of Remarkable Events.
London. 1827.
  b: LLL.

LONDON REVIEW. London. v1-2, F-N 1809.
q.
  a: ULS. / b: UCP; L; LdL; NwL.

LONDON REVIEW. London. v1-2, 1829-30.
  b: UCP.

LONDON REVIEW, and Biographia Literaria.
  (See New London Review; or, Monthly Report of Authors and Books.)

LONDON. Royal College of Physicians. Medical Transactions.
  (See Medical Transactions. Published by
  the Royal College of Physicians in London.)

LONDON SOCIETY for Promoting Christianity among the Jews. Jewish Records. London. no1-33, Midsummer, 1818-Ladyday, 1828.
  a: ULS.

LONDON SOCIETY for Promoting Christianity among the Jews. Report. London. 1809-
date.
  a: ULS. / b: UCP.

LONDON SPY; a Weekly Magazine of In-
structing and Amusing Literature. London.
v1-3, 1831-32. w.
  a: ULS. / b: L.

LONDON STAR. London. [?]-1805-1810-[?].
  a: IP 1805-Je 1806; 1807-10.

LONDON TELEGRAPH. London. no1-48,
My 31, 1824-Ap 25, 1825.
  b: L.

LONDON TELEGRAPH. London. no1, Ag
17, 1832.
  b: O.

LONDON. UNIVERSITY. King's College.
Science Society. Report of the Proceedings.
London. v1, 1822-83/?.
  a: ULS.

LONDON UNIVERSITY CHRONICLE. London. no1+, Ap 26, 1830-[?].
  (No issues known. Data from CBEL, III.
  836, and H. Hale Bellot, University College, London, 1826-1926, p. 184.)

LONDON UNIVERSITY MAGAZINE. London.
v1-2, 1829-30.
  a: ULS; ULSup. / b: C; L; O.

LONDON WEEKLY GAZETTE. London. no1-
68, Mr 13, 1822-Jl 2, 1823. w.
  b: L.

LONDON WEEKLY MAGAZINE.
  (See The Thief. A London, Edinburgh, and
  Dublin Weekly Journal, &c.)

LONDON WEEKLY MAGAZINE; or, Falstaff's Touch upon Nothing but Good Things.
London. no1-12, 1819.
  b: L.

LONDON WEEKLY REVIEW, and Journal of
Literature and the Fine Arts. London. v1-3,
1827-29. w.
  a: ULS. / b: UCP; E v1-2, L; O no1.

LONDON WEEKLY SCOTSMAN. London. no1-
2, My 29-Je 6, 1824. w.
  b: L.

LONDONDERRY CHRONICLE. Londonderry.
no1+, F 18-O 7, 1829.
  b: L.

LONDONDERRY JOURNAL. Londonderry.
1772-91-[?]. w.
  b: LoM Ja 4-D 27, 1791.
  Continued as
LONDONDERRY JOURNAL, and Donegal
and Tyrone Advertiser. Londonderry. [?]-
1793-1832-[1880].
  a: CSmH My 8, 1827; MiD-B O 24, 1797;
OClWHi N 1, 1803. / *b:* UCP; E S 8,
1795; L F 15, 1825-32, lacking F 25, 1832;
LoM Ap 1793-D 1794; (1798-1825); sc.nos.
1826-27; S 1828-D 1832, lacking Jl 17-S
25, 1832; LoP 1809.
  (Continued as *Derry Journal,* [1880]-date.)

LONDONDERRY SENTINEL. Londonderry.
no1+, S 19, 1829-date. w; t.w.
  b: L; LoLS.

THE LONDONER. London. 1820.
  b: L no1-2,4.

LONDONER DEUTCHES WOCHENBLATT.
London. no1-8, N 19, 1819-Ja 7, 1820/?. w.
  b: L.

THE LONGFORD, and Midland Advertiser.
Longford. [?]-1831/?. w.
  a: CSmH v4, no?, Je 25, 1831.

LONSDALE MAGAZINE, or Kendal Repository.
  (See *Lonsdale Magazine, or Provincial Repository.*)

LONSDALE MAGAZINE, or Provincial Repository. Kendal. v1-3, 1820-22. m. (In 1822
title changed to *Lonsdale Magazine, or Ken
dal Repository.*)
  a: ULS. / *b:* BdP; BwP; CsP; KdP; L.

THE LOOKER-ON: a Periodical Paper. London. 1792-93. s.w.;w.
  a: ULS; ULSup; MdBJ. / *b:* UCP; C; GeG;
L; LLL; MR.

LOOKING-GLASS; or Caricature Annual. London. v1-7, 1830-36. a.
  a: ULS; ULSup. / *b:* BkP; L.

LORD'S MUNSTER HERALD; or General
Advertiser. Cashel. no1+, Mr 24, 1788-D 31,
1789-[?].
  (No issues known after 1788. Data from
CBEL, II.737, and Madden, *The History
of Irish Periodical Literature,* II.244-46.)

THE LOUNGER. Advertisements for Monday.
London. 1814.
  b: BP no1.

THE LOUNGER'S COMMONPLACE BOOK,
being the third and last Number of the Eccentric Magazine. Aberdeen. 1821.
  (No issues known. Data from S N & Q, s1.
I.20.)

LOUNGER'S MISCELLANY; or the Lucubrations of Abel Slug, Esq. London. no1-20,
My 31, 1788-Mr 7, 1789.
  a: ULS. / *b:* UCP; L.

LOUTH FREE PRESS, and Ulster Reporter.
Dundalk. 1829-30. s.w.
  a: CSmH v2, no121, My 12, 1830.

LOW-FEN JOURNAL, and Local Miscellany;
comprising the Grand Level at Large,&c.
Lynn. 1812.
  b: L pp. 1-22.

LOYAL INTELLIGENCER; or, Lincoln, Rutland, Leicester, Cambridge and Stamford Advertiser. Stamford. [?]-no65, Je 10, 1794.
  (No issues known. Data from C & K, 1544a.)

LOYAL REFORMERS' GAZETTE. Glasgow.
v1-2, 1831-32.
  a: ULS. / *b:* UCP; E; GM; L; LE.
  Continued as
REFORMERS' GAZETTE. Glasgow. v3-5,
1832-35/?.
  a: ULS. / *b:* UCP; E; GM; L v3; LE v3.

LOYALIST. London. v1, no1, O 2, 1819. w.
  a: ULS. / *b:* UCP.

LOYALIST; containing Original and Select
Papers; intended to Rouse and Animate the
British Nation, during the Present Important
Crisis. London. v1, no1-20, 1803.
  a: ULS. / *b:* L; O.

LOYALIST; or, Anti-Radical; consisting of
three Departments: Satyrical, Miscellaneous
and Historical. London. no1-10, S 21, 1820-
F 1, 1821. ir.
  b: O.

THE LOYALIST; or, Anti-Radical. Containing the Principal Facts . . . Satyres, Jeu de
sprits [sic] . . . and Political Retrospects
published during the . . . Caroline Contest.
London. 1820. (A second titlepage reads *Loyalist's Magazine . . . containing the Principal Facts, Circumstances, Satyres, Jeu de
sprits [sic], &c.*)
  b: BP no1; L pp. 1-256.

LOYALIST'S MAGAZINE . . . containing the
Principal Facts, &c.
  (See *Loyalist; or Anti-Radical. Containing
the Principal Facts,* &c.)

LUNATIC ASYLUM OF EDINBURGH. Report. Edinburgh. 1814-19.
  b: UCP.

THE LYNX. London. no1-7, 1796.
  b: L.

M'CARTIE'S KERRY DISPATCH. Tralee.
1807. s.w.
  b: C no13, F 17, 1807.

M'DONNEL'S DUBLIN WEEKLY JOURNAL.
Dublin. 1785-95.
  b: UCP; MR v3, no50, for 1792.

M'KENZIE'S LOYAL MAGAZINE. Dublin.
no1, Ja 1800. m.
  b: DL.

MACLEOD'S GAELIC MESSENGER. Glasgow. 1830.
  b: EP.

McPHUN'S GLASGOW MAGAZINE. Glasgow.
v 1, 1824-25.
  b: GM; L no1-2.

MACCLESFIELD COURIER AND HERALD.
  (See *Macclesfield Courier, Stockport Express,* &c.)

MACCLESFIELD COURIER, Stockport Express, and Cheshire General Advertiser. Macclesfield. no1+, [1811]-1825-1827. w.
  a: CSmH S 15, 1827. / *b:* L no758+, Ja 1, 1825-D 1827.
  Continued as
MACCLESFIELD COURIER AND HERALD.
Macclesfield. Ja 1828-date. w.
  a: CSmH O 3, 1829. / *b:* L.

MACCLESFIELD HERALD and Congleton Gazette. Macclesfield. no1-121, S 3, 1825-D 29, 1827. w.
  b: L.
  (Incorporated with *Macclesfield Courier.*)

MAGAZINE AND REVIEW of Literature, Science, and the Arts. London. no1-5, Ja-My 1830. m.
  b: L.

MAGAZINE OF ANTS; or, Pismire Journal. London. no1-5, 1800/?.
  b: UCP.

MAGAZINE OF FEMALE FASHIONS of London and Paris. London. 1798.
  (No issues known. Data from CBEL, II. 683, and C & K, 1557.)

MAGAZINE OF FOREIGN LITERATURE. London. v1, 1823.
  b: UCP; L; LdL.

MAGAZINE OF IRELAND.
  (See *Bolster's Quarterly Magazine.*)

MAGAZINE OF NATURAL HISTORY, and Journal of Zoology, Botany, Mineralogy, Geology, and Meteorology. London. v1-9, 1829-36; ns, v1-4, 1837-40.
  a: ULS; ULSup. / *b:* UCP; BP; CPL; CrP; CsP; EP; HP; L; LR; LdP lacking v2; SP.
  (Merged into *Annals of Natural History;* later *Annals and Magazine of Natural History.*)

MAGAZINE OF THE BEAU MONDE; or Monthly Journal of Fashion. London. v1-12, 1831-42.
  a: ULS. / *b:* UCP; L.

MAGAZINE OF THE FINE ARTS, and Monthly Review of Painting, Sculpture, Architecture, and Engraving. London. v1, 1821. m.
  a: ULS. / *b:* UCP; L.

MAGAZINE OF USEFUL KNOWLEDGE and Co-operative Miscellany. London. no1-4, 1830.
  a: ULS. / *b:* UCP; L.

MAGEE'S WEEKLY PACKET; or, Hope's Lottery Journal of News, Politics, and Literature. Dublin. no1+, 1771-95.
  b: UCP; L Jl 11, O 10, 1789; Jl 3, Ag 7, 1790; Ag 4, N 10, 1792; Mr 3, Ag 10, 1793.

THE MAGIC AND CONJURING MAGAZINE, and Wonderful Chronicle. London. v1, pt1-4, 1795.
  b: L v1, pt1.

THE MAGIC LANTHORN. Belfast. v1-2, 1815-16. f.
  b: BlL v1, no6-7; v2, no12.

THE MAGICIAN. Glasgow. no1-2, 1832.
  b: GM.

THE MAGISTRATE; or, Sessions and Police Review, Critical, Humorous and Instructive. London. no1-3, My-Jl 1825.
  a: ULS. / *b:* L.

THE MAGNET, a General Repertory of Literature, Philosophy, Science, Arts, &c. London. no1, 1832.
  b: L.

THE MAGNET; or Plymouth Monthly Magazine. Plymouth. no1-12, 1822-23; ns, v1, no1-6, 1823-24. m.
  b: L no1-12; PlP ns, no5-6.

MAGNETISER'S MAGAZINE and Annals of Animal Magnetism. London. no1-2, Jl-Ag 1816. m.
  a: ULS. / *b:* L no1.

MAIDS, WIVES, AND WIDOWS MAGAZINE. London. v1, no1-40, O 27, 1832-Jl 27, 1833. w.
  a: ULS; ULSup. / *b:* UCP; DL; L; LLL.
  (Continued as *Weekly Belle Assemblée,* 1833-34; as *New Monthly Belle Assemblée,* 1834-70.)

MAIDSTONE GAZETTE. Maidstone. [?]-1822-1851. w.
  a: CSmH no1287, N 26, 1822; no2224, S 2, 1828. / *b:* L no1657+, Ja 5, 1830-32.
  (Continued as *South Eastern Gazette,* 1852-date.)

MAIDSTONE JOURNAL and Kentish Advertiser. Maidstone. no1+, 1786-1853. w.
  a: DLC D 31, 1793. / *b:* L no2294+, Ja 5, 1830-32; MsP.
  (Continued as *Maidstone and Kentish Journal,* 1853-1912. Incorporated with *South Eastern Gazette.*)

THE MAIL REVIEWED. Dublin. no1-2, N 29-D 13, 1823.
  b: DL.

MAITLAND CLUB, Glasgow. Publications. Glasgow. v1-75, 1829-59.
  a: ULS; ULSup. / *b:* UCP; EP.

THE MAN IN THE MOON. Edinburgh. no1, S 1, 1832/?.
  b: L.

THE MAN IN THE MOON. Consisting of
Essays and Critiques on the Politics, Morals,
Manners, Drama, &c., of the Present Day.
London. v1, no1-24, N 12, 1803-F 11, 1804.
s.w.
　　a: ULS; ULSup. / *b:* L.

MAN OF KENT, or Canterbury Political and
Literary Weekly Miscellany. Canterbury. v1-
2, no1-68, 1818-19. w.
　　b: CyP; L; WoP.

THE MAN OF LETTERS. London. no1-8, Ap
3-My 22, 1824.
　　b: L.

MANCHESTER ADVERTISER. Manchester.
1825.
　　b: L Ag 30, 1825.

MANCHESTER AND SALFORD Advertiser.
Manchester. no1+, 1828-48. w.
　　a: CSmH no125, Ap 2, 1831. / *b:* L no
　　113+, Ja 8, 1831-32; MP no114+, Ja 15,
　　1831-32.
　　(Incorporated with *Manchester Times*.)

MANCHESTER CHRONICLE. Manchester.
1762-81-[1792]. w. (Subtitle varies.)
　　b: MP.
　　Continued as
WHEELER'S MANCHESTER CHRONICLE.
Manchester. 1792-1843. w. (Dropped *Wheeler's* from the title in 1838.)
　　a: CSmH N 25, 1820; CtY Ja 7-S 29, N3-
　　D 29, 1792; MHi 1809; (1810); 1811-12;
　　MnU F 4, 1815-D 14, 1816. / *b:* C Ja 24,
　　1795; L 1806; sc.nos. 1807-30; 1831-32;
　　MCh 1819-32; SfP v39-46, F 6, 1819-Jl 15,
　　1826, lacking a few nos. in v40-46; MP.
　　(Incorporated with *Manchester and Sal-
　　ford Advertiser* in 1843.)

MANCHESTER COURIER. Manchester. no1+,
Ja 1, 1825-1916. w.
　　a: CSmH Ag 13, 1825; CtY 1825-27. / *b:*
　　L; MCh 1826-32; MP.

MANCHESTER EXAMINER. Manchester. 1823.
　　b: LUC pt2, for 1823.

MANCHESTER GAZETTE. Manchester. no
1+, [O 1795]-[?]. w.
　　b: MP.
　　Continued as
COWDROY'S MANCHESTER GAZETTE and
Weekly Advertiser. Manchester. [?]-1797-
Jl 31, 1824. w.
　　a: CSmH N 18, 1815. / *b:* L Ap 27, 1797;
　　9 sc.nos. 1801; Ja 25-S 1806; 1807-09; F
　　1810-11; 1813-N 1814; Ja-Je 1815; Ja-N
　　1816; Ap-D 1817; Mr 1818-Jl 1824; LLL
　　Ap 11, 18, 1818; MP; SfP v20-29, Mr 25,
　　1815-Mr 15, 1823, lacking a few nos. in
　　v20, 27-28.
　　Continued as
MANCHESTER GAZETTE. Ag 7, 1824-My
23, 1829. w.
　　b: L no1514-1691, Ag 7, 1824-D 29, 1827;
　　MP; SfP My 5, 1827-Ag 2, 1828, lacking
　　nos. 1666, 1689.
　　(Incorporated with *Manchester Times and
　　Gazette*.)

MANCHESTER GUARDIAN. Manchester. no
1+, My 5, 1821-date. w. (Subtitle varies.)
　　a: DLC 1823-32, lacking 8 sc.nos. / *b:*
　　L, lacking 1825-27, except Jl 8, 1826, and
　　Ap 28, 1827; MCh; MMG; MP; SfP lacking
　　a few nos. in v3-5, 7-8, 11.
　　(Manchester Reference Library in pro-
　　cess of having files microfilmed.)

MANCHESTER HERALD. Manchester. no1-
52, Mr 31, 1792-Mr 23, 1793. w.
　　b: L; MP.

MANCHESTER HERALD and Wednesday's
Commercial Advertiser. Manchester. [?]-
1815-1836. w.
　　a: CSmH no1096, D 2, 1826; WHi Ja 10,
　　1815-D 29, 1825. / *b:* L no1309+, Ja
　　1831-32; MP no1361+, Ja 4-D 1832.

MANCHESTER INSTITUTION for Curing Diseases of the Eye. Report. Manchester. v1-
19, [?]-1828-1835.
　　b: UCP.
　　(Continued as *Manchester Eye Hospital.
　　Report*, 1839-68; as *Manchester Royal
　　Eye Hospital. Report*, 1881-1907.)

MANCHESTER IRIS; a Literary and Scientific Miscellany. Manchester. v1-2, F 2,
1822-D 27, 1823. w.
　　a: ULS. / *b:* UCP; BkP lacking no10;
　　L; MP; MR; MCh; O F 22-Jl 13, 1822; ScP
　　lacking v1, no1.

MANCHESTER LITERARY and Philosophical Society.
　　(See *Literary and Philosophical Society
　　of Manchester*.)

MANCHESTER MAGAZINE; the Chronicle
of the Times, &c.
　　(See *Chronicle of the Times and Provin-
　　cial Magazine*.)

MANCHESTER MAGAZINE; or Provincial
Chronicle for the Counties of Chester, &c.
　　(See *Chronicle of the Times and Provin-
　　cial Magazine*.)

MANCHESTER MAIL. Manchester. no1-52,
Ja -D 23, 1805. w.
　　b: L.

MANCHESTER MECHANICS' INSTITUTION.
Report. Manchester. 1832-34.
　　b: UCP.

MANCHESTER MERCURY, and Harrop's
General Advertiser. Manchester. [?]-1776-
1830. w. (Preceded by *Harrop's Manchester
Mercury*, 1752-[?].)
　　a: CSmH Ja 8, 1828. / *b:* L 1799, lack-
　　ing Ja 22, 29, Mr 19; 1800, lacking D 30;
　　D 1, 1801; S 8, 22, 1807-D 6, 1808, lack-
　　ing Je 7; 1810-14; 1817-18; F 14, 1826;
　　MCh 1789-1825; MP.

MANCHESTER OBSERVER: or Literary,
Commercial and Political Register. Manchester. no1+, 1818-22. w.
　　a: CSmH Ag 7, 1819. / *b:* CsP N 6, 1819-

20; L lacking Je 5-19; Jl 3, 1819; MP 1818-Je 23, 1821; MR 1818-19; sc.nos. 1820-21.
(Incorporated with *Wooler's British Gazette.*)

MANCHESTER POLITICAL REGISTER; or, Reformers' Repository. Manchester. v1, no1-8, Ja 4-Mr 1, 1817.
a: ULS.

MANCHESTER SCHOOL for the Deaf and Dumb. Report. Manchester. 1826-96.
b: UCP.
(Continued as *Royal School for the Deaf and Dumb,* 1896-date.)

MANCHESTER THEATRICAL CENSOR.
(See *Theatrical Censor.*)

MANCHESTER TIMES. Manchester. 1819-20. w.
a: CSmH no31, My 16, 1820.

MANCHESTER TIMES. Manchester. no1+, O 17, 1828-1848. w. (Subtitle varies.)
b: L lacking N 1829-1830; MP.
(Incorporated with *Manchester Examiner.*)

THE MARAUDER. London. no1, 1829.
b: L.

MARINERS' MARVELLOUS MAGAZINE, or Wonders of the Ocean, &c. London. v1-4, 1809.
b: L.

MARK LANE EXPRESS. London. v1-131, 1832-1924. w.
a: ULS; CSmH no7, F 13, 1832.
(Continued as *Farmers Express,* 1924-29; merged into *Farm, Field, and Fireside,* 1929.)

MARSHALL'S CHRISTMAS BOX.
(See *Christmas Box; an Annual Present,* &c.)

MART AND PORT ADVERTISER. London. no1-4, S 28-O 19, 1818. w.
b: L.

MARVELLOUS MAGAZINE; or, Entertaining Pocket Companion. Dublin. v1-2, 1822.
a: ULS; ULSup. / *b:* UCP; DA v1; DL.

MARVELLOUS MAGAZINE and Compendium of Prodigies, &c. London. v1-4, 1802-03.
a: ULS. / *b:* DL v3.

MARWADE'S COMMERCIAL REPORT. London. Ag 18, 1820-D 14, 1821. w.
b: L.

MASONIC MIRROR. Edinburgh. no1, 1797.
b: UCP.

MASQUERADE. Southampton. [?]-1798.
(No issues known. Data from C & K, 1572.)

MATHEMATICAL AND PHILOSOPHICAL Repository and Review.
(See *Mathematical Repository.*)

MATHEMATICAL COMPANION.
(See *Companion to the Gentleman's Diary.*)

MATHEMATICAL, Geometrical and Philosophical Delights. London. v1-11, 1792-98.
a: ULS.

MATHEMATICAL REPOSITORY. London. v1-3, 1747-55; s2, v1-3, 1795-1804; s3, v1-6, 1806-35; (s2 originally pub. in 14 nos.: no1-8 as *Mathematical and Philosophical Repository;* no9-14 as *Mathematical and Philosophical Repository and Review.* The three parts have separate titlepages: *Mathematical Repository,* 1798-1804, 3v; *Philosophical Repository,* 1801-04, 2v; *Review of Mathematical and Philosophical Books,* 1804, 1v.)
a: ULS. / *b:* UCP; GeG 1806-09; NwL.

MAYO CONSTITUTION. Castlebar. [?]-1812-72-[?]. s.w.
a: CSmH My 3, 1827. / *b:* L D 24, 1812; Ja 3, 1828-32.

MAYO FREE PRESS. Castlebar. [?]-1830. w.
a: CSmH v4, no11, O 20, 1830.

MAYO WEEKLY MESSENGER. Castlebar. [?]-1827. w.
a: CSmH v2, no23, Je 9, 1827.

MECHANICS' CHRONICLE. London. no1-13, Ag 28-N 20, 1824. w.
a: ULS. / *b:* LP.

MECHANIC'S GALLERY of Science and Art. London. v1, 1825.
b: UCP.

MECHANICS' INSTITUTION, Sunderland. Report. Bishopwearmouth. 1826.
b: UCP.

MECHANIC'S LIBRARY. London. pt1-3, 1825.
b: O.

MECHANICS MAGAZINE. London. v1-97, 1823-73. (Subtitle varies.) w.
a: ULS. / *b:* UCP; BP; BdP lacking pt1, 1824, and 1831-32; BrP; CPL; EP; L; LGU lacking v8, 10-11; LLL; LP v1; MsP; NpP lacking v5, 9; NwL lacking v13; SP.
(Continued as *Iron,* 1874-93.)

MECHANICS' MAGAZINE, West of England. Reports of Lectures at Plymouth Mechanics Institute. Plymouth. 1826.
(No issues known. Data from librarian at PlP.)

MECHANIC'S NEWSPAPER.
(See *Journeyman and Artizan's London and Provincial Chronicle.*)

MECHANIC'S ORACLE, and Artisan's Laboratory and Workshop; explaining ... the ... Application of Practical Knowledge, in the Different Departments of Science and Art. London. no1-28, 1824-25.
a: ULS. / *b:* UCP; L; LP.

MECHANIC'S WEEKLY JOURNAL; or, Artisan's Miscellany of Inventions, Experiments, Projects, and Improvements in the Useful Arts. London. v1, no1-26, 1823-24. w.
    a: ULS; ULSup. / *b:* UCP; L; LP 24 nos.

Y MEDDYG; Family Physician. Merthyr. v1, no1-4, 1827.
    b: UCP.

MEDIATOR. London. 1798.
    (No issues known. Data from C & K, 1581.)

MEDICAL ADVISER, and Guide to Health and Long Life. London. v1-3, 1823-25; ns, v1-2, 1825.
    a: ULS. / *b:* UCP; L; LCP 1823-24; LS v1-2.

MEDICAL AND CHIRURGICAL REVIEW; containing a Copious Account of the various Publications in different Languages on Medicine and Surgery. London. v1-16, 1794-1808. m.
    a: ULS; ULSup. / *b:* UCP; L v1-12; LMA; LS.

MEDICAL AND CHIRURGICAL SOCIETY of London. Transactions. London. v1-18, 1809-33.
    a: ULS; ULSup. / *b:* UCP; LCP; LMA;LR.
    (Continued as *Royal Medical and Chirurgical Society of London*, 1834-1907.)

MEDICAL AND PHYSICAL JOURNAL; containing the Earliest Information on Subjects of Medicine, Surgery, Pharmacy, Chemistry, and Natural History. London. v1-32, 1799-1815. m.
    a: ULS. / *b:* UCP; L; LS.
    Continued as
  LONDON MEDICAL AND PHYSICAL Journal. London. v33-35, 1815-26; ns, v56-69, 1827-33. m.
    a: ULS. / *b:* UCP; L.

MEDICAL AND POLITICAL RECORD. London. no1-2, D 31, 1820-Ja 7, 1821. w.
    b: L.
    Continued as
  MEDICAL RECORD. London. no3-15, Ja 14-My 11, 1821. w. (The numbering of *Medical Record* began with no2 in consequence of the plan to form a no1 by reprinting the medical articles of *Medical and Political Record.*)
    b: L.

MEDICAL AND SURGICAL SPECTATOR. London. 1809/?.
    a: ULS.

MEDICAL ANNUAL, containing a Popular Account of all the New Discoveries in Medicine. London. v1-4, 1831-34.
    b: UCP; L.

MEDICAL BOTANY. London. v1-4, 1828-31.
    b: UCP.

MEDICAL COMMENTARIES. London. v7-s2, v10, 1780-95. q. (Preceded by *Medical and Philosophical Commentaries*, 1773-79.)

    a: ULS. / *b:* UCP; LCP; LMD; LR; LS.
    Continued as
ANNALS OF MEDICINE. Edinburgh. v1-8, 1796-1804. q.
    a: ULS. / *b:* UCP; LCP; LMA 1796-1802; LMD; LS.
    Continued as
EDINBURGH MEDICAL AND SURGICAL Journal. Edinburgh. v1-82, 1805-55. q.
    a: ULS; ULSup. / *b:* UCP; DRS; LCP; LMA; LS.
    (United with *Monthly Journal of Medicine* and continued as *Edinburgh Medical Journal.*)

MEDICAL COMMUNICATIONS of the Society for Promoting Medical Knowledge.
    (See *Society for Promoting Medical Knowledge.*)

MEDICAL EXAMINER. London. v1, no1-17, S 26, 1829-Ja 16, 1830. w.
    a: ULS. / *b:* L 1830.

MEDICAL EXAMINER. Glasgow. v1-2, 1831-32. (May be identical with *Glasgow Medical Examiner.*)
    b: GM.

MEDICAL EXTRACTS. London. v1-4, 1796-97. q.
    b: UCP.

MEDICAL FACTS AND OBSERVATIONS.
    (See *London Medical Journal.*)

MEDICAL INTELLIGENCER; or Monthly Compendium of Medical, Chirurgical, and Scientific Knowledge. London. v1-4, 1819-23. m. (Subtitle varies.)
    a: ULS; ULSup. / *b:* UCP; L; LS.

MEDICAL OBSERVER.
    (See *Medical Observer and Family Monitor.*)

MEDICAL OBSERVER; Essays on Medical Science, Empirical Medicines, &c. no1-12, 1806-08. m.
    b: L; LCP; LP 1806; NwL; O.

MEDICAL OBSERVER and Family Monitor; or London Monthly Compendium of Medical Transactions. London. v1-10, 1807-11/?. m.
    a: ULS; ULSup. / *b:* UCP; LMA 1807, 1811.

MEDICAL RECORD.
    (See *Medical and Political Record.*)

MEDICAL RECORDS AND RESEARCHES. Selected from the Papers of a Private Medical Association. London. pt1-2, 1798.
    a: ULS. / *b:* UCP; LS.

MEDICAL REGISTER; or Quarterly Journal of Medical and Surgical Science. London. v1, 1818. q.
    a: ULS.

MEDICAL REPORT of the Aberdeen Lunatic Asylum.
    (See *Aberdeen Lunatic Asylum.*)

MEDICAL REPORT of the House of Recovery in Cork Street, Dublin. Dublin. 1816-23.
b: UCP.

MEDICAL SOCIETY OF LONDON. Memoirs. London. v1-6, 1787-1805.
a: ULS. / *b:* UCP; LMA; LCP; LR v1-5; LS.

MEDICAL SOCIETY OF LONDON. Transactions. London. v1-s3, v2, 1817-62.
a: ULS. / *b:* UCP; LMA v1, pt1. LS.
(Continued as *Proceedings of the Medical Society of London, 1872-89.*)

MEDICAL SPECTATOR. London. v1-3, no1-48, 1791-96.
a: ULS. / *b:* UCP; LS.

MEDICAL STUDENT. London. no1, 1827.
b: L.

MEDICAL TRANSACTIONS. Royal College of Physicians. London. v1-6, 1768-1820.
a: ULS. / *b:* UCP; LMA; LS.

MEDICO-BOTANICAL SOCIETY of London. Minute Books. London. v1-9, 1821-53.
b: LMD.

MEDICO-BOTANICAL SOCIETY of London. Transactions. London. v1, no1-4, 1821-37.
a: ULS. / *b:* UCP; LCP 1832; LS.

MEDICO-CHIRURGICAL JOURNAL.
(See *Medico-Chirurgical Journal and Review.*)

MEDICO-CHIRURGICAL JOURNAL and Review. London. v1-5, 1816-18. m.
a: ULS. / *b:* UCP; LS.
Continued as
MEDICO-CHIRURGICAL JOURNAL. London. v1-2, 1818-20. m.
a: ULS. / *b:* UCP; LS.
Continued as
MEDICO-CHIRURGICAL REVIEW and Journal of Medical Science. London. v1-4, 1820-24; ns, v1-47, 1824-47. m.
a: ULS; ULSup. / *b:* UCP; DRS 1824-31; L; LCP; LS v1-4.
(United with *British and Foreign Medical Review* to become *British and Foreign Medico-Chirurgical Review, 1848-77.*)

MEDICO-CHIRURGICAL REVIEW and Journal of Medical Science.
(See *Medico-Chirurgical Journal and Review.*)

MEDICO-CHIRURGICAL SOCIETY of Edinburgh. Transactions. v1-3, 1824-29; ns, v1+, 1881-date.
a: ULS; ULSup. / *b:* LCP.

MEDLEY. London. 1797.
(No issues known. Data from C & K, 1584.)

MEDLEY. London. v1, no1-12, Ja 4-F 12, 1805. s.w.
b: L.

MEDUSA; or, Penny Politician, a Political Publication. London. v1, no1-47, v2, no1, F 20, 1819-Ja 28, 1820. w.
a: ULS. / *b:* UCP; O no1-47.

MELANCHOLY HOURS. London. 1825.
b: O.

MÉMOIRES SECRETS, ou Chronique de Paris, &c.
(See *Chronique de Paris, imprimée à Londres.*)

MEMOIRS OF SCIENCE and the Arts. London. v1-2, 1793-94.
a: ULS; ULSup. / *b:* UCP; LP; LR; LS.

MEMOIRS OF THE . . .
(In general, see the society, institution, or other group concerned. In UCP, however, see *Memoirs.*)
See especially (1) *Analytical Society;* (2) *Caledonian Horticultural Society;* (3) *Manchester Literary and Philosophical Society;* (4) *Medical Society of London;* (5) *Royal Astronomical Society of London;* (6) *Wernerian Natural History Society.*

MENTAL MAGAZINE; or, Young Lady's Repository of Arts and Sciences. Dublin. 1801.
b: DL.

MENTOR; or, Edinburgh Weekly Essayist; containing Dissertations on Morality, Literature, and Manners. Edinburgh. v1-2, 1817-18. w. (Also called *Edinburgh Weekly Essayist.*)
a: ULS. / *b:* UCP; GM; L.

MENTOR; or, St. Cecilia at School. London. [?]-1808-[?]. f.
(No issues known. Data from *Literary Annual Register, or Records of Literature,* 2 (F 1808) 73.)

MERCANTILE BAROMETER. London. no1-4, Mr 22-Ap 12, 1822.
b: L; O no1.

MERCANTILE CHRONICLE. London. no1+, Jl 20, 1821-Ja 10, 1823. t.w.
a: CSmH no232, Ja 10, 1823. / *b:* L.
(Incorporated with *London Packet and Lloyd's Evening Post,* Ja 13, 1823.)

MERCANTILE GAZETTE and General Intelligencer.
(See *Sarah Farley's Bristol Journal.*)

MERCANTILE GAZETTE, and Liverpool and Manchester Daily Advertiser. Liverpool. 1803. d.
b: L Prospectus only.

MERCANTILE GAZETTE, and Liverpool and Manchester Daily Advertiser. Liverpool. no1, Ag 6, 1811-[?]. d.
(No issues known. Data from CBEL, III. 801.)

MERCANTILE JOURNAL. London. no1+, Jl 13, 1830-Mr 8, 1831.
   a: CSmH v1, no1, Jl 13, 1830. / b: L.
   Continued as
NEW MERCANTILE JOURNAL. London. Mr 22-D 6, 1831.
   a: L.
   Continued as
LONDON MERCANTILE JOURNAL. London. D 13, 1831-1870.
   a: L.

MERCHANT TAYLORS' MISCELLANY. London. no1-9, 1831-32.
   a: ULS. / b: UCP; L.

MERCURE BRITANNIQUE; ou, Notices historiques et Critiques sur les Affaires du Temps. London. v1-5, no1-36, 1798-1800. (no1-3 of v1 entitled Essai Historique sur la Destruction de la ligue et de la Liberté Helvétiques.)
   a: ULS; ULSup. / b: UCP; L; LLL; MR.

MERCURE DE FRANCE; ou Recueil Historique, Politique et Littéraire. London. v1-6, 1800-01.
   b: L.

MERCURE DE LONDRES. London. 1826-27.
   b: L.

IL MERCURIO BRITANNICO; ossia, Notizie storico-critiche sugli affari attuali. London. v1-5, Ag 1798-Mr 25, 1800. (No nos. for Ag 25, S 10, 1799 and F 25, 1800.)
   a: ULS.

IL MERCURIO ITALICO; o sia, ragguaglio generale intorno alla letteratura, belle arti, utili scoperte, &c. London. v1-3, 1789-90.
   a: ULS; ULSup. / b: UCP; L v1-2.

MERLE'S CHURCH REGISTER. London. 1832.
   b: O no1, S 18, 1832.

MERLE'S COMMERCIAL REGISTER. London. 1832.
   b: O no1, N 18, 1832.

MERLE'S MEDICAL REGISTER. London. 1832.
   b: O no1, N 18, 1832.

MERLE'S SPORTING REGISTER. London. 1832.
   b: O no1, N 18, 1832.

MERLE'S (Clerical and Medical, Literary, and Political) Weekly Register. London. no1-20, N 18, 1832-Mr 31, 1833. w.
   b: L; O no1.

MERLINUS LIBERATUS; an Almanac for 1815(-1840?). London. [?]-1815-1840/?.
   b: LGU 1815, 1831.

METEOR; or, General Censor. London. 1817.
   b: O.

METEOR; or, Monthly Censor. London. v1-1, N 1813-Jl 1814. m. (No issue for Je 1814.)
   a: ULS. / b: O lacking F, My-Jl 1814.

A METEOROLOGICAL REGISTER, kept at Mansfield Woodhouse, in Nottinghamshire. Nottingham. 1785-1806 (pub. 1795-1806). a.
   b: UCP; L.

METEOROLOGICAL SOCIETY. Transactions. London. 1823 (pub. 1839) (Title varies: as, Meteorological Society of Great Britain.)
   a: ULS.

METEOROLOGICAL SOCIETY of Great Britain.
   (See Meteorological Society.)

METEORS. London. v1-2, N 30, 1799-My 3, 1800. f.
   a: ULS; ICU. / b: UCP; L.

METHODIST CONFERENCES. Minutes of ... from the First Held in London. v1-10, 1744-1847.
   b: UCP.

METHODIST MAGAZINE. Dublin. v1-39, [?]. 1816/?. m.
   a: ULS.

METHODIST MAGAZINE, being a Continuation of the Arminian Magazine.
   (See Arminian Magazine, &c.)

METHODIST MAGAZINE ... conducted by the Camp-Meeting Methodists known by the Name of Ranters, called also Primitive Methodists. Leicester. v1, 1819. m.
   b: L.
   Continued as
PRIMITIVE METHODIST MAGAZINE. Bemersley, London. v2-79, 1820-98.
   a: ULS. / b: UCP.
   (Continued as Aldersgate Primitive Methodist Magazine, 1899-date.)

METHODIST MAGAZINE; or, Evangelical Repository. Leeds. v1-25, 1798-1822.
   a: ULS.
   Continued as
NEW METHODIST MAGAZINE and Evangelical Repository. London. ns, v1-10 (also called v26-35), 1823-32. (Running title of some issues, New Wesleyan Methodist Magazine.)
   a: ULS.
   (Continued as Methodist New Connexion Magazine, 1833-1907. In ULS under this title.)

METHODIST MINISTERS. Minutes of the Several Conversations at their . . . Annual Conference. London. 1829-date.
   (No issues known. Data from CBEL, III. 844.)

METHODIST MISSIONARY SOCIETY of Leeds. Report of their first Meeting. Leeds. 1813.
   b: LdP.

METHODIST MONITOR; or, Moral and Religious Repository. Leeds. v1-2, 1796-97. m.
   a: ULS. / *b:* UCP.

METHODIST New Connexion Magazine.
   (See *Methodist Magazine; or, Evangelical Repository.)*

METHODISTS. Minutes of the Conference of.
London. 1794-date.
   b: UCP.

METROPOLITAN: a Monthly Journal of Literature, Science, and the Fine Arts. London.
v1-5, 1831-32. m.
   a: ULS; ULSup. / *b:* UCP; BP; GeG v2-5; L.
   (Continued as *Metropolitan Magazine,* 1833-50.)

METROPOLITAN, and Independent Trades' Journal. London. v1-13, 1831-35. w. (Subtitle varies.)
   a: CSmH no1, Ag 28, 1831. / *b:* DLL; L no1-13, Ag 28-N 20, 1831.

METROPOLITAN LITERARY JOURNAL and General Magazine of Literature, Science, and the Arts. London. v1, 1824. m.
   a: MH no3, Jl 1824. / *b:* UCP; L.

METROPOLITAN MAGAZINE.
   (See *Metropolitan; a Monthly Journal of Literature.)*

METROPOLITAN QUARTERLY MAGAZINE.
London. v1-2, 1826. q.
   a: ULS; OC v1-2. / *b:* UCP; L.

MICROCOSM OF LONDON. London. v1-3, Ja 1808-Ja 1810. m.
   b: O.

MICROSCOPE; or Minute Observer. London. v1-2, 1799-1800. m.
   b: UCP; BlL; BlU v1, no2-8.

MIDDLESEX JOURNAL, and London Evening Post. London. [?]-1783-1785-[1790?]. t.w. (Preceded by *Middlesex Journal; or, Chronicle of Liberty,* 1769-[1772]; *Middlesex Journal; or, Universal Post,* [1772-73]; *Middlesex Journal and Evening Advertiser,* [1773-1778]-[?].
   (No issues known. Data from CBEL, II. 710.)

MIDLAND CHRONICLE. Birmingham. no1+, Ja 5, 1811-D 26, 1812. w.
   a: ICU. / *b:* L v2, no70, 74, My 2, 30, 1812.

MIDLAND CHRONICLE and Westmeath Independent. Mullingar. v1-2, [?]-Ja 10-N 7, 1827.
   a: CSmH Je 6, 1827. / *b:* L v2, Ja 10-N 7, 1827.

MIDLAND MEDICAL and Surgical Reporter, and Topographical and Statistical Journal. Worcester. v1-3, no1-16, 1828-32.
   a: ULS. / *b:* UCP; BP v1; L; LS.

MIDLAND MERCURY.
   (See *Newark Herald.)*

MIDLAND REPRESENTATIVE and Birmingham Herald. Birmingham. no1+, Ap 23, 1831-Je 2, 1832.
   a: CSmH v1, no5, My 21, 1831. / *b:* BP D 3, 1831; L.

MILESIAN MAGAZINE; or Irish Monthly Gleaner. Dublin. no1-16, 1812-25. m.;q.;ir.
   a: ULS. / *b:* UCP; DL; L lacking pp. 3-6 of no15.

MILITARY MAGAZINE. London. v1, 1793.
   b: L.

MILITARY MAGAZINE. London. no1, 1811. m.
   b: O.

MILITARY PANORAMA, or Officer's Companion. London. v1-4, 1812-14. m. (Titlepages of v3-4 read *Royal Military Panorama.* In ULS under this title.)
   a: ULS; ULSup. / *b:* UCP; L.

MILITARY REGISTER. London. no1+, Mr 30, 1814-Ap 11, 1821. m.
   a: ULS. / *b:* L; O no1.

MINERVA MAGAZINE. Dublin. 1793.
   (No issues known. Data from CBEL, II. 688, and C & K, 1675.)

THE MINIATURE, a Periodical Paper. Windsor. no1-34, Ap 23, 1804-Ap 1, 1805. Another edn. has no1-40, Ap 23, 1804-My 6, 1805. w.
   a: ULS; MdBJ no1-34. / *b:* UCP; BP; EtS; L; O.

MINIATURE MAGAZINE, or Epitome of the Times. London. v1-3, Je 1818-Ja 1820. m.
   a: ULS; ULSup. / *b:* L.
   Continued as
MINIATURE MAGAZINE; or Monthly Epitome of the Times. London. v1, Jl-D 1820. m.
   a: ULS. / *b:* CrP.

MINIATURE MAGAZINE; or Monthly Epitome of the Times.
   (See *Miniature Magazine, or Epitome of the Times.)*

MINING REVIEW, and Journal of Geology, Mineralogy, &c.
   (See *Quarterly Mining Review.)*

MINUTES OF . . .
   (In general see the society, institution, or other group reporting its minutes. In UCP, however, entries are found under *Minutes.)*
   See especially (1) *Iron-Masters of York and Derby;* (2) *Medico-Botanical Society of London;* (3) *Methodist Conferences;* (4) *Methodist Ministers;* (5) *Methodists;* (6) *Political Economy Club;* (7) *Primitive Wesleyan Methodists;* (8) *Society for Philosophical Experiments and Conversations;* (9) *Society of Medical and Chirurgical knowledge;* (10) *United Associate Synod;* (11) *Wesleyan Methodist Church.*

MIROIR DE LA MODE. London. v1, no1-12, Ja-D 1803.
    a: ULS.

THE MIRROR. London. no1-88, O 21, 1821-Je 22, 1823. w.
    b: BP no3; L; O no1.

THE MIRROR: a Weekly Miscellany. Belfast. 1823.
    b: BlL.

MIRROR, late Bonner and Middleton's Journal.
    (See *Bonner and Middleton's Bristol Journal.*)

MIRROR. Monthly Magazine.
    (See *Mirror of Literature, Amusement, and Instruction.*)

THE MIRROR; or Weald of Kent Repository of Literature, Amusement and Instruction. Cranbrook, Kent. no1-24, 1824. s.m.
    b: WoP.

MIRROR and the Lounger. London. v1, 1825.
    a: ULSup.

MIRROR OF FASHION. London. 1807.
    b: SU v1, no12.

MIRROR OF LITERATURE, Amusement, and Instruction. London. v1-38, 1822-41; s2-4, 1841-47. w.
    a: ULS; ULSup. / *b:* UCP; BP lacking v1-4; BhP lacking v8; BrP 1830-32; CrP; KeP; L; LGU; LLL.
    (Continued as *Mirror. Monthly Magazine,* 1847-49.)

MIRROR OF PARLIAMENT. London. v1-36, 1828-37; ns, v1-24, 1838-41.
    a: ULS. / *b:* UCP; BP; BdP 1830-32; L; WmP.

MIRROR OF PHILANTHROPY, and Compendious Magazine. London. Jl 1812/?.
    (No issues known. Data from John Nichol, *Illustrations of Literary History,* v8,p.610.)

MIRROR OF THE STAGE. London. no1, 1803.
    b: O.

MIRROR OF THE STAGE; or, New Dramatic Censor. London. v1-5, 1822-24. f. (After v2 the titlepage reads *Mirror of the Stage and New Theatrical Inquisitor.*)
    a: ULS; ULSup. / *b:* L.

MIRROR OF THE STAGE and New Theatrical Inquisitor.
    (See *Mirror of the Stage; or, New Dramatic Censor.*)

MIRROR OF THE TIMES. London. no1-1391, 1796-1823. w.
    a: ULS; CtY Ja 19, 1799-Ap 16, 1803; sc. nos. Ja 2-D 28, 1805; MBAt Jl 28-Ag 4, 1804. / *b:* BP S 9-16, 1815; L no92-1391, Ja 6, 1798-F 23, 1823, lacking D 29, 1804-Ja 3, 1818.

MIRROR OF TRUTH. London. no1-2, O 10-N 7, 1817.
    b: UCP.

MISCELLANEA PERTHENSIS .... Containing a Number of Original Pieces of Prose and Verse, and Extracts from new Publications of Merit. Perth. 1801. a.
    b: E; EP; L.

MISCELLANEA SACRA, or the Theological Miscellany. Ewood Hall (near Halifax). 1797-99.
    b: BdP.

MISCELLANEOUS ANTIQUITIES.
    (See *Bibliotheca Topographica Britannica.*)

MISCELLANEOUS REPOSITORY; and Farmer's and Tradesman's Magazine. Gilmenton. 1803/?.
    a: ULS.

MISCELLANEOUS REPOSITORY, neu y Drysorfa Gymmsgedig. Carmarthen. v1, 1795-96.
    b: CrP.

THE MISCELLANIST OF LITERATURE. London. 1826.
    b: L 1826.

THE MISSIONARY; or, Stokesley and Cleveland Illuminator. Stokesley. no1-3, 1823.
    b: L.

MISSIONARY HERALD; containing Intelligence at Large of the Proceedings and Operations of the Baptist Missionary Society, &c. London. 1819-date. (v1-54, for 1819-72, appeared as a section of the *Baptist Magazine.* v88, for 1906, is the first numbered volume.)
    a: ULS; ULSup. / *b:* L 1819-21, lacking no1, 3-4, 8-9 of vol. for 1819, and no3 of vol. for 1821.

MISSIONARY MAGAZINE. Edinburgh. 1796-1814. w.
    a: ULS; ULSup; KyLx v3. / *b:* UCP; L 1796-99.
    Continued as
CHRISTIAN HERALD. Edinburgh. 1814-35. w.
    a: ULS. / *b:* O 1814-23.
    (Continued as *Scottish Congregational Magazine,* 1835-80; as *Scottish Congregationalist,* 1880-date.)

MISSIONARY MAGAZINE; or, an Apology for Faith. London. no1-2, 1814.
    b: O no2.

MISSIONARY NOTICES. London. v1-9, 1816-38.
    a: ULS. / *b:* UCP; L; LLL v6-9.
    (Continued as *Wesleyan Missionary Notices,* 1839-date.)

MISSIONARY PAPERS for the Use of the Weekly and Monthly Contributors to the Church Missionary Society. London. no1-54, 1816-29/?.
    a: ULS. / *b:* BP 1816-27.

MISSIONARY REGISTER ... containing an Abstract of the Proceedings of the Principal Missionary and Bible Societies throughout the World. London. v1-43, 1813-55.
  a: ULS. / *b:* UCP; CrP; L; LLL 1816-30.

MISSIONARY SKETCHES for the Use of the Weekly and Monthly Contributors to the Missionary Society. London. no1-89, 1818-39. ir.
  a: ULS.

MISSIONARY SOCIETY (afterwards *London Missionary Society*). Report. London. 1795-date. (In C & K as *Church Missionary Society Report.*)
  b: UCP.

MISSIONARY SOCIETY. Transactions. London. 1804-1814-[?].
  a: GeG v1, 1804; L v4, no2, 1814.

MITCHELL'S SUNDAY London Gazette and Weekly Monitor. London. 1790.
  b: C no16, Ag 22.

THE MODERATOR. London. 1808.
  (No issues known. Data from John Nichol, *Illustrations of Literary History*, v.8, p. 610.)

MODERN AND CONTEMPORARY Voyages and Travels. London. 1808. m.
  (No issues known. Data from *Literary Annual Register, or Records of Literature*, 2(Jan. 1808) 38.)

MODERN SPECTATOR; or Wallis's Minor Magazine. London. v1, no1-18, D 19, 1818-My 29, 1819. w.
  b: L; O.

MODERN TIMES, or the Age of Folly. London. no1, Mr 24, 1832.
  b: O.

LE MONDE ÉLÉGANT, or the World of Fashion.
  (See *World of Fashion and Continental Feuilletons.*)

MONITOR, a Collection of Essays on Various Subjects. London. v1, no1-47, 1817. q.
  b: L.

THE MONITOR, consisting principally of Original Essays, both in Prose and Verse. Bristol, London. 1790.
  b: L.

THE MONITOR; or, Framework-knitters' Magazine. Nottingham. ns, no1-10, Ja 1-Mr 12, 1818. w. (May be the successor to *Stocking-makers' Monitor and Commercial Magazine.*)
  b: NP ns, no1-10.

THE MONITOR, or Useful Miscellany. Dublin. no1, 1800.
  b: D.

MONMOUTHSHIRE ADVERTISER, and Newport Mercantile Presentment. Newport. [?]-1811/?.
  a: CSmH v3, no115, Ja 9, 1811.

MONMOUTHSHIRE MERLIN. Newport. no1+, My 23, 1829-1891. w.
  a: CSmH v1, no32, D 26, 1829. / *b:* CrP; L; NpP.

MONTHLY ARGUS and Public Censor.
  (See *Birmingham Argus and Public Censor.*)

MONTHLY ARMY LIST. London. 1798. m.
  b: L lacking pp. 25-30 for Je 1798.

MONTHLY BEAUTIES; or, the Cabinet of Literary Genius. London. 1793/?. m.
  a: ULS. / *b:* UCP.

MONTHLY BLOWING HEART'S EASE. Bristol. no1-12, 1822. m.
  b: L.

MONTHLY CENSOR; or General Review of Domestic and Foreign Literature. London. v1-2, Je 1822-F 1823. m.
  a: ULS. / *b:* UCP; L.

MONTHLY CHAMPION. London. 1822. m.
  b: O My 1822.

MONTHLY COLLECTOR of Elegant Anecdotes and other Curiosities of Literature. London. 1798. m.
  (No issues known. Data from CBEL, II. 683, and C & K, 1718.)

MONTHLY COMMUNICATIONS; being a Collection of Tracts on all Subjects. London. v1, 1793.
  b: L.

MONTHLY COMPENDIUM of Medicine, Surgery, Pharmacy, Chemistry, Midwifery, &c. London. v1, no1-4, 1809-10. m.
  a: ULS. / *b:* UCP.

MONTHLY CORRESPONDENT on Physical and Prognostic Astronomy, Chemistry, Botany, Agriculture, &c. London. no1-8, Ja-Ag 1814. m.
  b: UCP; L.

MONTHLY CRITICAL GAZETTE. London. v1-2, 1824-25. m.
  b: UCP; O.

MONTHLY ENTERTAINER; or, General Observer of the Times. Parsontown. no1, Ja 1814. m.
  b: DL.

MONTHLY EPITOME, or Readers their own Reviewers.
  (See *Monthly Epitome and Catalogue of New Publications.*)

MONTHLY EPITOME and Catalogue of New Publications. London. v1-5, 1797-1802. m.
  a: ULS*. / *b:* UCP; L.
  (*But ICN really has only v1-4, no6.)

Continued as
MONTHLY EPITOME, or Readers their own
Reviewers. New Series. London. v1-3, 1802-
04. m.
   a: ULS*; MdBJ v3. / *b:* UCP; L; O.
   (*But ULS errs in listing ICN.)
Continued as
LITERARY MAGAZINE; or Monthly Epitome of British Literature. London. v1-2,
1805-06. m.
   a: ULS*; MdBJ v1. / *b:* UCP; L v1 & v2,
   no13-15; O.
   (*But ULS errs in listing ICN and MB.)

MONTHLY EXTRACTS; or Beauties of Modern Authors. Consisting of elegant and interesting Selections, from new Books and
Pamphlets. v1-4. S 1791-N 1792.
   a: ULS. / *b:* BP L v1-2.

MONTHLY EXTRACTS from the Correspondence of the British and Foreign Bible Society.
   (See *British and Foreign Bible Society.
   Monthly Extracts.*)

MONTHLY EXTRACTS from the Correspondence of the Hibernian Bible Society.
   (See *Hibernian Bible Society.*)

MONTHLY GAZETTE OF HEALTH. London.
v1-17, 1816-32. Also called v1-15, 1816-30;
ns, v1-2, 1831-32. m. (Running title of v1-
15, *Gazette of Health;* of v16, *Monthly Gazette of Practical Medicine.*)
   a: ULS. / *b* UCP; LP.

MONTHLY INTELLIGENCE of the Proceedings of the London Society for Promoting
Christianity amongst the Jews. London. v1-
5, 1830-34. m.
   b: UCP.
   (Continued as *Jewish Intelligence and
   Monthly Account of the Proceedings of
   the London Society,* 1835-92; as *Jewish
   Missionary Intelligence,* 1893-date.)

MONTHLY JOURNAL; or, Dublin Literary
Repertory. Dublin. v1-2, O 1813-D 1814. m.
   (Listed by ULS, but apparently an erro-
   neous entry which properly should be
   *Monthly Museum; or Dublin Literary Rep-
   ertory.* See *infra.*)

MONTHLY JOURNAL of Popular Medicine.
London. v1-2, no1-12, Mr 1821-F 1822. m.
(Running title, *Journal of Popular Medicine.*)
   a: ULS. / *b:* L no1-5; LS no1.

A MONTHLY LIST of New Publications.
London. no1-31, Jl 1802-Ja 1805. m.
   b: O.
Continued as
MONTHLY LITERARY ADVERTISER. London. 1805-31. m.
   a: ULS; NNHi My 10, 1805-Ap 10, 1809.
   / *b:* UCP; L lacking no1-5 for 1805; O;
   WcP.
Continued as
BENT'S MONTHLY Literary Advertiser,
and Register of Engravings. London. 1832-
60. m.
   a: ULS. / *b:* UCP; L; O; WcP.

MONTHLY LITERARY ADVERTISER.
   (See *A Monthly List of New Publications.*)

MONTHLY LITERARY JOURNAL.
   (See *Literary Museum; containing Copious
   Extracts, &c.*)

MONTHLY LITERARY RECREATIONS; or,
Magazine of General Information and Amusement. London. v1-3, 1806-07. m.
   a: ULS*. / *b:* UCP; L lacking pp.1-16 of
   v3; SkP v1-2.
   (*Erroneously lists ICU; should be ICN.)

MONTHLY LITERARY REGISTER of Fine
Arts, Sciences, and Belles Lettres. London.
v1-3, My 1822-Ap 1823. m.
   b: UCP.

MONTHLY MAGAZINE. Chelmsford. 1800. m.
   (No issues known. Data from CBEL, II.
   684, and C & K, 1722.)

MONTHLY MAGAZINE; or, British Register
of Literature, &c.
   (See *Monthly Magazine and British Register.*)

MONTHLY MAGAZINE, or Literary Gleaner.
   (See *Pocket Magazine; or Literary Gleaner,
   &c.*)

MONTHLY MAGAZINE and British Register.
London. v1-63, 1796-1825.
   a: ULS; ULSup. / *b:* UCP; BP v1-2, 4,
   6; BdP lacking pt2 for 1819; 1820; CrP
   v1-7; EP v18-21, 23-24; GeG v1-6; L; LdL
   v1-4, 23-56; LvP v1-35; SwP v18-19, 51-
   52, 57-60; WcP v1-46.
Continued as
MONTHLY MAGAZINE; or, British Register
of Literature, Sciences, and the Belles-
Lettres. New Series. London. v1-18, 1826-
34; ns, v1, 1835. m.
   a: ULS. / *b:* UCP; BdP; L v1-2, 4, 8-18;
   RP v1-4; SwP ns, v2; WcP v2-10, 12.
   (Continued as *Monthly Magazine of Politics, Literature, and the Belles Lettres,*
   1835-38; as *Monthly Magazine,* 1839-43.)

MONTHLY MAGAZINE OF MUSIC. London.
v1, no1, 1823. m.
   a: ULS. / *b:* L; O.

MONTHLY MEDICO-CHIRURGICAL REVIEW
and Chemico-Philosophical Magazine.
   (See *Weekly Medico-Chirurgical and Philosophical Magazine.*)

MONTHLY MESSENGER of the Hebrew-
Christian Brethren. London?. v1, no1, Je
1831.
   b: BP.

MONTHLY MILITARY COMPANION; containing Communications relative to the Stand-
ing Orders, and Plans, and Treatises on
Fortifications, &c., for the Use of the Officers of the Army. Dublin. v1-2, 1801-02. (Also called *Ancell's Monthly Military Companion.*)
   b: L.

MONTHLY MIRROR; reflecting Men and Manners. London. v1-22, 1795-1806; ns, v1-9, 1807-11. m.
  a: ULS; ULSup; KyLx v12-22; ns, v4-7. / *b:* UCP; BP v1, 3; BrP v1-10; L lacking several pp. of ns, v1-2; LLL; MR.

MONTHLY MISCELLANY; or, Irish Review and Register. Dublin. no1+, Ap 1796-[Mr 1797]. m.
  b: DL no1-4.

MONTHLY MONITOR and Philanthropic Museum.
  (See *Cheap Magazine; or Poor Man's Fireside Companion.*)

MONTHLY MUSEUM; or Dublin Literary Repertory of Arts. Sciences, Literature, and Miscellaneous Information. Dublin. v1-2, O 1813-D 1814. m.
  a: ULS. / *b:* UCP; DL; L.

MONTHLY MUSICAL and Literary Magazine. London. no1-5, 1830. m.
  b: L; O no1-4.

MONTHLY NOTICES of the Royal Astronomical Society of London.
  (See *Royal Astronomical Society of London.*)

MONTHLY PANORAMA. Dublin. Ja-Je 1810. m.
  a: ULS. / *b:* DLL; L.
  (Incorporated with *Hibernia Magazine* to become *Hibernia Magazine and Dublin Monthly Panorama.* See *Hibernia Magazine* for library listings.)

MONTHLY PANTHEON; or, General Repertory of Politics, Arts, Sciences, Literature, and Miscellaneous Information. Dublin. v1-4, no1-18, Je 1808-N 1809. m.
  a: ULS. / *b:* UCP; BIL v1-2; DL.

MONTHLY PRECEPTOR; or, Juvenile Library. London. v1, 1800. m.
  b: L; O.
  Continued as
JUVENILE LIBRARY, including a Complete Course of Instruction on every Useful Subject. London. v2, 1801. m.
  b: L; O.
  Continued as
JUVENILE ENCYCLOPEDIA. London. v3-6, 1802-03. m.
  b: L; O.

MONTHLY PRECEPTOR and Youth's Manual. London. v1-2, 1830-31. m.
  b: L no1-10.

MONTHLY REGISTER and Encyclopedian Magazine. London. v1-3, Ap 1802-O 1803. m.
  a: ULS; MB. / *b:* L; LGU.

MONTHLY REGISTER OF LITERATURE; or Magazin des Savans. London. v1, Ja-Je 1792/?. m.
  a: ULS.

MONTHLY REPORTER. Edinburgh. no1, Ag 1826. m.
  (No issues known. Data from S N & Q, s2. VI.167.)

MONTHLY REPOSITORY and Review of Theology.
  (See *Monthly Repository of Theology and General Literature.*)

MONTHLY REPOSITORY OF THEOLOGY and General Literature. London, Hackney. v1-21, 1806-26. m.
  a: ULS. / *b:* UCP; BP; L; MR; SwP.
  Continued as
MONTHLY REPOSITORY and Review of Theology and General Literature. London, Hackney. ns, v1-11, 1827-37; s3, v1, 1837-38. m.
  a: ULS; ULSup. / *b:* UCP; BP; L; LLL; MR; SwP.

MONTHLY REVIEW. A Periodical Work giving an Account, with proper Abstracts of, and Extracts from, the new Books, &c. London. v1-81, 1749-89. m.
  a: ULS; ULSup; KyU. / *b:* UCP; BP; BdP; BrP; CrP; GeG; GrP; L; LGU; LLL; LP; LVA; MCh; MoM; PrH; WcP.
  Continued as
MONTHLY REVIEW; or, Literary Journal, Enlarged. London. s2, v1-108, 1790-1825. m.
  a: ULS; ULSup; KyLx v34-41; KyU lacking v49. / *b:* UCP; BP 1790-1821; BdP; BrP; CrP v1-96; GeG; GrP 1790-1824; L; LGU lacking 1809; LLL; LP; LVA; LvP lacking v17, 20-21, 57, 86, 96; MCh 1790-1821; MR 1792-1806, lacking v9-15; MoM; PrH; WcP.
  Continued as
MONTHLY REVIEW. New and Improved Series. London. s3, v1-15, 1826-30; s4, v1-45, 1831-45. m.
  a: ULS; ULSup. / *b:* UCP; BdP lacking pt1-2, 1826; pt2, 1827; 1828; pt1, 1829; pt1, 3, 1830; pt3, 1831; 1832; BrP; GeG; L; LGU; LIL v1-15; ns, v1-3; LP; MoM 1825-31; PrH; WcP.

MONTHLY REVIEW, or Literary Journal, enlarged.
  (See *Monthly Review. A Periodical Work,* &c.)

MONTHLY SCRAPBOOK; a Collection of Amusing, Instructive and Striking Pieces, with Monthly Instructions for Garden Work, and the Rising and Setting of the Sun. Dunfermline. Ja-D 1832. m.
  a: ULS. / *b:* DmP.

MONTHLY SPECTATOR. London. no1, F 1803. m.
  (No issues known. Data from John Nichol, *Literary Anecdotes,* v.9,p.711.)

MONTHLY TEACHER. Keighley. v1-8, 1829-36. m.
  b: BdP; L lacking v7; LdP v1-2, 4-7.

MONTHLY THEATRICAL REPORTER, or *Literary Mirror*. London. v1, O 1814-1815. m.
  a: ULS; ULSup. / *b:* UCP; L.

MONTHLY VISITOR.
  (No issues known. Data from S N & Q, s1. VI.120.)

MONTHLY VISITOR and Entertaining Pocket Companion. London. v1-11, 1797-1800. m.
  a: ULS; CtY. / *b:* UCP; DL; L.
  Continued as
MONTHLY VISITOR and New Family Magazine. New Series. London. v12-15; ns, v1-8, 1801-04. m.
  a: ULS; CtY 1801-03. / *b:* UCP; DL lacking v14; L.

MONTHLY VISITOR and New Family Magazine.
  (See *Monthly Visitor and Entertaining Pocket Companion.*)

MONTROSE, ARBROATH, AND BRECHIN Review, and Forfar and Kincardine Shires Advertiser. Montrose. Ja 18, 1811-1919.
  b: ArP 1812-32 impf.; DnP Ap-D 1825; MoP; MoMR; MoP no1-52, 1811; no105-208, 1813-14; no314-365, 1817; no418-70, 1819; no 471-522, 1820; no599, 622, 1822; no637-64, 1823.
  (Continued as *Montrose Review*, 1919-date.)

MONTROSE CHRONICLE, or Argus and Mearns Advertiser. Montrose. no1-176, N 19, 1819-Mr 27, 1823. w.
  a: CSmH Mr 30, 1827. / *b:* ArP N 19, 1819-D 15, 1820; GM N 19, 1819-F 15, 1822; MoP no3, 11, 13-28, for 1820; no 173-75, for 1823.

MONTROSE COURIER and General Advertiser for the Counties of Forfar and Kincardine. Montrose. no1-53, My 15, 1815-My 3, 1816. w.
  b: MoP lacking no1-2.

MONTROSE REVIEW.
  (See *Montrose, Arbroath, and Brechin Review, &c.*)

MONTROSE STANDARD. Montrose. [?]-1816-1821/?.
  (No issues known. Data from *Transactions of the Edinburgh Bibliographical Society*, I. 5. Sect. 10.)

MOON REVIEW.
  (See *Hibernian Review.*)

MOORE'S ALMANAC, Improved. London. 1815-33.
  b: LGU 1815, 1819, 1823-25, 1827-30.

MOORE'S PRICES of English and Foreign Funds. London. Ja 1827-D 1839.
  b: L.

MORAL AND LITERARY OBSERVER. Paisley. no1-12, F 15-My 3, 1823.
  b: GM; PsP.

MORAL AND POLITICAL MAGAZINE of the London Corresponding Society. London. v1, Je-D 1796.
  a: ULS. / *b:* UCP.

MORAL REFORMER and Protestor against the Vices, Abuses, and Corruptions of the Age. London. v1-3, 1831-33; s2, no1-23, 1838-39. (For a time known as *Liversey's Moral Reformer.*)
  a: ULS. / *b:* UCP; L.

MORALIST. Macclesfield. no1-14, Ap 20-Je 15, 1805.
  b: UCP.

MORALIST. London. v1, no1-16, 1823/?.
  a: ULS. / *b:* L.

MORAVIAN MISSIONS.
  (See *Periodical Accounts relating to the Moravian Missions.*)

MORISON'S PERTH and Perthshire Register . . . containing Accurate Lists of the Institutions, Public Officers, &c., in the City and County. Perth. 1812.
  b: L.

MORNING ADVERTISER. London. no1+, F 8, 1794-date. d.
  a: ULS; NNHi 6 sc.nos. 1796; 5 sc.nos. 1801; 2 sc.nos. 1802; NcD 1808, lacking 4 nos.; 1811, lacking Ja1; TxU 11 sc.nos. 1794-97. / *b:* BP S 18, 1826; L Je 21, 1804-1810; 1818-32.

MORNING CHRONICLE.
  (See *Morning Chronicle, and London Advertiser.*)

MORNING CHRONICLE, and London Advertiser. London. 1769-1862. d. (Subtitle dropped 1789 or 1790.)
  a: ULS; CtY (Ja 2-Mr 1789); 18 sc.nos. 1791-93; sc.nos. 1796; (Ja-Ap 20, 1797); (Ja 1-S 22, 1799); Ap 1, 1800-Ap 6, 1804; sc.nos. 1805-06; complete 1807-32; DLC 19 sc.nos. 1791-1806; (Jl 1-D 28, 1808; Ja 5-Je 30, D 12, 14, 27-28, 1809; 4 sc. nos. 1810-13; Ja 8-31, S20-O 16, 20, 22-28; 4 sc.nos. 1816; (1818-21); [1822-26]; (1827-32); ICU Mr-My 1789; Ap 13-16, 18, 1791; (1792-95); f.c. 1801-32; MB Ap 1, 1794-D 31, 1824; Ja 1, 1826-1832; MBAt (Ja-Mr 1789; Ja 5-My 13, 1807; F 5-Jl, 1808); Ag 31, 1814-S 1, 1817; 1820-32; MHi (Ag-D 1808); 1809-32; MdBJ sc.nos. 1791-92; MiU (Ja 15-Jl 3, 1823; S 15-28, 1824; 1825-32); MnU sc.nos. 1790-93; [1801-08]; 3 sc.nos. 1810-1813; 1817; (Jl-D 1818-Jl 1820, 1821-22); 1823-25; sc.nos. 1826-28; NNC Ja-O 1812, uncollated; NNHi 11 sc.nos. 1794-96; 10 sc.nos. 1799-1803; [N 21, 1804-O 11, 1805]; 10 sc.nos. 1807-08; 1 no. 1812; N 2, 1818-Ja 27, 1821; NcD 25 sc.nos. Ja-Mr 1789; f.c. Ja 1794-D 1800; (1801-S 1803; 1804); sc.nos. 1805-06; (1807-32); NjR 9 sc.nos. 1792-1801; 12 sc.nos. 1814-15; PPHi My 29-D 31, 1818; PU Je 14, 16-21, 23-25, 1806; V 2 sc.nos. 1793; WHi 10 sc.nos. 1802; 10 sc.

nos. 1813-20; 3 sc.nos. 1827. /   b: BP
widely sc.nos. 1795-1831; BiP Ja 23-Mr
15, 1790; sc.nos. Ap 6-D 25, 1790; 24 sc.
nos. 1791; 27 sc.nos. 1792-1830; BlU Je
27-Ag 5, 1795, impf.; Ja 15, 1812-D 31,
1816 impf.; C 1793-95, 1801, 1821-32; D
D 21, 1824-D 1829; E 1814, 1819, 1821-
24, 1828; EU 1820-32 impf.; ExD 1813-
32;LLL (1797, 1817-22); MR sc.nos. 1792-
94; O 1789-1815, impf.; PsP Je 1, 1798-
My 31, 1813, with 1809-10 slightly impf.;
SptP Ja 1-F 25, My 8-O 29, 1793; F 22-
Ag 30, 1794.

**MORNING CHRONICLE and Public Adver-
tiser.** Dublin. 1796-[1799].
  b: MR Ap 22, 1796.

MORNING COURIER and Dublin Journal.
Dublin. no1+, Jl 29-N 23, 1825.
  a: CSmH no30, S 1, 1825. / b: L.

MORNING HERALD (and Daily Advertiser).
London. no1+, 1780-1869. d. (Subtitle varies.)
  a: ULS; C-S Ag 26-S 9, O 30, 1797-Mr 16,
1798; CaM Mr 16, 18-24, Ap 2, 9-28, 1812;
CtY sc.nos. Ja-Je 1789; (F 4-D 1790); sc.
nos. 1791; (1792-97); 1798; (1799-1801);
(Ap 1805-Ap 1807); sc.nos. 1809-21; (N
12, 1822-1823); DLC (1798); [Ja 19-S 18,
1799]; (O 5, 1799-N 4, 1800); sc.nos. 1801-
02; F 9-Mr 24, 1803; 2 sc.nos. 1804; widely sc.nos. 1820, 1822, 1827-28; [Je 22-D
1830-1831]; ICU (Mr 14-Jl 1789; N 22-D
25, 1790; Ap 6-Je 4, 1791; My 31-Ag 15,
1792; S 19-D 1794; Ja-Ag 8, 1795; Ja-Ap
2, My 16-Jl 18, 1796; MBAt widely sc.nos.
1790, 1797-98; complete Mr 25-My 10, 1824;
sc.nos. N 1827; complete Je 23-D 26, 1828;
MHi (O 17-D 1823; Ja-S 3, 1824); MdBJ
widely sc.nos. 1790-92; MiD-B 15 sc.nos.
S-N 1800; MnU (Jl-Ag 1815); [1820]; sc.
nos. 1821 & 1825; N (1799); NN sc.nos.
My-Je 1790; Ja 1-Ag 3, 1793; widely sc.
nos. 1797; (1798); sc.nos. F-My 3, 1803;
NNHi widely sc.nos. 1799 & 1830; NcD
sc.nos. 1789-92; sc.nos. 1801-02; NjR sc.
nos. Mr-S 1815. / b: BP widely sc.nos.
1789-1831; BiP 1823-25; BlU sc.nos. 1813-
16; C N 11, 1813-My 9, 1814; Je 5-O 8,
1823; 1828-32; L 1789-90, 1792-1810,1818-
32, with vols. very impf. before 1801; LLL
(Ja 20,1817-O 28,1825); MR sc.nos. 1792-
94; O sc.nos. 1790-97; (1798-1832).

MORNING JOURNAL.
(See *New Times.*)

**MORNING NEWS-LETTER, and Daily Com-
mercial Advertiser.** Dublin. [?]-1831/?.
  a: CSmH no67, My 24, 1831.

**MORNING POST (;or, Cheap Daily Adver-
tiser).** London. no1+, 1772-1937. d. (Subtitle varies.)
  a: ULS; CU 1804-10; CaK widely sc.nos.
1805-06; sc nos. 1812-15; CtY (Ja 19-My
19, 1789); sc.nos. 1790-1803; (Ja-Je 1804);
sc.nos. 1804-06; sc.nos. 1810-14; sc.nos.
1819-20; sc.nos. 1831; DLC sc.nos. 1791;
sc.nos. 1804; sc.nos. 1811; sc.nos. 1817;
ICN Jl 2, 1794-D 30, 1797; Ja 1, 1799-

F 10, 1813; ICU 28 sc.nos. 1789-1811;
(1823-24; 1829-32); MH 5 sc.nos. 1820;
MdBJ sc.nos. 1791-92; MHi O 8-14, 1823;
MiD-B [Jl-O 9, 1800]; MnU F 9-Jl 3, 1813;
My 19, 1830-Ja 19, 1831; 1832; NIC Ja 1-
My 27, 1800; NNHi sc.nos. 1799-1800; sc.
nos. 1804-05; NcD sc.nos. Mr 20-Je 9,
1791; sc.nos. 1815; sc.nos. 1832; PPL
1789-93; TxU My 2, 1797; V 1796; 1798-
1808. / b: C widely sc.nos. 1789-95;
D O 18, 1792; E 1831; KkKJ sc.nos. 1791-
96; L 1789-96 very impf.; LLL 1818-32
impf.; O (Jl 1803-Je 1804); widely sc.nos.
1789-Je 1802; sc.nos. Jl 1804-1812; SptP
Ja 1, 1793-N 18, 29, 1794; F 18, 1795-D
31, 1796.

MORNING POST, or Dublin Courant. Dublin.
1788-96-[?]. w.
  b: BlU D 8, 1795; C Jl 1, 1794; DA 7 sc.
nos. for 1791-1792; MR v5, no11 for 1792.

MORNING REGISTER. Dublin. O 29, 1824-
1843.
  a: CSmH My 5, 1827. / b: D 1828-32; L.

MORNING STAR.
  (See *Stuart's Star and Evening Advertiser.*)

MORNING STAR. Dublin. [?]-1793-1794-[?].
  b: C no180, for 1794; DA F 13, 1793.

MORNING STAR. London. [?]-1806. w.
  b: L no58, Ja 23, 1806.

MORNING STAR. London. no1-15, 1832.
  b: L; O no1.

**MORNING VISITOR; or, Breakfast Table
Companion.** Dublin. no1-162, Ap 8-O 12, 1822.
  a: ULS; PPL. / b: UCP; DA; DL; DRS
no1-19; L lacking no116.

**MORNING WATCH; or, Quarterly Journal on
Prophecy, and Theological Review.** London.
v1-7, 1829-33. q.
  a: ULS. / b: UCP; L.

**MOTTLEY'S TELEGRAPH, and Portsmouth
Gazette.**
  (See *Portsmouth Telegraph; or, Mottley's
Naval Military Journal.*)

**THE MOUSE TRAP. A very Clever Work with-
out Distinction, Party or Prejudice!!!** Birmingham. no1-2, S 13-20. w.
  b: BP.

**MR. MATHEWS' COMIC ANNUAL ... as Pub-
lished by Him ... at the Adelphi Theatre.**
London. v1-4, 1830-33.
  b: L.

**MR. REDHEAD YORKE'S Weekly Political
Review.** London. v1-11, 1805-11. w. (Titlepage of v2-11, *Weekly Political Review of
Henry Redhead Yorke.*)
  a: ULS. / b: UCP; L.

MUDFORD'S CONTEMPLATIST.
  (See *Contemplatist; a Series of Essays,
&c.*)

MULTUM IN PARVO; or, Physicians and Doctors Reviewed. London. no1-2, 1825.
b: L.
Continued as
ANTI-LANCET; or, Physicians and Doctors Reviewed. London. no3-4, 1825.
b: UCP; L.

MUNSTER FARMERS' MAGAZINE. Cork. v1-6, 1812-19. q.
a: ULS. / *b:* UCP; DRS v1-3.

MUNSTER JOURNAL and Limerick Commercial Reporter. Limerick. no1-6, D 14, 1832-1833.
b: ULS.

MUNSTER OLIVE BRANCH. Cork. Ag 1814.
(No issues known. Data from John Power, *Irish Literary Periodical Publications,* p. 9.)

MUNSTER PACKET; or General Advertiser. Waterford. no1+, Ja 14, 1788-[1800]. (Incorporated with *Waterford Mirror.*)
(No issues known after 1788. Data from CBEL, II.738.)

MUNSTER TELEGRAPH, or Commercial Advertiser. Limerick?. [?]-1819-1821-[?].
(No issues known. See Robert Herbert, *Limerick Printers and Printing,* p. 54.)

LE MUSÉE DES VARIÉTÉS LITTÉRAIRES. London, Paris. v1-5, 1822-24.
b: L.

MUSEO UNIVERSAL de Ciencias y Artes. London. v1-2, 1825-26.
a: ULS. / *b:* L.

MUSEUM. Leicester. no1-12, 1795/?. w.
a: ULS.

MUSEUM. Cork. no1-23, Mr 9-D 14, 1796. ir.
b: DLL.

MUSEUM; or, Record of Literature, Fine Arts, Science, &c. London. no1-66, 1822-23. w.
(v1 entitled *Museum* on the titlepage; but each number bears the title *London Museum.* v2 entitled *Literary Museum,* though no33-66 are called *Museum.*)
a: ULS. / *b:* L; O.
Continued as
LITERARY MUSEUM and Register of Arts, Sciences, and General Literature. London. no67-88, 1823; ns, no1-6, 1824.
a: ULS. / *b:* L; O.

MUSEUM CRITICUM; or Cambridge Classical Researches. Cambridge. v1-2, 1813-26.
a: ULS. / *b:* UCP; L; LLL v2; LdL; MCh 1813-21.

MUSICAL BIJOU. London. 1831.
b: EP.

MUSICAL FORGET-ME-NOT. London. 1831-32.
b: UCP.

MUSICAL GEM. London. 1832-45/?. a.
(No issues known. Data from CBEL,II. 841.)

MUSICAL MAGAZINE; Review and Register. v1-2, 1809-10. m.
a: ULS.

MY TABLETS; or, the Dublin Weekly Gazette.
(See *Connoisseur; or Dublin Weekly Gazette.*)

MYER'S MERCANTILE ADVERTISER.Liverpool. no1-254,[?]-My 6, 1822-1838. w.
a: CSmH My 14, 1827; DLC sc.nos. 1823; (1824); [1825-26]; sc.nos. 1829-32; NNHi D 29, 1823-1832. / *b:* L 1825-32.
(Continued as *Liverpool Mercantile Gazette,* 1839-75.)

NATION. London. no1-65, My 10-Jl 24, 1824. d.
b: L.
(Incorporated in *Globe and Traveller.*)

NATIONAL ADVISER. London. no1-138, Ag 10, 1811-D 2, 1812. s.w.
b: L.

NATIONAL ADVOCATE. Dublin. no1, F 19, 1831.
b: DA.

NATIONAL INSTITUTION for the Education of Deaf and Dumb Children of the Poor in Ireland. Report. Dublin. 1817-36.
b: UCP.

NATIONAL IRISH MAGAZINE. Dublin. 1830-31.
(No issues known. Data from John Power, *Irish Literary Periodical Publications,* p. 13.)

NATIONAL JOURNAL. Dublin. 1792.
b: DA no5, Ap 4, 1792.

NATIONAL LIBRARY. London. 1830-32.
b: UCP.

NATIONAL MAGAZINE.
(See *Dublin Literary Gazette, or Weekly Chronicle,* &c.)

NATIONAL MAGAZINE and Dublin Literary Gazette.
(See *Dublin Literary Gazette, or Weekly Chronicle,* &c.)

NATIONAL MAGAZINE and General Review. London. 1826-27.
a: ULS. / *b:* UCP; L.
(United with *Inspector, Literary Magazine and Review* to form *Inspector and National Magazine.*)

NATIONAL OMNIBUS and General Advertiser; a Journal of Literature, Science, Music, &c. London. v1-2, no1-91, 1831-33; ns, no1-

30, 1833. (no69-91 have no volume numbering.)
   a: ULS; CSmH no11-82, 85-91; MHi D 30, 1831. / *b:* UCP; BP; L lacking no88 of v2 and no17-30 of ns.

NATIONAL REGISTER. London. no1+, Ja 3, 1808-My 12, 1823. w.
   a: ULS; ICU Ja 3-D 25, 1808. / *b:* IpP F 18-D 29, 1816; L; LGU 1809; LLL 1808-15, Monday edn.; O 1808-15.

NATIONAL SCHOOL MAGAZINE. London. v1-3, 1824-25.
   a: ULS. / *b:* L.

NATIONAL SOCIETY for Promoting the Education of the Poor in the Principles of the Established Church. Report. London. v1-100, 1812-1911.
   b: UCP.

NATIONAL VACCINE ESTABLISHMENT. Report. London. [1811.]
   b: UCP.

NATURAL HISTORY MAGAZINE and Journal of Zoology. London. 1828-38.
   b: EP.

NATURAL HISTORY SOCIETY of Northumberland, Durham, and Newcastle-upon-Tyne. Report. Newcastle-upon-Tyne. 1830-51/?.
   a: ULS. / *b:* LR.

NATURAL HISTORY SOCIETY of Northumberland, Durham, and Newcastle-upon-Tyne. Transactions. Newcastle-upon-Tyne, v1-2, 1830-38.
   a: ULS. / *b:* UCP; LR.

NATURALIST'S JOURNAL and Miscellany. Edinburgh. no1, Je 1832.
   b: L.

NATURALISTS' MISCELLANY. London. v1-24, 1789-1813. m.
   a: ULS. / *b:* DRS v1-3.
   Continued as
ZOOLOGICAL MISCELLANY. London. v1-3, 1814-17. m.
   a: DLC; MB; MH-Z. / *b:* UCP.

NATURALISTS' POCKET MAGAZINE; or, Compleat Cabinet of the Curiosities and Beauties of Nature. London. v1-7, 1798-1802. w.
   a: ULS. / *b:* UCP.

NATURALIST'S REPOSITORY, or Monthly Miscellany of Exotic Natural History. London. v1-5, 1823-27. m.
   a: NNM. / *b:* L.

NAUTICAL ALMANAC and Astronomical Ephemeris. London. v1-73, 1767-1859; v1-15, 1876-90.
   b: DRS 1800-32; LP 1789-1832, impf.; LR.

NAUTICAL MAGAZINE. A Journal of Papers on Subjects connected with Maritime Affairs. London. v1-39, 1832-70; s2+, 1871-date.

(Title varies slightly.)
   a: ULS. / *b:* C; L; LGU; LLL; LP.

NAUTICAL MAGAZINE and Naval Chronicle. (See *Nautical Magazine.*)

NAUTICAL REGISTER. London. no1-27, Je 26-D 25, 1822. w.
   a: CSmH Jl 31, 1822. / *b:* L.

NAVAL AND MILITARY MAGAZINE. London. v1-4, 1827-28. q.
   a: ULS; ULSup. / *b:* UCP; L; LvP; PmP v1-2.
   Continued as
UNITED SERVICE JOURNAL and Naval and Military Magazine. London. v1-37, 1829-41. q.
   a: ULS; ULSup. / *b:* UCP; BP; L; LGU; LLL; LdL; LdP 1831-32; LvP; MR.
   (Continued as *United Service Magazine,* &c., 1842-43; as *Colburn's United Service Magazine,* 1843-90; as *United Service Magazine,* 1890-1920. After 1920 united with *Army Quarterly.*)

NAVAL BIOGRAPHY; or the History and Lives of Distinguished Characters in the British Navy, from the Earliest Period of History to the Present Time. London. v1-2, 1800-05.
   a: CtY.

NAVAL CHRONICLE. Containing a General and Biographical History of the Royal Navy of the United Kingdom, &c. London. v1-40, 1799-1818. m.
   a: ULS; ULSup. / *b:* UCP; BP; BkP lacking v6, 20, 40; EP; L; LAt; LGU; LLL; LvA; PmP; SoP v1-3, 5, 10, 13-20, 23; WmP v1-28.

NAVAL MAGAZINE; or, Maritime Miscellany. London. v1-3, [1799]-1801. m.
   a: DLC v3.
   Continued as
BRITISH NAVAL MAGAZINE; or, Maritime Journal. London. v3, 1801. m.
   a: DLC Ap 1801.

NAVY ESTIMATES. Admiralty. London. 1810-date.
   b: UCP.

NAVY LIST. (Royal Navy List.) London. 1805-date.
   b: UCP; L Ja-My 1814; 1815; F 1816; Ja, Mr-Ap, Je-S, D 1817; 1818-Je 1819; Ag 1819-1820; F 1821-1824; F 1825-1832; LvP 1824-27, 1829-32.

NEGRO SLAVERY. Society for the Mitigation and Gradual Abolition of Slavery, &c. (See *Society for the Mitigation and Gradual Abolition of Slavery,* &c.)

THE NEPENTHES; or Liverpool Weekly Correspondent and Journal of Fashionable Literature. Liverpool. Ja 8-D 31, 1825.
   b: L; LvP.

THE NETTLE. London. 1809-10. f.
   b: O no1, 10, 12, 14.

NEW ABERDEEN ALMANACK and Complete Northern Register. Aberdeen. 1803-06.
  b: UCP.

NEW AGRICULTURAL AND COMMERCIAL Magazine, or General Depository of Arts, Manufactures, and Commerce. London. v1-2, 1811-12. m.
  a: ULS. / *b:* L; LGU; NwL v2.

NEW ANNUAL REGISTER, or General Repository of History, Politics and Literature. London. v1-46, 1781-1826. a.
  a: ULS; ULSup. / *b:* UCP; GeG 1791-97; L; LGU 1789-99, 1801-07, 1810-11; LdP 1789-1804; MR 1790, 1792; SwP 1789-1804, 1806-11.

NEW ANTI-JACOBIN REVIEW. London. no1-3, My-Je, 1827. f.
  b: L.

NEW BAPTIST MAGAZINE and Evangelical Repository. London. v1-2, 1825-26.
  a: ULS. / *b:* UCP; BP; CrP v2; L.
  Continued as
NEW BAPTIST MISCELLANY and Particular Baptist Magazine. London. v1-6, 1827-32.
  a: ULS; ULSup. / *b:* UCP; BP; CrP v5; L.
  (Incorporated with *Baptist Magazine.*)

NEW BAPTIST MISCELLANY and Particular Baptist Magazine.
  (See *New Baptist Magazine and Evangelical Repository.*)

NEW BON TON MAGAZINE, or Telescope of the Times. London. v1-6, 1818-21. m.
  a: ULS; ULSup. / *b:* L; LLL.

NEW BRITISH LADY'S MAGAZINE; or, Monthly Mirror of Literature and Fashion.
  (See *British Lady's Magazine and Monthly Miscellany.*)

NEW CALENDAR. London. 1791.
  b: UCP.

NEW CASKET; containing Gems of Amusement and General Instruction. London. v1-3, 1831-34.
  a: ULS. / *b:* L.

NEW COMIC ANNUAL. London. 1831. a. (Entitled in dedication and preface, *Falstaff's Annual.*)
  b: L.

NEW CONJUROR'S MUSEUM. London. v1-2, 1803.
  b: MR.

NEW COPPER PLATE MAGAZINE. London. 1795.
  a: ULS.

NEW CORK EVENING POST.
  (See *Cork Evening Post.*)

NEW CORNUCOPIA. Edinburgh. no1-5, Je-Jl 1832.
  b: ESL no5; GM.

NEW DUNDEE, PERTH AND CUPAR Advertiser.
  (See *Dundee Weekly Advertiser.*)

NEW EAST-INDIA KALENDAR. London. 1801.
  b: L.

NEW EDINBURGH REVIEW.
  (See *Edinburgh Monthly Review.*)

NEW EDINBURGH REVIEW. Edinburgh. 1832.
  b: EP.

NEW EDINBURGH WEEKLY CHRONICLE. Edinburgh. 1831. w.
  a: CSmH v1, no1, Mr 9, 1831.

NEW ENTERTAINING PRESS, and Instructive Magazine.
  (See *New Entertaining Press and London Advertiser.*)

NEW ENTERTAINING PRESS and London Advertiser. London. v1-2, 1832-33. (Title of v2, *New Entertaining Press, and Instructive Magazine.*)
  b: L; O no1, 36-37.

NEW EUROPEAN MAGAZINE. London. v1-4, 1822-24. m.
  a: ULS. / *b:* UCP; L.

NEW EVANGELICAL MAGAZINE and Theological Review. London. v1-10, 1815-24. m. (Binder's title: *Evangelical and Theological Review.*)
  a: ULS. / *b:* UCP; L v1, 4.

NEW FIGARO. London. no1-3, Mr 17-31, 1832. w.
  b: UCP; BoP; L no1, 3; O no1.

NEW, GENERAL, AND COMPLETE Weekly Magazine; or, Entertaining Miscellany. London. v1, 1796. w.
  b: O pp. 1-288 only.

NEW GLEANER; or Entertainment for the Fire-side.
  (See *Gleaner; or Instruction for the Fire-side.*)

NEW GLOBE. London. no1-132, F 3-Jl 5, 1823.
  a: CSmH no1. / *b:* L.

NEW GUIDE TO STAGE COACHES, Waggons . . . Vessels, &c. London. [?]-1803-1838-[?].
  b: L 1806-32; LGU 1803-04, 1808, 1812-13, 1816-18; 1821, 1823-24, 1828-31; LUC 1809, 1824-25, 1829, 1832.

NEW HIBERNIAN MAGAZINE. Dublin. v1-2, Jl 1820-Je 1821/?. m.
  a: ULS. / *b:* DL.

NEW IRISH MAGAZINE and Monthly National Advocate. Dublin. v1, Jl 1822-Ja 1823. m.
  a: ULS. / *b:* DA Jl-D, 1822; DL; DRS Jl-D 1822.

NEW JERUSALEM JOURNAL; or, Treasury of Divine Knowledge. London. v1, 1792. m.
a: PBr. / *b:* UCP.

NEW JERUSALEM MAGAZINE: or, a Treasury of Celestial, Spiritual,and Natural Knowledge. London. 1789-90. m.
a: ULS. / *b:* UCP; L Prospectus only.

NEW JERUSALEM MAGAZINE and Theological Inspector. London. v1-4, 1826-29.
b: UCP; L; O.

NEW JOURNAL. London. 1804-07.
(No issues known. Data from *Tercentenary Handlist of English and Welsh Newspapers, Magazines and Reviews.*)

NEW LADY'S MAGAZINE; or, Polite and Entertaining Companion for the Fair Sex. London. v1-10, 1786-95.
a: ULS. / *b:* BP (1791); L v1-8.

NEW LAPSUS LINGUAE; or, the College Tatler.
(See *Lapsus Linguae; or, the College Tatler.*)

NEW LAW LIST. London. v1-5, 1798-1802.
b: L.
Continued as
CLARKE'S NEW LAW LIST. London. 1803-40.
b: UCP; L; LGU 1817, 1821-30, 1832.
(Continued as *Law List*, 1841-date.)

NEW LIFE IN LONDON. London. no1-3, 1832/?.
a: ULS. / *b:* BP.

NEW LITERARY GAZETTE and Journal of Science and Fashion.
(See *New London Literary Gazette, &c.*)

NEW LOAF; or Food for the Mind. Edinburgh. no1-12, 1831.
b: EP.

NEW LONDON GLEANER; or Entertaining Register. London. v1-2, 1827.
b: DL.

NEW LONDON GLEANER; or General Repository. London. v1-2, no1-29, 1809/?.
a: ULS. / *b:* O.

NEW LONDON LITERARY GAZETTE, and Journal of Science, and Fashion. London. no1-27, 1827. (Also known as *New Literary Gazette and Journal of Science and Fashion.*)
b: UCP; L.

NEW LONDON MAGAZINE; being an Universal and Complete Monthly Repository of Knowledge, Instruction, and Entertainment. London. v1-9, 1785-93. (May succeed *London Magazine, Enlarged and Improved*, 1783-85.)
a: ULS. / *b:* UCP; L v1-5; LGU v1-8.

NEW LONDON MECHANICS' REGISTER, and Magazine of Science and the Useful Arts.
(See *London Mechanics' Register.*)

NEW LONDON MEDICAL JOURNAL. London. v1-2, 1792-93.
a: ULS. / *b:* UCP; LS.

NEW LONDON PRICE CURRENT. London. [?]-1786-1812-[?].
a: NNHi O 16, 1795-D 3, 1802; WHi N 7, 1806. / *b:* L My 9, 1812.
Possibly continued as
LONDON NEW PRICE CURRENT. [?]-1814-1870.
(No issues known. Data from CBEL,II.718.)

NEW LONDON RAMBLER'S MAGAZINE.
(See *Rambler's Magazine; or Annals of Gallantry, &c.*)

NEW LONDON REVIEW; or, Monthly Report of Authors and Books. London. v1-3, no1-18, 1799-1800. m.
a: ULS; ULSup. / *b:* UCP; L Prospectus only; NwL v3.
Continued as
LONDON REVIEW, and Biographia Literaria. London. v4, no19-20, Jl-Ag 1800. m.
a: ULS; ULSup.

NEW MAGAZINE. Strabane. no1-6, Ja-Je 1800. m.
a: ULS. / *b:* UCP; DL.
Continued as
STRABANE MAGAZINE. Strabane. no7-12, Jl-O 1800. m.
a: ULS. / *b:* UCP; BP v2; DL.

NEW MAGAZINE. The Dublin Museum.
(See *Dublin Museum, or Entertaining Pocket Companion.*)

NEW MAGAZINE. Ireland's Mirror; or, a Chronicle of the Times.
(See *Ireland's Mirror; or a Chronicle of the Times.*)

NEW MAGAZINE OF CHOICE PIECES; or, Literary Museum. Comprehending an Interesting . . . Assemblage of Entertaining Articles in every Branch of Human Knowledge. London. v1-2, 1810.
a: ULS. / *b:* DL; L.

NEW MAGAZINE OF KNOWLEDGE concerning Heaven and Hell and the Universal World of Nature. London. v1-2, no1-20, Ap 1790-O 1791/?. (Subtitle varies.)
a: ULSup. / *b:* UCP; O.

NEW MEDICAL AND PHYSICAL JOURNAL; or, Annals of Medicine, Natural History, and Chemistry. London. v1-10, 1810-15. m.
a: ULS; ULSup. / *b:* UCP; L v9-10, lacking Ja-Mr of v9; LS.

NEW MERCANTILE JOURNAL.
(See *Mercantile Journal.*)

NEW METHODIST MAGAZINE and Evangelical Repository.
(See *Methodist Magazine; or Evangelical Repository.*)

NEW MONTHLY MAGAZINE and Literary Journal.
(See *New Monthly Magazine and Universal Register.*)

NEW MONTHLY MAGAZINE and Universal
Register. London. v1-14, 1814-20. m.
  a: ULS; ULSup. / b: UCP; BP v1, 3-14
  with v4 impf.; BdP 1814-16, 1818-20, with
  1818 impf.; CrP; GrP v1-5, 14; HdP Jl-D
  1820; L; LLL; LVA; LdL; LvP v1-2, 4;
  MsP v2, 4-6; WcP v7, 11-12.
  Continued as
NEW MONTHLY MAGAZINE and Literary
Journal. London. v15-48, 1821-36. m.
  a: ULS; ULSup. / b: UCP; BP; BdP 1821-
  32, CrP v19-24; 31-37; EP; GeG; HdP 1821-
  25, 1831-32, with 1825, 1831 impf.; L; LGU
  1826-32; LLL; LVA; LdL; LvP; MR; SP
  1828-32; WcP.
  (Continued as New Monthly Magazine and
  Humorist, 1837-71; New Monthly Magazine, 1872-82; New Monthly, 1882-84.)

NEW MONTROSE REVIEW. Montrose. no1+,
1822.
  b: MoM no1, 10.

NEW NORTH BRITON.
  (See North Briton.)

NEW OBSERVER. London. no1-6, F 18-Mr
25, 1821. w.
  a: CSmH no2, F 25, 1821. / b: L.
  Continued as
INDEPENDENT OBSERVER. London. no1-
85, Ap 1, 1821-O 13, 1822. w.
  a: CSmH no84, O 6, 1822. / b: L.
  Continued as
SUNDAY TIMES. London. no1+, O 20, 1822-
date. w.
  a: CSmH no13, Ja 12, 1823. / b: C no56-
  57, 65; L.

NEW OPERA GLASS. Glasgow. no1-6, 1830.
  b: GM no2-3, 5-6.

A NEW ORIENTAL REGISTER and East-
India Directory . . . containing Accurate
Lists of the Company's Civil, Military, and
Revenue Establishments, &c. London. v1-2,
1800-02.
  b: L.

NEW, ORIGINAL, AND COMPLETE Wonderful Museum and Magazine Extraordinary. London. v1-6, 1802-08. (Also called Granger's
New, Original, and Complete Wonderful Museum.)
  a: ULS; ULSup.

NEW PENNY MAGAZINE, or Weekly Miscellany of Literature, Science and Art. London.
no1, S 22, 1832.
  b: O.

NEW PHOENIX. Dublin. [?]-1791/?.
  b: D v1, no59.

NEW PLAIN DEALER; or, Freeman's Bud-
gets. London. no1-5, 1792-96. ir.
  a: ULS. / b: UCP; L.

NEW POLITICAL CARICATURE MAGAZINE,
or Panoramic History of the Times. London.
[?]-1808/?. f.
  (No issues known. Data from Literary Annual Register, or Records of Literature,
  2 (Ja 1808) 35.)

NEW POLITICAL DICTIONARY. Glasgow.
no1-2, ca.1832.
  b: GM.

NEW PRINT MAGAZINE. Being a Collection
of Picturesque Views . . . in the several
Counties of England and Wales, &c. London.
1795.
  b: L.

NEW PROPHETIC ALMANACK. London.
1822-23.
  b: UCP.

NEW QUARTERLY REVIEW, and British
Colonial Register. London. 1811.
  b: L Prospectus only.

NEW REGISTER BOOK OF SHIPPING. London. 1799-[1833?]. a.
  (No issues known. Data from CBEL,II.
  718.)

NEW REVIEW; or Monthly Analysis of General Literature. London. v1-3, 1813-14. m.
  a: ULS. / b: UCP; NwL v1-2.

NEW SAILOR'S MAGAZINE.
  (See New Sailor's Magazine and Naval
  Chronicle.)

NEW SAILOR'S MAGAZINE and Naval Chronicle. London. Ja-D 1827.
  a: ULS; ULSup. / b: L.
  Continued as two separate publications,
  issued concurrently:
1. NEW SAILOR'S MAGAZINE. London. Ja
1828-D 1832. (Some titlepages for 1828-29
are entitled Soldier's and New Sailor's Magazine and Naval Chronicle.)
  a: ULS. / b: L.
2. SOLDIER'S MAGAZINE and Military
Chronicle. London. 1828-32.
  a: ULS. / b: UCP; L.
  (Superseded by Mariner's Church Soldier's
  and Sailor's Magazine.)

NEW SCOTS ALMANACK and British Register. Edinburgh. 1807.
  b: UCP.

NEW SCOTS ALMANACK and Town and
Country Register. Edinburgh. 1803.
  b: UCP.

NEW SCOTS MAGAZINE.
  (See Scots Magazine.)

NEW SPORTING MAGAZINE. London. v1-19,
1831-40; ns, v1-60, 1841-70.
  a: ULS; ULSup. / b: UCP; DL; E; L; LLL.

NEW SUNDAY TIMES. London. no1, Ja 4,
1829.
  a: CSmH. / b: L.

NEW THEOLOGICAL REPOSITORY. Liverpool. v1-5, 1800-02. m.
  a: ULS. / b: UCP.
  Continued as
THEOLOGICAL REPOSITORY. Liverpool.
v6; ns, v1-5, 1803-08/?.
  a: ULS. / b: UCP.

NEW TIMES. London. 1817-O 4, 1828. d. (According to CBEL,III.799, *New Times* was started before Easter, 1817, and soon absorbed *The Day;* was continued as *Day and New Times,* but the first part of the title was dropped before the end of 1817.)
  a: CSmH no6748, F 3, 1823; CU N 2, 1819-O 12, 1822; ICN Ap 1, 1817-S 26, 1818, not collated; ICU Jl 31, 1826-D 31, 1827; IU D 3, 1818; Ja 26-D 30, 1820; MB F 27-D 31, 1818; MHi (Jl 19-D 1821; Ja 22, 1822-O 6, 1823); NNHi Ap 9-N 6, 1827. / *b:* BP; L Ja 1, 1818-O 4, 1828; LGU S 19, 1825-O 4, 1828.
  Continued as
MORNING JOURNAL. London. O 6, 1828-My 13, 1830. d.
  a: CSmH Jl 24, 1829; ICU F 18-Ag 31, 1829, lacking F 19, Je 16. / *b:* BP; L; LGU.

NEW TOWN DISPENSARY, Edinburgh. Report of the Annual General Meeting. Edinburgh. v1-3, 1817-19.
  b: UCP.
  (Continued as *New Town Dispensary, Edinburgh,* 1821-42.)

NEW UNIVERSAL MAGAZINE.
  (See *Universal Magazine of Knowledge and Pleasure.*)

NEW VOYAGES AND TRAVELS; consisting of Originals, Translations, and Abridgements. London. v1-9, 1819-23.
  a: PPL. / *b:* L.

NEW WESLEYAN METHODIST MAGAZINE.
  (See *Methodist Magazine; or, Evangelical Repository.*)

NEW WIT'S MAGAZINE and Eccentric Calendar, consisting of Original Bon-Mots, Anecdotes, Puns, &c., of Living Public Characters. London. v1-3, no1-24, 1805. (Subtitle varies.)
  a: ULS; ULSup. / *b:* BP v1, no3.

NEW WONDERFUL AND ENTERTAINING Magazine; or Authentic Chronicle of Whatever is Curious, Extraordinary and Interesting in Nature, Providence, and Art. London. 1825.
  b: L.

NEW WONDERFUL MAGAZINE.
  (See *Wonderful Magazine of all that is Singular, Curious, and Rare in Nature and Art.*)

NEW WONDERFUL MAGAZINE; or, Marvellous Chronicle.
  (See *Wonderful Magazine and Marvellous Chronicle.*)

NEW WONDERFUL MAGAZINE, and Extraordinary Magazine, being a Complete Repository of all the Wonders, Curiosities, and Rarities of Nature and Art. London. v1-6, 1803-08. m.
  a: ULS.

NEW WONDERFUL MAGAZINE, containing Authentic Accounts, &c.
  (See *Wonderful Magazine and Marvellous Chronicle.*)

NEW YEAR'S GIFT and Juvenile Souvenir. London. v1-8, 1829-36.
  b: UCP; L.

NEW YOUTH'S MAGAZINE, compiled from the most Admired Writers. London. no1-10, 1824.
  b: L.

NEWARK HERALD. Newark. no1-156, O 5, 1791-O 1794. w.
  b: NkP O 5, 1791-S 1792. d.
  Continued as
MIDLAND MERCURY. Newark. no1+, O 1794-Mr 1795-[?]. w.
  (No issues known, and date of cessation not known. According to *Newark Herald* office, the present *Newark Herald* was revived some "seventy-eight years ago.")

NEWARK MAGNET. Newark. 1832.
  b: L no7, Ap 25, 1832.

NEWARK OBSERVER. Newark. 1832. w.
  b: L Ag 11, 18, 25, 1832.

NEWARK TIMES. Newark. no1-73, [?]-1830. w.
  a: CSmH v2, no66, S 29, 1830. / *b:* L no 41-73, Ap 7-N 17, 1830.
  Continued as
LINCOLN AND NEWARK TIMES. Newark. 1830-1931.
  b: L no76+, D 8, 1830-1832, lacking N 24, D 1, 1830.
  (Incorporated with *Stamford News.*)

NEWCASTLE ADVERTISER; or, General Weekly Post. Newcastle-upon-Tyne. 1788-1814.
  a: DLC D 10, 1812. / *b:* UCP; L no586-1350, Ja 4, 1800-Ag 30, 1814; LE 1795; NwP; NwS 1789-90; Ja 22-D 1791-1792; 8 sc.nos. 1793; (1794); 1795-96; [1797]; Jl 7-D 1798; 1799; sc.nos. 1813-14.
  (Transferred to Durham and changed to *Durham County Advertiser,* 1814-date. See the latter for details.)

NEWCASTLE CHRONICLE. Newcastle-upon-Tyne. 1764-1864. w.
  a: ULSup; CtY Ag 28, 1790; Ap 27, Ag 10, 1793; DLC 2 sc.nos. 1812; (Je-D 1813-Ja 21, 1815); ICU (Ja 3, 1795-Ja 23, 1796). / *b:* UCP; L 1789-1822, lacking Ag 19, 1797 & My 19, Jl 14, 1798; complete 1825-32; LLL (1790, 1794-96); NwEC 1789-94; 1798-99, 1806-10, 1815-17, 1820-32; NwL 1806-08, 1820-23; NwP (1789-1832); NwS sc.nos. 1789-90 & 1794-96; (1800); sc.nos. 1814-17 & 1824 & 1826; TmP sc.nos. 1795-1825; (F 1826-Jl 1827).
  (Continued as *Newcastle Weekly Chronicle,* 1864-date.)

NEWCASTLE COURANT. Newcastle-upon-Tyne. 1711-1884. w.;t.w.
  a: ULSup; CU 13 widely sc.nos. 1800-25; CtY (1789-93); [1797-1800]; DLC sc.nos. 1809 & 1811; [1812-21]; sc.nos. 1822-30. / *b:* UCP; L 1790; 1792; 1797-99; Ja 8-D 1803; 1805-07; S 23, D 16, 1809; 1819-22; 1824-32; LE 1795 impf.; NwEC; NwL 1804-06; 1815-26; NwP (1791-1831); NwS 10 sc.nos. 1790-95; (1796-1806); 1807-09; (1810-12); 1813-21; 1823; (1825); 1826-28; (1829-30); TmP 152 sc.nos. 1802-27.
  (Continued as *Newcastle Weekly Courant,* 1884-1902; as *Newcastle Weekly Journal and Courant,* 1902-10.

NEWCASTLE EYE INFIRMARY. Reports. Newcastle-upon-Tyne. 1822-36.
  b: UCP.

NEWCASTLE JOURNAL. Newcastle-upon-Tyne. no1+, My 12, 1832-1860. w.
  b: L; NwP sc.nos. My-D 1832; NwS.
  (Continued as *Newcastle Daily Journal,* 1861-1930; as *Newcastle Journal,* 1930-date.)

NEWCASTLE LITERARY MAGAZINE and Northern Chronicle. Newcastle-upon-Tyne. v1, 1824.
  b: NwS.

NEWCASTLE MAGAZINE, Newcastle-upon-Tyne. v1, S 1820-Ja 1821; ns, v1-10, 1822-31. m.
  a: ULS; ULSup. / *b:* UCP; L; LLL ns, v2; LP; NwL lacking ns, v10; NwS ns, v2-9; TmP ns, v1.

NEWCASTLE-UPON-TYNE and Northumberland Weekly Mirror of the Time, and Retrospect of Public Events. Newcastle-upon-Tyne. N 22, 1817/?. w.
  b: O N 22, 1817.

NEWCASTLE-UPON-TYNE Typographical Society. Publications. Newcastle-upon-Tyne. 1817-50.
  a: ULS. / *b:* UCP.

NEWGATE MONTHLY MAGAZINE; or, Calendar of Men, Things, and Opinions. London. v1-2, 1824-26. m.
  a: ULS. / *b:* L; LGU; O.

NEWMAN'S MORNING ECHO. London. 1809.
  b: L Prospectus only.

NEWMAN'S POLITICAL GLEANER, or Weekly Echo. London. 1809. w.
  b: L Prospectus only.

NEWRY COMMERCIAL TELEGRAPH. Newry. no1+, 1812-77. s.w.
  a: CSmH D 7, 1830; NjHi F 22, 1820. / *b:* L no55, My 25, 1813; Ja 1828-1832.
  (Continued as *Newry Telegraph,* 1877-date.)

NEWRY EXAMINER. Newry. no1+, Mr 17, 1830-Mr 23, 1844. w.
  a: CSmH, no11, My 26, 1830. / *b:* BlL Mr 17, 1830-Jl 2, 1831; L no129+, Ja 4-D 1832.

(Continued as *Newry Examiner and Louth Advertiser,* 1844-80; as *Dundalk Examiner and Louth Advertiser,* 1881-1930; as *Examiner,* 1935-date.)

NEWRY MAGAZINE, or, Literary and Political Register. Newry. v1-5, 1815-16. Every two months. (no1-5 have title *Newry Register.)*
  a: ULS. / *b:* UCP; BlL v1-4, L v1-2.

NEWRY REGISTER.
  (See *Newry Magazine; or, Literary and Political Register.)*

NEWS, a Weekly Paper, being a Faithful and Comprehensive Digest in Regular Series of every interesting Article of Foreign and Domestic Intelligence. London. no1+, 1805-35. w.
  a: ULS; ULSup; CtY D 4, 1814-16; 1818; 1820; 1829; DLC (1811-13); Jl 10, 1814-S 10, 1815; 11 sc.nos. 1816; 1817; sc.nos. 1818; (Ag 8, 1819-D 31, 1820); (1824); 1825-27; 1829-30; ICN (Ja 3-D 31, 1809); (Mr 24, 1822-1823); 1824-29; MnU 1816-28; OHi Ja-Ap 2, 1821; PPHi 1826-28. / *b:* BP Ja 1, 1815; D 24, 31, 1826; Mr 13, 1831; BiP 1812-13; L lacking 1806; LLL 1810-11, 1820-29.
  (Continued as *News and Sunday Herald,* 1835-37; as *News and Sunday Globe,* 1837-39.)

NEWS OF LITERATURE AND FASHION; or, Journal of Manners and Society, the Drama, the Fine Arts, Literature, Science, &c. London. v1-4, 1824-26.
  a: ULS. / *b:* UCP; L.

NEWTON'S LONDON JOURNAL of Arts and Sciences.
  (See *London Journal of Arts and Sciences.)*

NICHOLSON'S COMMERCIAL GAZETTE and Grocer's Register of Useful Knowledge. London. no1-165, Ap 7, 1832-1835. w.
  a: CSmH Mr 22, 1834. / *b:* L lacking no 15-16.

NICHOLSON'S JOURNAL.
  (See *Journal of Natural Philosophy, Chemistry, and the Arts.)*

THE NIC NAC, or Literary Cabinet . . . together with a Comprehensive History of the English Stage. London. v1-5, 1823-28. w. (Caption title of v1: *Nic-Nac; or Oracle of Knowledge.)*
  a: ULS; ULSup. / *b:* UCP; L; MR v1-2.

THE NIC-NAC; or Oracle of Knowledge.
  (See *Nic-Nac, or Literary Cabinet.)*

NIMROD.
  (See *English Gentleman.)*

NOBODY'S MAGAZINE. London. v1, no1-2, 1818. m. (Without titlepage or running title. Title inferred from preliminary address and superscription of letters to editor.)
  b: L.

NOLAN'S MAGAZINE; or, Weekly Miscellany of Knowledge. Dublin. no1, D 28, 1822.
(No issues known. Data from John Power, *Irish Literary Periodical Publications*, p. 11.)

NOLAN'S THEATRICAL OBSERVER.
(See *Theatrical Observer.*)

THE NON-DESCRIPT. Manchester. no1-20, 1805. w.
b: BkP; L; O.

THE NO-POPERY; consisting of Essays, Anecdotes, and Letters, illustrative of the Genius and Tendency of that System. London. no1-14, Ja 1-Jl 2, 1825.
b: UCP; L.

NORFOLK CHRONICLE; or, Norwich Gazette. Norwich. 1764-date. w. (Apparently succeeds *Norwich Gazette*, 1761-64.)
a: CtY 1791-96. / *b:* L 1789-97; Je 1802-1827; 1829-32; NrC (1789-1832); NrM sc. nos. 1820-25 & 1831; NrP.

NORFOLK YEOMAN'S GAZETTE. Norwich. no1-13, F 8-My 3, 1823. w.
a: CSmH no1. / *b:* C no4; L.

NORTH BRITISH ADVERTISER. Edinburgh. 1826-74. (In 1874 amalgamated with *Ladies' Own Journal.*)
(No issues known. Data from S N & Q, s1.VI.37.)

NORTH BRITISH GAZETTE. n.p. N 1, 1819-Mr 20, 1820.
a: NN.

NORTH BRITISH MAGAZINE AND REVIEW. Edinburgh. v1-3, Ja 1804-F 1805. m.
a: ULS. / *b:* E.

NORTH BRITISH REVIEW or Constitutional Journal. Edinburgh. no1-3, Mr-Jl 1814. Every two months.
(No issues known. Data from S N & Q, s2.VI.101.)

NORTH BRITISH SOCIETY of Halifax. Annals. n.p. v1-3, 1768-1903.
a: ULS.

NORTH BRITON. Edinburgh. 1830-32. s.w.
a: CSmH no101, My 11, 1831.
Continued as
NEW NORTH BRITON. London. 1832-33. s.w.
b: EP.

NORTH BRITON; a Weekly Political and Commercial Journal. Aberdeen. no1-3, S 9-23, 1825. w.
(No issues known. Data from S N & Q, s1,I.20.)

NORTH DEVON JOURNAL. Barnstaple, no1+, 1824-date. w. (Has varying subtitles.)
a: CSmH no117, S 22, 1826. / *b:* L no 132+, Ja 5, 1827-32.

NORTH DEVON MAGAZINE; containing the Cave and Lundy Review. Barnstaple. v1-3, 1824.
a: ULS; ULSup. / *b:* BaA v1-2; BddP; L v1-2.

NORTH DEVON MISCELLANY; or Magazine of the Muses. Barnstaple. v1, no1-3, Ap 2-Je 1, 1824/?. m.
a: ULS. / *b:* BddP no1, 3.

NORTH GEORGIA GAZETTE, and Winter Chronicle. London. no1-21, N 1, 1819-Mr 20, 1820. w.
a: ULS; ULSup. / *b:* UCP; BdP; L; MR; O.

NORTH STAR. Aberdeen. 1826.
(No issues known. Data from S N & Q, s1.I.21.)

NORTH WALES CHRONICLE. Bangor. no1+, O 4, 1827-date.
b: BnU O 4, 1827-1831; L.

NORTH WALES GAZETTE. Bangor. 1808-27. w.
b: BnU; L D 26, 1822-Je 21, 1827.

NORTH OF ENGLAND Medical and Surgical Journal. London, Manchester. v1, Ag 1830-My 1831.
a: ULS. / *b:* UCP; LMD; LS.

NORTHAMPTON FREE PRESS. Northampton. no1-130, Ja 4, 1831-Je 29, 1833. w.
a: CSmH no13, Mr 29, 1831. / *b:* L; NoP no37.
(Continued as *Northampton and Leamington Free Press*, 1833-34.)

NORTHAMPTON HERALD. Northampton. no 1+, N 12, 1831-1931.
a: CtY. / *b:* L; NoP.
(Amalgamated with *Northampton Mercury.*)

NORTHAMPTON MERCURY. Northampton. no1+, 1720-1931.
a: ULS; CSmH N 29, 1828. / *b:* L 1789, lacking Ag 22; 1790, lacking Ag 14; 1791-97; 1798, lacking Ag 11-S 22, O 27, N 10; 1799, lacking My 11, Je 29, S 14; 1800, lacking My 24, Je 21, Jl 19; 1801-03; 1812-32; NoMH 1793, 1798-1800, 1802-04, 1807-15, 1822-23, 1825-26, 1828, 1832; NoP; O sc.nos. 1789-91.
(Continued as *Mercury and Herald*, 1931-date, after merging with *Northampton Herald.*)

NORTHAMPTONSHIRE or County Magazine. Northampton. no1-6, Ja-Je 1820. m.
a: ULS.

NORTHERN AGRICULTURAL MAGAZINE. Elgin. 1828-29.
b: UCP.

NORTHERN CRUISER. Dundee. no1-4, Ap 22-Je 3, 1825.
b: DnP.

NORTHERN EXPRESS and Lancashire Daily Post. Manchester. no1+, D 1, 1821-F 1822/?. d.
b: SfP no5, D 6, 1821.

NORTHERN IRIS. Aberdeen. v1, no1-4, Mr 20-Jl 10, 1826.
   a: ULS. / *b:* UCP; EP; GM; L; O.

NORTHERN JOHN BULL; or, the English-man's Magazine.
   (See *Northern John Bull; or, Newcastle Pocket Magazine.*)

NORTHERN JOHN BULL; or, the Newcastle Pocket Magazine. Newcastle-upon-Tyne. v1, 1829.
   b: L.
   Continued as
NORTHERN JOHN BULL; or, the English-man's Magazine. Newcastle-upon-Tyne. v1-2, 1829-31.
   b: L; NwL v2, no4; SsP v1.

NORTHERN LOOKING GLASS. or Litho-graphic Album.
   (See *Glasgow Looking Glass.*)

NORTHERN MIRROR; or Inverness Maga-zine. Inverness. S 1830.
   (No issues known. Data from S N & Q, s1. II.52 and Inverness Burgh and County Public Library.)

NORTHERN OBSERVER, a Weekly Miscel-lany of Entertaining and Instructive Reading. Carlisle. v1, 1823-24.
   b: CsP; L.

NORTHERN REFORMER'S Monthly Magazine and Political Register. Newcastle-upon-Tyne. v1, no1-4, 1823.
   b: UCP.

NORTHERN REPORTER. Edinburgh. 1825-26. (Amalgamated with *Edinburgh Star,* Jl 8, 1826.)
   (No issues known. Data from S N & Q, s2. VI.66.)

NORTHERN STAR. Belfast. 1792-97. s.w.
   a: ICU (Ja 4, 1792-Je 12, 1794); NN Ja 4, 1792-D 30, 1796; NNHi Ja 4, 1792-D 30, 1796; NjP 1792-97 impf. / *b:* BP O 23-26, 1793; BlL; BlP; DA Mr-Je 1793; L Ja 4, 1792-D 29, 1794.

NORTHERN STAR, or Monthly Magazine.
   (See *Northern Star, or Yorkshire Magazine.*)

NORTHERN STAR, or Yorkshire Magazine; a Monthly and Permanent Register of the Statistics, Literature, Biography, Arts, Com-merce, and Manufactures of Yorkshire &c. London, Sheffield. v1-2, Jl 1817-Je 1818. m.
   a: ULS. / *b:* UCP; CfsP v1-2 impf.; HlP; L; LLL; LdL; LdP; O; SP.
   Continued as
NORTHERN STAR, or Monthly Magazine. London. v3, Jl-D 1818. m.
   a: ULS. / *b:* UCP; HlP; L; LLL; LdL; LdP; O; SP.

NORTHERN WHIG. Belfast. 1824-1920. w.;d.
   a: CSmH O 4, 1827. / *b:* BlL; BlNW 1824-29; BlP 1824-30 impf.; L no522+, Ja-D 1832.
   (Continued as *Northern Whig and Belfast Post,* 1920-date.)

NORTHERN YEARBOOK; or, Annual Regis-ter for the Counties of Northumberland, Dur-ham and Cumberland. Newcastle-upon-Tyne. 1829 [pub. 1830].
   b: UCP.

NORTHUMBERLAND ADVERTISER and South Shields Gazette. North Shields. no1+, Ag 16, 1831-1834.
   a: CSmH no1. / *b:* L; TmP (Ag 16, 1831-1832).

NORTHUMBERLAND AND NEWCASTLE Monthly Magazine. Newcastle-upon-Tyne. v1-2, 1818-19. m.
   a: ULS. / *b:* L; NwL; NwS v1; O; SsP; TmP.

NORTHUMBERLAND CHRONICLE of Lib-erty. Newcastle-upon-Tyne. no1-7, Ap 1-My 25, 1826/?.
   a: ULS.

NORTH-WEST OF IRELAND Society Maga-zine. Derry. v1-3, 1823-25-[?].
   a: ULS. / *b:* UCP.
   Continued as
NORTH WEST SOCIETY'S Magazine, a Pe-riodical Publication, intended to encourage and to improve Agriculture, Arts, Manufac-tures, and Fisheries. (North-West of Ireland Society). ns, v1-3, 1827-28.
   a: ULS. / *b:* DL.

NORTH-WEST SOCIETY'S Magazine, &c.
   (See *North-West of Ireland Society Maga-zine.*)

NORWICH AND BURY POST. Norwich. [?]-1784-1816/?.
   b: C 16 widely sc.nos. 1789-1816.

NORWICH AND YARMOUTH COURIER. Nor-wich. 1809/?.
   b: L Prospectus only.

NORWICH MERCURY. Norwich. 1725-date. (Succeeds *Weekly Mercury; or, the Protest-ant's Packet.* [1721-1752?].) (Subtitle varies.)
   a: CtY 1789-92. / *b:* C (1789-1832); L Ag 1789-D 24, 1790; 1829-32; NrC 1789-1804; (1805); 1806-32; NrM 1812-13; 1823, Ap-D 1827, 1828, 1831-32; NrP 1802-32.

NORWICH THEATRICAL OBSERVER and Dramatic Review.
   (See *Norwich Theatrical Observer and Ran-elagh Spectator.*)

NORWICH THEATRICAL OBSERVER and Ranelagh Spectator. Norwich. v1-2, F 10-O 3, 1827/?. (Title varies: no17-42 caption title as *Theatrical Observer;* v1 called *Norwich Theatrical Observer and Dramatic Review.* No37 was never published.)
   a: ULS; ULSup. / *b:* L v1.

NORWICH, YARMOUTH AND LYNN Courier, and General Norfolk Advertiser. Norwich. [?]-1818-23. w
   a: CSmH no452, Je 6, 1818. / *b:* C Ja 30, 1819; L no430-710, Ja 3, 1818-My 10, 1823.

THE NOSE. A Periodical Publication. London. Ja-Jl 1800. m.
  a: ULS. / *b:* UCP; L.

NOTTINGHAM AND NEWARK MERCURY. Nottingham. no1+, 1825-41. (Also as *Nottingham Mercury.)*
  a: CSmH no119, Ja 5, 1828. / *b:* L; NNG 1825-27; NP.
  (Continued as *Nottingham Mercury*, 1841-52.)

NOTTINGHAM GAZETTE. Nottingham. no1-127, Ja 1, 1813-Je 2, 1815. w.
  b: L; NP.

NOTTINGHAM HERALD. Nottingham. no1, S 13, 1826-[?].
  b: NP no1.

NOTTINGHAM JOURNAL. Nottingham. 1787-1887. w. (Also with varying subtitles. Preceded by *Weekly Courant*, 1710-[?]; *Ayscough's Nottingham Weekly Courant*, 1723-[?]; *Nottingham Courant*, 1732-[?]; *Creswell's Nottingham Journal*, [?]-1764-[?]; *Creswell and Burbage's Nottingham Journal*, [?]-1783-1787.)
  a: CSmH N 1, 1823; MeHi D 20-27, 1794. / *b:* L 1789; 1797-1812; N 26, 1814; Je 10, 1815-1817; 1827-32; MR sc.nos. 1797-1800; NNG 1789-1809; 1812-20; sc.nos. 1827-32; NNJ 1789-98; 1801-32; NP (1789-1832).
  (Incorporated with *Nottingham Daily Express.)*

NOTTINGHAM MERCURY. Nottingham. 1825-26. w.
  b: NNG.

NOTTINGHAM REVIEW. Nottingham. 1808-70. w. (Subtitle varies.)
  a: CSmH no208, My 22, 1812; CtY Jl 3, 1812. / *b:* L S 15, 1809; Ja 7, 1825; 1827-32; LLL Jl 17, 1818; NNG 1808-15; 1823-25; NP.
  (Incorporated with *Nottingham Daily Express.)*

NOVEL READER. London?. 1800.
  (No issues known. Data from CBEL,II. 683, and C & K, 1795.)

NOVITIATE'S PRECEPTOR; or, Religious and Literary Register for the New Church, &c. London. v1-3, 1827-29.
  a: ULS; PBr.

NURSERY AND INFANTS' School Magazine. London. 1830-32.
  a: ULS.
  (Continued as *Nursery Magazine*, 1833/?.)

NURSERY MAGAZINE.
  (See *Nursery and Infants' Magazine.*)

OBSERVADOR EN LONDRES. London. v1, no1, S 1819.
  a: ULS.

OBSERVER. London. no1+, D 4, 1791-date.
  a: CSmH Ag 20-O 1, 22, N 5, 19, 26, 1820; F 18, 1821; Ja 25, 1824; CtY D 28, 1806; sc.nos. 1820; (N 10, 1823-O 30, 1826); My 20, 1827-1829; My 20, 1830-1832; DLC O 27-D 15, 1805; ICU Ja 1809-Je 27, 1813, lacking Ja 8-29, F 19, 1809 & Ja 6, 1811; MBAt O 7, 1798; Je 3, 1804; Mr 2, 1806; NNHi Ag 9, 1807-N 1, 1812; Ja 3, 1820-D 30, 1822; sc.nos. 1830-31; NcD Ja 15, 29, 1832; NjR 4 sc.nos. 1813-15; V 4 sc.nos. 1793. / *b:* C 3 sc.nos. 1793-94; N 24, 1816; 5 sc.nos. 1823; EU Ap 1813-D 1816 impf.; L; LGU Ap 8, 1798; LLL (1817-18, 1829-32); SU 17 sc.nos. 1807-10; SfP (Jl 9-D 1820); 1821; (1822-23).

OBSERVER; or, a Delineation of the Times. Edinburgh. no1, S 28, 1793.
  (No issues known. Data from CBEL, II. 686, and C & K, 1803.)

OBSERVER; or, Essays on Various Subjects. Wisbech. no1-11, F 6-Ap 16, 1813. w.
  b: UCP.

OBSERVER OF THE TIMES. London. no1-52, Ja 7-D 30, 1821. w.
  a: CSmH no27. / *b:* L.
  Incorporated with *Aurora Borealis*, Ja 6, 1822, and continued as
OBSERVER OF THE TIMES and Aurora Borealis. London. no53-60, Ja 6-F 24, 1822. w.
  b: L.
  Continued as
OBSERVER OF THE TIMES. London. no61-103, Mr 3-D 29, 1822. w.
  b: L.
  (Incorporated in *The Constitution.*)

OBSERVER OF THE TIMES and Aurora Borealis.
  (See *Observer of the Times.*)

OBSERVER OF THE TIMES and Constitution.
  (See *Constitution.*)

OCCASIONAL. Buckingham. no1-13, N 30, 1821-F 22, 1822.
  b: UCP.

OCIOS DE ESPAÑOLES EMIGRADOS. London. v1-7, 1824-27.
  a: ULS. / *b:* L; MR.

ODD FELLOWS' MAGAZINE. Manchester. v1-ns, v6, 1824-42.
  b: UCP; L 1829-32.
  (Continued as *Odd Fellows' Quarterly Magazine*, 1842-47; as *Quarterly Magazine of the Independent Order of Odd Fellows*, 1857-83; as *Monthly Magazine of the Independent Order of Odd Fellows*, 1885-date.)

OECONOMIST; or, Englishman's Magazine. Newcastle-upon-Tyne. v1-2, no1-24, 1798-99. m. (Also known as *Æconomist.)*
  a: ULS; TxU. / *b:* UCP; BhP; L; NwS.

YR OES. Llanelli. v1-2, 1826-63.
b: UCP; CrP v1.

OFFICIAL KALENDAR. London. 1831.
b: L.

THE OGLIO. London. 1807-08. Every eighth day.
b: O no1-4, 8-10.

OHIO; or Museum of Entertainment. London. 1828-33.
(An error in UCP; should be *Olio; or Museum of Entertainment.*)

OLD BAILEY REPORTER. London. 1832.
b: O v1, no1, My 1832.

OLD BAILEY SESSIONS PAPER.
(See *The Whole Proceedings of the Sessions,* &c.)

OLD BRITISH SPY and London Weekly Journal. London. [?]-1779-1795/?. (Possibly succeeds *British Spy; or, New Universal London Weekly Journal.*)
b: NwS 1 no. for 1795.
(Incorporated with *Westminster Journal* and continued as *Westminster Journal and Old British Spy.* See *Westminster Journal* for details.)

OLD ENGLAND. London. no1-52, N 14, 1824-N 6, 1825. w. (Has varying subtitle.)
a: CSmH no15. / *b:* L.

OLD ENGLAND. no1+, Ap 14, 1832-1842. (Incorporated with *Alfred,* Ap 28, 1833. Publication suspended Mr 12, 1836-Je 15, 1839.)
a: CSmH D 23, 1832; Je 23, 1839. / *b:* L; MaP no14, Jl 15, 1832.

OLD ENGLISHMAN; and Anti-Jacobin Examiner. London. no1-17, D 5, 1798-F 10, 1799/?. s.w.; w.
a: ULS. / *b:* UCP.
Perhaps continued as
ENGLISHMAN; or, Sunday Express. London. [?]-1803-1834. w.
(No issues known. Data from CBEL,II.716.)

OLD ENGLISHMAN and Real Sentinel. London. no1-6, Mr 9-Ap 13, 1823. w.
b: L.

OLD POOR ROBIN. An Almanack, &c.. London. 1776-1826. a. (Succeeds *Poor Robin,* 1664-1776.)
b: UCP; LE 1790-99.

OLD SOLDIER. London. no1-10, D 26, 1828-Mr 8, 1829. w.
a: CSmH v1, no1. / *b:* L.

OLD WOMAN. London. no1-3, 1824/?.
a: ULS.

OLIO. London. 1792.
a: MdBJ. / *b:* UCP.

OLIO; or, Anything-Arian Miscellany.
(See *Proceedings and Debates of the Parliament of Pimlico.*)

OLIO; or, Museum of Entertainment. London. v1-12, 1828-33.
a: ULS; ULSup. / *b:* UCP (erroneously records it as *Ohio,* &c.); BoP; CrP v7; DL; HdP v3-11; L; LLL v1-5, with v5 impf.; O.

OLIVER AND BOYD'S Edinburgh Almanac. (See *Edinburgh Almanac.*)

OLLA PODRIDA. London. no1-6, 1825. m.
b: L no1-3; O no1-3, 5-6.

OLLA PODRIDA; being the Delectable Musings of the Trio. London. no1-2, Jl-Ag, 1816. m.
a: ULS.

OLLIER'S LITERARY MISCELLANY. In Prose and Verse. London. v1, no1, 1820. ir.
a: PP. / *b:* L.

OMNIUM GATHERUM: or, Bath, Bristol and Cheltenham Literary Repository. Bath. no1-7, O 15, 1814-F 1, 1815. f.
a: ULS. / *b:* BhP; BrP; GrP; LLL; O.

ONE PENNYWORTH OF PIG'S MEAT; or, Lessons for the Swinish Multitude, &c. London. v1, 1793. w.
a: ULS; ULSup. / *b:* UCP; L.
Continued as
PIG'S MEAT; or, Lessons for the Swinish Multitude. London. v2-3, 1794-95. w.
a: ULS; ULSup. / *b:* UCP; L.

THE OPERA. Edinburgh. 1832.
b: EP.

THE OPERA GLASS. A Series of Criticisms on the Performances of the Glasgow Stage. Glasgow. no1-27, D 19, 1829-Je 5, 1830. (Subtitle varies: e.g., *A Critique on the Performances of the Glasgow Stage.*)
a: ULS. / *b:* GM.

OPERA GLASS, for Peeping into the Microcosm of the Fine Arts, and more especially of the Drama. London. no1-26, O 2, 1826-Mr 24, 1827. w.
a: ULS. / *b:* L; O no1-9, 11-16.

THE OPPIDAN. Eton. no1-2, 1828.
b: EtS.

THE ORACLE. Tralee. no1, Jl 11, 1829.
b: O.

ORACLE. Bell's New World. London. no1+, Je 1, 1789-F 28, 1794. d.
a: CtY no32-295, Jl 7, 1789-My 10, 1790; no478-804, Ja 1-D 24, 1791 impf.; DLC Je 28, 30, Ag 1-13, 1791; ICU Je 13-Jl 18, 1789, lacking Je 24; Ag 23-24, 26, 30-31, 1790; My 31-Ag 15, 1792, lacking Je 8, 18, 28, Jl 17; MdBJ 12 sc.nos. 1790-91; (1792). / *b:* BP Ja-Je 1791; 33 sc.nos. Jl 1791-Jl 1792; L Je 1-D 31, 1789; Je 15, 1790; Je 3-D 15, 1791; 1792-94.
Incorporated with *Public Advertiser* and continued as
ORACLE AND PUBLIC ADVERTISER. London. Mr 1, 1794-[S 8, 1798]. d.

a: NcD My 9, 1798. (No other issues known. Data from CBEL, II.709.)
Incorporated with *Daily Advertiser* and continued as
ORACLE AND DAILY ADVERTISER. London. S 10, 1798-Mr 24, 1802. d.
(See under *Daily Advertiser* for library holdings, as well as for continuation titles: *Daily Advertiser and Oracle, &c.*)

ORACLE; Moral, Religious, and Literary. Northampton. v1-2, 1824-25/?.
a: ULS.

ORACLE; or Sunday Gazette. Dublin. 1796-97/?. w. (Probably succeeds *Sunday Gazette.*)
a: ICU no9, Jl 9, 1797. / *b:* UCP; L v2, no3, O 22, 1797.

ORACLE AND DAILY ADVERTISER.
(See *Daily Advertiser* and *Public Advertiser.*)

ORACLE AND PUBLIC ADVERTISER.
(See *Public Advertiser.*)

ORBISTON REGISTER. Edinburgh, Orbiston. 1825-27. f.
(No issues known. Data from S N & Q, s3. IX.223.)

ORIENTAL COLLECTIONS; consisting of Original Essays and Dissertations, Translations, and Miscellaneous Papers, illustrating the History and Antiquities, the Arts, Sciences, and Literature of Asia. London. v1-3, 1797-99. m.
a: ULS. / *b:* UCP; BP; L.

ORIENTAL HERALD and Colonial Review. London. v1-3, 1824.
a: ULS; ULSup. / *b:* UCP; GeG; L; LLL.
Continued as
ORIENTAL HERALD, and Journal of General Literature. London. v4-23, 1825-29.
a: ULS; ULSup. / *b:* UCP; GeG 1825, 1827-29; L; LLL lacking v6, 17-18, 23.

ORIENTAL HERALD, and Journal of General Literature.
(See *Oriental Herald and Colonial Review.*)

ORIENTAL QUARTERLY REVIEW. London. v1, no1-2, Ja-Ap 1830. q.
a: ULS. / *b:* UCP; GeG; L; O.

ORIENTAL REPERTORY. London. v1-2, 1791-97.
a: ULS; ULSup. / *b:* UCP; LR.

ORIENTAL SPORTING MAGAZINE. London. v1-2, 1828-33.
b: UCP.

ORIENTAL STAR. London. [?]-1816-[?].
a: DLC D 7, 1816.

ORIENTAL TRANSLATION FUND (Royal Asiatic Society). Miscellaneous Translations from Oriental Languages. London. v1-2, 1831-34.
a: ULS.

ORIENTAL TRANSLATION FUND (Royal Asiatic Society). Publications. London. v1-74, 1829-88; ns, v1+, 1891-date.
a: ULS; ULSup. / *b:* UCP.

ORIENTAL TRANSLATION FUND (Royal Asiatic Society). Report of the Proceedings for the General Meeting of the Subscribers. London. v1-5, 1828-34/?.
a: ULS. / *b:* UCP.

THE ORIGINAL; a New Miscellany of Humor, Literature, and the Fine Arts.
(See *The Original; or Weekly Miscellany of Humour.*)

THE ORIGINAL; or Weekly Miscellany of Humour, Literature and the Fine Arts. London. no1-22, Mr 3-Jl 28, 1832. (Subtitle varies slightly; for example, . . . *a New Miscellany, &c.*)
a: ULS; ULSup. / *b:* BP no1; DL; L; O.

ORIGINAL EDINBURGH ALMANACK and Universal Scots Register. Edinburgh. 1816.
b: UCP.

ORIGINAL RAMBLER'S MAGAZINE; or, Annals of Gallantry; an Amusing Miscellany of Fun, Frolic, Fashion, and Flash, &c. London. v1, 1827.
b: L.

ORIGINAL THEATRICAL OBSERVER.
(See *Theatrical Observer.*)

ORKNEY CLUB. Report. Edinburgh. v1, 1828.
b: UCP.

ORKNEY AND ZETLAND Charitable Society. Report. Edinburgh. v1-15, [?]-1830-1837.
b: UCP.

ORTHODOX CHURCHMAN'S MAGAZINE; or, Treasury of Divine Knowledge. London. v1-15, 1801-08. m. (May succeed *Clerical Review, or Impartial Report of Sermons,* 1800.)
a: ULS. / *b:* UCP; L; LdL v9-15.

ORTHODOX JOURNAL and Catholic Monthly Intelligencer. London. v1-12, 1813-30. m.
a: ULS. / *b:* UCP; BO 1813-24, 1829-30, 1832; L v4-5, 7-8, 11-12; SthC.
(Suspended after D 1830, but probably revived as *Weekly Orthodox Journal of Entertaining Christian Knowledge,* 1832-35. But see under this title for details.)

ORTHODOX PRESBYTERIAN. Belfast. v1-8; ns, v1-3, 1829-41. m.
a: ULS; ULSup. / *b:* UCP; BIL.

OSCOTIAN, a Monthly Literary Gazette of St. Mary's College. Oscott, Birmingham. v1-ns, v7, 1828-88. m.
a: ULS. / *b:* UCP; BO; BP v1-2; DCC v1-2; L v1-2; O v1-2.

OUTINIAN SOCIETY. Records and Proceedings. London. v1, no1-2, 1822. (No1 called *Report of Origin and Proceedings.*)
a: ULS.

THE OWL, or the Wandering of a Bird of
Night . . . Memoirs, Theatrical Critiques.
London. v1, 1831.
  b: L; O.

OXBERRY'S DRAMATIC BIOGRAPHY and
Histrionic Anecdotes. London. v1-7, no1-108,
1825-27. w.
  a: ULS. / *b:* L; MR.

OXBERRY'S DRAMATIC MIRROR. London.
v1, no1-24, 1828/?.
  a: ULS.

OXBERRY'S THEATRICAL INQUISITOR; or,
Monthly Mirror of the Drama. London. v1, no
1-6, 1828. m.
  a: ULS.
    Continued as
  STAGE; or, Theatrical Inquisitor. London.
  v1-2, no1-11, Ag 1828-F 1829. m.
    a: ULS. / *b:* BP v1 & v2, no8-10; L no2-
    6, 8-11.

OXFORD AND OXFORDSHIRE Auxiliary
Bible Society. Report. Oxford. v1-27, 1814-
45.
  b: UCP.

OXFORD AND OXFORDSHIRE Auxiliary Society for Promoting Christianity among the
Jews. Report. Oxford. v1-15, [?]-1832-42.
  b: UCP.

OXFORD ENTERTAINING MISCELLANY.
Oxford. v1, 1824. w.
  a: ULS. / *b:* UCP.

OXFORD GAZETTE and Reading Mercury.
  (See *Reading Mercury; or, Weekly Post.*)

OXFORD JOURNAL and County News.
  (See *Jackson's Oxford Journal.*)

OXFORD LITERARY GAZETTE. Oxford.
no1-6, 1829.
  b: O.

OXFORD MERCURY, and Midland County
Chronicle. Oxford. v1, no1-2, Ag 5-12, 1795/?.
w.
  a: ULS. / *b:* UCP; L Prospectus only.

OXFORD MISCELLANY AND REVIEW. Oxford. no1-2, 1820.
  b: L.

OXFORD QUARTERLY MAGAZINE. Oxford.
no1-2, Mr-Je, 1825. q.
  a: ULS. / *b:* UCP; DL; L; O.

OXFORD REVIEW, or Literary Censor, containing Analyses, Criticisms, and Notices
of New Books, Domestic and Foreign. Oxford. v1-3, 1807-08. m.
  a: ULS. / *b:* UCP; L lacking pp.417-32
  of O 1807; LdL v1-2.

OXFORD SPY. Oxford. 1819.
  b: O.

OXFORD UNIVERSITY and City Herald. Oxford. no1+, 1806-30. w. (Subtitle varies.)

  a: CSmH Ja 27, 1821; N 20, 1830; CtY no1-
  240, Mr 31, 1806-D 28, 1810. / *b:* L 1806,
  lacking Je 21-O; (1807-15); 1821-30; O no
  1-36; OPU lacking 1824-25.
    Continued as
  OXFORD UNIVERSITY CITY and County
  Herald. Oxford. 1831-52. w.
    b: L.
    (Continued as *Oxford University Herald*,
    1852-92.)

OXFORD UNIVERSITY CALENDAR for the
Year 1810(-date). Oxford. 1810-date.
  b: O; SP.

OXFORD UNIVERSITY City and County Herald.
  (See *Oxford University and City Herald.*)

THE OXONIAN. Oxford. no1-3, 1817.
  b: L no1; O.

THE PACIFICATOR. Edinburgh. 1818-22.
(No issues known. Data from S N & Q, IX.
145.)

PADDINGTON CANAL Boatmen's Magazine.
  (See *Canal Boatman's Magazine.*)

PADDY BULL. London. no1, Ap 6, 1823.
  b: L.

PADDY KELLY'S BUDGET; or, a Pennyworth of Fun. London. v1-4, no1-161, N 1832-
F 24, 1836; S 16, 1836-Je 4, 1859/?. w. (Subtitle varies. Volume nos. irregular. Sometimes called *The Budget.*)
  a: ULS. / *b:* BIL v1; L v1; O no1-3, 8-9,
  28, 30, 52.

O PADRE AMARO, ou Sovéla, Politica, His-
torica, e Literaria. London. v1-12, 1820-26.
  a: ULS. / *b:* L.

PAISLEY ADVERTISER. Paisley. 1824-44.
  a: CSmH no201, Ag 9, 1828. / *b:* PsP.

PAISLEY MAGAZINE; or, Literary and Antiquarian Miscellany. Paisley. v1, 1828.
  a: ULS; ULSup. / *b:* UCP; E; GM; L; O;
  PsP.

PAISLEY PHILOSOPHICAL INSTITUTION.
Report. Paisley. v1+, 1808-date. (Title varies slightly.)
  a: ULS.

PAISLEY REPOSITORY. Being chiefly a
Collection of Poetry, Original and Selected.
Paisley, no1-24, 1802-11. (The numbers published as of no date, so that they "might appear for ever young.")
  b: E; PsP 1809-11.

PALLADIUM. London. no1-98, F 6, 1825-D
17, 1826. w.
  a: CSmH no57, Mr 5, 1826. / *b:* L.

PALLADIUM. London. no1-2, Ap 5-12, 1829.
w.
  b: L.

THE PAMPHLET; or, Northern Scourge. Containing Political Disquisitions, Prominent Historical Narrations, and just Expositions of all Public Affairs. Durham. v1, no1, 1817.
 b: L.

THE PAMPHLETEER; dedicated to both Houses of Parliament. London. v1-29, 1813-28. ir.
 a: ULS; ULSup. / *b:* UCP; BrP; CrP; GrP; L; LLL; LdP; MR; MoM.

LE PANORAMA. Recueil littéraire Francais. Liverpool. v1, no1-18, 1829.
 b: L.

THE PANORAMIC MISCELLANY; or, Monthly Magazine and Review of Literature, Science, Arts, Inventions, and Occurrences. London. v1, no1-6, Ja 31-Je 30, 1826. m.
 b: UCP; L.

PAPER TRUMPET. [Edinburgh.] no1, [1832].
 b: EP; L.

PAPERS AND REPORTS of the Society for the Propagation of the Gospel.
 (See *Society for the Propagation of the Gospel.*)

PAPERS ON NAVAL ARCHITECTURE and other Subjects connected with Naval Science. London. v1-4, 1826-32; 1865. s.a. (Suspended after no13, in 1832, and not resumed until 1865, when it ran through no15.)
 a: ULS. / *b:* L; LP.

PAPERS PRESENTED TO PARLIAMENT. Foreign Relations. London. 1800-23.
 b: UCP.

PARENTAL MONITOR. London. no1-4, 1796.
 b: UCP.

PARENT'S CABINET; or, Amusement and Instruction. London. 1832-35.
 (No issues known.)

LE PAPILLON; or, the Bath Fashionable Trifler. Bath. no1-10, Ja 23-My 8, 1809. f.
 b: BhP; BrP.

THE PARIS MERCURY; and Continental Chronicle. London. no1+, My 28-Je 16, 1792/?. s.w.
 a: ICU My 28, Je 14-16, 1792.

PARIS PENDANT l'Année 1795(-1802). London. v1-35, no1-250, 1795-1802. w.; ir.
 a: ULS. / *b:* UCP; C; L; MR.

PARISIAN CHIRURGICAL Journal. London. v1-2, 1793-94. (Translation of *Journal de Chirurgie,* 1791-92.)
 a: ULS. / *b:* UCP; LS.

PARISIAN GEM OF FASHION. London. Ja-D 1832.
 b: L.

PARLIAMENT OF IRELAND. Transactions. Dublin. no1-5, 1792.
 b: UCP.

PARLIAMENTARY ABSTRACTS. London. v1-2, 1825-26.
 b: UCP.

PARLIAMENTARY DEBATES.
 (See *Cobbett's Parliamentary Debates.*)

PARLIAMENTARY HISTORY AND REVIEW. London. v1-2, 1825-26.
 b: UCP.
  Continued as
 PARLIAMENTARY REVIEW. London. 1826-27.
 b: UCP.

PARLIAMENTARY PAPERS. London. 1715-date.
 b: UCP; LIT.

PARLIAMENTARY POLL BOOK. London. 1832-date.
 b: UCP.

PARLIAMENTARY REGISTER; or, an Impartial Report of the Debates, &c.
 (See *Impartial Report of the Debates that occur in the Two Houses of Parliament.*)

PARLIAMENTARY REGISTER; or History of the Proceedings and Debates of the House of Commons (and the House of Lords), containing the most interesting Speeches, &c. London. v1-112, 1774-1813.
 b: L.

PARLIAMENTARY REGISTER; or, History of the Proceedings and Debates of the House of Commons of Ireland. Dublin. v1-15, 1782-95.
 b: UCP.

PARLIAMENTARY REVIEW.
 (See *Parliamentary History and Review.*)

PARLIAMENTARY WRITS. London. v1-3, 1827-34.
 b: UCP.

PARLOUR FIRE-SIDE; or, an Hour after Tea. Sheffield. no1-26, Mr 6-Ag 28, 1824. w.
 b: L; SP.

PARLOUR WINDOW. Dublin. no1-8, 1795.
 b: DA no1-7; DL; O no1-5.

PARNASSUS, a Weekly Compendium of Useful Knowledge and Polite Literature. Liverpool. no1, 1832.
 b: L.

THE PARROT, a Weekly Echo of the Literature, Fine Arts, &c. London. no1-21, 1832. w.
 b: O no1, 4, 21.

THE PARTHENON; a Magazine of Art and Literature. London. no1-16, Je 11, 1825-Ja 1826. w.
 a: ULS. / *b:* UCP; L; O.

PARTICULAR BAPTIST MAGAZINE. n.p. v1, 1827.
 b: UCP.

PARTINGTON'S SCIENTIFIC GAZETTE.
(See *Scientific Gazette; or, Library of Mechanical Philosophy.*)

THE PASQUIN; or, the General Satirist. London. 1821.
  b: O no1, F 24, 1821.

PASSATEMPO ITALICO. London. 1795-96.
(No issues known. Data from C & K, 1838.)

PASTORAL ADDRESS from the Ministers of the Synod of Ulster. Cookstown. 1803-09. a.
  b: UCP.
  Continued as
ANNUAL PASTORAL ADDRESS of the General Synod of Ulster. Belfast. 1831.
  b: UCP.
  (Continued as *Annual Address of the General Synod of Ulster to the Churches under that Care*, 1833.)

PASTORAL VISITOR. Bradford. no1-24, Ja 1815-D 1816. m.
  b: O.

PATRIOT. Dublin. 1792-93.
  b: UCP.

PATRIOT. London. 1793.
  b: O.

PATRIOT. Dublin. v1+, 1807-28.
  a: CSmH Je 19, 1823; IU O 5, N 23, D 29, 1819. / *b:* UCP; DA O 22, 1812; O 20, 22, 31, 1814; My 24, 1815; L no877+, My 29, 1813-O 31, 1828, lacking Je 1813-D 1822.
  Continued as
STATESMAN AND PATRIOT. Dublin. 1828-29.
  b: L N 24, 1828-My 4, 1829.

PATRIOT. Edinburgh. no1-7, O 9-N 20, 1819. w.
  b: GM.

PATRIOT. Manchester. no1, Ag 27, 1831. w.
  b: O.

PATRIOT. London. no1+, F 22, 1832-1866. w.;s.w.
  a: CSmH no1; CtY. / *b:* L.
  (Incorporated in *English Independent*, 1867-80.)

PATRIOT; a Collection of Political Essays. London. no1-16, My 12, 1792-Je 15, 1793.
  b: O.

PATRIOT . . . A Journal of Literature, Science, Theatricals, and the Fine Arts. London. no1, F 4, 1832. w.
  b: O.

PATRIOT: a Periodical Publication, intended to Arrest Progress of Seditious and Blasphemous Opinions too Prevalent in the Year 1819(-1820). Manchester. no1-19, 1819-20. w.
  a: ULS. / *b:* UCP.

PATRIOT; or Carlisle Advertiser. Carlisle. no1+, Je 3, 1815-D 1816. w.
  a: CtY. / *b:* CsCN; CsP.
  Continued as
CARLISLE PATRIOT; or Carlisle and Cumberland Advertiser. Carlisle. 1817-1910.
  a: CSmH O 31, 1829; CtY Ja 3, 1818; Ja 2-My 22, 1819; D 15, 1821; S 7-28, O 26, D 14, 1822; F 1-15, 1823. / *b:* CsCN; CsP 1820-24; Ja 22, 1825-26; F 10, 1827-1829; L My 7, 1831-1832; LLL (Ja 29, 1820-1821); WtP 1818-19; 1822-27.
  (Incorporated with *Cumberland News* and continued as *Cumberland News*, 1910-date).

PATRIOT; or Cork Daily News-Letter. Cork. 1809/?. d.
  b: C no32, Mr 21, 1809.

PATRIOT; or, Political, Moral, and Philosophical Repository. London. v1-3, 1792-93.
  a: ULS. / *b:* UCP; C v1; L.

PATRIOT AND GENERAL ADVERTISER.
(See *General Advertiser.*)

PATRIOTIC MAGAZINE; Political, Moral, Historical and Poetical. Cork. 1808-1809. f.
  a: ULS. / *b:* O no34.

PATRIOTICK MAGAZINE. Macclesfield, no1-10, O-D 1803. w.
  b: O lacking no4, 6, 9.

THE PATRIOTS; or, Palladium of British Liberty. Plymouth. [?]-1821-[?].
  b: PlP v1, no36, Ag 2, 1821.

PATRIOT'S CALENDAR. London. 1795.
  b: EP.

PATRIOTS' WEEKLY CHRONICLE. Edinburgh. 1794-96/?. w.
  a: ICU D 11-25, 1794; Ja 8, 1795.

PAUL PRY. London. v1, no1-26, F 18-Ag 12, 1826.
  a: ULS. / *b:* L no2-4, 7-11, 13-17; O no2-4, 22; StfS no9.

PAUL PRY. London. no1+, 1830-31.
  b: L lacking no1.
  (Incorporated with *Intelligence*, MR 20, 1831.)

PAUL PRY. Weekly Local Publication. Birmingham. no1-8, 1827. w.
  b: BP.

THE PAULINE. London. no1, N 1831.
  b: L.

PAYMENTS MADE. Ireland, Treasury Office.
(See *Treasury Office, Ireland.*)

PEACE SOCIETY. Publications. London. v1-98, 1817-1913/?.
  a: ULS.

THE PEDLAR: a Miscellany. London. 1796.
  b: O.

THE PEEPER. London. no1-34, 1796.
  a: ULS; PPL. / *b:* O.

THE PEERAGE (and Baronetage) of the British Empire. (Lodge's Peerage.) London. 1832-1912. a.
  b: D; SaU.

THE PEERAGE OF THE UNITED KINGDOM of Great Britain and Ireland. London. 1817-31.
  b: AU 1817, 1822-23, 1825, 1828-29, 1831; SaU 1809, 1817, 1822, 1825, 1828-29, 1831.
  (Continued as *Debrett's Complete Peerage,* 1834-36; as *Debrett's Peerage, Baronetage, Knightage, and Companionage.*)

PENNY COMIC MAGAZINE of an Amorous, Clamorous . . . and Glorious Society for the Diffusion of Broad Grins. London. no1, 1832.
  b: L.

A PENNY GEOGRAPHY AND GAZETTE. London. 1832. w.
  b: O no1, S 1, 1832.

PENNY LANCET. a Medical Magazine. London. no1-4, O 3-24, 1832.
  b: O.

PENNY MAGAZINE of the Society for the Diffusion of Useful Knowledge. London. v1-14, 1832-45. (Also called *Knight's Penny Magazine.*)
  a: ULS; ULSup; CSmH; WHi. / *b:* UCP; BP; BrP; CoP; CrP; DL; EP; LGU; LLL; LP; LdP; LvP; NwP; PeP; PsP.
  (Continued as *Knight's Penny Magazine.*)

PENNY NOVELIST, a Weekly Magazine of Tales, Fictions, Poetry, and Romance. London. 1832. (The issues undated. The year determined by internal evidence.)
  b: O.

PENNY ORTHODOX JOURNAL.
  (See *Weekly Orthodox Journal of Entertaining Christian Knowledge.*)

A PENNY PAPER FOR THE PEOPLE, by the Poor Man's Guardian, containing a Comprehensive Digest of all the Political Occurrences of this Week. London. 1830-31. w.
  a: ULS; CtY Ap 29-Jl 2, 1831. / *b:* UCP; BP; L; O Mr 1831.
  Continued as
POOR MAN'S GUARDIAN; a Weekly Paper for the People. London. v1-5, no1-238, Jl 9, 1831-1835. w.
  a: ULS; ULSup. / *b:* UCP; BP; L; O no 8, 15.

PENNY PULPIT.
  (See *Pulpit.*)

PENNY SCHOOL-BOOK. London. 1832. w.
  b: O no1, Ag 29, 1832.

A PENNY SHAKESPEARE, complete with Life, Glossary, &c., from the best Editions. London. 1832. w.
  b: O no1, S 8, 1832.

PENNY STORY-TELLER. London. 1832.
  b: O no9.

PENNY TRUMPET. London. 1832.
  (No issues known. Data from *Figaro in London,* 1 (O 20, 1832) 184.)

PENTATEUCH. Discourses on the Several Revelations of the Lord Jesus Christ, &c. London. no1, 1815.
  b: L.

THE PEOPLE. London. no1-15, Ap 19-Jl 26, 1819. w.
  a: ULS. / *b:* UCP; L.

PEOPLE OF ENGLAND. A Periodical Paper. London. no1-28, O 1-N 23, 1830.
  (No issues known.)

PEOPLE'S PRESS. London. 1830.
  a: CSmH D 15, 1830.

PERIODICAL ACCOUNTS of the United Brethren Missions.
  (See *United Brethren Missions.*)

PERIODICAL ACCOUNTS relating to the Moravian Missions. London. v1-34, 1790-1889; s2, v1+, 1890-date. (Title varies slightly.)
  a: ULS.

PERIODICAL ACCOUNTS relative to the Baptist Missionary Society. Clipstone, Dunstable, London, Kettering, Bristol. v1-6, 1800-17. a. (See also under *Baptist Missionary Society. Periodical Accounts.*)
  b: UCP; BP; L.
  Continued as
ANNUAL REPORT of the Committee of the Baptist Missionary Society . . . being a Collection of the Periodical Accounts. Bristol, London. 1819-date. q.
  b: UCP; L.

PERIODICAL CORN TABLES. n.p. no1, Mr 16, 1816.
  b: EU.

PERIODICAL DEVIL UPON TWO STICKS; or, a Peep at the Metropolis. London. v1, 1816.
  b: L v1, no3.

PERIPATETIC. London. v1-3, 1793.
  b: UCP.

PERRY'S BANKRUPT and Insolvent Gazette, containing a complete Register of English, Scotch, and Irish Bankrupts, Insolvents, Assignments, &c. London. v1-33, 1828-58.
  b: L lacking no1-36, 49-60, 193, 253-64, 290, 300, 307-25.

PERTH COURIER. Perth. F 1809-F 1822.
  a: C-S no6-585, Ag 10, 1809-Ap 22, 1819. / *b:* L My 28, 1812; PeP; PePA 1809-22 impf.
  Continued as
PERTHSHIRE COURIER and General Advertiser. Perth. F 1822-1929.

a: CSmH Je 17, 1825. / *b:* E 1829; PeP; PePA 1822-32 impf.
(Incorporated in *Perthshire Advertiser,* 1929.)

PERTH MISCELLANY of Literature, Agriculture, Gardening and Local Intelligence. Edinburgh. v1, no1-3, Ja-Mr 1830. m.
b: L; PeP.

PERTHSHIRE ADVERTISER and Strathmore Journal. Perth. 1829-1929.
b: PePA 1830.
(Combined in 1929 with *Perthshire Courier and General Advertiser* and continued as *Perthshire Advertiser,* 1929-date.)

PERTHSHIRE COURIER and General Advertiser.
(See *Perth Courier.)*

LE PETIT BIJOU POUR 1829. London. 1829. a.
b: UCP; L.

THE PETRISSEUR. Dublin. 1830.
(No issues known. Data from John Power, *Irish Literary Periodical Publications,* p. 13.)

THE PHENIX, or Griffith's New Morning Post. Dublin. 1789-90/?.
b: UCP; DA N 13, 18, 23, 25, 27, D 4, 1789; Ja 8, 1790.

THE PHILADELPHIAN MAGAZINE; containing a Great Variety of Important Matter... chiefly original, calculated to Promote true Religion and true Virtue. London. v1-2, no1-22, F 1788-N 1789. m.
a: ULS. / *b:* L v1.

THE PHILANTHROPE: after the Manner of a Periodical Paper. London. 1797.
a: PPL. / *b:* UCP.

LE PHILANTHROPE CHRETIEN, ou revue périodique des sociétés philanthropiques et reliquieuses de Londres. London. v1, no1, 1824.
b: L.

PHILANTHROPIC GAZETTE; a Weekly Journal of Intelligence. London. no 1+, Ja 1, 1817-Ag 27, 1823. w. (Subtitle varies.)
a: ULS; CSmH no25; OClWHi 2 sc.nos. Ag 1821. / *b:* L.
(Incorporated with *Baldwin's London Weekly Journal,* S 1823.)

PHILANTHROPIC MAGAZINE. Lindfield. no1-4, 1827-29.
b: O.

PHILANTHROPIC MAGAZINE. London. 1829.
b: E.

THE PHILANTHROPIST. Liverpool. 1826.
b: L no8.

THE PHILANTHROPIST; or, Philosophical Essays on Politics, Government, Morals, and Manners. London. v1, no1-43, Mr 16, 1795-Ja 25, 1796. w.
a: ULS; ULSup. / *b:* UCP; L no1-42.

THE PHILANTHROPIST; or, Repository for Hints and Suggestions calculated to Promote the Comfort and Happiness of Man. London, Lindfield. v1-7, 1811-19; ns, v1-2, no17, 1825-30. (Discontinued 1816-17, After ns, no17 had appeared, the work was discontinued but was revived in 1835-42 as *Lindfield Reporter; or Philanthropic Magazine.)*
a: ULS; OClWHi 1811-19. / *b:* UCP; L; LFS 1811-19.

PHILO-DANMONIAN; a Western Magazine of Matter chiefly original, &c. Plymouth. v1, no1-6, Ja-Je 1830. m.
a: ULS. / *b:* BddP; L no6.

PHILOLOGICAL MUSEUM. Cambridge. v1-2, 1832-33.
a: ULS; ULSup. / *b:* UCP; GM; L; LLL v1.

PHILOMATHIC JOURNAL, and Literary Review. London. v1-4, 1824-26.
a: ULS. / *b:* UCP.

PHILOSOPHICAL AND LITERARY Register. London. v1, 1792.
b: MR.

PHILOSOPHICAL AMUSEMENTS. London. 1790.
b: O.

PHILOSOPHICAL HERALD. London. 1795.
(No issues known. Data from C & K, 1869.)

PHILOSOPHICAL MAGAZINE. Comprehending the various Branches of Science, the Liberal and Fine Arts, Agriculture, Manufactures, and Commerce. London. v1-42, 1798-1813. m.
a: ULS; ULSup. / *b:* UCP; BP; CrP v33-42; DRS; L; LGU; LP; LR; MCh; NwL; SthC.
Absorbed *Journal of Natural History, Chemistry, and the Arts* and continued as
PHILOSOPHICAL MAGAZINE and Journal. London. v43-68, 1814-26. m.
a: ULS; ULSup. / *b:* UCP; BP; CrP v43-60; DRS; GeG; L lacking pp.225-40 of v45; LGU; LP; LR; MCh; NwL; SthC.
Absorbed *Annals of Philosophy; or Magazine of Chemistry,* &c., and continued as
PHILOSOPHICAL MAGAZINE; or, Annals of Chemistry, Mathematics, Astronomy, Natural History, and General Science. London. v1-11, 1827-32. m.
a: ULS; ULSup. / *b:* UCP; BO v1-9; BP; CrP; DRS; GeG; L; LGU; LP; LR; MCh; NwL; SthC.
United with *Journal of Science* and continued as
LONDON AND EDINBURGH Philosophical Magazine, and Journal of Science. London. v1-16, 1832-40. m.
a: ULS; ULSup. / *b:* UCP; BP; CrP; DRS; EP; L; LGU; LR; LS; MCh; NwL; SthC.
(Continued as *London, Edinburgh, and Dublin Philosophical Magazine,* 1840-date.)

PHILOSOPHICAL MAGAZINE; or, Annals of Chemistry, Mathematics, Astronomy, &c.
(See *Philosophical Magazine.*)

PHILOSOPHICAL MAGAZINE and Journal.
(See *Philosophical Magazine.*)

PHILOSOPHICAL REPOSITORY.
(See *Mathematical Repository.*)

PHILOSOPHICAL TATLER. Glasgow. 1826.
b: GM.

PHILOSOPHICAL TRANSACTIONS of the Royal Society.
(See *Royal Society of London.*)

PHILOSOPHY OF MEDICINE. London. 1799-1800.
a: ICU; VU.

PHOENIX; or, Blagdon's Weekly Chronicler. London. no1-16, F 14-My 29, 1808. w.
b: L; LE.
Continued as
PHOENIX AND PATRIOT; or, Blagdon's Weekly Chronicler. London. no17-46, Je 5-D 25, 1808. w.
a: CSmH no28. / *b:* L; LE no17-46.
Continued as
PHOENIX, PATRIOT AND ALBION. London. no80-136, 1809-10. w.
b: SU no80-102, 112-23, 125-28, 130-36.

PHOENIX; or, Manchester Literary Journal. Manchester. no1-25, Jl 5-D 19, 1828. w.
a: ULS. / *b:* L; MP; MR.

PHOENIX; or Weekly Miscellany Improved.
(See *Weekly Miscellany of Instruction and Entertainment.*)

PHOENIX AND PATRIOT; or, Blagdon's Weekly Chronicler.
(See *Phoenix; or, Blagdon's Weekly Chronicler.*)

PHOENIX, PATRIOT AND ALBION.
(See *Phoenix; or, Blagdon's Weekly Chronicler.*)

PHRENOLOGICAL JOURNAL and Miscellany. Edinburgh. v1-10, 1823-37.
a: ULS; ULSup. / *b:* UCP; BP; CrP v1-2; EP; L; LE 1823-29; LdP.
(Continued as *Phrenological Journal and Magazine of Moral Science*, 1838-47.)

PHRENOLOGICAL SOCIETY. Report of the Proceedings. n.p. [?]-1820-21-[?].
b: LdP F 22, 1820-Ap 23, 1821.

PHRENOLOGICAL SOCIETY. Transactions. Edinburgh. v1, 1820/23. [Pub. 1824]. (Also called *Edinburgh Phrenological Society.*)
a: ULS. / *b:* UCP; LS.

THE PHYSICIAN. London. v1, no1-2, N 3-10, 1832. w.
b: E no1; O.

PIANOFORTE MAGAZINE. London. no1-5, 1798/?. w.
a: ULS.

PIC NIC. A Literary Newspaper. London. no1-14, Ja 8-Ap 9, 1803. w.
a: ULS. / *b:* EP; L; O.
(Absorbed by *The Cabinet.*)

PICTURE OF LONDON; being a Correct Guide to all the Curiosities, Amusements, Exhibitions, &c. London. 1802-29.
b: LGU.

A PICTURE OF THE TIMES, . . . in a Series of Letters, addressed to the People of England by a Lover of Peace. London. no1-31, 1795. w.
a: ULS. / *b:* UCP; L.

PIERCE EGAN'S Book of Sports and Mirror of Life: embracing the Turf, the Chase, the Ring, and the Stage. London. v1, 1832.
b: L.

PIERCE EGAN'S Life in London and Sporting Guide. London. no1+, F 1, 1824-O 28, 1827.
a: CSmH no81, Ag 14, 1825. / *b:* L.
(Incorporated with *Bell's Life in London*, N 4, 1827.)

PIERCE EGAN'S WEEKLY COURIER. London. no1+, Ja 4-Ap 26, 1829. w.
a: CSmH no1. / *b:* BP Ap 19, 26, My 3, 10, 1829; L.

PIGOT AND CÓ.'S City of Dublin and Hibernian Provincial Directory. London. 1824.
b: DA.

PIGOT AND CO.'S London and Provincial New Commercial Directory. London. Manchester. 1826-27.
b: SaU.

PIGOT AND CO.'S Metropolitan Alphabetical Directory. London. 1828.
b: EU; SaU.

PIG'S MEAT; or, Lessons for the Swinish Multitude.
(See *One Pennyworth of Pig's Meat*, &c.)

THE PILOT. London. no1+, 1807-1815. d.
a: CSmH no1758, Ag 12, 1812; CtY Jl 16, 1812; ICU D 8, 10, 15, 1813; NcD Ja-F 17, Je 13, 1814; NNHi 12 sc.nos. 1808. / *b:* BP S 2, 1815; C Ap 14, 1809; L Mr 15, 1809-D 31, 1813; PlP N 27, 1811.

THE PILOT. Dublin. no1+, N 24, 1828-F 16, 1849.
a: CSmH Je 6, 1831. / *b:* L.

PIMLICO PARLIAMENTARY REGISTER. Hem! Hip! Hollo! Don't be Alarmed. The Pimlico Parliamentary Register. no1, 1808.
(May be a continuation of *The Olio; or, Anything-Arian Miscellany.*)
b: L.

PINDARIANA; or Peter's Portfolio. London. no1-26, 1795/?.
a: ULS.

THE PIONEER. Carlisle. 1818. f.
b: CsP no2-4, Je 3-Jl 1, 1818.

PLAIN DEALER. Dublin. no1-68, Je 9-O 4, 1832.
  b: L.

PLAIN DEALER. London. no1+, Ja 1-F 19, 1832.
  b: L.
  (Incorporated with *The Constitution,* Ja 22, 1832.)

PLAIN ENGLISHMAN; comprehending Original Compositions, and the Selections from the best Writers. London. v1-3, 1820-23. m.
  a: ULS. / *b:* UCP; BP; L; O.

THE PLANET. London. no1-3, 1831.
  b: L; O no1.

PLEASING ENTERTAINER, containing Choice Tales, Essaies, &c.
  (See *Weekly Entertainer or Companion to the Chester Courant.*)

PLEASING VARIETY. London. 1794.
  b: UCP.

PLEDGE OF FRIENDSHIP. London. v1-3, 1826-28. a.
  b: UCP; L.
  Continued as
  GEM: a Literary Annual. London. v1-4, 1829-32. a.
  b: UCP; HdP 1829; L.

THE PLINIAN SOCIETY. Transactions. Edinburgh. 1828-29.
  b: UCP.

PLYMOUTH AND DEVONPORT Weekly Journal and General Advertiser for Devon, Cornwall, Somerset, and Dorset. Plymouth. 1819-63.
  b: PIP no261 &c., Ag 19, S 9, 1824; Jl 7, N 17, D 22, 1825; O 19, D 28, 1826; Ja 22, 1829.
  (Incorporated with *Western Daily Mercury,* 1863.)

PLYMOUTH AND DOCK TELEGRAPH and Chronicle; or, Naval and Commercial Register. Devonport. no1+, Mr 19, 1808-33. w.
  a: CSmH no552, O 19, 1818. / *b:* PIP no1, Mr 19, 1808; no511, D 27, 1817.
  (Continued as *Devonport Independent,* 1833-91; as *Western Independent,* 1891-date.)

PLYMOUTH AND PLYMOUTH-DOCK Weekly Journal. Plymouth. no1+, 1819-23/?. w.
  a: CSmH no196, My 15, 1823.

PLYMOUTH CHRONICLE, and General Advertiser for the West of England. Plymouth. 1780-82; 1808-18. w. (Suspended 1783-1807.)
  b: E no451, N 5, 1816; PIP F 23, D 8, 1813; Ja 17, 1815.

PLYMOUTH, Devonport, and Stonehouse Advertiser. Plymouth. Mr 1831-Mr 1832.
  (No issues known. Data from *Plymouth City Library.*)

PLYMOUTH, Devonport, and Stonehouse Herald. Plymouth. no1+, 1820-76. w.
  (No issues known. Data from Plymouth City Library.)

PLYMOUTH GAZETTE. Plymouth. no1+, Ag 21, 1819-O 1820. w.
  a: CSmH no7, S 30, 1819.

PLYMOUTH HERALD and Devonshire Freeholder, &c.
  (See *Devonshire Freeholder,* &c.)

PLYMOUTH INSTITUTION. Transactions. Plymouth. 1819-30.
  b: UCP; LP 1830.

PLYMOUTH INSTITUTION and Devon and Cornwall Natural History Society. Transactions. Plymouth. 1819-30.
  a: ULS. / *b:* UCP.

PLYMOUTH JOURNAL. Plymouth. 1815.
  (No issues known. Data from Plymouth City Library and R.N. Worth's bibliography of Plymouth publications, 1872.)

PLYMOUTH LITERARY MAGAZINE. Plymouth. no1-6, 1814.
  (No issues known. Data from Plymouth City Library and James Davidson, *Bibliotheca Devoniensis.*)

PLYMOUTH MAGAZINE. Plymouth. v1-3, 1822.
  (No issues known. Data from Plymouth City Library and R.N. Worth's bibliography of Plymouth publications.

POCKET ALBUM and Literary Scrapbook. London. 1832. a.
  b: UCP; L.

POCKET ANNUAL REGISTER . . . of the History, Politics, Arts, Sciences, and Literature of the Year 1824. London. 1824.
  b: UCP; L.

POCKET-BOOK; or, Christian's Monthly Companion. Brixham. v1, no1, O 1829.
  b: BP.

A POCKET BOOK for the Use of Friends. London. 1808-09.
  b: LFS.

POCKET CALENDAR and Useful Remembrancer. London. 1790-94.
  b: LFS 1790-91, 1793-94.

POCKET MAGAZINE; or, Elegant Repository of Useful and Polite Literature. London. v1-3, Ag 1794-D 1795. m.
  a: ULS; MB 1794. / *b:* UCP; L.

POCKET MAGAZINE; or Literary Gleaner; being a Choice Collection of Interesting Tales, Anecdotes, Essays . . . Memoirs and Poetical Pieces. London. no1-8, Jl 1819-F 1820. m. (Head-title of each number, *Pocket Monthly Magazine;* running title, *Monthly Magazine, or Literary Gleaner.*)
  b: L.

POCKET MAGAZINE of Classic and Polite Literature. London. v1-13, 1818-24; ns, v1-5, 1824-26. m. (From 1818 through 1826 each volume has an additional titlepage which reads *Arliss's Pocket Magazine*.)
   a: ULS. / *b:* UCP; BP ns, v2-4; CsP v2-3, 5-7; L.
   Continued as
POCKET MAGAZINE. Robin's Series. London. v1-14, 1827-33. m.
   a: ULS. / *b:* UCP; BP v2; L.

POCKET MAGAZINE. Robin's Series.
   (See *Pocket Magazine of Classic and Polite Literature.*)

POCKET MONTHLY MAGAZINE.
   (See *Pocket Magazine, or Literary Gleaner,* &c.)

POCKET RACING CALENDAR. London, Newcastle-upon-Tyne. v1-4; 1821-24.
   b: L.

POETICAL MAGAZINE; or, Temple of the Muses. London. v1-2, N 1803-O 1804.
   a: ULS. / *b:* E.

POETICAL MAGAZINE; consisting of Poems, original and selected. Paisley. 1815.
   b: PsP.

POETICAL MAGAZINE; dedicated to the Lovers of the Muse. London. v1-4, 1809-11. m. (Also called *Ackermann's Poetical Magazine; dedicated to the Lovers of the Muse.*)
   a: ULS. / *b:* L; O.

POETICAL REGISTER, and Repository of Fugitive Poetry. London. v1-8, 1801-11. a.
   a: ULS. / *b:* UCP; C; L; O.

POETICAL REPOSITORY. Dundee. D 1832-1834. m.
   (No issues known. Data from S N & Q, s1. IV.231-32.)

POLAR STAR.
   (See *Extractor; or, Universal Repertorium of Literature,* &c.)

POLAR STAR AND EXTRACTOR.
   (See *Extractor; or, Universal Repertorium of Literature,* &c.)

POLAR STAR OF ENTERTAINMENT and Popular Science, and Universal Repertorium of General Literature. n.p. v1-10, 1829-32.
   b: GM.

POLICE-COURT. Report of the Interesting Proceedings. Edinburgh. 1830-31.
   b: L Jl 29, 30, O 23, 1830; Ja 14, 24, Mr 3, 7, 11, 1831.

POLICE GAZETTE; or, Hue and Cry.
   (See *Hue and Cry and Police Gazette.*)

POLICE INTELLIGENCER; or, Life in Edinburgh. Edinburgh. no1-204, Ag 16, 1831-Ap 9, 1832.
   b: L no13, 28-29, 35, 41, 49, 54, 58, 62, 110, 121, 204.

POLICE RECORDER. Edinburgh. no1, S 11, 1832.
   (No issues known. Data from S N & Q, s3. X.120.)

POLICE REPORTS; being Reports of the Interesting Proceedings in the Police Court. Edinburgh. Jl 28-O 23, 1830?.
   b: L has 7 unnumbered issues.

POLITICAL AND LITERARY ARGUS. London. 1823. w.
   b: O v1, no1-2, F 8-15, 1823.

POLITICAL AND LITERARY OBSERVER; or Strictures on some of the most Respectable Reviews. Edinburgh, v1, no1, Je 1815. q.
   a: ULS. / *b:* UCP; L.

POLITICAL ANECDOTIST and Popular Instructor. London. no1-4, 1831.
   b: UCP.

POLITICAL DIRECTOR. London. 1831.
   a: CSmH Ap 30, 1831. / *b:* O Ap 30, 1831.

POLITICAL ECONOMY CLUB. Minutes. London. 1821-1935.
   b: UCP.

POLITICAL ECONOMY CLUB. Proceedings. v1-6, 1821-1920/?. (Title varies slightly.)
   a: ULS.

POLITICAL GUARDIAN. Dublin. no1-3, 1810-11. m;f.
   a: ULS. / *b:* BIL no1; DL; L no1.

A POLITICAL GUARDIAN.

A POLITICAL GUARDIAN. London. 1831.
   b: O Ap 22, 1831.

POLITICAL INVESTIGATOR. London. no1-4, 1832. w.
   b: L; LU no1-2; O.

A POLITICAL LETTER. London. no1+, Je 4-Ag 13, 1831. w.
   a: CSmH no1. / *b:* L; O F 4, 1831.
   (Incorporated with *Ballot,* Ag 20, 1831.)

POLITICAL LETTERS AND PAMPHLETS, published for the avowed Purpose of trying with the Government the Question of Law, whether all Publications containing News are liable to the Imposition of the Stamp Duty. London. 1830-31. (Each no. has separate title, such as "*A Letter to the Duke of Wellington*".)
   b: L.

POLITICAL MAGAZINE. London. S 1794. m.
   b: L.

POLITICAL MAGAZINE.
   (See *Carpenter's Monthly Political Magazine.*)

POLITICAL MAGAZINE and Parliamentary, Naval, Military, and Literary Journal. London. v1-21, 1780-91. m.
   a: ULS; ULSup. / *b.* UCP; L.

POLITICAL MIRROR OF THE TIMES.
(See *Flower's Political Review and Monthly Register*.)

A POLITICAL MISCELLANY. London. 1830.
b: O D 9, 1830.

POLITICAL MONITOR. London. 1796.
(No issues known. Data from C & K, 1889a.)

POLITICAL OBSERVER. London. no1+, N 28, 1819-Ja 30, 1820. w.
b: L.

A POLITICAL OLIO. London. 1831. w.
b: O Mr 5, 1831.

A POLITICAL OMNIBUS. London. 1831.
b: O Ap 8, 1831.

A POLITICAL PAMPHLET. London. 1831.
b: O F 26, 1831.

A POLITICAL REFLECTOR. London. 1831.
b: O Mr 18, 1831.

POLITICAL REGISTER.
(See *Dublin Monthly Magazine, and Political Register*.)

A POLITICAL REPERTORY. London. 1831.
b: O Ap 1, 1831.

POLITICAL REPOSITORY, or Weekly Magazine; containing a Concise View of Public Affairs. Macclesfield. v1, no1-11, D 1803-Mr 1804; ns, Mr-Ap 1804. w.
b: L; O.

POLITICAL REVIEW and Monthly Mirror of the Times.
(See *Flower's Political Review and Monthly Register*.)

POLITICAL REVIEW, and Monthly Register . . . containing Remarks on the State of Public Affairs, &c. London. [?]-1807/?.
(No issues known. Data from *Literary Annual Register; or, Records of Literature*, 2 (Ja 1807) 5-6.)

POLITICAL REVIEW of Edinburgh Periodical Publications. Edinburgh. no1-7, Je 20-Ag 1, 1792. w.
a: ULS. / *b:* UCP; L.

POLITICAL SKETCHES. London. no1-2, 1805.
a: ULS.

POLITICAL STATE OF EUROPE. London. 1792-95. m.
a: ULS. / *b:* UCP; L Prospectus of no8, 1792.

POLITICAL UNION REGISTER. Birmingham. no1-3, 1832.
b: UCP; BP Mr 1832.

POLITICAL UNIONIST. London. no1-2, 1832.
b: UCP; L.

POLITICIAN. London. no1-4, D 13, 1794-Ja 3, 1795/?. w.
a: ULS.

POLITICIAN. London. no1-7, Mr 2-9, 1832.
(No issues known.)

POLITICS FOR THE PEOPLE; (or, Hog's Wash.)
(See *Hog's Wash; or, a Salmagundy for Swine*.)

POLONIA; or, monthly Reports on Polish Affairs. (Literary Association of the Friends of Poland.) London. no1-5, Ag-D 1832. m.
a: ULS. / *b:* UCP; L.

THE POLYHYMNIA, being a Collection of Poetry, Original and Selected. Glasgow. no1-20, ca.1799 or 1800.
b: GM.

POMOLOGICAL MAGAZINE; or, Figures and Descriptions of the most important Varieties of Fruit cultivated in Great Britain. London. v1-3, no1-38, N 1827-1830. m.
a: ULS. / *b:* UCP; L.

POOR MAN'S ADVOCATE, and Workman's Guide. Manchester. v1-2, no1-55, Ja 21, 1832-D 6, 1843/?. (Subtitle varies.)
a: ULS. / *b:* UCP; L no1-18, 25-30.

POOR MAN'S GUARDIAN; a weekly Paper for the People.
(See *Penny Paper for the People, by the Poor Man's Guardian*.)

POOR RICHARD'S JOURNAL for Poor People. London. no1-3, 1832.
b: L.

POPERY EXPOSER; being a Review of the Correspondence between the Rev. Dr. J. Kidd, of the Church of Scotland, and the Rev. C. Fraser, of the Church of Rome, &c. Aberdeen. no1-9, 1831. (No1 has title of *Popish Exposer*.)
b: L.

POPISH EXPOSER.
(See *Popery Exposer*.)

O POPULAR. Jornal politico, litterario e commercial. London. v1-4, 1824-26.
b: L.

PORCUPINE. London. no1-298, O 30, 1800-1801. d.
a: ULS; C-S; DLC 3 sc.nos. 1800-01. / *b:* L; O.
Continued as
PORCUPINE and Antigallican Monitor. London. no299-365, 1801. d. (Incorporated with *True Briton*, Ja 1, 1802.)
a: ULS; C-S. / *b:* L O no300-333.

PORCUPINE and Antigallican Monitor.
(See *Porcupine*.)

PORT OF HULL SOCIETY for the Religious Instruction of Seamen. Hull. v1-7, [?]-1826-28. w.
b: UCP.

PORTFOLIO; a Collection of Engravings from Antiquarian and Topographical Subjects. London. v1-4, 1823-24.
  b: BP v1-2; L.

PORTFOLIO; a Weekly Paper on Criticism and Manners. Edinburgh. no1-8, N 12-D 31, 1818. w.
  b: EP; O no1.

PORTFOLIO; or Selections from the best Fugitive Literature. Aberdeen. no1, D 25, 1830.
  (No issues known. Data from S N & Q, s1. I. 21.)

PORTFOLIO OF ENTERTAINING and Instructive Varieties in History, Science, Literature, the Fine Arts, &c. London. v1-6, no1-174, 1823-26; ns, v1-4, no1-116, 1826-28; s3, v1-2, 1828-29. w. (Subtitle varies.)
  a: ULS. / *b:* BP ns, no1-23; L v1-5, lacking no145 of v5; s3, no1-23; O no1-32, for 1823.

PORTFOLIO, Political and Literary. London. no1-9, N 2-D 28, 1816. w.
  b: L; O no1-2.

PORTSEA, PORTSMOUTH, AND GOSPORT Journal. Portsea. no1+, 1802-04. w.
  b: L no37-141, Ja 3, 1803-D 31, 1804, lacking 43 sc.nos.

PORTSMOUTH AND PORTSEA Literary and Philosophical Society. Report of the Proceedings. Portsea. 1827-32/?.
  a: ULS.

PORTSMOUTH CHRONICLE. Portsmouth. no1-36, My 1, 1802-Ja 1, 1803. w.
  b: L.

PORTSMOUTH GAZETTE, and Weekly Advertiser. Portsmouth. no1-449, Jl 8, 1793-F 8, 1802. w.
  a: CtY 5 sc.nos. 1798. / *b:* L; NwS 7 sc. nos. 1799-1800.
  (Incorporated with *Hampshire Telegraph.*)

PORTSMOUTH, PORTSEA, AND GOSPORT Herald. Portsmouth. no1-307, Ag 16, 1829-Je 27, 1835. w.
  a: CSmH no49, Jl 18, 1830. / *b:* L.
  (Incorporated with *Hampshire Advertiser.*)

THE PORTSMOUTH, Portsea, and Gosport Literary and Scientific Register. A Monthly Miscellany. Portsmouth. v1, Je 20, 1822-Ja 16, 1823. m.
  b: BP Ja-O 1822; L; O.

PORTSMOUTH TELEGRAPH; or, Mottley's Naval and Military Journal. Portsmouth. no1-122, O 14, 1799-F 8, 1802. w.
  a: MnU 1801. / *b:* L; PmHT.
  Continued as
MOTTLEY'S TELEGRAPH, and Portsmouth Gazette. Portsmouth. no123-124, F 15-22, 1802. w.
  b: L; PmHT.
  Continued as
HAMPSHIRE TELEGRAPH and Sussex

Chronicle. Portsmouth. no125+, Mr 1, 1802-date. w. (Subtitle varies.)
  b: BiP 5 sc.nos. 1811; [1812-16]; C Jl 12, 1802; L; PmHT; SoP no1016-1107, Mr 29, 1819-D 25, 1820.

O PORTUGUEZ: ou, Mercurio Politico, Commercial, e Literario. London. v1-15, 1814-25.
  a: ULS. / *b:* UCP; L.

PORTUGUEZ CONSTITUCIONAL em Londres. London. no1-13, 1832/?.
  a: ULS.

PORTUGUEZ EMIGRADO; ou, Realista Constitucional. London. no1-15, 1828-29/?.
  a: ULS.

POST OFFICE ANNUAL DIRECTORY (of Edinburgh and Its Environs). Edinburgh. 1805-45.
  b: EU lacking 1815/16.
  (Continued as *Post Office Edinburgh and Leith Directory*, 1846-date.)

POST OFFICE GLASGOW DIRECTORY. Glasgow. 1827-date.
  b: GU 1827, 1832.

POST OFFICE LONDON DIRECTORY. London. v1-41, 1799-1839. a.
  b: C impf.; SA U 1826-27, 1830, 1832.
  (Continued as *W. Kelly and Co. The Post Office London Directory*, 1840-date.)

POST OFFICE REGISTER.
  (See *Advertiser.*)

POTTERY GAZETTE, Newcastle-under-Lyme Express. Hanley, Shelton. 1809-28-[?]. w. (Subtitle varies: originally . . . *and Weekly Advertiser for Newcastle-under-Lyme.*)
  a: CSmH My 12, 1827. / *b:* BP no27-43, 45-52, for 1809; StfS (1809-10); sc.nos. 1826-28.
  (Probably incorporated with *Pottery Mercury* to form *Staffordshire Mercury, Pottery Gazette*, &c. For details, see *Pottery Mercury.*)

POTTERY MERCURY, and Staffordshire and Cheshire Advertiser. Hanley. v1-5, no1-228, 1824-29. w.
  a: CSmH S 1, 1827. / *b:* StfS.
  Probably incorporated with *Pottery Gazette, Newcastle-under-Lyme Express* to form
STAFFORDSHIRE MERCURY, Pottery Gazette, Newcastle Express, and Cheshire Advertiser. Hanley. 1829-34. w.
  a: CSmH Ag 23, 1828. / *b:* L no313-519, Ja 2, 1830-1832; StfS v5-8, no230-416, 1829-31.
  (Continued as *North Staffordshire Mercury*, 1834-45; as *Staffordshire Mercury*, 1845-48.)

POWER'S CLONMEL GAZETTE, and Munster Miscellany. Clonmel. v1, no1-91, 1801-1802/?. s.w. (May succeed *Clonmel Gazette*, [?]-1790-[?].)
  b: C v1, no91, O 6/9, 1802.

PRACTICAL MAGAZINE; or, Temple of the Muses. London. v1-2, [?]-1804.
  b: BP v2.

PRAYER-BOOK and Homily Society. Proceedings. London. v1-62, 181[?]-1874.
  b: UCP.

PREACHER, containing Sermons by Eminent Living Divines. London. v1-8, 1831-35.
  a: ULS. / b: UCP; GM; L.

PRECEPTOR. London. 1809.
  b: L S 15, 1809.

PRECEPTOR and Weekly Family Chronicle. London. 1809. w.
  b: L Prospectus only.

PRECIOS CORRIENTES DE GÉNEROS de las Fábricas de Algodon de la Gran Bretaña. London. no1, 1817.
  b: L.

PRÉCURSEUR. London. no1+, F 5, 1831-Ap 28, 1832.
  b: L.

PREIS COURANT. London. 1816.
  b: L.

PREMIER. Lanark. 1832.
  b: GM.

PREMIUMS Offered by the Highland Society of Scotland. Edinburgh. 1821-29.
  b: UCP.

PRESBYTERIAN MAGAZINE. Edinburgh, v1, 1832; ns, v1-4, 1833-36. m. (No issues for Jl-Ag 1832.)
  a: ULS. / b: UCP; DnP.

PRESBYTERIAN REVIEW and Religious Journal. Edinburgh. v1-21, 1831-48.
  a: ULS. / b: UCP; L.

THE PRESENT PEERAGE of the United Kingdom. London. v1-25, 1808-32. a. (Vols. for 1823-32 have a second title: Stockdale's Peerage of the United Kingdom.)
  b: L lacking 1809, 1811, 1818-19, 1829-30.

THE PRESS. Dublin. no1-69, S 28, 1797-Mr 13, 1798. t.w.
  a: ULS; IU. / b: UCP: BIL; L.

PRESTON CHRONICLE and Lancashire Advertiser. Preston. [?]-1829-1893.
  a: CSmH Jl 25, 1829. / b: L no957+, Je 1, 1831-1832.
  (Incorporated with Preston Guardian.)

PRESTON JOURNAL and Croft's Lancashire General Advertiser. Preston. 1746-1812-[?]. (Subtitle varies.)
  b: L O 13, 1810; PrH F 14, 1807; Ag 29, 1812.

PRESTON PILOT and County Advertiser. Preston. [?]-1827-1888. w.
  a: CSmH no106, Ja 6, 1827; L no314+, 1831-32; PrH Ja 6, 1827-1832.
  (Incorporated with Lytham Times.)

PRESTON REVIEW and County Advertiser. Preston. no1-43, Je 1, 1793-Mr 29, 1794. w.
  b: PrH lacking 17 sc.nos.

PRESTON SENTINEL and Lancaster County Advertiser. Preston. [?]-Ap 7, 1821-Mr 30, 1822-[?].
  b: PrH Ap 7, 1821; Mr 30, 1822.

PRICE CURRENT of British Cotton Manufacturers. London. 1817.
  b: L.

PRICES CURRENT. London. [?]-1826-1869.
  a: CSmH no2579, Ag 26, 1825; MHi sc.nos. 1822-24 & 1828-32; PPL 1823-24.

PRICES OF COAL at the London Coal Market.
  (See London Coal Market.)

PRICES of the English and Foreign Funds. London. Je 1, 1826-D 30, 1843.
  b: L.

PRIMITIVE METHODIST MAGAZINE.
  (See Methodist Magazine... conducted by the Camp-Meeting Methodists, &c.)

PRIMITIVE WESLEYAN METHODISTS. Minutes of the Annual Conference. London. 1829-date.
  b: UCP.

PRINCE'S (LONDON) PRICE CURRENT.
  (See London Price Current.)

PRIVATE ACTS. [Parliament.] 1st George IV-41st Victoria. London. 1821-77.
  b: UCP.

PRIVATE TUTOR, and Cambridge Mathematical Repository. Cambridge. v1-2, 1830-31. (Titlepage of v2 reads: A Supplement to Wood's Algebra, as given in the Private Tutor.)
  a: ULS. / b: UCP; L.

PRIX COURANT GÉNÉRAL, Londres. Londón. 1816.
  b: L Mr 8, 1816.

PRIX COURANT MERCANTILE de Londres. London. 1816.
  b: L.

PRIZE ESSAYS AND TRANSACTIONS of the Highland Society of Scotland.
  (See Highland Society of Scotland.)

PROCEEDINGS AND DEBATES of the Parliament of Pimlico in the Last Session of the Eighteenth Century. Dublin. no1-28, 1799-1800.
  b: UCP.
  Continued as
  THE OLIO; or, Anything-Arian Miscellany. Dublin. no1-6, 1800.
  a: ULS. / b: UCP; L.
  (See Pimlico Parliamentary Register, which may be a continuation of The Olio, &c.)

PROCEEDINGS . . .
See also *Annual Reports, Extracts, Minutes,* etc.; and in general the society, institution, or other group reporting its Proceedings. In UCP, however, entries are
generally under *Proceedings.*
But see especially (1) *Aberdeen Auxiliary Society for Improving the System of
Church Patronage in Scotland;* (2) *Association for preserving Liberty against Republicans and Levellers;* (3) *Association
for Promoting the Discovery of the Interior Parts of Africa;* (4) *Baptist Union;*
(5) *Berwickshire Naturalists Club;* (6)
Bristol Institution; (7) *Catholic Association in Dublin;* (8) *Church Missionary Society;* (9) *Co-operative Congress;* (10)
European Missionary Society; (11) *Fund
for the Relief of Widows and Children of
Burgh and Parochial Schoolmasters in
Scotland;* (12) *Geological Society of London;* (13) *Incorporated Society for the
Propagation of the Gospel in Foreign
Parts;* (14) *Outinian Society;* (15) *Political Economy Club;* (16) *Prayer-Book
and Homily Society;* (17) *Royal Dublin
Society;* (18) *Royal Society of Edinburgh;*
(19) *Royal Society of London;* (20) *Seamen's Friend Society and Bethel Union;*
(21) *Sheffield Shakespeare Club;* (22) *Society for Educating the Poor of Newfoundland;* (23) *Society for Improving the
Conditions of the Labouring Classes;*
(24) *Society for Improving the System of
Church Patronage in Scotland;* (25) *Society of United Irishmen:* (26) *Zoological
Society of London.*

THE PROJECTOR; a Periodical Paper, o-
riginally published in numbers, from Jan. 1802-
Nov. 1809. London. v1-3, 1802-09. [These
are essays originally appearing in the *Gentleman's Magazine.*]
a: ULS; ULSup; NRU. / b: UCP; L; LP;O.

PROMPTER. London. no1-19, O 24-D 10,
1789.
a: ULSup. / b: UCP; L.

PROMPTER. London. v1, no1-53, N 13, 1830-
N 12, 1831/?.
a: ULS. / b: UCP; GM; L.

PROMPTER; or, Theatrical Investigator.
Manchester. no1-19, N 1815-Mr 1816. w.
a: ULS. / b: L.

PROMPTER PROMPTED: or, the Theatrical
Investigator Dissected. Manchester. no1-5,
1816.
a: MB; NIC. / b: L.

PROPERTY LAWYER. London. v1-12, 1826-
29; ns, v1-3, 1830.
a: ULS. / b: UCP; L no1; LLN v1-12;
LLW.

THE PROTESTANT; a Weekly Paper, on the
Principal Points of the Controversy between
the Church of Rome and the Reformed. Glasgow. v1-4, no1-208, My 23, 1818-Jl 6, 1822.
w. (*Catholic Vindicator, a Weekly Paper,* is
a reply to *The Protestant,* &c.)
a: ULS. / b: UCP; GeG; L; O.

PROTESTANT ADVOCATE; or, a Review of
Publications relating to the Roman Catholic
Question, and Repertory of Protestant Intelligence. London. v1-4, 1812-16. m. (Continued as a department of *Anti-Jacobin Review.*)
a: ULS. / b: UCP; CrP v1-3; L.

PROTESTANT AND CATHOLIC JOURNAL.
Birmingham. F-Ap 1831.
b: BP.

PROTESTANT CONFEDERATE and Mirror
of Truth. Dublin. v1, 1826/?.
a: ULS.

PROTESTANT DISSENTER'S MAGAZINE.
London. v1-6, 1794-99. m.
a: ULS. / b: UCP; L.

PROTESTANT DISSENTERS' REGISTER.
[London.] D 1800.
b: BP.

PROTESTANT GUARDIAN   London, Preston. v1-2, 1827-28.
b: UCP; L.

PROTESTANT GUARDIAN, or an Attempt
to Expose some of the Principal Errors and
Practices of the Romish Church. Dundee.
no1-30, Mr 28, 1829-Ap 23, 1830. w.;f.;ir.
b: DnP.

PROTESTANT HERALD and Anti-Catholic
Review. London. v1, 1829.
b: L; LdL.

PROTESTANT JOURNAL; or, the true Catholic's Protest against the Modern Church of
Rome. London. v1-6, 1831-37; ns, no1-6, Je-
N 1837.
a: ULS. / b: UCP; DLM; L.

PROTESTANT ORPHAN SOCIETY. Reports.
Dublin. 1828-37. ir.
b: UCP.

PROTESTANT UNION; a Periodical issued
by the Protestant Union in London. London.
no1-11, 1813-14. (Some of the numbers have
special titlepages.)
a: ULS; ULSup. / b: UCP; L.

PROTESTANT VINDICATOR; or, a Refutation of the Calumnies contained in Cobbett's
History of the Reformation. London. no1-14,
1826.
b: UCP.

PROTESTANT VINDICATOR. Aberdeen?.
1831?.
(No issues known. Data from S N & Q, s1.
I.39.)

PROTESTANT WARDER. Stourport. v1, no1-
8, 1829.
b: L; O.

PROVINCIAL LITERARY REPOSITORY.
Spalding, London. v1-2, 1801-1802/?. m.
(The individual numbers in v1 are headed
*The Lincolnshire Magazine and Provincial
Library Repository.*)
a: ULS. / b: L.

PROVINCIAL MAGAZINE.
(See *Gleaner's Port-Folio, or Provincial Magazine, &c.*)

PROVINCIAL MAGAZINE AND REVIEW. London. no 1-3, 1825.
b: L; O.

PROVINCIAL MEDICAL AND SURGICAL Association. Transactions. London. v1-19, 1832-52.
a: ULS.
(Superseded by *British Medical Association.*)

PROVINCIAL MEDICAL GAZETTE. Winchester. v1, no1-2, 1829.
a: ULS.

PROVINCIAL SPECTATOR. Bury St. Edmunds. no1-8, 1821.
b: L.

PSALTER OF CASHEL; or Irish Cyclopedia. Cork. no1, Jl 1814. m.
b: C.

PUBLIC ADVERTISER. London. 1752-F 28, 1794. (Preceded by *General Advertiser*, 1744-52.)
a: ICU Mr 14-My 6, 8, 1789; MB Ja 25, 1791; MdBJ widely sc.nos. 1789-92; NjR 6 sc.nos. F-Mr 1791; 5 sc.nos. Ja-F 1792. / *b:* BiP D 18, 1792; L.
Incorporated with *The Oracle* and continued as
ORACLE AND PUBLIC ADVERTISER. London. Mr 1, 1794-1798.
a: ULS; CtY Ja 1-Ap 21, 1796; Je-S 8, 1798; ICU S 1-5, 8-20, 1794; D 4, 1795; (F 15-Ap 2, 1796). / *b:* L.
Incorporated with *Daily Advertiser* and continued as
ORACLE AND DAILY ADVERTISER. London. 1798-1802.
(See *Daily Advertiser* for details.)

PUBLIC ADVERTISER; or, Political and Literary Diary. London. 1793.
b: L Prospectus only.

PUBLIC CHARACTERS. London. v1-10, 1798-1810. a. (v1 also called *British Public Characters.*)
a: ULS; ULSup. / *b:* UCP; GeG 1798-1807; L.

PUBLIC CHARACTERS. Dublin. v1-3, 1799-1801. a.
b: L.

PUBLIC CHARACTERS. London. 1828.
b: UCP.

PUBLIC COMMUNICATOR, and General Advertiser. London. 1832.
b: O no1, Ja 1832.

PUBLIC GENERAL STATUTES. New South Wales. Sydney. 1824-74.
b: UCP.

PUBLIC GUARDIAN. London. v1, 1806.
b: CrP.

PUBLIC HUE AND CRY. Dublin. 1827. w.
b: CsP S 1-N 17, D 1-29, 1827.

PUBLIC LEDGER. London. 1760-date. d. (Varying subtitles.)
a: CtY 1812-17; DLC 5 sc.nos. 1819-22; 1 no.1825; 1 no.1828; MBAt Ag 28, S 19, 1806; 1807-O 1809; MH 1817; NcD (1808, 1817). / *b:* UCP; L 1789-1832 very impf. before 1805; TmP 8 sc.nos. 1815-26.

PUBLIC REGISTER: or, Freeman's Journal. Dublin. no1+, S 10, 1763-1807. s.w.: d.
b: DA My 9, 1789; F 18, 21, 23, Mr 3, 1792; Ja 26, F 9, Ap 6, 1793; DPK 1789-O 20, 1792 impf.; L 1785-1807 very impf.; MR sc.nos. 1789-92.
Continued as
FREEMAN'S JOURNAL. Dublin. 1807-1924. d. (Subtitle varies.)
a: CSmH Ja 1, 1821; D 17, 1828; CtY (Ja 9-D 16, 1808); DLC Mr 23, 1811. / *b:* C F 24, 1807; DA Ja 7, 1828; L 1807-19 very impf.; O 6, 1821-1831.

PUBLIC REPORTER, or Monthly Register of Events; containing a faithful Record of Public and Domestic Occurrences; an Impartial Review of Drama, &c. London. Ja 1-23, 1806. m.
b: L.

PUBLICATIONS ...
In general, see the institution, society, or other group reporting its Publications. See especially (1) *Association for Preserving Liberty and Property against Republicans and Levellers*; (2) *Bannatyne Club*; (3) *English Historical Society*; (4) *London Corresponding Society*; (5) *Maitland Club, Glasgow*; (6) *Newcastle Typographical Society*; (7) *Oriental Translation Fund*; (8) *Peace Society*; (9) *Record Commission*; (10) *Roxburghe Club*.

THE PUBLICIST.
(See *Catholicon; or, the Christian Philosopher*, &c.)

PUE'S OCCURRENCES.
(See *John Hillary's Pue's Occurrences.*)

THE PULPIT. London. v1-91, 1823-71. (Some nos. called *Penny Pulpit.*)
a: ULS; ULSup. / *b:* UCP; C; L.

PUNCH IN CAMBRIDGE. Cambridge. v1-4, 1832-35.
b: C.

PUNCH IN LONDON. London. no1-17, Ja 14, 1831-My 5, 1832. w.
a: ULS. / *b:* BP no1-3, 12, 14; L; O no1, 3-4, 16.

PUNCHINELLO! A Family Gazette of Fun, Fashion, Literature, and the Drama. London. no1-10, 1832.
b: C no6, 8-10; O no1-4, 7.

PUNCHINELLO! or Sharps, Flats and Naturals; a Family Gazette of Fun. London. no1-10, Ja 20-Mr 23, 1832. w.
a: ULS. / *b:* BoP; L; O no1.

QUARTERLY BIOGRAPHICAL MAGAZINE.
London. no1-2, My-Ag 1828. q.
  b: UCP; L.

QUARTERLY CHRONICLE of the Transactions of the London Missionary Society.
  (See *London Missionary Society.*)

QUARTERLY EXTRACTS . . .
  See also *Extracts* and in general the society, institution, or other group reporting. See especially (1) *British and Foreign School Society;* (2) *British Society for Promoting the Religious Principles of the Reformation;* (3) *Hibernian Bible Society;* (4) *Irish Society for Promoting the Scriptural Education of the Native Irish,* &c.

QUARTERLY JOURNAL OF AGRICULTURE.
Edinburgh. v1-13, 1828-43. q.
  a: ULS. / *b:* UCP; BP; DRS; EP; GrP; L; LP; NwL; PsP.
  (Continued as *Journal of Agriculture,* 1843-68; as *Country Gentleman's Magazine,* 1868-73.)

QUARTERLY JOURNAL OF EDUCATION.
London. v1-10, 1831-35. q.
  a: ULS; ULSup. / *b:* UCP; BP; GeG; LLL; NwL.

QUARTERLY JOURNAL of Foreign (and British) Medicine and Surgery. London. v1-5, 1818-23. q.
  a: ULS. / *b:* UCP; LCP; LS.
  Continued as
ANDERSON'S QUARTERLY JOURNAL of the Medical Sciences. London. v1-3, 1824-26. q. (Running title: *Anderson's Quarterly Journal of Medicine and Surgery.*)
  a: ULS. / *b:* UCP; LCP; LS.
  Continued as
QUARTERLY MEDICAL REVIEW. London. v1, 1827. q. (Also called *New Series. Quarterly Journal of Foreign and British Medicine and Surgery.*)
  a: ULS. / *b:* L; LMD.

QUARTERLY JOURNAL OF LITERATURE, Science and the Arts.
  (See *Journal of Science and the Arts.*)

QUARTERLY JOURNAL OF SCIENCE, Literature, and the Arts.
  (See *Journal of Science and the Arts.*)

QUARTERLY JUVENILE REVIEW. London. no1, 1827.
  b: L.

QUARTERLY MAGAZINE.
  (See *Knight's Quarterly Magazine.*)

QUARTERLY MAGAZINE AND REVIEW. Chiefly designed for the Use of the Society of Friends. London. v1, 1832. q.
  a: ULS. / *b:* UCP; L; LFS.

QUARTERLY MEDICAL REVIEW.
  (See *Quarterly Journal of Foreign (and British) Medicine and Surgery.*)

QUARTERLY MINING REVIEW. London. v1-2, 1830-32. q.
  a: ULS. / *b:* UCP; L; LP.
  Continued as
MINING REVIEW and Journal of Geology, Mineralogy, and Metallurgy. London. 1832-41. q.
  a: ULS. / *b:* UCP; L; LP.

QUARTERLY MUSICAL MAGAZINE and Review. London. v1-10, 1818-28. q.
  a: ULS; ULSup. / *b:* UCP; CrP; L; LdP.

QUARTERLY MUSICAL REGISTER. London. no1-2, Ja-Ap, 1812/?. q.
  a: ULS. / *b:* LCM.

QUARTERLY PAPER of the Scottish Missionary Society.
  (See *Scottish Missionary Society.*)

QUARTERLY REVIEW. London. 1809-date. q.
  a: ULS; ULSup; KyLx v1-24. / *b:* UCP; BO; BdP; BhP; BiP; BrP; BtP; CnP; ColP; CrP; DA; EP; ExP; GeG; GrP; HP; KeP; L; LAt; LDC lacking no40-41, 60-61, 80-81; LGU; LIT; LLL; LLW; LMT; LVA; LaP; LcP; LdL; LdP; LvA; LvP; MCh; MR; NpP; NwL; PrH; RP 1809-25, lacking My & Jl 1821; SP; SthC; WcP; WmP; WnP; YP v11-19, 22-30.

QUARTERLY THEOLOGICAL REVIEW and Ecclesiastical Record. London. v1-4, 1825-26. q.
  a: ULS. / *b:* UCP; CrP; GrP.
  (Incorporated with *British Critic* to form *British Critic, Quarterly Theological Review, and Ecclesiastical Record.* See *British Critic* for details.)

QUARTERLY VISITOR, containing Essays, Miscellaneous Pieces in Prose and Verse; &c. Hull. v1-2, 1814-15. q.
  a: ULS. / *b:* UCP; HlP v2, no1-6; L.

QUEEN BEE; or, Monarch of the Hive.
  (See *The Bee, Fireside Companion,* &c.)

THE QUIZ. London. v1-2, no1-51, 1796-98. w.;f.
  a: ULS. / *b:* UCP; L no1-50.

THE QUIZ, a Burlesque Review of the Follies of the Day. London. no1, Ja 1818. m.
  b: L.

QUIZZICAL GAZETTE and Merry Companion. London. v1, no1-21, 1831-32. (Subtitle varies.)
  a: ULS. / *b:* L lacking pp.143-44; O no1, 5, 13.

QUIZZICAL GAZETTE EXTRAORDINARY!!! And Wonderful Advertiser, For the Lovers of Wit, Whimsicality, Laughability, Comicality, and Eccentricity. London. no1-11, 1819-28. a. (Subtitle varies. Each no. is dated Ap 1 of each year.)
  a: ULS; MNS no1-7. / *b:* BP no1; L no1-8; O; StfS.

THE QUIZZING GLASS. Glasgow. no1-11, 1832.
  b: GM no1.

RACING CALENDAR. London. no1+, Ap 23, 1818-date. f.
  b: L.

RACING CALENDAR; containing an Account of the Plates, Matches, and Sweepstakes run in Great Britain and Ireland, &c. London. 1773-date.
  b: L; WmP.

THE RADICAL. London. no1-6, 1831.
  a: CSmH no2. / b: L; O no1.
   Continued as
  RADICAL REFORMER. London. no9-22, 1831-32.
  b: L.

RADICAL REFORMER.
  (See The Radical.)

RADICAL REFORMER; or, People's Advocate. London. v1, no1-2, S 15-22, 1819/?. w.
  a: ULS.

RADICAL REFORMER'S GAZETTE. Glasgow. no1-14, 1832-33.
  b: GM.

RAINBOW; a Weekly Periodical. Edinburgh. no1-12, Jl 7-S 15, 1821. w.
  a: ULS. / b: EP no1-2; GM.

THE RAMBLER; or, Fashionable Companion. London. v1-2, no1-15, 1824-25. (Caption title; Rambler's Magazine; or Fashionable Companion.)
  a: ULS. / b: C no1-8.

RAMBLER'S MAGAZINE; or Annals of Gallantry, Glee, Pleasure, and Bon Ton: a Delicious Banquet of Amorous, Bacchanalian, Whimsical, Humourous, Theatrical, and Literary Entertainment. London. v1-2, 1827-29. (Individual numbers entitled: New London Rambler's Magazine.)
  b: L.

RAMBLER'S MAGAZINE; or, the Annals of Gallantry, Glee, Pleasure and the Bon Ton; calculated for the Entertainment of the Polite World: &c. London. 1783-Je 1790.
  b: LLL v7, for 1789.

RAMBLER'S MAGAZINE; or, Fashionable Companion.
  (See Rambler; or, Fashionable Emporium, &c.)

RAMBLER'S MAGAZINE; or Fashionable Emporium of Polite Literature, the Fine Arts, Politics, Theatrical Excellencies, Wit, Humour, Genius, Taste, Gallantry, &c. London. v1-2, Ja 1, 1822-D 1, 1823. m. (Subtitle varies slightly.)
  a: ULS; ULSup; MH v2. / b: L v1.
   Continued as
  RAMBLER'S MAGAZINE; or Fashionable

Companion. London. v1-2, no1-15, Ap 1, 1824-Jl 1, 1825. m.
  a: ULS.

RAMSEY'S WATERFORD CHRONICLE. Waterford. [1789?]-[1844]. t.w. (Preceded by Waterford Chronicle, [1738?]-[1789?].
  a: CSmH D 13, 1828; Je 11, 1831; NN Ap 26-My 1, Je 19-28, Jl 10, 1800. / b: C Je 7, 1794; D Ag 14-S 15, 1792; Je 20, 1826-O 30, 1828; DL 11 widely sc.nos. 1795-1823; L 1811-12; My 29, 1813; 1816-17; 1819-22; Jl 14, 1827-1832.
   (Continued as The Chronicle, [1844]-[1849]; as Waterford Chronicle, [1849]-[ca.1910].

THE RANGER, a Collection of Periodical Essays. Brentford. v1-2, no1-40, Ja 1, 1794-Mr 21, 1795. w.
  a: ULS; ULSup. / b: UCP; L.

RANGER'S MAGAZINE; or, the Man of Fashion's Companion; being the Whim of the Month, and General Assemblage of Love, Gallantry, Wit, Pleasure, &c. London. v1, 1795.
  b: L.

RATIONAL REFORMER. London. v1, no1, 1832.
  b: UCP.

THE RATIONALIST. no1-11, 1830/?.
  b: L no11.

READING MERCURY. Reading. [1737]-date. w. (Several slightly varying subtitles.)
  a: CtY 1802-32; MnU (1802-06). / b: L 1789-1832 impf.; MaP widely sc.nos. 1814-32; RP; RRM.

THE REAL JOHN BULL. London. no1-437, Ja 21, 1821-Mr 21, 1824. w. (After no155 the title was changed to The Real John Bull and British Gazette.)
  a: CSmH no9. / b: L; LGU Ap 29, 1821-Mr 31, 1822.

THE REAL JOHN BULL and British Gazette.
  (See The Real John Bull.)

THE REASONER; or Controversial Magazine. London. no1-12, Je 1813-Je 1814. m.
  a: ULS; ULSup.

THE REASONER and Statistical Journal; an Independent Weekly Publication. London. no1-15, Ja 2-Ap 16, 1808. w.
  a: ULS. / b: UCP; L; O.

THE RECORD. London. no1+, Ja 1, 1828-date. s.w.; w.
  a: ULS; CSmH no17, F 26, 1828. / b: D.

RECORD COMMISSION. Publications. London. 1783-date.
  b: UCP.

RECORD OF PEACE: a Periodical of Religious Information. Warrington. no1-17, N 1830-Je 1831.
  b: WrP.

RECORD OF THE TRANSACTIONS of the
Home Missionary Board.
(See *The Home Missionary Magazine.*)

THE RECORDER; a Magazine of Religious
Intelligence. Edinburgh. v1-3, 1823-25.
  b: EP v3; L v1.

THE RECORDER; or, Judicial and Magisteri-
al Magazine. London. no1-3, F-Ap 1816. m.
  a: ULS. / *b:* L.

RECORDS AND PROCEEDINGS of the Outinian Society.
(See *Outinian Society.*)

RECORDS OF FASHION.
(See *Records of Fashion and Court Elegance.*)

RECORDS OF FASHION and Court Elegance.
London. v1, no1-10, Mr-D 1807. m.
  a: ULS.
  Continued as
RECORDS OF FASHION. London. v2, Ja-D
1808.
  a: ULS.

RECORDS OF LITERATURE.
(See *Literary Annual Register; or, Records
of Literature,* &c.)

RECORDS OF MINING. London. v1, 1829.
  a: ULS. / *b:* UCP; LP.

RECORDS OF THE R.A.S. CLUB. Royal Astronomical Society.
(See *Royal Astronomical Society.*)

RECREATIONS IN AGRICULTURE, Natural
History, Arts, and Miscellaneous Literature.
London. v1-6, 1799-1802. (v5-6 also as ns,
v1-2.) m.
  a: ULS; ULSup. / *b:* UCP; EP v1-4; KeP;
L; LP.

RECREATIVE MAGAZINE, or Eccentricities
of Literature and Life. Boston, London. v1,
no1-6, 1822. (Added titlepage: *Eccentricities
of Literature and Life; or the Recreative Magazine.* American edition of *Recreative Review.*)
  a: ULS; ULSup.

RECREATIVE REVIEW, or Eccentricities of
Literature and Life. London. v1-3, 1821-22.
m.
  a: ULS; ULSup; MB. / *b:* UCP; CrP v1-2;
L; LLL.

THE REFLECTOR.
(See *College Observer.*)

REFLECTOR. London. no1+, D 15-30, 1832.
  a: CSmH no1. / *b:* L.

REFLECTOR; a Collection of Essays, on
Miscellaneous Subjects of Literature and
Politics; originally published at the Commencement as a Quarterly Magazine and writ-
ten by the Editor of the "Examiner" with the
Assistance of Various Hands. London. v1-2,
no1-8, 1810-11. q.
  a: ULS. / *b:* UCP; BP; EU no1-4; HdP; L;
LLL; LVA v2; NwL.

THE REFLECTOR; or Carlisle Essayist.
Carlisle. no1-20, F 4-O 28, 1818. f.
  b: CsP.

REFLEXIONS HISTORIQUES, morales and
politiques.
(See *Argus politique.*)

THE REFORMER. London. no1-22, My 18-
Jl 28, 1810. s.w.
  b: O.

REFORMER. London. no1-4, Je 26-Jl 17,
1831. w.
  a: CSmH no4. / *b:* L.

REFORMER, or the Schoolmaster Abroad.
London. no1-3, 1832.
  b: L; O no1.

REFORMERS' GAZETTE.
(See *The Loyal Reformers' Gazette.*)

REFORMERS' POCKET COMPANION. Glasgow. Je 9, 1832.
  b: GM.

REFORMISTS' REGISTER. London. v1, no1-
18, S 8, 1811-Ja 25, 1812. w.
  a: ULS. / *b:* UCP.

REFORMIST'S REGISTER and Weekly Commentary. London. v1-2, F 1-O 25, 1817. w.
(Also known as *Hone's Reformist's Register.
Hone's Weekly Commentary* is merged in this,
and apparently appeared no1-2, Ja 18-25.)
  a: ULS; ULSup. / *b:* L; O; TaP.

REGAL RAMBLER. London. 1793.
  b: UCP.

REGENCY HERALD, or Weekly Critic. London. 1811.
  b: BP no1.

REGENERATOR; or, Guide to Happiness.
London. no1, Ag 22, 1832.
  b: UCP; L; O.

THE REGISTER. Edinburgh. [?]-1809-1851/?.
  (No issues known. Data from S N & Q, s1.
  V.150.)

THE REGISTER BOOK OF SHIPPING (i.e.
The Underwriters' Register). London. [1760]-
1769-1833.
  (No issues known. Data from CBEL, II.
  718.)
  (Continued as *Lloyd's Register of British and Foreign Shipping,* 1834-date.)

REGISTER FOR THE FIRST SOCIETY of
Adherents to Divine Revelation at Orbiston
in Lanarkshire, N.B. Edinburgh, Orbiston.
no1-34, N 10, 1825-S 19, 1827.
  a: ULS. / *b:* UCP; L.

THE REGISTER, Literary, Scientific, and
Sporting Journal.
(See *Weekly Register of General Informa-
tion, Elegant Amusement, and Popular
Sport.*)

REGISTER OF ARTS, and Journal of Patent
Inventions.
(See *Register of the Arts and Sciences.*)

REGISTER OF OCCURRENCES and Miscellany.
(See *The Argus; or, General Observer, &c.*)

REGISTER OF THE ACTINGS and Proceedings of the General Assembly (of the Church
of Scotland). [In manuscript.] 1690-1902.
b: UCP.

REGISTER OF THE ARTS AND SCIENCES.
London. v1-4, no1-104, 1824-27.
a: ULS. / *b:* UCP; GM; L; LGU; LR v1;
NwL.
Continued as
REGISTER OF ARTS, and Journal of Patent Inventions. London. ns, v1-7, 1827-32.
a: ULS. / *b:* UCP; L; LGU; NwL ns,
v1-4.

REGISTER OF THE TIMES, or Political Museum, containing a Select, Impartial and Interesting Collection of Public Transactions.
London. v1-6, 1794-95.
a: ULS. / *b:* UCP; BdP; L; O.
Continued as
REGISTER OF THE TIMES, and Literary
Review. London. v6-8, 1795-96.
a: ULS; ULSup. / *b:* UCP; L.

REGISTER OF THE TIMES, and Literary Re-
view.
(See *Register of the Times, or Political
Museum, &c.*)

RELIGIOUS MISCELLANY for the Year 1814
(-16). Cork. v1-2, no1-11, 1815-16. m.
b: BIL; L.

RELIGIOUS MONITOR; or, Scots Presbyterian Magazine. Edinburgh. v1-17, 1803-19. m.
a: ULS. / *b:* UCP.

RELIGIOUS OBSERVER. Glasgow. 1827.
b: GM.

RELIGIOUS REPERTORY ... being a Choice
Collection of Original Essays on various Religious Subjects, Extracts from the Holy
Fathers, and other approved Authors, Lives
of the Principal Saints, and other distinguished Catholics, &c. Cork. no1-18, 1814. m.
b: UCP; L no11-18; O no12-17.

RELIGIOUS REPOSITORY. Ayr. 1817.
b: AyP.

RELIGIOUS TRACT SOCIETY.
(See *United Society for Christian Literature, &c.*)

REMEMBER ME. London. 1825.
b: UCP.

REMEMBRANCE. London. 1831.
b: UCP.

REMEMBRANCER. Exeter. Ja-F 1797.
a: ULSup.

REMINISCENTIA. London. no1, Mr 1814/?.
(No issues known. Data from John Nichol,
Illustrations of Literary History, v8, p.610.)

RENFREWSHIRE MAGAZINE and Political
Register. n.p. O 8-N, 1819.
b: GM.

REPEALER AND TRADESMAN'S JOURNAL.
Dublin. no1+, Je 6, 1832-My 18, 1833.
b: L.

EL REPERTORIO AMERICANO. London.
v1-4, 1826-27.
a: ULS; ULSup. / *b:* UCP; L; MR.

REPERTORY OF ARTS and Manufactures;
consisting of original Communications, Spec-
ifications of Patent Inventions, and Selections of useful practical Papers from the
Transactions of the philosophical Societies
of all Nations. London, v1-16, 1794-1802. m.
a: ULS; ULSup. / *b:* UCP; BP; DRS; L;
LGU; LLL; LP; NwL; SP.
Continued as
REPERTORY OF ARTS, Manufactures, and
Agriculture. Second Series. v1-46, 1802-25.
m.
a: ULS; ULSup. / *b:* UCP; BP; DRS; L;
LGU; LLL; LP; NwL; SP.
Continued as
REPERTORY OF PATENT INVENTIONS,
and other Discoveries and Improvements in
Arts, Manufactures, and Agriculture. Lon-
don. 1825-62. m.
a: ULS; ULSup. / *b:* UCP; BP; DRS; L;
LGU; LLL 1825-26; LP; NwL; SP.

REPERTORY OF ARTS, Manufactures, and
Agriculture.
(See *Repertory of Arts and Manufactures,
&c.*)

REPERTORY OF PATENT INVENTIONS,
and other Discoveries and Improvements in
Arts.
(See *Repertory of Arts and Manufactures.*)

REPORTS ...
(In general, see the institution, society,
or other group reporting. In UCP, however,
entries are commonly under *Report(s).*)
See especially (1) *Aberdeen Infirmary;*
(2) *Aberdeen Infirmary and Lunatic Hospital;* (3) *Aberdeen Lunatic Asylum;* (4)
African Institution; (5) *Association for
Oxford and its Vicinity in Aid of the
Church Missionary Society;* (6) *Associ-
ation for the Improvement of Prisons and
of Prison Discipline in Ireland;* (7) *Asso-
ciation for the Relief of the Manufactur-
ing and Laboring Poor;* (8) *Auxiliary
Bible Society;* (9) *Baptist Missionary So-
ciety;* (10) *Bristol Auxiliary, British and
Foreign School Society;* (11) *British and
Foreign Bible Society;* (12) *British and
Foreign School Society;* (13) *British and
Irish Ladies' Society for Improving the
Conditions ... of the Female Peasantry
of Ireland;* (14) *British Association for
Promoting Cooperative Knowledge;* (15)
British Association for the Advancement

of Science; (16) British Society for Promoting the Religious Principles of the Reformation; (17) Canterbury Philosophical and Literary Institution; (18) Christian Knowledge Society; (19) Commissioners of H.M.'s Woods, Forests, &c.; (20) Commissioners of the Board of Education; (21) Commissioners. Report from ... on the Public Records of Ireland; (22) Committee for the Abolition of Slavery; (23) Committee of the General Assembly for Increasing the Means of Education and Religious Instruction in Scotland; (24) Continental Society; (25) Court of Common Pleas and Exchequer Chamber; (26) Deaf and Dumb Institution; (27) Deputy Clerk Register of Scotland; (28) Dublin Infirmary for Skin Diseases; (29) Dundee Lunatic Asylum; (30) East Lothian Bible Society; (31) Edinburgh Academy; (32) Edinburgh and Leith Orkney and Zetland Society; (33) Edinburgh Association for Relief of Destitute Imprisoned Debtors; (34) Edinburgh Asylum for Relief of the Indigent and Industrious Blind; (35) Edinburgh Institution for the Encouragement of Sacred Music; (36) Edinburgh Lunatic Asylum; (37) Edinburgh Magdalene Asylum; (38) Edinburgh Missionary Society; (39) Edinburgh Society for Promoting the Mitigating and Ultimate Abolition of Negro Slavery; (40) Edinburgh Society for the Relief of Destitute Sick; (41) Friendly Society of Iron Founders of England, Ireland, &c.; (42) Fund for the Widows and Children of the Ministers of the Church of Scotland; (43) Glasgow (Royal) Asylum for Lunatics; (44) Glasgow City Poor, Suppression of Mendicity, &c.; (45) Glasgow North American Colonial Society; (46) Glasgow Theological Academy; (47) Glasgow Youth's Society for Schools in the Highlands; (48) Gratis Sabbath School Society, Edinburgh; (49) Hibernian Auxiliary. Church Missionary Society; (50) Hibernian Bible Society; (51) Hibernian Society for the Diffusion of Knowledge in Ireland; (52) Hibernian Sunday School Society; (53) High Court (and Circuit Courts) of Justiciary in Scotland; (54) House of Commons; (55) House of Industry, &c.; (56) House of Recovery and Fever Hospital; (57) House of Recovery of the City of Cork; (58) House of Refuge for Juvenile Offenders; (59) Incorporated Society for Clothing, Maintaining, &c.; (60) Infant School Society; (61) Infirmary and Dispensary; (62) Institution for the Education of Deaf and Dumb Children; (63) Irish Auxiliary, London Society for Promoting Christianity among the Jews; (64) Irish Evangelical Society; (65) Irish Society; (66) Irish Society for Promoting the Education of the native Irish, &c.; (67) Irish Unitarian Christian Society; (68) James Murray's Royal Asylum for Lunatics; (69) Juvenile Deaf and Dumb Association; (70) Kildare Place Society for Promoting the Education of the Poor of Ireland; (71) Leeds Philosophical and Literary Society; (72) Leeds Temperance So-

ciety; (73) Leith Dispensary and Humane Society; (74) List of Office-Bearers, &c.; (75) Literary and Philosophical Society of Newcastle-upon-Tyne; (76) Literary and Philosophical Society of Portsmouth and Portsea; (77) Literary and Philosophical Society of Sheffield; (78) London Hibernian Society; (79) London Oriental Institution; (80) London Society for Promoting Christianity among the Jews; (81) London University, King's College; (82) Lunatic Asylum of Edinburgh; (83) Manchester Institution for Curing Diseases of the Eye; (84) Manchester Mechanics' Institution; (85) Manchester School for the Deaf and Dumb; (86) Mechanics' Institution, Sunderland; (87) Methodist Missionary Society of Leeds; (88) Missionary Society (afterwards London Missionary Society); (89) National Institution for the Education of Deaf and Dumb Children of the Poor in Ireland; (90) National Society for Promoting the Education of the Poor in the Principles of the Established Church; (91) National Vaccine Establishment; (92) Natural History Society of Northumberland, Durham, &c.; (93) New Town Dispensary, Edinburgh; (94) Newcastle Eye Infirmary; (95) Oriental Translation Fund; (96) Orkney and Zetland Charitable Society; (97) Orkney Club; (98) Outinian Society; (99) Oxford and Oxfordshire Auxiliary Bible Society; (100) Oxford and Oxfordshire Auxiliary Society for Promoting Christianity among the Jews; (101) Paisley Philosophical Institution; (102) Phrenological Society; (103) Police-court, &c.; (104) Port of Hull Society for the Religious Instruction of Seamen; (105) Portsmouth and Portsea Literary and Philosophical Society; (106) Protestant Orphan Society; (107) Royal Humane Society; (108) Royal Infirmary of Edinburgh; (109) Royal Institution for the Deaf and Dumb; (110) Royal Institution for the Encouragement of the Fine Arts in Scotland; (111) Royal Institution of Architects of Ireland; (112) Royal Jennerian and London Vaccine Institution; (113) Royal Public Dispensary and Vaccine Institution; (114) Royal Society of Literature; (115) Royal United Service Institution; (116) Sabbath School Union for Scotland; (117) School of Arts of Edinburgh, for the Education of Mechanics; (118) Scottish Missionary Society; (119) Scottish Naval and Military Academy; (120) Society established in London for the Suppression of Mendicity; (121) Society for Bettering the Condition and Increasing the Comforts of the Poor; (122) Society for Education in the Highlands; (123) Society for Promoting Christian Knowledge; (124) Society for Promoting the Education of the Poor in Ireland; (125) Society for the Improvement of Prison Discipline; (126) Society for the Mitigation and Gradual Abolition of Slavery in the British Dominions; (127) Society . . . for the Recovery of Persons Apparently Drowned, &c.; (128) Society for the Relief of the Destitute Sick, Edinburgh;

(129) *Society for the Support of Gaelic Schools;* (130) *Society for the Suppression of Beggars;* (131) *Society in Dublin for Promoting the Comfort of the Poor;* (132) *Surveyor General of H.M. Land Revenue;* (133) *Trustees for Bettering the Condition of the Poor of Ireland;* (134) *Wesleyan Methodist Missionary Auxiliary Society of Hull;* (135) *Wesleyan Methodist Missionary Society;* (136) *Wicklow Education Society;* (137) *Widows' Fund of Writers to the Signet;* (138) *Workington Agricultural Society;* (139) *Yorkshire Society for Educating, Boarding and Clothing Boys in Yorkshire,* &c.

REPORTER; or the General Observer. London. v1, 1797. f.
b: UCP.

REPOSITORY; containing various political, philosophical, literary, and miscellaneous Articles. London. v1-2, 1788-89. f.
a: ULS. / b: L.

REPOSITORY, and Review of Literature, Science, and the Belles Lettres. Bristol. no1-18, Jl 21-N 17, 1827/?.
a: ULS. / b: BrP.

REPOSITORY OF ARTS, Literature, Commerce, Manufactures, Fashions, and Politics. London. v1-14. 1809-15; ns, v1-14, 1816-22; s3, v1-12, 1823-28; s4, no1-9, 1829. m. (Also called *Ackermann's Repository of Arts, Literature,* &c.)
a: ULS. / b: UCP; CrP v1-2, s2, v3-13; KeP lacking s3, v3-4, 8; s4; L; LLL s3, v3-12; LP; LVA; WiP.

REPOSITORY OF FASHIONS.
(See *Ackermann's Repository of Fashions.*)

REPOSITORY OF MODERN LITERATURE. London. v1-2, 1823. (First no. of each vol. called *Weekly Magazine; or, Repository of Modern Literature.*)
a: ULS. / b: DL; L.

LE REPRÉSENTANT DES PEUPLES. London. v1-20, [?]-1830.
b: UCP.

REPRESENTATIVE. London. no1+, Ja 1822-Ap 13, 1823.
a: CSmH no63, Mr 16, 1823. / b: L.

REPRESENTATIVE. London. no1-160, Ja 25-Jl 29, 1826. d.
a: CSmH no160, Jl 29, 1826; ICU (Ja 25-Jl 29, 1826). / b: L.
(Absorbed by *The New Times,* July 31, 1826.)

REPUBLICAN. London. no1-6, F 23-Mr 30, 1817. w.
a: ULS. / b: UCP; L no1; O no1, 5.
Continued as
SHERWIN'S POLITICAL REGISTER. London. v1-5, 1817-19. w. (Caption title: *Sherwin's Weekly Political Register.*)
a: ULS. / b: UCP; BP v1-2; L v1-3; v4, no2; v5, no8; NwP; O v2, no7; v4, no6.

Continued as
REPUBLICAN. London. v1-14, 1819-26. w.
a: ULS. / b: UCP; BP; BuC; L.

REPUBLICAN. London. v1-3, 1831-32. (Has varying subtitles: as . . . or, *Voice of the People* and . . . *and Radical Reformer.*)
a: ULS. / b: UCP; L impf.

REPUBLICAN, a Weekly Historical Magazine. London. v1, no1-20, Ja 6-My 23, 1813. w.
a: ULS. / b: O no9.

REPUBLICAN; or, Voice of the People.
(See *The Republican.*)

REPUBLICAN AND RADICAL REFORMER.
(See *The Republican.*)

REPUBLICAN JOURNAL; and Dumfries Weekly Advertiser. Dumfries. [?]-1795-1796-[?]. w.
a: CtY My 2, 1795; PPL Ap 7, 14, 1796.

REPUBLICAN RUSH-LIGHT.
(See *The Rush-Light.*)

RESTITUTA; or, Titles, Extracts, and Characters of old Books, &c.
(See *Censura Literaria.*)

RETROSPECT OF DISCOVERIES.
(See *Retrospect of Philosophical, Mechanical, Chemical, and Agricultural Discoveries.*)

RETROSPECT of Philosophical, Mechanical, Chemical, and Agricultural Discoveries; being an Abridgement of the Periodical and other Publications, English and Foreign, relative to Arts, Chemistry, Manufactures, &c. London. v1-8, 1806-15. (Also called *Retrospect of Discoveries.*)
a: ULS. / b: UCP; CrP v1-3; L; LP; O v6, v8 impf.

RETROSPECTIVE REVIEW (and Historical and Antiquarian Magazine). London. v1-14, 1820-26; ns, v1-2, 1827-28. Also as v1-16. (Title varies slightly.)
a: ULS; ULSup. / b: UCP; BP; BrP lacking v11; ns, v1-2; CrP; EP; GeG v1-13; GrP; L; LGU lacking 1826; LLL; LLN; LVA; LdL; LvA; LvP; MCh; MoM; NwL; SP; WcP; WmP.

REVIEW. London. 1795.
b: UCP.

REVIEW AND SUNDAY ADVERTISER. London. no1+, 1789-97/?. w.
a: ICU Ja 8-Ap 16, 1797; IU F 10, 1793. / b: BiP Jl 4, 1790; C Ag 15, 1790; L Ag 14, 1791; Ag 24, 1794; Mr 22, 1795; MR no183.
Continued as
SUNDAY REVIEW. London. [1797?]-1815-[?]. w.
a: CtY O 2, 1814-D 31, 1815; ICU Ap 23-D 31, 1797; F 25-D 30, 1798; MBAt My 10, 1807; NNHi (Mr 23-Ag 31, 1806). / b: L O 28, 1804; 8 sc.nos. 1808-09.

REVIEW OF MATHEMATICAL and Philosophical Books.
(See *Mathematical Repository*.)

REVIEW OF PUBLICATIONS OF ART. London. v1, 1808. q.
   b: BP; L; LLL.

THE REVIEWER. London. 1832. w.
   a: CSmH v1, no1, Ja 1, 1832.

REVIVALIST: exclusively devoted to the Revival and Extension of Evangelical Religion.
London. 1832-43.
   b: UCP; CrP; L.
   (Continued as *An Anglo-American Magazine*, 1844.)

REVOLUTION. London. no1+, My 4-Jl 20,
1822.
   b: L.

REVOLUTIONARY MAGAZINE: History of
the French Revolution. London. no1-7, 1795.
(Title varies slightly.)
   a: ULS. / *b:* L Prospectus only.

REVUE GÉNÉRAL DES THÉÂTRES de Londres et de Paris, London. no1-6, 1819.
   a: ULS; ULSup.

RIDER'S BRITISH MERLIN.
(See *Court and City Register*.)

RIDER'S SHEET ALMANACK. London. [?]-
1789-1790-[?]. (Issued with *London Kalendar*.)
   b: DA 1789-90.

RIFLEMAN. London. no1+, Ja 4-D 27, 1812.
w.
   a: DLC. / *b:* L; O no9.

RIGHTS OF INDUSTRY. London. no1, 1831.
   b: UCP.

RIGHTS OF IRISHMEN, or National Evening
Star. Dublin. 1791-93. t.w.
   b: UCP; DA N 10, 1791-Mr 12, 1793 impf.;
   L no214-15, Mr 21, 23, 1793.

RING THE ALARUM BELL! London. no1-4,
Ag 13-S 3, 1803. w.
   b: L.

THE RIVAL CANDIDATES. no1-7, 1832.
   b: AU no2-7.

ROBIN'S LONDON AND DUBLIN Magazine.
(See *Dublin and London Magazine*.)

ROBSON'S London Commercial Directory.
London. [?]-1830/?.
   b: SaU.

ROCHDALE RECORDER. Rochdale. no1-65,
Ja 6, 1827-Mr 29, 1828. w.
   b: RdP.

ROCHESTER GAZETTE and Kent Weekly
Advertiser. Rochester. no[?]-432-746, [?]-
1829-1835. (Title varies slightly.)
   a: CSmH no432, Je 30, 1829. / *b:* L no
   459-746, Ja 5, 1830-Jl 7, 1835.
   (Continued as *Rochester, Chatham and
   Stroud Gazette*, 1835-68.)

ROCKINGHAM AND HULL Weekly Advertiser. Hull. no1-1057, 1808-28. w.
   a: CSmH Ja 19, 1822; MnU Ap 15, 1820-N
   23, 1822. / *b:* C Ja 11, 1812-D 30, 1815;
   HP; L 1808-19; 1823; 1826-28.
   Continued as
HULL, ROCKINGHAM and Yorkshire and
Lincolnshire Gazette. Hull. no1058-1893,
1828-1844.
   b: HP; L.

ROMAN CATHOLIC EXPOSITOR, and Friend
of Ireland. (Society for promoting religious
Inquiry in Ireland.) Dublin. F 21, 1825-Ja 1,
1827/?.
   a: ULS. / *b:* O no1-11.

ROMSEY WEEKLY REGISTER. no3, D 16,
1816.
   (No issues known. See F.A. Edwards, "A
   List of Hampshire Newspapers," *Hampshire Antiquary and Naturalist*, I(1891)96.)

ROOPE'S WEEKLY LETTERS to the Free-
men of Norwich. Norwich. no1-14, 1810. w.
   b: L.

ROSCIUS; consisting of Original Memoirs of
the Principal Actors and Actresses, Strictures on the Drama and Its Interests, Original Essays, Green-room Gossips, &c. London. v1, no1-7, Ja 4-Ag 9, 1825/?. f.
   a: ULS.

ROSCOMMON AND LEITRUM GAZETTE.
Boyle. no1+, Ap 27, 1822-1882. w.
   a: CSmH My 13, 1827. / *b:* L.

ROSCOMMON JOURNAL and Western Reporter. Roscommon. no1+, Jl 12, 1828-1927.
   b: L.

ROSCREA SOUTHERN STAR; or, General
Advertiser. Roscrea. v1, no1, Ag 19, 1795.
   b: UCP.

ROXBURGHE CLUB. Publications. London,
Oxford. 1814-date.
   a: ULS; ULSup. / *b:* UCP; EP.

ROYAL ACADEMY OF ARTS. Catalogue of
the Exhibition. London. 1769-date.
   a: UCP; LdP 1827-28.

ROYAL ASIATIC SOCIETY of Great Britain
and Ireland. Transactions. London. v1-3,
1823-33. (Superseded by its *Journal*.)
   a: ULS; ULSup. / *b:* UCP; LAt 1827-32.

ROYAL ASTRONOMICAL SOCIETY. Records
of the R.A.S. Club. Oxford, London. 1820-
date.
   b: UCP.

ROYAL ASTRONOMICAL SOCIETY of London. Memoirs. London. 1821-date. (Originally as *Astronomical Society of London*.)
   a: ULS. / *b:* CPL; CrP 1822/25; DRS v1;
   LP; LR.

ROYAL ASTRONOMICAL SOCIETY of London. Monthly Notices. London. 1827-date.
   a: ULS; ULSup.

ROYAL BLIND ASYLUM.
(See *Edinburgh Asylum for Relief of the Indigent, &c.*)

ROYAL BLUE BOOK; or Fashionable Directory. London. 1822-date. a.
  b: C 1822, 1824-28, 1830-31; LGU; SaU 1822, 1825/27, 1830.

ROYAL COLLEGE OF PHYSICIANS. Medical Transactions.
(See *Medical Transactions. Royal College of Physicians.*)

ROYAL COLLEGE of the Physicians of Ireland.
(See *Association of Fellows and Licentiates, &c.*)

ROYAL COMPANY OF ARCHERS, Edinburgh. List of Members. Edinburgh. [?]-1819-1935/?.
  b: EP 1819.

ROYAL CORNWALL GAZETTE, Falmouth Packet, and Plymouth Journal.
(See *Cornwall Gazette and Falmouth Packet.*)

ROYAL DEVONPORT TELEGRAPH and Plymouth Chronicle.
(See *Royal Dock.*)

ROYAL DOCK. Devonport. 1808-[?].
(No issues known. Data from Plymouth City Library and R.N. Worth's bibliography of Plymouth materials.)
Continued as
ROYAL DEVONPORT TELEGRAPH and Plymouth Chronicle. Devonport. [?]-1827-1833. w.
  a: CSmH no1018, S 15, 1827. / *b:* L no 999+, My 5, 1827-Je 29, 1833.
  (Continued as *Devonport Telegraph and Plymouth Chronicle*, 1833-51; as *Devonport and Plymouth Telegraph*, 1851-63. Incorporated with *Western Weekly News*, 1863.)

ROYAL DUBLIN SOCIETY. Proceedings. Dublin. v1+, 1764-date.
  a: ULS. / *b:* DRS.

ROYAL DUBLIN SOCIETY. Transactions. Dublin. v1-6, 1799-1810.
  a: ULS. / *b:* UCP; DRS; LR v1-2, 4, 6.

ROYAL GAZETTE and Sierra Leone Advertiser. Freetown. [?]-1821-[?].
  b: CsP no184, D 8, 1821.

ROYAL GEOGRAPHICAL SOCIETY, London. Journal. London. v1-50, 1830-80.
  a: ULS; ULSup. / *b:* UCP; BP; CrP; DRS; EP; HdP; KeP; LGU; LdP; NwP; PsP; SP 1832; WmP.
  (Continued as *Geographical Journal*, etc., 1880-date.)

ROYAL GEOLOGICAL SOCIETY of Cornwall. Transactions. Penzance. 1818-date.
  a: ULS. / *b:* DRS; LCP; LP; LR.

ROYAL HORTICULTURAL SOCIETY of London. Transactions. London. v1-7, 1805-29; s2, v1-3, 1831-48.
  a: ULS; ULSup. / *b:* BP; CPL 1811-32; CrP v1-7; DRS; LGU 1815-32; LP 1812-32; LdP.

ROYAL HUMANE SOCIETY. Reports. London. 1774-1878.
  b: L; LP 1816-32; LR 1789-1812, 1827-30, 1832; LS.

ROYAL INFIRMARY OF EDINBURGH. Report by the Managers. Edinburgh. 1801-23.
  b: UCP.

ROYAL INSTITUTION for the Deaf and Dumb. Report. Edinburgh. 1815-45.
  b: UCP.

ROYAL INSTITUTION for the Encouragement of the Fine Arts in Scotland. Report. Edinburgh. 1826-28.
  b: UCP.

ROYAL INSTITUTION of Architects of Ireland. Report. Dublin. v1-10, 1814-24.
  b: UCP.

ROYAL INSTITUTION OF CORNWALL. Annual Report. Truro. v1-45, 1818-63. (Continued in its *Journal.*)
  a: ULS.

ROYAL INSTITUTION OF GREAT BRITAIN. Journal.
(See *Journal of Science and Arts.*)

ROYAL INSTITUTION OF GREAT BRITAIN. Journals. London. v1-2, Ap 5, 1800-My 1803.
  a: ULS; ULSup. / *b:* DRS; LP.
  (See also *Journal of Science and Arts.*)

ROYAL IRISH ACADEMY. Transactions. Dublin. v1-33, 1787-1906.
  a: ULS. / *b:* BP; CPL; CrP lacking 1792-99; DRS; LP; LR; LVA; MCh.

ROYAL JENNERIAN and London Vaccine Institution. Report. London. [?]-1817-1851/?. (1803-[?] as *Royal Jennerian Society.*)
  a: ULS.

ROYAL KALENDAR. London. 1767-1893.
  b: DA 1789-90, 1806; LGU.

ROYAL LADY'S MAGAZINE, and Archives of the Court of St. James's. London. v1-5, 1831-33; ns, v1-3, 1834-35/?.
  a: ULS. / *b:* UCP; E v1-5; L.

ROYAL MAGAZINE.
(See *Liverpool and Manchester Quarterly Magazine.*)

ROYAL MEDICAL AND CHIRURGICAL Society of London.
(See *Medical and Chirurgical Society of London.*)

ROYAL MILITARY CHRONICLE; or, the British Officers' Monthly Register, Chron-

icle and Military Mentor. London. v1-7, 1810-
14; ns, v1-6, 1814-17.
   a: ULS; ULSup. / *b:* UCP; DL; KeP
v1-2, lacking no 11 of v2; L; LLL.

**ROYAL MILITARY PANORAMA, or Officer's
Companion.**
   (See *Military Panorama, or Officer's Com-
panion.*)

ROYAL NAVY LIST.
   (See *Navy List.*)

**ROYAL PUBLIC DISPENSARY and Vaccine
Institution. Report.** Edinburgh. 1822-46.
   b: UCP. .

**ROYAL REGISTER, Genealogical and His-
toric.** London. 1831.
   b: L.

**ROYAL SCOTTISH ACADEMY. Exhibitions.
Catalogues.** Edinburgh. no 1+, 1827-date.
   b: EP.

**ROYAL SCOTTISH SOCIETY OF ARTS.
Transactions.** Edinburgh. v 1-19, 1832-1925.
   b: LP.
   (Continued as *Edinburgh Journal of Science, Technology, and Photographic Art,*
1926-date.)

ROYAL SOCIETY OF ARTS . Transactions.
London. v1-57, 1783-1851.
   a: ULS; ULSup. / *b:* LP.

**ROYAL SOCIETY OF EDINBURGH. Pro-
ceedings.** Edinburgh. 1832-date. (1783-1803
in its *Transactions,* v1-5.)
   a: ULS; ULSup. / *b:* EP; L; LR; MCh.

**ROYAL SOCIETY OF EDINBURGH. Trans-
actions.** Edinburgh. v1+, 1783-date.
   a: ULS; ULSup. / *b:* BP; CPL; GeG 1789-
1805; LCP; LP; LR.

**ROYAL SOCIETY OF LITERATURE. Re-
port of the Proceedings.** London. v1, 1823.
   b: UCP.
   Continued as
**ROYAL SOCIETY OF LITERATURE. Re-
port.** London. v2+, 1824-date.
   b: UCP.

**ROYAL SOCIETY OF LITERATURE of the
United Kingdom. Transactions.** London. v1-
3, 1823-38; s2, v1-37, 1840-1919.
   a: ULS. / *b:* UCP; BP; LdP.
   (Continued as *Essays by Divers Hands.
Being the Transactions of the Royal Society of the United Kingdom,* 1920-date.)

**ROYAL SOCIETY OF LONDON. Abstracts
of the Papers printed in the Philosophical
Transactions.** London. v1-4, 1800-43.
   a: ULS. / *b:* UCP; BP; LAt; LR; WhP;
WmP.
   (Continued as *Abstracts of the Papers
Communicated to the Royal Society,* 1843-
54; and continued ultimately as *Proceedings.*)

**ROYAL SOCIETY OF LONDON. Catalogue
of Scientific Papers.** London. 1800-1900.
   b: LP.

**ROYAL SOCIETY OF LONDON. Philosoph-
ical Transactions.** London. 1665-date. (For
further bibliographical details, see ULS.)
   a: ULS; ULSup. / *b:* BP; CPL 1812-32;
DRS; GeG 1789-1800; L; LAt lacking 1819;
LCP; LdP v1-6, 8-10, 47-160, 171-72; WiP.

**ROYAL SOCIETY OF LONDON. Proceed-
ings.**
   (See *Royal Society of London. Abstracts
of the Papers,* &c.)

ROYAL STANDARD. London. v1, no1-20,
1803. w.
   a: ULS.
   Continued as
**ROYAL STANDARD and Loyal Political
Register.** London. v2, no1-18, Ja 7-My 5,
1804. w.
   b: UCP.

**ROYAL STANDARD and Loyal Political Reg-
ister.**
   (See *Royal Standard.*)

**ROYAL UNITED SERVICE INSTITUTION.
Report of the Naval and Military Library and
Museum.** London. v1-2, 1832-33.
   b: UCP.

ROYAL YORK. London. no1+, My 13-S 16,
1827.
   a: CSmH no3, My 27, 1827. / *b:* L.

**ROYAL ZOOLOGICAL SOCIETY of Ireland.
Annual Report.** v1+, 1832-date.
   a: ULS.

RUMP CHRONICLE. London. no1-6, F 26-
Mr 3, 1816. d.
   a: ULSup. / *b:* L; O no1-5.

THE RUSH-LIGHT. Glasgow. v1, no1-6, F
15-Ag 30, 1800. ir.
   a: ULS; ULSup. / *b:* GM no1-5.
   Continued as
REPUBLICAN RUSH-LIGHT. Glasgow. v2,
no1, 1801/?. (Also called no7.)
   a: ULS; ULSup.

THE RUSH LIGHT. Glasgow. no1-10, 1824.
   b: GM.

**THE RUSHLIGHT; a weekly Literary Publi-
cation.** Belfast. v1, no1-41, 1824-25. w.
   b: BlL; DL no2-4.

RYE AND HASTINGS ADVOCATE. Rye. no1-
5, Je 30-Jl 28, 1827.
   b: L.

**THE SABBATH; containing morning and
evening Prayers, original Sermons, Illustrations of Holy Writ.** London. no1-24, 1823.
   b: L; O.

THE SABBATH GLEANER. Sheffield. no1-8, Je 1832-Mr 1833.
b: SP.

THE SABBATH REMEMBRANCER. London. v1-2, 1831.
b: O.

THE SABBATH SCHOOL MAGAZINE for Scotland. Glasgow. v1-4, [?]-1824.
b: GM v3-4, 1824.

SABBATH SCHOOL UNION for Scotland. Report. Edinburgh. v[1]-6-11,[?]-1822-1827.
b: UCP.

SACRED OFFERING, a Poetical Annual. London, Liverpool. 1831-35. a.
b: UCP.

SAILOR'S MAGAZINE and Nautical Intelligencer. (British and Foreign Seaman's Society.) London. v1-10, 1820-29; ns, v1-15, 1830-53/?. m. (Also called *Sailor's Magazine and Naval Miscellany.*)
a: ULS; ULSup.

SAILOR'S MAGAZINE and Naval Miscellany. (See *Sailor's Magazine and Nautical Intelligencer.*)

THE ST. ANDREWS' UNIVERSITY Magazine. Dundee. D 3, 1825-Mr 31, 1826. f.
(No issues known. Data from S N & Q, s1. III.150. and s1.VI,107.)

ST. GEORGE'S CHRONICLE and Granada Gazette. St. George. [?]-1790-1840/?.
a: ULS. / *b:* E 1799-1813.

SAINT JAMES' CHRONICLE. London. no1+, 1761-1866. t.w. (Subtitle varies, *General Evening Post* was incorporated with this on F 2, 1822.)
a: ULS; CtY sc.nos. Je-Jl 1789; (Jl 8, 1790-Mr 19, 1793; Ap 30, 1793-Mr 22, 1794); Ja-Ap, Je 4-D 1820; ICU 4 sc.nos. 1789; 7 sc.nos. 1791-95; (Ja 1797-D 1798); 4 sc. nos. 1819; MBAt S 22-O 13, N 15, 1791; MH Ap 20-D 1830 impf; Ja 1-Ag 4, 1831 impf.; MdBJ Ja 3-5, 1792; MiD-B Ag 1803-D 1804, Mr-D 1805, F 1808-Jl 1809, O 1809-O 1810, Ja-O 1811, Ja 1812-D 1813 all uncollated; NNHi S 28, 1816-D 30, 1819; NcD 6 sc.nos. 1790-92. / *b:* C Ag 28-30, 1792; N 24, 1795; D 1791 impf.; EP 1828; L lacking 1816-18; LGU 1789-1827; O 1789-1805 impf.; OPU 1804, 1806-23.
(Continued as *Press and St. James' Chronicle.*)

ST. JAMES'S ROYAL MAGAZINE, and Monthly Gazette of Fashion.
(See *English Spy; an original Work*, &c.)

THE SALAD; a Periodical of Taste and Elegant Literature. Stockport. no1-8, Ja 22-Mr 12, 1830. w.
b: ScP.

THE SALE-ROOM. Edinburgh. no1-28, Ja 4-Jl 12, 1817. w.
a: ULS. / *b:* UCP; EP; L; O.

SALISBURY AND WINCHESTER JOURNAL. Salisbury. 1772-date. w. (Preceded by *Salisbury Journal; or, Weekly Advertiser*, 1738-50; by *Salisbury Journal*, 1750-72.)
a: ULS; CSmH Ja 7, 1828; CtY 1789-91; 1795-1806; (1807-09); 1810-32; ICU Ja 6, 1800-D 27, 1802, lacking Mr 3, Ag 11, 1811 & Je 21, 1802; KyU; MnU Jl 10, 17, 1815; N 6, 1820. / *b:* DcrN D 1796-1809; 1811-16; 1819-20; 1822-25; 1828-29; 1831-32; DvW 1789-95; 1809-31; L 1824-32; SbSW.

SALMAGUNDI. London. 1823.
b: O no1, My 17, 1823.

SALOPIAN JOURNAL.
(See *Salopian Journal and Courier of Wales.*)

SALOPIAN JOURNAL and Courier of Wales. Shrewsbury. no1+, Ja 29, 1794-1803. w.
a: CtY 5 sc.nos. 1798-1803. / *b:* L no1; SrP 1794-96, 1798-1800.
Continued as
SALOPIAN JOURNAL. Shrewsbury. 1803-43. w.
a: CSmH My 14, 1828. / *b:* BP 19 sc.nos. 1802-15; CrP 1826-31; L Mr 6, 1822-1832; SrP 1806-32.
(Incorporated with *Eddowes's Journal.*)

SALOPIAN MAGAZINE and Monthly Observer. Shrewsbury. v1-3, 1815-17. m.
a: ULS. / *b:* UCP; BP; C; CrP; L; LGU; O; SrP.

THE SALT-BEARER. London. no1-33, My 1820-Ap 1821.
a: ULS. / *b:* BiP; L; O.

SAMS'S ANNUAL PEERAGE of the British Empire. London. v1-2, 1827.
b: EU; L.

THE SANS PAREIL; or, Curiosities of Literature. London. no1, Mr 17, 1832.
b: L; O.

SARAH FARLEY'S BRISTOL JOURNAL. Bristol. [1777]-[1806]. w. (Succeeds *F. Farley's Bristol Journal*, [1743]-1744-1748; *Farley's Bristol Journal*. 1748-[?]; *Bristol Journal*, [?]-1748-1774-[1777].)
b: BrP 1789-99 impf.; L Ag 3, 1793; O 8, 1796.
Continued as
MERCANTILE GAZETTE and General Intelligencer. Bristol. [1806]-[1807]. w.
(No issues known. Data from CBEL,II. 721.)
Continued as
WESTERN STAR and Bristol Mercantile Gazette. Bristol. [1807]-[1809].
b: WcBW S 12, 19, 26, O 17, 24, 1807.

THE SATCHEL. A Repository of Wit, Whimsies, and What-Not. Croydon [printed]. London. no1-9, Mr 5-Ap 30, 1831. w.
  b: CrP; DL; L; O.

THE SATELLITE; or, Repository of Literature. Consisting of Miscellaneous Essays, &c. Carlisle, Newcastle-upon-Tyne. v1-3, N 1798-Je 1800.
  a: ULS. / *b:* CsP; DL; L.

THE SATIRIST; or, Monthly Meteor. London. v1-14, 1807-14. Also v11-14 known as ns, v1-4.) m.
  a: ULS; ULSup; MdBJ v1-3. / *b:* BdP lacking v4, 11; CrP v1-2; DL v1-11; L; LAt v1-4, with v3-4 impf.; LGU v1-2; LLL v1-13; LdP v1-9; O v1-4.
  Continued as
THE TRIPOD; or, New Satirist. London. no1-2, Jl-Ag 1814. m.
  a: ULS; ULSup.

SATIRIST; or, the Censor of the Times. London. no1-924, Ap 10, 1831-1849. w.
  a: ULS; CSmH no6. / *b:* L.

SATURDAY MAGAZINE. London. [?]-1823/?.
  b: O no34.

SATURDAY MAGAZINE. Published under the Direction of the Committee of General Literature and Education, &c. London. v1-25, 1832-44. w.
  a: ULS; NcD. / *b:* UCP; CrP; EP; L; LLL; LP; SP; WhP.
  (Superseded by *Parker's London Magazine.*)

SATURDAY NIGHT; comprising a Review of new Publications, Biography, Essays on Literature, the Arts and Sciences, Anecdotes, typographical Descriptions, Sketches of Society, &c. London. v1-2, no1-60, 1824. w.
  a: ULS. / *b:* UCP; L; O.

THE SATURDAY REGISTER.
  (See *Edmond's Weekly Recorder and Saturday Advertiser.*)

SATURDAY'S ADVERTISER.
  (See *Liverpool Saturday's Advertiser.*)

SATURDAY'S MANCHESTER COURIER.
  (See *The Courier; or, Manchester Advertiser.*)

SAUNDERS' NEWS-LETTER and Daily Advertiser. Dublin. 1784-1878. d. (Succeeds *Saunders' News-Letter,* 1745-84.)
  a: DLC 1823-24, 1830-32; ICU 14 sc.nos. 1793-1804; MBAt Ap 28, 30, My 7, 1807; NN Ap 10, 1810. / *b:* C Mr-D 1799; D D 12, 1791-D 29, 1792; Ja-Je 1797; 1798-Je 1800; 1802; 1816-32; DA Je 3, 1789; F 8, D 17, 1823; O 4, 10, 1827; O 19-20, 1829; DLL Ja 1794-Je 1805; 1806-Je 1808; L 1789; 1793; Ja-N 1794; 1795; 1797-1811; 1813-15; 1817-32; MR D 20, 1792.
  (Continued as *Saunders' Irish Daily News,* 1878-79.)

THE SAUNTERER; a Periodical Paper. Newcastle-upon-Tyne. no1-50, 1804-05.
  a: ULS; MdBJ. / *b:* UCP; C; CsP no1-44; O no1-44.

SCALPEL. London. v1, no1-18, O 25, 1823-F 21, 1824. w.
  a: ULS. / *b:* UCP.

SCARBOROUGH COLLECTOR; and Journal of Olden Time. Scarborough. 1826.
  b: UCP; LdL.

SCARBOROUGH Philosophical (and Archaeological) Society. Annual Reports. Scarborough. 1831-1909/?. a.
  b: LdP 1831.

SCARBOROUGH REPOSITORY and Mirror of the Season. Scarborough. v1, no1-8, 1824/?.
  a: ULS. / *b:* L; LdP; O.

THE SCHOOL MAGAZINE. London. no1, O 1809/?.
  (No issues known. Data from John Nichol, *Illustrations of Literary History,* v8,p.610.)

SCHOOL OF ARTS OF EDINBURGH, for the Education of Mechanics. Report. Edinburgh. v1-19, 1822-45.
  b: UCP; EP 1822-28.

SCHOOLMASTER, a weekly Essay; the Subject of which is to point out the Errors and Defects of the present System of Education, &c. London. v1-2, 1829-30.
  a: ULS. / *b:* L.

THE SCHOOLMASTER, and Edinburgh Weekly Magazine. Edinburgh. v1-2, no1-48, Ag 4, 1832-Je 29, 1833. w.
  a: ULS; ULSup. / *b:* EP; L; O.
  (Continued as *Johnstone's Edinburgh Magazine,* 1833-34, and then incorporated *Tait's Edinburgh Magazine.*)

THE SCHOOLMASTER AT HOME. London. no1-6, Je 9-Jl 14, 1832. w.
  a: ULS. / *b:* BoP; L; O no1-2.

SCIENCE OF SOCIETY and Gnomian Review. London. 1802.
  b: LU no5.

SCIENTIFIC GAZETTE; a weekly Record. London. v1, no1, 1830/?.
  a: ULS.

THE SCIENTIFIC GAZETTE; or, Library of Mechanical Philosophy, Chemistry and Discovery. London. v1-2, no1-31, 1825-26. (Sometimes called *Partington's Scientific Gazette.*)
  a: ULS. / *b:* UCP; BP no1; L; LP.

SCIENTIFIC MAGAZINE and Freemason's Repository.
  (See *Freemason's Magazine, or General and Complete Library.*)

SCIENTIFIC MIRROR, a Literary, Mathematical . . . Repository. Bolton. no1-2, 1829-30. s.a.
   a: ULSup. / *b:* UCP; O.

SCIENTIFIC RECEPTACLE. Holbeach. v1, 1825.
   a: ULS. / *b:* UCP.

SCIENTIFIC RECEPTACLE; containing Problems, Solutions, Queries, Enigmas, Rebuses, Charades, Anagrams, &c. London. v1-3, no1-26, 1791-1819.
   a: ULS. / *b:* UCP; L v1-2.

SCOTCH CHEAP REPOSITORY, containing moral and religious Tales. Dumfries. no1-12, 1808.
   b: GM.

THE SCOTCHMAN. To be continut frae time to time. Paisley. no1-11, 1812-13.
   h: L no1-5; PsP.

THE SCOTISH [SIC] BEACON, or Advice from an old Scotchman to his Countrymen. Edinburgh. no1-4, Ag 1-Ag 29, 1803.
   (No issues known. Data from S N & Q, s3. IX.88.)

THE SCOTISH [SIC] REVIEW.
   (See *Edinburgh Monthly Magazine and Review.)*

SCOTS CHAMPION and Aberdeen Free Press. Aberdeen. v1, no1, O 11, 1832.
   b: AU.

SCOTS CHRONICLE. Edinburgh. no1-559, 1796-1801/?. s.w.
   b: EP (no1-559).

THE SCOTS DIGEST of Scots Appeals in the House of Lords from 1707. Edinburgh. 1800-date.
   b: EP.

SCOTS LAW CHRONICLE.
   (See *Law Chronicle.)*

SCOTS MAGAZINE. v11-55, 1748-94. m. (Succeeds *Scots Magazine. Containing a general View of the Religion, Politicks,* &c. 1739-48.)
   a: ULS; ULSup. / *b:* UCP; L; LLL; MR; PsP.
   Continued as
SCOTS MAGAZINE; or Repository of Literature, History, and Politicks. Edinburgh. v56-65, 1794-1803. m.
   a: ULS; ULSup. / *b:* UCP; BP; L; LLL; MR; PsP.
   United with *Edinburgh Magazine, or Literary Miscellany* and continued as
SCOTS MAGAZINE, and Edinburgh Literary Miscellany, being a General Repository. Edinburgh. v66-79, 1804-17.
   a: ULS; ULSup. / *b:* UCP; BP; EP; L; LLL; LdL v71-79; MR; NwL v76-79; PsP.
   Continued as
EDINBURGH MAGAZINE, and Literary Miscellany; a New Series of Scots Magazine.

Edinburgh. ns, v1-18 (os, v80-97), 1817-26. m.
   a: ULS; ULSup. / *b:* UCP; BP; EP; GeG ns, v1-3, 8-16; L; LLL; LdL; MR; NwL 1817-25; PsP.
   Continued as
NEW SCOTS MAGAZINE. Edinburgh. v1-2, 1828-1830. m.
   a: ULS; ULSup. / *b:* UCP; L; LLL.
   Continued as
SCOTS WEEKLY MAGAZINE; a Repertory of Literary Entertainment. Edinburgh. 1832-33.
   a: ULS; ULSup. / *b:* UCP; E; EP; GM; L.

SCOTS MAGAZINE; or Repository of Literature, History, &c.
   (See *Scots Magazine.*)

SCOTS MECHANICS' MAGAZINE. Glasgow. v1, 1825/?.
   a: ULS.

SCOTS MECHANICS' MAGAZINE. Glasgow. v1, 1827.
   b: UCP.

THE SCOTS TIMES. Glasgow. v1-7, 1825-32. s.w.
   a: CSmH no360, Mr 19, 1831. / *b:* GM.

SCOTS WEEKLY MAGAZINE.
   (See *Scots Magazine.*)

THE SCOTSMAN; or, Edinburgh Political and Literary Journal. Edinburgh. no1+, 1817-date. w.;d. (Title varies slightly.)
   a: ULS; CtY Ja 25, 1817-F 14, Ag 22, 1818; DLC (Ja 25, 1817-D 28, 1822); Mr 6, 1830; MnU 1821; NjP Je 14, 1817-D 19, 1818 impf. / *b:* UCP; E; EP; ESL; ETS; L; SaU 1817-30.

SCOTTISH ADVOCATE of Scriptural Principles. Edinburgh. no1-12, 1832-34.
   h: UCP; GM.

SCOTTISH BEACON. Edinburgh. no1-4, 1803/?.
   b: EP no1, 3-4.

SCOTTISH CONGREGATIONAL Magazine.
   (See *Missionary Magazine.)*

SCOTTISH CONGREGATIONALIST.
   (See *Missionary Magazine.*)

SCOTTISH EPISCOPAL REVIEW and Magazine.
   (See *Literary and Statistical Magazine for Scotland.*)

SCOTTISH GUARDIAN. Glasgow. 1832-61. s.w.
   a: CSmH no84, N 2, 1832; CtY Ja 17-D 28, 1832. / *b:* UCP.

SCOTTISH JURIST, containing Reports of Cases decided in the House of Lords, Courts of Session, Teinds and Exchequer, and in the Jury and Justiciary Courts. Edinburgh. v1-46, 1829-73. (After v7 entitled *Reports of*

Cases decided in the Supreme Courts of Scotland, &c.)
  a: ULS; ULSup. / *b:* UCP; L.
  (Incorporated with *Cases decided in the Court of Sessions*, 1873.)

SCOTTISH MISSIONARY and Philanthropic Register. Edinburgh. v1-27, 1820-46. m.
  a: ULS.

SCOTTISH MISSIONARY CHRONICLE. Edinburgh. 1832-36/?. (As *Scottish Missionary Society Chronicle*, 1833-34.)
  a: ULS.

SCOTTISH MISSIONARY REGISTER. . .containing the Proceedings of the Scottish Missionary Society, &c. Edinburgh. v1-27, 1820-46. m.
  b: UCP.

SCOTTISH MISSIONARY SOCIETY. Quarterly Paper. Edinburgh. 1819/?.
  (No issues known. Data from S N & Q, s2. II.40.)

SCOTTISH MISSIONARY SOCIETY. Report. Edinburgh. 1823-25.
  b: UCP.

SCOTTISH NAVAL AND MILITARY Academy. Report. Edinburgh. 1826-29.
  b: UCP.

SCOTTISH NEWS.
  (See *Edinburgh Evening Courant*.)

SCOTTISH PULPIT. Glasgow. v1-5, 1832-36. w.;m.
  a: ULS. / *b:* GM.

SCOTTISH REGISTER; or, General View of History, Politics, and Literature . . . with philosophical, critical, and miscellaneous Papers, &c. Edinburgh. v1-6, 1794-95. q.
  a: ULS. / *b:* UCP; E; EU; L v1-4; PsP.

SCOURGE; or, Literary, Theatrical, and Miscellaneous Magazine.
  (See *Scourge; or, Monthly Expositor of Imposture and Folly*.)

SCOURGE; or, Monthly Expositor of Imposture and Folly. London. v1-6, 1811-13. m.
  a: ULS. / *b:* UCP; BP v1; L; LLL v1-2.
  Continued as
SCOURGE; or, Literary, Theatrical and Miscellaneous Magazine. London. v7-11, 1814-16.
  a: ULS. / *b:* UCP; BP v9, pt1; L v7-10.
  Continued as
SCOURGE AND SATIRIST; or, Literary, Theatrical, and Miscellaneous Magazine. London. v12, 1816. m.
  a: ULS.

SCOURGE AND SATIRIST.
  (See *Scourge; or, Monthly Expositor of Imposture and Folly*.)

THE SCRAP BOOK; a Series of original and selected Papers on Literary and Scientific Subjects. Manchester. v1, no1-35, Ja 29-S 21, 1822.
  a: ULS. / *b:* L; WrP no1-34.

THE SCRAP BOOK of Literary Varieties, Entertaining, Instructive, &c. London. ns, v1-2, Ap 23, 1831-Ag 18, 1832.
  a: ULS. / *b:* GM; L; O no1.

SCRAPIANA; or, a brief Chronicle of the Times; being a summary of the Contents of the London daily Newspapers and the Prices of Stocks each Day, &c. Durham. 1819.
  b: L.

THE SCRIBBLER; Weekly Essays on Literary Subjects. n.p. v1-2, 1823.
  b: GM v2.

SCRIPTURE EXTRACTS, accompanied with Notes and Observations, from some of the most striking Historical Parts of Holy Scriptures. Plymouth. v1-2, no1-24, 1823.
  b: L.

THE SCRIPTURE MAGAZINE. Edinburgh. v1-6, 1809-14. m.
  a: ULS. / *b:* UCP.

THE SCRUTATOR, a Series of weekly Papers addressed to the Students of the Hon. E.I. College, &c. Hertford. pt1-3, no1-46, 1820-21. w.
  b: L.

SEAMEN'S FRIEND SOCIETY and Bethel Union, Bristol. Proceedings at the Anniversary. Bristol. v1-8, [?]-1828.
  b: UCP.

THE SEARCHER; or, an Inquiry after Truth. As an Antidote to the little Nostrums and big Blunders of Political Quacks. Birmingham. no1-6, Mr-My 1817. f.
  a: ULS. / *b:* BP no1-2; L.

SELECT DISCOURSES from the "American Preacher," &c. Edinburgh. v1-2, 1796-1801.
  b: UCP.

THE SELECT MAGAZINE, for the Amusement and Instruction of young Persons. Wellington, v1-5, 1822-24.
  a: ULS. / *b:* UCP; DL no1; L; O no1.

SELECT PAPERS. Belfast Literary Society.
  (See *Belfast Literary Society. Select Papers*.)

SELECT SPECTATOR. Stourbridge. v1-2, 1789.
  b: UCP.

SELECTIONS from the most celebrated Foreign Literary Journals, and other Periodical Publications. London. v1-2, 1798/?.
  a: ULS; CtHT; ICN; NN.

THE SELECTOR. Peterhead. no1-13, Ja 6-N 21, 1817. f.
  (No issues known. Data from S N & Q, s1, II.147.)

THE SELECTOR. London. no1-3, 1820. w.
 b: L no1, 3.

THE SELECTOR; a Cabinet of Prose and
Poetry. Newcastle-upon-Tyne. v1-4, 1827-28.
 b: L.

THE SELECTOR: a Periodical Paper Consisting of Familiar Essays. Manchester. no1-
12, Je 1-Ag 17, 1816. w.
 b: MP.

THE SELECTOR; or Cornish Magazine. Falmouth. v1-2, 1826-27.
 b: UCP; L v1.
   Continued as
 THE CORNISH MAGAZINE. Falmouth. v3-
4, 1828-29.
 b: UCP; L v4.

THE SELECTOR; or Magazine of Useful and
Literary Information. Plymouth. no1-3, My 30-
S 1, 1809. ir.
 b: L.

THE SELECTOR; or, Political Bouquet. Birmingham. no1-14, 1819.
 b: BP no1-10, 12-14.

SELECTOR; or, Say's Sunday Reporter. London. 1799-1808. w.
 a: ULS; CtY sc.nos. 1799; 1800 complete;
 ICU 1801-02. / b: UCP; L Ja 10, 1802;
 Ap 27, 1806; Jl 31, 1808; O 1801-06.

SEMANARIO DE AGRICULTURA Y ARTES.
London. no1-127, Jl 2, 1829-D 15, 1831/?.
 a: ULS.

THE SENATE; containing the Debates in
both Houses of Parliament and Parliamentary
Papers. London. v1, 1831.
 b: L.

THE SENATOR: or, Chronicle of the Proceedings and Debates of the Imperial Parliament.
 (See The Senator; or Clarendon's Parliamentary Chronicle.)

THE SENATOR; or, Clarendon's Parliamentary Chronicle. London. v1-27, 1790-1800. w.
 a: ULS. / b: UCP; BP; L; LLL.
   Continued as
 THE SENATOR; or, Chronicle of the Proceedings and Debates of the Imperial Parliament. London. v1-5, 1801-02. w.
 a: ULS. / b: UCP; BP; LLL.

THE SENTIMENTAL AND MASONIC Magazine. Dublin. v1-6, 1792-95.
 a: ULS. / b: UCP; L.

SENTINEL. London. no1-8, Ja 5-Mr 2, 1823.
 b: L.

THE SENTINEL; or, British Miscellany and
Review. London. 1804.
 b: BP Jl-D 1804.

SEREN GOMER; neu, Gyfrwng Gwybodaeth
cyffredinol. Abertawe, Caerfyrddin. v1+,
1818-1931.
 a: ULS. / b: UCP; CrP; L; SwP.

SEREN GOMER. Neu Hysbysydd wythnosol
cyffredinol dros holl Dywysogaeth Cymru.
Abertawe. v1-2, 1814-15. w.
 b: UCP; CrP; L v1, no1-53.

THE SESSION OF PARLIAMENT for 1825;
exhibiting the State of Parties . . . the Debates and Enactments, and the whole Proceeding of both Houses, &c. London. 1825.
 b: L.

SESSIONS CASES. Edinburgh. 1821-date.
 b: UCP.

SESSIONS PAPER . . . held at Justice Hall,
in the Old Bailey.
 (See The Whole Proceedings of the Sessions, &c.)

SHADGETT'S WEEKLY REVIEW of Cobbett,
Wooler, Sherwin, and other Democratical and
Infidel Writers, &c. London. v1-2, no1-78,
1818-19. w.
 b: UCP; L.

SHAKESPEARE CLUB of Sheffield.
 (See Sheffield Shakespeare Club.)

SHAMROC. Dublin. no1-4, 1799. w.
 b: UCP.
   Continued as
 TAAFE'S NATIONAL SHAMROC. Dublin.
 no5-10, 1799. w.
 b: UCP.

SHAMROG. Waterford. 1808-09.
 b: UCP.

SHARPE'S LONDON MAGAZINE. London.
no1-3, 1829. m.
 a: ULS. / b: UCP; L lacking a few pages
 of pt3 of no1.

THE SHARPSHOOTER. London. no1-31,
1808-10. Every 8th day.
 b: O no4, 19, 21, 31.

THE SHASTONIAN. Shaftesbury. no1-2, 1826.
 b: O no2.

SHEFFIELD ADVERTISER.
 (See Sheffield (Public) Advertiser.)

SHEFFIELD COMET. Sheffield. no[?]-57-
104, [?]-Ag 1, 1828-Jl 13, 1835.
 (No issues known.)

SHEFFIELD COURANT.
 (See Sheffield (Public) Advertiser.)

SHEFFIELD COURANT, and Rotherham,
Barnsley and Chesterfield Advertiser. no1+,
Jl 6, 1827-Je 13, 1834. w. (Subtitle varies.)
 a: CSmH no7, Ag 17, 1827. / b: L no57+,
 Ag 1, 1828-1832; SP Jl 1827-Jé 1829; sc.
 nos. 1828-31; SU 1827-32 impf.

SHEFFIELD INDEPENDENT and Yorkshire
and Derbyshire Advertiser. Sheffield. no1+,
D 11, 1819-1839. w.
 a: CSmH no176, Ap 26, 1823. / b: L no
 452+, Ag 2, 1828-1832; SP; SST impf.
 (Continued as Sheffield and Rotherham
 Independent, 1839-1901; as Sheffield

Daily Independent, 1901-09; as *Sheffield Independent*, 1909-32; as *Daily Independent*, 1932-date.)

SHEFFIELD IRIS.
(See *Sheffield Register, Yorkshire, Derbyshire . . ., Advertiser.)*

SHEFFIELD LITERARY and Philosophical Society.
(See *Literary and Philosophical Society of Sheffield.)*

SHEFFIELD MERCURY. Sheffield. no1+, Mr 28, 1807-1848. w. (Also with varying subtitles.)
a: CSmH no1132, D 27, 1828; DLC (Ap 16, 1814-D 30, 1815). / *b:* L no773+, Ja 5, 1822-1832; SP Ap 1812-1832; SST 1810-32 impf.; SU (1812); 1813-19; (1820); 1821-23; (1826); 1827; (1828); 1832.
(Incorporated with *Sheffield Times.)*

SHEFFIELD (PUBLIC) ADVERTISER. Sheffield. 1760-Je 7, 1793.
b: SP 1790-92; sc.nos. 1793.
Continued as
SHEFFIELD COURANT. Sheffield. Je 10, 1793-Ag 4, 1797.
b: SP (Je 10, 1793-S 1794); Ja 1796-Ag 4, 1797.

SHEFFIELD REGISTER, or Yorkshire, Derbyshire, and Nottinghamshire General Advertiser. Sheffield. no1+, Je 1787-Je 26, 1794.
b: MR 22 sc.nos. 1793-94; SP 1789-Je 1794 impf.; SST 1790-1794 impf.; SU 1790-Je 1794.
Continued as
IRIS: or Sheffield Advertiser. Sheffield. Jl 3, 1794-S 27, 1825.
a: ULS; CtY 1799-1801; (1813-16). / *b:* BP 10 sc.nos. 1804-15; L Ja 6-D 29, 1807; SP; SST 1794-1808 impf.; SU Jl 4, 1796-S 27, 1825 impf.
Continued as
SHEFFIELD IRIS. Sheffield. O 4, 1825-1848/?.
a: CSmH S 25, 1827. / *b:* L Ag 5, 1828-1832; SP O 4, 1825-1832, with 1831-32 impf.; SST 1825-32 impf.; SU 1831-32 impf.

SHEFFIELD SHAKESPEARE CLUB. Proceedings. Sheffield. 1819-1829-[?].
b: LdP 1819-29.

SHERBORNE, Dorchester and Taunton Journal.
(See *Dorchester and Sherborne Journal, &c.)*

SHERIDAN'S COMIC OFFERING. London. 1831-35.
b: O.

SHERWIN'S POLITICAL REGISTER.
(See *The Republican.)*

SHERWIN'S WEEKLY POLITICAL Register.
(See *The Republican.)*

SHIELDS MONTHLY MIRROR and Provincial Register. North Shields. v1, no1-12, Jl 1819-Je 1820. m.
a: ULS. / *b:* DrC; NwS; SsP; TnP.

SHIPPING LIST. London. 1817. d.
a: NcD Ap 15-16, Ag 25, 1817.

SHOPKEEPER'S AND TRADESMAN'S Assistant; being a . . . List of . . . Stage-coaches, Carriers, Coasting-vessels, &c. London. 1768-1807.
b: L 1790, 1796, 1799-1801, 1805-07; LGU 1789, 1792, 1794, 1797-98, 1801-03.
Continued as
KENT'S Shopkeeper's and Tradesman's Assistant. London. 1810-13.
b: C 1813; L 1810; LGU 1810-11.
Continued as
KENT'S Original Tradesman's Assistant. London. 1814-28/?.
b: C 1816; L 1814-21, 1827; LGU 1816, 1818-20, 1823, 1825-28.

SHREDS AND PATCHES; or the College Microcosm. Edinburgh. N 16, 1825-D 1828.
b: EU no1-11, for 1825.

SHREWSBURY CHRONICLE. Shrewsbury. 1772-date. w. (Also with varying subtitles.)
a: CSmH Ag 26, 1825. / *b:* BP sc.nos. 1794-1814; D N 4, 1791; L Ja 2, 1829-1832; SrSC.

SICKLE. Manningtree. no1-15, S 4-D 11, 1828. w.
b: L.
Continued as
COLCHESTER COURIER. Manningtree. no 1-17, Ja 6-Ap 28, 1829. w.
b: L.

SILURIAN. Hereford. no1-3, 1832. w.
b: HfP.

SIMPSON'S SALISBURY GAZETTE. Salisbury. Ja 4, 1816-Je 24, 1819. w.
a: CSmH no137, Ag 13, 1818. / *b:* DvW; DvWG.
Continued as
DEVIZES AND WILTSHIRE GAZETTE. Salisbury. Je 24, 1819-1909.
a: CSmH no291, Jl 26, 1821. / *b:* L no 416+, Ja 1, 1824-1832; DvW 1820-26, 1829-31; DvWG.
(Continued as *Wiltshire Gazette*, 1909-date.)

THE SIR JOHN FALSTAFF; alias the Sir John Barleycorn; alias the Social Fellow. Nottingham. Ja 7, 1832.
b: NP.

SIR PATRICK DUN'S HOSPITAL, Dublin. Annals. Dublin. v1, 1831. a.
b: LCP.

THE SIZAR; a Rhapsody. Cambridge. no1, 1799.
b: LVA.

THE SKETCH WRITER. London. no1-3, 1832. w.
b: BP no1-3; O no1, Jl 20, 1832.

A SLAP AT SLOP, and the Bridge Street Gang. London. no1, 1821.
b: L.

A SLAP AT THE CHURCH! London. no1-17,
Ja 21-My 12, 1832. w.
   a: ULS. / *b:* BP; BoP; L; O.

A SLAP AT THE TIMES. London. 1830.
   b: UCP; BoP; L; O.

SLIGO JOURNAL. Sligo. [1771?]-1813-1866.
w.;s.w. (Also with varying second- and subtitles.)
   a: CSmH no2705, S 14, 1827. / *b:* UCP;
   L no1238, My 24, 1813; O 9, 1828-1832.

SLIGO MORNING HERALD. Limerick. [?]-
1793-[?].
   (No issues known. Data from C & K, 2002b,
   and CBEL,II.738.)

SLIGO OBSERVER. Sligo. no1+, O 9, 1828-
F 10, 1831. w.
   a: CSmH no121, F 3, 1831. / *b:* L.

SMEETON'S WONDERFUL MAGAZINE.
   (See *Wonderful Magazine of all that is Singular, Curious, &c.*)

SMITH'S ANGUS AND MEARNS REGISTER.
   (See *Angus and Mearns Register.*)

SMITH'S COURT CALENDAR and Pocket
Almanack. Dublin. 1832.
   b: DA.

SMITH'S WEEKLY MAGAZINE and Historical Register. Dublin. 1793.
   a: ULS.

THE SNOB: a Literary and Scientific Journal.
Cambridge. v1, no1-11, 1829. w.
   a: ULS; CSmH. / *b:* C; L.
   Continued as
THE GOWNSMAN, (formerly called "The
Snob") a Literary Journal. Cambridge. v2,
no1-17, 1829-30. w.
   a: ULS. / *b:* C; L; O no1-14, 16.

SOCIAL MAGAZINE; or, Monthly Cabinet
of Wit. London. 1800. m.
   (No issues known. Data from C & K, 2003,
   and CBEL,II.683.)

SOCIETY ESTABLISHED IN LONDON for
the Suppression of Mendicity. Report. London. v1-10, 1819-28.
   b: UCP.

SOCIETY FOR BETTERING the Condition
and Increasing the Comforts of the Poor. Report. London. no1-40, 1797-1817.
   a: ULS. / *b:* UCP; EP no7-12; LR 1797-
   1800.

SOCIETY FOR EDUCATING the Poor of
Newfoundland. Proceedings. London. v1-3,
[?]-1825/26.
   a: ULS.

SOCIETY FOR EDUCATION in the Highlands. Report. Inverness. 1819-30.
   b: UCP.

SOCIETY FOR IMPROVING the Conditions
of the Labouring Classes. Proceedings. London. v1, 1832/?. (Also known as *Labourer's
Friend Society.*)
   a: ULS.

SOCIETY FOR IMPROVING the System of
Church Patronage in Scotland. Account of the
Proceedings. Edinburgh. v1-3, 1825-29/?.
(Also known as *Anti-Patronage Society of
the Church of Scotland.*)
   a: ULS.

SOCIETY FOR PHILOSOPHICAL Experiments and Conversations. Minutes. London.
Ja 25-Je 21, 1794.
   a: ULS. / *b:* L; LCP; LMD; LP.

SOCIETY FOR PROMOTING CHRISTIAN
Knowledge. Report. London. 1811-date.
   b: UCP.

SOCIETY FOR PROMOTING MEDICAL
Knowledge. London. Medical Communications. London. v1-2, 1784-90.
   a: ULS. / *b:* UCP; L; LCP; LS.

SOCIETY FOR PROMOTING the Education
of the Poor of Ireland. Report of the Proceedings. London. 1813-39.
   a: ULSup. / *b:* UCP.

SOCIETY FOR THE DIFFUSION of Useful
Knowledge. Penny Magazine.
   (See *Penny Magazine of the Society for the
   Diffusion, &c.* See also *Quarterly Journal
   of Education.*)

SOCIETY FOR THE ENCOURAGEMENT of
Arts, Manufactures, and Commerce. Transactions. London. v1-57; ns, v1-2, 1783-
1850/51. (Afterwards *Royal Society of Arts,
Manufactures, and Commerce.*)
   a: ULS. / *b:* UCP; BP; DRS; GrP 1789-
   1829.

SOCIETY FOR THE IMPROVEMENT of Medical and Chirurgical Knowledge. Transactions. London. v1-3, 1793-1812.
   a: ULS; ULSup. / *b:* UCP; LCP; LMA;
   LMD; LS.

SOCIETY FOR THE IMPROVEMENT of Prison Discipline. Report. London. 1820-27.
   b: UCP.

SOCIETY FOR THE MITIGATION and Gradual Abolition of Slavery in the British Dominions. Negro Slavery. London. no1-17, 1824-
1830/?. (Also known as *Anti-Slavery Society.*
In UCP under *Negro Slavery.*)
   a: ULS. / *b:* UCP.

SOCIETY FOR THE MITIGATION and Gradual Abolition of Slavery in the British Dominions. Report of the Committee. London.
v1-3, 1823-25.
   a: ULS. / *b:* UCP.

SOCIETY FOR THE PRESERVATION of
Public Footpaths. Journal. Glasgow. no1-2,
1832-33.
   b: GM.

SOCIETY FOR THE PROPAGATION of the Gospel. Papers and Reports. London. 1825-date.
b: UCP.

SOCIETY FOR THE PROPAGATION of the Gospel in Foreign Parts. Abstract of the Charter and Proceedings. London. [?]-1701-1912/?. (Title varies.)
a: ULS.

SOCIETY FOR THE RECOVERY of Persons Apparently Drowned. (Afterwards *Royal Humane Society.*)
b: UCP.

SOCIETY FOR THE RELIEF of the Destitute Sick, Edinburgh. Reports. Edinburgh. 1816-72/?.
b: EP 1816-17, 1819.

SOCIETY FOR THE SUPPORT of Gaelic Schools. Report. Edinburgh. v1-21, 1811-32.
b: UCP; EP.

SOCIETY FOR THE SUPPRESSION of Beggars, &c. Report. Edinburgh. v1-14, 1814-29.
b: UCP; EP 1814-16, 1827-28, 1831.

SOCIETY IN DUBLIN for Promoting the Comfort of the Poor. Report. Dublin. v1-5, 1800-02.
b: UCP.

SOCIETY OF ANTIQUARIES of Newcastle-upon Tyne.
(See *Archaelogia; or, Miscellaneous Tracts relating to Antiquity.*)

SOCIETY OF ANTIQUARIES of Scotland, Edinburgh.
(See *Archaelogia Scotica; or, Transactions of the Society of Antiquaries of Scotland.*)

SOCIETY OF DILETTANTI, London. Antiquities of Ionia. London. v1-5, 1769-1915. (v1 as *Ionian Antiquities.*)
a: ULSup.

SOCIETY OF FRIENDS IN GREAT BRITAIN. An Account of the Times and Places of Holding the Meetings for Worship, and the Quarterly Meetings. London. 1789-1889.
b: L 1811, 1818, 1821, 1828-32; LFS 1789, 1800-01, 1810-32.

SOCIETY OF INCORPORATED ARTISTS. Catalogues of Exhibitions. Edinburgh. [?]-1808-1813/?.
b: EP 1808-13.

SOCIETY OF MEDICAL and Chirurgical Knowledge. Minute Books. London. 1793-1818.
b: LMD.

SOCIETY OF UNITED IRISHMEN, Dublin. Proceedings. Dublin. 1791-95.
a: ULS; ULSup. / *b:* UCP.

SOLDIER'S AND NEW SAILOR'S Magazine and Naval Chronicle.
(See *New Sailor's Magazine and Naval Chronicle.*)

SOLDIER'S COMPANION; or, Martial Recorder. London. v1, 1824/?.
b: UCP.

SOLDIER'S MAGAZINE and Military Chronicle.
(See *New Sailor's Magazine and Naval Chronicle.*)

SOLDIER'S POCKET MAGAZINE, containing . . . Information respecting the Practical Discipline, and Scientific Learning of Cavalry, Infantry, Artillery, and Marine, &c. London. no1-3, 1798.
b: L.

SOMERSET HOUSE GAZETTE and Literary Museum; or, Weekly Miscellany of the Fine Arts, Antiquities, and Literary Chit Chat. London. v1-2, 1823-24. w.
a: ULS. / *b:* UCP; L; LGU; LLL; MR; O.

SOMERSET HOUSE WEEKLY MISCELLANY. London. 1823.
b: BP no1.

SOMETHING NEW OF MEN AND MANNERS. Hailsham. 1828.
b: O.

SONGSTER'S JEWEL; or, Annual Harmonist, being a compleat Collection of the favourite Songs, &c. London. 1823.
b: L.

SONGSTER'S MULTUM IN PARVO; or Mirth in Miniature for the Love of Harmony. London. v1-6, 1808-10/?; ns, v1-3, 1812-13/?. (Subtitle varies.)
a: ULSup.

SOUTH AFRICAN QUARTERLY JOURNAL. (The South African Institution.) Cape Town, London. v1, O 1829-S 1830.
b: UCP; SaU.

SOUTH BUCKS Christian Reporter and Sunday School Journal. London. v1-2, 1830-31.
b: L v1, no2-10; v2.

SOUTHAMPTON and Isle of Wight Mercury. Southampton. no1-36, Mr 27-N 27, 1830.
a: CSmH no17, Jl 17, 1830. / *b:* L.

SOUTHAMPTON COUNTY CHRONICLE and Isle of Wight; or, Weekly Advertiser for Hampshire, the adjoining Counties and the Islands of Guernsey and Jersey. Southampton. no1-127, Ap 4, 1822-S 4, 1824. w.
b: SoP.

SOUTHAMPTON HERALD and Isle of Wight Gazette. Southampton. no1, Jl 28, 1824. (No issues known. Probably continued as *Southampton Town and County Herald, Isle of Wight Gazette, and General Advertiser.* For details, see F.A. Edwards, "A List of Hampshire Newspapers," *Hampshire Antiquary and Naturalist,* I (1891) 96.)

SOUTHAMPTON LUMINARY and County Chronicle, Isle of Wight, Portsmouth, &c., Gazette. Southampton. no3, Ap 28, 1822; no 16, Jl 29, 1822.
(No issues known. For details, see F.A. Edwards, "A List of Hampshire Newspapers," *Hampshire Antiquary and Naturalist,* I (1891) 96.)

papers," *Hampshire Antiquary and Naturalist,* I (1891) 96.)

SOUTHAMPTON TOWN AND COUNTY Herald. Southampton. 1825-1826-[?]. w.
a: CSmH no155, Jl 10, 1826.
(Probably continued as *Hampshire Advertiser.* See the latter for details.)

SOUTHERN MIRROR. Dumfries. no1-20, Ja 14-My 19, 1832. w.
b: DsD no2-20, some nos. impf.; E no3-5, 17-18.

SOUTHERN REPORTER. Cork. no1+, Je 1807-1871. t.w.
a: CSmH Ag 12, 1817. / *b:* UCP; L My 29, 1813; Ja 2, 1823, 1832.
(Continued as *Irish Daily Telegraph,* 1871-73. Incorporated with *Waterford Mail.*)

SOUTHWARK SENTINEL and General Advertiser, a Journal of Literature and Science. Southwark. no1-18, 1832.
b: L.

THE SOVEREIGN. London. no1-14, Ap 17-Jl 18, 1825. w.
a: CSmH no1. / *b:* L; O no1.

SOWERBY'S ENGLISH BOTANY.
(See *English Botany; or, Coloured Figures,* &c.)

SPECTATOR, a weekly Journal of News Politics, Literature and Science. London. no1+, Jl 5, 1828-date. w.
a: ULS; ULSup. / *b:* BP N-D 1830; 1831; Jl-D 1832; EP lacking v3; L; LdP.

SPECTRUM; or Edinburgh Miscellaneous Register. Edinburgh. no1-6, Je 1-Jl 6, 1826. w.
b: UCP; EP.

SPECULATOR. London. no1-26, Mr 27-Je 22, 1790.
a: ULS; CtY. / *b:* UCP; L; LLL.

SPECULATOR. London. no1-2, S 25-O 2, 1824. w.
b: O.

SPECULATOR, containing Essays on Men and Things. London. no1-2, Mr 21-28, 1801. w.
a: ULS. / *b:* L no1; O no1.

SPECULUM ACADEMICUM, or Edinburgh Miscellany. Edinburgh. no1-6, 1824.
a: ULS. / *b:* L.

THE SPHYNX; Journal of Politics, Literature and News. London. v1-4, no1-116, Jl 8, 1827-Ap 25, 1829. w. (Subtitle varies: . . . *London News Gazette; . . . Politics, Literature and News.*)
a: ULS; ICU Ap 2, 1828-Je 28, 1828. / *b:* BP; BdP; DL; L.

SPIRIT AND MANNERS OF THE AGE (; a Christian and Literary Miscellany). London. v1-4, Ja 7, 1826-D 29, 1827; ns, v1-2, Ja 1828-1829. m. (First series lacks subtitle.)
a: ULS; ULSup. / *b:* UCP; CrP ns, v1-2; DL; L.
Continued as
BRITISH MAGAZINE; a Continuation of "The Spirit and Manners of the Age." London. no1-10, 1830.
b: O.

SPIRIT OF LITERATURE. London. v1, 1830.
a: MH no2, Je 5, 1830. / *b:* L.

SPIRIT OF PARTRIDGE; or, Astrologer's Pocket Companion and General Magazine. London. no1-17, Ag 5, 1824-Ja 15, 1825.
a: ULS. / *b:* L; MR.

SPIRIT OF THE MAGAZINES; or, Beauties of Modern Periodical Literature. London. v1-3, 1820-21.
a: ULS.

SPIRIT OF THE PRESS. London. 1832.
a: NNHi S 15, 1832.

SPIRIT OF THE PRESS, and Advocate of Public Freedom. London. no1-9, N 23, 1816-Ja 18, 1817. w.
b: O no1, 3-7, 9.

SPIRIT OF THE PUBLIC JOURNALS. Being an Impartial Selection of Essays, Jeu d' Esprit, &c. London. v1-18, 1797-1814; ns, v1-3, 1823-25. a. (Title varies slightly. Suspended 1815-22.)
a: ULS; TxU v1-3. / *b:* UCP; EP v1-8; L 1797-1814; 1824-25; LLL v1-17; LLN v1-18; O.

SPIRIT OF THE TIMES; or, Universal Mirror. A Monthly Compendium of Intelligence, Foreign and Domestic. London. v1-2, no1-10, 1818.
b: L Ja-Je, 1818; O.

SPIRIT OF THE TIMES; concentrating every Week, all that is worthy of being preserved from the whole of our periodical Literature. London. v1-2, no1-10, 1825-26. w. (Title varies.)
a: ULS; ULSup. / *b:* UCP; BP no1; CrP; L.
Continued as
BEAUTIES OF THE MAGAZINES and Spirit of the Times, containing choice Selections from the whole of the Periodical Literature, &c. London. v1, no1-24, S 8, 1827-F 16, 1828. w.
b: L.

SPIRIT OF THE TIMES; in a Series of Observations on the Important Events of the Age. London. no1-8, 1790/?. w.
  a: ULS.

SPIRIT OF THE TYNE AND WEAR; or, the Master's and Workman's Guardian. Hetton. no1, D 1832. w.
  b: DrC.

SPIRIT OF THE UNION. Glasgow. no1-11, O 30, 1819-Ja 8, 1820. w.
  b: GM lacking no4-5.

SPIRITUAL MAGAZINE; or, Saints' Treasury. London. v1-13, 1825-37.
  a: ULS. / *b:* E v3-13; L.
  (Continued as *Spiritual Magazine and Zion's Casket,* 1838-77. In ULS under this title.)

SPIRITUAL MAGAZINE; or the Christian's Grand Treasure ... in a Series of Dialogues. London. v1-3, 1802. (Also known as *Allen's Spiritual Magazine.)*
  b: UCP.

THE SPIRITUAL TIMES. A Monthly Magazine. London. no1-10, 1829-30. m.
  b: L.

SPORTING MAGAZINE. London. v1-15, 1831-40; ns, v1-9, 1841-45/?.
  a: ULS.

SPORTING MAGAZINE; or, Monthly Calendar of the Transactions of the Turf, Chase, &c. London. v1-50, 1792-1817; s2, v51-100, 1817-42; s3, 1843-70. m.
  a: ULS; ULSup. / *b:* UCP; C 1824-32; DL; L; LLL 1826, 1828-32.

SPORTING REPOSITORY, containing Horseracing, Hunting, Coursing, &c. London. v1-2, 1822.
  a: ULS. / *b:* UCP; L.

SPORTSMANS AND BREEDERS vade mecum. York. v1-12, 1786-97.
  b: L lacking v10-11.

SPORTSMAN'S CABINET, and Town and Country Magazine. London. v1-2, 1832-33/?.
  a: ULS; ULSup.

SPORTSMAN'S MAGAZINE; or, Chronicle of Games and Pastimes. London. v1-3, no1-20, Ag 1823-Ja 1825/?.
  a: ULS; ULSup. / *b:* DL D 1823-Jl 1824.

THE SPRIG OF SHILLELAH: or, Humorous Magazine. Cork. no1-5, Jl 3-Ag 12, 1817. ir.
  b: DA.

THE SPY. London. Ap 4, 1808.
  (No issues known. Data from John Nichol, *Illustrations of Literary History,* v8, p. 610.)

THE SPY. A Periodical Paper of Literary Amusement and Instruction. Edinburgh. no1-52, S 1, 1810-Ag 24, 1811. w.
  a: ULS; ULSup. / *b:* UCP; EP; L; O.

THE SPY; or Political Inspector. Sheffield. v1, no1-16, 1795.
  b: SP.

THE SQUIB. London. no1-2, Jl 13-20, 1820. w.
  b: O.

THE SQUIB. Aberdeen. no1, Mr 12, 1832. (No issues known. Data from S N & Q, s1. I.40.)

THE SQUIB; being a Satire on passing Events in Lancashire. Manchester. no1-37, Jl 28, 1832-Ap 20, 1833. w.
  a: ULS. / *b:* MP; MR.

ST. ———————
  (See "Saint.")

STAFFORD COUNTY HERALD. Stafford. no1-57, O 10, 1831-N 5, 1832.
  b: L.

STAFFORDSHIRE ADVERTISER. Stafford. no1+, Ja 3, 1795-date. w. (Subtitle changes prior to 1809.)
  a: CSmH O 20, 1827. / *b:* BP sc.nos. 1795-96; sc.nos. 1803-05; sc.nos. 1807-09; sc.nos. 1817; 1818; sc.nos. 1819; (1820-22); sc.nos. 1823-24; 1825; sc.nos. 1826-29; 1830-31; L Ja 11-Ag 15, 1812; Jl 2, 1814; Ja 9, 1830-32; StfP 1808-16, 1819-22, 1831-34; StfS; StfSA.

STAFFORDSHIRE GAZETTE. Stafford. no1+, Jl 6, 1831-S 5, 1832. w.
  a: CSmH Jl 20, 1831. / *b:* L.

STAFFORDSHIRE MERCURY. Stafford. v1-2, 1814-15-[?].
  b: StfS.
  (Probably combined with *Pottery Gazette* in 1829 in order to form *Staffordshire Mercury, Pottery Gazette.)*

STAFFORDSHIRE MERCURY, Pottery Gazette, and Newcastle Express.
  (See *Pottery Mercury, and Staffordshire and Cheshire Advertiser.)*

THE STAGE. London. v1-3, N 17, 1814-D 23, 1815; ns, v1, D 30, 1815-Je 22, 1816. w.
  a: ULS. / *b:* UCP; L.

STAGE; a Theatrical Paper. Dublin. v1, no1-30, Ap 9-My 12, 1821. d.
  a: ULS. / *b:* L lacking no22.

STAGE; or, Theatrical Inquisitor.
  (See *Oxberry's Theatrical Inquisitor.)*

STAGE; or, Theatrical Touchstone. London. Jl 20-S 28, 1805.
  a: ULS.

STAMFORD CHAMPION.
(See *Champion of the East.*)

THE STANDARD. London. no1+, My 21, 1827-1916. d.
a: CSmH no66, Ag 4, 1827; DLC sc.nos. Mr 14-Ag 6, 1829; [F-D 1830]; sc.nos. Ja-F 1831; (Mr 10-D 1832). *b:* BP Jl 4, 1832; C; E 1832; L.
(Continued as *Evening Standard,* 1916-date.)

STAR. London. D 6, 1788-O 15, 1831. d. (Also known as *Stuart's Star* and as *Morning Star* during 1789. Preceded by *Star and Evening Advertiser,* 1788.)
a: C-S S 16, 1793-1795; 1802; Jl-D 1805; CaM Jl 13-D 27, 1805; CtY sc.nos. 1789; sc.nos. 1791; (O-D 1792); (1793); (Ja 21-Jl 30, 1794; S 1797); sc.nos. 1798; sc.nos. 1806-07; 1810; My 11-D 30, 1812; Ja-Je 1813; DLC 9 sc.nos. 1791-92; (1793; O 9-D 31, 1794); sc.nos. N 1795; 64 sc.nos. 1815-18; ICU 22 sc.nos. 1789; 12 sc.nos. Ag-D 1790; Ap 4-Je 4; 1791; sc.nos. 1792-97; (1800-07); (Ja 1-My 23, Je 17, 1808); 2 sc.nos. 1822; MH 6 sc.nos. Ja-Je 1811; (Jl-D 1811); 75 sc.nos. 1812-19; MdBJ 2 sc.nos. 1791-92; MnU Ja 10, 1799; D 1, 1801; NNHi Jl 1-D 31, 1793; Ja 1-My 23, 1795; sc.nos. N-D 1804; 5 sc.nos. 1805; Jl 1, 1807-F 17, 1808; 6 sc.nos. 1812; NcD 135 sc.nos. 1791-98; 36 sc.nos. 1801-02; (1810); 1813; (1816-17); PPL (1798); / *b:* BP sc.nos. 1798-1831; BIU 9 sc.nos. 1805; 3 sc.nos. 1806; C D 24, 1792-My 6, 1828; EP S-D 1805; Ja-D 1807; O 1, 1803; EU O 5-12, 1789; F 1791-D 1802; 1803-10; L 1789-N 15, 1830, very impf. before 1793; LLL Jl 1798-1807; 1811; 1814-15; MR sc.nos. 1792-99; NwS 28 sc.nos. 1797;, O sc.nos. 1789-92; (1793-1805); PIP 7 sc.nos. 1801-02; WcBW 5 sc.nos. 1807.
Incorporated with *Albion* and continued as
ALBION AND STAR. London. O 17, 1831-1835. d.
b: C Mr 18, 1832; L.
(See also under *Albion.*)

STAR CHAMBER. London. pt1, no1-9, Ap 19-Je 7, 1826. w.
a: ULS. / *b:* L; LGU; O.

STAR CHAMBER: or, a Panorama of the Moral Assassins of the Metropolis. London. 1825.
b: UCP.

STAR OF BRUNSWICK. Dublin. no1+, 1828-29. w.
a: CSmH no17, Mr 21, 1829; CtY no1-57, N 29, 1828-D 26, 1829. / *b:* L N 29, 1828-N 21, 1829.

STATE OF THE ESTABLISHMENT and other Changes of Government. (Ireland. Accountant-General's Office.) Dublin. 1789-91.
b: UCP.

STATE TRIALS. London. [?]-1817-1892/?.
b: O 1817.

THE STATESMAN. London. no1+, F 26, 1806-F 18, 1824. d.
a: CSmH My 12, 1812; CtY Ag 14, 1809; DLC 16 sc.nos. 1811; 5 sc.nos. 1812-13 & 1815; ICN Ja 2-D 29, 1808, lacking My 25, O 3, N 7; Ja 2-Je 26, 1809, lacking Je 2; MBAt Ag 15, 27, S 3, 1806; Ap 4, My 8, 1807; NcD (1811); NNHi Ap 19-My 31, 1808; WHi [Jl-D 1806]. / *b:* UCP; L 5 sc.nos. 1806-08; Je 19, 1809-F 18, 1824, lacking D 31, 1810-Ap 1, 1813 and D 30, 1815-Ja 1, 1818.
(Incorporated in *Globe and Traveller.*)

STATESMAN AND PATRIOT.
(See *Patriot.*)

STATISTICAL REPORT on the Health of the Navy. London. 1830-date.
b: UCP; LS.

STATUTES AT LARGE of Parliament (Acts and Rules), 1215-1869. London. 1769-1869.
b: LP.

STATUTES AT LARGE Passed in the Parliament held in Ireland. Dublin. v1-20, 1786-1800.
b: UCP.

STATUTES OF THE REALM. London. v1-11, 1810-28.
b: UCP.

STATUTES OF THE UNITED KINGDOM. London. 1801-69.
b: UCP.

STEEL'S Original and Correct List of the Royal Navy. London. v1-19, 1782-1809. m.;q. (Preceded by *A Complete List of the Royal Navy.*)
b: UCP; L impf.
Continued as
STEEL'S Original and Correct List of the Royal Navy, and the Hon. East India Company's Shipping. London. 1809-16.
b: C impf.; L impf.

STEWART'S TELEGRAPHIC DISPATCH. Dublin. no1+, N 12, 1832-1835. d. (Also with varying second- and subtitles.)
a: CSmH no8, N 20, 1832. / *b:* L.

STIRLING ADVERTISER and General Intelligencer for the Counties of Stirling, Clackmannan, Kinross and Perth. Stirling. no1+, D 28, 1827-Ag 2, 1833. w.
a: CSmH no157, Ja 7, 1830. / *b:* StlSJ.
(United Ag 9, 1833, with *Stirling Journal and General Advertiser* and continued as *Stirling Journal and Advertiser,* 1833-date.)

STIRLING JOURNAL and General Advertiser for the Counties of Stirling, Clackmannan, Kinross and West of Perthshire. Stirling. no1-680, Jl 13, 1820-Ag 9, 1833. w.
a: CSmH no391, Ja 24, 1828. / *b:* StlP 1820-32, lacking 17 nos.; StlSJ.
(United Ag 9, 1833, with *Stirling Advertiser* and continued as *Stirling Journal and Advertiser,* 1833-date.)

STOCKDALE'S BARONETAGE of the United Kingdom . . . with the Arms of the Baronets. London. 1831-32.
  b: L.

STOCKDALE'S BUDGET of "all that is Good, and Noble, and Amiable in the Country." London. no1-26, D 13, 1826-Je 5, 1827.
  a: ULS. / *b:* L.

STOCKDALE'S PEERAGE of the United Kingdom.
  (See *The Present Peerage of the United Kingdom.*)

THE STOCKING-MAKERS' MONITOR and Commercial Magazine. Nottingham. no1-10, O 18-D 24, 1817. w.
  b: NP no2-10.
    (May be continued as *The Monitor; or, Framework-knitters' Magazine.*)

STOCKPORT ADVERTISER, and Cheshire, Lancashire, and Derbyshire Weekly Journal. Stockport. no1+, Mr 29, 1822-date. w. (Also without the subtitle.)
  a: CSmH Je 17, 1825. / *b:* L S 5-19, N 28, 1823; Ja 23, Ag 20, 1824; 1825-32; ScP; SfP O 25-N 15, 1822.

STOCKTON BEE; or, Monthly Miscellany. Stockton. v1-3, 1793-95. m.
  a: ULS; MdBJ lacking S 1794-O 1795. / *b:* UCP; DrC v1-2; L.

THE STORM, being a Periodical Paper containing . . . no Name . . . but such as are notoriously known to be of that exterminating Banditti called Orange-men. Dublin. no1, 1798.
  b: L.

THE STORY-TELLER; A Journal of Fiction. London. no1, 1832.
  b: O.

STOURBRIDGE AND DUDLEY Messenger and Worcestershire General Advertiser. Stourbridge. 1813-14.
  b: BP no26, O 29, 1813; no71, S 9, 1814.

STRABANE JOURNAL. [1771?]-1785-1801-[?].
  b: C v18, no1218, for 1795.

STRABANE MAGAZINE.
  (See *New Magazine.*)

STRABANE MORNING POST. Strabane. [?]-1821-1837.
  a: CSmH no497, Je 12, 1821. / *b:* L no 580+, Ja 7, 1823-1832.

STRAGGLING ASTROLOGER of the Nineteenth Century.
  (See *Astrologer of the Nineteenth Century,* &c.)

STRAKER'S SELECT LIST. A Catalogue of Books. London. Mr-S 1830.
  b: L.

STRATFORD THEATRICAL REVIEW and Stage Reporter. Stratford-upon-Avon. no1-10, 1827-28.
  a: ULS. / *b:* L.

STUART'S STAR and Evening Advertiser. London. no1-64, F 13-Ap 27, 1789. d.
  b: UCP.
    Continued as
  MORNING STAR. London. no65+, Ap 28-O 1789/?. d.
  b: UCP.

THE STUDENT. London. no1-3, 1821. m.
  b: O.

THE STUDENT: a Periodical Paper, consisting of Essays and Observations on Subjects of Literature and Morality. Glasgow. no1-20, Ja 18-My 31, 1817. w.
  a: ULS. / *b:* UCP; GM; L.

THE STUDENT; containing many Curious Essays, Receipts, and Preparations . . . in Arts and Sciences. Liverpool. no1-4, 1797-1800. a.
  a: ULS. / *b:* UCP; LvP no1-3.

SUBURBAN MAGAZINE and Parochial Censor. London. no1, 1832.
  b: L.

SUBURIAD; or Poems from the Cottage. London. 1813.
  b: L.

SUFFOLK CHRONICLE and Ipswich Advertiser. Ipswich. no1+, Ap 4, 1801-Jl 17, 1802. w.
  a: CtY no1, Ap 4, 1801. / *b:* IpP; L Ap 4-Je 6, 1801.
    Ceased and then revived as
  SUFFOLK CHRONICLE; or Weekly General Advertiser and County Express. Ipswich. no1+, My 5, 1810-Ag 26, 1815. w.
  a: DLC My 2, 1812-My 7, 1814. / *b:* ColP; IpP; L lacking Ja-My 1814.
    Continued as
  SUFFOLK CHRONICLE; or Ipswich General Advertiser and County Express. Ipswich. no1+, S 2, 1815-date.
  b: BurC 1816-19, 1825; ColP 1815-17, 1819-21, 1826-27, 1829-30; IpP; L 1815-27, 1830.

SUFFOLK HERALD. Bury St. Edmonds. no1-66, Mr 28, 1827-Je 25, 1828. w.
  b: BurC Mr 28, 1827-Ja 1828; C Mr 28, 1827-Ap 23, 1828; L.
    Continued as
  BURY AND SUFFOLK HERALD. Bury St. Edmunds. no67-1184, Jl 2, 1828-D 26, 1849. w. (Also with varying subtitle.)
  a: CSmH no122, Jl 22, 1829. / *b:* BurC My-D 1832; L.
    (Incorporated with *Bury and Norwich Post.*)

THE SUN. London. 1793-1876. d.
  a: ULS; C-S N 3, 1796-Ag 25, 1797; Ja 17-Mr 16, 1798; CSmH Je 5, 1797; Ap 10-15, 18-19, 1822; Ag 13-D 25, 1811; CtY 1 no. 1791; Ap 12-D 31, 1793; [Ag-D 1794];

(1795-O 1796); 1797; (Ag 10-N 8, 1798);
1799;[My-D 1800-1802];sc.nos. Jl-D 1803;
complete F 16-19, 21; Ag 9-D 31, 1805;
1813;1831; Ja-Mr 3, 1832; DLC O 1, 1792-
D 31, 1805, with 9 nos. missing; sc. nos.
1811-18; sc.nos. 1827; sc.nos. 1831; ICU
(Ag 27, 1794-Ag 10, 1795; Mr 10-Jl 18,
1796; 1799); 28 sc.nos. 1809-23; MH (O
1792-D 1801; Jl 1803-D 1807); MdBJ 7 sc.
nos. Jl 1794; MeHi (Ja 5-D 16, 1800); MnU
1796; 1798; Ja-Je 1800; 1802-05; NN 7 sc.
nos. 1794; (F-Mr, Je-D 1795); 80 nos.1796-
1802; NNHi Jl 1798-D 31, 1806; My 1-2,
9-12, 14-16, 28-30, 1810; NcD 225 sc.nos.
1797-1801; 1808; (1810-11); PU Mr 13-D
1797, 1799-1821; TxU 18 sc.nos. 1794-96.
/ b: BP Ja 1792-Je 1802; 1803; Jl 1805-
Je 1807; 1808-16; Jl 1817-1820; 11 sc.nos.
1821-31; C widely sc.nos. 1794-1812; E
1831-32; EU 1798-1807; 1831; L sc.nos.
1793; complete 1794; F 7-Je 11, 1795; 13
sc.nos. 1797; complete 1798-1832; MR sc.
nos. 1793; NpP Ja 1-Je 30, 1795; NwS 10
sc.nos. 1795; O sc.nos. 1793-1810; SaU
1827-28.

**THE SUN. The Last Speech and Dying Words,
with the Birth . . . Life . . . and Behaviour
of that Notorious . . . British Imposter, known
by the Nickname of the Sun, who was burnt
at the Stake . . . for . . . a false . . . Attack
upon the House of Commons of Ireland.** Dublin. 1799.
  b: L.

SUNDAY ADVERTISER. London. no1-739,
1807-21. w.
  b: L no555-739, Ja 4, 1818-Ag 5, 1821.
  On Ag 12, 1831, absorbed *Weekly Regis-
ter* and continued as
**SUNDAY ADVERTISER and Weekly Regis-
ter.** London. Ag 12, 1821-Ja 5, 1823. w.
  (In 1822 run in conjunction with *Morning
Post.)*
  a: CSmH Je 10, 1821. / *b:* L.
  Continued as
WEEKLY REGISTER. London. Ja 12, 1823-
D 30, 1827. w.
  a: CSmH Ag 28, 1825. / *b:* L.
  Continued as
SUNDAY HERALD. London. Ja 6, 1828-F
8, 1829. w.
  a: CSmH Ag 17, 1828. / *b:* L.
  (Incorporated with *The News.)*

SUNDAY ADVERTISER and Weekly Register.
(See *Sunday Advertiser.)*

SUNDAY CHRONICLE. London. no1+, Mr 30,
1788-Je 20, 1790-[?].
  b: L Je 7, 1789; Je 20, 1790.

SUNDAY CHRONICLE. London. no1-2, 1832.
  b: L; O no1.

SUNDAY GAZETTE. Dublin. no1+, Je 3,
1796-Jl 9, 1797-[?]. w.
  (No issues known. Data from CBEL, II.
736.)
  (Probably continued as *Oracle; or Sunda;
Gazette.)*

SUNDAY HERALD. London. [?]-1790-[?]. w.
  (No issues known. Data from CBEL, II.
716.)

SUNDAY HERALD.
  (See *Colonist and Commercial Weelly Advertiser.)*

SUNDAY HERALD.
  (See *Sunday Advertiser.)*

SUNDAY HERALD. London. no1-16, 1832.
  b: L.

SUNDAY LONDON GAZETTE.
  (See *Ayre's Sunday London Gazette.)*

SUNDAY MONITOR.
  (See *E. Johnson's British Gazette and
Sunday Monitor.)*

**SUNDAY MORNING; being a Repository of
Religious, Moral, Biblical, Historical, Biographical, Critical, and other Entertaining
Readings.** London. v1-2, 1823-24.
  a: ULS. / *b:* L.

SUNDAY MORNING HERALD. London. no1-
13, Mr 2-Je 8, 1824.
  b: L.

SUNDAY NEWS. London. no1-18, Je 1-S 28,
1823. w.
  b: L.

SUNDAY OBSERVER. London. [?]-1792/?. w.
  (No issues known. Data from C & K, 2024a.)

SUNDAY OBSERVER. Dublin. no1+, D 11,
1831-My 27, 1832.
  b: L.
  Continued as
DUBLIN OBSERVER. Dublin. Je 2, 1832-
Ja 16, 1836.
  b: L.

**SUNDAY PAPERS, on the Importance of Re-
ligion.** London. S 13, 1807-Ja 31, 1808. w.
  b: L no6; O.

**SUNDAY REFORMER and Universal Regis-
ter.** London. no1+, Ap 14, 1793-Mr 3, 1799-
[?].
  a: V 1 no for 1793. / *b:* UCP N 1, 1795;
L no11-13, 17, 22, 38, 102, 120, for Je 23,
30, Jl 7, Ag 4, S 8, D 29, 1793; Mr 22, Ag
9, 1795.
  (Perhaps incorporated with *London Recorder.)*

SUNDAY REVIEW.
  (See *Review and Sunday Advertiser.)*

**SUNDAY SCHOLAR'S MAGAZINE, or Monthly
Reward Book.** London. v1-2, 1821-22. m.
  a: ULS. / *b:* CrP; L no1; O impf.

**SUNDAY SCHOOL REPOSITORY; or, Teach-
er's Magazine.** London. v1-2, 1813-16. q.
  b: UCP; L v1, no8; v2.
  Continued as
**SUNDAY SCHOOL TEACHERS' MAGAZINE
and Journal of Education.** London. ns, v1-
s4, v18, 1816-67. q.
  a: ULS. / *b:* UCP; L.
  (After 1867 incorporated with *Sund
School Teacher.)*

SUNDAY SCHOOL TEACHERS' MAGAZINE and Journal of Education.
(See *Sunday School Repository*, &c.)

SUNDAY TIMES.
(See *New Observer*.)

SUNDERLAND AND DURHAM General Shipping Gazette. Sunderland. no1-16, Ja 29-O 7, 1831.
b: L; SuP Ja 29-S 30, 1831.

SUNDERLAND HERALD and Shields and Stockton Observer. Sunderland. no1+, My 28, 1831-1838. w.
a: CSmH no1. / *b:* L; SuP.
(Continued as *Sunderland and Durham County Herald*, 1838-80; as *Sunderland Daily Herald*, 1880-81; as *Sunderland Herald and Daily Post*, 1881-1902; as *Sunderland Daily Post*, 1902-date.)

SUNDERLAND LITERARY MISCELLANY. Sunderland. no1-12, Ja-D 1815. m.
b: UCP; L no1-11.

SUPERNATURAL MAGAZINE . . . containing Ancient and Modern Supernatural Experience, in Testimony to the Truth of Revelation. Dublin. v1, Je-S 1809. m.
a: ULS. / *b:* UCP; L; MR.

SURREY DRAMATIC SPECTATOR; or, Critical Remarks on the daily Performances, with the Bills of the Plays. London. no1-113, 1827-28/?. d.
a: ULS. / *b:* L no70, 93, 102, 108, 113.

SURREY HERALD. London. no1+, D 20, 1826-Mr 4, 1828.
b: L.

SURREY, Southwark, Middlesex, Sussex Gazette. London. 1809-1820. w.
a: CSmH no41, O 13, 1810. / *b:* L no419+, Ja 3, 1818-F 5, 1820.

SURVEYOR GENERAL of H. M. Land Revenue. Report. London. v1-4, 1797-1809.
b: UCP.

SUSSEX ADVERTISER.
(See *Sussex Weekly Advertiser*.)

SUSSEX AND SURREY CHRONICLE. London. no1+, Ag 20, 1823-Je 16, 1824.
b: L.

SUSSEX COURIER of Literature and Athenaeum of Arts and Science. Brighton. 1827.
b: BiP no2, Ja 20, 1827.

SUSSEX EVANGELICAL GLEANER.
(See *Evangelical Gleaner; containing interesting Narratives*, &c.)

SUSSEX WEEKLY ADVERTISER; or, Lewes Journal. Lewes. 1746-1811. w.
b: BiP 1789-My 1806; 1807-11; L (1789-92); Ja-Ag 1793; Je 22-D 1795; sc.nos. 1799; Ja-S 1800; (1803); 1804; LLL 1789-97 impf.
Continued as

SUSSEX ADVERTISER. Lewes. 1811-1904. w.
a: CSmH F 1, 1813. / *b:* 1811-12, lacking S 7-28, 1812; 1813-14, lacking S 26-D 1814; (1815-16); 1817-18 mutilated; (1820); Ja 1823-O 4, 1824; 1825-32.

SWEEPINGS OF MY STUDY. London. 1824.
b: O.

SWINNEY'S Birmingham and Warwickshire Chronicle and Staffordshire Advertiser. Birmingham. [?]-1789-1827/?. w. (Title varies. Known as *Birmingham Chronicle* and *Swinney's Birmingham Chronicle*. Preceded by *Warwickshire Weekly Journal*, 1769; by *Warwickshire Journal*, 1769-70; by *Warwickshire Journal and Hereford Mercury*, 1770; by *Birmingham Chronicle and Warwickshire Journal*, 1770-[1773]; by *Swinney's Birmingham and Stafford Chronicle*, [1773]-1775-1781-[?].
a: CSmH Ag 13, 1818; MHi O 26, 1815. / *b:* BP sc.nos. 1789-1806; Ap 29-D 30, 1819; F 5, 1824; L 8 widely sc.nos. 1791-1814; S 9, 1819-D 26, 1822; Ja 1, 1824-Ap 19, 1827; MR sc.nos. 1792-94.

SYLE'S BARNSTAPLE HERALD. Barnstaple. no1-52, [1825]-1826.
b: L no21-52, Ja 5-Ag 8, 1826.

SYLPH. London, Deptford. no1-40, S 22, 1795-Ap 30, 1796. s.w.
a: ULS. / *b:* UCP; L.

SYLPHID. London. no1-14, 1799.
b: O.

Y SYLWEDYDD. Caernarfon. v1, 1831.
b: UCP; CrP.

TAAFFE'S NATIONAL SHAMROC.
(See *Shamroc*.)

TABLE BOOK.
(See *Every-Day Book*.)

TABLEAU DE NOS POETES VIVANS. London. v1, 1789.
b: MR.

TABLES OF THE DUTIES, Bounties, and Drawbacks, of Customs to be paid, or allowed, on all Goods, Wares, or Merchandise, either imported, exported, or carried Coastwise, in the United Kingdom. London. 1827-1830.
b: L.

TABLES OF REVENUE, Population, Commerce, &c., of the United Kingdom and its Dependencies. London. v1-22, 1820-52.
b: UCP.

TAGGART'S MERCANTILE JOURNAL. Belfast. 1816-21.
(No issues known. Data from Albert Campbell, *Belfast Newspapers, Past and Present*, p. 5.)
Continued as

BELFAST MERCANTILE REGISTER. Belfast. 1822-185[?].
(No issues known. Data from Albert Campbell, *Belfast Newspapers, Past and Present,* p. 5.)

TAIT'S EDINBURGH MAGAZINE. Edinburgh. vl-4, 1832-34; ns, vl-28, 1834-61. (In Je 1834 incorporated with *Johnston's Edinburgh Magazine.)*
a: ULS; ULSup. / *b:* UCP; BP; CrP v2; EP; GeG; L; LLL.

THE TALISMAN. London. vl, nol-13, Je 24-S 13, 1820. w.
a: ULS.
Continued as
THE TALISMAN; or, Literary Observer. London. v2, S 20, 1820-Ja 24, 1821. w.
a: ULS.

THE TALISMAN. London. vl-2, 1829-31.
(No issues known. Data from CBEL,III. 840.)

THE TALISMAN; or, Literary Observer.
(See *The Talisman.*)

THE TALISMAN; or Monkland and Bothwell Literary Melange. Edinburgh. vl, nol-6, Ja-Je 1829.
a: ULS.

THE TATLER. A Daily Journal of Literature and the Stage. London. vl-4, 1830-32; ns, vl, 1833. d.
a: ULS; CSmH; MBAt. / *b:* UCP; HdP vl-2; L; LVA; O.

THE TATLER. A Record of Books, Fine Arts, Music, Theatricals, and Improvement. London. 1832.
b: O ns, nol, Ap 2, 1832.

TAUNTON COURIER and Western Advertiser. Taunton. nol+, 1808-1936. w.
a: CSmH Ag 4, 1830. / *b:* L no803+, Ja 7, 1824-1832; TaP 1819; 1821-32; TaS (1808-32).

TAYLOR'S BUILDER'S PRICE BOOK.
(See *Builder's Price Book,* &c.)

AN TEACHDAIRE GAELACH; o Bhealltuinn 1829. Glasgow. vl-2, 1830-31.
b: UCP; CrP; E; GM; L..

TEACHER'S OFFERING; or the Sunday School Monthly Visitor. London. 1823-64/?. m.
a: ULSup. / *b:* BP vl; CrP ns, v2, for 1829.

TECHNICAL REPOSITORY; containing practical Information on Subjects connected with Discoveries and Improvements in the Useful Arts. London. vl-11, 1822-27.
a: ULS; ULSup. / *b:* UCP; DRS; L; LP.
Continued as
GILL'S TECHNOLOGICAL REPOSITORY . . . being a Continuation of his Technical Repository. London. vl-7, 1827-30.
a: ULS. / *b:* UCP; DRS; L vl-6; LCP; LP.

THE TELEGRAPH, London. nol+, D 30, 1794-Mr 18, 1797-[?]. d. (Also called *Daily Telegraph.)*
a: ULS; C-S Ap-O, 1796; ICU sc.nos. 1795-96; / *b:* BiP F 15, 1797; C Ja 4, 1796; L D 30, 1794; Mr 23, Je 17-N 27, 1795; My 13, 1796-Mr 18, 1797; O Ja 2, 1796.
(Incorporated with *The Morning Post.)*

THE TELEGRAPH. London. nol-11, My 30-Jl 5, 1826.
b: L.

TELEGRAPH, or Connaught Ranger. Castlebar.nol+, S 22, 1830-1870.
b: UCP; L.

TELESCOPE. London. nol-53, D 12, 1824-D 11, 1825. w.
b: UCP; L.

TELESCOPE DRAMATIQUE; ou, Revue générale des Spectacles de Londres et de Paris. London. vl-2, My 1817-Mr 5, 1818/?.
a: ULS.

THE TELL-TALE. Bath. nol-6, 1810. w.
b: BrP.

TELL-TALE, Fireside Companion, and Amusing Instructor. London. vl, 1824.
a: ULS. / *b:* UCP; L.

TEMPERANCE MAGAZINE and Review. London. vl-2, Mr 1832-My 1833. m.
a: ULS. / *b:* L.

TEMPERANCE SOCIETY of Leeds. Reports.
(See *Leeds Temperance Society.*)

TEMPERANCE SOCIETY RECORD. Glasgow. vl-6, 1830-35/?.
a: ULS. / *b:* UCP; GM nol-4, 6, 8.

TEMPLAR; or, Monthly Register of Legal and Constitutional Knowledge. London. vl-2, F 1788-Ja 1789. m.
a: ULS. / *b:* UCP; L; LLN.

THE TEN POUNDER. Edinburgh. nol-16, Ag 4-D 30, 1832. w. (Publication suspended O 6-17.)
a: ULS. / *b:* UCP; EP nol-2, 7, 11, 14; GM; L; O.

TERRIFIC REGISTER; or, Record of Crimes, Judgments, Provinces and Calamities. London. vl-2, 1825.
b: BP vl; L.

TEST-ACT REPORTER; or Report of Proceedings in the late Application to Parliament for the Repeal of the Corporation and Test-Acts: including Parliamentary Debates and Public Documents. London. vl, 1829.
b: L.

TEST-BOOK for the Year . . . 1823. London. nol-2, 1823.
b: L no2.

TEWKESBURY Yearly Register and Magazine. Tewkesbury. 1830-33.
b: O.

THALIA'S TABLET and Melpomene's Memorandum Book; or, Orpheus's Olio, or the Album of All Sorts. London. no1, D 8, 1821. w.
  a: MH.

THANET MAGAZINE. Margate. v1, Je-D 1817. m.
  b: L.

THE THEATRE. Edinburgh. no1-8, N 17, 1813-Ja 1814. w.
  b: L.

THEATRE. London. v1, no1-13, O 4-D 27, 1828/?. w.
  a: ULS; ULSup. / b: L.

THE THEATRE. A Review of the Performances at the Theatre Royal. Edinburgh. 1831.
  b: EP.

THE THEATRE; or, Daily Miscellany of Fashion. Dublin. no1-13, 1822; s2, v1-2, D 2, 1822-Ja 22, 1823/?.
  a: ULS. / b: L lacking no14 of s2, v2.

THE THEATRE; or, Dramatic and Literary Mirror. London. v1-2, no1-23, F 20-O 30, 1819. w.; f. (According to the Bodleian Hope Collection Catalogue, the publication was extended to 28 nos. but I know of no copies of no24-28.)
  a: ULS. / b: BP no5; L no2-3, 5, 7, 12; O.

THE THEATRIC MAGAZINE; or, General Repository. Dublin. no1-2, D 30, 1805-Ja 13, 1806. ir.
  b: DL.

THEATRICAL ARGUS. Birmingham. 1830.
  b: BP no1, My 3, 1830.

THEATRICAL CENSOR. Manchester. no1-6, My 24-Je 28, 1828/?. w.
  a: ULS.

THEATRICAL EXAMINER; or, Critical Remarks on the Daily Performances, with the Play Bills of the Play. London. v1-9, 1823-31/?.
  a: ULS. / b: L v1, no86, 137; v2, no1, 23, 35, 59, 73, 130, 157, 196, 209, 214, 221, 227, 237, 255; v3, no19, 61, 165, 352, 356; v4, no4, 7; v6, no121.

THEATRICAL EXAMINER for Sheffield. Sheffield. v1, O 28, 1824, Ja 24, 1825.
  a: ULS. / b: L; LdP; SP.

THE THEATRICAL GAZETTE. London. 1815-16. d. (No dates and no numbering. On cover: *Dramatic Manual . . . Being an Abstract of the Performances at Covent Garden and Drury Lane Theatres.*)
  a: MH; NN. / b: L no1.

THEATRICAL GAZETTE; or, Nightly Reflector of the Theatres Royal, Covent Garden, and Drury-Lane. London. no1, 1818. d.
  b: L.

THEATRICAL GUARDIAN. London. no1-6, Mr 5-Ag 9, 1791. w.
  a: ULS. / b: UCP; L no1-4.

THEATRICAL GUIDE; or, Daily Chronicle of Public Amusements. London. no1-4, 1822. d.
  b: L no4.

THEATRICAL INQUISITOR; or, Literary Mirror. London. 1812-13. m.
  a: ULS; ULSup. / b: UCP; MR.
  Continued as
THEATRICAL INQUISITOR. and Monthly Mirror. London. v2-16, 1813-20; ns, v1, 1821. m. (Title varies slightly.)
  a: ULS. / b: UCP; BP v5, 8-9, 11-12; L. (Incorporated with *Gold's London Magazine.*)

THEATRICAL INQUISITOR, and Monthly Mirror.
  (See *Theatrical Inquisitor; or, Literary Mirror.*)

THEATRICAL JOHN BULL. Birmingham. v1, no1-21, My 29-O 16, 1824. w.
  a: ULS. / b: L.

THEATRICAL JOHN BULL, and Weekly Journal of Amusements. London. 1822. w.
  b: O no1, O 12, 1822.

THEATRICAL LOOKER-ON. Birmingham. v1-2, My 27, 1822-N 21, 1823.
  a: ULS; ULSup. / b: BP; DL v2; L.

THEATRICAL MAGAZINE. London. 1800/?. m.
  (No issues known. Data from C & K,2042.)

THEATRICAL MINCE PIE. London. v1, no1-8, Ja 1-F 19, 1825. w.
  a: ULS.

THEATRICAL MIRROR; or, Daily Bills of the Performances. London. v1, no1-36, O 1-N 10, 1827/?. d.
  a: ULS.

THEATRICAL NOTE-BOOK. Birmingham. v1, no1, Je 28, 1824/?.
  a: ULS. / b: BP.

THEATRICAL OBSERVER.
  (See *Norwich Theatrical Observer and Ranelagh Spectator.*)

THEATRICAL OBSERVER. Dublin. v1-7, Jl 19-D 3, 1821.
  a: ULS.
  Continued as
ORIGINAL THEATRICAL OBSERVER. Dublin. v7-13, D 3, 1821-Ag 13, 1822/?.
  a: ULS. / b: DL v8, no1-37.

THEATRICAL OBSERVER. Dublin. v1-19, Ja 19, 1821-Ag 2, 1825/?. d. (Caption title of some nos.: *Nolan's Theatrical Observer.*)
  a: ULS. / b: DL v1-14; DLL; L v1-4; no 22 of v6; v8.

THEATRICAL OBSERVER; and Daily Bills of the Play. London. 1821-76. (From Ja 1, 1825, compiled from *Theatrical Observer.)*
  a: ULS; CSmH 1821-30. / *b:* BP no148, My 7, 1822; E Ja 3, 13, 1827; EP no2919, Ap 25, 1831; L.

THEATRICAL OBSERVER; or Thespian Critique. Glasgow. no1, Jl 22, 1820.
  b: BP.

THEATRICAL RECORDER. London. v1-2, 1805-06. m.
  a: ULS. / *b:* BP; L; MR;

THEATRICAL REPERTORY, or Weekly Rosciad, containing Criticisms on the Performances . . . at Drury Lane and Covent Garden, &c. London. v1, no1-28, S 19, 1801-Je 28, 1802. w. (Dropped subtitle after no24, Mr 1, 1802.)
  a: ULS. / *b:* L.

THEATRICAL REPORTER. Aberdeen. no1, D 1, 1832.
  (No issues known. Data from S N & Q, s1. I.40.)

THEATRICAL REVIEW. London. no1-3, 1807. m.
  a: ULS.

THEATRICAL REVIEW.
  (See *Bath Theatrical Review,* &c.)

THEATRICAL ROD! A Weekly Journal of the Stage, Literature, and General Amusement. London. no1-3, 1831/?.
  a: ULS.

THEATRICAL SPECTATOR. London. no1-11, Ap 7-Je 23, 1821/?. w.
  a: ULS.

THEATRICAL SPECULUM and Musical Review. Edinburgh. no1-9, Je 18-Ag 13, 1831. w.
  b: EP.

THEATRICAL SPY. Plymouth. 1829.
  (No issues known. Data from Plymouth City Library.)

THEATRICAL TATTLER [sic]. Birmingham. v1, no1-3, 1830/?.
  a: ULS. / *b:* BP no2-3.

THEOLOGICAL and Biblical Magazine.
  (See *Theological Magazine.)*

THEOLOGICAL and Political Comet.
  (See *Theological Comet; or, Free-thinking Englishman.)*

THEOLOGICAL COMET; or, Free-thinking Englishman. London. no1-5, Jl 24-Ag 21, 1819. w.
  a: ULS. / *b:* L.
  Continued as
  THEOLOGICAL and Political Comet. London. no6-17, Ag 28-N 23, 1819. w.
  a: ULS. / *b:* L.

THEOLOGICAL INQUIRER; or, Moral Religious, and Metaphysical Miscellany. London. v1, Je 1817-Ap 1818/?. (Subtitle varies.)
  a: ULS.

THEOLOGICAL INQUIRER; or, Polemical Magazine; being a General Medium of Communication on Religion, Metaphysics, and Moral Philosophy. London. Mr-S 1815. m. (Running title: *Theosophical Inquiry; or,. Polemical Magazine.)*
  b: L.

THEOLOGICAL MAGAZINE. London. v1, 1801. m.
  a: ULS.
  Continued as
  THEOLOGICAL MAGAZINE and Review. London. v2-3, 1802-03. m.
  a: ULS.
  Continued as
  THEOLOGICAL and Biblical Magazine. London. v4-7, 1804-07. m.
  a: ULS. / *b:* BrP; CrP v4; L Prospectus only.

THEOLOGICAL MAGAZINE and Review.
  (See *Theological Magazine.)*

THEOLOGICAL MISCELLANY; and Review of Books on Religious Subjects. London. v1-6, 1784-89. m.
  a: ULS. / *b:* UCP; BrP; L.

THEOLOGICAL REPOSITORY.
  (See *New Theological Repository.)*

THEOLOGICAL REVIEW. London. [?]-1808-[?]. m.
  (No issues known. Data from *Literary Annual Register; or, Records of Literature,* 2 (Ja 1808) 37-38.)

THEOSOPHICAL INQUIRY; or, Polemical Magazine, &c.
  (See *Theological Inquirer; or, Polemical Magazine.)*

THESPIAN. Liverpool. v1, no1-91, Ag-D 1821.
  a: ULS.

THESPIAN. Bristol. v1, no1-15, 1823.
  a: ULS. / *b:* BrP; L.

THESPIAN CENSOR; or Weekly Dramatic Journal. Edinburgh. no1-3, 1818. w.
  b: EP.

THESPIAN CRITIQUE, or Theatrical Censor. Edinburgh. no1-5, O 1816-N 25, 1816. ir.
  b: EP.

THESPIAN MAGAZINE and Literary Repository. London. v1-4, 1792-94.
  a: ULS; ULSup. / *b:* UCP; L.

THESPIAN REVIEW; an Examination of the Merits and Demerits of the Performers on the Manchester Stage. Manchester. no1-6, 1806.
  b: L.

THESPIAN SENTINEL; or Theatrical Vade-
mecum.London. v1-3, S 26, 1825-Mr 18, 1826.
d.
 a: ULS. / b: L lacking v1, no26; v2, no2,
43; v3, no45.

THESPIAN TELEGRAPH. London. 1796.
(No issues known. Data from C & K, 2045.)

THE THIEF. A London, Edinburgh, and Dublin Weekly Journal of Literature and Science.
London. no1-26, 1832-33. w. (Also known as
London Weekly Magazine.)
 a: ULS. / b: BP no4: L; LLL; O no1, 5,
14.
 (Continued as *London Weekly Magazine,*
1833.)

THISTLE. London. no1-9, Mr 10-My 5, 1822.
b: L.

THISTLE; or, Literary, Theatrical, and Police Reporter. Glasgow. v1-3, 1829-32.
b: GM lacking no1 & 66.

TICKLER; a Weekly Periodical. Paisley.
no1-13, O 15, 1827-Ja 12, 1828. w.
 b: PsP.

TICKLER; or, Monthly Compendium of Good
Things. London. v1-6, 1818-24. m.
 a: ULS. / b: UCP; L.

THE TIME-PIECE. London. no1, 1826.
 b: O.

TIME'S TELESCOPE, or a Complete Guide
to the Almanac. London. v1-21, 1813-34. m.
 b: UCP; EP 1819; LGU 1820, 1822, 1824,
1828; LP; LdP 1814-26, 1829-30; O 1828-
30, 1832.

THE TIMES. London. 1788-date. d. (Preceded by *Daily Universal Register,* 1785-87;
by *The Times; or, Daily Universal Register,*
1788.)
 a: CSmH (F-D 1809; Ag-D 1810, 1811, 1814-
15, 1819-20, Ja-Je 1821, 1822-23, Ja-Je
1824, 1825); CSt Ja 1811-D 1822; CU 1789-
1832 f.c.; CtY (Je 12-Ag 21, 1789); sc.nos.
O, D 1789; F 8-Je 30, 1790; 11 sc.nos.
1791-98; complete 1799; 5 sc.nos. 1800-
06; complete Ap 10, 1807-N 11, 1822; Ap
1, 1830-1832; DLC 1789-1832 f.c.; also
Ja 21, F 15, 1791; (Jl 4-D 31, 1791); (1796);
1797; (1798); 1799-1802; (1803-04); 1805;
1806-08; 1809-13; (1814); 1815-18; (1819);
1820-26; (1827); 1828-29; (1830-31); 1832;
ICN Ap 5, 1828-1832; ICU 1789-1832 f.c.
& also some good runs, especially 1829-
31; IU 7 sc.nos. 1799; (Ja-My 1800); (Je-
D 1817); 1820-21; 1823; Mr 29-D 1824; Ja-
D 15, 1825; (O-D 1831); sc.nos. 1832; MB
1789-1812 & 1824 f.c.; 1809-23 & 1825-32
original issues; MBAt [Je 29-D 1790];
widely sc.nos. 1793-1806; Mr 25-Ap 10,
1807; 1824; 1830-32; MH widely sc.nos.
1789-1824; My 1824-1827; sc.nos. 1829-
32; MHi [N-D 1802-Ja-Mr 1803]; [Ag-D
1815]; (1816); (Ja-Mr 1817); F-D 1818;
1819-Jl 1821); sc.nos. 1822-23; MdBP
1789-1832 f.c.; MdCP 1814; 1821; 1827-
32; MiU (1819-32); MnU 1789-1832 f.c.;

NN widely sc.nos. 1793-1801; complete
O 25, 1805-Mr 14, 1806; (Mr 17-D 31, 1806;
1807-11); (1814); 1815; (1816); 1817-32;
NNC (Ag 23-D 1, 1792; Ag 1-D 5, 1793);
[Ja 20-D 5, 1794]; (Je 3-D 31, 1795); [F-
O 1796; 1797-99; 1831]; NcD 1789-1832
partly f.c.; NjP 1812-32; OCl 1824; Ja-O
1828; Ja-O 1830; OU 1789-1832 f.c.; PPHi
Ja 4-S 30, 1815; PPL 1804-N 7, 1825;
1831-32; PU Jl 1818-Je 1819. / b: BP
sc.nos. 1790-99; complete 1800; sc.nos.
1804-09; 1810-17; 1819-32; B1U 26 sc.
nos. 1806-15; C 1789-1832 f.c. & impf.
set of original issues, 1791-1832; D Jl 1-
N 20, 1789; 1830-32; ETS; GU 1789-1832
f.c.; KeP 1811-18, 1829-32; L 1789-1832
f.c., plus original issues as follows: (Ja-
My 1789); sc.nos. 1790-92; (1793); 1794-
1832; LGU 1806-32; LIT 1811-32; LLL
1817-25 impf.; 1829-32; LLW 1795-1804;
1806-32; LTT lacking ca. 30 nos.; LU
(1813-18); 1830; (1831); 1832; LcP 1812-
32; LvP 1789-1832 f.c.; NwP 1815-32; O
1808-32; WmP.

TIMES EXPRESS. London. no1-188, 1823-
26. w.
 a: CSmH no175, S 3, 1826. / b: L no
171-88, Ag 6-D 3, 1826.

TIPPERARY FREE EXPRESS. Clonmel.
no1+, D 23, 1826-1881. s.w.
 a: CSmH no130, Mr 19, 1828. / b: L.

TO THE PEOPLE OF ENGLAND. London.
no1-28, O 1-N 23, 1830. (The numbers have
separate titles and distinct pagination.)
 b: L.

TOBY IN CAMBRIDGE. Cambridge. v1-4,
1832-36.
 b: UCP.

THE TOCSIN. Birmingham. 1832.
 b: BP no6, D 8, 1832.

TOILET; a Weekly Collection of Literary
Pieces Principally designed for the Amusement of the Ladies. Charlestown. no1-8, Ja
17-Mr 7, 1801/?. w.
 a: ULS.

THE TOMAHAWK; or, Censor General. London. no1-113, O 27, 1795-Mr 7, 1796. d.
 a: ULS; NPV. / b: UCP; L.

THE TOPOGRAPHER. Salisbury. [?]-1821/?.
 b: L pt1 of v5.

TOPOGRAPHER for the year . . . containing a Variety of Original Articles, illustrative of the local History and Antiquities of
England. London. v1-4, 1789-91.
 a: ULS. / b: UCP; BP; EP; L; LGU; LLL
 Continued as
TOPOGRAPHICAL MISCELLANIES, containing Ancient Histories and modern Descriptions of Mansions, Churches, Monu-
ments, and Families . . . throughout England. London. v1, 1792.
 a: ULS. / b: UCP; BP; L.

TOPOGRAPHICAL MISCELLANIES, containing Ancient Histories, &c.
  ((See *Topographer for the Year*, &c.))

TORCH; or, a Light to enlighten the Nations of Europe in their way towards Peace and Happiness. Dublin. no 1, 1798.
  b: L.

TORCH; or, Glasgow Museum. Glasgow. no 1-5, Ja 13-Mr 10, 1796/?.
  b: GM.

TORY. London. no 1-7, Je 17-Jl 29, 1827. w.
  a: CSmH no 1. / *b:* L.

TOURIST; a Literary and Anti-Slavery Journal. London. v 1, no 1-44, 1832-33. w. (Caption title: *Tourist; or, Sketch Book of the Times.)*
  a: ULS. / *b:* UCP; DL; L no 1, 3-6; LFS.

TOURIST; or, Sketch Book of the Times.
  (See *Tourist; a Literary and Anti-Slavery Journal.)*

THE TOWN. London. no 1-134, Ja 1, 1832-Jl 20, 1834. w.
  a: CSmH no 8. / *b:* BP Mr 18, 1832; L.
  (Incorporated with *United Kingdom.)*

TOWN; a Monthly Satire on Men, Manners, and Things. London. no 1, 1825. m.
  b: L.

TOWN; or Dublin Evening Packet.
  (See *Dublin Evening Packet.)*

TOWN, or Weekly Spectator; containing Essays on Literature, Morality, general Politics, and familiar Life. London. v 1, no 1-25. w.
  a: ULS; CtY. / *b:* L Prospectus only.

TOWN AND COUNTRY ALMANACK. Edinburgh. [?]-1781-1800/?.
  b: UCP.

TOWN AND COUNTRY MAGAZINE, or Universal Repository of Knowledge, Instruction and Entertainment. London. v 1-28, 1769-96.
  a: ULS; ULSup. / *b:* UCP; BP v 1-22; CrP lacking v22; EP v21; L v 1-24; LLL v 1-22.

TOWN TALK.
  (See *Town Talk; or, Living Manners.)*

TOWN TALK. London. no 1-18, Ja 6-My 5, 1822. w.
  b: L.
  Continued as
 TOWN TALK and Observer of the Times. London. no 19, My 12, 1822. w.
  b: L.

TOWN TALK; or Living Manners. London. v 1-6, 1811-14. (Also called v 1-5; ns, v 1. Caption title of v2: *Town Talk.)*
  a: ULS. / *b:* L; O no 1-22 for 1811.

TOWN TALK and Observer of the Times.
  (See *Town Talk.)*

TOWNSEND'S Monthly Selection of Parisian Costumes.
  (See *Townsend's Quarterly Selection of French Costumes.)*

TOWNSEND'S Quarterly Selection of French Costumes. London. no 1-9, 1822-24. q.
  a: ULS. / *b:* L no 2-9; LLL.
  Continued as
 TOWNSEND'S Monthly Selection of Parisian Costumes. London. no 1-336, 1825-52; ns, no 1-417, 1853-88. m.
  a: ULS. / *b:* L

TOWNSMAN, addressed to the Inhabitants of Manchester, on Theatricals. Manchester. no 1-26, 1803-05. t.w.;w.;t.w.
  a: ULS; CSmH no 1-18. / *b:* L.

TRACT MAGAZINE; or Christian Miscellany. London. v 1-6, 1824-29; ns, v 1-4, 1830-33; s3, v 1-13, 1834-46.
  a: ULS. / *b:* UCP; L lacking ns, v3.
  (Continued as *Penny Tract Magazine and Christian Miscellany,* 1847; as *Tract Magazine and Christian Miscellany,* 1848-91; as *Light in the Home and Tract Magazine,* 1892-date. In ULS under *Light in the Home.* &c.)

TRACTS OF THE ASSOCIATION for Preserving Liberty and Property against Republicans and Levellers.
  (See *Association for Preserving Liberty and Property,* &c.)

TRADES' EXAMINER; or Political and Literary Review. Edinburgh. no 1-2, N 17-D 1, 1832. f.
  b: L.

TRADES FREE PRESS.
  (See *Trades Newspaper and Mechanic's Weekly Journal.)*

TRADES NEWSPAPER and Mechanic's Weekly Journal. London. no 1-106, Jl 17, 1825-Jl 22, 1827. w.
  a: CSmH no 3. / *b:* L; O no 1.
  Continued as
 TRADES FREE PRESS. London. Jl 29, 1827-Ag 16, 1828. w.
  a: CSmH v3, no 135, F 17, 1828. / *b:* L.
  Continued as
 WEEKLY FREE PRESS. London. Ag 23, 1828-Ap 2, 1831.
  a: CSmH-v5, no 210, Jl 18, 1829. / *b:* L.

TRADESMAN; or, Commercial Magazine. London. v 1-15, 1808-1815. m. (Also as v 1-9; ns, v 1-6.)
  a: ULS. / *b:* UCP; BP v 1-5; L; LP v 2-5.

TRADESMAN AND FARMER'S GUIDE; or, Improved Pocket-Book. Belfast. 1827.
  b: BIL.

TRALEE MERCURY. Tralee. no 1+, F 14, 1829-1839. s.w.
  a: CSmH Je 25, 1831. / *b:* L.

TRANSACTIONS . . .
(In general, see the institution, society, or other group reporting. In UCP, however, entries are commonly under *Transactions*.) See also *Annual Reports, Reports, Extracts, Minutes, Proceedings*, &c. See especially (1) *Apothecaries and Surgeon-Apothecaries of England and Wales*; (2) *Arboricultural Society of Ireland*; (3) *Association of Fellows and Licentiates of the King's and Queen's College of Physicians in Ireland*; (4) *Berwickshire Naturalists' Club*; (5) *Cambridge Philosophical Society*; (6) *Cymmrodorion, or Metropolitan Cambrian Institution*; (7) *Entomological Society of London*; (8) *Gaelic Society of Dublin*; (9) *Geological Society of London*; (10) *Highland Agricultural Society of Scotland*; (11) *Horticultural Society of London*; (12) *Hull Literary and Philosophical Society*; (13) *Iberno-Celtic Society*; (14) *Kings and Queens College of Physicians in Ireland*; (15) *Leeds Philosophical and Literary Society*; (16) *Linnean Society of London*; (17) *Literary and Antiquarian Society of Perth*; (18) *Literary Society of Bombay*; (19) *Literary Society of Madras*; (20) *London Missionary Society*; (21) *Medical and Chirurgical Society of London*; (22) *Medical Society of London*; (23) *Medico-Botanical Society of London*; (24) *Medico-Chirurgical Society of Edinburgh*; (25) *Meteorological Society*; (26) *Missionary Society*; (27) *Natural History Society of Northumberland, Durham*, &c.; (28) *Parliament of Ireland*; (29) *Phrenological Society*; (30) *Plinian Society*; (31) *Plymouth Institution*; (32) *Plymouth Institution and Devon and Cornwall Natural History Society*; (33) *Provincial Medical and Surgical Association*; (34) *Royal Asiatic Society of Great Britain and Ireland*; (35) *Royal Dublin Society*; (36) *Royal Geological Society of Cornwall*; (37) *Royal Irish Academy*; *Royal Scottish Society of Arts*; (38) *Royal Society of Arts*; (39) *Royal Society of Edinburgh*; (40) *Royal Society of Great Britain and Ireland*; (41) *Royal Society of Literature of the United Kingdom*; (42) *Royal Society of London*; (43) *Society for the Encouragement of Arts, Manufactures, and Commerce*; (44) *Society for the Improvement of Medical and Chirurgical Knowledge*; (45) *Trifontial Scientific Society*.

TRANSLATOR. Original Translations from Various Languages, Ancient and Modern. London. no1-3, 1825.
b: L.

TRAVELLER. London. no1+, 1800-22. d.
a: CSmH My 24, 1808; S 5, D 2, 1820; Ap 1-8, 10-16, 18-24, 26-29, 1822; DLC 10 sc.nos. 1811-15; WHi 39 sc.nos. Ja-Ag 1805; 27 sc.nos. Ag-D 1806. / *b:* BP O 27, 1800; O 14, 1815; Je 27, 1820; BIU Ja 8, 28-D 31, 1806 impf.; BnU My-Je 1806; C no2035, S 24, 1806; L no5519+, Ja 1, 1818-D 28, 1822; LLL 1811, lacking 4 nos.
(Incorporated with *True Briton*, N 13, 1822.)

TREASURE OF KNOWLEDGE, Literature, Instruction, and Amusement. London. v1-2, 1829-30.
a: ULS. / *b:* CrP; L.

TREASURY OFFICE, Ireland. Abstracts of Receipts and Payments. Dublin. 1788-92.
b: UCP.

TREASURY OFFICE, Ireland. Payments Made. Dublin. 1789-92. (In UCP under *Payments Made.)*
b: UCP.

TREBLE ALMANACK. Dublin. v1-41, 1793-1833.
b: UCP.

TREWMAN'S EXETER FLYING POST. Exeter. 1770-1887; resumed 1902-17. (Preceded by *Exeter Mercury; or, West-Country Advertiser*, 1763-65; *Exeter Evening Post*, 1765-67; *Exeter Evening Post; or, Plymouth and Cornish Advertiser*, 1767-69; *Trewman's Exeter Evening Post*, 1769-70.)
a: CSmH Jl 3, 1828; WHi Jl 17, 1806. / *b:* ExD 1813-32; ExWT; L Ja 4, 1827-1832.

THE TRIBUNAL. Glasgow. no1-16, Je-N 1816. m.
b: GM.

THE TRIBUNE. A Periodical Publication consisting chiefly of the Political Lectures of J. Thelwall. London. v1-3, no1-50, Mr 1795-Ap 15, 1796. w.
a: ULS; ULSup. / *b:* UCP; L; LGU no1-7, 18-25; LLL.

TRIBUNE OF THE PEOPLE. London. no1-3, 1832.
b: L.

THE TRIFLER. [London.] v1-3, 1822-23.
b: L lacking v2, no1.

THE TRIFLER. London. no1-30, Mr 1-S 8, 1817. w.
a: ULS; MdBJ. / *b:* DLL; O.

THE TRIFLER. A New Periodical Miscellany. London. no1-43, Mr 31, 1788-Mr 21, 1789. w.
a: ULS; ULSup. / *b:* UCP; EP; L; LGU.

THE TRIFLER, a Periodical Paper. Edinburgh. 1795-96. w.
b: EP; L.

TRIFONTIAL SCIENTIFIC SOCIETY. Transactions. Edinburgh. 1821-26.
b: EP.

TRINITARIAN BIBLE SOCIETY. Annual Report. London. v1+, 1831-date. (Title varies.)
a: ULS. / *b:* UCP.

TRIPOD; or, New Satirist.
(See *Satirist; or, Monthly Meteor.)*

TRUE BLUE; or, Loyal Brunswick Repertory. Dublin. no1-2, 1828.
b: UCP.

TRUE-BORN IRISHMAN. Dublin. no1-30, 1803-04.
b: UCP; L D 10, 27, 1803; Ja 28, 1804.

TRUE BRITON. London. no1+, Ja 1, 1793-180 3. d. (Incorporated Ja 1, 1803, with *Porcupine;* and sometimes known as *True Briton and Porcupine.)*
a: ULS; CSmH O 22, 1798; ICU F 27-Ag 10-S 21, 23-D 12, 1795; Ap 4-Je 6, 8-Jl 18, 1796; Ja 13, 1802; NcD O 30, N 11, 1793; NjR F 1, My 14, 17, Je 2, 9, 14, 1803; WHi N 2, 3, 7, 1820. / *b:* L Ja 5, 7, 28, 30-D 27, 1793; Jl 5, 1794-D 31, 1803, lacking many nos. for 1801; MR sc. nos. 1793; O no1-122, Ja 1-My 22, 1793, lacking no49, 81, 90; Ja 1794-D 1795. (Incorporated with *Daily Advertiser and Oracle,* Ja 1, 1804.)

TRUE BRITON. Boston. no1-27, Je 9-D 8, 1819.
a: ULS.

TRUE BRITON. London. no1+, Jl 1, 1820-N 13, 1822. d.
a: CSmH N 21, 1820; DLC sc.nos. 1795-96; (1797); sc.nos. 1798-1802; ICU O 8, 1822. / *b:* L; StfS no2-767 for 1820-22. (Incorporated with *Traveller* N 13, 1822.)

TRUE BRITON AND PORCUPINE.
(See *True Briton*)

TRUE HALF-PENNY MAGAZINE, of a Society for the Diffusion of Useful Knowledge. London. no1-20, My 4-S 14, 1832. w. (Title varies slightly.)
a: ULS. / *b:* BP no1-2, 11; L no1-10, 16, 19; O no1-2.

TRUE HERALD; or, Annual Racing Calendar. London. v1, 1824.
b: L lacking pp. 109-120.

TRUE PATRIOT. London. no1-10, 1824.
b: UCP; L.

TRUE SUN. London. no1-442, Mr 5, 1832-D 23, 1837. w.
a: CSmH no14, Mr 20, 1832; CtY. / *b:* L.

TRUMPETER. Aberdeen. 1832.
(No issues known. Data from S N & Q, s1. I. 39-40.)

TRUSTEES for Bettering the Conditions of the Poor of Ireland. Report. Dublin. 1825-26.
b: UCP.

THE TRUTH! London. no1+, Ag 22, 1832-F 3, 1833. w.
b: O no1.
(Continued as *The Truth; a Weekly Radical Christian and Family Newspaper,* 1833/?.)

TRUTH TELLER. London. no1-52, S 23, 1824-S 17, 1825.
b: L.
Continued as
THE TRUTHTELLER; A Weekly Political

Pamphlet. New Series. London. v1-16, 1825-28.
a: ULS. / *b:* C v1-5; L v1-5; O.

TRUTH'S ADVOCATE against Popery and Fanaticism. London. v1-2, Ja 1822-S 1823.
b: L lacking S 1823.

TRYSOR I BLENTYN. Llanfair Caereinion, Llanidloes. v1+, 1825-42.
b: UCP; CrP v2-4, 8-9.

TRYSORFA.
(See *Trysorfa Ysprydol.)*

TRYSORFA EFANGYLAIDD. Caerfyrddin. v1, 1806.
b: UCP; CrP.

TRYSORFA GWYBODAETH. Caernarfon. v1, 1807-08.
b: UCP.

TRYSORFA I'R YSGOL SABBOTHOL. Dolgellan. 1826-29.
b: UCP.

TRYSORFA YSPRYDOL. Caerlleon. v1, 1799-1801. q.
a: ULS. / *b:* UCP; CrP; L.
Continued as
TRYSORFA. Bala. v2-4, 1809-27.
a: ULS. / *b:* UCP; CrP 1809-22.
Continued as
Y DRYSORFA. Caerlleon. 1831-date.
b: UCP.

THE TUAM GAZETTE. Tuam. Je or Jl 1799-Ag 7, 1824.
(No issues known. Data from *Galway Reader,* v1, no3 (Winter, 1948) 31.)

TURF GUIDE; or, Sportsman's Vade Mecum. London. v1-4, 1825-28.
b: C.

TURF HERALD; or, Annual Racing Calendar. London. v1-5, 1824-28. a.
b: UCP.

TYNE MERCURY; or, Northumberland and Durham and Cumberland Gazette. Newcastle-upon-Tyne. no1-2280, 1802-46.
a: CtY N 9, 1819; DLC N 22, 1814; F 7, 1815. / *b:* L 1802-22, 1825-32; NwL 1809-20, 1823-32; NwS (1813); 1814; (1817-18); sc.nos. 1826-27; TmP 62 sc.nos. 1811-27. (Incorporated with *Newcastle Guardian.)*

TYWYSOG CYMRU. Caernarfon. v1-2, 1832-34.
b: UCP; CrP.

ULSTER FARMER AND MECHANIC. Belfast. v1, F 1824-F 1825.
b: DL.

ULSTER MAGAZINE. Belfast. v1-2, 1830-31.
b: DL; BlL no1, Ja 1830.

ULSTER MAGAZINE; or, Edifying and Interesting Magazine. Lurgan. v1, Ja-Je 1804. m.
  b: BIL; BIP; DL.

ULSTER MONTHLY MAGAZINE. Belfast. v1-2, 1830-31.
  b: BIL.

ULSTER REGISTER, a Political and Literary Magazine. Belfast. v1-5, 1816-18. w.
  b: UCP; BIL v1-4; DL; L v1, no1-2, 4; v2, no23; v3, no59; O v2, no33; v3, no49.

THE UMPIRE. London. no1-10, Ja 4-Mr 9, 1823. w.
  a: ULS. / *b:* L no3-10; O.

THE UNDERGRADUATE. Oxford. no1-6, F 8-Mr 20, 1819. w.
  a: ULSup. / *b:* BP no2; L no1, 3-6; O.

UNION. London. no1-10, N 26, 1831-Ja 28, 1832. w.
  a: ULS. / *b:* UCP; O no1.

UNION, Monthly Magazine.
(See *Union Magazine of Politics, Literature and General Intelligence.*)

UNION MAGAZINE. London. v1-2, Ja-D 1801. m.
  a: ULS. / *b:* L.
  Continued as
UNION MAGAZINE, and Imperial Register. London. v2-3, Ag 1801-Je 1802. m.
  a: ULS. / *b:* UCP.
  Continued as
UNION MAGAZINE; or, Agricultural and Commercial Register. London. v4, Jl-D 1802. m. (Also with running title of *Union Magazine; or, Commercial Register.*)
  a: ULS. / *b:* L.

UNION MAGAZINE; or, Agricultural and Commercial Register.
(See *Union Magazine.*)

UNION MAGAZINE; or, Commercial Register.
(See *Union Magazine.*)

UNION MAGAZINE, and Imperial Register.
(See *Union Magazine.*)

UNION MAGAZINE OF POLITICS, Literature and General Intelligence. London. v1. 1831-32/?. (Individual numbers entitled *Union, Monthly Magazine.*)
  a: ULS. / *b:* UCP; L.

UNION PILOT, and Cooperative Intelligencer. Manchester. v1, no1-14, 1832/?.
  a: ULS.

UNION STAR. Dublin. no1-2, 1798.
  b: L.

UNIQUE. London. v1, 1824.
  b: UCP.

UNITARIAN CHRONICLE and Companion to the Monthly Repository. London. v1-2, 1832-33.

  a: ULS. / *b:* UCP; L; LLL.
(Continued as *Unitarian Magazine and Chronicle,* 1834-35.)

UNITARIAN FUND REGISTER. Hackney. no1-5, 1822-24.
  b: L.

UNITARIAN REPOSITORY. London. v1, 1823.
  b: UCP; O.

UNITED ASSOCIATE SYNOD. Minutes of. Glasgow. 1820-46.
  b: UCP.

UNITED BRETHREN MISSIONS. Periodical Accounts. London. v1-4, 1790-1806.
  b: O.

UNITED BRETHREN'S SOCIETY for propagating the Gospel in Ireland. Extracts from the Journals of the Scripture Readers. London. no1-38, My 1831-Mr 1848/?.
  a: ULS.

UNITED KINGDOM. London. no1-168, O 30, 1830-Ja 2, 1834/?. (Incorporated with *Sunday Herald.* Absorbed *The Town.*)
  b: L.

UNITED KINGDOM GAZETTE. London. no 1+, Ja 6, 1827-D 27, 1832. w.
  a: CSmH no224, Ap 14, 1831. / *b:* L.

UNITED SERVICE JOURNAL and Naval and Military Magazine.
(See *Naval and Military Magazine.*)

UNITED SOCIETY for Christian Literature. Annual Report . . , and Missionary Society's Digest. London. v1+, 1800-date.
  a: ULS.

UNITED TRADES' Co-operative Journal. Manchester. no1-27, Mr 6-S 4, 1830/?.
  a: ULS.

UNIVERSAL CORN REPORTER. London. no1+, F 6, 1832-D 26, 1836.
  b: L lacking Ap 2, 1832.
(Continued as *Corn Reporter,* 1837-70.)

UNIVERSAL LONDON PRICE CURRENT. London. [1784]-1787-1789-[?].
  b: L sc.nos. 1789.

UNIVERSAL MAGAZINE. Dublin. v1, no1, Ap 1798. m.
  b: DL.

UNIVERSAL MAGAZINE. Edinburgh. no1-4, Mr 24-Ap 14, 1832. w.
  b: EP.

UNIVERSAL MAGAZINE (and Entertaining Miscellany). Dublin. Mr-My 1802. m.
  b: UCP; L.

UNIVERSAL MAGAZINE, and Court and Fashionable Gazette. London. no1-10, Ja 4-Mr 8, 1823. w.
  b: L.

UNIVERSAL MAGAZINE and Parlour Library.
(See *Daily Magazine and Parlour Library.*)

UNIVERSAL MAGAZINE AND REVIEW; or,
Repository of Literature. Dublin. v1-9, 1789-
93/?.
  a: ULS. / *b:* UCP; CoP v1, 7-8; DLL v1-
  8; L v1-8; MR v1.

UNIVERSAL MAGAZINE of Knowledge and
Pleasure. London. v1-113, 1747-1803. m.
  a: ULS; ULSup. / *b:* UCP; CrP v84-103,
  107, 110-12; L; MsP v92-95; PrH 1789-
  1801.
  Continued as
UNIVERSAL MAGAZINE. New Series. London. v1-21, 1804-14. m.
  a: ULS; ULSup. / *b:* UCP; CrP v2; L.
  Continued as
NEW UNIVERSAL MAGAZINE. London. v1-
3, 1814-15. m.
  a: ULS; ULSup. / *b:* UCP; L.

UNIVERSAL MEDLEY; containing Selections
from the best English Authors; Translations
from the most esteemed Italian and French
Writers, &c. Barnstaple. v1, no1-3, Ja 12-
Mr 1, 1824/?. m.
  a: ULS. / *b:* BddP.

UNIVERSAL MONTHLY INTELLIGENCER.
(See *Historical Register; or, Edinburgh
Monthly Intelligencer.*)

UNIVERSAL POLITICIAN, and Periodical
Reporter of the most interesting Occurrences
which happen throughout the World. London.
no1+, Jl-D 1796.
  b: UCP; DLL.

UNIVERSAL REVIEW, or Chronicle of the
Literature of all Nations. London. v1-2,
1824-25. m.
  b: UCP; L.

UNIVERSAL SCOTS ALMANACK. Edinburgh.
1764-98/?.
  b: UCP.

UNIVERSAL THEOLOGICAL MAGAZINE
and Impartial Review.
(See *Universalist's Miscellany; or, Philanthropist's Museum.*)

UNIVERSALIST'S MISCELLANY; or, Philanthropist's Museum. Intended chiefly as an
Antidote against the Antichristian Doctrine
of Endless Misery. London. v1-9, 1797-1803.
m.
  a: ULS. / *b:* UCP; CrP v4; L v1-5.
  Continued as
UNIVERSAL THEOLOGICAL MAGAZINE
and Impartial Review. London. v1-4, 1804-
05. (v2-4 also called ns, v1-3). m.
  a: ULS. / *b:* UCP; O v1.

UNIVERSITY MAGAZINE. Cambridge. no1-
2, Ja-F 1795. m.
  b: UCP.

THE UNSESPECTED [SIC] OBSERVER.
London. v1-2, 1792.
  b: UCP.

UPHOLDER'S MAGAZINE. London. v1, no1-
3, Ja-Mr 1823/?. m.
  a: ULS.

URANIA; or, the Astrologer's Chronicle and
Mystical Magazine. London. no1, 1825.
  b: UCP; L.

USEFUL HINTS FOR THE LABOURER.
London. no1-115, 1832-41. (Also known as
Labourer's Friend Society. Also see *Society
for Improving the Conditions of the Labouring Classes.*)
  a: ULS.

UXBRIDGE NOTE-BOOK. Uxbridge. no1-12,
N 1, 1827-O 1, 1828. m.
  b: O no1. 12.

VACHER'S PARLIAMENTARY COMPANION.
London. 1832-date.
  a: ULS.

IL VAGABONDO, a Terminal Miscellany.
Oxford. no1-8, 1816. w.
  a: ULS. / *b:* L lacking no4; O lacking
  no8.

VAN DIEMEN'S LAND ALMANACK. Hobart
Town. 1830-31.
  b: UCP.

VARIEDADES; ó Mensagero de Londres,
periodico trimestre. London. v1-2, 1823-25.
(No nos. issued F-D 1823.)
  a: ULS. / *b:* UCP.
  Continued as
CORREO LITERARIO POLITICO de Londres; periodico trimestre. London. v1, no1-
4, Ja-O 1826.
  a: ULS.

VARIETY. London. no1, S 10, 1814.
  b: O.

VAUXHALL OBSERVER; or Critical Remarks on the Amusements at the Gardens,
with an Account of the Songs, &c. London.
no1-51, My 19-N 8, 1823. t.w.
  b: L lacking no47, 50.

THE VEHICLE OF FREE INQUIRY; or
Monthly Medium of Impartial Discussion,
&c. Glasgow. v1, 1813. m.
  b: GM; L.
  Continued as
GLASGOW Universalist's Miscellany; or
Monthly Medium of Impartial Discussions,
&c. Glasgow. v1-2, 1814. m.
  b: GM; L.

VEHICLE OF GENIUS, Literature, Science,
Information, &c.
(See *Humorous Delineator; or, Vehicle of
Genius, Literature, Information, &c.*)

THE VENUS, or Luminary of Fashion. London. 1810.
  b: L Prospectus only.
  (According to John Nichol's *Illustrations
  of Literary History*, v8, p.610, no1 appeared S 15, 1810.)

DER VERKUNDIGER; eine Zeitschrift politiscnen, literarischen, und vermischten Inhalts. London. v1-12, 1811-14.
  b: L.

VERULAM. A Scientific, Literary, and Political Newspaper. London. no1-12, Mr 1-My 17, 1828. w.
  a: CSmH no1. / *b:* L.
  (Incorporated with *Athenaeum*, My 17, 1828.)

VETERINARIAN. London. v1-5, 1828-32. m.
  a: ULS. / *b:* C; L; LMD; LP.
  (Continued as *Veterinarian: a Monthly Journal of Veterinary Science*, v6-s4, v75, 1833-1902.)

VETERINARY EXAMINER: or Monthly Record of Physiology, Pathology and Natural History. London. no1-3, 1832-33.
  b: L.

VETUSTA MONUMENTA. (Society of the Antiquaries of London.) London. v1-7, 1747-1906.
  a: ULS; ULSup. / *b:* UCP.

VILLAGE INSTRUCTOR. Sherborne. no1-5, My 1-29. 1820. w.
  b: L; O.

VILLAGE MAGAZINE; or, Wath Repository. Wath-upon-Dearne. v1-3, 1831-32.
  b: UCP; L v2; LdP; RtP; SP.
  (Apparently revived for a short time in 1839.)

VIRTUE'S FRIEND; consisting of Essays. Stockport. v1-2, no1-48, Ap-S 1798. s.w. (Republished 1808 and 1816 at Ormskirk.)
  b: UCP; L.

THE VIRTUOSO; or, Monthly Preceptor of Drawing. London. pt1-2, 1814. m.
  b: L.

THE VISIONARY. Edinburgh. no1-3, 1819.
  b: O.

THE VISITOR. Bristol. no1-30, 1823.
  b: BrP; L.

THE VISITOR. Paisley. no1-12, 1832/?.
  b: L no12.

THE VISITOR; a Literary Miscellany. Greenock. v1-2, 1817-18. a.
  b: GM; O.

VOCAL MAGAZINE. London. no1, 1832/?. w.
  (No issues known. Data from *Figaro in London*, 1 (My 5, 1832) 88.)

VOCAL MAGAZINE, consisting of Canzonets, Madrigals, Songs, Duets, &c. London. 1808/?.
  (No issues known. Data from *Literary Annual Register; or, Records of Literature*, 2 (F 1808) 116.)

VOCAL MAGAZINE, containing a Selection of the most esteemed English, Scotch, and Irish Songs. Edinburgh. v1-3, 1797-99. m.
  a: ULS. / *b:* GM 1797.

VOICE OF HUMANITY. London. 1831-33/?.
  a: ULS. / *b:* LUC v4.

VOICE OF THE COUNTRY and General Provincial Politician. A Monthly Magazine. London, Liverpool. 1832. m.
  b: L.

VOICE OF THE PEOPLE. Manchester, London. v1-2, Ja 1-S 24, 1831.
  b: L.

THE VOICE OF TRUTH. Bolton, Clithero. os, Ja 1830-32; ns, 1832-D 1833.
  b: BoP ns, v1; L ns, v1.

VOTES OF THE HOUSE OF COMMONS. London. 1690-date. (Daily during the sitting of Parliament.)
  b: L.

VOX STELLARUM; or, a Loyal Almanack for the Year of Human Redemption. London. 1702-1907. a.
  a: ULS. / *b:* EP 1811; IpP 1789-1826.
  (Continued to date as *Old Moore's Almanac.*)

WAKEFIELD AND HALIFAX JOURNAL. (See *Wakefield Journal*.)

WAKEFIELD JOURNAL. Wakefield. 1801-[?].
  (No issues known. Data from the Office of the *Wakefield Express*.)
  Continued as
WAKEFIELD AND HALIFAX JOURNAL. Wakefield. [?]-1828-1833.
  a. CSmH My 9, 1828. / *b:* HiHC 1825-26; HiP Ag 24, 1832; L Ag 1, 1828-1832.
  (Continued as *Wakefield and Dewsbury Journal*, 1833-34.)

WAKEFIELD STAR, and West-Riding Register. Wakefield. [?]-1806/?.
  a: MBAt no143, Ag 15, 1806.

WAKEFIELD'S Merchant and Tradesman's General Directory for London, Westminster, Borough of Southwark, and twenty-two Miles circular from St. Paul's, for the Year 1790. London. 1790.
  b: L.

WALKER'S HIBERNIAN MAGAZINE. Dublin. v1-26, 1786-1811. m. (Preceded by *Hibernian Magazine; or, Compendium of Entertaining Knowledge*, 1771-85.)
  a: ULS; ULSup. / *b:* UCP; BP v12-13, impf.; CoP Ja-Je 1791; O 1795; Ja-Je 1797; Ja-My 1798; 1803-05; Jl-D 1806; Ja-Je 1810; L.

THE WALSALL NOTE BOOK. Walsall. no1-12, 1830-31.
  b: BP.

THE WANDERER. London. 1803.
(No issues known. Data from John Nichol, *Literary Anecdotes*, v9, p.711.)

THE WANDERER, a Thing of Shreds and Patches. Glasgow. no1-21, 1818-19. f.
b: E; GM; L.

THE WANDERER, a Weekly Journal of Literature, Science, Theatricals, and the Fine Arts. London. no1, 1832. w.
b: BP; L; O.

THE WARBLER. London. 1808.
b: LGU.

THE WARDER. London. v1-2, Ap 14, 1827-D 27, 1828. w.
b: LGU.

THE WARDER; or Constitutional Observer. Dublin. 1821-28. w.
a: CSmH no343, Je 21, 1828; CtY no42-45, O 19-N 9, 1822. / *b:* O no10.

WARDLE'S MANCHESTER OBSERVER. Manchester. no1-5, Je 5-Jl 3, 1819. w.
b: L no1-3, 5; MP; MR no5.
Continued as
WARDLE'S MANCHESTER OBSERVER; or, Literary and Political Register. Manchester. no1-2, Jl 10-17, 1819. w.
b: L; MP; MR.

WARRINGTON OBSERVER; a Weekly Journal of Literary, Religious, and Miscellaneous Information. Warrington. no1-8, Je 2-Jl 21, 1830.
b: WrP.

WARRINGTON OLIO: a Weekly Periodical of Amusing Literature. Warrington. no1-7, Ag 21-O 2, 1830/?. w.
b: WrP no1, 7.

WARWICK AND WARWICKSHIRE Advertiser. Warwick. no1+, Ja 4, 1806-date. (Title varies, as *Warwick and Warwickshire General Advertiser and Leamington Gazette*.)
a: CSmH Ja 20, 1827; ICU N 24, 1827-D 31, 1831. / *b:* BP; L no1, Ja 4, 1806; F 5-19, O 22, 29, 1814; Jl 29, Ag 26, D 30, 1815; Ja 6, 1816; Ja 3, 1824-1832; WwWW.

WARWICKSHIRE CHRONICLE. Warwick. no 1-88, Ap 19, 1826-D 19, 1827. w.
b: BP; L.

THE WASP. Birmingham. v1, no1-4, 1832.
b: BP no1; O'no4.

THE WASP. A Literary Satire. Containing an Exposé of some of the most notorious Literary and Theatrical Quacks of the Day. London. v1, no1-12, S 30-D 16, 1826. w.
a: ULS. / *b:* L.

THE WATCHMAN. London. v1-2, no1-64, Mr 11, 1827-My 25, 1828. w.
a: ULS; CSmH no23. / *b:* L.

THE WATCHMAN. Bristol. no1-10, Mr 1-My 13, 1796. w.
a: ULS. / *b:* UCP; BrP; L; LVA; MR.

THE WATCHMAN; or, Protestant Guardian. Dublin. v1, N 1826-Ap 1827. w.
b: DL.

THE WATCHMAN; or Protestant Guardian, a Weekly Paper. Dublin. 1812. w.
b: DA v2, My-O 1812.

THE WATCHMAN; or Theological Inspector. London. no1-10, N 1809-S 1810. m.
b: L Prospectus only; O.
Continued as
THE CHRISTIAN WATCHMAN; or Theological Inspector. London. no11-12, S-O 1810. m.
b: O.

WATCHMAN AND JAMAICA Free Press. London. 1829-32.
b: UCP.

WATCHMAN AND POLICE RECORDER. London. no1, 1826.
b: L.

WATCHMAN, containing the most interesting Cases tried in the Police Courts. Glasgow. 1831.
b: L no4.

THE WATER KELPIE. Aberdeen. no1, F 3, 1827.
(No issues known. Data from S N & Q, s1. I.21.)

WATERFORD CHRONICLE
(See *Ramsay's Waterford Chronicle*.)

WATERFORD HERALD. Waterford. no1+, 1791-1796/?.
b: UCP; KkKJ sc.nos. 1791-96; L no567, S 16, 1794; no907, Mr 10, 1796.

WATERFORD MAIL. Waterford. no1+, Ag 16, 1823-1870.
a: CSmH My 5, 1827. / *b:* DL no1; L.
(Continued as *Waterford Daily Mail*, 1870-74; as *Waterford Mail*, 1874-86; as *Waterford Daily Mail*, 1886-date.)

WATERFORD MIRROR, and Munster Packet. Waterford. no1-6610, 1801-46. t.w. (Dropped subtitle in 1803.)
a: CSmH Jl 21, 1828; NN My 5, Je 9, 12, Jl 7, 1802. / *b:* C no26, Jl 8, 1801; DL 13 sc.nos. 1801-06; Ja 3-D 3, 1807; Ag 5, 1812; F 8, 1813; L no1129+, Ag 1, 1808-Jl 1809; My 29, 1813; 1827-32; WtfP.
(Later became *Waterford Mirror and Tramore Visitor* and continued until 1910.)

WATSON'S GENTLEMAN'S and Citizen's Almanack. Dublin. [?]-1805-1832-[?].
b: DA 1805, 1830, 1832.

WATSON'S LIMERICK CHRONICLE.
(See *Limerick Chronicle*.)

WATT'S NEW YEAR'S GIFT and Juvenile Souvenir. London. 1830-39.
  b: O 1830-31.

Y WAWR-DDYDD; sef Cyrfwng Gwybodaeth i'r Ieuengctyd. Caernarfon. no1-7, 1830.
  b: UCP; L no1-7, no1 impf.

THE WAYFARER. Paisley. no1-4, O 2-23, 1824. w.
  b: PsP.

THE WEAVER'S MAGAZINE and Literary Companion. Paisley. v1-2, no1-12, S 1818-Ag 1819. m.
  a: ULS. / *b:* E; GM; L no1-6; PsP.

THE WEDNESDAY PACKET. Edinburgh. Ja 3, 1798-D 30, 1801. w.
  (No issues known. Data from CBEL, II.. 732; C & K, 2111.)

WEDNESDAY TIMES.
  (See *Dissenter's Gazette of Politics, Commerce*, &c.)

WEEKLY BILL OF MORTALITY. London. [?]-1602-1840. w.
  (No issues known. Data from CBEL, II. 720.)
  (Continued as *Returns of the Registrar General*, 1840-49.)

WEEKLY DISPATCH. London. no1+, S 27, 1801-1928. w.
  a: CSmH N 9, 1823; CtY 7 sc.nos. 1817-19; ICN F 27, 1825-1832; NPV My 19, Je 9, 1816-Mr 9, 1817; Je 15, 1817-F 22, 1818. / *b:* L Ja 22, 1804; Jl 5, S 6, 1807; Ja 4, 1818-1832; LGU My 25, 1823-D 26, 1824; LSD; LU 7 sc.nos. 1824-25; O My 8, 1803; Ja 3, 1830-1832; SU no295, (no 377-480).
  (Continued as *Sunday Dispatch*, 1928-date.)

WEEKLY DRAMATIC CHRONICLE and Entertaining Miscellany. London. no1-10, N 27, 1824 Ja 29, 1825. w.
  b: EP no1-5; L.

WEEKLY DRAMATIC REGISTER, a concise History of the London Stage. London. v1-3, 1825-27/?. w.
  a: ULS. / *b:* L no22.

WEEKLY DRAMATIC REVIEW. Edinburgh. no1-6, Jl 7-Ag 11, 1828. w.
  b: EP.

WEEKLY ENTERTAINER; or, Agreeable and Instructive Repository. Sherborne. v1-59, 1783-1819. w. (Preceded by *Weekly Miscellany; or Instructive Entertainer*, &c. 1773-82.)
  a: ULS. / *b:* UCP; L v3-6, 13, 15, 17, 30, 32-34, 37, 39, 42.
  Continued as
WEEKLY ENTERTAINER, and West of England Miscellany. Sherborne. v1-12, 1820-25. w.
  a: ULS. / *b:* UCP; L.

WEEKLY ENTERTAINER or Companion to the Chester Courant. London. no1-7, S 12-O 24, 1814. w. (Reprinted as *Pleasing Entertainer, containing Choice Tales*, &c.)
  a: BkP; L.

WEEKLY ENTERTAINER, and Dumfries and Galloway Literary Miscellany. Dumfries. v1, no1-9, D 31, 1823-F 25, 1824. w.
  b: DsD.

WEEKLY ENTERTAINER, and West of England Miscellany.
  (See *Weekly Entertainer; or Agreeable and Instructive Repository*.)

WEEKLY FREE PRESS.
  (See *Trades Newspaper and Mechanic's Weekly Journal*.)

WEEKLY FREEMAN'S JOURNAL.
  (See *Public Register; or Freeman's Journal*.)

WEEKLY GLOBE. London. no1+, Ja 4, 1824-Mr 20, 1825. w.
  a: CSmH no 3. / *b:* L.
  (Incorporated with *Common Sense* and continued as *Common Sense and Weekly Globe*. See *Common Sense* for details.)

WEEKLY INTELLIGENCE. London. no1-143, Ja 7, 1816-S 27, 1818. w.
  a: ICU Ja 7, 1816-D 28, 1817. / *b:* L; O.
  Incorporated with *British Luminary* and continued as
WEEKLY INTELLIGENCER and British Luminary. no1-139, 1818-21. w.
  a: ULS; CSmH N 5, 1820; CtY Jl 11-N 7, 1819, lacking 2 nos.; IU Ja 21, 1821. / *b:* BP F 6, 1820; L no96-139.
  Continued as
BRITISH LUMINARY and Weekly Intelligencer. London. no1-145, 1821-23. w.
  a: CSmH Ap 6, 1823. / *b:* L.

WEEKLY INTELLIGENCER and British Luminary.
  (See *Weekly Intelligencer*.)

WEEKLY LITERARY MAGNET.
  (See *Literary Magnet of the Belles Lettres, Science*, &c.)

WEEKLY MAGAZINE. Boston. 1798.
  b: UCP.

WEEKLY MAGAZINE. London. v1, no1-6, Ja 6-F 10, 1816. w.
  b: UCP; L.

WEEKLY MAGAZINE, or Literary Observer; containing original Reviews of new Publications, original Poetry, &c. London. v1, 1824. w.
  b: L.

WEEKLY MAGAZINE; or, Repository of Modern Literature.
  (See *Repository of Modern Literature*.)

WEEKLY MAGAZINE and Historical Register. Dublin. no1-7, F 3-Mr 16, 1793. w.
  a: ULS. / *b:* DL no7.

WEEKLY MEDICO-CHIRURGICAL and Philosophical Magazine. London. v1-3, 1823-24. w. (No49-52 are entitled *Weekly Medico-Chirurgical Review and Philosophical Magazine.*)
   a: ULS. / *b:* UCP.
   Continued as
MONTHLY MEDICO-CHIRURGICAL Review and Chemico-Philosophical Magazine. London. ns, v1, no1-5. w.
   b: UCP.

WEEKLY MISCELLANY; or, new National Magazine of Instruction and Amusement. London. no1-5, 1832.
   b: L; O no1, Jl 7, 1832.

WEEKLY MISCELLANY of Instruction and Entertainment. Glasgow. v1-6, no1-156, 1789-92. w.
   a: ULS. / *b:* UCP; GM.
   Continued as
THE PHOENIX; or Weekly Miscellany Improved. Glasgow. ns, v1-4, no1-104, 1792-94. w.
   a: ULS. / *b:* UCP; GM.
   Continued as
THE ASYLUM, or Weekly Miscellany. Glasgow. 1794-96. w.
   b: EP 1794; GM; O no53, 78, for 1795.

WEEKLY MONITOR; a Series of Essays on Moral and Religious Subjects. Charleston, U.S.A.; reprinted in London. 1815. w.
   b: UCP; O.

WEEKLY MUSEUM. London. 1788-1795-[?]. w.
   (Listed by C & K, 938; but is really a New York publication.)

WEEKLY MUSEUM of Politics and Literature. Edinburgh. no1-5, N 19-D 17, 1831. w.
   b: EP.

WEEKLY NEWS and General Advertiser. London. no1-2, Ja 11-18, 1818. w.
   b: L.

WEEKLY ORTHODOX JOURNAL of Entertaining Christian Knowledge. London. v1-4, no1-143. 1832-35/?. w. (Caption title of no1, *Penny Orthodox Journal;* no2-78, *Andrews' Penny Orthodox Journal;* no79+, *Andrews' Weekly Orthodox Journal.*) (This journal may be a revival of *Orthodox Journal and Catholic Monthly Intelligencer.*)
   a: ULS. / *b:* SthC.
   (Continued as *London and Dublin Orthodox Journal of Useful Knowledge.*)

WEEKLY PANTHEON, or General Repertory of Politics, Arts, Science, Literature, &c. Dublin. Je 1801-D 1809. w.
   (No issues known. Data from John Power, *Irish Literary Periodical Publications,* p. 6.)

WEEKLY POLITICAL REVIEW of Henry Redhead Yorke.
   (See *Mr. Redhead Yorke's Weekly Political Review.*)

WEEKLY POLITICIAN and Literary Review. London. no1-17, 1811. w.
   b: L Prospectus only; O no17, N 2, 1811.

WEEKLY PRESS. London. Ag 23, 1823-Ap 2, 1831. w.
   (No issues known. Data from CBEL, III. 813.)

WEEKLY RECORDER and General Commercial Intelligencer. Manchester. 1819. w.
   b: MP no3, My 20, 1819.

WEEKLY REGISTER. London. no1-193, Ap 11, 1798-D 23, 1801/?. w.
   a: ULSup; CtY no2-89. / *b:* BP no63; L Prospectus only; LLL; MR no62.

WEEKLY REGISTER.
   (See *Sunday Advertiser.*)

WEEKLY REGISTER and Political Magazine; including a Digest of Politics, Literature, and Fine Art. London. v1-3, no1-70, 1809-11. w.
   b: L.

WEEKLY REGISTER of General Information, Elegant Amusement, and Popular Sport. Stafford. v1, no1-21, 1827. w.
   b: BP; StfS.
   Continued as
THE REGISTER, Literary, Scientific and Sporting Journal. Stafford. v1, no22-v2, no56. w.
   b: BP; StfS.

WEEKLY REGISTER of the Fine Arts, Sciences, and Belles Lettres.
   (See *Literary Register of the Fine Arts, Sciences, &c.*)

WEEKLY REPOSITORY of Letters on Historical, Moral, and Theological Subjects. London. 1792. w.
   b: UCP.

THE WEEKLY REVIEW. London. no1-7, My 5-Je 16, 1821. w.
   b: L.

THE WEEKLY REVIEW; or. Literary Journal. London. 1799. w.
   (No issues known. Data from CBEL, II. 683, and C & K, 2151.)

WEEKLY SATIRIST. London. no1-4, Jl 28-Ag 18, 1827. w.
   b: O.

WEEKLY SCOTSMAN.
   (See *Scotsman; or, Edinburgh Political and Literary Journal.*)

WEEKLY SELECTOR; or Sligo Miscellaneous Magazine. Sligo. F 4-Ag 4, 1812. w.
   b: BIL.

WEEKLY SHOW-UP; or, Practical, Satirical, and General Humourist. London. no1-6, Je 30-Ag 4, 1832. w.
   b: BoP; L; O no1-3, 5-6.

WEEKLY TIMES. London. no1-357, Je 3, 1826-My 5, 1833. w. (Published as *The Liberal*, Ap 26-D 27, 1829.)
    a: CSmH no140, 148. / *b:* ExWT no59-357; L.
    (The proprietors decided to run an Exeter edition; thus we have *Exeter Weekly Times and West of England Advertiser* from O 6, 1827. See this title for details.)

WEEKLY VISITOR; and London Literary Museum, London. no1+, Ja 21, 1832-1833. w.
    a: CSmH no3, F 4, 1832. / *b:* BoP no1-15; L; O no1-3, 9.

WEEKLY WATERFORD CHRONICLE. Waterford. [?]-1831. w.
    a: CSmH no194, Je 11, 1831.

WELSHMAN. Carmarthen. no1+, Ja 13, 1832-date.
    b: L.

WERNERIAN NATURAL HISTORY Society. Memoirs. Edinburgh. v1-8, 1808-38.
    a: ULS; ULSup. / *b:* UCP; CrP v1-2, 4-5; DRS; EP; GeG 1808-16; L; LR; MCh 1811-32.

WESLEY PROTESTANT METHODIST Magazine. London. v1-2, 1829-30/?.
    a: ULS.

WESLEYAN METHODIST CHURCH. Minutes of several Conversations at the yearly Conference. Leeds, London. 1744-1818/?. a.
    b: CrP; LdP 1789-1804, 1818.

WESLEYAN METHODIST MAGAZINE. Third Series.
    (See *Arminian Magazine; consisting of Extracts,* &c.)

WESLEYAN METHODIST MISSIONARY Auxiliary Society [of Hull]. Hull. [?]-1821-1827-[?].
    b: LdP no7-9, 12-13, for 1821-27.

WESLEYAN METHODIST MISSIONARY Society. Report. London. 1804.
    b: UCP.

WESLEYAN MISSIONARY NOTICES.
    (See *Missionary Notices.*)

WESLEYAN PREACHER, containing Sermons by the most Eminent Ministers in the Connexion. London. v1-5, 1831-39/?.
    a: ULS. / *b:* UCP; L.

WESLEYAN PROTESTANT MAGAZINE. Leeds. v1-3, 1829-31.
    a: ULS. / *b:* LdP v1, 3.

WEST BRITON and Cornwall Advertiser. Truro. no1+, Jl 20, 1810-date. w. (Dropped second half of title in 1944.)
    a: CSmH O 5, 1827. / *b:* BiP N 14, 1817; CbP 27 sc.nos. 1813; (1814-15, 1817-19); L; TrWB 1810-16, 1819-32.

WEST INDIAN REPORTER. London. no1-45, Ja 1827-Ag 1831.
    a: ULS. / *b:* BP no12.

WEST-INDIAN SKETCHES, drawn from authentic Sources. London. no1-8, 1816-17.
    a: ULS. / *b:* UCP.

WEST OF ENGLAND and South Wales Magazine. Bristol. v1-2, 1832-33. (v1, no2-9, have title *Bristol, West of England and South Wales Magazine.*)
    b: CrP.

WEST OF ENGLAND MAGAZINE. Bath. 1813. m.
    b: L Prospectus only; LP.

WESTERN ARGUS and Ballinasloe Independent. Ballinasloe. no1+, Ap 30, 1828-1833. s.w.
    a: CSmH Je 25, 1831. / *b:* L Ap 30, 1828-1832, lacking Ja, Ap 14-Jl 14, 1830.

WESTERN ARGUS and Galway Commercial Chronicle. Galway. [?]-1832-[?].
    (No issues known. Data from *Galway Reader*, v1, no4 (Spring, 1949) 40.)

WESTERN CHRONICLE, or Connaught Advertiser. Tuam. [?]-1805-N 13, 1813-[?].
    (May succeed *Connaught Advertiser.*)
    (No issues known. Data from *Galway Reader*, v1, no3, (Winter, 1948) 31.)

WESTERN COUNTY MAGAZINE. Salisbury. v3-6, 1790-92. (Preceded by *County Magazine*, 1786-88.)
    a: ULS. / *b:* L.

WESTERN FLYING POST; or, Sherborne and Yeovil Mercury. Sherborne. no1+, 1749-1867. w. (Formed by amalgamation of *Sherborne Mercury*, founded 1736, and *Western Flying Post or Yeovil Mercury*, founded 1743.)
    a: CSmH S 8, 1827; MBAt My 18, 1807. / *b:* DcrN D 1796-D 1816; L sc.nos. 1796-99; 1800-10; Ja 5, 1829-32; TaP (Je 1800-D 1806); TmP My 28, 1827; YeWG 1789-1823.
    (Amalgamated with *Western Gazette*, founded 1863, and continued as *Western Gazette and Flying Post*, 1867-date. Second half of title dropped.)

WESTERN LUMINARY, or Glasgow Literary and Scientific Gazette. Glasgow. no1-26, 1823-24.
    b: E no4; GM no1-10; PsP.

WESTERN LUMINARY; the Family Newspaper of the Nobility and Gentry, Farmers and Traders, &c. Exeter. no1+, 1813-ca. 1860. w. (Also known as *Flindell's Western Luminary.*)
    a: CSmH S 28, 1813; My 11, 1827. / *b:* ExD O 1813-1831; ExP 1813-17, 1819-20; L O 17-24, 1820; [1821]; sc.nos. 1822; 1827-28; (1829-30); PlP F 1, 1820; S 21, 1824.

WESTERN MERCURY; or, Kerry Herald. Tralee. 1793.
  b: UCP.

WESTERN STAR. Glasgow. 1807-09.
  b: GM no1, N 13, 1807; no126, Ja 24, 1809.

WESTERN STAR.
  (See *Sarah Farley's Bristol Journal.*)

WESTERN TIMES.
  (See *Exeter Weekly Times.*)

WESTMEATH JOURNAL. Mullingar. [1783]-1834. w.
  a: CSmH My 3, 1827. / *b:* C Ag 15, 1795; L My 27, 1813; Ja 2, 1823-1832.

WESTMINSTER EVENING HERALD. London. 1790-[?].
  a: MdBJ S 11-14, 1790.

WESTMINSTER JOURNAL and London Political Miscellany. London. [1764]-[1794]. w. (Preceded by *New Weekly Miscellany,* 1741; *Westminster Journal; or, New Weekly Miscellany,* 1741-59; *Royal Westminster Journal and London Political Miscellany,* 1763-64.)
  a: IU. / *b:* L My 24, 1794.
    Continued as
WESTMINSTER JOURNAL and Old British Spy. London. [1794]-1812. w.
  a: CtY Ja 5, 1811-1812; IU 1794-96. / *b:* L S 7, 1805-D 29, 1810.
    Continued as
WESTMINSTER JOURNAL and Imperial Weekly Gazette. London. 1813-[14]. w.
  a: CtY 1813-Ja 1, 1814.
    Incorporated with *Imperial Weekly Gazette* and continued as
IMPERIAL WEEKLY GAZETTE and Westminster Journal. [1814?]-1825.
  (See *Imperial Weekly Gazette* for library holdings and other details.)

WESTMINSTER JOURNAL and Imperial Weekly Gazette.
  (See *Westminster Journal and London Political Miscellany.*)

WESTMINSTER JOURNAL and Old British Spy.
  (See *Westminster Journal and London Political Miscellany.*)

WESTMINSTER REVIEW. London. v1-181, 1824-1914.
  a: ULS; ULSup. / *b:* UCP; BP; BdP 1824-27 & parts of 1828-30, 1832; CnP; EP; GeG lacking v2; L; LLL; LLW; LdL lacking v14, LvA; LvP 1829-32; MCh; NpP; NwL; NwP; SP.

WESTMORLAND ADVERTISER and Kendal Chronicle. Kendal. no1+, 1811-34.
  a: CSmH Mr 29, 1828. / *b:* CsP Ja 13, 1821-D 27, 1823; KdP 1811-19. 1829-31; KdWG 1817-27 impf.; L Ja 3, 1829-1832; LLL sc.nos. 1818.
    (Continued as *Kendal Mercury and Westmorland Advertiser,* 1834-40; as *Kendal*

Mercury and Northern Advertiser, 1841-80; as *Kendal Mercury and Times,* 1880-1913; as *Westmorland Mercury and Times,* 1913-17.)

WESTMORLAND GAZETTE and Kendal Advertiser. Kendal. no1+, My 23, 1818-date. w.
  a: CSmH Ja 14, 1826. / *b:* KdP 1818-30; KdWG; L 25 sc.nos. 1818-19; complete 1829-32; LLL (My-D 1820); WtP 1819, 1822-27, 1830.

WEXFORD CHRONICLE. Wexford. [1782]-[before 1798].
  (No issues known. Data from CBEL, II. 739.)

WEXFORD CONSERVATIVE. Wexford. no1+, S 19, 1832-1846.
  b: L.

WEXFORD EVENING POST. Wexford. no1+, Mr 7, 1826-Mr 23, 1830. s.w.
  a: CSmH Je 5, 1827. / *b:* L.

WEXFORD FREEMAN. Wexford. no1+, My 30, 1832-1837.
  b: DA no4; L.

WEXFORD HERALD. Wexford. [1788]-1832. w.;s.w.
  a: CSmH My 5, 1827. / *b:* C no100, for 1794; L My 27, 1813; 1828-32; WxC no211-417, Ap 7, 1808-Mr 1810.

WEXFORD INDEPENDENT. Wexford. no1+, D 17, 1830-1843. w. (May succeed *Wexford Journal,* 1769-[?].)
  a: CSmH F 1, 1831. / *b:* L; WxOC D 21, 1831-1832.
    (Continued as *Independent,* 1843-70; as *Wexford Independent,* 1870-1906.)

WHEELER'S HAMPSHIRE and West of England Magazine. Winchester. v1, no1-12, Ja-D 1828. m.
  b: L; PmP; SoP.
    (Afterwards combined with *Crypt* and continued under title of *Crypt and West of England Magazine.* For details, see *Crypt.*)

WHEELER'S MANCHESTER CHRONICLE.
  (See *Manchester Chronicle.*)

WHIG WARBLER. Edinburgh. no1-2, 1820. d.
  b: E.

THE WHIM; a Periodical Paper. Canterbury. no1-12, D 31, 1810-Je 3, 1811. f.
  a: ULS. / *b:* C; CyP D 31, 1810-My 20, 1811; L; LLL; O.

THE WHISPERER; or, Tales and Speculations. London. no1-24, My 28-N 1795. w. (Pub. in vol. form 1798.)
  b: UCP; L; SP.

WHITBY LITERARY AND PHILOSOPHICAL Society. Annual Reports. Whitby. 1827-1925/?.
  b: LdP.

WHITBY MAGAZINE and Monthly Literary Journal. Whitby. v1, 1827/?. m.
  a: ULS. / *b:* BdP; L.

WHITBY REPOSITORY and Monthly Miscellany: religious, sentimental, literary, and scientific. Whitby. v1-6, 1825-30; ns, v1-3, 1831-33. m.
  b: L; LdP v1-2, 4.

WHITE DWARF; or General Miscellany of Political, Moral, and Entertaining Essays. London. no1-22, N 29, 1817-Ap 28, 1818/?. w. (Subtitle varies; ULS records it as a *London Weekly Publication.)*
  a: ULS. / *b:* L no1-13; O.

THE WHITE HAT. London. v1, no1-9, O 16-D 11, 1819. w.
  a: ULS. / *b:* E; L.

WHITEHALL EVENING POST, or London Intelligencer. London. no1-8487, 1746-1801.
  a: ULS. / *b:* C D 9-12, 1797; O 1789-98.
  (Incorporated with *English Chronicle* and continued as *English Chronicle and Whitehall Evening Post,* 1802-43. For details, see *English Chronicle.)*

WHITEHAVEN GAZETTE. Whitehaven. no1+, Ap 1819-1826-[?]. w.
  a: CtY 1821-25; Ja 3-24, 1826. / *b:* CsP Ap 1819-Ap 1823, lacking no78, 179, 185, 188, 191, 196, 198, 208; WtP 1819-26.

WHITEHAVEN HERALD and Cumberland Advertiser. Whitehaven. no1+, Ag 30, 1831-1878.
  b: CsP; L.
  (Incorporated in *West Cumberland Guardian.)*

WHOLE PROCEEDINGS of the Sessions of the Peace, and Oyer and Terminer for the City of London and County of Middlesex. London. [?]-1674-1824. a.;q. (Also known as *Old Bailey Sessions Paper.)*
  (No issues known. Data from CBEL, II. 720.)
  Continued as
SESSIONS PAPER . . . held at Justice Hall, in the Old Bailey. London. 1825-33.
  (No issues known. Data from CBEL, II. 720.)
  (Continued as *Central Criminal Court. Minutes taken in Shorthand,* 1835-date.)

WICKLOW EDUCATION SOCIETY. Report. Dublin. v1-4, 1819-22.
  b: UCP.

WIDOWS' FUND of Writers to the Signet. (Society of Writers to H.M.'s Signet in Scotland.) Report by the Collector. Edinburgh. 1811-17.
  b: UCP.

WIGAN HERALD. Wigan. no1-12, 1829.
  b: WiP no1-8, 10-12.

WIGAN MIRROR and Literary and Scientific Journal. Wigan. no1-12, My 27-Ag 12, 1825.
  b: WiP.

WIGTON SCHOOL REPORT. Wigton. 1816-32.
  b: LFS.

WILKINSON'S WANDERER. London. v1-2, 1795.
  b: O.

WILLIAM FLYNN'S Hibernian Chronicle. (See *Flynn's Hibernian Chronicle.)*

THE WILLIAM PITT. London. 1814. w.
  a: CSmH no13, N 13, 1814.

THE WILLIAMITES' MAGAZINE; or Protestant Advocate for Civil and Religious Liberty. Dublin. no1-8, Ja 31-Mr 14, 1823. w.
  b: DL; L.

WILLIAMSON'S LIVERPOOL ADVERTISER. Liverpool. My 1756-D 1793.
  b: LvP 1789-93 impf.
  Continued as
BILLINGE'S LIVERPOOL ADVERTISER and Marine Intelligencer. Liverpool. Ja. 1794-D 1828.
  a: CSmH My 21, 1822; MBAt My 7, 1804; F 4, S 9, 1805; Je 30, Jl 14, 1806; Jl 11, 1820; N My 8, 1827; WHi sc.nos. 1805-06. / *b:* BP Je 27, 1814; O 2, 1815; C Jl 9, 1795; Ap 17, 1809; L 1823, 1826-28; LvP Ja 1794-D 1802; Ja 1818-D 1828.
  Continued as
LIVERPOOL TIMES, and Billinge's Advertiser. Liverpool. Ja 6, 1829-1856. w.
  a: CSmH My 25, 1830; DLC Jl 20, 1830. / *b:* L; LvP.

WILSON'S DUBLIN DIRECTORY. Dublin. 1765-1848.
  b: D.

WILTSHIRE REGISTER. Melksham. 1825.
  b: L; O.

WINDSOR AND ETON EXPRESS. Windsor. no1+, 1812-date. w. (Title varies slightly; finally becoming *Windsor, Slough and Eton Express.)*
  b: L no189+, 1816-F 1832, lacking Mr 1816-F 1829; WdWS.

WINTER EVENINGS. London. v1-2, 1790.
  b: UCP.

WINTER'S WREATH, a Collection of Original Contributions in Prose and Verse. London, Liverpool. v1-5, 1825-32.
  b: UCP; L.

WISEHART'S SONGSTER'S OLIO, and Play House Companion. Dublin. 1825-26.
  b: DL no8, 11-36.
  Continued as
WISEHART'S SONGSTER'S OLIO. New Series. Dublin. no1-24, N 10, 1827-S 27, 1828. f.
  b: DPK.

WIT'S MAGAZINE, and Attic Miscellany. London. v1-2, 1818.
  a: ULS.

THE WIZARD. Glasgow. no1, 1826.
  b: L.

WIZARD OF THE TOWER. Portobello. no1-
12, Ja-Je, 1832.
  b: GM; O.

WOLVERHAMPTON CHRONICLE. Wolverhampton. no1+, 1789-1930. w. (Also with
varying subtitles.)
  a: CSmH D 13, 1826; CtY Ag 8, 1792. /
  b: BP Ag 26, 1812; S 14, 1831; L Ja 6,
  1830-1832; StfS 1811-20; WvP S 2, 1789-
  Je 12, 1793; 1811-32.

WONDERFUL AND SCIENTIFIC MUSEUM,
or Magazine of Remarkable Characters.
  (See *Kirby's Wonderful and Eccentric Museum,* &c.)

WONDERFUL MAGAZINE, and Marvellous
Chronicle; or, New Weekly Entertainer. London. v1-5, 1793-94. m.;w. (This is a duplicate of *The New Wonderful Magazine, containing Authentic Accounts,* &c., except for
alteration in titlepage and preliminary matter.)
  a: ULS. / *b:* UCP; L.

WONDERFUL MAGAZINE of all that is Singular, Curious, and Rare in Nature and Art.
London. no1-19, 1830. (Cover title of no1-11,
New Wonderful Magazine; cover title of no12-
19, *Smeeton's Wonderful Magazine.)*
  a: ULS. / *b:* L.

WONDERS OF THE UNIVERSE; or, Curiosities of Nature and Art. London. v1-2, 1827/?.
(Added titlepage has title of *Wonderful Magazine; or Curiosities of Nature and Art.* Running title of *Curiosities of Nature and Art.)*
  a: DLC.

WOODFALL'S PARLIAMENTARY REPORTS.
  (See *Impartial Report of the Debates that
  Occur in the Two House of Parliament.)*

WOOLER'S BRITISH GAZETTE. Manchester.
no1-259, Ja 3, 1819-D 14, 1823. w. (Also
with subtitle.)
  a: CSmH Ap 2, 1820; CtY Jl 18, 1819.
  b: L; MP S1, 8, 1821; MR no1.

WOOLMER'S Exeter and Plymouth Gazette.
Exeter. [1791]-1864. w.;d. (Succeeds *Exeter
Gazette,* 1772.)
  a: CSmH My 12, 1821. / *b:* ExD 1813-32;
  ExDE Je 21, 1792-1832; ExP Ja 1, 1814-
  Jl 13, 1822; L Ja 6, 1827-1832.
  (Continued as *Exeter and Plymouth Ga-
  zette,* 1865-85; as *Devon and Exeter
  Daily Gazette,* 1885-92; as *Daily Ga-
  zette,* 1892-95; as *Devon and Exeter
  Gazette,* 1895-date.)

WORCESTER HERALD. Worcester. no1+, Ja
4, 1794-1930. w.
  a: CSmH S 15, 1821. / *b:* BP My 5, 1804;
  sc.nos. 1819-32; L 1808-14; 1816; 1818-
  20; 1822-32; WcP (1794-1832).

WORCESTERSHIRE MISCELLANY. Worcester. no1-5, 1829-31.
  b: BP; L.

WORKER'S BRITISH GAZETTE. London.
[?]-1819-[?].
  a: CtY Jl 18, 1819.

WORKING BEE; or, Caterer for the Hive.
  (See *Bee, Fireside Companion,* &c.)

WORKING MAN'S FRIEND. Bolton. v1, no1-
14, F 1-Ap 14, 1832/?.
  b: BoP.

WORKING MAN'S FRIEND, and Political
Magazine. London. no1-33, 1832-33.
  a: ULS. / *b:* UCP; L; O.

WORKINGTON AGRICULTURAL SOCIETY.
Reports (Rules, Proceedings, and Reports).
Workington. 1805-14.
  b: UCP.

THE WORLD. London. 1787-1832/?. d. (Preceded by *The World; Fashionable Advertiser,*
1787.)
  a: CSmH Jl 25, 1827; My 4, 1827-Mr 28,
  1832; CtY (1789-My 13, 1790); DLC O 15,
  21, 22, 1791; ICN (1789-Je 30, 1794);
  ICU (Mr 14-Jl 18, 1789); MdBJ (1789-91);
  Ja 1792; NjR Jl 2, 1789. / *b:* L 1789-
  1791; F 27-Mr 17, Ap 3-D 13, 1792; Jl 1,
  1793-Je 30, 1794.
  (It is possible that the library holdings
  listed above for the 1780's and 1790's
  are for a different paper than that for the
  1820's.)

WORLD. London. no1-38, Ja 4-O 4, 1818. w.
  b: L.

WORLD. London. no1+, My 4, 1827-Mr 28,
1832.
  b: L.
  (Incorporated in *The Patriot.)*

WORLD AT WESTMINSTER, a Periodical
Publication. London. v1-2, no1-30, 1815-16.
s.w.
  a: ULS; ULSup. / *b:* UCP; L; O.

WORLD OF FASHION and Continental
Feuilletons. London. v1-28, 1824-51. m.
  a: ULS. / *b:* UCP; BP Je 1825; L; LVA
  v8.
  (Continued as *Ladies Monthly Magazine.
  The World of Fashion,* 1852-79; as *Le
  Monde Elégant, or the World of Fashion,*
  1880-91.)

THE WREATH; or Nottingham Literary Miscellany. Nottingham. v1, no1-12, O 1832-S
1833. m. (Entirely distinct from the following
entry.)
  b: NP.

THE WREATH; or, Nottingham Monthly Miscellany of Original Prose and Poetry. Nottingham. v1, no1-12, O 1832-S 1833. m. (Entirely different from the preceding entry.)
  b: NP.

WREATH FROM THE EMERALD ISLE. A New Year's Gift. Dublin. 1826. a.
b: UCP; L.

THE WREATH OF FRIENDSHIP.
(See *The Keepsake for the Young*, &c.)

WRIGHT'S LEEDS INTELLIGENCER.
(See *Leeds Intelligencer.*)

WRIGHT'S LITERARY MAGNET.
(See *Literary Magnet of Belles Lettres, Science*, &c.)

THE WRONGS OF CHILDREN; or, a Practical Vindication of Children; from the Injustice done them in early Nurture and Education, &c. London. no1-2, 1819. ir.
b: L.

YARMOUTH HERALD: or, Norfolk, Suffolk, and Essex Advertiser. Yarmouth. 1804. w.
a: CSmH no3, N 24, 1804.

YEAR BOOK of Daily Recreation and Information. London. 1832.
(No issues known. Data from CBEL, II. 841.)

THE YELLOW DWARF, a Weekly Miscellany. London. no1-21, Ja 3-My 23, 1818. w.
a: ULS. / *b:* BP no15; L; O.

THE YORK ALBUM of Literature and Science. York. no1-2, 1829/?.
b: L no2.

YORK CHRONICLE and General Advertiser. York. 1777-1840. w. (Preceded by *York Chronicle, and Weekly Advertiser*, 1772-73; *Etherington's York Chronicle*, 1774-77.)
a: CSmH Ag 27, 1829; ICU Ja 7, 1808-N 23, 1809; Ja 1810-D 1817. / *b:* L 1817; 1819; 1828-32; LE 1807-10; O 1793-1804; YP 1790-98; 1803-14; 1816-32.
(Incorporated with *Yorkshire Gazette.*)

YORK COURANT. York. 1725-1848. w.
a: CSmH Jl 17, 1827. / *b:* L 1789-1801; 1803, lacking My 9; 1804; 1806-07; S 9, 1811; 1828-32; YP 1797-1802; YYH (1789-1832).
(Incorporated with *York Herald*, 1848.)

YORK HERALD. York. no1+, 1790-1889. w.
a: CSmH Je 2, 1827; DLC (1813); [1814-19]; sc.nos. 1820-21; [1822]. / *b:* UCP; L 1801; 1803-20; 1823-32; YP 1790-93; 1799-1807; YYH.
(Continued as *Yorkshire* (later *York*) *Herald*, 1890-date.)

YORK RETREAT. Annual Report. York. 1792-1832. a.
b: LFS.

YORKSHIRE AND DERBYSHIRE Magazine. Sheffield. v1, 1824.
b: UCP; L; LdL; SP.

YORKSHIRE GAZETTE. York. no1+, 1819-date. w.
a: CSmH My 29, 1830; ICU Jl 19-D 27, 1828; Ja 3, 1829-D 31, 1831, lacking Ja 24, 31, 1829, Mr 20, 1830, & Ap 17, Je 12, 19, 26, 1830. / *b:* L no194+, Ja 4, 1823-1832; YP.

YORKSHIRE INSTITUTION for the Education of Deaf and Dumb Children. Annual Report. Doncaster. [?]-1831-1885-[?].
b: LdP 1831.

YORKSHIRE JOURNAL and General Weekly Advertiser. Doncaster. 1786-1796/?. w.
b: DcDG.
(Absorbed by *Doncaster, Retford and Gainsborough Gazette*, probably in 1796. For details, see *Yorkshire, Nottinghamshire and Lincolnshire Gazette*, &c.)

YORKSHIRE LITERARY ANNUAL. London, Leeds. 1832. a.
b: L; LdP; SP.

YORKSHIRE, Nottinghamshire and Lincolnshire Gazette and Universal Advertiser. Doncaster. 1794-95.
b: DcDG.
Continued as
DONCASTER, Retford and Gainsborough Gazette. Doncaster. 1795-97.
b: DcDG.
Absorbed *Yorkshire Journal and General Weekly Advertiser*, probably in 1796, and continued as
DONCASTER, Nottingham and Lincoln Gazette; Yorkshire, Nottinghamshire and Lincolnshire Advertiser. Doncaster. 1797-1882.
a: ICU 22 sc.nos. 1797-99; (1800-01); [1802]; MH Ja 14-D 30, 1814; (F 10-N 10, 1815); 17 sc.nos. 1826-32. / *b:* DcDG; DcP 1828-32; L Ag 1, 1828-1832.
(Continued as *Doncaster Gazette*, 1882-date.)

YORKSHIRE OBSERVER. York. no1-31, N 2, 1822-Je 14, 1823. w.
a: ULS. / *b:* L; LdP.

YORKSHIRE PHILOSOPHICAL SOCIETY. Annual Report of the Council. York. 1822-date.
a: ULS; ULSup. / *b:* LR 1827-32; LdP 1824-32.

YORKSHIRE SOCIETY for Educating, Boarding and Clothing Boys born in Yorkshire, or one of whose Parents were born there. Report of the Committee. York. [?]-1822-1869-[?].
b: LdP.

YORKSHIREMAN, a Religious and Literary Journal. Pontefract. v1-5, 1832-37.
a: ULS.

YOUNG GENTLEMAN'S AND LADY'S Magazine, or Universal Repository of Knowledge, Instruction and Amusement, &c. London. v1-2, 1799-1800. m.
a: ULS. / *b:* BiP v1, no1; L.

THE YOUNG MISSES MAGAZINE. Edinburgh.
v1-2, 1791.
   b: GM.

THE YOUNG MISSES MAGAZINE, containing
Dialogues between a Governess and several
young Ladies of Quality. Glasgow. v1-2,
[?]-1800.
   b: GM v2, no18-29.

THE YOUTH'S INSTRUCTOR and Guardian.
London. v1-39, 1817-55.
   a: ULS; ULSup. / *b:* CrP v1, 4; L.

YOUTH'S MAGAZINE; or Evangelical Miscellany. London. v1-10, 1805-15; s2, v1-12,
1816-26; s3, v1-10, 1828-37; s4-s7, 1838-
67. m.
   a: ULS. / *b:* UCP; BP s3, v2-3 impf.;
   CrP v10; ns, v8; L.
   (After D 1867 incorporated with *Bible
   Class Magazine.*)

THE YOUTH'S MISCELLANY of Knowledge
and Entertainment.
   (See *Youth's Monthly Visitor, or Instructive and Entertaining Miscellany,* &c.)

THE YOUTH'S MONTHLY VISITOR, or Instructive and Entertaining Miscellany of
Useful Knowledge. London. v1-3, 1822-23.
m. (Also known as *Youth's Miscellany of
Knowledge and Entertainment.*)
   a: ULS. / *b:* L.

LO ZINGARO; or, Literary Rambler. London.
no1, Ja 1, 1828.
   b: L.

ZION'S BANNERS. London. no1-11, 1825-26.
   b: UCP.

ZION'S RECORDER and Truth's Advocate.
London. no1, 1824.
   b: L; O.

ZION'S TRIUMPH. Bristol. 1798-1800-[?].
   (Listed by C & K, 2182. No issues known,
   but apparently a title error: intended to be
   Zion's Trumpet.)

ZION'S TRUMPET, a Theological Miscellany.
Bristol. v1-4, 1798-1801. m.
   a: ULS. / *b:* UCP; BrP; L.
   Continued as
CHRISTIAN GUARDIAN; a Theological
Miscellany. Bristol. v1-10, 1802-06; ns, v1-
2, 1807-08. m.
   a: ULS. / *b:* UCP; BrP 1803-05, 1807; L.
   Continued as
CHRISTIAN GUARDIAN and Church of Eng-
land Magazine. London. v1-41, 1809-49. ir.
   a: ULS. / *b:* UCP; BrP 1809-21; CrP
   1821-32; L.
   (Continued as *Christian Guardian and
   Churchman's Magazine,* 1850-52.)

ZOOLOGICAL ILLUSTRATIONS. London.
v1-3, 1820-23; s2, v1-3, 1829-33.
   a: ULS.

ZOOLOGICAL JOURNAL. London. v1-5,
1824-34.
   a: ULS. / *b:* UCP; CPL; DRS; L; LR;
   NwL; O.

ZOOLOGICAL KEEPSAKE; or, Zoology, and
the Garden and Museum of the Zoological
Society. London, Edinburgh. 1829-30/?. a.
   b: UCP; L 1829.

ZOOLOGICAL MAGAZINE, and Elegant Museum of the Curiosities and Rarities in Nature. London. 1808/?.
   (No issues known. Data from *Literary Annual Register, or Records of Literature,*
   2 (F 1808) 67-75.)

ZOOLOGICAL MISCELLANY.
   (See *Naturalists' Miscellany.*)

ZOOLOGICAL MISCELLANY. London. no1-
6, 1831-44.
   a: ULS. / *b:* L.

ZOOLOGICAL SOCIETY of London. (Committee of Science and Correspondence.) Proceedings. London. v1-2, 1830-32.
   a: ULS. / *b:* UCP; CPL; L; LR.
   (Continued under slightly varying titles,
   1833-90.)

O ZURRAGUE POLITICO das Cortes Novas,
publicado por huma Sociedade amiga do Rei
e da Patria. London. no1-2, 1821.
   b: L.

SELECTED BIBLIOGRAPHY

Bailey, J. "Lancashire Periodicals. Bibliographical Notes," *Manchester City Notes and Queries*, V (1883), 121-122.

Bellot, H. Hale, *University College, London, 1826-1926*. London, 1929.

Berkeley, Mrs. R. "A Sketch of Early Provincial Journalism," *Associated Architectural Society Reports and Papers*, XXIV (1898), 550-573.

Bulloch, J.M. *Chronological List of Aberdeen Newspapers*. Aberdeen, 1829.

———"Files of the Local Aberdeen Press, Past and Present," *Scottish Notes and Queries*, IX (1896), 170.

Cambridge Bibliography of English Literature. Edited by F.W. Bateson, New York and Cambridge, England, 1941. 4 vols.

Campbell, A. Albert. *Belfast Newspapers, Past and Present*. Belfast, 1921.

——— "*Irish Presbyterian Magazines, Past and Present. A Bibliography*. Belfast, 1919.

Casaide, Seámus ó. *A Guide to Old Waterford Newspapers*. Waterford, 1917.

Catalogue of a Collection of Early Newspapers and Essayists formed by the late John Thomas Hope, and Presented to the Bodleian Library by the late Rev. Frederick William Hope. Oxford, 1865.

Catalogue of Newspapers (in the Nichols Collection of the Bodleian Library). MS. copy in the Bodleian Library.

Catalogue of Periodicals contained in the Bodleian Library. Oxford, 1878-1880. 2 vols.

Couper, W.J. *The Edinburgh Periodical Press. Being An Account of the Newspapers, Journals, and Magazines issued in Edinburgh from the Earliest Times to 1800*. Stirling, 1908. 2 vols.

Craig, Mary Elizabeth. *The Scottish Periodical Press, 1750-1789*. London, 1931.

Crane, R.S. and F.B. Kaye. *A Census of British Newspapers and Periodicals, 1620-1800*. Chapel Hill, 1927.

Davidson, James. *Bibliotheca Devoniensis: A Catalogue of the Printed Books relating to the County of Devon*. Exeter, 1852; Supplement, 1862.

Davies, R. *A Memoir of the York Press in the XVIth, XVIIth, and XVIIIth Centuries.* Westminster, 1868.

Dix, E.R. McC. "The Earliest Periodicals Published in Dublin," *Proceedings of the Royal Irish Academy*, 3rd ser., VI (1900-1902), 33-35.

—— "List of Books, Pamphlets and Newspapers printed in Drogheda, Co. Louth, in the Eighteenth Century," *Irish Bibliographical Pamphlets*, No. III (1904).

—— "List of Books, Pamphlets and Newspapers printed in Ennis, Co. Clare, in the Eighteenth Century," *Irish Bibliographical Pamphlets*, No. VIII (1912).

—— "List of Books, Pamphlets and Newspapers printed in Limerick to 1800," *Irish Bibliographical Pamphlets*, No. V (1912). 2nd ed.

—— "List of Books, Pamphlets and Newspapers printed in Monaghan in the Eighteenth Century," *Irish Bibliographical Pamphlets*, No. IV (1908).

—— "List of Books, Pamphlets and Newspapers printed in Strabane, Co. Tyrone, in the Eighteenth Century," *Irish Bibliographical Pamphlets*, No. I (1901).

—— *List of Books, Pamphlets and Newspapers printed in the City of Cork in the XVIIth and XVIIIth Centuries.* Cork, 1904. 13 parts.

—— "Rare Ephemeral Magazines of the Eighteenth Century," *Irish Book Lover*, I (1910).

—— *Tables Relating to some Dublin Newspapers of the Eighteenth Century.* Dublin, 1910.

Edwards, F.A. *The Early Newspaper Press of Hampshire.* Southampton, 1869.

—— "A List of Hampshire Newspapers," *Hampshire Antiquary and Naturalist*, I (1891), 94-97; II (1892), 77-78.

Fenton, W.A. *Cambridge Periodicals, 1750-1931. (Cambridge Public Library Record and Book List,* March, 1931.) Cambridge, 1931.

Fletcher, Rev. John R. "Early Catholic Periodicals in England," *Dublin Review*, No. 397 (1936), 284-310.

The Galway Reader. (Issued by the Galway County Council Public Libraries). Athlone, No. 2-3 (1948).

Graham, M. *The Early Glasgow Press.* Glasgow, 1906.

Graham, Walter. *English Literary Periodicals.* New York, 1930.

Hawgood, J.A. "University College and Its Magazines," *University College Magazine*, June, 1927.

Holden's Triennial Directory for 1805, 1806, 1807. 4th ed. (Contains a list of London and County Newspapers.)

Hunt, W. *Hull Newspapers.* Hull, 1880.

Lamb, A.D. "Bibliography of Dundee Periodicals," *Scottish Notes and Queries,* III (1889), 98-100.

Lefanu, W.R. *British Periodicals of Medicine.* Baltimore, 1938.

Leiper, R.T. and others. *Periodicals of Medicine and the Allied Sciences in British Libraries.* London, n.d.

Lewis, H. "The Beginnings of the Bath Newspaper Press," *Proceedings of the Bath Natural History and Antiquities Field Club,* V (1885), 8-21.

Local Catalogue of Material concerning Newcastle and Northumberland. Newcastle-upon-Tyne, 1932.

M'Bain, J.M. *Bibliography of Arbroath Periodical Literature and Political Broadsides.* Arbroath, 1889.

Madden, Richard Robert. *The History of Irish Periodical Literature, from the end of the 17th Century to the middle of the 19th.* London, 1867. 2 vols.

Milford, R.T. and D.M. Sutherland. *A Catalogue of British Newspapers and Periodicals in the Bodleian Library, 1622-1800.* Oxford, 1936.

Morley, J. Cooper. *The Newspaper Press and Periodical Literature of Liverpool.* Liverpool, 1887.

Nichols, John. *Illustrations of the Literary History of the Eighteenth Century.* London, 1817-1858. 8 vols.

—— *Literary Anecdotes of the Eighteenth Century.* London, 1812-1815. 6 vols.

Noble, H. *A Bibliography of Inverness Newspapers and Periodicals. Edited with Notes by J. Whyte, with an Appendix by W. Mackay.* Stirling, 1903.

Norris, William. *Edinburgh Newspapers, Past and Present.* Earletown, 1891.

Parson, William, and William White. *History, Directory, and Gazeteer of . . . Cumberland and Westmoreland.* Leeds, 1829.

Patterson, Alexander. *Yorkshire Journalism, Past and Present.* Barnsley, 1901.

Periodical Press of Great Britain and Ireland. An inquiry into the State of the Public Journals, chiefly as regarded their moral and political influence. London, 1824.

Pierpont, R. "Newcastle and Durham Papers," *Notes and Queries*, March, 1923.

Porter, W.S. "Old Sheffield Newspapers," *Transactions of the Hunter Archaeological Society*, I (1914), 110-111.

Power, John. *Irish Literary Periodical Publications*. London, 1866.

Scottish Notes and Queries. Aberdeen, 1887+.

Sinclair, G.A. "[Scottish] Periodical Literature in the Eighteenth Century," *Scottish Historical Review*, II (1904), 136-159.

Slade, J.J. and Mrs. H. Richardson, "Wiltshire Newspapers—Past and Present," *Wiltshire Archaeological and Natural History Magazine (Devizes)*, XL, XLI (Dec. 1917-June, 1922), XL: 37-74, 129-141, 318-351; XLI: 53-69, 479-501.

Sper, Felix. *The Theatrical Press of London: Theatrical and Literary (excluding the daily Newspaper)*. Boston, U.S.A., 1937.

Symon, J.D. "The Earlier Oxford Magazines," *Oxford and Cambridge Review*, No. 13 (1911).

Tercentenary Handlist of English and Welsh Newspapers, Magazines and Reviews. Edited by J.G. Muddiman, London, 1920. (For additions and corrections see *Notes and Queries*, January 29, February 5, 26, March 26, 1921; March 11, 18, 1922.)

Union Catalogue of the Periodical Publications in the University Libraries of the British Isles, with their Respective Holdings, excluding Titles in the World List of Scientific Periodicals. London, 1937.

Union List of Serials in Libraries of the United States and Canada. Second Edition. Ed. by Winifred Gregory, New York, 1943.

Union List of Serials in Libraries of the United States and Canada. Second Edition. *Supplement*, January, 1941-December, 1943. Ed. by Gabrielle Malikoff. New York, 1945.

Wallace, E. *Early Scottish Journalists and Journalism*. Stirling, 1899.

Wightman, H. *A List of the Newspapers in Lancashire, Yorkshire, and Cheshire*. Liverpool, 1887.

Worth, R.N. *The Three Towns Bibliotheca: A Catalogue of Books, Pamphlets, Papers, &c.* Plymouth, 1873.

CO-OPERATING LIBRARIES†

AAJ	Aberdeen (Scot.) — Office of *Aberdeen Journals*	**BurC**	Bury St. Edmunds (Eng.) — Cullum Library
***AU**	Aberdeen (Scot.) — Aberdeen University Library	**BwP**	Barrow-in-Furness (Eng.) — Public Library
ArP	Arbroath (Scot.) — Public Library		
AyAA	Ayr (Scot.) — Office of *Ayr Advertiser & Galloway Journal*	***C**	Cambridge (Eng.) — Cambridge University Library
AyP	Ayr (Scot.) — Public Library	**CPL**	Cambridge (Eng.) — Cambridge Philosophical Society
AybA	Aylesbury (Eng.) — Buckinghamshire Archaeological Society	**CPU**	Cambridge (Eng.) — Public Library

---

NOTE TO USERS OF THIS INDEX

This *Index* is designed for use not only with the *Union List of Serials* (ULS) and the *Union Catalogue of the Periodical Publications in the University Libraries of the British Isles* (UCP) but also with the forthcoming *British Union Catalogue of Periodicals* (BUCOP). Cross references are given to ULS and UCP only, but when BUCOP has been published, the user of this *Index* may assume that the cross references to UCP are valid also for BUCOP. Furthermore, he may assume that in many cases BUCOP, which will list the holdings of many British libraries not covered by UCP, records titles not found in UCP and hence should be consulted even in the absence of a cross reference.

Certain precautions which the user of this *Index* should take when associating symbols with libraries (and especially those preceded by an asterisk) are set forth at the end of this list of co-operating libraries.

BBW	Birmingham (Eng.) — Office of *Birmingham Weekly Post*	**C-S**	San Francisco, Cal. (USA) — California State Library, Sutro Branch
BO	Birmingham (Eng.) — Oscott College Library	**CSmH**	San Marino, Cal. (USA) — Henry Huntington Library
BP	Birmingham (Eng.) — Public Library	**CSt**	Stanford Univ., Cal. (USA) — Stanford University Library
BaA	Barnstaple (Eng.) — North Devon Athenaeum	**CU**	Berkeley, Cal. (USA) — University of California Library
BbP	Blackburn (Eng.) — Public Library		
BdL	Bradford (Eng.) — Bradford Library and Literary Society	**CaK**	Kingston (Canada) — Queen's University Library
BdP	Bradford (Eng.) — Public Library	**CaL**	London (Canada) — University of Western Ontario Library
BddP	Bideford (Eng.) — Public Library		
BedP	Bedford (Eng.) — Public Library	**CaM**	Montreal (Canada) — McGill University Library
BerBA	Berwick-on-Tweed (Scot.) — Office of *Berwick Advertiser*	**CbP**	Camborne (Eng.) — Public Library
BhP	Bath (Eng.) — Municipal Library	**ChlP**	Chelsea (Eng.) — Public Library
BlBH	Brighton (Eng.) — Office of *Brighton & Hove Herald*	**ChsCCh**	Chester (Eng.) — Office of *Chester Chronicle*
BiP	Brighton (Eng.) — Public Library	**ChsCCo**	Chester (Eng.) — Office of *Chester Courant*
BkP	Birkenhead (Eng.) — Public Library	**CiP**	Cirencester (Eng.) — Bingham Public Library
BlBN	Belfast (No. Ire.) — Office of *Belfast News-Letter*	**CmC**	Carmarthen (Wales) — Carmarthenshire County Museum
BlL	Belfast (No. Ire.) — Linen Hall Library		
BlNW	Belfast (No. Ire.) — Office of *Northern Whig and Belfast Post*	**CnP**	Croydon (Eng.) — Public Library
		CoP	Cork (Eire) — Municipal Library
BlP	Belfast (No. Ire.) — Public Library	**ColCG**	Colchester (Eng.) — Office of *Colchester Gazette*
BlU	Belfast (No. Ire.) — Queen's University		
BmP	Bournemouth (Eng.) — Public Library	**ColEC**	Colchester (Eng.) — Office of *Essex County Standard*
BnU	Bangor (Wales) — University College of North Wales Library	**ColP**	Colchester (Eng.) — Public Library
BoP	Bolton (Eng.) — Public Library	**CpFH**	Cupar (Scot.) — Office of *Fife Herald and Journal*
BrBW	Bristol (Eng.) — Office of *Bristol Western Daily Press* &c.	**CrP**	Cardiff (Wales) — Public Library
BrP	Bristol (Eng.) — Public Library	**CsCN**	Carlisle (Eng.) — Office of *Cumberland News*
BrU	Bristol (Eng.) — Bristol University Library	**CsP**	Carlisle (Eng.) — Public Library
BtP	Battersea (Eng.) — Public Library	**CsfP**	Chesterfield (Eng.) — Public Library
BtlP	Bootle (Eng.) — Public Library	**CtHT**	Hartford, Conn. (USA) — Trinity College Library
BuC	Bury (Eng.) — Co-operative Society Library		

† To these libraries should be added those in ULS and UCP which are not listed here, since cross references are given to these volumes. For a full explanation of this fact see the second paragraph of the Foreword.

CtP	Cheltenham (Eng.) — Public Library
CtY	New Haven, Conn. (USA) — Yale University Library
CvCS	Coventry (Eng.) — Office of *Coventry Standard*
CvP	Coventry (Eng.) — Public Library
CyKG	Canterbury (Eng.) — Office of *Kentish Gazette and Canterbury Press*
D	Dublin (Eire) — Trinity College Library
*DA	Dublin (Eire) — Royal Irish Academy Library
DCC	Dublin (Eire) — Central Catholic Library
DCU	Washington, D. C. (USA) — Catholic University of America Library
*DL	Dublin (Eire) — National Library of Ireland
DLC	Washington, D. C. (USA) — Library of Congress
DLL	Dublin (Eire) — King's Inn Law Library
DML	Dublin (Eire) — Marsh's Library
DPK	Dublin (Eire) — Public Library, Kevin Street
DRC	Dublin (Eire) — Representative Church Body Library
DRS	Dublin (Eire) — Royal Dublin Society Library
DSA	Dublin (Eire) — Royal Society of Antiquaries in Ireland Library
DcDG	Doncaster (Eng.) — Office of *Doncaster Gazette*
DcP	Doncaster (Eng.) — Public Library
DcrN	Dorchester (Eng.) — Dorset Natural History and Archaeological Society Library
DeP	Derby (Eng.) — Public Library
DlP	Darlington (Eng.) — Edward Pease Public Library
DmP	Dunfermline (Scot.) — Public Library
DnCA	Dundee (Scot.) — Office of *Courier and Advertiser*
DnP	Dundee (Scot.) — Public Library
DrC	Durham (Eng.) — County Libraries
DrDC	Durham (Eng.) — Office of *Durham County Advertiser*
DrU	Durham (Eng.) — Durham University Library
DsD	Dumfries (Scot.) — Dumfriesshire Libraries
DuC	Duns (Scot.) — Berwickshire County Library
DvW	Devizes (Eng.) — Wiltshire Archaeological and Natural History Society Library
DvWG	Devizes (Eng.) — Office of *Wiltshire Gazette*
*E	Edinburgh (Scot.) — National Library of Scotland
EEG	Edinburgh (Scot.) — Office of *Edinburgh Gazette*
EP	Edinburgh (Scot.) — Public Library
ER	Edinburgh (Scot.) — Royal Society of Edinburgh Library
ESL	Edinburgh (Scot.) — Signet Library
ETS	Edinburgh (Scot.) — Office of *The Scotsman*
EU	Edinburgh (Scot.) — Edinburgh University Library

ElEC	Elgin (Scot.) — Office of *Elgin Courant and Courier*
EnnIR	Enniskillen (No. Ire.) — Office of *Impartial Reporter and Farmer's Journal*
EtS	Eton (Eng.) — School Library
ExD	Exeter (Eng.) — Devon and Exeter Institution Library
ExDE	Exeter (Eng.) — Office of *Devon and Exeter Gazette*
ExP	Exeter (Eng.) — Public Library
ExWT	Exeter (Eng.) — Office of *Western Times*
FoP	Folkestone (Eng.) — Public Library
GGH	Glasgow (Scot.) — Office of the *Glasgow Herald*
GM	Glasgow (Scot.) — Mitchell Library
*GU	Glasgow (Scot.) — Glasgow University Library
GeG	Greenock (Scot.) — Greenock Library
GmP	Grimsby (Eng.) — Public Library
GrGJ	Gloucester (Eng.) — Office of *Gloucester Journal*
GrP	Gloucester (Eng.) — Public Library
HP	Hull (Eng.) — Public Library
HdP	Hampstead (Eng.) — Central Library
HdS	Hampstead (Eng.) — Hampstead Subscription Library
HfP	Hereford (Eng.) — Public Library
HlHC	Halifax (Eng.) — Office of *Halifax Courier and Guardian*
HlL	Halifax (Eng.) — Literary and Philosophical Society Library
HlP	Halifax (Eng.) — Public Library
HnA	Haddington (Scot.) — East Lothian Antiquarian Society Library
HnP	Haddington (Scot.) — Public Library
HsP	Hammersmith (Eng.) — Central Carnegie Library
HtHM	Hertford (Eng.) — Office of *Hertfordshire Mercury & County Press*
HtP	Hertford (Eng.) — Public Library
HwV	Harrow (Eng.) — Vaughan Library
ICN	Chicago, Ill. (USA) — Newberry Library
ICU	Chicago, Ill. (USA) — University of Chicago Library
IHi	Springfield, Ill. (USA) — Illinois Historical Society Library
IP	Peoria, Ill. (USA) — Public Library
IU	Urbana, Ill. (USA) — University of Illinois Library
InIC	Inverness (Scot.) — Office of *Inverness Courier*
InP	Inverness (Scot.) — Burgh and County Public Library
InR	Inverness (Scot.) — Raigmore
IpP	Ipswich (Eng.) — Public Library
IpSC	Ipswich (Eng.) — Office of *Suffolk Chronicle and Mercury*
IsP	Islington (Eng.) — Islington Public Libraries

KAS	Atchison, Kans. (USA) — St. Benedict's College Library
KdP	Kendal (Eng.) — Public Library
KdWG	Kendal (Eng.) — Office of *Westmorland Gazette*
KeP	Kensington (Eng.) — Public Library
KiP	Kilmarnock (Scot.) — Dick Institute Public Library
KkKJ	Kilkenny (Eire) — Office of *Kilkenny Journal*
KyLx	Lexington, Ky. (USA) — Public Library
KyU	Lexington, Ky. (USA) — University of Kentucky Library
*L	London (Eng.) — British Museum Library
LAt	London (Eng.) — Athenaeum Club Library
LCM	London (Eng.) — Royal College of Music Library
LCP	London (Eng.) — Royal College of Physicians Library
LDC	London (Eng.) — Dulwich College Library
LE	London (Eng.) — London School of Economics Library
LFS	London (Eng.) — Friends Society Library
LGI	London (Eng.) — Gray's Inn Library
LGU	London (Eng.) — Guildhall Library
LIT	London (Eng.) — Inner Temple Library
LLG	London (Eng.) — Office of *London Gazette*
LLL	London (Eng.) — London Library
LLlL	London (Eng.) — Office of *Lloyd's List and Shipping Gazette*
LLN	London (Eng.) — Lincoln's Inn Library
LLW	London (Eng.) — Law Society Library
LMA	London (Eng.) — British Medical Association Library
LMD	London (Eng.) — Royal Society of Medicine Library
LMT	London (Eng.) — Middle Temple Library
LNHT	New Orleans, La. (USA) — Howard Memorial Library
*LP	London (Eng.) — Patent Office Library
LR	London (Eng.) — Royal Society Library
*LS	London (Eng.) — Royal College of Surgeons Library
LSD	London (Eng.) — Office of *Sunday Dispatch*
LTT	London (Eng.) — Office of *The Times*
*LU	London (Eng.) — London University Library
LUC	London (Eng.) — University College Library
LVA	London (Eng.) — Victoria and Albert Museum Library
LaP	Lambeth (Eng.) — Tate Central Library
LcLC	Leicester (Eng.) — Office of *Illustrated Leicester Chronicle*
LcLM	Leicester (Eng.) — Office of *Leicester Mercury*
LcP	Leicester (Eng.) — Public Library
LdL	Leeds (Eng.) — Leeds Library
LdP	Leeds (Eng.) — Public Library
LdYP	Leeds (Eng.) — Office of *Yorkshire Post*
LmLC	Limerick (Eire) — Office of *Limerick Chronicle*
LmP	Limerick (Eire) — Municipal Public Libraries
LnLR	Lincoln (Eng.) — Office of *Lincoln, Rutland and Stamford Mercury*
LnP	Lincoln (Eng.) — Public Library
LoLS	Londonderry (No. Ire.) — Office of *Londonderry Sentinel*
LoM	Londonderry (No. Ire.) — Magee University College Library
LoP	Londonderry (No. Ire.) — Public Library
LrC	Lismore (Eire) — Waterford County Libraries
LsP	Lancaster (Eng.) — Public Library
LvA	Liverpool (Eng.) — Athenaeum Library
LvP	Liverpool (Eng.) — Public Library.
MB	Boston, Mass. (USA) — Public Library
MBAt	Boston, Mass. (USA) — Boston Athenaeum Library
MCh	Manchester (Eng.) — Chetham's Library
MH	Cambridge, Mass. (USA) — Harvard University Library
MH-Z	Cambridge, Mass. (USA) — Harvard Museum of Comparative Zoology
MHi	Boston, Mass. (USA) — Massachusetts Historical Society Library
MMG	Manchester (Eng.) — Office of *Manchester Guardian*
MNS	Northampton, Mass. (USA) — Smith College Library
MP	Manchester (Eng.) — Public Library
MR	Manchester (Eng.) — John Rylands Library
MWA	Worcester, Mass. (USA) — American Antiquarian Society Library
MaP	Maidenhead (Eng.) — Public Library
MdBE	Baltimore, Md. (USA) — Enoch Pratt Free Library
MdBJ	Baltimore, Md. (USA) — The Johns Hopkins University Library
MdBP	Baltimore, Md. (USA) — Peabody Institute Library
MeB	Brunswick, Me. (USA) — Bowdoin College Library
MeHi	Brunswick, Me. (USA) — Maine Historical Society Library
MiD-B	Detroit, Mich. (USA) — Detroit Public Library, Burton Historical Collection
MiU	Ann Arbor, Mich. (USA) — University of Michigan Library
MiU-C	Ann Arbor, Mich. (USA) — University of Michigan Library, William Clements Library of American History
MnU	Minneapolis, Minn. (USA) — University of Minnesota Library
MoM	Montrose (Scot.) — Montrose Library
MoMR	Montrose (Scot.) — Office of *Montrose Review*
MoP	Montrose (Scot.) — Public Library
MoU	Columbia, Mo. (USA) — University of Missouri Library
MsP	Maidstone (Eng.) — Public Library
N	Albany, N. Y. (USA) — New York State Library
NIC	Ithaca, N. Y. (USA) — Cornell University Library
NN	New York, N. Y. (USA) — Public Library
NNC	New York, N. Y. (USA) — Columbia University Library

*NNG	Nottingham (Eng.) — Office of *Nottingham Guardian*
NNHi	New York, N. Y. (USA) — New York Historical Society Library
NNJ	Nottingham (Eng.) — Office of *Nottingham Journal*
NP	Nottingham (Eng.) — Public Library
NPV	Poughkeepsie, N. Y. (USA) — Vassar College Library
NRU	Rochester, N. Y. (USA) — University of Rochester Library
NcD	Durham, N. C. (USA) — Duke University Library
NcU	Chapel Hill, N. C. (USA) — University of North Carolina Library
NjHi	Newark, N. J. (USA) — New Jersey Historical Society Library
NjP	Princeton, N. J. (USA) — Princeton University Library
NjR	New Brunswick, N. J. (USA) — Rutgers University Library
NkP	Newark-on-Trent (Eng.) — Gilstrap Public Library
NoMH	Northampton (Eng.) — Office of *Mercury and Herald*
NoP	Northampton (Eng.) — Public Library
NpP	Newport (Eng.) — Public Library
NrC	Norwich (Eng.) — Private Library of Mrs. Colman (Inquire at NrM or NrP)
NrM	Norwich (Eng.) — Castle Museum Library
NrP	Norwich (Eng.) — Public Library
NwEC	Newcastle-upon-Tyne (Eng.) — Office of *Evening Chronicle*
NwL	Newcastle-upon-Tyne (Eng.) — Literary Philosophical Society Library
NwP	Newcastle-upon-Tyne (Eng.) — Public Library
NwS	Newcastle-upon-Tyne (Eng.) — Society of Antiquaries Library
O	Oxford (Eng.) — Bodleian Library
OC	Cincinnati, O. (USA) — Public Library
OCl	Cleveland, O. (USA) — Public Library
OClWHi	Cleveland, O. (USA) — Western Reserve Historical Society Library
OHi	Columbus, O. (USA) — Ohio State Archaeological and Historical Society Library
OMA	Oxford (Eng.) — Manchester College Library
OPU	Oxford (Eng.) — Public Library
OU	Columbus, O. (USA) — Ohio State University Library
PBr	Bryn Athyn, Pa. (USA) — Academy of the New Church
PHC	Haverford, Pa. (USA) — Haverford College Library
PPAP	Philadelphia, Pa. (USA) — American Philosophical Society Library
PPHi	Philadelphia, Pa. (USA) — Historical Society of Pennsylvania Library
PPL	Philadelphia, Pa. (USA) — Library Company of Philadelphia
PPPrHi	Philadelphia, Pa. (USA) — Presbyterian Historical Society Library

PU	Philadelphia, Pa. (USA) — University of Pennsylvania Library
PeP	Perth (Scot.) — Sandeman Public Library
PePA	Perth (Scot.) — Office of *Perthshire Advertiser*
PlP	Plymouth (Eng.) — Central Library
PmHT	Portsmouth (Eng.) — Office of *Hampshire Telegraph*
PmP	Portsmouth (Eng.) — Public Library
PrH	Preston (Eng.) — Harris Public Library
PsP	Paisley (Scot.) — Public Library
RP	Reading (Eng.) — Public Library
RRM	Reading (Eng.) — Office of the *Reading Mercury*
RdP	Rochdale (Eng.) — Public Library
RiP	Richmond (Eng.) — Public Library
RtP	Rotherham (Eng.) — Public Library
SP	Sheffield (Eng.) — Public Library
SU	Sheffield (Eng.) — Sheffield University Library
SaU	St. Andrews (Scot.) — St. Andrews University Library
SbSW	Salisbury (Eng.) — Office of *Salisbury and Winchester Journal*
ScP	Stockport (Eng.) — Public Library
ScSA	Stockport (Eng.) — Office of *Stockport Advertiser and Guardian*
SfP	Salford (Eng.) — Public Library
SkP	Southwark (Eng.) — Public Library
SnP	Stoke Newington (Eng.) — Public Library
SoP	Southampton (Eng.) — Public Library
SptP	Southport (Eng.) — Public Library
SrP	Shrewsbury (Eng.) — Public Library
SrS	Shrewsbury (Eng.) — Shrewsbury School Library
SrSC	Shrewsbury (Eng.) — Office of *Shrewsbury Chronicle*
SsP	South Shields (Eng.) — Public Library
StP	Stoke-on-Trent (Eng.) — Public Library
StfP	Stafford (Eng.) — Public Library
StfS	Stafford (Eng.) — William Salt Library
StfSA	Stafford (Eng.) — Office of *Staffordshire Advertiser*
SthC	Stonyhurst (Eng.) — Stonyhurst College Library
StlP	Stirling (Scot.) — Public Library
StlSJ	Stirling (Scot.) — Office of *Stirling Journal and Advertiser*
StmLR	Stamford (Eng.) — Office of *Lincoln, Rutland, and Stamford Mercury*
SuP	Sunderland (Eng.) — Public Library
SwI	Swansea (Wales) — Royal Institution of South Wales Library
SwP	Swansea (Wales) — Public Library
SyP	Stepney (Eng.) — Public Libraries
TaP	Taunton (Eng.) — Public Library
TaS	Taunton (Eng.) — Somerset Archaeological and Natural History Society Library
TmP	Tynemouth (Eng.) — Public Library
ToP	Tottenham (Eng.) — Public Library
TrP	Truro (Eng.) — Public Library

TrRC	Truro (Eng.) — Office of *Royal Cornwall Gazette and County News*		**WiP**	Wigan (Eng.) — Public Library
TrWB	Truro (Eng.) — Office of *West Briton*		**WmP**	Westminister (Eng.) — Public Library
TuP	Tunbridge Wells (Eng.) — Public Library		**WnP**	Winchester (Eng.) — Public Library
			WoP	Woolwich (Eng.) — Public Library
			WrP	Warrington (Eng.) — Municipal Library
V	Richmond, Va. (USA) — Virginia State Library		**WtLE**	Whitehaven (Eng.) — Lowther Estates Library
VU	Charlottesville, Va. (USA) — University of Virginia		**WtP**	Whitehaven (Eng.) — Public Library
			WtfP	Waterford (Eire) — Municipal Library
			WvP	Wolverhampton (Eng.) — Public Library
			WwP	Warwick (Eng.) — Public Library
WHi	Madison, Wis. (USA) — University of Wisconsin Library		**WwWW**	Warwick (Eng.) — Office of *Warwick and Warwickshire Advertiser*
WcBW	Worcester (Eng.) — Office of *Berrow's Worcester Journal*		**WxC**	Wexford (Eire) — County Libraries
WcP	Worcester (Eng.) — Public Library		**WxOC**	Wexford (Eire) — Office of M. J. O'Connor, Solicitors
WdWS	Windsor (Eng.) — Office of *Windsor, Slough and Eton Express*		**YP**	York (Eng.) — Public Library
WhP	West Ham (Eng.) — Public Library		**YYH**	York (Eng.) — Office of *Yorkshire Herald*
			YeWG	Yeovil (Eng.) — Office of *Western Gazette*

Note 1:

Fortunately my adoption of the library symbols employed by ULS and BUCOP did not lead to a single case of duplication when the American and British libraries co-operating with this *Index* were combined into one list. In seven instances, however, libraries listed in ULS (but not in this *Index*) have the same symbols as other libraries which co-operated with this *Index* and BUCOP. It is unlikely that confusion will arise because of this duplication, but a word of caution can hardly be amiss.

AU	Aberdeen University	is also Alabama University in ULS
C	Cambridge University	is also California State Library in ULS
DA	Royal Irish Academy	is also U.S. Department of Agriculture in ULS
DL	National Library of Ireland	is also U.S. Department of Labor in ULS
GU	Glasgow University	is also University of Georgia in ULS
LU	London University	is also University of Louisiana in ULS
NNG	Office of *Nottingham Guardian*	is also General Theological Seminary in ULS

Note 2:

A possible source of confusion (especially for British users) arises from the fact that the symbols to be used in the forthcoming BUCOP (and hence the symbols in this *Index*) do not always signify the same libraries that they do in UCP. Five of these symbols are used in this *Index*. (When BUCOP is published, this problem, of course, will cease to exist.)

E	National Library of Scotland in this *Index* and BUCOP, but Edinburgh University in UCP
L	British Museum in this *Index* and BUCOP, but London University in UCP
LP	Patent Office in this *Index* and BUCOP, but School of Pharmacy in UCP
LS	Royal College of Surgeons in this *Index* and BUCOP, but School of Slavonic Studies in UCP
LU	London University in this *Index* and BUCOP, but University College in UCP